Camp Nelson, Kentucky

Camp Nelson, Kentucky

A Civil War History

Richard D. Sears

THE UNIVERSITY PRESS OF KENTUCKY

Publication of this volume was made possible in part by a grant
from the National Endowment for the Humanities.

Editorial and Sales Offices: The University Press of Kentucky
663 South Limestone Street, Lexington, Kentucky 40508-4008

06 05 04 03 02   5 4 3 2 1

Cataloging-in-Publication data available
from the Library of Congress

ISBN 0-8131-2246-5 (cloth: alk. paper)

This book is printed on acid-free recycled paper meeting
the requirements of the American National Standard
for Permanence in Paper for Printed Library Materials.

Manufactured in the United States of America.

This work is dedicated to John and Sandra Bolin,
in gratitude for their support and encouragement
and our long-continued friendship.

Contents

Illustrations insert follows page 172

Preface

Sources

My debt to the monumental works in the series *Freedom: A Documentary History of Emancipation 1861-1867* is both deep and obvious. The idea of compiling a documentary history of Camp Nelson, Kentucky, had already occurred to me before I ever saw *Freedom*, but my original idea was simply to convey Camp Nelson's story through the letters of the American Missionary Association (AMA) workers at the camp, especially Rev. John Gregg Fee. These sources—which had become familiar to me during my research into Berea history over a period of more than a decade—present a very clear picture of the growth and development of the Refugee Home at Camp Nelson, but they begin *in medias res* and then jump to the dissolution of Camp Nelson after an inexplicable hiatus that can only be filled by other sources. I wanted to convey a much wider impression of Camp Nelson, partly because it had always been subordinated to Berea in my earlier works. So I added two major archival sources to my research. The military records of the Civil War in the National Archives tell the story of Camp Nelson's origins and functions before the missionaries arrived, and, in addition, provide a totally different perspective on the entire life span of General Ambrose Burnside's supply depot, the black recruiting station, the refugee camp, the National Cemetery, and so on. The records of the Freedmen's Bureau, also in the National Archives, complete the story with a highly detailed account of the official breaking up of Camp Nelson.

Generally speaking, AMA records, supplemented by original letters in the Berea College Archives, present stories of Camp Nelson from a social and religious point of view, specifically from the perspective of evangelical Christians, devoted to social reforms, abolition in general (all AMA workers were abolitionists), and social equality in particular (in the case of John G. Fee). The Records of the United States Army Continental Commands, 1821-1920 (RG 393 in the National Archives) and the portions of it that have been published in *The War of the Rebellion: A Compilation of the Official Records of the Union and Confederate Armies* (this compilation is in 130 large, small-print volumes, but it is only a part—perhaps a small part—of Record Group 393) operate perforce with almost wholly military and political points of view, although a number of pieces in the army's inspection reports, telegrams, and general correspondence reveal surprisingly personal slants from some writers. The Records of the Bureau of Refugees, Freedmen, and Abandoned Lands (RG 105;

abbreviated as BRFAL) are usually not particularly military, but bureaucratic, with strong emphasis on sociological and economic issues. Among the Freedmen's Bureau documents, however, are many affidavits from slaves and former slaves, missionaries, soldiers, and slaveholders—some of the most personal and intimate of all the narratives presented in this collection. Rounding out the perspectives represented are the published reports of the United States Sanitary Commission, the voluntary public health organization associated with the American Civil War (analogous to and based upon the British version, which had originated during the Crimean War); the officials of this group naturally take a medical point of view, but their observations range far beyond the general questions of health, sickness, and injury that might be predicted. The result of putting these widely separated records together is, I believe, a very diverse, well-rounded depiction of how slavery ended at Camp Nelson, in Kentucky, in the United States.

In addition to the more general military records mentioned above, this work includes many items from the Records of the Office of the Quartermaster General (RG 92), Records of the Adjutant General's Office (RG 94), Records of the Office of the Inspector General (RG 159), all in the National Archives, and the Orlando M. Poe Papers in the collection of Central Michigan University. A special source in Record Group 94, "The Negro in the Military Service of the United States," is a typescript copy of many compiled documents relating to black recruitment and service, along with occasional actual documents that were removed from original record series at the time of compilation. This resource also exists in a microfilm copy (M858, five rolls), which is the version I used.

Personal documents from Civil War soldiers themselves include letters written by Robert Audley Browne (in the Archives of the U.S. Army Military Institute at Carlisle Barracks, Carlisle, Pennsylvania), W.H. Chapman (in the Tennessee Historical Society), Joseph Rabb (in the Indiana Historical Society), Abram McLellan (in the Ohio Historical Society), and J.C. Currier (in the Filson Club Library in Louisville); and an unpublished diary by Oliver C. Haskell (in the Indiana Historical Society). An unpublished journal of a Kentucky slaveholder, Rev. William Pratt—in the Division of Special Collections and Archives of the Margaret I. King Library, University of Kentucky—is quoted in two brief entries mentioning Camp Nelson. In addition, two memoirs by former slaves, Elijah P. Marrs and Peter Bruner, report various experiences connected to Camp Nelson, and a published excerpt from the diary of Frances Dallam Peter in Lexington also refers directly to the camp.

I should not conclude this brief description of sources without saying—for the benefit of subsequent researchers—that tremendous amounts of material concerning Camp Nelson remain to be studied. In the relatively small areas that I personally researched, I passed over literally thousands of pieces without transcribing them; in the many records groups that I never looked at still more thousands of records await the scholar's scrutiny: RG 110, for example, Records of the Provost Marshal General's Bureau (Civil War); or RG 77, Records of the Office of the Chief of Engineers. Or the dozens of volumes of hospital records from Camp Nelson that I never had time to examine or even locate in the record groups.

Coverage and Principles of Selection

In choosing what materials to include from the wealth available, I established several simple, but important standards. Virtually every document included in this collection mentions, emanates from, or was received at Camp Nelson. Documents were systematically chosen to cast light on the daily life and general operations of Camp Nelson, providing a general context for all historical developments, and/or to present chronologically the major events in which Camp Nelson was involved or which took place at the camp, with preference given to those incidents that actually occurred within its borders. (For that reason, for example, the Battle of Saltville is presented in only a couple of documents; although black soldiers from Camp Nelson fought in that engagement, it was not exactly a Camp Nelson incident. For the same reason, the founding of Berea College receives only a few notes in this volume, even though Berea and Camp Nelson had many connections.)   Every significant event at the camp itself is represented by some document or documents, whereas "outside" events are usually presented in the book's introduction. Since the most important historical events at Camp Nelson involved the recruiting of black soldiers and the freeing of former slaves, the selected documents concerning those subjects are extremely numerous, exactly as they are in all the major sources. The emphasis on the ending of slavery in this book is not due to some peculiar predilection of my own selections: no faithful representation of the history of Camp Nelson could emphasize anything else without seriously skewing the historical record.

I have selected from the major sources in widely varying proportions: from the AMA collection I transcribed and interpreted all the letters that had anything to do with Camp Nelson (a task that took a couple of years) and every major event mentioned in those letters is represented in the collection of documents. I only used about half of the letters because they are very repetitive, and some deal with subjects other than Camp Nelson. A great many of the AMA letters—the majority of them— were written by John G. Fee, who was the first missionary at Camp Nelson, the leader of all the AMA missionaries, and the chief reporter to that organization; many of his letters are partly devoted to Camp Nelson and partly devoted to Berea because he was founding schools, churches, and villages in both places at the same time. For this particular work, the Berea passages have been systematically omitted. But, to repeat, every mention of Camp Nelson in the AMA Archives has been taken into account.

Likewise, the BRFAL records concerning the states of Tennessee and Kentucky have been searched through the entire nineteen reels of microfilm, and every document pertaining to Camp Nelson was transcribed. Most of those records have been included in this book because the presence of the Freedmen's Bureau at the camp, although brief, was absolutely crucial, resulting in the destruction of all the institutions put in place during the war. A large of majority of the Camp Nelson letters in the Freedmen's Bureau series were written by R.E. Farwell, the special agent sent by the Bureau to "break up the camp."

From the *Official Records*, I have extracted every document mentioning Camp Nelson or Hickman Bridge; since my final search was conducted by computer on a website (Cornell University's magnificent Making of America site at <http://moa.cit.cornell.edu/>) with a photographic image of every page of the 130 volumes of the *Official Records*, I am certain that I have copied every reference to Camp Nelson in that monumental work. I have not included all of the documents, of course, but through this special study, which took many weeks, I am assured that I have viewed sources about every military operation and function in which Camp Nelson was involved. Most of these are discussed in the introduction because no battle ever took place at the camp itself.

In RG 393, Records of the United States Army in the National Archives, I have been through every page (many volumes and hundreds of pages) of the Camp Nelson post records. Every one of the documents in this series relates to Camp Nelson, but I transcribed by hand only selected reports, orders, telegrams, and letters, because the materials in this area were very repetitive, extraordinarily detailed, and frequently mundane and trivial. (In two of my week-long visits to the National Archives the single photocopier capable of copying large volumes of records was broken; everything had to be done by hand!) I tried to select representative correspondence and typical orders, while at the same time I paid special attention to interesting or significant events, following some of them as they developed through a series of chronological documents. In effect, I combed through everything in this area, but used only a very small percentage of the available texts.

In other records groups—Quartermaster General (RG 92), Adjutant General (RG 94), Inspector General (RG 159)—I was aided by the research of Professors Stephen and Kim McBride, who generously allowed me to use the documents they had dug out of the National Archives in their own lines of Camp Nelson projects. This material was invaluable to me, but I cannot claim that I examined whole archival collections in the process of locating it. I have no idea how much more Camp Nelson material exists in those record groups, but I am reasonably certain that the McBrides were very thorough in their searching.

Forms of Documents

The National Archives resources I have used appear in several different record groups, all of which are relatively difficult to locate within the repository itself. Researchers are interviewed and assisted by experts who guide them through large reference volumes describing the record groups, with their categories (parts), sub-categories (entries), and sub-sub-categories. I have tried to keep faithful and accurate records for citation of these materials, but subsequent researchers are hereby warned that the National Archives can change its filing systems (some records are designated in a palimpsest fashion, with the numbers and references of older systems still confusingly visible) and that the original system of military filing sometimes gives a better means of pinpointing particular sources than any of the later ones.

Most of the records I researched from Record Group 393 were materials from the Department of the Ohio series, more specifically, records of the District of Kentucky and, more specifically still, the post records from Camp Nelson. For the district and for the camp, records primarily took the form of large bound volumes of varying sizes (some of which, I believe, had scarcely been examined since the Civil War), mostly with printed page numbers of their own. Citations to these sources incorporate information from the National Archives filing system, plus the original volume numbers and page numbers, which were used in the original military filing systems. Some of these volumes are very easy to read, having been kept by adjutants with excellent handwriting and dependable supplies of pens and ink. (The post records of Camp Nelson display the handwriting of a great many different clerks, since clerks usually changed whenever commandants changed, and sometimes Camp Nelson got a new commandant every few days!) Some volumes, however—particularly those containing press copies—are terribly difficult to decipher. (Press copies are produced by wetting an original letter or order and pressing it upon a kind of onion skin paper to leave an impression; occasionally, such copies are smeared and unreadable on the day of production, much less some 130 years later.) In volumes of military orders, some documents are copied by clerks in their entirety with the designation "(Signed)" at the end followed by the name but not the original signature of the sender of the order. Some volumes, however, contain documents nearly all of which are signed by the commandant (or sender) himself, presumably at the time when he was checking the record book.

In Record Group 94, the Records of the Adjutant General's Office, a series within the Generals' Papers category contains the correspondence of Gen. Ambrose E. Burnside. Unlike the district and camp records mentioned above, these letters, orders, reports, and telegrams received are filed as individual pieces in boxes. The Quartermaster General and Inspector General records are also boxed. In its rules for citation of its holdings, the National Archives advises against giving box numbers because the filing system is liable to change (Nevertheless, I have given box numbers for some pieces, such as the collections consolidated under the names of Theron E. Hall and Mrs. Mary Scott, because they would otherwise be so difficult for any other researcher to find.)

Some of the records of the Bureau of Refugees, Freedmen, and Abandoned Lands are also individual pieces filed in boxes, but most of the Freedmen's Bureau materials I have transcribed are included in nineteen rolls from the microfilmed series M999, Records of the Assistant Commissioner for the State of Tennessee, Bureau of Refugees, Freedmen, and Abandoned Lands, 1865-1869. Rolls 1 through 19 of this 34 roll set contain all the Kentucky records (the Assistant Commissioner of Tennessee had jurisdiction over Kentucky from July 1865 until June 1866). Unlike the original documents in the National Archives, the microfilmed resources can be cited with absolute precision, to the very page, since each frame of microfilm has a number. A citation to the Freedmen's Bureau records from this source will include the microfilm symbol (M999), followed by a roll number, followed by a frame number: for example, M999:4:123 indicates the 123rd frame of the 4th roll of Microfilm Publication 999 of the National Archives.

Another important microfilmed resource is the AMAA in the Hutchins Library at Berea College, which owns the Ohio and the Kentucky series. The originals of the AMA letters are now housed in the Amistad Research Center in New Orleans, although they were once part of the collection of Fisk University in Nashville. Every piece of correspondence, arranged chronologically by state, in the AMA archives is stamped with a locating number; so a citation to one of these letters will read something like this: AMAA 44057. Unlike some of the military records mentioned above, the AMA letters were not written by people with dependable supplies of good-quality paper and reliable ink (many must have been almost unreadable for the original recipients), and they were not recorded once in a volume that was then safely closed. The AMA letters have all been in the U.S. mail, traveling from place to place, subject to wind and weather. A few have clearly been wet; some have been torn; pages may be missing; they have been handled by various people for well over a century; in short, many of the documents in this series are very difficult to decipher. If that were not enough of a problem, there is John G. Fee's extraordinarily difficult handwriting (concerning which I must now be the world's primary expert). I have been over some items of the AMA correspondence literally dozens of times to reach a conclusive reading, scanning some pieces with magnification and poring over individual letters of the alphabet. I have to say that I am very proud to see how few brackets containing the word "Indecipherable" remain in the AMA letters.

Editorial Method

Most of the pieces in this book are based on my own transcriptions from archival material, either the original documents (for most of the National Archives holdings) or microfilm.

My editorial method is based on the practices employed by the transcribers and editors of *Freedom: A Documentary History*, but with some innovations of my own. Since the items in my work are very numerous and diverse, it has proven impossible to imitate all of *Freedom*'s standards. For example, I have frequently presented only excerpts from longer letters and reports, and I have a system of my own for designating what has been left out. Three ellipses indicates that a portion of a single sentence has been omitted; four ellipses means a whole sentence is gone. A series of four asterisks stands for the omission of at least one full paragraph. In most instances, the four asterisks symbol are followed by brackets within which the number of missing paragraphs is reported. Especially in some personal letters, it may be important to have a sense of the length of the document, but for many reports and other military forms determining the exact size of the document may be impossible, and is not particularly useful anyway. I had originally planned to provide a summary of all omissions, but that proved to be impractical for two reasons: it would have taken up too much space, and it would have resulted in manifold irrelevant subjects being introduced. Over one hundred signing correspondents are represented in this book; their range of interests is vast, and what they write about in addition to the subjects in excerpted portions of their letters would fill several other books to whose hypothetical authors I feel little obligation.

For considerations of space, the place and date (spelled and punctuated as in the original) of all correspondence always appear together on the first line of the document, no matter where they appeared in the original. The signature and title(s) (as in the original) always appear together on the last line of the document. Complimentary closes, usually some variation of "Your obedient servant"—which can become as long as "I am General very sincerely your very humble and obedient servant," for example—are eliminated and their absence is marked by a single asterisk. In a few instances where a complimentary close was really original or otherwise meaningful in some way, it has been retained. Thus, for example, John G. Fee's "In haste" sometimes appears.

Other than the exceptions mentioned above, all documents from manuscript or microfilmed manuscript sources are transcribed exactly, with original capitalization, original punctuation (whether correct or not) or lack thereof, original spelling or misspelling, original paragraphing, and original underlining or double underlining (as in the common nineteenth-century method of providing emphasis). On occasion, when a writer has crossed out a word or passage, the material is printed as ~~canceled type~~. In cases where no punctuation occurs, sentence breaks are indicated by the addition of extra spaces. No *sic*'s appear in the text and no corrections unless the form of a word is so puzzling that no ordinary reader could figure it out. When bracketed material appears in the text it may take two different forms. If it is in standard typeface, a word in brackets is a highly probable reading of a word that actually appears in the original document; if it is in standard type but followed by a question mark, then the reading is problematic, but still represents what the text contains. Italics in brackets within the text always represent material that is not in the document itself, either a probable missing word or words, or an explanation that some passage is indecipherable with an estimation of the number of words involved, or some other editorial interpolation.

Documents written on letterhead or on official printed forms of some kind are given special treatment. In the case of letterhead, the form is indicated in brackets in italics [*Letterhead.*], and the printed words are presented in italics, but not in brackets. The same practice is followed with printed forms, such as those for telegrams: all the non-handwritten words are in italics, but not in brackets.

All documents are accompanied by citations to original sources in notes following each document, and—in many cases—by information notes identifying individuals or institutions mentioned in the texts, or providing general information for context or interpretation. An individual is identified in an information note only upon first mention, but any particular note can be found by consulting the index. No attempt has been made to identify absolutely everybody, for three reasons: (1) sometimes it is impossible, particularly if a person is mentioned only by surname and/or title; (2) sometimes it is irrelevant, because all the information about the person already appears in the text; (3) sometimes it is irrelevant, because the person is so well-known that any encyclopedia (or the Internet, for that matter) will give all the necessary information.

It is important to note that the items from the *Official Records* do not require complete formatting in the style described above, since that publication had formatting standards of its own. The words of each text from this source are reproduced precisely as in the published version, except where I have omitted passages originally included. The same is true for all other published texts, including "The Negro in the Military Service" (at least, in all its typescript pages), Newberry's report on the United States Sanitary Commission, the Marrs and Bruner memoirs, and Frances Dallam Peter's diary.

The documents that follow tell a consecutive story of life in Camp Nelson for the most dramatic and crucial years of its existence. My primary purpose in assembling this material was simply to allow the people who lived and worked, triumphed and suffered at Camp Nelson to speak for themselves, to tell their own tales, state their own opinions, and express their own emotions. Their voices are a permanent part of my consciousness.

Acknowledgments

I wish to express my gratitude to the employees of Berea College who helped me with various aspects of my research and writing over an extended time. The Professional Growth Committee funded many of my research trips for this project; Dean John Bolin offered encouragement and support for years; Eileen Hart and other members of the Hutchins Library staff gave me continual assistance with such mundane items as microfilm readers and photocopiers; Phyllis Gabbard gave me invaluable advice about computers, printers, ink cartridges, and so on. To all much thanks.

My special thanks go to Stephen and Kim McBride, whose scholarly generosity and expertise have delighted and helped me immeasurably.

I also wish to thank the Ohio Historical Society for permission to quote eight letters from the Abram McClellan Papers, the Tennessee State Library and Archives for permission to quote a letter in their Chapman Papers, and the Indiana Historical Society Library for permission to quote from the Joseph M. Rabb Papers and the diary of Oliver C. Haskell. As far as I am able to determine, all other works quoted in this book are either in the public domain or government documents requiring no permission.

Historical Introduction

Camp Nelson is very quiet now, very peaceful. But this is a place where many people suffered and died, where young black women wailed aloud for their dead and dying children, Rachel who could not be comforted. In this field an ardent and impassioned abolitionist preacher raised his voice again and again, encouraging throngs of young black men in uniform, urging them to fight for their own freedom and their own dignity. Here they cheered him on, ecstatic to hear his encouragement. Here the country's newest citizens heard their first news about voting and citizenship and equality.

The tramp of many soldiers marching, officers barking orders, the neighing and braying, hoof beats of thousands of horses and mules rounded up to supply the regiments on their way to battle in Tennessee. The sound of children's voices reciting their ABCs in the first schoolroom they have ever seen, a cold, empty barracks in a military camp.

It's midnight. A quaking old man stands behind a locked door listening to the curses of a band of drunken guerrillas; out in the torchlit street they are threatening his life, threatening his children's lives, setting his house on fire, because he's a white abolitionist and he is keeping a "nest of niggers."

There is the sound of spontaneous rejoicing, black people singing for joy. They have come by the thousands—13,322, to be exact—to receive their freedom papers at Camp Nelson.

One can imagine the crack of whips as benighted Union soldiers, like plantation overseers, drive the refugee slaves out of camp, hundreds of women and children, almost naked, shoeless, homeless, shivering with cold and starving. . . .

Camp Nelson is a haunted place.

Halfway through the Civil War, Union operations in the Western Theater had stalled under the leadership of Gen. William S. Rosecrans, commander of the Army of the Cumberland. Although Gen. Ulysses S. Grant's Army of the Tennessee had captured Nashville and won West Tennessee in February 1862, a large population of East Tennessee loyalists continued to suffer greatly under Confederate rule. Determined to liberate these loyal Southerners, Abraham Lincoln appointed Gen. Ambrose E. Burnside[1] as commandant of the Department of the Ohio[2] on March 16, 1863. Burnside, who enjoyed both the favor and trust of Lincoln, was to march upon

Knoxville from Lexington, Kentucky, with Rosecrans moving upon Chattanooga from Murfreesboro.[3]

Headquartered in Cincinnati, Ohio, Burnside firmly fixed his attention upon Kentucky, the offensive and defensive crux for the Department of the Ohio. The state's location made it the only possible launching site for an invasion of East Tennessee, as well as a vulnerable target for Confederate invaders. Kirby Smith had already successfully invaded Kentucky: his triumph at the Battle of Richmond in August 1862 led to temporary Confederate occupation of the state until the Union victory at Perryville in October. When Burnside took command the following spring, many politicians and military leaders believed that the Confederates would invade again soon, probably coming from East Tennessee through the Cumberland Gap and from southwestern Virginia through numerous mountain passes such as Pound Gap and Stone Gap.

Gen. Horatio G. Wright,[4] whose resignation resulted in Burnside's appointment, also considered an invasion likely, since the Kentucky division of the Department of the Ohio was very short on soldiers. The only time the department as a whole saw any significant action was when the enemy chose to cross the border into Kentucky, but when Kentucky was not being invaded, the state's forces were simply scaled back and sent to other states, some of which were relatively secure. As Wright pointed out, the Departments of the Tennessee and of the Cumberland, both massively involved in actual fighting, relied heavily on the Department of the Ohio for men and supplies, which could be moved to the appropriate destinations only through Kentucky.[5] Of course the Rebels wanted to invade Kentucky, virtually undefended and crucial to Union efforts in Tennessee and even farther south. Such an invasion, Kentucky's governor James F. Robinson cautioned, would be much more likely than Kirby Smith's to result in the Union's permanent loss of the state, because now, after the Emancipation Proclamation, Kentuckians were not so inclined to be loyal; they would welcome the Confederates, support them, shelter them, and supply them.[6]

Early on, Burnside was advised to consider a preemptive offense. Less than a week after assuming command of the department, he received a long letter from Henry W. Halleck,[7] General-in-Chief in Washington, urging him to invade East Tennessee; rather than waiting for the Confederates to invade Union territory, he should give them something else to think about, by taking Knoxville and by seizing and fortifying Cumberland Gap, perhaps other gaps as well. On the defensive side, Burnside was urged to concentrate his forces, including those from other states, somewhere in central Kentucky to protect crucial roads and railroads and to command the army breadbasket (and horse and mule farm) called the Bluegrass.[8] Halleck neglected to emphasize the immense difficulty of the operation he was suggesting. General Wright had stated only a week before Halleck's letter that he regarded "an invasion of East Tennessee by any of the direct routes through Kentucky as an impossibility," because an army from Kentucky going south into Tennessee would be forced to sustain itself with supplies from central Kentucky, "over a country of bad

roads, nearly destitute of forage and subsistence, and where everything is to be supplied by wagons from the rear." Since the distance involved would be at least two
hundred miles, it would be impossible because a wagon could "scarcely take the
forage necessary for its teams, leaving nothing for subsistence, ammunition, camp
equipage, &c."[9] Subsequent events bore out most of Wright's analysis. He was absolutely right about all the difficulties, but he was mistaken in thinking the invasion
was "impossible." He did not reckon with the (perhaps foolhardy) courage of Ambrose
E. Burnside.

     Burnside, whose previous service had included some signal successes in North
Carolina and a major defeat at Fredericksburg, Virginia, was simply determined to
invade East Tennessee; Lincoln had personally entrusted him with liberating the
region.[10] He never swerved from his goal, even in the face of monumental difficulties. Burnside began his mission by creating his Army of the Ohio, combining the
Ninth Army Corps[11] and the Twenty-third Army Corps.[12] The Ninth, en route
from the Army of the Potomac in Virginia to rejoin their former general, consisted
of seasoned regiments recruited early in the war from Massachusetts, Rhode Island,
New Hampshire, Pennsylvania, New York, and Michigan; whereas the Twenty-third,
with regiments drawn from within the Department of the Ohio, had troops—some
of them very green—from Michigan, Indiana, Illinois, and Ohio, as well as Tennessee and Kentucky.[13]

     So eager was Burnside to begin his campaign that on the second day of his
command he ordered troops "to keep constantly on hand three days' cooked rations
and sixty rounds of ammunition . . . when they are ordered to march."[14] While
awaiting the arrival of his Ninth Army Corps and making the numerous preparations required by the proposed invasion, Burnside took offensive action by sending
Brig. Gen. Julius White[15] into West Virginia and Col. W.P. Sanders[16] into East Tennessee. Sanders, laying waste to much enemy materiel and numerous railway bridges,
led "one of the boldest and longest raids made during the war" to gain valuable
information on possible routes for later attacks on the region.[17]

The Site for Camp Nelson

The formidable tasks of establishing and operating a suitable camp preoccupied
Burnside between March 25, when he took command, and August 16, when he
actually marched off with his regiments toward Tennessee. Four closely related stra-
tegic objectives influenced the site selection for the camp that would become (as
intended) one of the Union Army's most important supply depots and, shortly
thereafter (and patently not as intended), Kentucky's largest recruiting station for
black soldiers: the first objective was to protect Hickman Bridge; the second, to
prepare for the potential invasion of Tennessee; the third, to seize the Cumberland
Gap; and the fourth, to consolidate troops in central Kentucky.

     A covered wooden structure built in 1838 and the only bridge crossing the
Kentucky River above Frankfort, Hickman Bridge[18] was essential to any invasion of

Tennessee through Kentucky. Gen. John Hunt Morgan and five hundred of his raiders had threatened to burn the vulnerable bridge in their raid of October 1862,[19] prompting the military brass of the Department of the Ohio to fortify it with defensive batteries by January 1863.[20] The most serious threat to the bridge virtually coincided with Burnside's spring arrival in the Department of the Ohio. Confederate generals John Pegram[21] and Humphrey Marshall[22] were raiding central Kentucky in March 1863; some of their forces were ensconced in Garrard County, and the Union forces, under command of Col. Frank Wolford[23] across the river in Jessamine County, believed that the Confederate numbers were so large they could not be successfully attacked. Capt. Samuel Boone, commander of a company of the First Kentucky Cavalry, reported: "At Hickman Bridge . . . we were housed up from the 24th, of March, 1863, until the morning of the 28th. The floor of the fine arched turnpike bridge, which had stood the storms of twenty-five years unscathed, was taken up, and the bridge ordered to be burned in certain contingencies."[24] So Colonel Wolford was poised to burn the bridge to prevent an attack by the Rebels crossing the Kentucky River to the northern side.

Two Unionist sympathizers in Lancaster, Mrs. Dr. H. Jackman[25] and Mrs. Margaret G. Vaughan, learned accidentally—by overhearing Confederate officers boasting—that the number of Confederate troops in Garrard County was really quite small, only some twenty-five hundred. The women undertook two days of riding on horseback and crossing a swollen river (they could not cross on Hickman Bridge, which was guarded by Rebels on the southern side) to inform Wolford, who quickly pursued the not-so-strong Rebels and drove them out of Kentucky. And he did not torch the bridge, but rather ordered the flooring replaced.[26]

In addition to defending the all-important Hickman Bridge, Burnside needed to establish a camp of instruction in central Kentucky that was suitable for gathering, training, and quartering large numbers of soldiers and also capable of serving as a fortified supply depot for troops moving into the relatively barren, forageless territory of East Tennessee and southeastern Kentucky's Cumberland Gap. On April 25, 1863, when Burnside sent out officers to select a site, all the elements for their choice were clearly established.[27] In a report headed "Surveys for Military Defenses," James H. Simpson,[28] major of engineers wrote: "Between the 27th and 29th of April, by direction of Major-General Burnside, I, with Captain Dickerson,[29] chief quartermaster, selected a site for a large depot, 6 miles beyond Nicholasville, between a bend of the Kentucky River and Hickman Creek,[30] on its west side, distant from Lexington on the Danville pike 18 miles. Lieutenant-Colonel Babcock,[31] assistant inspector-general and chief engineer, District of Central Kentucky, has been directed to me, under instructions from Major-General Burnside, to fortify the area, embracing about 4 ¼ square miles."[32]

In hindsight, his choice of a site seems almost inevitable: Camp Nelson, named for the recently murdered Union general, would be located in southern Jessamine County, on the north side of the palisades of the Kentucky River, at Hickman Bridge on the Lexington-Danville Turnpike, near Nicholasville, Danville, Lancaster, Lexington, Lebanon, Richmond—close to the many routes south to Tennessee, the many roads leading to the gaps. It was a hub, really a perfectly central spot.

Morgan's Raid of July 1863

While Burnside waited to begin his larger offensive against East Tennessee—one of the most dramatic periods of the entire war, with the siege of Vicksburg and the Battle of Gettysburg[33]—Gen. John Hunt Morgan[34] and his raiders swept, unpredictably, through Kentucky on their way to "invade" Indiana and Ohio. Apparently, Morgan had intended this eccentric and ultimately pointless military exercise when he left his base in East Tennessee, but no one could have predicted it, not even his commanding officer, who had forbidden such a foolhardy enterprise. Throughout the month of July 1863, Morgan and his Confederates kept the Kentucky district of the Department of the Ohio constantly on the alert and occasionally in battle. General Burnside and all his subordinate generals were determined to track Morgan down and destroy him, and the raiders were repeatedly sighted and rumored to be in various locations: in Campbellsville, Lebanon, Harrodsburg, Springfield, Bardstown, within fifteen miles of Danville, moving it was believed toward Lexington, in Bloomfield, in Columbia, in Brandenburg, and so on. On July 6, Morgan was reported to be on his way from Danville to Hickman Bridge. "After destroying Government stores there," the reporter, one Major Elisha Mix of the Eighth Michigan Cavalry, stated, "he was going with his whole command to Louisville."[35] The truth is that Union officers usually did not know where quixotic Morgan and his troops were located or where they intended to go.

Wherever he was, Morgan was being chased indefatigably—Burnside's ordered his troops to pursue Morgan "to the extremity of endurance of . . . horses and men." He advised his generals—Gen. George L. Hartsuff at Camp Nelson, Gen. Jeremiah T. Boyle at Louisville, and Gen. Edward H. Hobson at Lebanon—". . . After ascertaining as near as possible the direction of General Morgan's route, you will endeavor to overtake him or cut him off. . . . You are authorized to subsist your commands upon the country and impress the necessary horses to replace the broken down ones. . . . Morgan ought to be broken to pieces before he gets out of the state."[36] Morgan did get out of the state, advancing into Indiana by July 8, thence into Ohio on the 13th, and into captivity on July 26.

All this action took place within the Department of the Ohio and all of it occupied Gen. Ambrose Burnside. But even in the midst of the turmoil, he had ordered "the whole available command in the State [to be] put in readiness for a rapid movement as soon as Morgan is driven out."[37] The buildup at Burnside's new supply depot at Hickman Bridge had continued throughout the July furor, with work proceeding on roads and fortifications. Morgan's Ohio Raid, a very dramatic, drastic, and frightening event, received a lot of attention, but it really did not delay Burnside's projected invasion of Tennessee, except by putting some Union regiments out of position for a few days.

Waiting for the Ninth Corps

Although Burnside announced that he was ready to move toward East Tennessee on June 3, the Ninth Corps[38] was ordered out of Kentucky on the same day to assist General Grant at the siege of Vicksburg,[39] effectively stalling the attack on Tennessee until August 16. When a Union victory ensued in Mississippi one day after the July 3, 1863, Gettysburg triumph, Burnside set off from Cincinnati for central Kentucky on August 11 expecting his regiments to be marched back to spearhead his own operation. Apparently, he had not yet realized that he was awaiting a few thousand very sick men suffering from malaria and other illnesses that plagued Northern armies when they reached the Deep South; the Ninth Corps that Burnside had loaned to Grant was coming back to Kentucky all right, but more than eight thousand men had been sent off, and barely six thousand were returning, greatly delayed and "too sick for any but the lightest duty."[40]

Gen. Ambrose Burnside, the putative founder of Camp Nelson, spent less than a week at Camp Nelson,[41] arriving late on the evening of August 11 and departing on August 16. During that time he issued many orders from the camp, including the optimistic order of August 13 informing Rosecrans that he would "endeavor" to start three brigades of cavalry and one infantry division by August 15.[42] While at the new supply depot, Burnside received the news that Ninth Corps commander Gen. John Parke had reached Cincinnati, a message that put the general in a very good humor. So that Parke could join him, Burnside immediately countermanded his order that the staff be ready to leave for Tennessee within an hour. Instead of the planned departure, a party was held at Camp Nelson on Saturday night, August 15. Burnside's assistant adjutant general described the festivities: "After tea we all went down to the cabins & had a real old fashioned dance—three old nigger fiddlers & a nigger prompter Mrs Capt Bell, Mrs Col Hanly & the young ladies from the cottage together with the General & staff danced two or three cottillins & then the niggers had a break down."[43] After the party was over, Burnside returned to his lodging, where he found Parke, looking very ill and bearing the desperately disappointing news that the rest of the corps was as sick as he. Burnside regretted having summoned Parke to Camp Nelson from Cincinnati and sent the ailing general back to the city the next morning.[44] These incidents in Burnside's personal experience at Camp Nelson symbolize the much larger pattern of Camp Nelson's development as a supply depot for the Army of the Ohio: the first part optimistic, even enthusiastic; the second, almost totally disappointing.

The invasion of Tennessee had to begin anyway. On August 16, Burnside and his army of almost fifteen thousand men launched their march from the new supply depot and camp of instruction that the general had founded, a camp that had been built up throughout the time of rather frantic arrivals and departures of regiments, throughout the period of near hysteria because of Morgan's raid.

Struggling toward East Tennessee

In spite of its special location and the care with which it was selected, Camp Nelson virtually failed in fulfilling most of the military goals that called it into being. It did succeed in averting any potential raid on Hickman Bridge and on itself; despite many episodes when Camp Nelson was supposedly threatened with enemy attack, such an attack never came. But when General Burnside actually invaded East Tennessee, the supply lines from Camp Nelson to his troops, some two hundred miles distant, were so bad, as predicted, the muddy roads so nearly impassable for so long, as predicted, that the whole enterprise was endangered; food and provisions were almost impossible to deliver, as predicted. Although Camp Nelson itself was sometimes incredibly well equipped, hundreds of the animals that the camp was designed to provision starved to death, and many of the men who depended on supplies from Camp Nelson suffered great hardships and deprivations during their sojourn in Knoxville, Cumberland Gap, and other sites in Tennessee.

Supplying soldiers with materiel was always the chief concern, but horses and mules constituted Camp Nelson's biggest responsibility (by far) during the first year of its operation. Very early on, even before the invasion of Tennessee began, Camp Nelson was having difficulty supplying horses and feed. On August 4, 1863, Capt. T.E. Hall[45] sent a telegram to General Burnside that was a harbinger of many more to come. At that point, Camp Nelson was not prepared to issue any horses, although Hall had a mule train ready, and he was generally hopeful, even though forage was coming in too slowly.[46] Six days later, Hall telegraphed Col. Charles Goulding[47] that he had no forage on hand, although a large amount was due from Covington, and a "large train of Corn" had been sent to Stanford the day before.[48]

At first, mules were more readily available than horses. On August 11, Camp Nelson had 550 mule teams on hand (each was a 4-mule team), and 348 teams on detached service taking supplies out to regiments; the quartermaster's department had issued 175 6-mule teams, and, in addition, there were 600 serviceable mules at the camp.[49] In a cable sent that day, however, Hall described how the horse problem was being compounded: not only was he required to provide horses for the troops preparing to invade East Tennessee, horses by the hundreds were being sent back from the front to Camp Nelson with the expectation that they would immediately be replaced with fresh mounts. On the night of August 11, Hall received requisitions for 1,500 horses and 800 mules from one division of the Twenty-third Army Corps;[50] these requests not only exceeded the number of horses available, but even the number of mules. And the invasion had not yet begun.

Still, John H. Dickerson, chief quartermaster of the Department of the Ohio, was able to ship Hall 1,500 horses from Cincinnati two days later, and he expected 600 more, although he remarked, "there appears to be some difficulty in getting Horses at Louisville." But at Camp Nelson the demand for horses continued unabated; on August 17, Hall needed 233 more, and he asked Burnside if he could buy "poor horses at an extravagant price." Meanwhile, more and more mule trains were being sent out from the camp, about 175 loaded with commissary stores on the seventeenth. With the invasion of East Tennessee exactly two days old, the crisis was already becoming clear: on August 18, Hall was expecting 1,000 horses that very night, but he was still purchasing "Every Horse I can get my hands on." His department, he reported, was "crippled for want of transportation" because now "nearly Every serviceable team" (that is, every mule team) was gone.[51]

Then a new problem emerged: on August 20, Hall had five hundred horses at Camp Nelson ready to go. "I have on hand more horses than men to receive them   what shall I do with them?" he asked Burnside. This problem—having what was needed without the means to deliver it—became, from that point on, the main one. And it was not just a matter of horses. For example, on September 8, a train of fifteen wagons loaded with ammunition was stalled in London waiting for its forage to arrive from Crab Orchard.[52]

On September 11, Hall cabled to Gen. Robert B. Potter:[53] "General Burnside wants 3,000 horses. I have no way of sending them to him. Can you assist me in any way?" Then he cabled to Burnside to say he was about to start 3,000 horses toward Tennessee and to ask if a guard could meet the herd at Crab Orchard "or at wherever they can." But simultaneously he was wiring General Potter again to report that he had no men to take the horses to Burnside. Gen. Speed S. Fry, commanding the post, was forced to order men from the Convalescent Camp out as drivers because it was "impossible to procure a sufficient number of teamsters to take charge of teams required to transport stores to front."[54] The situation was so serious that Secretary of War Edwin M. Stanton had issued a direct order at the end of November to employ Kentucky slaves as teamsters.[55] By Christmas day, teamsters were so important that it was forbidden to enlist them, since "the necessity for teamsters [was] as pressing as that for soldiers."[56]

The men in the field were all too aware of the transportation problems. Capt. William W. Buckley participated in the march to East Tennessee across the Cumberland Mountains, which began on August 16 and ended (for his unit) on September 4, with his arrival at Loudon, Tennessee; he reported that the march was 230 miles long, "extremely hard on both men and animals." By mid-October, as Buckley returned to Knoxville, he "lost 12 horses from no other cause than their being totally exhausted for want of rest and food."[57] By mid-November he described the roads as being in "dreadful condition." It was almost impossible to move artillery, because the horses were completely worn out. Burnside ordered ten mule teams turned over to Buckley's artillery unit, which burned the wagons the mules had been pulling; but artillery was still almost impossible to move, because axles were breaking on the caissons. By early December, Buckley reported, "A great many of my horses were burned as unserviceable, as I could not get forage for them." In addition, the troops were running low on ammunition; they had "drawn no clothing of any kind since leaving Cincinnati," and some of them were barefooted. The weather was becoming quite cold, but it was impossible to get anything over the mountains, whether the roads were muddy or frozen. Buckley's men had "not drawn over one-half rations of coffee and sugar since the 28th day of August, and a great part of that time it [had] been but one-quarter rations, and sometimes none at all." They had a little hard bread; their diet consisted of flour and fresh beef. "The flour," Buckley complained, "they can only cook to make it hardly eatable, as they have nothing to mix with it." They had had no beans, rice or vegetables since leaving Cincinnati, and "only in a great while, candles and soap."[58]

Writing from Cumberland Gap, late in November, Gen. Orlando B. Willcox described the situation to his wife: "After a rain storm the weather has turned severely cold & frozen up the roads & the dreadful mud, but the men & the horses & mules suffer both with the cold & short rations. . . . The men have been sometimes two & three days without bread & a few scanty ears of corn without hay have to do for the horses."[59] In Knoxville also the situation was very grave. Maj. Gen. John G. Foster, commanding the Department of the Ohio from its Tennessee headquarters, reported on December 14: "The infantry force is very much reduced in numbers by sickness arising from want of supplies, both in kind and quantity, of camp equipage, and of medicines. The vacant buildings of this town are full of sick. Of the Twenty-third and Ninth Corps, only 10,000 men are able to march and fight. I would, therefore, request that my old division, of the Ninth Corps, may be ordered from Virginia (Old Point Comfort) to Camp Nelson, whence I can order it where most needed."[60]

The most graphic and disturbing descriptions came from Gen. Jacob D. Cox, who was ordered on December 2 "to report in person to the general commanding in East Tennessee." His eight-day journey from Lexington to Knoxville gave him, he wrote,

> a vivid appreciation of the impossibility of supplying an army in East Tennessee by wagon trains over the mountains. . . . The forage was exhausted all along all the routes, and till grass should grow large trains of supplies were not to be thought of. The effort to force trains through in the autumn had been most destructive to the teams. Noticing how the way was lined by the carcasses of dead horses and mules, we kept an accurate count one day of the number of these. In the twenty miles of that day's journey we counted a hundred and fifty dead draught animals.[61]

Among the men, according to Cox,

> The want most felt was that of clothing and shoes. The supply of these had run very low by the time Burnside had marched through Kentucky and Tennessee to Knoxville, and almost none had been received since. Many of the soldiers were literally in rags, and none were prepared for winter . . . . Their shoes were worn out, and this, even more than their raggedness, made winter marching out of the question. The barefooted

men had to be left behind, and of those who started the more poorly shod would straggle, no matter how good their own will or how carefully the officers tried to enforce discipline and keep their men together. (89)

Despite the difficulties, General Burnside had taken Knoxville on September 3. General Cox wrote an eyewitness account of Burnside's reception as a great liberator:

> The advent of the army into East Tennessee was, to its loyal people, a resurrection from the grave. Their joy had an exultation which seemed almost beyond the power of expression. Old men fell down fainting and unconscious under the stress of their emotions as they saw the flag at the head of the column and tried to cheer it! Women wept with happiness as their husbands stepped out of the ranks of the loyal Tennessee regiments when these came marching by the home. These men had gathered in little recruiting camps on the mountain-sides and had found their way to Kentucky, traveling by night and guided by the pole-star, as the dark-skinned fugitives from bondage had used to make their way to freedom. Their families had been marked as traitors to the Confederacy, and had suffered sharpest privations and cruel wrong on account of the absence of the husband and father, the brother, or the son. Now it was all over, and a jubilee began in those picturesque valleys in the mountains, which none can understand who had not seen the former despair and the present revulsion of happiness. (528–29)

Burnside and his troops seized Cumberland Gap on September 9, attacking it simultaneously from both the north and the south. Taking Knoxville and Cumberland Gap was the easiest part of the Burnside's campaign; holding on to them was a greater challenge, and, in some cases, simply enduring was the greatest of all. Although the total operation was ultimately successful, contributing significantly to the Union victory in the war of the West, Burnside's invasion of East Tennessee very nearly failed on the basis of the *misplacement* of his depot at Camp Nelson.

Camp Nelson certainly contributed, in a desperate and frustrating way, to this victory, in spite of being almost totally inadequate—hampered by virtually every possible condition that could not be helped: distance, weather, seasons, terrain, conditions of roads, absence of railroads—through no fault of anyone except its planners. Burnside himself (who was certainly the individual most responsible for the choice of Camp Nelson's location) reported to General Grant the "great difficulty in transporting supplies over the long lines between [Knoxville] and Camp Nelson."[62] As bad as its record was, there may not have been a place in Kentucky that could have rendered better service in Camp Nelson's difficult mission.

With the victory the tide of horses and mules literally turned in January 1864. Special Orders No. 24—sent to Headquarters of the Department of the Ohio, now in Knoxville, where the siege had ended—specified what the occupying army was to do with its animals. All horses fit for cavalry duty were to be turned over to dismounted men, but "all other serviceable wagons and animals" were to be "made up, as fast as possible, into trains and sent to Camp Nelson, Ky., for supplies." (Refugees who wanted to leave the country were furnished transportation on such trains, as were sick and disabled soldiers.) The rest of the horses and mules would be inspected and those judged capable of recuperation were to be sent to Kentucky for rest and relaxation, while those that were condemned should be sold to local citizens.[63] In short, most of the surviving mounts that had been sent from Camp Nelson to Knoxville were going back.

By the end of January, Capt. T.E. Hall, assistant quartermaster at Camp Nelson, had to start one thousand horses to General Willcox "to remount the cavalry"; but Willcox reported that his men were low on ammunition, and "suffering for food." Unfortunately, "the road to Camp Nelson had become impassable for wagons," and Willcox had to scatter his command "for forage and subsistence." Capt. W.G. McCreary, chief signal officer of the Department of the Ohio, declared that all of his signal wagons had broken on his journey into Tennessee; the first one broke going down Wild Cat Mountain, and he "requested a returning train to take it back to Camp Nelson to be repaired if possible."[64] In report after report, the story is the same.

In April 1864 Quartermaster General M.C. Meigs summarized precisely how bad the situation with horses and mules had been. "Operations last fall and winter," he reported, "destroyed or broke down in Tennessee and Georgia not less that 30,000 draft animals and an unknown number of cavalry horses." There had been more animals "in East Tennessee than it was possible to feed," and even by the time of his report "the animals sent to the rear from East Tennessee and Chattanooga [were] not yet fit for service," although 1,000 mules had been sent to Nashville from Camp Nelson on April 12.[65]

Grant and Sherman's Assessments of Camp Nelson

Despite decisive Union victories in the Chattanooga Campaign in November 1863, the suffering of the soldiers in the region was far from over. Gen. Ulysses S. Grant, the victorious Union commander, went in person to inspect the state of affairs in East Tennessee, reaching Knoxville on December 30. There he saw plainly "that the great problem . . . was the clothing and subsistence of the troops. . . ." Determined to form his own judgment, he rode over the mountains from Tennessee to Kentucky by way of Cumberland Gap to see for himself if the supply route was really impassable. He traveled on horseback in sub-zero temperatures; "the weather had hardly moderated at all when he left . . . on the 4th of January."[66] Reporting the results of his visits to Knoxville and into Kentucky, Grant stated "that he found the troops so destitute of clothing and shoes that not more than two-thirds of them could march; that the difficulty of supplying them even with food was so great that it was not advisable to send reinforcements. . . . Of his own journey he said, 'From the personal inspection made, I am satisfied that no portion of our supplies can be hauled by teams from Camp Nelson.'"[67]

In the spring of 1864, when Camp Nelson itself was inspected for General Grant, the site was in grave danger of being "broken up entirely" at his command. The military operation that it had been established to support had been successfully executed, partly in spite of Camp Nelson, and all of its most noteworthy features now seemed, in Grant's assessment, "a wasteful extravagance"[68]; the supply depot had basically lost its original function, while assuming a great many others, some of which now seemed pointless.

Gen. William Tecumseh Sherman recommended gradually diminishing Camp Nelson, rather than discontinuing it "absolutely": provisions for Knoxville and the rest of East Tennessee were no longer such a problem once Chattanooga with its railroad was in the hands of the Union. Eastern Kentucky, according to Sherman, would be better supplied from a camp near Prestonsburg, but it would prove impossible to construct a large-scale supply depot there. Camp Nelson remained in place, eventually trying to cope with a military emergency in Eastern Kentucky on the line to Cumberland Gap, which would once again tax the camp's resources, although not as drastically as the Tennessee Campaign had done. It would continue as a supply depot of sorts until the last soldier posted there had departed.

More than anything else, the exigencies of black recruitment extended Camp Nelson's military significance and its official existence. Once the enlistment of Kentucky's slave men was in full swing, Camp Nelson quickly became the biggest black recruitment center in the whole state (and third largest in the nation), and after that no one recommended closing the camp until the war was over.

But in the wake of the success of the East Tennessee invasion, after the subsidence of the big military emergency that had created such insurmountable problems for Camp Nelson, there was a growing chorus of hostile criticism, severe disapproval of Camp Nelson's "extravagant" development, its size, its numerous buildings, its multifaceted operations. Why was Camp Nelson so big and so costly? Army inspectors asked, apparently forgetting that virtually every structure at the camp had been expressly ordered for a sufficient military reason, that its accumulations of stores and equipment had once been deemed absolutely necessary, that its functions had all been adopted by command.

Buildings and Fortifications

Because it was so crucial at first, Camp Nelson was built up rapidly, expensively, and expansively: it quickly and probably inevitably became a huge operation. The sheer numbers of horses and mules, for example, were simply staggering; add to the animals everything to equip them: harness, bridles, saddles, horseshoes, horseshoe nails, packs, wagons; everything to feed them: corn, hay, forage, mountains of forage to be obtained and somehow transported over long, rough, muddy, precipitous, almost impassable roads. And, of course, the soldiers had to be fed, clad, shod, armed, trained, assembled, sheltered, sometimes imprisoned, and/or hospitalized. The list becomes unimaginable, and for all these requirements the only recourse seemed to be—in the emergency of the moment—to add to the camp, stables, factories, blacksmith shops, corrals, officers' quarters, mess halls, barracks, hospitals, tent cities, Soldiers' Home, prison, bakery, laundry, sawmills, waterworks, more and more.

The growth of Camp Nelson's physical plant and the increase in its functions were trajectories that continued from its inception through the arrival of Freedmen's Bureau agents who intended to close the Refugee Camp, Camp Nelson's final wartime purpose. In the rather wild and disorganized beginnings of the camp, the supply depot burgeoned, always growing to meet increasing demands, and more increasing demands, and then different demands, and so on. One pattern of operation could never suffice. It was not possible simply to adopt the most efficient, orderly means of supplying horses and mules, for example, and then repeat it indefinitely. Nor was it possible to feed the animals on a simple, regular schedule. Even the soldiers themselves could not be provisioned adequately—with food, clothing, or shelter—on a *regular* basis, no matter what anyone did.

Construction continued indefinitely. Through virtually every month of Camp Nelson's existence as an active military installation, something was being built there, including, of course, the camp's extensive fortifications. In addition, Camp Nelson became the center of a network of sub-depots, which also had to be (in some cases) constructed, supplied, and supervised, including Camp Burnside, Paris, London, Cumberland Gap, Nicholasville, Frankfort, Lexington, and Crab Orchard.[69]

Even a partial listing of the building projects at Camp Nelson during its first year conveys both the extent and variety of its physical structures and the magnitude of its responsibilities in the war effort. On June 8, 1863, General Burnside himself directed Capt. T.E. Hall (as he is always called in official documents) to "take charge of the construction of the Depot at Hickmans Bridge relieving Capt J.H. Pratt A Q M."[70] About a month later (July 14), Hall was instructed to go beyond the usual buildings for a supply depot—perhaps for the first time—by erecting a prison. Wondering how many prisoners to expect (there were already 160 "of different grades" at the camp), Hall telegraphed to Burnside to ask for directions.[71] The order to erect a "Military Prison and Barracks" within the lines of the camp" became official on August 5, and the construction was to be undertaken "as speedily as possible."[72] At about the same time (on July 29), Burnside ordered Hall to "erect the necessary buildings for a Hospital at Hickmans Bridge Kentucky, in conformity with the plans furnished by Surgeon Shumard, U S Vols."[73]

By August 21, two warehouses, one for quartermasters and one for subsistence stores, were required.[74] On September 1, General Burnside directed that "barracks be erected at Camp Nelson capable of accommodating five hundred invalids," thus formally providing for the Convalescent Camp. Two days later, Gen. Speed S. Fry ordered "an office built at these Head Quarters at the earliest practicable moment, Dimensions of office 20 ft by 30 ft."[75]

Special Orders No. 58 commanded Capt. Hall to construct a waterworks for

Camp Nelson immediately, because "the General Commanding can see no other way by which troops at this post can receive a sufficient supply of water."[76] This particular construction was to win Hall and Camp Nelson a great deal of criticism; again and again, Hall would be forced to defend himself for having built the water-works and having spent money in the process. In February 1864 the surgeon in charge of the Nelson United States General Hospital at Camp Nelson, Daniel Meeker, urged the construction of a laundry since the existing facilities were "totally inad-equate."[77] The same month, quarters for the commanding officer, a mess room for the men and "a suitable store-room for the public property" were ordered.[78]

During the winter of 1863–64, the Soldiers' Home[79] at Camp Nelson was under construction for the use of the United States Sanitary Commission; it was nearly complete by February, when its initials occupants were refugees, starving, poverty-stricken people from East Tennessee and southeastern Kentucky. When it had become obvious that for military reasons Burnside might have to abandon the Knoxville region, loyal citizens who had been rejoicing were suddenly stricken with terror. The Confederates would regain the territory and make Union sympathizers suffer even more than they had suffered before their supposed rescue. According to Cox, "the terror in East Tennessee, when it became known that they were likely to be abandoned, was something fearful" (542). People swarmed north by the thou-sands, fleeing from the hardships they had incurred from both armies. All along the escape route of the armies, food was scarce, partly because the ill-equipped soldiers had been forced to pillage. General Foster reported from Knoxville: "The people of this country, from the presence of hostile armies in their midst since the opening of the war, are rendered nearly destitute. These armies have rarely paid for what has been taken by foraging parties. Over $100,000 in claims are now here for settle-ment, and more than this is outstanding."[80] One of the places the impoverished refugees found succor was Camp Nelson, squarely on the route of the Union sol-diers coming back from Tennessee, where food and shelter were provided for hun-dreds. A report of the United States Sanitary Commission described the situation at Camp Nelson:

> Very soon after the establishment of this military post, and after General Burnside's army had opened the region of Southeastern Kentucky and East Tennessee, nearly every Quartermaster's train brought more or less families from their poverty-stricken homes into camp. The war, as con-ducted by the rebels, soon made property and homes of the South unten-able to high and low, rich and poor of her own people, and uncovered to the gaze and sympathy of the world the enormous ignorance and wretch-edness of scores of thousands of her poor citizens. . . . The refugees were in many instances compelled to leave their homes and all they possessed to save their lives, while the majority started for this "city of refuge" because their fathers, husbands and brothers were in the army, and no men were left to afford them protection and provide them subsistence.[81]

Some of these people were sent out of the camp soon after they arrived, typically to Cincinnati, but many of them were too needy and debilitated to go any farther, and they remained, cared for by Sanitary Commission workers and grudgingly sustained by the Union Army. Of all the denizens of Camp Nelson, these people were—perhaps surprisingly—on the lowest social level, ignored and disregarded by virtually everyone. Although the later masses of black refugees received a great deal of attention, favorable and unfavorable, from officials in the camp, military brass, missionaries, and reporters throughout the United States, as well as from Camp Nelson's letter writers, the Appalachian refugees went almost unmentioned.[82]

The first soldiers to benefit from the Soldiers' Home, designed expressly for their comfort, arrived on March 1: the Fourth Kentucky Volunteer Infantry, which had left "all their camp equipage" in Georgia. The staff of the Home, given only a few hours warning, stuffed bed sacks, rearranged furniture, and at the end of a dark, cold, snowy day, welcomed almost three hundred men, who otherwise would been "left to crawl into sundry open buildings, where cattle might be content to remain and suffer." This visit Thomas Butler of the U.S. Sanitary Commission identified as "the Soldiers' Home's natal hour," from which time the facility would rescue thousands of soldiers from "hunger and a shelterless bed."[83]

In March more new buildings were ordered: "barracks for the accommodation of the companies of the Second Ohio Heavy Artillery at Camp Nelson," as well as "buildings for commissary stores sufficient to store two millions of rations, . . . corrals and feeding sheds sufficient to feed and care for the necessary number of animals to provide for the Army of the Ohio, . . . work shops, and all other needful buildings therefore."[84]

During the same construction period, work was proceeding apace on the fortifications at the camp. Even before Camp Nelson was begun, General Burnside had been informed that the fortifications he contemplated would have to be constructed "by the troops and contrabands."[85] All the troops, as it turned out, were needed in actual military operations, and that left contrabands. From the beginning the primary laborers on Camp Nelson's fortifications were black men. When Lt. Col. Orville E. Babcock presented the first proposal (May 19, 1863) for an entrenched camp at Hickman Bridge, he already expected to procure "a large gang of negroes to do this work."[86]

On June 22, 1863, Capt. Orlando M. Poe, chief engineer of the Twenty-third Army Corps proceeded to Hickman Creek to commence work "upon the Entrenched Camp at that place."[87] In addition to workers, Poe needed equipment, some of it rather difficult to come by on short notice. For example, on July 8, Poe was shipped "1 Bdle containing 4 cross cut Saws 1 Rip Saw and 6 Bdls Twine, with the *prospect* [my emphasis] of shipping 100 Wheel Barrows to day, but regret very much to inform you that it has been impossible for me to ship them. . . ."[88] Of more military significance, a requisition "for guns to arm the fortifications at Camp Nelson" was approved on July 30.[89] According to a report of July 31, both Fort Nelson and Fort Jackson, in spite of the difficulties involved in constructing them, were already defensible, and a new battery had been commenced; Captain Poe was now in charge of an engineer battalion, already numbering 150 men, being formed from infantry regiments in the Twenty-third Army Corps. His black laborers, some of whom had been temporarily returned to their masters to work in the harvest, were still doing all the strenuous toil involved in the project.[90] In addition, "Hickmans Bridge" was considered "a proper place to sentence prisoners to work at hard labor by Court Martial."[91]

As they had on the entrenchments and forts, contrabands, impressed slaves, and prisoners served as the chief laborers on the road and railroad projects. In the same report announcing that the site for Camp Nelson had been chosen, J.H. Simpson, Major of Engineers, discussed some of the roads: "The direct road from Crab Orchard toward Cumberland Gap I have had, by direction of General Burnside, examined as far as a point 18 miles beyond London, with a view, if possible, to its being metaled or planked." Wagon roads between Camp Nelson and Cumberland Gap, "about Somerset, and thence to Jamestown, Columbia, Campbellsville, and Lebanon" were inspected "with a view to ascertain the best route for forwarding supplies." There was plenty to be done on the roads now that they were military routes, and on August 10, 1863, General Orders No 41 was issued commanding the impressment of 6,000 laborers "from the negro population" to do the work. These impressed slaves were to be concentrated at Camp Nelson.[92]

Railroads also required workers; on August 17, General Boyle requested that contrabands from various points in Tennessee, especially runaways from Kentucky, be sent to Camp Nelson as part of the railroad gang. The next day, Gen. Speed S. Fry seconded Boyle's request, in a telegram to Burnside stating: "I learn there is a great many runaway Slaves in the different Camps of the Army of the Ohio not in Ky   If consistent with your views I should like to have an order to get them & place them on the public works at this Post on R R" On August 20, General Burnside ordered General Boyle to impress 8,000 slaves to construct a railroad going toward East Tennessee. When work on the railroad began in September, Boyle reported: "since the negroes have been impressed and part of them collected, it is not so popular, and there is more signs of dissatisfaction." According to Boyle, "many of the best men in the country" were urging that the work be abandoned.[93] In any case, the War Department expressed doubts that the new railroad could be finished in time to be significant in the war effort.[94] By mid-October only 3,000 of the proposed 8,000 slaves had been impressed, and Maj. J.H. Simpson reported to Burnside "that the number will not reach 5000." By December 1863 Burnside's successor as commander of the Department of the Ohio, Gen. John G. Foster, ended the use of impressed slaves to build railroads, and designated them instead "to work on the wagon roads through south Kentucky into east Tennessee." In February 1864 Gen. Stephen G. Burbridge, newly appointed commandant of the District of Kentucky, "extended to still more counties the impressments of slaves ordered by Boyle the previous August."[95]

Early on, Camp Nelson was set up to provide food, clothing, shelter, training, tools, and discipline for large forces of these workers. As stated earlier, the use of black men as teamsters had quickly emerged as imperative also. Thus, the initial crises of Camp Nelson underscored the importance of black men in Union military operations in the state before the decision to recruit Kentucky's slaves as soldiers was ever made.

Recruiting Black Kentuckians

Camp Nelson had been conceived as a recruiting station for white soldiers from the beginning, and because of the depot's role in Burnside's campaign the first regiments formed there were composed of young men who were refugees from East Tennessee. From June 30 to August 14, 1863, five companies of the Fifth Regiment of East Tennessee Cavalry were organized at Camp Nelson for the Tenth Tennessee Cavalry, but in August the regiment was assigned to the Eighth Tennessee Cavalry, along with seven companies that had been organized in Tennessee at large. It became part of the Twenty-third Army Corps, and spent most of its service time in East Tennessee after Burnside's invasion. The Eighth Tennessee Infantry, organized at Camp Dick Robinson and Camp Nelson from November 11, 1862 to August 11, 1863, served first in the District of Central Kentucky, then became part of the Twenty-third.[96]

In addition, four Kentucky regiments were formed at Camp Nelson either wholly or in part: (1) Battery "E" Light Artillery, organized at Camp Nelson from October to December 1863, was attached to the District of North Central Kentucky, First Division, Twenty-third Army Corps, Department of the Ohio. Although it was shifted to other Kentucky districts, Battery "E" performed garrison duty at Camp Nelson and Camp Burnside until June 1864. The battery participated in Stoneman's Raid into southwestern Virginia and the Battle of Saltville, among other engagements, but spent most of its war time on duty at Lexington and Camp Nelson until being mustered out on August 1, 1865. (2) The Twenty-sixth Kentucky Infantry had been organized originally at Owensboro from July to November 1861, but while the regiment was on furlough at Camp Nelson in January and February of 1864, 239 new recruits were added to its ranks. (3) The Forty-seventh Kentucky Infantry, organized at Irvine and Camp Nelson, enlisted over 222 men at Camp Nelson, mostly in three increments, in October and December 1863 and March 1864. The Forty-seventh participated in several battles with Morgan's Raiders, including those at Mt. Sterling and Cynthiana in June 1864. This regiment was on duty at Camp Nelson and on the line of the Kentucky Central Railroad through most of its term of service until April 1865. (4) The Forty-Ninth Kentucky Infantry, organized at Camp Nelson on September 19, 1863, enlisted over 600 of its troops there. As part of the Twenty-third Army Corps, it served at Somerset, Camp Burnside, Lexington, and Camp Nelson until mustered out on December 26, 1864.[97]

The enlistment of slaves into the Union Army began very late in Kentucky; the first black soldiers to serve in Federal forces were recruited in the summer of

1862, fully two years before such recruitment was enacted in Kentucky. Lincoln and his administration handled Kentucky and its loyalist slaveholders with kid gloves; nothing could be done that might disturb slavery and its proponents in the most important, difficult, and exposed of all the border states. By the next summer (after the Emancipation Proclamation of January 1863), the enlistment of black soldiers was a major element of Union war policy, with recruitment fully under way in the free states and in parts of the Confederacy under Union occupation. But, of course, Kentucky was still exempt—since the Emancipation Proclamation, by design, did not apply there, and at least for the sake of a legal fiction, all Kentucky slaves were regarded as belonging to masters loyal to the Union. The prevailing attitude in Kentucky toward the mere possibility of black recruitment was little short of hysterical, if the reactions of its leading generals are any indication. "The enrollment act of March 3, 1863"—preparatory to the summer's recruitment drive—"included among those liable to draft all male *citizens* of the prescribed ages. This category was interpreted to include free Negroes, and the act was applied accordingly by the War Department. Enforcement of the provision met instant opposition in Kentucky."[98]

Opposition was spearheaded by Generals Boyle and Burnside. Briefly—from June 25 to June 27—Burnside was completely distracted from his military preparations by this issue. From Camp Nelson, Boyle cabled him the distressing news, received from the governor himself, that "the War Dept have ordered the Enrollment & Enlistment of Negroes into the U S service Especially free negroes. . . . If true," Boyle asserted, "Ky will never see another day of peace."[99] On the same day, Boyle also wrote to Col. James B. Fry, Provost-Marshal-General, to protest "the enrollment of free negroes for military service in Kentucky." After all, he estimated fewer than 700 men would be gained for the army, but the state would be "revolutionized" and "infinite and inconceivable harm" would be done. "I am sure this is all wrong," Boyle wrote, "and there is not an honest, loyal man in the State in favor of it, and it will meet with decided opposition. For the peace and quiet of the country I beg you will change your order on the subject."[100] Meanwhile, Burnside wired President Lincoln himself: "I am satisfied from my knowledge of Kentucky that it would be very unwise to enroll the free negroes of this State. It would not add materially to our strength, and I assure you it would cause much trouble. I sincerely hope this embarrassment to the interest of the public service will not be placed in our way." Boyle also cabled Lincoln. A reply from James Fry explained that the enrollment of free blacks was "simply taking the census of persons between the ages of twenty and forty-five." The government was merely seeking information. Then, turning to satire, Fry added: "I don't see why infinite and inconceivable harm . . . should be done by my ascertaining and informing the Government how many free negroes there are between those ages in the different States, and their names, and I have a better opinion of Kentucky than to think she would be revolutionized if such information is sought for by me as it has been by the Census Bureau without revolution . . . and to use your language, I do not see how any honest, loyal man in the

State can oppose it." In his cable, Lincoln wrote soothingly, "There is nothing going on in Kentucky on the subject of which you telegraph except an enrollment." Before receiving Lincoln's reassuring telegram, Burnside composed another, longer letter of protest, reiterating that the military draft in Kentucky should be from white people only—and the drafting of free blacks and slaves especially should be for labor only. "I was just about issuing an order drafting all the free able-bodied negroes in the State for labor on a military road . . . Kentucky is in good order now."[101] Then the Lincoln telegram was issued again verbatim, and the matter ended. For the moment.

In October 1863, all the border states—Maryland, Missouri, Tennessee, and Delaware—except Kentucky, became liable for black enlistment. The War Department exempted Kentucky this time because the state's slaves were being impressed by the army to labor on military roads. Secretary of War Edwin S. Stanton justified the decision by arguing that, since there was no rebel attack going on in Kentucky, "it is not essential that they [black men] should be enlisted as troops in that State, as they should be employed in labor for the supply of other troops."[102]

By January 1864 recruitment of Kentucky's slaves began in the western portion that was a part of Department of Tennessee, but not in the Department of the Ohio, where slaveholders were more and more fearful of the encroaching practice of enlisting and freeing slaves of loyal Kentuckians. Also in January, Kentucky governor Thomas E. Bramlette protested the attempt of a Federal government agent to recruit "able-bodied negroes of Ky. into the '1st Michigan colored regiment' for the U.S. army."[103] The governor stated that such recruiting would not be tolerated, that Kentucky would furnish white men to fill the quota required of the state, that Kentucky would not enlist colored men, and so on through a list of statements slated to be overturned virtually as soon as the impassioned official uttered them.

Less than a month later, Bramlette had a great deal more to protest, as President Lincoln on February 1 upped the draft ante to five hundred thousand men to be in uniform by March 10. On February 5, right on schedule, the Kentucky legislature protested the enlistment of Kentucky blacks into the U.S. Army, requesting "the President to remove negro-soldiers camps from the limits or borders of the state."[104] A new national enrollment act on February 24, 1864, declared that "all able-bodied male colored persons, between the ages of twenty and forty-five years, resident in the United States, shall be enrolled. . . ."[105] Now, not only free blacks but slaves were included, and "such legislation was not passed without the bitterest opposition from Kentucky legislators." The act was finally passed, but only with provisions for compensation, similar to those that had already been in place for loyal owners of slaves impressed for labor in the army. These slaveholders had been entitled to a compensation of $300 "in lieu of the future services of each slave thus employed. The new legislation extended this grant to the loyal masters of all enlisted slaves. When a slave was drafted the master received a hundred-dollar bounty due to drafted men and the slave received his freedom. For slaves who volunteered, loyal masters were allowed a remuneration of as high as $300, in which case also the slave was to secure freedom."[106]

At the end of February, "James B. Fry, U.S. provost marshal general, [ordered] the enrollment, without delay, of all colored males of military age" and the next week, "all impressed negroes" were ordered to be "released from their work and sent home to their owners," so that they could all participate in the draft. A spokesman for the resisting loyalists in Danville wrote President Lincoln to remonstrate: recruiting black soldiers in Kentucky, he stated, was

> eminently distasteful and obnoxious to the largest portion of the loyal people of the State, and there is no small danger of its producing an outbreak of a portion of our loyal people, and I dreadfully fear a conflict between the Federal and State authorities.
>
> Are such evils and dangers as these to be incurred for the sake of the few frightened and unwilling soldiers to be obtained by drafting the negroes?[107]

In April, with white enlistment dwindling, the new Commander of the District of Kentucky, Gen. Stephen G. Burbridge,[108] ordered recruitment of black men throughout the state. In General Orders No. 34, Burbridge limited enlistment to free blacks and slaves whose masters requested that their property be recruited. In addition, only provost marshals were permitted to recruit in order to avoid "mobile enlistment parties" of the sort that had been organized in Missouri and Maryland. All blacks enlisted had to be sent out of the state immediately to be organized and trained elsewhere.[109]

Both negative and positive responses soon altered Burbridge's careful policies. The widespread brutality and violence of the reactions of slave owners shocked military officials, but the slaves' determination to enlist suggested that policies to protect them and take advantage of their manifest eagerness to join the war effort and procure their own freedom would result in significant additions to the manpower of the Union Army.[110] By June 1864, all restrictions had been lifted.[111] Any black man who presented himself at a recruiting station could be enlisted, whether he was free or slave, with or without the knowledge and consent of his owner. Adj. Gen. Lorenzo Thomas[112] designated eight permanent centers in Kentucky, including Camp Nelson, where black regiments would be formed, and he also ordered that "as early as possible colored troops will be used . . . for recruiting purposes, and will be distributed among the different camps of reception."[113]

A tiny trickle of volunteers at Camp Nelson (only 8 in May 1864) quickly became a flood. In June 1864, legally unrestricted at last, 574 black men enlisted at Camp Nelson, their numbers increasing to 1,370 in July, dropping down to 444 in August, climbing again to 1,199 in September, dropping again to 376 in October. And, at that point, after the warm months were over, recruitment at Camp Nelson virtually ground to a halt, with fewer than 50 men recruited from November 1864 to April 1865, when the last 4 recruits were mustered in.[114] Altogether approximately 5,405 slaves enrolled in the Union Army at Camp Nelson (minus perhaps 20 white men who signed up as officers in the regiments and were thus counted).[115]

The whole recruiting episode lasted a surprisingly short time, but it was very dramatic and on some days it must have been simply overwhelming. On the biggest day (July 25, 1864), 322 black men enlisted at Camp Nelson; on four separate days out of the five significant months of recruitment (June through October 1864) over 150 men assembled at the camp, and 99 or more appeared on fourteen days during that period. The last six months of the recruiting period (November 1864 through April 1865), however, certainly did not strain Camp Nelson's resources in any way: 16 men in November, 4 in December, 15 in January, 1 in February, 1 in March, and, as stated above, 4 in April.

Many of Kentucky's black regiments were populated and formed at Camp Nelson. Six companies of the 5th U.S. Colored Cavalry (573 men in all) took shape at Camp Nelson in August and September; most of four companies of the 6th U.S.C.C. (243 men) formed primarily in September, with additions throughout October. The 114th United States Colored Infantry enlisted 514 men in June and July, while the 116th enlisted 720 (mostly in June).[116] Infantry units, including the 123rd and the 124th (with 427 and 382 members respectively) continued to be formed in September and October. The largest regiment recruited at Camp Nelson was the 12th United States Colored Heavy Artillery, which enlisted men continually from June 1864 to April 1865 (including the single day record of 322), for a total of 1,418.

Morgan's Last Raid and Its Effect on Camp Nelson

The plan to consolidate troops in one central Kentucky location never worked out exactly as planned: troops arrived at Camp Nelson in great numbers, and departed in great numbers, in such an erratic way that it was from time to time virtually depopulated of all save its civilian operatives, who were forced at one point to arm themselves, drill, and man various posts and guns in an effort to defend the camp against Morgan's raiders. This incident, whatever else it revealed, was symptomatic of the fact that Camp Nelson was a considerable miscalculation.

From June 8 through June 13, 1864, great excitement reigned in central Kentucky: a reported troop of twenty-five hundred rebel raiders led by Gen. John Hunt Morgan threatened Mount Sterling, Winchester, Richmond, Lexington, and particularly—it was thought—Camp Nelson. The actual order of events took one trajectory, while rumors and reports frequently took others.

Toward the end of May in 1864, Gen. Stephen G. Burbridge was informed that Gen. John Hunt Morgan was planning an attack into Kentucky from southwestern Virginia through Pound Gap.[117] Burbridge immediately launched an offensive intended to destroy Morgan's Raiders in their base camp. Delayed by a lack of rations and forage (a familiar story), Burbridge did not reach Pound Gap in time to stop Morgan from breaking through. With two thousand cavalrymen, eight hundred of whom were on foot, Morgan entered Kentucky on June 1.[118] He sent out several advance detachments in various directions, to cut off communications and transportation, and (perhaps most importantly) to confuse the enemy. On the morning of June 8, he captured Mount Sterling and received (erroneous) reports from his scouts to the effect "that Burbridge's entire force had gone into Virginia to attack the salt mines" (218). Assuming there was no immediate danger, Morgan set out for Lexington—his main objective because of the horses there—with a mounted brigade, leaving two brigades of dismounted men behind in Mount Sterling. There Burbridge, who had been marching day and night, fell upon them at 4 o'clock in the morning and inflicted heavy casualties. Meanwhile, Morgan had reached Winchester; hearing that Mount Sterling was under attack, he waited for the brigades at Mount Sterling to rejoin his forces. The reunited raiders left Winchester on the night of July 9, reaching Lexington at dawn. "Following a brief skirmish with a small Union force, his men seized hundreds of valuable thoroughbreds, more than enough to mount every raider on a fresh horse" (220). From Lexington, Morgan sent a company on a scout to Frankfort, but the main column rode to Georgetown (at 11 a.m. on the tenth), then departed that night; he began his successful attack on Cynthiana at daylight on Saturday, June 11. He had one day in which to revel in his great military achievement—his conquest of Mount Sterling, Lexington, Maysville, and Cynthiana, and much more—then, at 2:30 in the morning of Sunday, June 12, Burbridge caught up with Morgan and defeated him in the Battle of Cynthiana.[119]

Throughout the time of Morgan's Last Raid in central Kentucky, from June 9 through the thirteenth, Camp Nelson was receiving reams of information and misinformation; the people there were laboring under constant apprehension and misapprehension of an impending attack on Kentucky's largest supply depot, which quickly became desperately undermanned. Wiring from Lexington at 2 a.m. on June 9, J. Bates Dickson, captain and assistant adjutant-general, announced that Morgan had entered the state and captured Mount Sterling the previous morning; immediate steps were to be taken to protect Camp Nelson "and, if possible, Lexington also." A commissary of subsistence at Danville with 2,500 cattle "and no guard for them" was directed "to send them to Camp Nelson and its vicinity." By 10:20 a.m., the "enemy [appeared] to be making for Camp Nelson."[120] A rebel column had crossed Clay's Ferry road, ten miles from the camp, at daylight. The same day more Union soldiers were ordered to Camp Nelson from the direction of Lebanon.[121] However, these men and other troops were being sent to the camp, not to defend it, but to be provided there with "arms and equipments, ammunition, etc."[122]

At Camp Nelson, officers took steps in the camp's own defense. The guard at Hickman Bridge was immediately increased by thirty men, and two pieces of artillery were planted in the road near Hickman "so as to defend that side of the camp."[123] Then the civilians were mustered in front of Captain Hall's office and a commissioned officer placed in command of them.[124] The guard on the bridge was quickly increased to one hundred men (it was still the same day: June 9).[125]

By evening, the official word was still that Morgan intended an attack on either Lexington or Camp Nelson on the next day. His main force was said to be at Winchester, with another troop of four hundred threatening Paris.[126] Meanwhile, the rebels reportedly had burnt a train of wagons in Richmond at 2 o'clock in the morning[127]—a report that was immediately denied by Dickson, who announced once more that the "main force [was] at or near Winchester, intending an attack [on Lexington] or at Camp Nelson to-morrow"; in another report he said "the main rebel forces [were] moving toward Camp Nelson from Mount Sterling."[128] The rebels that had crossed the Clay's Ferry road were reported "near Tate's Creek Road, stealing horses."[129]

On the tenth, the commanding officer (unnamed) of the Thirtieth Kentucky at Camp Nelson was "ordered to detail sufficient men . . . to take all the horses in [his] command to Lexington." The commanding officer of the forty-seventh Kentucky was likewise ordered to relieve "all men belonging to [his] command that [were] on duty in the fortifications" at Camp Nelson in order to send them to Lexington.[130]

The next day a courier from General Burbridge in Paris brought orders to "protect Camp Nelson at all hazards," which was rather ironic since virtually every soldier there had just been sent away, but the general instructed in another order "that every person at Camp Nelson capable of assisting in its defense should be armed." General Fry responded to this message half an hour later: "Every man for whom I have a gun is under arms and on the fortifications. We will do the best we can in case of an attack. We had but few arms and they not of the best quality." Somewhat later, in an even less confident tone, Fry wrote to Dickson: "Should you ascertain that an attack upon this place is contemplated by anything like a formidable force, I should like, if you could spare them from Lexington, to have some 400 or 500 sent here, either cavalry or infantry. A large portion of the men upon whom I have to depend are clerks and employés in quartermaster's and commissary departments, very few of whom have ever been drilled or disciplined for military duty."[131]

On the twelfth of June, Camp Nelson reported in divergent veins: at 1:20 in the morning Col. Andrew H. Clark, commanding the post, ordered Major H.C. Edgerly to "have Evry armed man in [his] com'd sent immediately to the Fortifications" because General Fry had "received information that lead him to expect an attack from the Rebels";[132] later in the day, Fry wired Dickson to report, "Everything is quiet here. No enemy anywhere near, that we can hear of. Scouts are sent out every day."[133]

In the meantime, Burbridge moved out from Paris, attacked Morgan at Cynthiana in the early morning of June 12, and won a "complete victory."[134]

On June 13, information reached Camp Nelson that "Rebel force [was] within a short distance from Camp"; in response to this message, the Seventh Ohio Cavalry was sent "on a scout."[135] A more specific report placed "the Rebels . . . within two or three miles of Camp and 1600 strong." Major Edgerly was "directed to get

[his] troops in shape to move at a moment's notice and also see that [his] Command on the fortifications & at the Bridge [were] promptly at their Posts & on a sharp look out."[136]

The Confederates never reached Camp Nelson, but many more messages did, including further warnings. Brig.-Gen. Speed Smith Fry had grown so accustomed to alarming and conflicting accounts of the enemies' numbers, location, and movements that he dismissed a report of one thousand rebels "making off toward the mouth of Paint Lick, on [the] Kentucky [River]" as inflated. "Excitement is apt to exaggerate," he wrote. "The report is too big."[137] In fact, he was hopeful that some of the rebels would be stopped from crossing the river. "With the force sent from Lexington and from this camp," he announced, "I think that some of the rascals will be caught." A little later, after reading a courier's dispatch, Fry reported that the rebels were moving very rapidly across the river toward Richmond, "anxious to get away."[138] His scouts had seen "the rebels crossing seven miles east of Lancaster, going toward Crab Orchard or Stanford. Our forces are still in pursuit. . . . The rebels are reported nearly worn out, both men and horses. I hope our forces will overtake them to-night." All day on the thirteenth, Fry continued reporting from Camp Nelson, growing more confident dispatch by dispatch. "Rebels in Lancaster at 2 p.m. This I think reliable. Our men in pursuit, in hopes they will overtake them to-night. Rebels and their stock much worn down. Many of them arrived with nothing but revolvers. Would it not be best to keep them divided? We have every man in pursuit that could be mounted and armed." In the next dispatch Fry reported the taking of a prisoner, who turned out to be "very ignorant" about the number of troops in the retreat, reckoning fifteen hundred.[139]

After 7 p.m. on June 13, Fry was finally informed that General Burbridge had arrived in Lexington and that the rebels had lost at Cynthiana, "300 killed and 400 prisoners, besides wounded. Morgan's force [was] scattered, out of ammunition, totally demoralized."[140] After the Union victory at Cynthiana, Morgan's last raid in Kentucky was basically over.

According to Maj. C.E. Compton, who inspected Camp Nelson during these trying days, "the post was threatened by a large force of the enemy. . . . The military force stationed there was entirely inadequate to its defense"; so volunteers were called for, whereupon "all employees came forward and offered their services for the defense of the place." Six hundred men were armed, that being the number of arms on hand in the depot, and they "performed duty" on the line of fortifications "for six consecutive nights." Compton thought that it was, in some measure, "due to [these civilians] that the depot was saved from capture and destruction."[141] It seems much more likely that the camp was saved because Morgan and his raiders never showed up there, and perhaps never intended to show up there, even if they had not been pressed so hard by General Burbridge and others. Of course, Morgan's seasoned soldiers would have been very impressed when they heard that the clerks, cooks, and teamsters of Camp Nelson were all being armed! But it is doubtful that they ever heard anything about it.

Reverend John Gregg Fee

In 1863, the last year of his forced exile from Kentucky, Rev. John G. Fee[142] was preoccupied with the impact of the war upon the black population. "There are <u>reasons</u>," he wrote, "why the colored people of this nation—the freed men offer one of the most promising fields for good now open to missionary effort." He was convinced that the outcome of the Civil War would "turn greatly upon the shoulders of the black man," who might gain by his participation in the war the position that "we from moral principles ought to have given."[143]

Fee's major goals were three: (1) to find a way to work among freed people himself; (2) to promote the drafting of slaves in Kentucky; and (3) to foster immediate emancipation.

Fee tentatively suggested to the American Missionary Association,[144] the benevolent society that had sponsored his work for years, that he might go to Memphis and Corinth in Tennessee to work among the freedmen there, but Morgan's guerrilla raids and a severe illness prevented him from traveling.[145] In any case, Fee really wanted to investigate the situation in his native state, the place he had always considered his primary mission field. He was afraid no one within Kentucky was looking after the contrabands, but he was not sure that "the field there [could] be cultivated even to a small degree."[146] Certainly it could not be cultivated by John G. Fee, since he was unable to return to his home in Berea upon threat of death.

A fellow abolitionist turned Union Army officer, G.P. Reiley, reported to Fee that conditions of contrabands revealed "the deep wickedness & meaness [sic] of Ky[.] in a light little known or understood by the north." Former slaves from Alabama and Tennessee had followed the Union Army northward to Kentucky, where they had been imprisoned and quickly resold into slavery, although many died as a result of their treatment in Louisville jails, where "the water they had to drink was so filthy & loathsome that it was their poison." Reiley wanted Fee's help in winning the freedom of these black men so they could be enlisted in an Ohio regiment commanded by Reiley: to this project Fee devoted months of travel, consultation, and labor, although he would have preferred to be working with Kentucky slaves and forming Kentucky regiments.[147]

Fee was concerned that Kentuckians who were inclined to free slaves would adopt gradual emancipation and "imitate the wise Economical and humane policy of surgeons who cut off the dogs tail inch by inch." In fact, by Christmas of 1863, Fee was convinced that Kentucky would resist the ending of slavery and "make emancipation as gradual as possible."[148] He himself was enthusiastically promoting immediate emancipation, trying to establish emancipation leagues, and planning to attend a border state convention where he could speak out effectively against gradualism.[149]

For his own prospects of working among the freed people, Fee counted on the continuing sponsorship of the AMA, but he was somewhat disturbed to discover that his friend and fellow abolitionist leader, Levi Coffin, had founded an alternative benevolent organization, the Western Freedmen's Aid Commission, serving some of the same territory as the AMA and eager to share or take over the newest, potentially the most fundable, missionary field: educating contrabands.[150] But he was heartened to learn that new government policies favored selecting teachers and preachers for the freedmen from "those sent by the various Missionary societies," insuring that religious instruction would be an integral part of the freed people's education.[151]

In April John G. Fee, having at last returned to Berea, surveyed the Kentucky scene with distress. "Here," he wrote, "where armies have passed over and over again, is great destitution." He informed an AMA official, safe in his office in New York City, that "nothing but an experience where there has been the desolutions of war and that carelessness which slavery & war engenders could enable you to comprehend the difficulties. House, garden, well, fencing, stables, every thing to repair." To add insult to injury, he had lost a carriage wheel in crossing the Licking River, where the bridge had been burned. He and his household were living "in constant expectancy of rebel raids."[152]

On June 6, 1864, Simeon S. Jocelyn,[153] a chief officer of the AMA, urged Fee to visit "the Camps of the Colored Soldiers," labor for their good, and secure "Rights as to Chaplains." The organization promised to "send a quantity of Books for the teaching of the soldiers to read, cypher, write &c." and asked that Fee "Report at once whether there [was] a call for teaching and whether 'Eating & shelter' [would] be supplied to any teachers [and] missionaries."[154]

More than a quarter century later, writing his *Autobiography*, Fee recalled his decision to go to Camp Nelson:

> . . . Whilst sitting in my study, thinking of the political and social conditions around me, these words came to me with wonderful force, "Prepare thy work without, and make it fit for thyself in the field; and afterwards build thine house." Prov. 24: 27. I did not remember to have seen the text before; but of course I had, in general reading, though at that moment I was not reading my Bible. The text came to me in such manner and with such force, that I could not but regard it as from the Spirit of God; and therefore a call to the work indicated. The thing indicated to me was this: Until the work on the battlefield shall be first settled, there will be no permanency, or marked progress in your work here [Berea], either in school or church;—go do your part. That part, as I then believed, was moral, religious; rather than physical,—the actual bearing of arms. I had hitherto no confidence that the government would succeed, until it began to "break every yoke and let the oppressed go free"; until it began to enlist men as men,—and not merely as white men. I also knew that just at that time colored men were being enlisted in Kentucky. I believed I knew more about the movements of the government and the feelings of the people North, than these colored men did, and that there were reasons why I could instruct, comfort and en-

courage them,—reasons why they would hear me, and also reasons why loyal white men would hear me.

Without counsel from, or commission from any board, I immediately prepared to go; took my eldest son, my dear Burritt,[155] then living, and on the next Saturday started for Camp Nelson, thirty-five miles distant.

I found there two regiments[156] of colored men, forming,—not complete. The next day, Lord's day, I mingled freely with these colored soldiers and their officers; and at night preached to a large assemblage of them. This was to me, and to many of these men, a melting occasion. We saw then, in its first unfolding what we had long and anxiously prayed for, — "the beginning of the end"—the freedom of men, white and colored; freedom in such manner as would give prestige to the latter and sympathy from the former." (173–75)

Fee arrived at Camp Nelson for the first time on or about July 4, 1864, and immediately initiated the missionary labors there that would occupy him—off and on—for the rest of his life. On the day he arrived he agreed—somehow—to provide religious instruction, schools, and clothing for the black people at Camp Nelson. While he waited for the AMA to send teachers (or even answer his letters), he organized and taught a school himself for the black men who were then being organized into regiments, and he preached to "a thousand at a time," the largest, most responsive audiences he had ever addressed.[157]

Teachers and Missionaries

Two new preaching, teaching missionaries, commissioned by the AMA at Fee's behest, arrived in Camp Nelson on August 19, 1864, William L. and John B. Lowrey,[158] who had experienced an arduous journey from Pittsburgh, Pennsylvania, to Nicholasville, Kentucky. But they plunged into their new work: William "preached to the Colored Soldiers in the school room" and "to White soldiers at the Soldier's Home"; John preached "in the Military Prison" and also "to a congregation of colored soldiers" in the schoolroom. Before the week was out, John Lowrey was in charge of the school, "thinly attended, owing to the small number of troops quartered" at Camp Nelson at that moment, troops who had virtually no time for educational pursuits, in any case, because they had "to drill several hours extra each day."[159]

Along with the Lowreys, the new school for black soldiers had also received, at Fee's request, "a magnificent Bell for church & school purposes," paid for by a friend in Cincinnati. It cost $115, but Fee paid the freight, $4.60, himself.[160]

Large numbers of troops, potential students, were expected in late August.[161] And they arrived, 700 of them, according to John B. Lowrey's report to the AMA for that month. He stated that the school (designated "Camp Nelson School for colored Soldiers") had been established on July 13, and had been "kept" on twenty-seven days with two sessions per day. The largest number of students present for any one session was 150, the average attendance for the month 80. Of the 700 students, 692 were males, 8 were females, all students over the age of 16. Three hundred and fifty of the groups were studying reading and spelling, 150 studying "mental arithmetic," 1 pursuing written arithmetic, 500 writing, none studying geography. Along with the 700 African-Americans "one white boy" (probably Burritt Fee) was being taught. Lowrey answered "No" to the printed, standardized AMA form's question, "Do the mulattoes show any more capacity than the blacks?"[162]

According to John Lowrey's accompanying letter, John G. Fee had been in charge of the school himself from July 13 until the first of August, John Vetter[163] from the first to the twentieth, John Lowrey after that. He was assisted "by five teachers from the convalescent camp," and "Vetter [had] just started a night school." "The scholars," Lowrey reported, "are making rapid progress in reading, spelling and writing." He expected more adult females to come into classes (he had taught seven the morning of the report) and more little boys between the ages of ten and twelve (he already had a class consisting of eleven of them). Most of all he expected "an immediate increase" in the numbers of soldier-students because "fifteen hundred colored [men] had just come into camp."[164]

So Fee's school for soldiers was already "organized & supplied" when the Western Freedmen's Aid Commission at Cincinnati tried to get the school under its control in the second week of September. They wrote to Fee at the camp proposing "to organize the school & send the teachers." Then they dispatched their agent, John M. Walden, to Camp Nelson to claim the territory for themselves, but finding Fee already there, Walden perceived that "the land was occupied."[165]

On October 4, 1864, William L. Lowrey reported on the school's condition. It was well attended, he said, and "the scholars manifested a great desire to learn."[166] John Lowrey, in the formal report for the month of September, stated that the school had made "good progress . . . in reading and writing." However, the usual problems persisted: for example, "the regiment lying near the schoolroom [had] been on drill for 8 hours a days for the past month," which—not surprisingly—had "prevented most of them from attending school." Hundreds of recruits arrived each week and left nearly as fast as they arrived. Lowrey thought that the only soldiers who would actually remain in camp were the guards. He was not looking for any increase in the numbers of soldiers in the school "until winter when it [would] be too muddy to drill."

The average attendance included "25 non-commissioned officers in a day school and 60 soldiers and officers in night school." The average attendance of women and children, however, was on the increase, with "40 young women and girls and 30 boys." A separate schoolroom was being planned for the civilians. Lowrey saw an obvious need for more teachers, since the staff now consisted of John B. Lowrey, the principal, William L. Lowrey, his assistant, and two convalescent soldiers who were monitors.

The school report claimed 400 different pupils had been in attendance, 350 of them males, with a total of 48 sessions, averaging 95 students each. The largest number present for any session was 130—which would certainly be a large group of students learning to read and write even with two teachers and two monitors. Some of the students, by this time, were apparently old men—since eight of the students were designated as "Uncles."[167]

The Lowrey brothers left Camp Nelson after a few weeks because of ill health, but other AMA workers arrived to help Fee in the new field, notably Rev. Abisha Scofield, who came at the end of September 1864, and Rev. Gabriel Burdett,[168] a former slave preacher from Garrard County, now a soldier, who became Fee's personal assistant and pupil.

Fee was very active in trying to recruit teachers and missionaries for the work at Camp Nelson, but even without him the black military camp would have drawn a crowd of white philanthropists. Black soldiers, now freedmen, attracted missionaries, teachers, preachers, administrators, clerks, religious controversialists and reformers from all over the country. And they attracted sponsoring societies as well. In Camp Nelson's case these were represented first by the American Missionary Association, which arrived in the person of Rev. John G. Fee, and just a little later the Western Freedmen's Aid Commission. This society, founded by Levi Coffin ("Father of the Underground Railroad"), also sent workers—teachers especially—to Camp Nelson, which was much easier for the Cincinnati-based WFAC to access than for the AMA with its headquarters in New York City and its commissioned workers drawn almost wholly from Ohio and the Northeast.

The Battle of Saltville and Stoneman's Raid in Southwestern Virginia

Records other than school reports are grim reminders that black soldiers in the classroom were the same men participating in the war, moving straight from their primers to the battlefield. Within a few days of William B. Lowrey's last school report dealing with the same men as students, Gen. Stephen G. Burbridge spoke "in the highest terms of the gallantry of the Fifth Colored Cavalry," who were, he said, "doing better service than any other regiment." They had recently lost "4 officers and 116 men killed and wounded."[169]

On October 2, in an action fought at Saltville, Virginia, the Fifth U.S. Colored Cavalry, one of the first black regiments organized at Camp Nelson, participated with distinction. The Surgeon in Chief of the First Division, District of Kentucky, reported on October 4 that the Fifth had twenty-two killed, thirty-seven wounded, and fifty-three missing, but he also stated that his list was not accurate because the recording surgeons had been left on the field with the wounded.[170]

General Burbridge reported what sounded like a full-scale victory: "We whipped the rebels in every engagement," he wrote, "fighting from the Virginia line up to the salt-works, where we had a heavy engagement with from 6,000 to 10,000 rebels. . . ."[171] But, in reality, his mission had failed in its main goal: destroying the Confederate salt-works near Saltville. In any case, the primary significance of this particular engagement was probably not what happened during the battle, but what happened immediately afterward.

William H. Gardner, of the Thirtieth Kentucky Infantry and one of the surgeons who had been left behind with the wounded, was captured with them. Upon his release, he reported that "on Monday morning, October 3, there came to our field hospital several armed men . . . [apparently] soldiers in the Confederate service, and took 5 men, privates, wounded (negroes), and shot them." Four days later at Emory and Henry College Hospital, Washington County, Virginia, where the captive Union wounded had been taken, "several armed men entered the said hospital at about 10 p.m. and went up into the rooms occupied by the Federal wounded prisoners, and shot two of them (negroes) dead in their beds." The next day several armed men dressed in Confederate uniform returned, shot one white officer, and "called out for the other Federal officers confined there . . . swearing that they intended to kill all of them." Gardner was fortunately removed to safety, but seventy wounded prisoners were left behind and apparently suffered similar atrocities.[172]

On October 14, Col. Thomas D. Sedgewick, commanding at Camp Nelson, was warned to hold all his "available men in readiness to repel any attack" and "to keep scouting parties, under picked officers, out a few miles on the different approaches to the camp."[173] Information had been received that the post was "in danger of an attack by guerrillas," who were then at Shakertown. Speed S. Fry appealed to the commander of a brigade of cavalry at Nicholasville to send any men he could spare to Camp Nelson, since the camp had only a small force of about 100 men "for the protection of a vast amount of Government property." At Camp Nelson, the incident quickly became very reminiscent of Morgan's Last Raid. Special Orders No. 36, dated October 17, 1864, commanded:

> The Employees of the Quarter Master's, Commissary, Ordnance and Engineer Departments at Camp Nelson will be organized by Companies as Infantry and held in readiness in case of any emergency requiring their Services in the defence of the Camp. Each Company will elect its officers, non Commissioned Officers will be appointed by the Captains of the Companies. The Post Commandant at Camp Nelson, thro' the different Chiefs of departments will exercise general Supervision and Control over the force, each Company will be required to drill one hour daily and none will be excused from drilling unless by written permission of their Captain approved by the head of their respective departments. A Consolidated return of the several Companies organized under this order will be made on the 1st 10th and last days of each month.[174]

Once again, no enemy appeared. It was the last time Camp Nelson would seem to be under a serious military threat, either real or imagined.

In November and December 1864, however, in a period quite reminiscent of the East Tennessee Campaign, Camp Nelson functioned (again) as supply depot and way station for a multitude of troops being sent via Crab Orchard to join Gen. Stephen G. Burbridge's forces at Cumberland Gap. He was to command a brigade of cavalry as part of General Stoneman's raid[175] in southwestern Virginia, but like Burnside before him, he first had to assemble the scattered regiments that would serve under him. Their gathering point and launching ground was, of course, Camp Nelson.

On November 17, Camp Nelson had to deliver ten days rations for five regiments[176] ordered to Crab Orchard, "with 100 rounds of ammunition per man, and, in addition, 150 rounds per man" to be taken in wagons. The Twelfth Kentucky Cavalry was to be equipped at Camp Nelson, and any horses on hand at the camp were to be issued to this regiment.[177] The First Battalion of the Fifth U.S. Colored Cavalry was ordered immediately to Crab Orchard.[178]

On November 21, Camp Nelson, along with Lexington and Nicholasville, was ordered to "clear out . . . all officers and men. . . . There must be no delay," General Burbridge stated, "Let all move, night and day, and have them armed and equipped and supplied with ammunition; draw from Camp Nelson."[179] Regiments were pouring into Camp Nelson—the Thirtieth Kentucky on the twenty-first, followed by the Thirty-ninth and Forty-fifthth—being equipped and then pushing "on to Cumberland Gap by forced marches." All available horses at Camp Nelson were taken, "all horses in wagons and ambulances, and in possession of officers and attachés."[180] On the twenty-third, Brig.-Gen. N.C. McLean informed Burbridge that all the troops had left Camp Nelson but the Thirty-ninth Kentucky, which was pressing horses for the command in preparation to leave from the camp the next morning. McLean was going to Camp Nelson himself "to insure the marching of every available mounted man from the place."[181]

Burbridge rather peremptorily ordered McLean to send him the whole of the Fifty-third and to use in place of them—among other choices—the Fifteenth U.S. Colored Infantry or else the Sixth Colored Cavalry, both from Camp Nelson. The Fifty-third was expected at the camp on November 25, but McLean informed S.S. Fry that Camp Nelson was running short of horses; consequently, Fry sent messages asking how many more would be wanted. Once again Burbridge summoned the Fifty-third, commanding Fry to "hurry them forward night and day; listen to no excuse," but have them gone from Camp Nelson by the next morning.[182] The Fifty-third Kentucky Volunteers was stationed at Paris guarding bridges, but a black regiment was sent to relieve them so that all men "armed and unarmed" could set out for Camp Nelson.

On the morning of the November 26 all of the Fifty-third—190 wanting arms and 350 needing horses—had still not reached Camp Nelson. From Lexington three hundred horses were sent to Camp Nelson for the troops and four hundred bridles. Brigadier General Fry was ordered to see that the men were "armed and equipped and mounted immediately on arrival and marched at once to Crab Orchard." Some stragglers of the Thirty-ninth were to be placed with the Fifty-third—"the 53rd must march by forced marches, without the usual halts to Cumberland Gap."[183]

On December 5, Colonel J.W. Weatherford, stationed at Camp Nelson, was instructed to send "a good officer with 50 men" of his regiment to Crab Orchard "with instructions to patrol the telegraph line with squads to Cumberland Gap"; Weatherford was reluctant to undertake the mission, noting there was "no subsistence for men between Cumberland Gap and Crab Orchard."[184] On December 9, all the men "able for duty" from Lexington and Camp Nelson were ordered to Cumberland Gap in support of Burbridge's operations — "except telegraph guards."[185]

The raid was a notable success, resulting in the final victory over the last remnant of John Hunt Morgan's force, when "a battalion of the Sixth U.S. Colored Cavalry, 300 strong, attacked and whipped Duke's brigade, of 350" on December 13.[186] On December 20 and 21, Federals in Stoneman's command captured and destroyed the saltworks in and around Saltville, thus completing the mission Burbridge had left unfinished in the first battle of Saltville. On January 2, 1865, Burbridge and his men returned to Kentucky as victors.[187] From this point on, all of the military engagements that involved Camp Nelson were brief and relatively insignificant, small guerrilla raids and small offensive forays. Never again would the immense Union supply depot have occasion for a massive effort of receiving and dispatching troops and materiel for the war. But while the personnel of Camp Nelson were deeply involved in preparations for Stoneman's Raid, another challenge, perhaps the greatest challenge of all, was arising.

The Refugees, Their Expulsions, and the Refugee Home

White Kentuckians resisted the recruitment of black Kentuckians with all their strength and, it must be said, with remarkable malice, cruelty, and violence. They stopped at nothing: torturing, maiming, and even murdering their victims.[188] In spite of the manifold difficulties put in their way, black men responded to the call to arms in great numbers; in approximately a year, more than half of the eligible black men in Kentucky joined the Union Army.

As in all states where slave men were enlisted, their wives and children, sometimes their parents and other dependents, followed them to recruiting centers and pressed to stay near them at training camps. Villages of contrabands had sprung up in Tennessee, Mississippi, Louisiana, and so on; it was much the same in Kentucky, but here the situation was desperately complicated since Kentucky technically had no contrabands. The women and children of black soldiers in Kentucky were not free, because they belonged to loyal Union supporters, not to rebels. They had not been freed by the Emancipation Proclamation, and they were not freed by the recruitment process in the state. They were property of loyal citizens, many of whom were leaders in the state government and in the military.

Slaves found themselves in an uncomfortable and often tragic limbo between freedom and bondage. Since women and children were not "legal," their reception in Union Army camps, Camp Nelson or any other, was not legal either, although it occurred over and over. Like their counterparts in other states, they gathered by the hundreds, even by the thousands—especially at Camp Nelson. There they were frequently treated like cattle and repeatedly they were driven out of the lines of the camp to be reclaimed by their owners. But the slaveholders, now deprived of the services of their male property, were of two minds about the women and children. Some owners redoubled their efforts to hang on to their "servants," virtually imprisoning them to prevent their running away, often beating and torturing them as a way of punishing slave soldiers by proxy. Under those circumstances, many women—with or without their children—ran away to Camp Nelson as soon as they had a chance. Other owners, punishing the black soldiers in a different way, turned their wives and children out, refusing to support them, sometimes tearing their cabins down around them, putting them out on the road without clothing, without shoes, without food. These people too drifted to Camp Nelson.

The army tried to get rid of them; some officials knew they were not legitimate contrabands, but others simply found them continually bothersome and—to put it baldly—in the way. At various points in the summer and autumn of 1864, the women and children at Camp Nelson and its sub-depots were driven out. On June 18, Col. Andrew H. Clark, "Comd. Post," cited "standing orders" that directed "all negroes that are found in camp without authority from their owners to be placed beyond the lines." On July 6, Speed S. Fry ordered that "all negro women and children & men in camp unfit for service [should] be delivered to their owners." On July 16, Lorenzo Thomas found at Camp Nelson "a number of old men, women, and children, which . . . should be sent to their homes. . . ." On August 13, General Burbridge ordered "that all women children & men unemployed in Camp Nelson be expelled." All the black women in the camp were sent out by General Orders Number 19 on August 23. "All negro women and children, except those who have written permits from these Head Qurs, to remain within the limits of this Camp," were expelled on September 19. Moving beyond the supply depot itself, on October 29, the commander of Point Burnside was ordered by the commander of Camp Nelson: "Preparatory to the Regiments moving you will turn out of Camp all Negro women and children."[189]

When the expulsion of November 1864 took place, it was certainly not a brand-new kind of incident; in fact, it was at least the eighth expulsion. In late November, as noted above, Camp Nelson was in the midst of its last military furor, the preparation for Stoneman's Raid in Virginia; regiments were coming and going; horses and mules had to be procured; forage provided. And there were four hundred slave women and children in the way and no one—it seemed—had time to notice that this expulsion was different from the earlier ones because the temperature was below freezing. The incident resulted in instant notoriety for Camp Nelson, a great deal of suffering, and many deaths. The November expulsion must be acknowledged as one of the darkest incidents in the history of Kentucky, much less of Camp Nelson.[190]

On the basis of the hardships and tragedies that this incident caused and through the combined efforts of Rev. John G. Fee and Capt. Theron E. Hall, an official, government-sponsored Refugee Home was opened at Camp Nelson, with buildings erected under the supervision of Capt. Hall. At the Home, black women and children who had male relatives serving as soldiers were legally entitled to sanctuary. Thousands took advantage of this new opportunity to escape from slavery and, more precisely, from the cruelty of their masters. They still were not necessarily free, but for a brief time they were safe from the savage persecution they had been suffering.

From disease and death, however, they were not safe. Even as the refugees assembled, they began to sicken and die, especially the children. Because most of Kentucky's slaveholders had owned only a few slaves, most of the black refugees had never been exposed to common communicable diseases. In fact, most of them had probably never been in a crowd of people before. Beyond that, many of the refugees had been starved, beaten, and half-frozen; their lives had been in turmoil for months. A report concerning the women and children in the Refugee Home, giving statistics for every five-day period from April 11 through July 16, reveals the full extent of the tragic problem. During the three months covered, the number of women increased at the camp steadily from 728 to 1408, almost doubling; the number of children increased from 813 to 1392. The number arriving far exceeded the number being discharged, obviously, but by a figure much larger than might be expected because there were so many deaths; 969 women arrived and 196 were discharged, while 1,030 children arrived and 105 were discharged. The death statistics are staggering, as evidenced by the following table[191]:

Week of	Deaths, women	Deaths, children
April 16	9	11
April 21	5	22
April 26	4	26
May 1	5	29
May 6	8	29
May 11	2	24
May 16	4	26
May 21	10	21
May 26	4	13
June 1	13	23
June 6	3	23
June 11	3	17
June 16	8	15
June 21	1	25
June 26	3	32
July 1	7	28
July 6	6	21
July 11	5	17
July 16	3	7

In a period of approximately three months, 103 women and 409 children died.

For the entire duration of the Refugee Home's operation, nothing could be done to stop the high mortality, although military officials tried to help. For example, "Medical Officers at Camp Nelson" were ordered "to furnish medical supplies for colored refugees on proper requisition approved by Camp Commander."[192] Unfortunately, the most significant words in this order may very well have been "on proper requisition approved by Camp Commander." In the context of the mortality among the refugees, some of the bureaucratic controversies that raged among the administrators of the Home and among the officials of the Union Army and the Freedmen's Bureau seem pointless indeed.

Controversies at the Refugee Home

From the opening of the Camp Nelson Refugee Home in January 1865 to its closing in March 1866 (no one predicted such a brief span of operation when the expensive enterprise began) the people who worked there—teachers, missionaries, and administrators—were deeply embroiled in controversies concerning policies and staffing. Upon Fee's return to Camp Nelson from Berea in January 1865, he immediately began pressing for his particular short-term goals: to have the AMA, rather than the WFAC, in charge of educational and religious work (although the WFAC, conveniently based in Cincinnati, might be permitted to dispense clothing and books); to have Rev. Abisha Scofield appointed superintendent of the Home rather than Rev. John Vetter or Rev. Lester Williams Jr. The latter was Capt. Hall's choice, probably because Williams had been a friend of Hall's even before the war; they both came from the same small town of Holden, Massachusetts.[193] Hall and Fee agreed to put Lester Williams in the position "on trial," under the oversight of a board of directors, consisting of Fee for certain and two others, upon whom they could not yet agree.[194]

After an absence from Camp Nelson to visit his rather neglected home in Berea, Fee returned to camp—having been delayed by "eruptions" (hemorrhoids and saddle sores) and "ice in the streams"—only to find new and growing enmities among the missionaries.[195] Rev. Williams was still superintendent, with Rev. Vetter in his employ as clerk, receiving pay from the government. This arrangement aroused passionate jealousy in Rev. Scofield, who had coveted the superintendency of the Home and now regarded Vetter, whom he had previously befriended, as a traitor. The new quartermaster of Camp Nelson, E.B.W. Restieaux,[196] disturbed by these personal conflicts, was unwilling to consider replacing Williams with Scofield; Fee reported to Whipple on February 3 that Restieaux deemed Scofield "too old for the post." Fee disagreed and was much exercised as well because the quartermaster objected to the plan for a three-man board of directors. Still, Fee thought the matter would be resolved. "I think," he wrote, "we can give Bro. Scofield the school & Bro. Williams the general superintendence and both will be satisfied."

Fee wanted the AMA to appoint a superintendent and then apply for governmental confirmation. A new committee of three was proposed: Fee "for religious care . . . & order," Williams to "manage the school" at the Refugee Home, Scofield "in another part of the camp" to teach the black soldiers. Fee would be chairman of this committee. General Fry, in the meantime, urged Fee himself to accept the general superintendency of the Home and the soldiers' schools, because, as Fee stated, "The colored people know me as their friend and I know their habits."[197] Fee refused—on the basis that he wanted to devote himself to preaching, but he would continue to do a great deal more than preach.

Another controversy was growing because Fee objected to Hall's ward system at the Refugee Home. "Much labor is being expended," Fee complained in his February 7 letter to Whipple, "in putting up 4 wards, 25 ft. by 75, aisle between bunks — these three berths high — unhandy. 125 persons in one continuous babel, children crying, mothers fretting." He urged the construction of "little cottages, 16 by 12 feet, room for 8 or 10 persons in neat rows [the cottages, not the persons]." As with most Camp Nelson issues, this one was most urgent; in this case, because 5,000 troops were expected in camp by the middle of April.

April was two months away, but even by the next day (February 8), Camp Nelson had received "parts of three regiments of colored soldiers" and nearly eight hundred women and children (and still more coming—seventy-seven on the previous day alone). Scofield was to be in charge of the school for the soldiers, Williams in charge of superintending the women and children—as agreed. But in the meantime, on February 7, Capt. Hall had gone to Lexington "& had himself appointed general superintendent." Gen. Burbridge had obligingly made the appointment, even though he had already assured John G. Fee that "some benevolent society" (the AMA) would be allowed to nominate the general superintendent. Fee was irked at Burbridge's thoughtlessness, but he was uncommonly angered by Hall's action. "And this he did," Fee fumed, "after he had proposed a <u>board</u> of directors."

It was hard for Fee to accept, even though he acknowledged that Capt. Hall was a devoted abolitionist. "But [he] does not serve God for naught," Fee said. "He is artful and ambitious." Fee wondered if he should have accepted the position himself when he had the chance, "so as to have kept it within the direction of the Am. Miss. Associa." Still, Fee was willing to work with Hall, believing that the captain might "wield this for Good." So Fee proposed another committee to Hall— one to select teachers and matrons. Hall generously suggested that Fee "assume the whole" himself, but Fee refused: "principle not right," he explained, objecting to one-man rule, even if he was the man. Thus it was back to the idea of a committee of three (Fee, Williams, and Scofield), subject to the approval of the distant AMA, of course, from which responses were never timely. There was an inverse proportion between the dire urgency of the work at Camp Nelson and the slowness and difficulty of administrative decisions concerning it. On the housing front, Fee was convinced that Capt. Hall would adopt his cottage plan and put an end to the "noise, feuds, disease, and disgust . . . engendered" in the wards.[198]

Hall and Fee, the most prominent leaders in the refugee section of the camp, continued to disagree about whether the work should be supported primarily by the AMA, the WFAC, or by both. Hall regarded the services of the WFAC as especially important because it could deliver physical donations—clothing, furniture, cutlery for the dining room, even, in a sense, teachers—much more quickly and efficiently than the AMA could, as Fee grudgingly agreed at last.[199] Fee was very upset with the "cooperative movement"[200] between the AMA and the WFAC because he had, as he wrote to AMA officials, stayed at Camp Nelson "at great sacrifice of feeling & family interest . . . for the sake of turning all into your society . . . and for the Kingdom of Christ." Now it seemed that all would slip through the slack fingers of the AMA. "If I have ungodly helpers," Fee protested, "I shall be hindered."[201]

He was convinced he already had ungodly helpers. Many, including Capt. Theron E. Hall, neglected their worship opportunities. In fact, few of them attended Rev. Fee's church services. Rev. Lester Williams was the most reprehensible, since he lived within "ten steps" of the Dining Hall where church was held, and habitually slept in on the Sabbath. Once Fee checked up on the recalcitrant Baptist minister after preaching was over and was shocked to discover him "in bed — not sick."[202]

Nevertheless, Williams had sufficient energy to weigh in on the side of the WFAC in the mission society controversy. He wrote to the AMA to point out— quite accurately—that that unresponsive organization had provided no teachers for Camp Nelson at all when they were being begged to do so. In the wake of the power struggle with its rival organization, the AMA suddenly *wanted* to supply teachers. Your letter, Williams wrote sarcastically, "unveils to me an interest in the instruction of the colored refugees at this place that I did not suppose existed in connection with the Miss. Asso. I have good reason for thinking that this regard was small." This letter was written at a time when the camp had ten new teachers, five from the WFAC, four sent by the Quakers' yearly meeting in Indiana, and one who had simply volunteered on her own. The WFAC had even offered three more, who had to be refused because all the schoolrooms were in use.[203]

Gen. Clinton B. Fisk[204] of the Freedmen's Bureau thought all the teachers should be hired from the same source—namely, the convenient one, WFAC. However, when asked for its "will . . . in reference to [this] proposition, the AMA promptly replied with a resounding, NO.[205] Visiting Camp Nelson in July 1865, Fisk decided to put all under military rule, probably as opposed to the rule of warring aid society advocates, but asked John G. Fee to nominate a suitable man (that is, a military man) to be general superintendent of the camp. It was a privilege that Fee would not have time to use. He was deeply concerned about his nominating assignment and wrote many letters analyzing and pondering potential candidates and possible outcomes, but none of his work and worry would come to fruition, because the camp would soon be closed. The newly established Freedmen's Bureau had jurisdiction over all the black civilians at the Refugee Home, and the Bureau's single-minded policy was simply to disperse them. No one living at Camp Nelson—neither missionaries, teachers, nor former slaves—knew that the facility was doomed.

For a few months, Fee had been not just the primary letter writer and controversialist at Camp Nelson, but also its most productive planner by far: he wrote separate proposals for virtually every aspect of the freed peoples' future—for their health, employment, land ownership, housing, education, religious training, political advancement, etc.; had these proposals been gathered together, they would have comprised a coherent overall plan for the advancement of former slaves. Many of his ideas never had any practical fruition because they were meant for a Camp Nelson that did not endure. Some of his most notable principles, however, were actually put into practice—albeit on a greatly reduced scale—in his work at Berea College, but never really at Camp Nelson, where a small school was established under his guidance, a school that was never more than a grade school and Normal school for local young people who all happened to be black.[206] It was almost a contradiction of Fee's most revolutionary plan, because his central goal was social equality among the races.

When John G. Fee introduced into the camp a young woman of African descent as a teacher, insisting that she be treated as an equal by all the other staff, the resulting controversy put everything else in the shade. In his *Autobiography* Fee remembered how the whole episode began. He was visiting Danville, helping the local black people start a school; on Sunday, of course, he attended church, a black church, which was perfectly usual for him, whenever he was away from home. "I saw in the congregation (colored) a young woman of light complexion, whose manner, as she came to the altar to partake of the Lord's Supper, favorably impressed me. I inquired of the pastor who she was. He told me she was a member of that church, with fair education and good parentage. Immediately it occurred to me that she was the woman with whom to test the caste question among the teachers at Camp Nelson, and set the precedent of giving positions to colored persons as fast as prepared for such" (180). Fee, expecting the full support of the AMA in his decision, apparently had not expected the outrage that his action would arouse among the Camp Nelson teachers and administrators.

Maybe he should have foreseen the local reaction. But how could he have known, more generally, that ". . . segregation was not uncommon in AMA educational facilities"? In many AMA freedmen's schools in the South, white teachers and black teachers were advised not to board in the same households. In North Carolina, for example, an AMA educator "contended that boarding black and whites together would create an intolerable situation for the white teachers" because they were already being "charged with endeavoring to bring about a condition of social equality between the blacks and the whites," and, even worse, "charged with teaching the blacks that they have a right to demand from the whites social equality."[207]

Fee expected or hoped for more institutional imprimaturs than he ever received. The AMA and the WFAC more or less supported Fee's position, while decrying his action, but the Freedmen's Bureau, from which Fee wanted some support, never took a public position at all. If it had, Fee probably would not have been pleased, for "Bureau leaders from the commissioner on down were especially anxious to counteract allegations that teachers openly practiced 'social equality,' a breach of Southern racial etiquette that [Oliver Otis] Howard considered one of the chief causes of local resistance."[208]

A sample of the ordinary contemporary response to Fee's testing of social equality appears in a comment written by a Bureau clerk performing his usual task of summarizing a letter's contents: assessing the social equality crisis at Camp Nelson, the clerk calls it "a small family quarrel over the <u>victuals</u> whereon Fee expends much rhetoric — and is finally of the opinion that 'Faith can wait.'"[209] For Fee, however, the matter was absolutely crucial; when James Jaquess, then superintendent of the Refugee Home, ordered Fee to take Belle Mitchell[210] out of the dining hall, Fee refused; threatened with Jaquess's authority, Fee said, "Very well, I will risk all on the issue."[211]

Was it trivial, as some of Fee's contemporaries believed, or was it, as he clearly thought, worth staking everything for? What was all the struggle for if the equality of black people and white people was not to be recognized? It was for nothing, in Fee's opinion. The war, the end of slavery, the effort to teach and minister, all for nothing, unless practical recognition of the brotherhood and sisterhood of all people sprang from it.

The Belle Mitchell incident at Camp Nelson completely divided the former abolitionists who worked there, basically pitting Fee and his few supporters against everyone else. The administrative structure that the founding of the Refugee Home had inspired crumbled even as the Freedmen's Bureau approached the camp with the avowed intention of dissolving the whole enterprise.

The Freedmen's Bureau and the Closing of Camp Nelson

The formation of the Refugee Home was a turning point in Camp Nelson's history; now much more than a military post, recruiting station, or a supply depot, Camp Nelson was suddenly the focus of dreams and plans for the future of the black race in Kentucky and beyond. The facilities attracted thousands of black people and raised enormous expectations in the minds of the white workers among them. There would be a permanent gathering place, they thought, even a flourishing town perhaps, with spectacularly well-equipped schools. The physical plant was already there. When the war ended, Camp Nelson would be the largest center for black progress—of every sort—in the state of Kentucky. John G. Fee, a ringleader in planning for such an enlightened prospect, was not the only person to suffer from this delusion. Hundreds of people had their hopes tied to it: high hopes, doomed to come crashing down.

When the Refugee Camp was in full swing, Camp Nelson was at the height of its population and its building boom. Thousands of people, hundreds of buildings, hundreds of workers—all these within a military post that was vast, a huge operation, four thousand acres in all, with more than eight hundred acres in use as the core of the camp, more than three hundred wooden buildings besides numerous tents. In addition, ninety-seven cottages had been built specifically for the refugees. But at Camp Nelson's high point of population and structures, it was already all over. When the war ended in April 1865 virtually everything that had been built up at Camp Nelson had to go. The soldiers went first, leaving only a token military presence at Camp Nelson for a brief interlude, then disappearing altogether. All of the WFAC and most of the AMA workers departed for other teaching assignments.

But to the dismay of Federal officials, the refugees stayed, insisted on staying, kept staying, were sometimes ejected and then returned. The Freedmen's Bureau, the government's solution to the problem of four million freed people suddenly thrust into American society, had been formed on March 3, 1865, and the policy of the Bureau was to break up all gatherings of black people at military installations. Camp Nelson had to go: the Refugee Home had to be destroyed.

On June 26, 1865, Clinton B. Fisk took office as assistant commissioner of the Freedmen's Bureau for Tennessee and Kentucky. This appointment by Gen. Oliver Otis Howard seems to have stretched the authority of the Bureau, "for Kentucky had not been one of the Confederate states, and only they were supposed to have assistant commissioners."[212] But R.E. Farwell,[213] the Bureau's Special Agent, their designated Superintendent of the Refugee Camp at Camp Nelson, was charged with the monumental and heartbreaking task of breaking up the camp. By October 6, 1865, the week before Farwell's arrival at Camp Nelson, all but one of the camps in Kentucky and Tennessee had already been closed:[214] the only one remaining was Camp Nelson. Gen. Clinton B. Fisk had already decided "to cease offering rations," which had been one of the Freedmen's Bureau's primary functions; Generals Howard and Fisk agreed that closing the camps and denying rations to those people living within former camps would "[force] the idle to work or starve."[215]

Even before Farwell's work began, the Bureau had been reducing the numbers of women and children in the camp. On September 14, Miss Annie Hager, who had been a volunteer teacher at the camp under the WFAC, now working for the Freedmen's Bureau, was on the road with forty-seven Camp Nelson refugees she was escorting to their new home in Springfield, Ohio. En route she bought their meals, paid for their transportation, including a seven dollar fee to cross the Ohio River, and purchased dresses, shoes, stockings, and underclothing, plus a straw tick, sheets, bolster and pillow cases, a blanket, a stove, and a supply of wood. Upon their arrival in Springfield, Hager paid the rent and started back to Camp Nelson to organize another group.[216]

On October 1, Annie Hager was traveling again, this time with a group of seventy-five black women and children from Camp Nelson. Hager had searched for homes for these people in various Ohio towns: Urbana, Mechanicsburg, Landau, Xenia, among others. This trip was much more expensive than the previous one, with outlays for skirts (seven of them), blankets, ticking, diaper flannel (twenty yards of it), seven chemises to go with the seven skirts, wood, beef, coffee, tea, sixty-nine loaves of bread, and one month's rent for two rooms ($9.00). Hager's escorting trips continued throughout October and November 1865, and during each of them she procured and paid for basic food, clothing, and shelter for dozens of people. The trips must have been very demanding: on one journey, for example, Hager had five nursing mothers in tow. Illnesses among the travelers were frequent; some of Hager's expenses on almost every trip were for medicine. An expense item on November 5 was "Tea & provisions for the Sick & dying." In the middle of October she had to pay $12.75 for a coffin and burial for one Martha Carr; on the fifteenth of November, $13.80 to bury Mary Bowen on the way to Toledo, Ohio; on the twenty-eighth of November, $14.20 "Funeral Expenses of Beverlin Hay."

Hager's organizational skills and her patience must have been incredible. On November 11 she was beginning a trip with 103 people; she paid for their supper at Nicholasville, Kentucky, their hotel bills for two days in Covington, and their rail-road fares to various points in Ohio. Eventually, she presented an expense account for $959.77 to the Freedmen's Bureau, the total of her expenditure in the process of relocating some 450 homeless people from Camp Nelson.

It was only a small percentage of the thousands who had to be turned out and away from Camp Nelson. Farwell had been supposed to get the job done in days or at most a few weeks, but it necessarily stretched on for months, in order to be "consistent with humanity."[217] The Bureau's policy involved uprooting a few thousand homeless people (again), mostly women and children, and sending them away from a place of comparative security to—well, who knows where? That was the problem. Where were the people to go? They had no jobs, no education to speak of beyond what little they had learned in their all-too-brief schooling at Camp Nelson, no experience of the world, no money, no land . . . the list could be extended.

Farwell was ordered to make life at the camp so unpleasant that the people would go of their own free will; government rations were reduced to beans and split peas. Still many refugees stayed. Buildings had to be torn down around them to induce some to depart.

Eventually, inevitably, the camp was almost emptied. Some refugees struck off on their own; some made rapprochements with their former owners and returned to situations frighteningly like what they had known before the war; many migrated to big cities, Cincinnati especially. Some trekked off with Annie Hager, as we have seen; some families and individual soldiers accepted John G. Fee's invitation to settle in his new experimental colony at Berea, Kentucky, where they could buy land, attend an integrated school and church, and live on a basis of equality with white neighbors. Some—rather horrifyingly—were impressed into work gangs, much against their will, and shipped to a plantation in Mississippi owned by Gen. Stephen G. Burbridge and a business partner, who was, according to the Massachusetts-born Farwell, "a very good specimen of the swell head whiskey drinking Southern planter"; it was said the black people on this journey were to become "free" workers.[218] Most of the refugees left Camp Nelson by the grimmest possible route; they went to the cemetery. None of the other departing groups approached the numbers of the dead.

Some few refugees remained in camp.

Months behind his original schedule, Farwell filed his last report from Camp

Nelson on March 14, 1866. From that day on, no official refuge for former slaves existed in Kentucky—and the official "protection" provided for them by the Freedmen's Bureau soon ended as well. At the site of the former Refugee Home, the black people remaining would become the inhabitants of a little village known first as Ariel, then as Hall, or merely Camp Nelson.

Ariel and Afterwards

After all the other teachers and administrators had gone, Fee, his friends Rev. Abisha Scofield and Rev. Gabriel Burdett, through a series of hardships and setbacks that would have deterred most people, established a school (called Ariel Academy or simply Camp Nelson School) and provided leadership for the little group of black people who still lived where the Refugee Home had been. For a brief time, Scofield and his family lived at the camp and continued teaching the local people, now the citizens of Camp Nelson, but in December 1866 he was violently driven from his home by a mob of pro-Confederate ruffians. He appealed to the Freedmen's Bureau and to the Union Army for protection, but to little avail. The Scofield family left Camp Nelson. In April 1867 the American Missionary Association listed its new workers at Camp Nelson, Rev. Gabriel Burdett, Rev. A. Scofield, and Miss Scofield, but a note at the bottom of the page stated that the Scofields had been "driven out by rebel 'regulators.'"[219] They would never return.

A small, scattered village grew up, sponsored by John G. Fee, who had, with great difficulty and at a considerable financial loss, purchased the land where the refugee camp had been located and "parceled the whole" out into town lots to be purchased by the former slaves who stayed on. For the whole year of 1868, John and Matilda Fee sold nine lots in Ariel for a total of $417; in May 1869 they sold one lot for $115, the only sale for that year. In April 1869 Charles Burdett and John Tracy, both of Ariel, were empowered "to collect rents from tenants occupying tenements belonging to John G. Fee in the town of Ariel." In 1870 the Fees sold two lots for a total of $135, in 1871 one lot for $67, in 1872 one for $62. And so it continued: two or three sales in 1875, and then none at all for five years: one lot sold to "Henry Clay (colored) of Ariel" for $18 in 1880. Throughout the 1880s and 90s, Fee was still selling lots from his original purchase of Camp Nelson, which he had really expected to sell off completely in 1868. The last piece that Fee actually sold himself was on August 27, 1900, a few months before his death.[220]

For years, Rev. Gabriel Burdett was a leader in the Ariel community, minister of the church that had been founded by Fee, and even trustee and superintendent of the academy, although his own writing remained at the grade school level where Fee's brief instruction had left it; but Burdett was the only continuous presence at the school for a decade. On March 10, 1869, John G. Fee reported to the AMA that the school at Camp Nelson "ran up from 16 to 106 within three months."[221] It never got much higher than that, but it frequently fell lower. Teachers at Camp Nelson were, apparently, easy to find and very hard to retain.

The workers at Camp Nelson in May 1869, "commissioned at Cincinnati and supported by the Western Freedmen's Aid Commission and the A.M.A." were Rev. Gabriel Burdett and Mr. and Mrs. Isaac M. Newton.[222] The Newtons, a couple from Kinsman, Ohio, taught at Ariel Academy for only a few months in 1869. But their primary interest in life was Temperance, with a capital T. For the *American Missionary*, they wrote a glowing report of the school and their work, promising a further account because their readers "would also like to hear whether . . . the Temperance Society succeeds in breaking up the Distillery one mile from here but is now making $1,000 worth of whiskey per day." They recommended that their readers "pray that the songs & prayers of these children may be uppermost in causing those formidable stone walls to tumble and fall, never more to rise."[223] The distilleries are still there, looming, hideous eyesores at the intersection of Highway 27 and Hall Road, but the Newtons "fled Camp N." by December 1869, having been "indiscreet"; perhaps they had been intemperate about temperance.[224]

By June of the next year, the Newtons had been replaced by Rev. and Mrs. William H. Butler of Camp Nelson, who had likewise disappeared by the next report in January 1871; the job was then taken by Mr. Enoch Seales, the new single and sole schoolteacher, who claimed an enrollment of 18 in the school, 6 of whom were over 16, and who was no longer at Camp Nelson by May 1872.[225] Superintendent Gabriel Burdett reported: "We have a School now going on at this point though the number was not veary large last month yet we have a great many more this month than came lasst month And our sunday school is increasing. And or Church is still growing some. And the temperance band or band of hope is increasing."[226]

Seales was replaced by B.A. Imes, whom Burdett described as "a splended teacher from Oberlin Ohio."[227] Meanwhile, Burdett had begun setting up local schools for black children, taught by former students of Ariel, and had launched himself into an enthusiastic career as a prohibition speaker.[228] Fee was very impressed with Gabriel's new mission: "White men who are good judges tell me no man in the county spoke with such power & effect as did Burdett to immense audiences white & colored White men opened [the] Court House then churches & own tables to him — many of the best men of [Garrard] county."[229]

Throughout 1873, Burdett continued "geting up Schools" for former Academy students to teach in a ten or twelve mile radius around Camp Nelson.[230] In 1873, Burdett was the sole AMA worker again (and so he remained until 1877), although teachers continued to come to the school under other auspices.[231] A Quaker friend of Levi Coffin's (Coffin had been an Ariel Academy trustee) and his wife were the new teachers early in 1874.[232]

The Friends were followed by the man who would be the school's most popular and successful teacher, Howard S. Fee,[233] John G. Fee's second son. Howard, like his older (now dying) brother Burritt, had taught soldiers in Camp Nelson when he himself was still a very young teenager; now he returned, all grown up and determined to do his best for his father's ancient project. Under his leadership, both the school and the church grew in numbers. "Our School is in better condition than it ever has been," Burdett wrote in February 1875; the enrollment was up to 115 pupils, and Eugene Fairchild, son of the Berea College's president, was pressed into service to help his friend Howard with the work. Ariel Academy Normal School was advertised with a real promotional leaflet for the fall term of 1875: "The School will be conducted by Howard S. Fee, a graduate from Berea College, who has had experience as a teacher . . . Special attention will be given to the Normal Department— the work of preparing teachers for the work of teaching."[234]

On September 30, 1876, John G. Fee's son Burritt, in his father's words, "came home to die & was in great distress."[235] When he was only fifteen, Burritt had taught black soldiers at Camp Nelson in the earliest days of his father's sojourn there. In the pestilential atmosphere of Camp Nelson, Burritt had become extremely ill, and he remained sick or sickly all the rest of his brief life. At his death, it must have seemed to John G. Fee that he had now sacrificed as much for the work at Camp Nelson as human flesh could endure.

Gabriel Burdett also was sacrificing more than he could bear. By the end of 1876, he was beginning "to think that the colorade people of this state can never do much in this camp, and especialy in this State. We are in a hopeless minority here and I fear we will not be able to accomplish much with all the impediments that will of corse, be thrown in our way." The church was in debt and so was Burdett; "many days," he wrote, "I have to do almost without any thing to eat and I am getting entirely without Clothing suitble to wear away from home." On May 12, 1877, he confessed to the AMA that he was considering going to Kansas. "And at this time," he stated, "there seames to bee a great upriseing of the colorade people to that end all over the state of Kentucky   Hundreds of them are going from this county and Fayet and Garrard counties and many other portions of the state." He begged the officers of the AMA not to blame him for his decision; "for I know," he said, "if you were to see my little ones around my feet and hear them asking where we will get the next bread to eat, you would say go and trust the Lord for he is in Kansas as well as Kentucky."[236]

On May 15, 1877, Gabriel Burdett wrote his last letter from Camp Nelson, expressing his sorrow at leaving the state where he had spent "more than forty seven years of my life 34 of it a slave and 2 of it a soldier in order to free myself and wife and children, and the rest of it as a freedman and Missionary."[237] So after years of grinding poverty and increasingly pointless struggles with the church and school, Burdett gave up his hope that black people might make recognizable progress in his native Kentucky, abandoned his work, and left with a number of black families from Camp Nelson and surrounding areas to resettle in Kansas. "Shall I give my influence," he asked, "in behalf of my people remaining where they will be oppressed all of their life and where it will be imposible for them to rise any higher than mear mud sills. . . ?" The February 1878 edition of the *American Missionary* still printed the heading "CAMP NELSON. *Minister*" followed by a blank where Gabriel Burdett's name had appeared for ten years.

The church that had been under his ministry for a decade found a series of new preachers; for a few years, Howard S. Fee continued to teach at Ariel Academy. In 1878 Berea College sponsored a pamphlet advertising the Normal School at Camp Nelson, addressed "To the friends of Christian Education"; President Edward Henry Fairchild of Berea extolled the work of Camp Nelson's principal, H.S. Fee; John A.R. Rogers, professor at Berea, gave the Normal School work his imprimatur. And Fee himself, under the heading "Words of a Life Worker in the Cause of Freedom," contributed the following reflection: "Camp Nelson was the rendezvous of soldiery and the birthplace of liberty to Kentucky. It is hallowed in the minds of thousands. I felt during the war and do now, that God has marked it out as a place for a school—a fountain of intellectual and moral good to the State. Faith and earnest effort can make it such."[238]

It sounded like a eulogy, and, in effect, it was. After Gabriel Burdett's departure, the Camp Nelson school continued its moderately successful, small-scale operation for almost thirty years, but the days were long past when anyone really expected great things of it. In 1902, when Ariel Academy, in need of financial support and students, was very near failure, its trustees applied to Berea College, requesting that Ariel become a part of Berea. John Rogers, a close associate of Fee's in the founding of Berea, urged President William Goodell Frost of Berea not to accept the proposal from Camp Nelson on the grounds that it might lead black people of Kentucky to think of "Camp Nelson . . . [as] the colored part of Berea College."[239] Ironically, the Day Law of 1904, the very year of Ariel Academy's closing, would eventually drive Berea College to the formation of a segregated "colored part." By that time, the school at Camp Nelson no longer existed. Then nothing connected with wartime institutions remained at Camp Nelson except a national cemetery.

In 1912, the Board of Missions for Freedmen of the Presbyterian Church in the United States of America, a corporation duly organized under the laws of the Commonwealth of Pennsylvania, city of Pittsburgh, sold part of its real estate from Camp Nelson Academy to Charles Clay for twenty-five dollars. The last piece of real estate associated with the school was sold in 1915 to Jack Isom of Jessamine County for thirty dollars.[240]

John G. Fee did not live to see the end of his Camp Nelson work. He died on January 11, 1901, and as part of the settlement of his estate, his surviving children were still selling portions of the Camp Nelson land he had purchased *to sell* in 1868; the last lot was sold in 1904.

In 1872 Fee had written, "I have just returned from a very fatiguing & exhausting trip, through rain & cold to & from Camp Nelson. That work is a great burden to me. I have not sold a lot during the year — have collected 155 dollars rent — have paid near one hundred for repairs. Have a debt of over 12 hundred dollars there." And in 1873 he had written, "Camp Nelson has been a great burden on my shoulders. I do not see the end; yet my purpose was to do good and had men met their pledges to Gabriel Burdett I should not have been embarrassed." He was "embarrassed" (which meant "financially disabled" in contemporary usage) for years to come, but still—not exactly hopeful—faithful in his support of Ariel Academy. In his will he left a bequest to the Camp Nelson school, directing that his remaining property at Camp Nelson should be sold and "the proceeds [should] go to the benefit of the Camp Nelson Academy. If it shall not then be in operation as an accademy it shall go to the benefit of the Church there . . . [if it is still] undenominational and teaching as now, Faith in the Lord Jesus Christ, the son of God and baptism in his name and the Bible as the source of teaching and guide in good works."[241]

John G. Fee—who never lived in Camp Nelson after 1865, when he decided to make Berea his life's work—nevertheless maintained his connection with Camp Nelson from the day he first arrived there (the Fourth of July in 1864) until his dying day in 1901. Eventually, he was the only person associated with the wartime work at the camp who was still engaged there, still engaged in the project of trying to help former slaves enter the mainstream of American society. Rev. John G. Fee, the first missionary to arrive at Camp Nelson, was the last to go.

Notes to Introduction

1. Ambrose Everett Burnside (1824–1881), a native of Indiana, began his military career in the Mexican War. He is generally identified as the founder of Camp Nelson because he started the process of building it when he took command of the Department of the Ohio. *CWD*; Marvel, 268–69.

2. The Department of the Ohio had been formed, reorganized, reformed and abolished several times before its revival on August 19, 1862, to encompass Illinois, Indiana, Ohio, Michigan, Wisconsin (very briefly), and Kentucky east of the Tennessee River, including Cumberland Gap. The headquarters for this version of the military division were in Cincinnati (an earlier Department of the Ohio had headquarters in Louisville). *CWD*, 606.

3. Cox, 449.

4. Horatio Gouvernour Wright (1820–1899), Union general from Connecticut, was commander of the Department of the Ohio from August 23, 1862, until March 25, 1863, when Burnside took over. *CWD;* Dyer, 1:112, 524; *GIB; HR*, 1:1062.

5. Wright to Cullum, 15 Mar. 1863, *OR*, Series 1, Vol. 23, Part 2, pp. 143–46. (Hereafter, records from *OR* abbreviated as "*OR*, [series number], [volume number], pt. [part number], [page numbers]"; eg, *OR*, 1, 23, pt. 2, 143–46.) Wright claimed he had sent off so many men from the department that there were "left only enough to protect the State of Kentucky from inroads of the enemy in the winter season, while the roads were nearly impassable." He had only six thousand available men in central Kentucky "to keep off raids from the most fertile portion of the State."

6. Robinson to Wright, 1 Mar. 1863, *OR*, 1, 23, pt. 2, 96–97. James Fisher Robinson became acting governor of Kentucky after Beriah Magoffin resigned; Robinson's brief term lasted from August 18, 1862, until September 1, 1863. *KE*, 777.

7. Henry Wager Halleck (1815–1872), a career soldier from New York, was commander of Missouri, of Mississippi, of the Armies of the United States, and of Virginia, and ultimately Lincoln's military adviser and General-in-Chief until Grant's promotion in March 1864. *CWD;* Dyer, 1:71; *GIB; HR*, 1:491.

8. Halleck to Burnside, 23 Mar. 1863, *OR*, 1, 23, pt. 2, 162–64. Halleck's advice was basically the experienced wisdom that Gen. Horatio G. Wright had formulated upon the occasion of his resignation as commander of the Department of the Ohio. But Wright had mentioned the invasion of East Tennessee as a military idea that was basically impossible; Halleck conveyed the same notion to Burnside, while urging its possibility.

9. Wright to Cullum, 15 Mar. 1863, *OR*, 1, 23, pt. 2, 145.

10. Cox, 475.

11. The Ninth Army Corps had been created on July 22, 1862, from troops in the Department of the South and the Department of North Carolina; the latter had been Burnside's Expeditionary Corps in his North Carolina operations. The corps was first assigned to the Army of the Potomac under General Burnside's command until September 3, 1862, when he was replaced. The corps was under Burnside's direct command again very briefly (two days) after he was appointed commandant of the Department of the Ohio, but various other generals (Parke, Willcox, and Potter) actually commanded the Ninth when it was part of Burnside's Army of the Ohio. Ordered to Kentucky, the corps had two months of occupation

duty there, then participated in Grant's siege of Vicksburg, Mississippi, before embarking on Burnside's Knoxville Campaign. In April 1864, the Ninth was moved back to the East and rejoined the Army of the Potomac, with Burnside once again as commandant (from April 13 to August 14, 1864). The Ninth Army Corps was so mobile that it was called "a wandering corps, whose dead lie buried in seven states." *CWD*, 192; Dyer, 1:313–18.

12. The Twenty-third was organized April 27, 1863, from regiments stationed in Kentucky and placed under the command of Gen. George L. Hartsuff. *CWD*, 199–200; Dyer, 1:528–37.

13. During its first year of operations (actually for more than a year), Camp Nelson was mostly populated by troops of the Ninth and the Twenty-third Army Corps in various configurations as they arrived and departed and sometimes arrived again. Kentucky soldiers were always a very small proportion of the population at the camp, until the recruitment of slaves in the state began.

14. Burnside to Gillmore, 26 Mar. 1863, *OR*, 1, 23, pt. 2, 179.

15. Julius White (1816–1890), a native New Yorker, was the general in command of the Fourth Division of the Twenty-third Army Corps, Department of the Ohio. He had begun his military career as colonel of the Thirty-seventh Illinois Infantry. *CWD; Dyer*, 1:110; *GIB; HR*, 1:1028.

16. William Price Sanders (1833–1863) was colonel of the Fifth Kentucky Cavalry from March 4, 1863. He was promoted to brigadier general in October 1863 and appointed chief of the cavalry for the Department of the Ohio, but he was mortally wounded in the East Tennessee Campaign in November of the same year. Burnside named Fort Sanders at Knoxville for this fallen comrade. *CWD*.

17. Cox, 492.

18. Hickman Bridge or Hickman's Bridge: both versions appear equally often in the original texts. It is also occasionally called "Wernwag Bridge" in honor of Lewis Wernwag of Pennsylvania, who constructed the two-hundred foot covered bridge at a cost of thirty thousand dollars. The south entrance of the bridge, in Garrard County, bore the inscription "Erected A.D. 1838, L.V. Wernwag, Architect." It stood for ninety years. Apparently, the bridge originally had solid walls, but windows were added to "allow enough light for safe passage." Lancaster Women's Club, 275.

19. Report of Maj. Charles B. Seidel, Third Ohio Cavalry, 19 Oct. 1862, *OR*, 1, 16, pt. 1, 1147. At the time, Morgan was participating with his Second Kentucky Cavalry in the Confederate invasion of Kentucky under Gen. Braxton Bragg. Hickman Bridge was protected from his supposed intentions by one battalion of the Fourth Ohio Volunteer Cavalry. On another occasion, according to local legend, the bridge barely escaped destruction when retreating Confederates prepared a bonfire in the bridge, but "a Garrard County comrade," Captain Michael Salter of Company E, Third Kentucky Cavalry (South), prevailed upon them "to spare the structure as it was the only outlet north for the citizens and it might never be restored." Kinnaird, 15.

20. Officers of the Engineers Corps who inspected the site found rebel batteries already in place on the south side of the river, left there after Bragg's invasion. Anderson to Simpson, 4 Jan. 1863, Orlando M. Poe Papers, CMU. (Collection hereafter abbreviated as Poe Papers.)

21. John Pegram (1832–1865) was Kirby Smith's chief of staff during the Confederate invasion of Kentucky. *GIG*.

22. Humphrey Marshall (1812–1872), a Kentuckian, became a brigadier general in the Confederate Army; he had also participated in Kirby Smith's earlier Confederate invasion. *GIG*.

23. Frank Wolford (1817–1895) was colonel of the First Kentucky Cavalry. *KE*, 963.

24. Kinnaird, 16.

25. A native of Garrard County, Jackman's maiden name was Louisa West; apparently, Wolford readily believed her because she was a relative of Capt. Thornton K. Hackley, who was part of Wolford's command. In addition, Mrs. Vaughn had two sons in Hackley's Company G, a fact which makes it plain that she, at least, was not a young woman at the time of this heroic incident. See the following note for sources.

26. Telling substantially the same story with slightly differing details, three histories of Garrard County, Kentucky, recount these incidents: Calico, 149–52; Lancaster Women's Club, 275–283; Kinnaird, 15–16.

27. Special Orders No. 141, 25 Apr. 1863, *OR*, 1, 23, pt. 2, 350.

28. James Hervey Simpson (1813–1883), a native of New Jersey, was chief engineer of the Department of the Ohio; he was promoted to the rank of lt. colonel on June 1, 1863. *CWD*; *HR*, 1:888.

29. Capt. John H. Dickerson, U.S. Army, was chief quartermaster for the Department of Ohio, with his headquarters in Cincinnati. A native of Ohio, he began his military service in an Indiana regiment. *HR*, 1:372.

30. This formation undoubtedly contributed to the choice of site. On May 16 Simpson wrote, "The Kentucky River and Hickman Creek, on account of the precipitous character of their bluffs, will doubtless form a considerable natural defense. . . ." Simpson to Babcock, 16 May 1863, Poe Papers.

31. Orville E. Babcock (c. 1836–1884) was chief engineer of the Central District of Kentucky at the date of this letter; he participated in Burnside's East Tennessee Campaign and subsequently served as chief engineer for the Department of the Ohio from January 23 to March 20, 1864. *CWD*.

32. Simpson to Totten, 20 May 1863, *OR*, 1, 23, pt. 2, 349. Lt. Col. Babcock's proposal for "defenses of Depot between Hickman Creek and the Kentucky River" was approved by Burnside on the next day, and the general directed "that the work be pushed forward by the Military available . . . or hired labor." Simpson to Babcock, 21 May 1863, Poe Papers.

33. In the same period, on July 18, the Fifty-fourth Massachusetts, one of the first official black regiments in the Union Army, made its tragic charge at Fort (or Battery) Wagner, Charleston Harbor, South Carolina: the subject of the climactic battle scene in the well-known film *Glory*. The New York City draft riots took place in the same time frame.

34. Morgan (1825–1864), one of Kentucky's most famous Civil War figures, was born in Huntsville, Alabama, but spent most of his life in Lexington, Kentucky. His guerrilla raids in and from Tennessee made him one of the most hated and feared of Confederate generals. He participated in Braxton Bragg's invasion of Kentucky and later led raids into Kentucky in July 1863 and June 1864. *GIG*; *KE*, 650–51.

35. Mix to Burnside, 6 July 1863, *OR*, 1, 23, pt. 1, 699. Elisha Mix, a major in 1863 and a Connecticut native, eventually was promoted to the rank of brevet brigadier general. *HR*, 1:718.

36. Burnside to Hartsuff, Boyle, and Hobson, 6 July 1863, *OR*, 1, 23, pt. 1, 693–94.

37. Burnside to Hartsuff, 6 July 1863, *OR*, 1, 23, pt. 1, 697.

38. The diary of Capt. Ralph Ely of the Eighth Michigan Infantry, part of the Ninth Army Corps from the corps' inception, gives a day-by-day account of the events between the Ninth's arrival in the Department of the Ohio ready to start to Tennessee, its trip into Mississippi, and then its return to Kentucky and actual movement toward East Tennessee. Ely was actually at Camp Nelson only one day, September 7, 1863, before moving on to Camp Dick Robinson and points south. See George M. Blackburn, ed., *With the Wandering Regiment: The Diary of Captain Ralph Ely of the Eighth Michigan Infantry* (Mount Pleasant: Central Michigan University Press, 1965).

39. Cox states: "By the 1st of June he [Burnside] was ready to leave in person for the front, and on the Third was at Lexington, definitely committed to the movement into East Tennessee. There he was met by an order from Halleck to send 8000 men at once to reinforce General Grant at Vicksburg. The promise was made that they should be returned as soon as the immediate exigency was over, but the order was imperative. Burnside never hesitated in obedience" (478).

40. Marvel, 267. According to Cox, ". . . the advanced division of the Ninth Corps, returning from Vicksburg reached Cincinnati on the 12th [of August], and although the troops were wholly unfit for active service by reason of malarial diseases contracted on the 'Yazoo,' they could relieve some of the Kentucky garrisons, and Burnside was thus enabled to increase his moving column to about 15,000 men" (520).

41. Burnside visited Hickman Bridge early in June 1863, before appointing Capt. T.E. Hall to be in charge of building the supply depot there (on June 8) and before the proposed installation was given a name on June 12.

42. Burnside to Rosecrans, 13 Aug. 1863, *OR,* 1, 30, pt. 3, 22.

43. Entry for Saturday, 15 Aug. 1863, in Daniel R. Larned's journal, D.R. Larned Papers, Library of Congress. Daniel R. Larned, Burnside's assistant adjutant-general, had traveled with the general to Camp Nelson. The young women, seventeen or eighteen years old, were Capt. T.E. Hall's daughter and Mrs. Hanly's granddaughter, Miss Bonner.

44. Referring to D.R. Larned's journal, August 10–16, Marvel states: "Though he ought to have taken medical leave, Parke remained in the city a while, culling the Ninth Corps for its few able men and sending them on to Kentucky. His occasional reports grew gradually worse, instead of better, describing units with two-thirds of their muster rolls on the sick list and officers dying on the job from chills and fever. The corps would obviously not be able to follow Burnside south any time in the near future"(269).

45. Theron Edmond Hall was born November 8, 1821, in Sutton, Massachusetts, the son of Edmund Trowbridge Hall and Abigail Slocomb. A resident of Holden, near Worcester, Massachusetts, he became first lt. adjutant in the Twenty-first Massachusetts Infantry, a part of Burnside's Ninth Army Corps, on September 18, 1861, and was promoted to captain on July 22, 1862. Under General Burnside's command, Hall was given the primary responsibility for constructing Camp Nelson, where he was assistant quartermaster for the crucial year of 1863–1864. At his suggestion and under his direction, the Soldiers' Home was constructed for the United States Sanitary Commission. With Rev. John G. Fee, he was one of the founders and planners of the Camp Nelson Refugee Home, and once again construction was under his direction. Subjected to constant criticism from the military and hostility from the local community, he left Camp Nelson in a storm of controversy. But after he gave up his Camp Nelson post, he was promoted to the rank of brevet colonel on March 13, 1865. He resigned from the Quartermaster Department on December 5, 1865, and died on August 3, 1880, in San Diego, California. Many of his friends and a few relatives from the region of Worcester, Massachusetts, figured prominently in Camp Nelson affairs, and he himself was certainly a central figure in Camp Nelson's development. Civil War Archive at www.ancestry.com; *HR,* 1:490; *OAR,* 1:179.

46. Hall to Burnside, 4 Aug. 1863; Generals' Papers: Burnside; RG 94.

47. Charles N. Goulding, born in New York, first enlisted in an Ohio regiment and served as lt. colonel and quartermaster from May 5 to December 8, 1863. *HR,* 1:466.

48. Hall to Goulding, 10 Aug. 1863; Generals' Papers: Burnside; RG 94.

49. Hall to Burnside, 11 Aug 1863; Generals' Papers: Burnside; RG 94. The six hundred additional animals, not yet sorted into teams, were not enough.

50. Hall to Burnside, 11 Aug 1863; Generals' Papers: Burnside; RG 94.

51. Dickerson to Burnside, 13 Aug. 1863; Generals' Papers: Burnside; RG 94; Hall to Burnside, 17 Aug. 1863; Generals' Papers: Burnside; RG 94; Fry to Burnside, 17 Aug. 1863; Generals' Papers: Burnside; RG 94; Hall to Burnside, 18 Aug. 1863; Generals' Papers: Burnside; RG 94.

52. Hall to Burnside, 20 Aug. 1863; Generals' Papers: Burnside; RG 94; Hall to Potter, 8 Sept. 1863, *OR,* 1, 30, pt 3, 473.

53. Potter (1829–1887), a native of Massachusetts, participated in Burnside's North Carolina Expedition as lt. colonel of the Fifty-first New York Infantry; he was promoted on March 13, 1863, to brigadier general, and became commander of the Second Division, Ninth Army Corps, when it was still part of the Army of the Potomac. He retained his command of the Second Division as the Ninth was transferred to the Department of the Ohio and thence to the Army of Tennessee. On August 25, 1863, he was named commander of the Ninth Army Corps, Department of the Ohio, a position he held until January 17, 1864. Thus, he was one of the primary generals in Burnside's East Tennessee Campaign. His middle name is given both as "Brown" and as "Barnwell" in standard sources. *GIB; HR,* 1:802; *OAR,* 2:498.

54. Hall to Potter, 11 Sept. 1863, *OR,* 1, 30, pt. 3, 556; Hall to Burnside, 12 Sept. 1863;

Generals' Papers: Burnside; RG 94; Hall to Robert B. Potter, 12 Sept. 1863, *OR*, 1, 30, pt. 3, 591; Fry to Lewis Richmond, 14 Oct. 1863; Generals' Papers: Burnside, Telegrams Received; RG 94. Captain Hall requested that the convalescents, who were presumably not in the best of health, be allowed to return to Camp Nelson in wagon trains.

55. Stanton to Boyle, 30 Nov. 1863, *OR*, 3, 3, 1104–5; Boyle to Stanton, *OR*, 1, 31, pt. 3, 284.

56. p. 13; Entry 906; Part 4; RG 393.

57. Report of Capt. William W. Buckley, *OR*, 1, 30, pt. 2, 600–601. Buckley was commander of Battery D, First Rhode Island Light Artillery, which was attached to the Twenty-third Army Corps.

58. Ibid., 347–49.

59. Scott, 486. Orlando Boliver Willcox (1823–1907), a native of Michigan, was commander of the First Division of the Ninth Army Corps and commander of the District of Central Kentucky, both in the Department of the Ohio, in the six months before Burnside's East Tennessee Campaign. During that operation, Willcox commanded the Left Wing Forces of the Department of the Ohio in many engagements. *CWD;* Dyer, 1:111, 528; *HR,* 1:1038; *OAR,* 8:304.

60. Reports of Maj. Gen. John G. Foster, 14 Dec. 1863, *OR*, 1, 31, pt. 1, 282–83.

61. Cox, 67; 83, 84. Jacob Dolson Cox had commanded in the Ninth Army Corps before becoming commander of the Twenty-third Army Corps in the Department of the Ohio, a position he held during the latter part of the East Tennessee Campaign. Late in his life Cox composed his *Military Reminiscences of the Civil War*, which was published in 1900, the year of his death. A personal assessment of the military aspects of the war, it discusses much of Burnside's contribution as commander of the Department of the Ohio, presented from the point of view of an eyewitness with impeccable military and academic credentials: Cox was a graduate of Oberlin College with advanced degrees from Denison, North Carolina, and Yale. *CWD;* Dyer, 1:58; *GIB;* [*Oberlin*] *Alumni Register Graduates and Former Students, Teaching and Administrative Staff 1833–1960* (Oberlin, 1960), 5 (hereafter abbreviated "*Oberlin Register*"); *HR,* 1:331.

62. Burnside to Grant, 20 Oct. 1863, *OR*, 1, 31, pt. 1, 680.

63. Special Orders No. 24, 24 Jan. 1864, *OR*, 1, 32, pt. 2, 205.

64. Willcox to Lewis Richmond, 23 Jan. 1865 [Date of filing report], *OR*, 1, 31, pt. 1, 402–6; Report of William G. McCreary, 10 Oct. 1863, *OR*, 1, 30, pt. 2, 573–74.

65. Meigs to George H. Thomas, 20 Apr. 1864, *OR*, 1, 32, pt. 3, 423.

66. Cox, 101; 104.

67. Ibid., 108, 109; Cox quotes Grant to Halleck, 15 Jan. 1864, *OR*, 1, 32, pt. 2, 100–101.

68. Grant to Schofield, 17 Mar. 1864, *OR*, 1, 32, pt. 3, 83–84.

69. Report of Maj. Charles E. Compton to James A. Hardie, 23 June 1864; June 1864 Inspection, Box 2, File C–10 (1864), Entry 15; Inspector General's Records, RG 159.

70. Dickerson to Hall, 8 June 1863; Camp Nelson, Box 720; Consolidated Correspondence File, 1794–1915, Entry 225; RG 92. (Hereafter, "Camp Nelson, Box 720; . . . ; RG 92" abbreviated as "Box 720; RG 92.") [N.B.: The National Archives warns against using box numbers because they may be changed when materials are reorganized; in the meantime, this whole box is full of quartermaster records from Camp Nelson]. Like Capt. Hall, James Hervey Pratt was a native of Massachusetts, who began his army career in the Eighteenth Michigan Infantry. Captain and assistant quartermaster from February 19, 1863, he was the first officer to be placed in charge of construction at Camp Nelson. After being replaced by Hall, he became assistant quartermaster at Camp Burnside as early as June 1864. *HR,* 1:804.

71. Hall to Burnside, 14 July 1863; Generals' Papers: Burnside, July 1863; RG 94. On August 4 Burnside received a telegram (by U.S. military telegraph from Camp Nelson) from one Mrs. Martha Thomson asking that she be allowed to see her son, "a Prisoner at this Place." He endorsed the request: "If Mrs Thomson is a loyal person she can see her son." Thomson to Burnside, 4 Aug. 1863; Generals' Papers: Burnside; RG 94.

72. Boyle to Fry, 5 Aug. 1863; Box 720; RG 92. Capt. S.K. Williams furnished the plan for the prison's construction; as assistant quartermaster, Capt. Hall was ordered to "furnish Carpenters, Lumber &c." Special Orders No. 18, 5 Aug. 1863; Box 720; RG 92.

73. Goddard to Hall, Special Orders No. 285, 29 July 1863; Box 720; RG 92. Surgeon George Getz Shumard, a native of New Jersey, was medical director in the Department of the Ohio, from his post in Louisville. *HR,* 1:885.

74. Special Field Orders No. 9, 21 Aug. 1863; Box 720; RG 92.

75. Dickerson to Hall, 1 Sept. 1863; Box 720; RG 92; Special Orders No. 41, 3 Sept 1863; Box 720; RG 92.

76. Special Orders No. 58, 21 Sept. 1863; Box 720; RG 92.

77. Meeker to Shumard, 19 Feb. 1864; Box 720; RG 92. Meeker, a native of New York, had been a surgeon in the Ninth Indiana Infantry and then in the U.S. Volunteers; he became a brevet lieutenant colonel for his "faithful and meritorious service." *HR,* 1:701.

78. Swords to Hall, 26 Feb. 1864; Box 720; RG 92.

79. On December 22, Hall was "authorized to erect a building suitable for the accommodation of small detachments of troops passing Camp Nelson"; this authorization probably refers to the Soldiers' Home. Dickerson to Hall, 22 Dec. 1863; Box 720; RG 92.

80. Reports of Maj. Gen. John G. Foster, 14 Dec. 1863, *OR,* 1, 31, pt. 1, 282–83.

81. Newberry, 529–30.

82. The white Appalachian refugees at Camp Nelson have been the best kept secret of its history. They continued to be a presence at the camp until its official closing as a military post in 1865. Throughout the period when black refugees were flocking to the camp, white refugees were arriving as well, although very few contemporary sources mention them.

83. Newberry, 382–83. Thomas D. Butler, superintendent of the United States Sanitary Commission at Camp Nelson, was in charge of the Soldiers' Home. His reports for the Sanitary Commission, including several vivid descriptions of life at Camp Nelson, were published in 1871.

84. Special Orders No. 9, 5 Mar. 1864; Box 720; RG 92; Special Orders No. 20, 7 Mar. 1864; Box 720; RG 92.

85. Halleck to Burnside, 12 Apr. 1863, *OR,* 1, 23, pt. 2, 234. Technically, contrabands were slaves from states in rebellion who were freed by the Emancipation Proclamation. "Contrabands" was not a term that could be applied to Kentucky's slaves, who were, nevertheless, soon to join contrabands as part of the Union Army's workforce.

86. Babcock to Simpson, 19 May 1863, Poe Papers; also in Entry 3541; Part 1; RG 393. Orville Ellis Babcock, a native of Vermont, served as chief engineer of the Ninth Army Corps from February 6 to April 10, 1863, when he became chief engineer of the Central District of Kentucky, a position he held until June 9, 1863; in both capacities, he was the official primarily responsible for constructing the first entrenchments and fortifications at Camp Nelson. He served with the Ninth Corps at Vicksburg and in the East Tennessee Campaign. After fighting at Knoxville, he was chief engineer of the Department of the Ohio from January 23 to March 20, 1864, when he became General Grant's aide-de-camp. *CWD; HR,* 1:178.

87. Drake to Poe, 20 June 1863, Special Orders No. 7, Poe Papers. Orlando Metcalfe Poe (1832–1895) was born in Ohio, but became a colonel in the Second Michigan Infantry. By 1863 he was commander of the First Brigade, First Division, Ninth Army Corps; by May of that year he had been appointed chief engineer of the Twenty-third Army Corps and soon after chief engineer of the Army of the Ohio. Orlando M. Poe's Papers, in the Special Collections of Central Michigan University at Mount Pleasant, Michigan, are an important source of Camp Nelson history. The sender of the order to Poe, George Bernard Drake, began his military career in the Twelfth Massachusetts Infantry; he was a native of the same state. In June 1863, he was a lt. colonel and assistant adjutant general. *HR,* 1:382.

88. Simpson to Poe, 6 July 1863, and George P. Webster to Poe, 8 July 1863, Poe Papers. George Parmalee Webster, born in Connecticut, became a captain and assistant quartermaster in a Kentucky regiment on May 12, 1862. *HR,* 1:1013.

89. Simpson to Poe, 30 July 1863, Poe Papers. In the same letter, Simpson approved of

Poe's proposal for naming the forts at Camp Nelson. "It strikes me," he wrote, that "the appellations are appropriate."

90. Simpson to Totten, 11 Aug. 1863, *OR*, 1, 23, pt. 2, 608, 609. Poe's original report, dated 31 July 1863, is in Entry 3541; Part 1; RG 393.

91. Willcox to Burnside, 5 Aug. 1863; Generals' Papers: Burnside; RG 94.

92. Simpson to Totten, 20 May 1863, *OR*, 1, 23, pt. 2, 349; General Orders No. 41, 10 Aug. 1863; pp. 206–7; Entry 2177; Part 1; RG 393.

93. Fry to Burnside, 18 Aug. 1863, Generals' Papers: Burnside, Entry 159; RG 94; Burnside to Boyle, 20 Aug 1863, *OR*, 1, 30, pt. 3, 92–93; Boyle to Burnside, 8 Sept. 1863; Generals' Papers: Burnside, Entry 159; RG 94. Evidently, Burnside preferred impressing Kentucky slaves on the spot, close to their labor assignments, over exploring far afield for contrabands who would have to be transported to central Kentucky.

94. *OR*, 1, 30, pt. 3, 786–87, 810, 942.

95. Simpson to Burnside, 15 Oct. 1863; Generals' Papers: Burnside, Entry 159; RG 94; Berlin et al., *Freedom,* series 1, *The Destruction of Slavery* (hereafter abbreviated "*The Destruction of Slavery*"), 587; ibid., cited from *OR*, 1, 32, pt. 2, 479.

96. (Fifth Regiment) Dyer 1:230–31; (Eighth Tennessee) ibid., 1:232.

97. (Battery "E") Dyer 2:1196–97; (Twenty-sixth Kentucky) ibid., 2:1208; (Forty-seventh Kentucky) ibid., 2:1211; (Forty-ninth Kentucky) ibid., 2:1212. The total enlistment of white Kentuckians at Camp Nelson was 1,117, about one-fifth of the number of black recruits.

98. Shannon, 2:731.

99. Boyle to Burnside, 25 June 1863, General's Papers: Burnside, Letters Received May-June 1863; RG 94.

100. Boyle to Fry, 25 June 1863, *OR*, 3, 3, 416. James Barnet Fry (born 1827 in Carrollton, Illinois; died 1894) became provost marshal general after a long career in the United State Army, beginning in an Illinois regiment in the 1840s. *ANB; CWD; GIB; HR,* 1:439. Unfortunately, Boyle—of all these telegram writers—was the most nearly correct in his assumptions about what black recruitment would bring about. "Infinite and inconceivable harm" would indeed result for black Kentuckians (men, women and children, free and enslaved, soldiers and civilians) because of the attitudes of white Kentuckians.

101. Burnside to Lincoln, 26 June 1863, *OR*, 3, 3, 418. Burnside's expertise concerning the state of things in Kentucky was based on a very brief sojourn there. Fry to Boyle, 26 June 1863, *OR*, 3, 3, 418–19; Lincoln to Burnside, 27 June 1863, *OR*, 3, 3, 419; Burnside to Lincoln, 27 June 1863, *OR*, 3, 3, 419–20.

102. *The Destruction of Slavery,* 510n 26. The slaves were impressed under an order of August 1863. Stanton quote cited from *OR*, 3, 3, 855–56.

103. Collins, 103. Thomas Elliott Bramlette (1817–1875), Kentucky's governor from 1863 to 1867, had been commissioned a major general in the Union Army in 1863, but resigned his commission to accept the Union Democrats' nomination for governor. Throughout his term in office, he was a dedicated Unionist, but a strong proponent of slavery. He angrily resisted the enlistment of Kentucky's blacks into the Union Army, opposed both the Fourteenth and Fifteenth Amendments to the U.S. Constitution, and protested the establishment of the Freedmen's Bureau in Kentucky. *KE*, 112–13.

104. Collins 131, 132.

105. *U.S. Statutes at Large*, 13:11.

106. Shannon, 164, 165.

107. Collins, 132; Jacobs to Lincoln, 13 Mar. 1864, *OR*, 3, 4, 176.

108. In addition to his ordinary duties as commander of the District of Kentucky, Burbridge had been charged by the War Department "with a general superintendence of the execution of the acts of Congress for raising troops in Kentucky by voluntary enlistment and by drafting." Special Orders No. 140, 6 Apr. 1864, *OR*, 4, 218.

109. Berlin et al., series 2, *The Black Military Experience,* 193; *OR*, 3, 4, 233–34; 248–49. Tennessee and Indiana received many of Kentucky's black recruits for organization and train-

ing. One thousand Kentucky blacks were recruited at Evansville, Indiana; nine hundred were sent to Gallatin, Tennessee. *OR,* 3, 4, 733.

110. On May 14, 1864, Burbridge threatened Kentucky with martial law because "in some parts of this District attempts have been made to prevent the enlistment of persons desiring to enter the service of the United States." General Orders No. 42, 14 May 1864, Printed leaflet included in *NIMSUS,* 4:2546; also in *OR,* 1, 39, pt. 2, 27.

111. *OR,* 3, 4, 422.

112. Brig. Gen. Lorenzo Thomas (born 1804 in New Castle, Delaware; died March 2, 1875) was adjutant general of the U.S. Army 1861–1869; on March 23, 1863, he took over the organization of colored troops. *ANB; CWD; GIB; HR,* 1:954.

113. General Orders No. 20, 13 June 1864, Printed leaflet in *NIMSUS,* 4:2611–12; also in *OR,* 3, 4, 428–29. Each of the eight recruiting centers served a single congressional district, except Camp Nelson which served two: the seventh and the eighth. Besides Camp Nelson, the centers were Paducah (First Congressional District), Owensboro (Second), Bowling Green (Third), Lebanon (Fourth), Louisville (Fifth), Covington (Sixth), and Louisa (Ninth).

114. Winter weather undoubtedly discouraged black enlistment at Camp Nelson, but probably the November expulsion of slave families caused an even larger drop in numbers. After all, ten thousand more Kentucky slaves were added to Union forces after the summer of 1864, and fewer than fifty of those had enrolled at Camp Nelson.

115. These statistics and subsequent data concerning regiments were derived from my own study of the *Report of the Adjutant General of the State of Kentucky.* During the summer of 1864, 14,000 black men volunteered, almost 5,400 of them at Camp Nelson, and by the time enlistment ended in May 1865, almost 24,000 had joined the Union forces. As the editors of *The Destruction of Slavery* point out, "more than half the black men of military age in the state" had been recruited (512).

116. An incredible array of details about the 116th U.S. Colored Infantry is available in Lt. Col. Charles Kireker's regimental history, the complete title of which tells it all: *History of the 116th Regiment U.S.C. Infantry from its organization in the early part of the spring and summer of 1864, to the present time, giving a list of names of all officers and enlisted men who have ever belonged to the regiment, and remarks attached to each name, noting the dates of all appointments and promotions, &c; and to the enlisted men place and date of enlistments, deaths, discharges, desertions, &c* (Philadelphia: King & Baird, Printers, 1866).

117. At the time of the Civil War, the longest road through the eastern mountains of Kentucky was the Mt. Sterling-Pound Gap Road. For troop movement between central Kentucky and Virginia, it was the primary route. *KE,* 658.

118. "Morgan was counting on the raid itself to provide horses and equipment for his command." Ramage, 213.

119. This account is drawn from "The Last Kentucky Raid," a chapter in *Rebel Raider,* 208–25. Morgan's first official report of this raid was an account of his victories—at Mount Sterling, Lexington, and Cynthiana, among other triumphs. A postscript to this report stated: "Since the above I learn that the force which entered Va. under Gen'l Burbridge to attack the salt works & lead mines has returned and is moving to attack me." John Hunt Morgan official report, 11 June 1864, quoted in Ramage, 222.

120. Dickson to Campbell, 9 June 1864—2 a.m., *OR,* 1, 39, pt. 2, 90; Dickson to Fry, 9 June 1864—9:30 a.m., *OR,* 1, 39, pt. 2, 91; Dickson to Hobson, 9 June 1864—10:20 a.m., *OR,* 1, 39, pt. 2, 90.

121. Hobson to Dickson, 9 June 1864—12 midnight, *OR,* 1, 39, pt. 2, 90.

122. Hobson to Dickson, 9 June 1864—7 p.m., *OR,* 1, 39, pt. 2, 91.

123. Hanaford to Edgerly, 9 June 1864, p. 117; Entry 902; Part 4; RG 393; quotation from Hanaford to Gillis, 9 June 1864, p. 133; Entry 902; Part 4; RG 393.

124. Hanaford to Edgerly, 9 June 1864, p. 133; Entry 902; Part 4; RG 393.

125. Ibid., 134.

126. Dickson to Hobson, 9 June 1864—8:20 p.m., *OR,* 1, 39, pt. 2, 91.

127. Fry to Dickson, 9 June 1864, *OR,* 1, 39, pt. 2, 91, 92.

128. Dickson to Fry, 9 June 1864—9:03 p.m., *OR,* 1, 39, pt. 2, 92; Dickson to John Boyle, 9 June 1864, *OR,* 1, 39, pt. 2, 92.

129. Garrard to Dickson, 9 June 1864, *OR,* 1, 39, pt. 2, 93.

130. Hanaford to Commanding Officer of Thirtieth Kentucky Volunteers, 10 June 1864, p. 152; Entry 902; Part 4; RG 393; Hanaford to Commanding Officer of Forty-seventh Kentucky Volunteer Infantry, 10 June 1864, p. 154; Entry 902; Part 4; RG 393.

131. Dickson to Henry B. Carrington, 11 June 1864—10:15 p.m., *OR,* 1, 39, pt. 2, 101; Dickson to Fry, 11 June 1864—10:30 p.m., *OR,* 1, 39, pt. 2, 99; Fry to Dickson, 11 June 1864—11 p.m., *OR,* 1, 39, pt. 2, 100; Fry to Dickson, 11 June 1864, *OR,* 1, 39, pt. 2, 100.

132. [Hanaford, unsigned] to Edgerly, 12 June 1864—1:20 a.m., p. 183; Entry 902; Part 4; RG 393. Andrew Hamilton Clark (born March 29, 1835, in Clay County, Kentucky), was the son of William Clark, also a native of Clay County, and Tabitha Evans. As colonel of the Forty-Seventh Kentucky Volunteers, he was enrolled and mustered in on January 1, 1864, for a period of one year, during which he was commandant of the post at Camp Nelson. At one point, he wanted to take troops to avenge the death of his father, deputy provost marshal in Owsley County, at the hands of rebel guerrillas. He was mustered out December 26, 1864, in Lexington. *OAR,* 4:1292; *RAGK,* 459; genealogical details from IGI at www.familysearch.org. Henry Clay Edgerly, thirty years old, enlisted on June 19, 1861 in the Eighth Michigan Cavalry. He became a post inspector and commanded the camp of distribution at Camp Nelson. *Record of Service of Michigan Volunteers 1861–65* (1903) on Civil War Archives at www.ancestry.com.

133. Fry to Dickson, *OR,* 1, 39, pt. 2, 103.

134. Dickson to Fry, 12 June 1864, *OR,* 1, 39, pt. 2, 103. President Lincoln honored Burbridge for this victory with a promotion to "major-general by brevet" on July 4, 1864. Stanton to Burbridge, 4 July 1864, *OR,* 1, 39, pt. 2, 162.

135. Hanaford to Commanding Officer of Seventh Ohio Volunteer Cavalry, 13 June 1864, p. 190; Entry 902; Part 4; RG 393.

136. Hanaford to Edgerly, 13 June 1864, p. 191; Entry 902; Part 4; RG 393.

137. Fry to Dickson, 13 June 1864, *OR,* 1, 39, pt. 2, 110.

138. Fry to Dickson, 13 June 1864—10:10 a.m., *OR,* 1, 39, pt. 2, 111.

139. With the exception of the two preceding citations, all of the quotations from this paragraph are from a series of separate telegrams from Fry to Dickson, 13 June 1864, *OR,* 1, 39, pt. 2, 111.

140. Dickson to Fry, 13 June 1864—7 p.m., *OR,* 1, 39, pt. 2, 112. The victory was decisive: "General Burbridge telegraphs from Cynthiana: We attacked Morgan at this place this morning and gained a complete victory." Dickson to Campbell, 12 June 1864, *OR,* 1, 39, pt. 2, 103.

141. Report of Maj. Charles E. Compton to James A. Hardie, 23 June 1864; June 1864 Inspection, Box 2, File C–10 (1864), Entry 15; Inspector General's Records, RG 159. In 1864 Maj. Charles Elmer Compton commanded the Forty-Seventh U.S. Colored Infantry (organized at Lake Providence, Louisiana), but he was promoted to colonel of the Fifty-Third U.S. Colored Infantry (organized at Warrenton, Mississippi) later the same year. He also had time to inspect Camp Nelson. *HR,* 1:319; *OAR,* 8:220, 226.

142. John Gregg Fee (born September 9, 1816, in Bracken County, Kentucky; died January 11, 1901, in Berea, Madison County, Kentucky), son of John Fee and Sarah Gregg, was reared in a slaveholding family, but became an ardent evangelical abolitionist while he was attending Lane Theological Seminary in Cincinnati. In December 1859 Fee, his family, and all other abolitionists in Berea were exiled from Kentucky by irate slaveholders of Richmond in Madison County. They were unable to return to their homes in Berea on a permanent basis until central Kentucky was in Union hands five years later (see my book *The Day of Small Things: Abolitionism in the Midst of Slavery, Berea, Kentucky 1854–1864* [Lanham, Md: University Press of America, 1986] for a complete account of the Berea exiles).

Fee's fight against slavery lasted until the Civil War was over, but his stand for social equality among the races was literally lifelong. In the course of his dedicated life, Fee founded many churches, one of which was at Camp Nelson (it did not last), two schools, one at Berea (which lasted), one at Camp Nelson (which did not), a town which lasted (Berea) and a village which did not (Ariel at Camp Nelson). Once Fee became connected to Camp Nelson (July 4, 1864), he never gave up the work there, no matter how discouraging it became.

143. Fee to Whipple, 13 Jun. 1863, AMAA 111267.

144. The American Missionary Association (hereafter abbreviated in the text as AMA), a society of very devout and active evangelical Christian abolitionists, was organized at Syracuse, New York, in 1846, with William Jackson of Massachusetts as president, George Whipple, corresponding secretary, and Lewis Tappan, treasurer. Its mission work was "conducted with special purpose to bear decided testimony against slavery and sin of caste." The organization was an outgrowth of the Amistad Committee—organized by Simeon S. Jocelyn, Joshua Leavitt, and Lewis Tappan in 1839 "for the defense of a group of slaves who killed the master of a 'slaver,' the *Amistad*." Swint, 11–12.

145. Fee to Whipple, 21 June 1863, AMAA 111270; Fee to Whipple, 6 Aug. 1863, AMAA 111302.

146. Fee to Whipple, 21 June 1863, AMAA 111270.

147. Reiley to Fee, 17 June 1863, AMAA 43974–7.

148. Fee to Simeon S. Jocelyn, 24 Nov. 1863, AMAA 111422; Fee to AMAA, 23 Dec. 1863, AMAA 111444.

149. Fee to Jocelyn, 22 Oct. 1863, AMAA 111394; Fee to Jocelyn, 30 Dec. 1863, AMAA 111449.

150. Fee to Jocelyn, 9 Jul. 1863, AMAA 111283. Levi Coffin (1798–1877), a Quaker from North Carolina, became known as the "Father of the Underground Railroad" for his work—mostly in Indiana—on behalf of escaping slaves. A well-known abolitionist and reformer, he was a longtime friend and supporter of John G. Fee. He served on the executive committee of the American Freedmen's Union Commission, cofounded the Western Freedmen's Aid Commission, based in Cincinnati, and for several years was a trustee of Ariel Academy at Camp Nelson; *ANB;* Swint, 149.

The Western Freedmen's Aid Commission (hereafter abbreviated as WFAC) was organized in Cincinnati, Ohio, on January 19, 1863, by Levi Coffin, J.M. Walden, and C.B. Boynton. Its purpose was not only to relieve "the present physical wants of the Freedmen," but to provide "for their general welfare" and fit them "for their new condition." Like the AMAA, the WFAC sent out "missionaries to evangelize as well teachers to instruct freedmen." Swint, 20.

151. Fee to Jocelyn, 15 Jul. 1863, AMAA 111287.

152. *AM* 8, no. 4 (April 1864): 94, 95; Fee to Jocelyn, 28 Apr. 1864, AMAA 43995; ibid.

153. Simeon S. Jocelyn (1799–1879), as chairman of the Amistad Committee, assisted in the organization of the AMA, "in which he held various offices for over thirty years." He had begun his career as minister of a black church in New York. "In 1829 he and Arthur Tappan proposed the organization of a Negro college at New Haven. In support of this project, Jocelyn and Tappan called a national convention of free Negroes, which . . . was [called] the first 'organized expression of Negro solidarity in the nation.'" Swint, 155.

154. Jocelyn to Fee, 6 June 1864, BCA.

155. John G. Fee's eldest son, Burritt Hamilton Fee (born May 1, 1849, in Lewis County, Kentucky), was named for abolitionist Elihu Burritt, and all his brief life was spent preparing himself for a missionary career like his father's. A member of Berea College's first graduating class in 1873, Burritt attended Oberlin Theological Seminary (1873–75), but he died on October 1, 1876, after many years as a semi-invalid. In his extreme youth, aged fifteen, he worked long and hard at Camp Nelson; he began teaching black soldiers by February and March 1865, and he was teaching them again in the autumn of 1865. At Camp Nelson, he contracted the illness, probably tuberculosis, that recurred throughout his life.

156. Three regiments were being formed when Fee arrived at Camp Nelson: the 114th and 116th U.S. Colored Infantries and the 12th U.S. Colored Heavy Artillery. On July 20, Lorenzo Thomas stated that two infantry regiments were "fully organized, clothed, and armed"

and the heavy artillery was "well under way." Thomas to Stanton, 20 July 1864, *OR*, 3, 4, 528–29.

157. Fee to Jocelyn, 12 July 1864, AMAA 44007. The exact day of Fee's arrival is not specified, but in this first letter written by him from Camp Nelson, postmarked on July 12, he says he had been at Camp Nelson several days the week before.

158. The two men were presumably brothers—they traveled together to Camp Nelson (presenting precisely the same expense account)—not father and son, as Fee thought they might both be too young to be superintendent of the school.

159. William L. Lowrey to Whipple, 27 Aug. 1864, AMAA 44025 and John B. Lowrey to Whipple, 27 Aug. 1864, AMAA 44026.

160. Fee to Strieby, 29 Aug. 1864, AMAA 44030. Fee took this bell to Berea when his new school became established there. It now hangs in the belfry of the Church of Christ in Berea.

161. Ibid.

162. Monthly school report of John B. Lowrey to AMAA, Aug. 1864, AMAA 44031.

163. Rev. John Vetter (sometimes written as Vetters) was graduated from Oberlin College in the class of 1859, from the seminary in 1862. A Congregational clergyman, he served as clerk for Rev. Lester Williams at Camp Nelson and became chaplain of the Fifth U.S. Colored Cavalry on March 14, 1865. *Oberlin Register*, 7–8; *OAR*, 8:145.

164. John B. Lowrey to Whipple, 6 Sept. 1864, AMAA 44034.

165. Fee to Strieby, 10 Sept. 1864, AMAA 44035. Rev. Mr. John Morgan Walden (born 1831, near Lebanon, Ohio; died 21 Jan. 1914) served as secretary of Cleveland's Freedmen's Aid Commission, of the Northwestern Freedmen's Aid Commission, of the American Freedmen's Commission, and of the Western Freedmen's Aid Commission in Cincinnati. *DAB;* Swint, 168.

166. William L. Lowrey to Whipple, 4 Oct. 1864, AMAA 44041.

167. Monthly school report of John B. Lowrey to AMAA, 5 Oct 1864, AMAA 44042–3.

168. Gabriel Burdett, born a slave c. 1829 or 1830, became the black minister at the Forks of Dix River Baptist Church, where he was given the authority to hold services "among his brethren." Mustered in Company I, 114th U.S. Colored Infantry on September 30, 1864, he became a friend and protégée of Fee's at Camp Nelson. Fee taught him to read and write and ordained him. At Fee's urging, he became a trustee of both Berea College (the first black to serve in that capacity) and Ariel Academy; after Fee left Camp Nelson, Rev. Burdett became the next minister of the church Fee had founded there. Gabriel was married as a slave and had five children (one of whom, born in 1867, was named John G. Burdett), but his household also included his sister-in-law, Clarissa Burdett, and nine nephew and nieces. A political activist, Burdett participated in the State Convention of Colored Men, held at Lexington in 1867, and he was an active campaigner and canvasser for the Republican Party, attending the Republican National Convention, held in Ohio in 1876, as a delegate. *KE,* 142; *RAGK,* 59.

169. Burbridge is quoted in Thomas to Stanton, 10 Oct. 1864, *OR*, 1, 39, pt. 3, 200. The first enlistments for the 5th occurred on August 12, 1864. The regiment's beginnings coincide exactly with the Lowreys' school reports. Other black soldiers from Camp Nelson participated in the Battle of Saltville: Companies D, E, G, and H of the 116th U.S.C.I. Kireker, 64, 73, 95.

170. Report of Surgeon James G. Hatchitt, 4 Oct. 1864, in *OR*, 1, 39, pt. 1, 553, 554.

171. Burbridge to Schofield, 10 Oct. 1864, *OR*, 1, 39, pt. 1, 552, 553. For Burbridge, of course, this campaign represented the resumption of a military objective that Morgan's last raid into Kentucky had interrupted. His "victory" report is rather reminiscent of Morgan's premature triumph at Cynthiana. Schofield's report to General Sherman definitely sounds a different note: "General Burbridge has returned to Kentucky," he wrote, "having failed in his expedition. His troops will require rest for some time before they will be fit to take the field again." Schofield to Sherman, 11 Oct. 1864, *OR*, 1, 39, pt. 1, 219.

172. Report of Surgeon William H. Gardner, 26 Oct. 1864, *OR*, 1, 39, pt. 1, 554, 555.

173. Dickson to Sedgewick, 14 Oct. 1864, *OR*, 1, 39, pt. 3, 283. Thomas D. Sedgewick, colonel of the 114th U.S. Colored Cavalry, mustered in at Camp Nelson on July 5, 1864; he became superintendent in charge of organizing colored troops, then commander of the United States Colored Troops at Camp Nelson; he was relieved from duty at Camp Nelson on November 29, 1864. He served as commander of the 22nd Brigade, 4th Division, Army of the Ohio; commander of the 1st Brigade, 2nd Division, 21st Army Corps, Army of the Cumberland; commander of the 1st Brigade, 1st Div., 4th Army Corps, Army of the Cumberland. In the *Official Army Register*, Thomas D. Sedgewick is listed as colonel of 114th U.S.C.I. on July 5, 1864, while Thomas S. Sedgewick is listed as lieutenant colonel of the same regiment on September 8, 1864—it seems they were not the same person. Dyer, 1:1739; *OAR*, 8:295; *RAGK*, 53.

174. Fry to Horace Capron, 14 Oct. 1864, *OR*, 1, 39, pt. 3, 283. (This letter was actually sent by C.M. Holt, lieutenant and aide-de-camp, on Fry's behalf, "the general being absent.") Special Orders No. 36, 17 Oct. 1864; Entry 1030; Part 2; RG 393.

175. George Stoneman (1822–1894) commanded the Department of the Ohio from November 17, 1864 to January 17, 1865. At least four raids were named after him. *CWD.*

176. The five regiments of cavalry were the Eleventh Michigan, Thirteenth Kentucky, Twelfth Ohio, Thirtieth and Thirty-ninth Kentucky Mounted Infantry. Dickson to McLean, 17 Nov. 1864, *OR*, 1, 45, pt. 1, 931–932. The cavalry of the Department of the Ohio had been reorganized "under Stoneman at or near Camp Nelson" much earlier by command of General Sherman on April 2, 1864. Sherman to Grant, 2 Apr. 1864, *OR*, 1, 32, pt. 3, 221.

177. Dickson to McLean, 17 Nov. 1864, *OR*, 1, 45, pt. 1, 931–932.

178. Butler to Commanding Officer First Battalion, Fifth U.S. Colored Cavalry, 18 Nov. 1864, *OR*, 1, 45, pt. 1, 941. The Fifth United States Colored Cavalry was at Ghent, Kentucky, when it was ordered to join Burbridge's brigade.

179. Burbridge to McLean, 21 Nov. 1864, *OR*, 1, 45, pt 1, 980.

180. Burbridge to McLean, 21 Nov. 1864, *OR*, 1, 45, pt. 1, 981, 982. Not the same letter as the foregoing.

181. McLean to Burbridge, 23 Nov. 1864, *OR*, 1, 45, pt. 1, 1010.

182. Burbridge to McLean, 24 Nov. 1864, *OR*, 1, 45, pt. 1, 1031; McLean to Fry, 25 Nov. 1864, *OR*, 1, 45, pt. 1, 1053; Fry to Butler, 25 Nov 1864, *OR*, 1, 45, pt. 1, 1054; Burbridge to Fry, 25 Nov. 1864, *OR*, 1, 45, pt. 1, 1054.

183. Butler to Fry, 26 Nov. 1864, *OR*, 1, 45, pt. 1, 1074.

184. Butler to Weatherford, 5 Dec. 1864, *OR*, 1, 45, pt. 2, 68; Weatherford to Butler, 6 Dec. 1864, *OR*, 1, 45, pt. 2, 81. James W. Weatherford, who enlisted on September 8, 1862, in Russellville, Kentucky, was a major in the Eighth Kentucky Cavalry and then a colonel in the Thirteenth. He was mustered out at Camp Nelson on January 10, 1865. *HR*, 2:159; *RAGK*, 352.

185. Butler to Lt. Col. Ferguson, Thirty-ninth Kentucky Infantry, 9 Dec. 1864, *OR*, 1, 45, pt. 2, 128.

186. Thomas to Stanton, 2 Jan. 1865, *OR*, 1, 45, pt. 2, 494–95. Basil Wilson Duke (1838–1916) was John Hunt Morgan's brother-in-law and one of Morgan's ablest commanders. *GIG.*

187. Thomas to Stanton, 2 Jan. 1865, *OR*, 1, 45, pt. 2, 494–95.

188. James M. Fidler, captain and provost marshal of the Fourth District, reported: "In several counties colored men desiring to enlist have been severely handled. Two were lately caught in Marion County, and their left ears cut off." Fifteen Negroes had been whipped for trying to enlist in Lebanon. Fidler to James B. Fry, 31 May 1864, *NIMSUS*, 4:2600.

189. Clark to Dickson, 18 June 1864; p. 129; Entry 902; Part 4; RG 393; Fry to Hanaford, 6 July 1864; p. 24; Entry 904; Part 4; RG 393; Thomas to Stanton, 16 July 1864, *OR*, 3, 4, 501–2; Hamilton to Fry, 13 Aug. 1864, p. 46; Entry 904; Part 4; RG 393; General Orders No. 19, 23 Aug. 1864, p. 78; Entry 904; Part 4; RG 393; General Orders No. 23, 16 Sept. 1864, p. 87; Entry 905; Part 4; RG 393; Sedgewick to Andrew J. Hogan, 29 Oct. 1864, p. 191; Entry 904; Part 4; RG 393.

190. Since this expulsion is presented in a chapter containing a number of highly detailed eyewitness accounts, I will not describe the same incidents in this introduction.

191. [Report by Lester Williams, Superintendent of Refugee Home, undated, but after 11 July 1865]; M999: Roll 6: Frame 1040; BRFAL, RG 105. (Hereafter, the words "Roll," "Frame(s)," and "BRFAL" will be omitted from M999 references; e.g., M999:6:1040; RG 105.)

192. Dickson to Restieaux, 4 Feb 1865, p. 393; Entry 2168; Part 1; RG 393.

193. Hall to Whipple, 9 Jan [1865], AMAA 43987. This letter is misdated as 1864. Rev. Lester Williams Jr. was a Baptist minister from Holden, Massachusetts. Born July 24, 1823, in West Springfield, Massachusetts, he married Ann Eliza Warren about 1865. He became superintendent of the Refugee Home at Camp Nelson, and his wife also entered the administration of the camp. Both husband and wife were friends with Theron E. Hall, but both fought vehemently with John G. Fee about various policies at Camp Nelson, including social equality. Genealogical details from IGI at www.familysearch.org.

194. Fee to Whipple, 10 Jan. 1865, AMAA 44070.

195. Fee to Whipple, 3 Feb. 1865, AMAA 44073–4.

196. Edward Boylston Walter Restieaux, a native of Massachusetts, became a captain and assistant quartermaster on February 19, 1863. He succeeded Capt. Theron E. Hall as assistant quartermaster at Camp Nelson, holding the position by November 1, 1864. His surname is misspelled in many different ways in the Camp Nelson documents and in modern texts as well. He may have been born in 1832 in Chelsea, Massachusetts; he died in 1878; *HR,* 1:824; IGI.

197. Fee to Whipple, 7 Feb. 1865, AMAA 44076.

198. Ibid.

199. Hall to Strieby, 22 May 1865, AMAA 44135; Fee to Whipple, 1 Jul. 1865, AMAA 44151.

200. Hall to Strieby, 22 May 1865, AMAA 44135.

201. Fee to Whipple, 6 Jul. 1865, AMAA 44153.

202. Fee to Strieby, 2 May 1865, AMAA 44126.

203. Williams to Strieby, 24 Jul. 1865, AMAA 44167.

204. Clinton Bowen Fisk (born December 8, 1828, in western New York) had careers as an abolitionist reformer and as a Union Army officer. He began his military career as colonel of the Thirty-Third Missouri Infantry on September 5, 1862; he became commander of various departments and sub-departments in Missouri and Tennessee before becoming commander of the Thirteenth Division of the Thirteenth Army Corps in Tennessee. As a reformer he served on the executive board of American Missionary Association, and as vice-president of the Freedmen's Aid Society of the Methodist Episcopal Church. He was breveted as a major-general on March 13, 1865, and on June 26 took office as assistant commissioner for the Freedmen's Bureau in Kentucky and Tennessee; as an administrator of the Freedmen's Bureau, he founded Fisk University in Nashville, Tennessee. He died on July 9 in 1890. *CWD; DAB;* Dyer, 1:65; *GIB; HR,* 1:421; Swint, 151–52.

205. Williams to Strieby, 17 Jul. 1865, AMAA 44158.

206. No big plans for Camp Nelson ever worked out after the Federal government abandoned it.

207. Morris, 126, 127.

208. *CWD.* Oliver Otis Howard (1830–1909), Union general from Maine, had a distinguished military career, but he was probably best known for his (some would say "disastrous") postwar work as commissioner of the Freedmen's Bureau, a position he assumed on May 12, 1865. He founded Howard University in Washington, D.C., and served as its president from 1869 through 1874.

209. Freedmen's Bureau clerk's file summary; M999:7:190; RG 105.

210. E. Belle Mitchell (born c. 1847 in Perryville, Boyle County, Kentucky), daughter of Monroe Mitchell and his wife Mary E., had never been a slave. With one-quarter black ancestry, the educated eighteen-year-old woman of good family was chosen by John G. Fee

as the person to test the caste feeling of Camp Nelson's all-white teaching staff; most of them failed the test, and Belle was quickly expelled from their midst. She became a teacher in Lexington's first freedmen's school; attended Berea's Normal School, 1868–73; and married one of Lexington's most successful black businessmen, Jordan Jackson, a black trustee of Berea College (and father, by his first marriage, of another). She was co-founder of the Lexington Orphan's Home. Genealogical details from IGI at www.familysearch.org.

211. Wheeler to Whipple, 31 Aug. 1865, AMAA 44187–8.

212. Bentley, 60.

213. Although Fisk sometimes addresses R.E. Farwell as "Captain" Farwell, the term was probably honorific rather than military. No standard source for Civil War soldiers has any reference to R.E. Farwell. Apparently, he was a civilian appointee to the Freedmen's Bureau; Fee refers to him as a Massachusetts Yankee, but nothing further is known about his background.

214. Farwell previously had been employed by the Bureau in Tennessee; in August 1865, for example, he was instructed to break up the camp at Clarksville "at the earliest possible day." Cochrane to Farwell, 29 Aug. 1865; M999:4:718; RG 105.

215. Bentley, 77.

216. Account of Hager; M999:10:351–55; RG 105.

217. In a letter to John G. Fee, Bureau chief Clinton B. Fisk said his instructions from Washington were to break up the camp "at the earliest possible day consistent with humanity." Fisk to Fee, 4 Aug. 1865, 4 Aug. 1865, AMAA 44174–5.

218. Farwell to Fisk, 22 Dec. 1865; M999:7:373.78; RG 105.

219. *AM* 11, no. 4 (April 1867): 76.

220. [1868 sales] Jessamine County Deed Book W, 37, 155; Deed Book V, 779, 780; Deed Book 3, 384; Deed Book 13, 347; [1869 sale] Deed Book 3, 265; [1869 rental] Deed Book W, 95; [1880 sale] Deed Book 2, 343; [1900 sale] Deed Book 15, 292.

221. Fee to Whiting, 10 Mar. 1869, AMAA 44588.

222. *AM* 13, no. 5 (May 1869): 103. The two missionary societies had combined forces toward the end of their joint service at Camp Nelson.

223. Ibid.; Isaac M. Newton and Mrs. M.M. Newton to the AMA, 18 Mar. 1869, AMAA 44595–7.

224. Scofield to Fee, 27 Dec. 1869, BCA.

225. *AM* 14, no. 6 (June 1870): 125; *AM* 15, no. 5 (May 1871): 99; *AM* 16, no. 5 (May 1872): 99.

226. Burdett to Cravath, 28 Feb. 1871, AMAA 44741.

227. Burdett to Cravath, 1 Feb. 1872, AMAA 44915.

228. Burdett to Cravath, 19 Feb 1872, AMAA 44919.

229. Fee to Cravath, 7 May 1872, AMAA 44938.

230. Burdett to Cravath, 5 Dec. 1873, AMAA 45075.

231. *AM* 17, no. 11 (November 1873): 250.

232. Burdett to Cravath, 13 Dec. 1873, AMAA 45078.

233. Howard Samuel Fee (born August 25, 1851, in Lewis County, Kentucky), son of John G. Fee and Matilda Hamilton, was one of the first students at Berea College, graduating with the class of 1874. For several years in the 1870s, he was principal of Ariel Academy at Camp Nelson, where he began to teach in 1875. He had first taught at the Camp Nelson School for Colored Soldiers in the autumn of 1865, when he was fourteen! He died in Whittier, California, on October 15, 1904. Fee Collection, BCA.

234. Burdett to Cravath, 2 Feb. 1875, AMAA 45148; Ariel Academy leaflet, 10 Aug. 1875, AMAA 45168.

235. Fee to Strieby, 26 Dec. 1876, AMAA 45237.

236. Burdett to Strieby, 19 Nov. 1876, AMAA 45232; Burdett to Strieby, 3 May 1877, AMAA 45243; Burdett to Strieby, 12 May 1877, AMAA 45246; Burdett to Strieby, 3 May 1877, AMAA 45243.

237. Burdett to Strieby, 15 May 1877, AMAA 45248.

238. [*Camp Nelson*] Normal School promotional leaflet, AMAA 45271.

239. Rogers to Frost, 21 Nov 1901, BCA.

240. [1912 sale] Jessamine County Deed Book 26, 351; [1915 sale] Deed Book 29, 326.

241. Fee to Cravath, 1 Feb. 1872, AMAA 44915; Fee to Cravath, 20 Jan. 1873, AMAA 44997. Fee's will, dated 18 Oct. 1895, proved 4 Mar. 1901, is recorded in Madison County, Kentucky, Will Book 2, 326–28.

Abbreviations

Abbreviations within the Notes

AM	*American Missionary* [Magazine]
AMAA	American Missionary Association Archives
ANB	*American National Biography*
BCA	Berea College Archives
BRFAL	Bureau of Refugees, Freedmen, and Abandoned Lands
CMU	Central Michigan University
CWD.	Boatner, Mark Mayo. *The Civil War Dictionary* (New York, 1959).
DAB	*Dictionary of American Biography*
Dyer	Dyer, Frederick H. A. *A Compendium of the War of the Rebellion.* 2 vols. (Des Moines, 1908).
GIB	Warner, Ezra J. *Generals in Blue: Lives of the Union Commanders* (Baton Rouge, 1964).
GIG	Warner, Ezra J. *Generals in Gray: Lives of the Confederate Commanders* (Baton Rouge, 1959).
HR	Heitman, Francis B. *Historical Register and Dictionary of the United States Army from its organization, September 29, 1789, to March 2, 1903.* 2 vols. (Washington, D.C., 1903).
KE	Kleber, John, ed. *Kentucky Encyclopedia.* (Lexington, Ky., 1992).
NA	National Archives
NIMSUS	Woodward, Elon A., ed. "The Negro in the Military Service of the United States: A Compilation of the Official Records, State Papers, Historical Extracts, Relating to His Military Status and Service, from the North American Colonies." 7 vols. Typescript. (National Archives, 1888). RG 94. Also published on microfilm (M858).
OAR	Secretary of War. *Official Army Register of the Volunteer Force of the United States Army for the Years 1861, '62, '63, '64, '65.* 8 vols. (Washington, D.C., 1865–1867).
OR	U.S. War Department. *The War of the Rebellion: A Compilation of the Official Records of the Union and Confederate Armies.* 128 vols. (Washington, D.C., 1880–1901).

RAGK   *Report of the Adjutant General of the State of Kentucky.* 2 vols. (Frankfort, 1867).
RG 92   Records of the Office of the Quartermaster General [NA]
RG 94   Records of the Adjutant General's Office [NA]
RG 105   Records of the Bureau of Refugees, Freedmen, and Abandoned Lands [NA]
RG 159   Records of the Office of the Inspector General [NA]
RG 393   Records of the United States Army Continental Commands, 1821–1920 [NA]

Abbreviations within the Documents

Please note that many of the following abbreviations appear in the documents in a variety of forms: capitalized, partially capitalized, or uncapitalized, punctuated, partially punctuated, or unpunctuated, and in various combinations of the foregoing possibilities.

A.A.A.G.	Acting Assistant Adjutant General
A.A.G.	Assistant Adjutant General
A.C.	Army Corps
A.C.	Assistant Commissioner (of the Freedmen's Bureau)
Act., Actg.	Acting
A.D.C.	Aide-de-Camp
Adjt.	Adjutant
A.G.	Adjutant General
Agt.	Agent
A.I.G.	Assistant Inspector General
A.Q.M.	Assistant Quartermaster
Asst.	Assistant
A.S.A.C.	Assistant Subassistant Commissioner (Freedmen's Bureau)
BG	Brigadier General
BGC	Brigadier General Commanding
BBG	Brevet Brigadier General
BGV	Brigadier General of Volunteers
BMG	Brevet Major General
Brig.	Brigadier
Bvt.	Brevet
Capt.	Captain
Cav.	Cavalry
Co.	Company
Col.	Colonel
col^d, cold., col.	colored
comdg., cmdg.	Commanding
Comdr., Commr.	Commander

Comr.	Commissioner (Freedmen's Bureau)
C.S.	Commissary of Subsistence
C.S.A.	Confederate States of America
Dep	Deputy
Dept.	Department
Dist.	District
D.P.M.	Deputy Provost Marshal
Engr.	Engineer
Gen., Gen'l	General
Inf.	Infantry
Insp.	Inspector
inst.	*instant* (the current month of the year)
J.A.	Judge Advocate
Lt., Lieut.	Lieutenant
Maj.	Major
MG	Major General
ord.	ordnance
P.M.	Provost Marshal
P.M.G.	Provost Marshal General
Pro. Mar.	Provost Marshal
prox.	*proximo* (the next month of the year)
Q.M.	Quartermaster
Q.M.D.	Quartermaster's Department
Regt.	Regiment
R.Q.M.	Regimental Quartermaster
S.A.C.	Subassistant Commissioner (Freedmen's Bureau)
Sergt., Sgt.	Sergeant
Supt.	Superintendent
Sur., Surg.	Surgeon
ult., ult°	*ultimo* (the preceding month of the year)
USCA Lt	U.S. Colored Artillery (Light)
USCA Hvy	U.S. Colored Artillery (Heavy)
USCC	U.S. Colored Cavalry
USCHA	U.S. Colored Heavy Artillery
USCI	U.S. Colored Infantry
USCLtA	U.S. Colored Light Artillery
USCT	U.S. Colored Troops
U.S.A.	U.S. Army
V, Vols.	Volunteers
V.R.C.	Veteran Reserve Corps

Chapter One

The Establishment of Camp Nelson and the Invasion of East Tennessee

Head Quarters 1ˢᵗ Tenn Battery[1]   Hickman Bridge Ky   May 30ᵗʰ 1863
Lᵗ Col. [*Orville E.*] Babcock. Chief Engr.

Col   I wrote you a short time since asking for more specific instructions in relation to entrenching this Post but have not received them. I am at a loss what to do
not knowing what kind of defenses you propose making. I have taken every precaution possible to insure the safety of the bridge from fire by accident or by our enemies. I have made a casual survey of the country surrounding and examined the
points where defence is practicable. I have a force at work clearing the undergrowth
and brush from adjacent heights on opposite side of the river. I can in a short time
place light pieces on the commanding points. A company of Infantry for guard at
Bridge is necessary. The guard now detailed weakens the force of my Battery very
much   There are four companies of Infantry at Camp Dick Robinson belonging
to the 8ᵗʰ Tennessee doing no duty whatever. This force could be used advanta-
geously in completing any works you may wish erected at this post and from them
a Bridge Guard could be detailed leaving my command to mount the gun. My
Battery is at present parked one mile this side of the Bridge on the nearest ground
suitable   I have received complete armament & equipments   my rifled guns
are fine. I have done some splendid shooting with the concussion shells   Please to
forward me instructions as to what I shall do further *

R. Clay Crawford[2]   Capt Comdg 1ˢᵗ Tenn Battery[3]

1. The supervisor during the first days of Camp Nelson's establishment, Assistant Quartermaster James H. Pratt (T.E. Hall's predecessor) stated: "When I arrived at Camp Nelson
in May 1863 there were no troops there except a Battery of East Tenn troops commanded by
Capt R Clay Crawford   they were encamped near Mrs Scotts house and were guarding the
bridge across the Ky River." Pratt to Fry, 18 Feb. 1866; Entry 225; Consolidated Correspondence File (1794–1915); Box 1012 (Mary Scott); RG 92. (Hereafter, "Entry 225; . . . Box
1012 (Mary Scott); RG 92" abbreviated as "Box 1012; RG 92.")
2. R. Clay Crawford, who first served in the Fifth Tennessee Infantry, became captain of
the First Battalion of Tennessee Light Artillery. By November 1, 1863, he had been promoted to the rank of lieutenant colonel. All Tennessee troops in Kentucky were reporting to

him by December 1863; by January 1, 1864, he commanded the First East Tennessee Heavy Artillery. *OAR*, 4:1205.

3. Crawford to Babcock, 30 May 1863, Orlando M. Poe Papers, CMU.

Cincinnati, May 31, 1863.

General Willcox, Lexington, Ky.:

Give orders to have your officers' baggage cut down to the lowest possible amount. In my staff I have limited it to 30 pounds baggage. The men should not be allowed to take more than one change of underclothing and an extra pair of shoes; the remainder of their clothing should be nicely packed, marked distinctly, and sent to the depot at Hickman Bridge.[1] Let this be seen to by the regimental officers to-morrow, and surplus baggage all arranged and started to the rear on Tuesday morning. The officers should see that every package is distinctly marked. Men should be required on starting to carry in haversacks three days' provisions, and in the surplus room in knapsacks five days' hard bread and small rations. . . . [*They*] can send their surplus things to Lebanon, and thence by rail, under charge of an officer and two or three men, to Nicholasville, via Louisville, and thence to camp at Hickman Bridge.[2]

A.E. Burnside, Major-General.[3]

1. Camp Nelson developed an important function as a way station; its location at Hickman Bridge made it an invariable route for troops fanned out on either side of the Kentucky River.

2. A spur from Lebanon connected to the Louisville-Nashville Railroad; another line (Louisville-Frankfort-Lexington) ran east from Louisville to Lexington; and the Kentucky Central ran south from Covington through Lexington to its terminus at Nicholasville. Of course, the distance from Lebanon to Camp Nelson is much shorter than the circuitous route Burnside prescribes for his men's "surplus things." But the inconvenient rerouting is symptomatic of a major transportation problem for Camp Nelson and Kentucky as a whole. None of the state's railroads during the Civil War connected to Camp Nelson or to East Tennessee.

3. Burnside to Willcox, 31 May 1864, *OR*, 1, 23, pt. 2, 376. When he wrote this message, Burnside expected to lead his troops into East Tennessee in a matter of days; in fact, he announced that he was ready on June 3, but the Ninth Corps was deflected to Vicksburg and Burnside's movement was delayed for over a month. Nevertheless, this letter makes it clear that Burnside planned to march his troops quickly, with no extra burdens of supplies and personal possessions—the supplies were to follow the men, and Camp Nelson was to provide them. The depot also was designated as the storage center for personal possessions.

Head Quarters   District of Western Kentucky   Louisville   June 2, 1863
Genl. Fry[1] Comdg Camp of Instruction near Hickman Bridge Ky

* * * *

In reply to your inquiry as to your exact command, the Gen[l] directs me to say that you are in Command of a Camp of organization and instruction with all the authority incident thereto. The troops in your Camp are under military authority and are to be used as other troops, for guards, protection of public property &c.

General Burnside is about to establish his Head Quarters in your immediate vicinity and will therefore himself approve your requisitions.

The necessary blanks, instructions &c for recruiting officers will be obtained, on application to the Adjutant General of the State.[2] *

J.M. Wright[3]   Major & A.A.A.G.[4]

1. Speed Smith Fry (1817–1892), a native of Boyle County, attended Centre College and was generally involved in the region of Central Kentucky all his life. As Commander of the First Division, North Central Kentucky, Twenty-third Army Corps, Department of the Ohio, he was the first commandant of Camp Nelson, even when it was only a nameless "Camp of Instruction near Hickman Bridge"; relieved of the command for a time, he would return to Camp Nelson by June 1864 to take charge of training black recruits. He has become notorious in Kentucky history as the general who issued the tragically inhumane order to expel all black women and children from the camp in November 1864. *CWD;* Dyer, 1:66; *GIB; OAR,* 5:1248.

2. Later in June 1863, Fry received an express package containing "six copies Infantry Tactics, one of Cavalry Tactics and three copies Army Regulations." John M. Wright to Fry, 24 June 1863; Vol. 62/105, Letter no. 64; Letters Sent, May-Sept. 1863, Entry 2164 [Part 1 of 4]; General Records: Correspondence, District of Kentucky, Part 1; RG 393. (Hereafter, letters from Vol. 62/105 cited as "Vol. 62/105, [letter number]; Letters Sent; RG 393.")

3. John Montgomery Wright, a native of New York, became a major and assistant adjutant general in 1862 and resigned from the service in January 1864. The extra A in his title above apparently means he was acting assistant adjutant general. *HR,* 1:1063.

4. Wright to Fry, 2 June 1863; Vol. 62/105, 30; Letters Sent; RG 393. General Speed Smith Fry was already in command of a camping site at Hickman Bridge when Camp Nelson began to spring up around him. Fry had written Burnside to inquire about the nature of his command of the still unnamed camp; how much power the commander of Camp Nelson might really exercise never became exactly clear, and sometimes it was not even clear who the commander was.

Headquarters, Cincinnati, Ohio, June 3, 1863.

Maj. Gen. H.W. Halleck, General-in-Chief:

Your dispatch received. Rosecrans[1] is now relying upon my advance into Tennessee, and I am all ready. If I do not go there, some 8,000 or 10,000 men might be spared for Grant.[2] Rosecrans has just telegraphed me that he is moving, and wants me to push on. I leave for Hickman Bridge at daylight to-morrow. Telegraph me at Lexington.

A.E. Burnside, Major-General.[3]

1. William Starke Rosecrans (1819–1898), commanding the Army of the Cumberland, was engaged in a crucial but protracted campaign in Tennessee; Burnside's invasion of East Tennessee was intended to facilitate the operations that Rosecrans had been engaging in (and sometimes delaying) for months. The two commanders had already agreed upon the nature of their joint campaigns, but both had expected Burnside to march into Knoxville much sooner than he did. Rosecrans was decisively defeated by the Confederates at the Battle of Chickamauga in September 1863 and subsequently lost his command. *CWD.*

2. Ulysses Simpson Grant (1822–1885) was engaged in the Vicksburg campaign at this time. The Ninth Army Corps was ordered to his support in Mississippi on the date of this dispatch, June 3, 1863, thus spoiling Burnside's plan to advance into Tennessee immediately. After winning at Vicksburg, Grant would turn his own attention to Tennessee, winning decisive victories around Chattanooga.

3. Burnside to Halleck, 3 June 1863, *OR,* 1, 23, pt. 2, 384.

Hd. Qrs. Dept of the Ohio   June 12, 1863

[*Memorandum only.*] Camp near Hickman's Bridge Ky will be called <u>Camp Nelson</u> in honor of the memory of the late Maj. Genl. Wm Nelson[1]

[*Unsigned.*][2]

    1. William Nelson (1824–1862) had been murdered in public by Gen. Jefferson C. Davis (not to be confused with the Confederate president) less than a year before his memory was honored by having Camp Nelson named for him. Just before his death, he had been defeated by Kirby Smith at the Battle of Richmond, Kentucky. In the more positive phase of his military career, he had served, at President Lincoln's behest, as the primary recruiting officer for the Union Army in Kentucky, and he had established Camp Dick Robinson in Garrard County. *CWD; GIB.*

    2. Memorandum in Theron E. Hall papers, 12 June 1863; Box 720; RG 92. [N.B.: The National Archives warns against using box numbers because they may be changed when materials are reorganized; in the meantime, this whole box is full of Quartermaster Records from Camp Nelson].

U.S. Military Telegraph[1]   1130 am July 1st *1863*   *By Telegraph from* Lexington
To **Gen Burnside**

    The officer who had charge of the repairs of the Road from Stanford to Somerset is here   the Contrabands he had were taken from him by order of Capt Williams[2] & sent I believe to Hickman Bridge   the road has become since the rain so nearly impassable that teams can haul scarcely more than their rations & the troops cannot be supplied   When it begins to dry it can be made passable if there is work enough to fill the holes & make the other repairs   if not it will remain impassable   Immediate action is necessary   if the Contrabands cannot return I must detail soldiers & they ought not to be spared

Geo L Hartsuff M G[3]

    1. Military telegrams from Record Group 94 are generally recorded on printed forms. The part of the text that appears in print is given in italics.

    2. Samuel K. Williams was a member of the Veteran Reserve Corps. *HR*, 2:161.

    3. Hartsuff to Burnside, 1 July 1863; Generals' Papers: Burnside; Entry 159; RG 94. From May 28, 1863, to September 24, 1863, Gen. George L. Hartsuff (1830–1874) was commander of the Twenty-third Army Corps, Department of the Ohio. He was at Camp Nelson June 6–8 preparing to move his troops. A native of New York, Hartsuff began his military service in a Michigan regiment. *CWD;* Dyer, 1:72; *GIB; HR,* 1:507.

U.S. Military Telegraph   3:45 Pm July 8th *1863*   *By Telegraph from* Camp Nelson
To **Gen Burnside**

    Made a rapid inspection here today   the line along Hickman Creek is Easily assailable in several places   there are many Points on the opposite side of the creek that command the position here. The Gorge between the Creek & River is only partially closed in consequence of the impossibility of getting workmen in

sufficient numbers   There has been a great deal of looseness & maladministra-
tion in the affairs of the Q Mrs Dept between this & Cincinnati   things here
generally lack system greatly but seem to be reducing themselves to it fast as circumstances will permit   I will do all that lies within power & province — . . . .

Geo L Hartsuff   Maj Gen[1]

1. Hartsuff to Burnside, 8 July 1863; Generals' Papers: Burnside; Entry 159; RG 94.

Camp Nelson   July 13 1863
Major J.M. Wright

Maj.   Some ten days since I received a dispatch from Genl Boyle[1] through
you directing me to take command of all Tennessee Troops[2] at this place with a view
of having them properly organized and drilled.

Prior to the reception of that dispatch these Troops had all been placed under
Command of Col Mott[3] by order of Major Genl Hartsuff. I immediately sent the
dispatch to Genl Sturgis[4], who was then here with the request that he cause to be
issued an order in compliance with that dispatch.

The Genl declined doing so, saying it was not in his power to sit aside an
order issued by Genl Hartsuff, but would refer the matter to him. He did and Genl
Hartsuff promised to have it attended to. It has never been done and the matter still
stands in an unsettled condition. Genl Burnside seems to be laboring under the
impression that these Troops are under my command. He is constantly dispatching
me in regard to them. I sent Genl Boyle a dispatch, some days since, asking him to
have the matter settled one way or the other, but suppose it did not reach him, as
the news came in a very short time after that the wire had been cut. I should like to
have it definitely settled one way or the other, so that I may know exactly what to
do. Every thing here so far as the Command of the Post is concerned is in great
confusion. I was relieved of the Command of the Post by order of Major Genl
Hartsuff and Col Stockton[5] of the 8th Michigan Cavalry[6] succeeded me. since that
time Col Mott commanding a Brigade under Genl Hartsuff has been sent here to
assume command and it is now a difficult matter for me or any one else to tell who
commands the Post. No order that I have seen has been issued superceding Col
Stockton. They do not seem to know themselves who is in Command and the
consequence is that every thing is in great confusion. I have command of nothing
except my own troops the recruits being raised

If I could see the Genl and have a talk with him I could explain more fully the
nature of the troubles and difficulties that exist here. they are not a few. I cannot
give them air in the space of a short letter. I do not like to trouble the Genl with
matters that do not come within the immediate scope of his command, but as the
officers here seem to make no effort to rectify the evils that exist here I felt it my
duty to report them to him believing that he would interest himself [*indecipherable*]
to see that some steps are taken to remove them. As an example of the evils that exist
here, I learn from many and good sources that the Quarter Master who has had, up

to this time, the superintendance of the buildings in process of erection, has in many instances refused to pay men for their work and in some instances has destroyed the papers showing how long they had worked and what was done. I am also told that the paying clerk has been charging the laborers interest upon their wages alledging that it was to pay the public revenue. This is done in cases where the mans wages would not amount to more than $300

This same clerk has heretofore, I am told, been paying the slaves of loyal masters the wages due for their work.[7] This however I have stopped. There are other things which I could mention, but I will not persist at this [history? listing?] — If the Genl requires it I will give him in detail all that has come to my Knowledge in regard to them   *

Speed S Fry   Brig G[8]

1. Jeremiah Tilford Boyle, born 1818 in Mercer County, Kentucky, had studied law at Transylvania and was a Whig slave owner in Boyle County, Kentucky. He helped organize the defense of Kentucky and became the state's military governor from 1862 to 1864; he served as commander of the First Division of the Twenty-third Army Corps, Department of the Ohio, and as commander of the District of Kentucky (among many military assignments). He died on July 28, 1871. *ANB; CWD;* Dyer, 1:51; *GIB; HR,* 1:236; *KE,* 109.

2. Several East Tennessee regiments were organized and trained at Camp Nelson while military operations in Tennessee were still in progress. The Eighth Tennessee Infantry was organized at Camp Dick Robinson and Camp Nelson from November 11, 1862, to August 11, 1863. Five companies of the Fifth East Tennessee Cavalry (also known as the Eighth Tennessee Cavalry) were formed at Camp Nelson from June 30 to August 14, 1863. In addition, the Tenth, Twelfth, and Thirteenth Tennessee Cavalry regiments were placed under General Fry's command, along with Battery E of the First Tennessee Light Artillery. Dyer, 1:1636–47.

3. Samuel Rolla Mott, a Union officer from Ohio, commanded various brigades in the Twenty-third Army Corps; he was stationed at Camp Nelson in June and July of 1863. *CWD;* Dyer, 1:88.

4. Samuel Davis Sturgis (1822–1889) was a brigadier general from Pennsylvania who been commander of the District of Central Kentucky during June 1863. He became commander of the Cavalry Corps of the Department of the Ohio. *CWD;* Dyer, 1:104, 528; *GIB.*

5. When he began his very brief term as (maybe) the commandant of Camp Nelson, Col. John Stockton of the Eighth Michigan Cavalry was sixty-five years old. He was dishonorably discharged on April 15, 1864, for misuse of funds. *Record of Service of Michigan Volunteers 1861–1865* (1903) in Civil War Archive at www.ancestry.com.

6. The Eighth Michigan Cavalry had been ordered to Hickman Bridge shortly before June 22, 1863, as part of the Second Brigade, Fourth Division, Twenty-third Army Corps. Dyer.

7. Masters of slave laborers were legally entitled to their earnings.

8. Fry to Wright, 13 July 1863; Generals' Papers: Burnside; Entry 159; RG 94.

Camp Nelson   July 15ᵗʰ 1863.
(Private)
Brig Genl J.T. Boyle   Louisville Ky.

Dear Genl. * * * * [*One paragraph.*]

I am Sir litterally annoyed to death by the constant complaints of Citizens and the Employess at the Depot   That which appears to me the most infamous, is that some of the Officers and their Clerks in the Commissary and Quarter Master's Departments seem to look upon all Kentuckians as rebels and treat them with more contempt than you would the meanest negro in the land

They seem to make it a rule to show them as little favor as possible and actually take delight in keeping Ky Mechanics and Laborers out of their honest wages, in some instances, I have been told, actually sending them home to their suffering families without one cent of pay, and I am truly sorry to say they are receiving encouragement in their conduct from very high sources. To convince of the truth of what I say, two or three days since two very clever farmers from Garrard County came to me and asked the privilege of looking in the Camp for some cattle they had lost, one of them stating that he knew his were here that he had seen them a pair of oxen. The man acted in such a way as to satisfy me that the cattle were his, but did not wish to take them without making proof of ownership. I told him to go home, bring his proof and I thought he would have no trouble in getting them. I had the day before addressed a note somewhat in the shape of an order to Capt Bell C.S.[1] saying that if Mr Scott[2] proved his property in the cattle he should give them up.

The Capt immediately dispatched Genl Hartsuff asking if I had any right to give him orders and the following answer was returned.

"Genl Hartsuff directs me to say that you are not subject to the orders of Genl Fry and he can exercise no control whatever over your department. If you are satisfied that Cattle belong to Citizens, I should advise delivering them over, but not otherwise. I don't see any necessity of investigation on my part."

Signed   J.M. Ellis[3]   Lt Col and Chf. C.S.   23. A.Cr

The underscoring is mine. You can see why I did it.

This dispatch ended the matter so far as these two men were concerned. they went home minus the cattle. . . . * * * * [*Five paragraphs; last page or pages missing from letter.*]

[*Speed Smith Fry.*][4]

1. Captain Molyneux Bell was commissary of subsistence at Camp Nelson.
2. Mr. Scott was probably Thomas B. Scott, one of the two sons of Mrs. Mary Scott, owner of much of the land upon which Camp Nelson was located.
3. James Marsh Ellis, a native of Massachusetts, was a lieutenant colonel and commissary of subsistence of the Twenty-third Army Corps.
4. [Fry?] to Boyle, 15 July 1863; Generals' Papers: Burnside; Entry 159; RG 94.

August 3, 1863.

General Hartsuff, Lexington, Ky.:

I do not care to have any permanent changes made in the troops now in Kentucky, as I propose to move them as soon as possible. Let all the troops that have been on the move be concentrated at Lebanon and Hickman Bridge, and there be fitted out. Have all the cavalry ready to move by Saturday night, and all the deficiencies supplied. I shall organize the main body into a separate command. Only keep enough cavalry at the front to scout the country well to the Cumberland River. The Ninth Corps[1] will be here in a few days, but it is very much reduced in numbers. I want to increase its divisions by adding some new regiments and transferring some of the regiments now in Kentucky. The cavalry is being shipped to Hickman Bridge[2] as fast as it arrives. There are plenty of horses here, if they are needed at Hickman Bridge. I am giving the necessary instructions to the cavalry that are in Ohio.

A.E. Burnside, Major-General.[3]

1. The Ninth Corps had finished its service in Mississippi, but its return to Kentucky was slowed by the illness and fatigue of the men.
2. In his correspondence, Burnside never calls Camp Nelson by its name; he always refers to Hickman Bridge or to the camp at Hickman Bridge.
3. Burnside to Hartsuff, 3 Aug. 1863, OR, 1, 23, pt. 2, 590.

Lexington, Ky., August 10, 1863.

General H.W. Halleck, General-in-Chief:
    The mounted force in this department will amount to 8,000 men as soon as all of the organizations are perfect, which will be in a very few days. I leave for Hickman Bridge at once.

A.E. Burnside, Major-General.[1]

1. Burnside to Halleck, 10 Aug. 1863, OR, 1, 23, pt. 2, 603.

[*Excerpt from U.S. Sanitary Commission*[1] *report*] SOLDIERS' HOME, CAMP NELSON, KY.

    In 1863 a large military force was gathered in Central and South-eastern Kentucky, as a defense against invasion, and in preparation for an advance upon Knoxville. At this time Camp Nelson was made the most important military center, and the base of supplies for the army south of that point. Numerous large buildings were erected from the Commissary and Quartermaster's Departments, water works constructed, and other improvements of the most substantial character made, such as fitted it to become a large and permanent military encampment. At this time an Agency of the Sanitary Commission was established there, under the superintendence of Mr. Thomas Butler, who was already experienced in our work. This Agency was at first simply a depot of supplies, and from thence Sanitary stores were distributed to the camps and hospitals in that section of the State.[2]

1. The United States Sanitary Commission, inspired by the British Sanitary Commission of the Crimean war and "an outgrowth of various women's organizations," was organized in April 1861. Its aim "was to do for the soldiers what the government did not do, and this included raising the hygienic standards of the camps and diet, caring for the wounded, coor-

dinating the program to send food and supplies to the soldiers, and compiling a directory of the sick and wounded in army hospitals." *CWD*, 720.

   2. Newberry, 379–80.

Louisville, Ky., August 10, 1863
General Orders No 41.

     I. The construction of military roads in the State being a necessity, by the order of the Major General commanding the Department, six thousand laborers from the negro population of the country through which the roads pass will be impressed.

     II. The negro laborers will be impressed first from the following counties: Harrison, Bourbon, Scott, Clarke, Fayette, Woodford, Jessamine, Mercer, Boyle, Garrard, Lincoln, Marion, Washington, and Nelson.

     III. Male negroes from the ages of sixteen to forty-five both inclusive, are subject to this impressment.

     IV. In order that the impressment may not hinder and materially injure the cultivation of and the harvesting and gathering the crops for the subsistence of the country, it is ordered that when a citizen has but one male negro laborer he will not be impressed under this order. In case a person has more than one and less than four, one is to be impressed. In case a person has four male laborers and over, one-third of them are impressed by this order.

     V. Brig. Gen. S.S. Fry is charged with the execution of this order, and is directed to appoint officers from the 1st Division of the 23d Army Corps to assist him, and to employ citizens to take charge of said negro laborers.

     VI. The negroes hereby impressed are required to be delivered by the owners at the points to be designated by the the 20th August inst., or at such time thereafter as Brig. Gen. S.S. Fry shall appoint officers or persons to take charge of them. Persons failing to comply with this order will have taken all their negroes of the ages designated.

     VII. He will concentrate the negroes impressed by this order at Camp Nelson, or such other place as may be directed, and have them subsisted as laborers in the Quartermaster's Department; requiring complete rolls to be kept, with the names of the negroes, their owners, and place of residence.

     VIII. All owners will be paid for the services of the laborers, and at the expiration of each month proper vouchers will be furnished to the persons entitled thereto. The negroes taken under this order will be delivered to their owners after the expiration of the time for which they are impressed.

     IX. Brig. Gen. Fry is ordered to take immediate action for the execution of this order, and report to these Head Quarters the number of laborers collected, for information, that further orders may be issued to secure the quota of laborers required, and to distribute the impressment as equitably as practicable over the country to be mainly benefited by the proposed improvement.

By order of Brig. Gen. Boyle[1]

1. Berlin et al., *Freedom*, series 1, *The Destruction of Slavery,* 585, 586. (Hereafter abbreviated "*The Destruction of Slavery.*")

Office Chief of Engineers, Dept. of the Ohio, Cincinnati, Ohio, August 11, 1863. [To] Brig. Gen. Joseph G. Totten, Chief of Engineers, U.S. Army, Washington, D.C. Capt. O.M. Poe, chief engineer Twenty-third Army Corps, in charge, reports, July 31:

The intrenchments at Camp Nelson have been pushed forward as rapidly as the number of men at my disposal for work would admit. Fort Nelson has one face finished and the other in a defensible condition. Fort Jackson (occupying the site of the central point of the line) has all the revetment completed, and the parapet more than half done. The rifle-pits are completed to connect Fort Jackson with the river. A new battery, 200 yards to the eastward of Fort Jackson, has been commenced, and good progress made upon it. This work I propose to build entirely with the engineer battalion of the Twenty-third Army Corps, and will devote particular attention to their instruction while engaged upon it, thus making it a drill for them.

. . . . During the month of July about three thousand days' work were expended upon those intrenchments. Now that the harvest is over, I am in hopes that the negroes which had been returned to their owners will be returned to me for work. * * * * [*Two paragraphs.*]

About the 18th of July, General Hartsuff, upon my suggestion, directed that an engineer battalion, to number 300 men and 8 officers, be organized by detail from infantry regiments in the Twenty-third Army Corps. About 150 of these men have already reported to me at Camp Nelson, and are at work there. The details report quite irregularly on acount of the recently disturbed condition of affairs. I hope to render this battalion very efficient. I have been trying to select from the corps officers for the battalion, but as yet have not been as successful as I could wish, but expect to obtain them from time to time, as I can discover a good man. General Hartsuff's orders upon the subject are very explicit, and certainly should be very satisfactory to the department which we represent. If a similar organization be made in the Ninth Army Corps, it will give an engineer brigade of 600 picked men.

I take great pleasure in speaking of the ready assistance which has thus far been given me by the quartermaster's department at Camp Nelson. It has furnished me all the lumber I have thus far required for revetment, but, in view of any possible difficulty, I would respectfully request you to obtain from the department commander an order directing that the lumber be furnished me. It is impossible to procure anything like sods or gabions enough near the camp to do even a small portion of the revetment. * * * *[1]

[From] J.H. Simpson, Major & Chief Engineers, Dept. of the Ohio.[2]

1. The report goes on to discuss, at some length, stockades on the Kentucky Central Railroad.
2. Report of Capt. Orlando M. Poe, included in Simpson to Totten, 11 Aug. 1863, *OR*, 1, 23, pt. 2, 608, 609. Poe's original report, dated 31 July 1863, is in Entry 3541; Part 1; RG 393.

Nicholasville, Ky.   Aug 11" 1863   Teusday 9 1/2 A.M.

My own dear wife, * * * * [*One paragraph.*]
We arrived here 1/2 an hour ago. Our departure from Covington[1] was postponed till dark, which gave us the discomfort of a night trip. I don't feel very brisk after it; but having got my face washed, I conclude I would feel about right if I now had a cup of coffee, as I soon will have. We had 3/4 hour halt at Lexington. Col. D. & I lunched there on bread, milk, & pie.
We have now on our debarkation stacked muskets under the shade of locust trees which ornament the extensive ground of a citizen just opposite to the R.R. depot. The men, tired with their journeyings including last night's ride, are reclining very quietly in groups under the shade while coffee is in course of preparation   I am seated under a locust leaning against it, while a grateful breeze fans me, & a pleasant shade lies around. I will mail this here. Our departure yesterday prevented our procuring any letters the evening mail . . . . They will now follow us to "Camp Nelson" as the Hickmans Bridge camp is called. . . . * * * * [*Three paragraphs.*] [*No closing.*]
[*Robert Audley Browne*][2]

1. Various pieces of the Ninth Army Corps were arriving at Covington and traveling to Camp Nelson from there. Some of the corps had already arrived at Camp Nelson, while other troops were still in Covington waiting for transportation. On August 16 Burnside received a message stating that "a great many complaints [were] being made of the conduct of the Ninth Army Corps, while waiting for transportation in Covington," where they were assembling without a general officer of the corps. William P. Anderson to Burnside, 16 Aug. 1863, *OR*, 1, 30, pt. 3, 54.
2. Browne to Mary E. Browne, 11 Aug. 1863, Civil War Miscellaneous, Robert A. Browne, Chaplain, 100th Pennsylvania Infantry Regiment, Letters, Browne and family, May 23, 1860 to Nov. 11, 1863, Archives, U.S. Army Military Institute, Carlisle Barracks, Carlisle, Pa.

Camp Nelson, Jessamine Co. Ky.   Teusday Aug 11 1863
Mrs Mary E. Browne   New Castle Pa

My own, We arrived here near 3 o'clock. Our canvas Village is up, but not finished, tho' busy workmen are hastening in completion. We left Nicholasville near the noon hour. . . . Our march would have been pleasant but for the dust. The climate is, oh, so superior to Miss but the refreshing breeze wafted clouds of limestone dust from the turnpike over our clothes   To these & beards the dust seemed to have a wonderful tenacity, as also to the drops of perspiration. All bearded men seemed to have grown many years older during our march of 2 or 3 hours, powdered over as they were with fine whitish limestone particles: & they were really amusing to look upon. Arrived here a good wash, & change of shirt & a good brushing have operated like a rejuvenation. . . . . Ever man of our mess including the servants, seem to have to have bethot him to buy a box of blacking   For a week or two therefore specially after the arrival of the Pay Master we may expect stylish times. Gen. Burnside is going to have his headqrs. here also for a time & there will be withal the painful & onerous details of camp ceremonies, I presume, on the arrival of our corps. . . . * * * * [*Two paragraphs.*]

Robt Audley Browne   Chapl. 100" Reg P.V.   9" A.C.[1]

1. Ibid.

Louisville, August 11, 1863.

Capt. Charles R. Thompson,[1] Aide-de-Camp:
General Burnside has left Lexington for Camp Nelson this evening.

G.W. Tyler.[2]

1. Captain and aide-de-camp Charles Robinson Thompson, born in Maine and enlisted in Missouri, became a colonel in the Twelfth U.S. Colored Infantry less than a week after this letter was written. *HR,* 1:956.
2. Tyler to Thompson, 11 Aug. 1863, *OR,* 1, 30, pt. 3, 8.

Camp Nelson, Ky. Hickmans Bridg   Aug 12th 1863

Dear father   . . . .   Hoping these few lines may find you all well and doing well dear father I have not heard any thing you since I left home   I would be glad to Hear from you   it would gratify me very much to hear from you and to hear what the Rebels has done and what they are doing   I have had my health very well since i have been hear with the aception of a bad Cold and a bowel Complaint but I am well of that now   i dont think it will be very Long before we can get to come home   our forces is gathern up here for some purpose a nother   i supose you heard of morgans capitulations in ohio him and all his force. The rebels Lost agreat many of their men while they were on their raid   our men Captured about seven hundred of them and sent them to Camp chaise where morgans men was   They done some damage while they were in here but not as much as could have been expected from the force they had. They were keener to get out than they were to Come in for they like not to have got out at all for they were persued briefly   You all need not be uneasy about me for I will promise you that I will take good care of my self for i am along Ways from home one hundred and forty miles   it is not as far as some have been but i call it a good-piece off but we can soon ride it once we draw our horses   we will consider it no piece when once we start home   . . . .   all the boys sends their bes respects to all thier enquiring Friends   There is agreat force in Kentucky they it seems is moving towards Tennessee   i expect there is not short of fifty thousand well drilled men in here of diferent sections   . . . .

Dear father i had a toilsome Journey in geting here   it took us five days to come here hard walking at that   i can inform you that i have volunteered in the 9th Tennessee cavalry in care of Colnel Jo parson from Knox County Tennessee   dear father i also can inform you that there is agreat many of our neighbour boys here boys that I have been raised with from campbell County. . . . our regment is blessed so far with good health   there is not more than three or four sick ones in our regment and they have bad Colds mostly   that is the principle disease   when i left home i didnot have much notion of volunteering for Ii not know hardly what i would do but i thought it best to volunteer because i could not stay at home * * * * [*One paragraph.*]

B F. Mozings sends his best respects to all of the family and wants see you all very bad and also wants you all to write to him and he says if ever he lives to get back to Tennessee he will bring aunt delila a fine pipe.

So no more at present. But remains your Dear son untill death   so fare well to all

W H Chapman To John Chapman Fincastle Tennessee Campbell County[1]

1. W.H. Chapman to John Chapman, 12 Aug. 1863, Tennessee State Library and Archives, Nashville, Chapman Papers, Box 1, Folder 9, Microfilm Acc. No. 1256.

Headquarters Department of the Ohio, Camp Nelson, August 12, 1863.

W.S. Rosecrans:

I arrived at Hickman's Bridge yesterday, and have been expecting to hear from you again, as your dispatch indicated there will be a delay of two or three days on account of forage and supplies. How are you progressing? We can hasten our movements if it is necessary.

A.E. Burnside, Major-General.[1]

1. Burnside to Rosecrans, 12 Aug. 1863, *OR*, 1, 30, pt. 3, 16.

[*Excerpt from the memoirs of Peter Bruner*]

Burnside was at Camp Nelson just preparing to start out and I thought if I could only make it to that place I would be all right. Previous to this I had overtaken some more men and they were going along with me. Just as we were putting our shoes on after we had been wading the river, some five or six men came and captured them all but me and I escaped by taking refuge under some bushes. I do not know who the men were. After they had been gone about a half hour I thought I would proceed so I went on until I had gone about a half mile, then I climbed over a fence and laid down in some tall weeds. When I awoke some men were cutting the weeds over me and some of them said kill the d——n nigger. Then they took me up to an old blacksmith's shop where they had the remaining part of the crowd. Then they took us from there to Nickleville [*Nicholasville*] which was about eighteen miles below Lexington. There they took us before the Magistrate and swore that we were runaway slaves. They then took us to jail. In the room I occupied were twenty-four more slaves all running off trying their very best to get free. Oh, how hard some of us poor slaves labored to gain our freedom.[1]

1. Bruner, 32–33. Bruner, a Kentucky slave who tried repeatedly to escape from a sadistic master, here recalls a futile attempt made when he was seventeen or eighteen.

U.S. Military Telegraph.   Aug 13 186[3]   *By Telegraph from* Stanford
To Maj Genl Burnside

Your despatch in regard to pack mules rec^d   I doubt the practcability of relying on pack mules as a means of transportation unless they are trained & have Experienced packers   I have heard of about one or two men in the command who have any Knowledge of the business   The supplies to be carried securely or indeed at all without greatly injuring the mules should be made up in proper packages & that would probably require more time than can now be spared   I have used pack mules but once and then with only partial success   when wagons can be used I think they are preferable unless perhaps with trained mules & Experienced muleteers   I have heard today that Forrest[1] H^dQuarters are at Kingston Tenn

S P Carter[2]   BG.[3]

1. Brig. Gen. Nathan Bedford Forrest (1821–1877) was the foremost leader of cavalry in the Confederate Army, and one of the great impediments to the Union's military progress in Tennessee. He began as a private in the Seventh Tennessee Cavalry and eventually rose to the rank of lieutenant general in command of all cavalry. Forrest served brilliantly in the Tennessee campaign, and he exceeded John Hunt Morgan as a military commander in every respect, except possibly undeserved fame. *GIG.*
2. Native Tennesseean Samuel Powhatan Carter (1819–1891) commanded various divisions of the Twenty-third Army Corps, including the First and the Fourth, and finally of the whole Twenty-third; earlier, he commanded the First Brigade of the District of Central Kentucky. *CWD;* Dyer, 1:55; *GIB; HR,* 1:288.
3. Carter to Burnside, 13 Aug. 1863; Generals' Papers: Burnside; Entry 159; RG 94.

[Date illegible; filed with letters dated August 13, 1863]

Gen Burnside
We only asked for such number of Horses as are required   those sent to Camp Nelson were inspected & turned over for most part for Treatment & rest. If the Second & seventh Ohio & the detachments which were left in Ohio Bring with them Horses for Whole Command we will require fewer Horses by that number

from Camp Nelson   I am from head Quarters & have not with me Exact number of Horses required but Capt Lynch[1] Division Quarter Master is at Camp Nelson & has the Number needed   Ammunition some springfield Rifle about 80 of latter & clothing in small quantitys are needed   Some corn in Ear will probably be in tomorrow from vicinity of Harrodsburg but we are feeding on sheaf oats & Hay   a few feeds of corn will be of great service to the Horses as they are growing thin on present forage rations   I think the number of arms you mention will be sufficient for I think but few men will be left in the Country two (2) weeks hence unless they are protected from Rebels   Numbers are arriving daily & I hear of many more on the way to Ky   I shall do all In my Power to be ready but the time will depend on the promptness with which requisitions are filled at Camp Nelson   Men have left to attempt the work mentioned in despatch of yesterday

S P Carter   BG.[2]

1. Evidently Captain Lynch was John Arthur Lynch. Born in Ireland, Lynch served in an Ohio regiment and became a captain and assistant quartermaster in November 1862. *HR,* 1:649.
2. Carter to Burnside, illegible date; Generals' Papers: Burnside; Entry 159; RG 94.

Headquarters, Camp Nelson, Ky., August 13, 1863.

Major-General Rosecrans:

Shall endeavor to start Saturday [15th] moving a brigade of cavalry from Glasgow, a division of infantry from Danville, and two brigades of cavalry from Stanford. I already have one brigade of cavalry at Somerset.

We shall go into East Tennessee with the understanding that we are to live on the country, and as the entire command will not be over 14,000 strong, we shall value very much your assistance and co-operation and hold ourselves in readiness to co-operate with you in every possible way. Our destination will be as you suggest, and the time necessary for the march will be about what I have already notified you.

A.E. Burnside, Major-General.[1]

1. Burnside to Rosecrans, 13 Aug. 1863, *OR,* 1, 30, pt. 3, 22.

Office C.S.   Camp Nelson Ky   August 14th 1863
[Addressee illegible; perhaps General Burnside, but discernible letters do not appear so]

General.   Agreeable to your instructions, I have the honor to report; that I have thoroughly enquired into the subject of procuring Flour, and baking both Hard and Soft Bread in this camp; thereby making it in this particular self sustaining and have arrived at the conclusion that the plan is not only feasible but that it would result in great benefit to the Government.

In the first place the grain crop this season has been enormous in Kentucky and all over this section of the country the Farmers are most anxious to dispose of the fruits of their richly laden fields, somewhere in their own vicinity.[1] * * * * *[Two paragraphs.]*

From nearly two months experience of manufacturing and baking Soft bread at "Camp Nelson" I am happy to state that it has proven a most signal success. Our soldiers appreciate it, and it is considered generally, very excellent, and healthy bread. * * * * [*Three paragraphs.*]

As an addend to the foregoing I would also state to the Commanding General that there are great quantities of Potatoes now in the ground hereabouts which must soon be gathered. To purchase them on the spot would save to the Government much money, which is now expended in transportation for hundreds of miles. *

Molyneux Bell   Capt & CS[2]

1. This report of the bountiful harvest in Kentucky is very ironic considering the circumstances that were soon to arise, with the soldiers who relied on provisions from Kentucky going hungry.
2. Bell to General ?, 14 Aug. 1863; Generals' Papers: Burnside; Entry 159; RG 94.

Hdqrs. Army of the Ohio, In the Field, Camp Nelson, Ky., August 14, 1863. General Field Orders, No. 2.

I. The general commanding calls upon all members of his command to remember that the present campaign takes them through a friendly territory, and that humanity and the best interests of the service require that the peaceable inhabitants be treated with kindness, and that every protection be given by the soldiers to them and to their property.

II. Officers will enforce the strictest discipline to prevent straggling, any ill treatment of citizens, depredations, or willful destruction of private property, and each officer will be held strictly responsible for offenses of such nature committed by men under his command.

III. No prisoners will be liberated on parole, but will be conducted under guard to the authorities appointed to receive them.

IV. It must also be distinctly understood that this war is conducted for national objects, and that any desire which may exist on the part of soldiers to avenge their private wrongs must yield to a proper observance of the well-established usages of civilized warfare.

V. Prisoners of war, particularly the wounded, will be treated with every consideration consistent with their safe-keeping, and any ill treatment or insults offered to them will be severely punished.

VI. Whenever regimental evening dress parades are held, it shall be the duty of the commanding officer to see that the chaplain, or some proper person in his absence, holds some short religious service, such as the reading of a portion of the Scriptures, with appropriate prayers for the protection and assistance of Divine Providence.

By order of Major-General Burnside:
Lewis Richmond,[1] Assistant Adjutant-General.[2]

1. Lewis Richmond was a Union officer from Rhode Island; an assistant adjutant general in the Army of the Ohio, he arrived at Camp Nelson with Burnside to write the general's dispatches. He was brevetted for his "gallant and meritorious service" during the campaign in East Tennessee at the siege of Knoxville. *CWD; HR,* 1:829.

2. General Field Orders No. 2, 14 Aug. 1863, *OR,* 1, 30, pt. 3, 30–31.

Hdqrs. Army of the Ohio, Camp Nelson, Ky., August 14, 1863.
General Field Orders, No. 3.

The commanding general welcomes back to the department the veterans of the Ninth Corps. The inscriptions, "Vicksburg" and "Jackson,"[1] they bring with them on their banners, bear testimony to their valor and to the faithfulness with which they have fulfilled their mission and sustained the high reputation of a name already prominent in the annals of patriotism.

By command of Major-General Burnside.
Lewis Richmond, Assistant Adjutant-General.[2]

1. The Ninth Corps had fought at both Vicksburg and Jackson in Mississippi.
2. General Field Orders No. 3, 14 Aug. 1863, *OR,* 1, 30, pt. 3, p. 31.

U.S. Military Telegraph.   **August 15** *1863*   *By Telegraph from* **Stanford**
To **Gen Burnside**

We will have today I hope about 5 Days forage of shelled grain   We are now Engaged in threshing Wagons   have gone to vicinity of Harrodsburg for 1000 Bushels shelled corn & will be back Tomorrow Night   Will send you Just as soon as I can get reports the number of Rations here & amount of transportation. The Commissary has returned from Camp Nelson   If we take six (6) Days Forage of grain for five thousand (5000) animals in Wagons at only ten (10) pounds Each per Day It will require one hundred & twenty (120) wagons for that alone Putting 2500 pounds in each   But one Days forage can be carried on Horses which will reduce the wagons to 100   as men are constantly arriving I cannot state the exact number of Animals we shall have   I want no more wagons to look out for than are absolutely necessary for I count them a great encumbrance

Carter   BG.[1]

1. Carter to Burnside, 15 Aug. 1863; Generals' Papers: Burnside; Entry 159; RG 94.

U.S. Military Telegraph.   **Aug 15** *1863*   *By Telegraph from* **Danville**
To **Gen Burnside**

Despatch recd   · I did not mean that the wheels of Phillip Batty[1] were in bad condition but referred to the hind wheels of many of the Wagons in the supply train & suggested that while the train is being loaded the wheels might be replaced by taking some from other wagons that are to be left back at Camp Nelson   I have never recd notice that any wagons had been turned over to me beside the 60 I got, of Col Gilbert & supposed my Q M would have to get the remainder of train at Camp Nelson   The reason why I speak of a requisite train is that I have never been Informed where I am going or the nature of the campaign   If we have got to take along 14 Days Rations & forage for all the animals of the train & Div I dont think 100 wagons will do it   of this however you can Judge better than myself as you know where we are going & what the resources of the Country are which we pass   I am informed that after the first 2 or 3 days out the Country is entirely destitute of any Kind of supplies so we will have to transport not only rations but forage for twelve (12) or fourteen hundred (1400) animals. I had two (2) Batteries with my Command before the Phillips Batty arrived . . . 2 Batteries is all I need with my Div   Do you intend the Phillips Battery to go with me   Genl Hartsuff has ordered it in reserve at Camp Nelson.

Milo S. Hascall[2]   BG.[3]

1. Phillip's Battery was Battery M, under the command of Lt. George W. Reed, of the Second Illinois Artillery.
2. Milo Smith Hascall, a native New Yorker who became colonel of the Seventeenth Indiana Infantry, was a brigadier general of volunteers by April 25, 1862. *HR*, 1:509.
3. Hascall to Burnside, 15 Aug. 1863; Generals' Papers: Burnside; Entry 159; RG 94.

Camp Nelson, August 15, 1863.

Major-General Parke,

The general wishes to see you particularly. Please come down on the 2 o'clock train, and an ambulance will meet you at the depot in Nicholasville. It will not be necessary for the staff to accompany you unless you wish it. General Potter's[1] division is to go through Cincinnati. The news of the death of General Welsh[2] was received here with the greatest regret as a severe loss to the cause.

Lewis Richmond, Assistant Adjutant-General.[3]

1. Robert B. Potter, subject of note 53, introduction.
2. General Thomas Welsh (born 1824 in Pennsylvania), commander of the First Division of the Ninth Army Corps, had died on August 14, 1863, from malaria contacted during the Vicksburg campaign. *CWD; Dyer*, 1:109; *GIB; HR*, 1:1018.
3. Richmond to John G. Parke, 15 Aug. 1863, *OR*, 1, 30, pt. 3, p. 45.

**Head Qtrs Convalescent Camp.   Camp Nelson Ky.   Aug 21st 1863.
Brig Gen'l M.C. Meigs,[1] Q.M. Gen'l.   Washington D.C**

Sir.   I have the honor to state that I have recently been ordered to take command of this Camp. in doing so I have reciepted to the retiring Commandant for (400) Four Hundred Blankets many of which are so worn as to be nearly worthless. I would also state that men are being constantly sent to this Camp and sometimes without Descriptive Lists or Blankets. Will you please inform me if in such cases, I ought to furnish them Government Blankets during their stay or issue Blankets, and send the acc't to their Company Commanders. And will the soldiers signature on a clothing reciept roll be sufficient voucher for such issue on my part   Can I have worthless Blankets now in my possession condemned and Ordered to be dropped from my return by a board of survey.

I would also enquire how Prisoners of War and deserters and stragglers &c who are in my charge and destitute of Clothing ought to be supplied   *

H.H. Richardson[2]   Maj. Commandant of Convals't Camp and

Provost Master   Camp Nelson Ky.[3]

1. Montgomery Cunningham Meigs, a native of Georgia, began his military career in Pennsylvania. By May 15, 1861, he was a brigadier general and quartermaster general, a position which he held for over twenty years. *HR*, 1:702.

2. Henry H. Richardson was a major in the Twenty-first Massachusetts Infantry. *HR*, 2:141.

3. Richardson to Meigs, 21 Aug. 1863; Box 720; Records of the Office of the Quartermaster General, RG 92.

Headquarters Ninth Army Corps, Lexington, Ky., August 23, 1863.
Col. John De Courcy,[1] Comdg. Third Brigade, Second Division, Camp Nelson:

Colonel: The general commanding corps requests that you will please inform these headquarters of the whereabouts of the different regiments and of the battery of your brigade.[2] If they are not yet assembled at Camp Nelson, you will please order them at once to that point to await the arrival of the general commanding division, to whom you will report for duty with your brigade. *

Saml. Wright,[3] Assistant Adjutant-General.[4]

1. John F. De Courcy was colonel of the Sixteenth Ohio Infantry and commander of the Third Brigade of the Second Division of the Ninth Army Corps at this time. *HR*, 2:94.

2. About a week earlier, Col. De Courcy, commander of the 16th Ohio Volunteer Infantry, had been ordered to organize a brigade to attach to the 9th Army Corps at Camp Nelson; the brigade was to be composed of the 86th Ohio Volunteer Infantry, 129th Ohio Volunteer Infantry, Neil's Ohio Volunteer battery, plus the 1st Battalion of East Tennessee Cavalry and the 9th East Tennessee Cavalry. Special Field Orders No. 3, 15 Aug. 1863, *OR*, 1, 52, pt. 1, 438.

3. Samuel Ives Wright was born in New York, but his military service began in Michigan. He became a captain and assistant quartermaster on February 27, 1863. *HR*, 1:1063.

4. Wright to De Courcy, 23 Aug. 1863, *OR*, 1, 30, pt. 3, 143–44.

Camp Nelson Near Nicholasville Ky.   August 30th 1863

Dear Cousin Louisa, This is an age of excitement — and a soldiers life comes in for its shares of excitement and turmoil and during the last three months, we have had plenty of it. But we are again settling down into our old routine of camp life — viz — Reveille at 6 a.m. Breakfast — at 7 — Drill at 8 1/2 — Tactics at 10 1/2 Dinner at 12 — Recreation till 4 — Inspection at 4 1/4 Dress Parade at 5 1/2 p.m. Etc.

This life comes as natural now as though I had always followed it — Indeed the longer I stay here — the more attracted I become to military life — The very hardships of campaigning gives me a new impulse — For every new movement is a rich experience for me — I would not exchange my three months experience at Vicksburg and Jackson for three <u>years camp</u> life in Kentucky and yet have no desire to go over the same scenes again I <u>assure you</u>. * * * * [*Four paragraphs.*]

This camp is a regularly organized institution   Transportation can readily be obtained, being only 4 miles from Nicholasville   therefore we get supplies in any quantity. We shall be content to remain here for a long time — Indeed the Corps is in no condition for active service   large numbers have fallen by the malarious diseases arising from the swamps of the Farm — A great many of these sick ones have been taken since we came back, the poison in their systems not taking effect until lately — I have not been effected very badly yet so think I shall escape —

Our healthy camp and the cool breezes of September undoubtedly will have an excellent effect on the sick ones — During the last three days we have had remarkably cool weather and we find our blankets not uncomfortable. . . . * * * * [*Two paragraphs.*]

Your aff Cousin   J.C. Currier[1]

1. Currier to Louisa ? [his cousin], 30 Aug. 1863, Filson Club Library, Louisville, Ky. Currier's regiment was a part of the Ninth Corps that went to Vicksburg and Jackson under the command of a Colonel Harrison.

Head Qrs. 100" Regt P.V   Camp near Crab Orchard Ky   Sept 1, '63

* * * * [*Two paragraphs.*]

. . . . We have no sick in hospital since arriving here. The regt left 112 sick & convalescent at Camp Nelson on the morning it marched for this place (28") All now here with few & slight exceptions are improving; & in good spirits. While I was at the Smith's, Joseph Kennedy of Co. D died. He was not in the regimental hospital at Camp Parke but in general hospital Camp Nelson left there at our former move. His disease took the congestive form.* * * * [*Two paragraphs.*]

Robt Audley Browne[1]

1. Robert Audley Browne to Mary E. Browne, 1 Sept. 1863, Civil War Miscellaneous, Robert A. Browne, Chaplain, 100th Pennsylvania Infantry Regiment, Letters, Browne and family, May 23, 1860 to Nov. 11, 1863, Archives, U.S. Army Military Institute, Carlisle Barracks, Carlisle, Pa.

Cumberland Ford, September 7, 1863.

Brigadier-General Potter:

My force is all across the Cumberland River. My spies just in say that the enemy is very busy preparing to defend the gap. Just received a telegram informing me that there are no trains with rations or ammunition for me, and the commissary and quartermaster officers at Crab Orchard have not been sober for many days. The telegram further states that I must not depend upon receiving supplies from either Camp Nelson or Crab Orchard, so long as the men now in these two places remain there. What is to be done? My men will begin to get sick before many hours for want of bread. Little corn here, and I have only ammunition enough to bluster with and persuade the enemy to evacuate or capitulate if he be so inclined, but I cannot make a serious attack. If the enemy is disposed and strong enough to resist, I do not intend to retire until compelled, but the commissary and quartermasters have put a retreat on my cards.

John F. De Courcy, Colonel, Commanding Brigade.[1]

1. De Courcy to Robert B. Potter, 7 Sept. 1863, *OR*, 1, 30, pt. 3, 435.

[*Excerpt from the diary of Oliver C. Haskell*]

Wednesday morning September 9th rained very hard this morning & the water ran down under our beds which rousted us up in double quick time   We started about 9 oclock for Nicholasville   The road and country between Lexington & Nicholasville looks natural   we traveled it a little over one year ago on foot   we passed through Nicholasville about noon and stoped and fed about 2 oclock   after we had fed our horses & made some coffee we took up the line of march and arrived at Camp Nelson about 6 oclock. this camp is 8 miles south of Nicholasville on the Ky river. There are a great many squads of soldiers camped here but not many full companies or regts. The fortifications here are very good. we went into camp here   don't know how long we will remain here   probably three or four days.

This is military headquarters of Ky

Thursday morn. Sept 10th weather warm and foggy, looks very much like rain   we piched our tents this morning those of us who did not pich last night

We went down to the river to water our horses this morning. The hills or small mountains along the river where the pike crosses it at Hickmans Bridge are magnificent. I was more interested in this scenery than any I have seen in Ky   the gradual slope together with the perpendicular sides of the mountains   the ledges of rock which hang over the road far above it the trees which cover the rock and mountains all strike the individual with wonder and delight and leaves an impression that there is a great and all powerfull being who created the universe and formed these things thus

Friday morn Sept 11th

nothing of importance this fore noon, in the afternoon Co A & B moved to a new camp near the Generals Headquarters. We are Gen Frys Body guard. we are in the woods completely.

Sat. Sept 12th

In the evening it rained very hard and the most of us got wet in our tents   when it ceased raining a little we drawed 2 rations   got soft bread. we don't get much of this Kind of bread.

1. Oliver C. Haskell diary, SC0707, Folder 3, Indiana Historical Society. Sgt. Oliver C. Haskell, a soldier in the Sixth Cavalry (formerly the Seventy-first Indiana Infantry), was part of a detail assigned as a bodyguard to Gen. Speed S. Fry. Their travels eventually brought them to Camp Nelson again in November 1863. While there Haskell recorded on November 4 that he drew rations and took care of other tasks for his squad. The next day he turned over four unserviceable horses. In 1864 Haskell found himself again in the vicinity when the regiment moved through Camp Nelson on their way to Danville; this time he was encamped three and one-half miles east of Nicholasville from April 18 until April 29. His diary covers the years 1862–1864.

U.S. Military Telegraph. [No date, but telegram is filed next to one dated September 12, 1863] By Telegraph from **Camp Nelson**
To **Maj Genl Burnside   Knoxville**

There has been no delay here of Telegraph material   Everything has been forwarded as fast as rec^d . . . the road between Crab Orchard & Mt Vernon is getting impassible   would it not be well to order a part of the forces on the route to repair them   do you get supplies promptly   if you do not it is not the fault of this depot   all well here   ladies send regards

T E Hall   Capt AQM[1]

1. Hall to Burnside, no date [filed in Sept. 1863]; Generals' Papers: Burnside; Entry 159; RG 94.

London, Ky., September 13, 1863.

Brigadier-General Potter:
    Will need the men's overcoats now at Camp Nelson. What has been done with reference to sending for drafted men? Regimental commanders are very anxious to send. Will leave here in the morning; will reach Barboursville on Tuesday. If you are sending more troops this way, send 6–mule teams, for it is almost impossible to get along with 4 experience teaches.

E. Ferrero,[1] Brigadier-General.[2]

1. Edward Ferrero, born in Spain, became a colonel in the Fifty-first New York Infantry and was promoted to the rank of brigadier general on September 10, 1862. During the siege of Vicksburg, he commanded the Second Brigade of the Second Division of the Ninth Army Corps; at Knoxville he commanded the First Division of the Ninth. *CWD;* Dyer, 1:64; *GIB; HR,* 1:417; *OAR,* 2:498.
    2. Ferrero to Potter, 13 Sept. 1863, *OR,* 1, 30, pt. 3, 618, 619.

Sabath Sept 13th 63
    This is a lonesome Sabath   don't seem like Sunday to me. . . .
Tuesday Sept 15th
    This afternoon we drawed Clothing and among the rest we drawed Boots.
    Wednesday Sept 16th rained very heard this afternoon. Len & I carried slabs & raised our tent higher. Slept tonight with wet pants on and a wet blanket over me. have been about half sick today.

Thurs. Sept 17ᵗʰ Clear and very warm this morning. I am cooking today. The boys are cleaning up the quarters this afternoon. I don't feel any better today than I did yesterday.[1]

1. Oliver C. Haskell diary, SC0707, Folder 3, Indiana Historical Society.

Cincinnati, September 17, 1863.

Captain Hall, Assistant Quartermaster, Camp Nelson, Ky.:
    Three regiments of infantry, the One hundred and fifteenth, One hundred and seventeenth, and One hundred and eighteenth Indiana,[1] about 800 strong each, and two batteries of artillery, will arrive at Nicholasville as rapidly as the quartermaster's department can forward the same from here. They will all receive wagons to move from Nicholasville. They have been assigned to the Ninth Corps. It is of the utmost importance that they be furnished with wagons and pushed forward at once.
By command of Major-General Burnside,
W.P. Anderson,[2] Assistant Adjutant-General.[3]

1. All these Indiana regiments (115th, 117th and 118th) were brand-new, having been organized in Indianapolis and Wabash in August 1863 to participate in the East Tennessee campaign. All were sent to Willcox's division, Left Wing Forces of the Twenty-third Corps in the Department of the Ohio; apparently, their assignment to the Ninth Corps was either very brief or Anderson's error. Dyer, 1:139.
2. William P. Anderson served in the Sixth Ohio Infantry; he was promoted to captain and assistant adjutant-general on September 15, 1862. *HR*, 1:165.
3. Anderson to Hall, 17 Sept. 1863, *OR*, 1, 30, pt. 3, 719.

[Excerpt from a letter of Joseph Rabb to his sister Ella Rabb.]

We are now encamped about two miles from Camp Nelson. There is no other troops near us. . . . I suspect that we will start for East Tenn. today as body guard to Gen. Parke   Ell this kind of life just suits me   we get to forage all we want to so you may bet that we dont starve   we go out about every day and milk a cow and steal a lot of peaches   then we stew the peaches and have splendid mess.   the other night bob Stephens John Miller Sam Smith Geo Beauchamp and me went out on a chicken hunt   we hunted a round along while in the dark before we found any   at last we found a coopful but it was so strong that we could not get it open so we sent and woke the old darkey up but he hadent the keys and we couldent get the old man of the house up so we got the old darkey to tell us where we could find some   so we went to another house about a quarter of a mile off and there we found a coop that we could get into   so me and John got into it and handed out the chickens to Sam and George while bob stood guard   after we had got about done an old Darkey stuck his head out of the door and began to call the dogs and Bob cocked his gun and told him to go back or he would shoot him and you ought to have seen him hunt his hole   we dident get enough here to make a mess for us so we went back to the house that we first got them and John Pryed off a board and I got in and handed out about a dozen   we then skedadled for Camp and we left the place the next morning. Ell direct your letters to Camp Nelson to the 1st Battalion 6 Ind Cav.

[*Joseph Rabb.*][1]

1. Joseph Rabb to Ella Rabb, 18 Sept. 1863, Joseph Rabb Papers, M0557, Indiana Historical Society. Rabb (1846–1925), like Oliver C. Haskell, was a soldier in the Sixth Indiana Cavalry.

[*Excerpt from the diary of Oliver C. Haskell*]

Sat. September 19th rained very hard Thursday night turned cold Friday was a cold and cloudy day. this morning we packed up & took up the march for Cumberland gap. Our Co and Co B went over the river to the camp where Co. K was   we fed our horses here and ate our dinners   we traveled all the after noon. This is a very cool chilly day cool enough for over coats and we have none   We Camped at Lancaster tonight. This is a cold night froze considerable   some of the boys slept very cold tonight[1]

1. Oliver C. Haskell diary, SC0707, Folder 3, Indiana Historical Society.

Camp Nelson, Ky., September 20 /'63

My darling Wife,
    This is Sunday evening, not much like the Sunday evenings at home. I have been full of business all day, superintending the outfit of a large command of troops, wagon trains, etc., for a long march.
    The prisoners from Cumberland Gap passed here to-day on their way north. Gen'l Burnside paroled Gen. Frazer & his staff & they went by alone, much to the disgust of the Union people who consider how differently our own captured people are treated by the Confederates. The other officers & men were under guard. . . .
    Gen. Parke passed on yesterday. The mess have an excellent cook; he was head waiter at the Bates House,[1] & is named Alexis — colored. . . .

Thine, O.B.W.[2]

1. Bates House, presumably a hotel, was in Indianapolis, Indiana. In any case, Willcox habitually stayed there when he was in that city. The question of how a head waiter from Indianapolis became a cook at Camp Nelson remains to be answered. Scott, 457.
2. Willcox to Marie Farnsworth Willcox, 20 Sept. 1863, in Scott, 476. In a letter written four days later, Willcox remarked: "There are many darkies laboring at this depot. I can hear them singing this morning. They all confidently expect their freedom . . ." (477).

Cincinnati, Ohio, October 1, 1863 (Received 1.50 p.m.)

Hon. E.M. Stanton,[1] Secretary of War:
    Colonel Parsons' Ninth Tennessee,[2] 800 strong, at Camp Nelson, has neither

guns nor horses, and is ordered forward. General Burnside gave them orders for horses and arms, but they are not here. Can you send them carbines?

W.G. Brownlow.[3]

1. Edwin M. Stanton was secretary of war in Lincoln's cabinet.
2. Col. Joseph H. Parsons commanded the Ninth Tennessee Cavalry, which became part of the Ninth Army Corps. *OAR*, 4:1185.
3. Brownlow to Stanton, 1 Oct. 1863, *OR*, 1, 30, pt. 4, 25.

U.S. Military Telegraph. **Oct 15** *186*[*3*] *By Telegraph from* **Camp Nelson** *To* **Genl Burnside**

Sir   in accordance with verbal understanding with you while here I made an arrangement with Mr Pond[1] who went to Knoxville with my wagon train to get clothing & supplies to the employees at the Post to avoid the necessity of issuing soldiers clothing   Genl Fry has seized the stock & ordered it to be confiscated & informed me that they will not allow one to Keep it here for that purpose except as sutler   Mr Pond acting in good faith, ought not to loose his stock   I have applied to Genl Fry to revoke his order told him you had [*indecipherable*] sanction in matter   I dislike to trouble you but feel that injustice has been done mr Pond as well as myself   Genl Fry has also ordered Buckley & Gould to leave at once or he will confiscate their stock not withstanding Buckley showed him your permit

T E Hall   Capt & aqm[2]

1. Mr. Pond was one of the many people marketing clothing and other supplies at Camp Nelson. Some of these people were semi-official sutlers authorized from time to time by various officers in command, although the right hand never seemed to know what the left hand was doing. Buckley and Gould, for example, apparently approved by General Burnside, were kicked out by General Fry, who had sutlers of his own to protect.
2. Hall to Burnside, 15 Oct. 1863; Generals' Papers: Burnside; Entry 159; RG 94.

U.S. Military Telegraph.   **Oct 17** *186*[*3*]   *By Telegraph from* **Camp Nelson 1863.** **To Maj Gen Burnside**

Despatch received   I am well aware that complaints are made by officers of 23rd A C & I know that they are instigated by Col Goulding   I am sorry to have you embarassed by my remaining at the post & will cheerfully give way at any time you desire   if I have committed errors it has been from an ardent desire to aid you at the front even if it is to the inconvience of troops stationed in Kentucky   I have no desire to remain longer in the service & will write out my resignation & send it to you by mail   trust you will approve any moment when you think the service or yourself will be benefitted by my withdrawing from the service   your word shall be law to me if you will indicate in what respect you desire me to change my course

T E Hall   Capt & A Q M[1]

1. Hall to Burnside, 17 Oct. 1863; Generals' Papers: Burnside; Entry 159; RG 94.

U.S. Military Telegraph.   **Oct. 19** *1863*   *By Telegraph from* **Camp Nelson 1863.**
To **Gen Burnside**

I start today for Knoxville 1020 shelter Tents 5000 Caps & covers 1025 Blouses 144 Hatchets & handles 755 pairs Cary Trousers 2700 blankets 3600 Pairs Bootees 156 pairs boots 600 Cav Great Coats 1010 pairs Infantry trousers 340 artillery Jackets 196 Cavalry Jackets   I shall load another Train tomorrow if I can get men to drive   Capt Stuart desires transportation for Ord Stores   which do you wish sent first Clothing Commissary Stores or Ordnance Stores   Please Keep me Informed what you want most & I will send them first

T E Hall   Capt Q M[1]

1. Hall to Burnside, 19 Oct. 1863; Generals' Papers: Burnside; Entry 159; RG 94.

Camp Nelson, October 24, 1863.

Major-General Burnside:

When you left Kentucky there seemed to be some objections to the proposition to introduce contraband negroes from the South into the State to labor on military roads. Since that time the subject has been thoroughly canvassed, the advantages and disadvantages have all been fully weighed, and, as far as I can now learn, it is almost the unanimous feeling and opinion with slave owners in this region that no serious difficulty will arise from using them. I have before me a petition from a large number of slave owners in the counties of Lincoln, Boyle, and Mercer, praying that slaves be immediately taken to improve the State; a sufficient number of them to prosecute the work and military road, and completing at the least possible period.

The great difficulty presented by the opposers of the movement was that slaves in Kentucky would become demoralized and worthless by coming in contact with the contrabands. To prevent this, it is now proposed that the contrabands be placed upon the road south of Danville, and the impressed negroes upon the road between Nicholasville and Danville, thus keeping them entirely separate. I am satisfied that unless something of this sort is done, the work will not progress as rapidly as you and its friends desire. The impressed hands will not amount to more than 2,500; to divide them between the two roads now in process of construction, will not give to each sufficient force to complete the work in any reasonable time, and to impress slaves from the counties upon which the call has been made, would be doing great injustice to the farming interests of the country.

I have consulted with Major Simpson upon the subject, and he gives it as his opinion that it is the only way by which the work can be successfully prosecuted. . . . If this arrangement could be effected, there would be no difficulty in completing the Central Kentucky road between Nicholasville and Danville. Besides all this, there is a great deal of work to be done at a depot, and on the fortifications at this place, and I shall be compelled to keep a portion of the impressed negroes here for a time to complete that work. Had it not been for the impressed hands, the depots and fortifications would have been very far short of completion.

Owing to the scarcity of hands in the country, this difficulty, and in getting teamsters, I have been compelled to give up all the free negroes impressed to work the railroad to Captain Hall to drive teams to East Tennessee. He is yet in need of more, and where we are to get them I cannot tell. The greatest and most important consideration with us all is, to feed and clothe your army; and this cannot be done without teamsters.

If the railroad is to be pushed forward, we must be supplied with hands from some other quarter to do the work here yet unfinished, and to drive teams; they can be obtained from no other quarter than the South. I have strained every point and used every means in my power to secure laborers and teamsters enough without encroaching upon impressed slaves, and I now, in the name of the people of this region of the country, who have cheerfully given us all the aid in their power, appeal to you. If you can do so consistently with propriety, ask the privilege from War Department to send to Nashville, Memphis, and other points for as many contrabands as may be necessary to carry on the work at this post, and on the railroad. Rest assured it will meet with the hearty approbation of the people in this portion of the country.

Speed S. Fry, Brigadier-General.[1]

1. Fry to Burnside, 26 Oct. 1863, *OR,* 1, 31, pt. 1, 723–24. [Generals' Papers: Burnside, Telegrams Received; Entry 159; RG 94.]

Frankfort, October 26, 1863.

Captain Anderson:
    The guerrillas overrun the border and rob banks, sack towns, and pillage the people; all for want of horses, horse equipments, and arms. We have more than 3,000, and can clear the country, if the men be mounted and equipped. Can you have horses &c., furnished? Go to Camp Nelson now.

J.T. Boyle, Brigadier-General.[1]

1. Boyle to Anderson, 26 Oct. 1863, *OR,* 1, 31, pt. 1, 750.

U.S. Military Telegraph   Oct 26 *1863*   *By Telegraph from* Camp Nelson
To Gen Burnside

Do you intend to use both the Cumberland Gap & Somerset Roads in transportation of Supplies to your Army this fall & Winter   if only the Somerset Road We will withdraw the five hundred & fifty Negroes now on the Cum Gap Road & place them on the Somerset South of Hall Gap   Gen Garrard[1] can be sent forward to superintend & press forward the work while Laborers to some

extent can be procured if they can be assured of payment of one Dollars to one &
half Dollars per day   Do you desire Provisions & supplies concentrated at
Somerset   Shall fortifications be erected to protect the place   a large amount of
Supplies can be concentrated there before the Roads become bad   presume you
will establish Depot at Somerset or some Point near & the old Pontoons have been
looked up   they are here & at Nicholasville   More will be made   All the
Negroes that have been engaged on Military R R south of Danville is four hundred
& fifty (450) men now scattered by recent raids but are being Collected
again   besides these there are two hundred & fifty (250) on the fortifications
available which will be forwarded when they are ready for them thus making whole
number seven hundred (700)   on the Lebanon Extension There are about six
hundred (600)

J T Boyle   BG & J H Simpson Maj & Engr.[2]

1. At this time, General Theophilus Toulmin Garrard (1812–1902) was in command of
the District of Somerset. He was born and died in the same house near Manchester, Kentucky. *GIB.*
2. Boyle & Simpson to Burnside, 26 Oct. 1863; Generals' Papers: Burnside; Entry 159;
RG 94.

U.S. Military Telegraph   [*October*] *27 186*[*3*]   *By Telegraph from* C Nelson
To Gen Burnside

I find all right here   Capt Hall & Genl Fry are well agreed & Capt Hall is
pushing matters with great energy   he lacks mules & wagons but is procuring
them as fast as possible   with exception of one defect in Capt Hall which I mentioned he is first rate officer   his work is an immense one & very few men could
do it better   I believe he is disposed to do his duty & obey orders   your dispatches to him did much good to him. . . .

J T Boyle   B G[1]

1. Boyle to Burnside, 27 Oct. 1863; Generals' Papers: Burnside; Entry 159; RG 94.

U.S. Military Telegraph   Oct 28 *186*[*3*]   *By Telegraph from* Camp Nelson
To Gen Burnside.

Gen Boyle & Capt Hall think with me that the Easiest mode of settling with
Masters for Impressed Negroes would be to allow not exceed 15 Dolls per Month
according to value of service & to charge to the Master in Every Instance Clothing
issued   the R R sutler might be ordered to Keep Negro clothing on hand & furnish it the Cost to be charged to the Negro on the Rolls — Gen Boyle Informs me
he has authorized Capt Hall to appoint some Individual to Keep on hand & supply
to the Employees negroes & others suitable citizens clothing to be paid for by the
Employees   I have directed Gunn to report to you the result of his reconnaisance

between Somerset & the Cumberland Including proper place for Pontoon Bridges   Please telegh me at Cincin

J H Simpson   Maj & chf Engrs[1]

1. Simpson to Burnside, 28 Oct. 1863; Generals' Papers: Burnside; Entry 159; RG 94.

U.S. Military Telegraph. Oct 28 186[3] By Telegraph from Camp Nelson To Gen Burnside

Gen Fry & Maj Simpson are confident that sufficient labor force cannot be gotten from the Negroes of the state & are anxious to procure Contrabands   Will you order Maj Simpson to go & see Gen Grant to procure order for 2 or 3000 of them to put on the R R & plant Roads   Mr Guthrie will be able to complete the Lebanon Extension by January If he get the Iron in time   if we had 2000 or 3000 Contrabands, the Road could be completed to Somerset or North of Big South fork   Mr Gunn has gone to River to select Route & arrange for pontoons. Gen Garrard leaves here today for Somerset. Maj Simpson returns to Cincinnati today

J T Boyle   B Gen[1]

1. Boyle to Burnside, 28 Oct. 1863, Generals' Papers: Burnside; Entry 159; RG 94.

U.S. Military Telegraph   Oct 29 1863   By Telegraph from Camp Nelson To Maj Gen Burnside

As far as I can perceive Capt Hall is conducting everything here with industry & energy & accomplishing a very great work. I know no one who could do it so well   he deserves great credit for the amount & manner in which he has done his work   his business capabilities & energy are wonderful & the work he has performed regarding his rare business qualifications entitles him to promotion I trust you may award to him   the sixth N.H.[1] is here on guard duty and Col Griffin[2] I have made commandant of which will give Greater security & enable Capt Hall to facilitate his operations — I have ordered Capt Hall to be prepared to establish depot at somerset soon as I hear from you   I trust you will signify your wishes on subject — Hands have been sent to Road to push it as ordered by you —

Gen Garrard has gone to superintend push forward the work   hope to hear from you —

J T Boyle   B.G.[3]

1. The Sixth New Hampshire Infantry had been part of Burnside's Expeditionary Corps in North Carolina and later part of the Ninth Army Corps, both in the Army of the Ohio and the Army of the Tennessee. By October of 1863 it was part of the Twenty-third in the North Central District of Kentucky. Dyer, 1:176.
2. Simon Goodell Griffin (born in Nelson, New Hampshire, in 1824; died in 1902) was

lieutenant colonel of the Sixth New Hampshire when he accompanied Burnside's North Carolina expedition in 1861/62. He became commander of the First Brigade, Second Division, Ninth Army Corps, and briefly commanded the post at Camp Nelson. *CWD;* Dyer, 1:69–70; *GIB; HR,* 1:479; *OAR,* 1:76.

   3. Boyle to Burnside, 29 Oct. 1863; Generals' Papers: Burnside; Entry 159; RG 94.

Co Ky.   O.V.H.A [*Ohio Volunteers Heavy Artillery*]
Camp Nelson Ky   November 5th 1863

   Dear wife   I suppose you will be supprised to learn that I am at this place but the change is a good one for we have a nice place here and a much better place than that at Covington   I was a little surprised when I got to Covington to find that the company was gone   they went on Thursday before I came   you recollect that I told [*you*] that I saw a notice in the paper of an rail road accident on the lexington road   our company was on the train at the time   thare was three of them hurt but none that you know   one of the other companies sufered the most as they were on the cars that was thrown   thare was four cars thrown of   thare was one man was killed instantly   he belonged to Co L and about 20 wounded   two or three have died since   the boys had hard time on friday   it rained all day and they marched out to camp a bout 8 miles from the rail road through the rain and layed in the mud that night but they are all right now except George Carter   he is sick   we think he is taking the fever   . . . . Forshee had taken care of my gun a[*nd*] Blankets for me   all the rest of my things were lost   I will get a new over coat   the boys took care of some of my things my knife and tobacco box but my portfolio with all the letters that I got from you and one shirt that I left when I come home   our stove was left at the quarter Master in covington   the Lieut. is going to send a man Back to day to hunt up and bring all the things that belong to the company   when we started from Cov thare was five of us . . . . we got our things haul to camp and I got to ride on a load of hay. this is a very large Camp   thare is two thousand acrs of land in it   thare is a lar[*g*]e number of soldiers here   it is the nicest place I ever saw for a camp and I think it will be a very healthy place   it is very high and dry   I think the company will do better here than they did in Cov for they can not get any whisky or any thing that would do them any harm   I would rather have stayed in Cov this winter on one account   that is I would be nearer home if you would send for me but I can come from here if I can get to come at all. . . . Remember that I am   Yours in love

Abram McLellan[1]

   1. Mss. 26. Abram McClellan Papers, Letter from Abram McClellan, 5 November 1863: Ohio Historical Society. (Hereafter abbreviated as "Mss. 26, [date of letter].") Abram McLellan (as he invariably spells his last name, putting him in basic disagreement with the Ohio Historical Society) was a soldier in Battery D, First Ohio Heavy Artillery. His collected letters and papers range from 1858 to 1879.

Co K   1st O V H.A.   Camp Nelson Ky   Nov 14th /63

Dear wife   . . . . I have got cold since I came down by laying on the ground but I have almost got over it now   I have been busy for a week building chimneys and fixing up for winter   I commenced Capt chimney this morning but it rained and I had to stop   I will go at it soon

Sunday morning.

we have a heavy rain this morning mixt with snow but it is not very cold. I suppose that thare will be a heavy snow up thare to day. we have our tent fixt tolerable comfortable all but a fire place   we have a kind of a little chimney inside of the tent but it smokes us out sometimes   Forshee calls it a crawfish house and he is the only one that can build a fire in it that will do any good at all   we [*have*] some great times here   we can go any where with in the picket line three or four miles of a range so you see that we are not bound up so close as we were at covington and the mess are better satisfied than they were before   we have quit drilling infantry and will drill nothing but artilery hereafter   the duty is not near so hard here as we have had   I have been on gard once since I come here. I am detailed to build chimneys and fix up things a bout the camp   I do not have to stand gard nor anything else in the way of military duty   it suits me very well   these wet nights I can go to bed and sleep dry and nice and if it is raining I do not have to work   so I do not have it very hard now. . . . I need my tools very badly but if I can get my trowel I can do very well. we expect to be pay to morrow   we would have been payd at the time I spoke of in my last letter but the pay Rolls were not right and had to be made out new. I did not get to sign the pay Roll but I will get my money any how   I was please with the way that you wrote your last letter   I do not like to hear of you and the children being sick but I am glad to hear you say that you are willing to do the best you can under the present circumstances. I hope I can send you some money soon. . . . thare is 25 men gone out of our camp to Columbus to gard prisoners   they come though our camp from Noxville Tenn   thare was 250 of them and the hardest set of fellows I ever see in my self [*apparently, he means "life," not "self"*] I will close for this time   write soon my love   to you all hoping that you may fare well

I send this present to you. Yours in love

A. McLellan[1]

1. Mss. 26, 14 November, 1863.

Camp Nelson, Ky., November 19, 1863 (Received 4.20 p.m.)

Hon. E.M. Stanton:

I have the honor to report that we have in store here over 600,000 rations. We can daily, if necessary, throw to this place from Cincinnati from 400,000 to 500,000 rations. There is great want of transportation from this to Knoxville, and the very bad state of the roads forces me to the belief that unless some other route than that now used, by the Cumberland Gap, be substituted, there will be great danger of our troops in East Tennessee suffering from the want of commissary supplies. A telegram this morning is received from General Burnside, directing all stores, &c., en route from this to Knoxville to be turned back to this place, as the enemy was encamped around him. I go to Louisville to-day.

J.P. Taylor.[1]

1. Taylor to Stanton, 19 Nov. 1863, *OR,* 1, 31, pt. 3, 195. Joseph Pannel Taylor, a Union officer from Kentucky, became brigadier general and commissary general of subsistence on February 9, 1863. He had entered the army in 1813; he died on June 29, 1864. *CWD; GIB; HR,* 1:947–48.

Louisville, November 22, 1863.

Major-General Foster:[1]
    Dispatch dated to-day 8 p.m., from General Willcox, at Cumberland Gap, just received, says:

> It is important that my line of communication with Camp Nelson should be strongly guarded, especially at London, near which there is a large quantity of Government stores. General Burnside is holding out heroically, and I hope will hold Knoxville. Firing was going on at 11 o'clock to-day. Is there any news from General Grant?
> O.B. Willcox, Brigadier-General.

No communication between the gap and Knoxville.
J.T. Boyle, Brigadier-General.[2]

1. John Gray Foster (1823–1874), a native of New Hampshire, had served under Burnside in the North Carolina expedition. In the autumn of 1863, he participated in the operations to aid Burnside at Knoxville, and he succeeded Burnside as commander of the Department of the Ohio on December 11, 1863, serving in that capacity until February 9, 1864, when he was relieved in order to recover from injuries. *CWD;* Dyer, 1:65, 524; *GIB; HR,* 1:431.
2. Boyle to Foster, 22 Nov. 1863, *OR,* 1, 31, pt. 3, 226.

Military Post Office   Nicholasville Ky   Camp Nelson   Nov 24th /63

Dear wife   . . . .   well I shall have to give you some of the news concering the camp   thare are some talk of us being mustered out and sent home and all the rest of the new companies that are in the regiment for being enlisted under false pretence   we will know in the course of a month   the word is that the colonel is under arrest now. but this may be all camp talk but we are led to believe that thare is some truth in it for we hear some of the officers talking about it. unless thare is some changes made in the co. soon thare will be a mighty effort to break it up as thare is a great deal of dissatisfaction among the officers and considerable among the men   I feel very well satisfied under the circumstances but not so much so if everything went of in good feeling   I dont believe I should be satisfied out of the service if the company should break up but feel it my duty to stay with my family until they were in better condition to leave   I will be able to give you something more certain a bout the concerns of the company in my next. I am still on detail duty yet and do not know how long it will last. I am busy every day that it is not raining   I made a tabl for the captian to day and a door to our tent   I built a chimney for capt last week   all that I have built does very well but hard winds down here are hard on stick chimneys   we have our tent fixed up pretty well   we have it raised up three feet of the ground with slabs stood up end wise and dirt throwed up all around with a good fire place   the chimney is not high enough   I will build it higher to morrow   we have sixteen in our mess now   we do our own cooking. . . . I want to when I get time to draw a map of this camp and send it to you to show you a bout how we are fixt here   I [am] going to get a company roll printed and send it also   I subscribed for one yesterday as will cost 75 cts   I have not time to write as I would like to to night it is late and I shall have to go to bed. I have not got my clothes and things that were lost but expect as soon as Cline comes back as that was his busines to Covington to see after our things but my things were lost on the road down here my overcoat and hat and haversack and such things   I dont know what is the cause of me not geting them yet   I guess it is because it has not been attended to by the officer   if it gets very cold I shall be in need of a overcoat   I will see some thing a bout it to morrow   you must excus this for it was written in haste   good Bye. Yours in love

Abram McLellan

Mage McLellan
[*indecipherable*]
    I finished my letter last night but did not get it mailed so I though I would [*indecipherable word*] it eraly this morning so it would get out to day   it was quite windy last night and the wind blew so that we could not have any fire in our tents so we slept pretty cool. I have charge of our mess and I have a great time with my family   They want to take the job easy but they cant   I have them to take thir turn in curring watter but some of them want to get clear but have to come to it   we have no regular cook   John Knott did cook until he got sick   dave is doing it part of the time   bob miler is ruptured but he helps to do some of the work   George Carter is not much better   Forshee says he looks very bad but thinks he will get well although he is not out of danger. I shall have to go to breakfast as they are calling me   write soon and give me all the news that you can think off   tell Jessie that pa will come some time   the boys must be good boys and go to school[1]

1. Mss. 26, 24 November, 1863.

Camp Nelson Ky   Dec 2ᵈ 1863

Dear wife   . . . . I have been sick since I wrote last   I feel better now only my throat is some sore & dont think it will be very bad   last thursday I took a chill which lasted all the afternoon   at night I was very sick nearly all night with a fever. the next day I had a slight chill and some fever but not so much as they day before   I took some pills and salts and have been better since. . . . I am tinkering around all the time   I have been appointed Artificer . . .   I wont have any more gard or drill to do   it suits me very well these cold nights and rainy weather   . . . .   lately we have a good deal of gard to do   we began to gard the Military Prison to as the regt that was doing the garding thare was ordered to Noxvill to day   thare is not any talk of us leaving here this winter for some time   I wrote you that thare was some talk of us being mustered out of the service   I only told you what was then talked of in camp   I then told you that it is camp talk, that we could not tell what was going to be done. bob Hill got a letter to day   his wife wrote that I had wrote to you that we were going to be mustered out in a month and would be at home. I did not intend to have it understood that we would be dismissed in a month   I only give it as rumors of camp   now the talk has all disappeared   we don't hear any thing of it any more. Dont know what will come up next. we have a nice mess as all the noisy ones has been taken out   we still have 13 in the tent yet   . . . .   I have had charge of our mess for two weeks   I have to see to having every thing cleaned up when the officer of the gard comes around twice a day to inspect the Quarters   I have to attend to drawing our rations and good many thing generaly & we have [*to*] get our stove from covington so we have a stove and fire place both. . . .

Abram McLellan[1]

1. Mss. 26, 2 December 1863.

[*From the diary of Frances Dallam Peter*[1]]
Sunday Dec 13th [1863]

. . . The darkies met with a great mishap this evening. Just as their churches [*in Lexington*] were being dismissed a number of soldiers who had been stationed out side rushed upon the unsuspecting negroes capturing all the men they could lay hands on. The darkies in great terror ran in all directions, some jumping out of the church windows and all doing their best to elude pursuit, sometimes in a most laughable manner, stout, hale men pretending to be crippled & hobbling along with their canes. The soldiers however caught a good many whom they sent off to Camp Nelson to work on the wagon road they are going to make to Cumberland Gap until they can get hands enough to finish the railroad. It was right mean of them to be 'pressing' the darkies on Sunday and all dressed in their 'go to meetin' clothes, and not even give them time to take off the latter. . . .

One old fellow from Camp Nelson had his hand in a kind of a sling and when Dr. Bush[2] came to examine it, held it out with the fingers all cramped up, pretending he could not straighten them. Dr. Bush pretended to examine them with a great deal of attention. At last he turned to one of the soldiers near him and told him to bring his dissecting knife, for said he 'I shall have to cut the tendons of this man's hand.['] He had no sooner said this than a most wonderful cure was effected. The man's fingers straightened themselves instantly and he became well enough to be sent to his regiment. There have been two cases of this kind in the hospital lately, sneaking fellows who pretend to be disabled, so they may get a discharge, and make money by hiring themselves for substitutes or by reinlisting. But the doctors here have seen enough of such tricks to know pretty well how to detect them.[3]

1. Frances Dallam Peter was born in Lexington, Kentucky, on January 28, 1843, and died in the same town on August 5, 1864. She was the daughter of Dr. Robert Peter, a prominent physician, who served as the chair of chemistry and pharmacy at Transylvania University's Medical Department. Her familiarity with the experience of local doctors is quite obvious in this passage from her diary. See introduction to *A Union Woman in Civil War Kentucky*, ix-xxxiii.

2. Dr. James M. Bush was active, along with Dr. Robert Peter, in the Transylvania Medical College. *A Union Woman in Civil War Kentucky*, 15n. 1, 178n. 3.

3. Peter, *A Union Woman in Civil War Kentucky*, 177.

Headquarters Army of the Ohio, Knoxville, Tenn., December 14, 1863.

Brig. Gen. J.D. Cox, Commanding District of Kentucky:

General: The major-general commanding directs that the following instructions govern you in the exercise of your new command, and that you give immediately your personal, undivided, and most energetic attention to their execution, viz:

First. Make all necessary repairs on roads between your main supply depot, Camp Nelson, and Cumberland Gap, via Crab Orchard and London; also between Camp Nelson and the Tennessee line via Somerset.

Second. You will be responsible for the forwarding of supplies within the limits of your district.

Third. You will establish necessary forage depots on supply routes at convenient points.

Fourth. Forage for these depots must be obtained from the surrounding country by means of energetic and responsible agents, who can be selected from the inhabitants, employed and paid by the quartermaster's department, as being most familiar with the country and its resources; or if necessary other appointments, to be made at your discretion.

Fifth. So far as practicable arrangements for hauling the forage to depots must be made with the seller; or with neighboring farmers having disposable transportation. The object of this being to economize in public transportation and wear and tear of roads. In some cases public wagons and teams may be loaned to reliable farmers, but not drivers.

Sixth. Officers of the quartermaster's department, with ample funds, must be kept moving through the country, paying promptly certificates of indebtedness against the Government for supplies purchased by your order.

Seventh. You will reduce the garrisons of all posts on the Ohio River, and others of like comparative unimportance, to the minimum number necessary, to consist of invalids as far as possible.

Eighth. Block-houses on line of railroads and other important points must be adequately garrisoned, but not in excess of actual requirements of service.

Ninth. After reorganizing and establishing the required posts and garrisons for depots, you will concentrate at Camp Nelson all scattered troops within your district, and have them reorganized, equipped, drilled, and disciplined. *

George E. Gouraud,[1] Captain and Aide-de-Camp.[2]

1. George Edward Gouraud of the Third New York Cavalry became captain and aide-de-camp in June 1863. *HR,* 1:466.
2. Gouraud to Jacob D. Cox, 14 Dec. 1863, *OR,* 1, 31, pt. 3, 407, 408.

Office Provost Marshal   Camp Nelson Ky   Dec 29 1863
Capt Denis, A.A.G., Disct No Central Ky

Captain. I received on the 26th inst a communication from Col S.G. Griffin Comdg Post written by Genl Fry in regard to Citizen Harvey Padget, and thinking there might be some misunderstanding in regard to my action in the matter I respectfully request the attention of the General to . . . the following statement.

I have positive proof that this man has repeatedly, during the last month sold whiskey to soldiers and Government Employees & he has been notified by my order three times to stop selling whiskey in this camp.

Christmas eve he was again notified to keep quiet the next day. — Early the following morning a complaint was made at this office of drunken soldiers and men at Padgetts — Sent an orderly to quiet the disturbance — while obeying my instructions, Padget drew a pistol, placed it against the orderly's breast and threatened to shoot him. I immediately had Padget arrested. Confined him one night in jail.

His daughter's reputation is bad — the citizens in the vicinity of Hickman state that Padget is protected by officers in this Camp who enjoy his daughter's favours. Padget is perfectly well aware of his daughters mode of life.

I endeavour not to act hastily in matters of his kind. I satisfied myself of this mans guilt before ordering himself and family to leave camp (in five days)

In my opinion these were improper people to stay in this camp   *

S. Hovey, Jr[1]   Capt   Provost Marshal   Camp Nelson Ky[2]

1. Solomon Hovey Jr. (born ca. 1836 in Boston; died 1931 in Boston) served in the Twenty-first Massachusetts Infantry. Civil War Archive at www.ancestry.com.
2. Hovey to Capt. Denis, 29 Dec. 1863; Vol. 237/576, pp. 34, 35; Letters Sent by the Provost Marshal, Nov. 1863-Sept. 1865, Entry 1660; Camp Nelson, Ky., 1863–65, Part 4; RG 393.

[*Excerpt from*] **REPORTS OF MR. BUTLER.** CARE OF THE SANITARY COMMISSION FOR WHITE REFUGEES AT CAMP NELSON.

Very soon after the establishment of this military post, and after General Burnside's army had opened the region of Southeastern Kentucky and East Tennessee, nearly every Quartermaster's train brought more or less families from their poverty-stricken homes into the camp. The war, as conducted by the rebels, soon made property and homes of the South untenable to high and low, rich and poor of her own people, and uncovered to the gaze and sympathy of the world the enormous ignorance and wretchedness of scores of thousands of her poor citizens. The cavaliers of secession everywhere took the bread from the children and devoured it like dogs, and age and helplessness were driven without compunction from the shelter of their own roofs. No property, however sacred, escaped their cupidity; no man, however decrepit, helpless or innocent, was safe from their violence; and no woman, in bloom or decay, in sickness or destitution, but had ample reason to dread their presence by night or day.

The refugees were in many instances compelled to leave their homes and all they possessed to save their lives, while the majority started for this "city of refuge" because their fathers, husbands and brothers were in the army, and no men were left to afford them protection and provide them subsistence. . . . Orders were issued for the distribution of subsistence to needy refugees at all important military points, of which Camp Nelson was one, and though from its position the number of objects of military charity who gathered there was less than at some localities further South, in the aggregate they amounted to thousands. The number of refugees who pilgrimed as far as this point, or others similarly designated, was by no means the sum total of such refugees from oppression. In one journey through East Tennessee I came in contact with hundreds who sternly contested every mile they placed between themselves and their hearthstones. Often merely concealing themselves in the nearest caves or forests; or, for awhile seeking asylum in more populous neighborhoods, ever and anon they returned to their homes and remained in their accustomed routine of life until another approach of their enemies again drove them away in pursuit of personal safety. The privations and sufferings of those who encountered the long journey to this camp were extremely severe, many dying on the rocky hills or by the dreary roadside, and in nearly every instance the sight which nearly every family on arriving presented, was intensely pitiable. Humanity could not look on its own kind so unfortunate and wretched without instant promptings to relieve their wants, and at least temporarily to provide them food and shelter. For some months, until provision for their reception and care was instituted, they were allowed to remain in the wagon camps until they could find some building which they could occupy. The Post Commandant, however, felt his responsibility to these people, and sought as far as possible to meet it. Buildings were set apart for their use. Rations were issued, an officer appointed to devote himself solely to their care, a surgeon and hospital appropriated, and access opened to the seat of authority at all times.

Thus all possible measures were adopted by the representatives of the Government to express its design to provide for such people as were refugees by necessity of their fidelity and loyalty, as far as possible to relieve the sufferings which had been thereby occasioned.[1]

1. Newberry, 529–31.

Camp Nelson Ky   January 10th /64

Dear wife

After a few days delay I now write you a few lines to let you know that I am well and full of life   . . . .   I did not have any trouble on my way   only a[t] the river I like to not got over the river   the Ice was runing so the ferry boats had all stoped but one and that could just make it with dificulty but I got over all right and stayed at Head quarters. . . . it has been very cold here   thare was 18 men froze to death mostly Teamsters and rebel prisoners   thare was a few soldiers but none in our Battalion   smithson froze his toes and several others of our company. we are very much croweded in our tent   have 16 in now   we are under marching oders for Knoxville but will not go until the weather is better   if that is not until spring it is certain that we will go some time but how soon I do not know   I had rather go thare or some place else than to stay here on suspence   we will not have things fix comfortable until we are permanently settled. I made one dollar since I come   I made the doctor a bunk   I would send it in this letter but they say the pay master is here   if that is so we will be payed to morrow   then we will send our money all to gether. . . . you will excuse this hasty letter and write soon   I hope you will get along better   Yours as ever

A McLellan[1]

1. Mss. 26, 10 January 1864.

Headquarters Military Division of the Mississippi, Nashville, Tenn., January 15, 1864. Maj. Gen. H.W. Halleck, General-in-Chief, Washington, D.C.:

General: I reached here the evening of the 12th on my return from East Tennessee. I felt a particular anxiety to have Longstreet[1] driven from East Tennessee, and went there with the intention of taking such steps as would secure this end. I found, however, a large part of Foster's command suffering for want of clothing, especially shoes, so that in any advance not to exceed two-thirds of his men could be taken. The difficulties of supplying these are such that to send re-enforcements at present would be to put the whole on insufficient rations for their support. Under these circumstances I only made such changes of position of troops as would place Foster nearer the enemy when he did get in condition to move, and would open to new foraging grounds and diminish those held by the enemy. Having done this, and seen the move across the Holston at Strawberry Plains commenced, I started on my return, via Cumberland Gap, Barboursville, London, and Richmond, to Lexington, Ky. The weather was intensely cold, the thermometer standing a portion of the time below zero; but being desirous of seeing what portion of our supplies might be depended upon over that route, and it causing no loss of time, I determined to make the trip. From the personal inspection I made, I am satisfied that no portion of our supplies can be hauled by teams from Camp Nelson. While forage could be got from the country to supply teams at the different stations on the road, some supplies could be got through in this way; but the time is nearly at an end when this can be done. On the first rise of the Cumberland 1,200,000 rations will be sent to the mouth of the Big South Fork. There I hope teams will be able to take [them]. The distance to haul is materially shortened, the road is said to be better than by the Cumberland Gap, and it is a new route and will furnish forage for a time.

In the mean time troops in East Tennessee must depend for subsistence on what they can get from the country and the little we can send them from Chattanooga. The railroad is now complete into Chattanooga, and in a short time (say three weeks) the road by Decatur and Huntsville will be complete. Steamers then can be spared to supply the present force in East Tennessee well, and to accumulate a store to support a large army for a short time if it should become necessary to send one there in the spring. This contingency, however, I will do everything in my power to avert. Two steamers ply now tolerably regular between Chattanooga and Loudon. From the latter place to Mossy Creek we have railroad. Some clothing has already reached Knoxville since my departure. A good supply will be got there with all dispatch. Then, if necessary, and subsistence can by possibility be obtained, I will send force enough to secure Longstreet's expulsion. * * * * [*Four paragraphs.*]

U.S. Grant, Major-General.[2]

1. Lt. Gen. James Longstreet (1821–1904), one of the Confederate Army's high command, was largely responsible for the Rebel victory at Chickamauga in September 1863, but unsuccessful in an attempt to take Knoxville from Burnside.
2. Grant to Halleck, 15 Jan. 1864, *OR*, 1, 32, pt. 2, 100, 101.

Camp Nelson Ky   January 17th /64

Dear wife   I wrote to you a week ago and am looking for an answer but the river has been so full of ice that the ferry could not get across so I suppose you did not get the letter as soon as at other times   . . . .   I am well and as harty as ever I was in my life   we are still making preparations to march and expect to go some time this week   it will be a farely hard march but if all the men was as able as I am I would like it better   I dont believe thare is half of the men in the company that can walk through   some of the men have sent one of thir Blankets home and other clothing but I believe that I will keep mine   I know that I will need all that I have and will take them as far as I can and if I give out I will lay down by them   the 44th regt is in camp now   they have reenlisted and are going home on furlough   thare is only 28 left that did not enlist again . . . . Yours in love

Abram McLellan[1]

1. Mss. 26, 17 January 1864.

Camp Nelson Ky   Jan. 21 1864

Dear wife   I received your letter this evening and was very well pleased to do so   I am well and harty and enjoying my self the best I can   considering all I am geting along very well   since I come back thare has not been any thing for me to do so I have had easy times but I expect to have rough times between this and Spring if we march to Noxvill and the way things look at present we will move in a few days   we have got all of our equipment and clothes all ready and waiting for the word to go   if we were thare I would not care   the forty fourth boys say that if we get thare once we will have pretty good times to what they had   thare will be more to eat and thing will be fixt up in better shape than they were three months ago   as I said before I did [not] know when we would go   it may be that it will be the first of April as the roads are almost impassable to all kind of traveling but if we do start soon I think that I can go it if any of them can   the most objection that I have as I have to go is on account of the mail   it takes for ever for a letter to come or go   some of the 44 men did not hear from home for three months at a time   when we write it will have to be in newspaper style   we will have to write three or four sheets at a time and tell all we know betwen times. thare is several of the men are going back to covington such as cannot stand the march. . . . thare is a good deal of measels in the regiment and some fever but considering the cold damp weather that we have the men are in good health   thare was one hundred rebs prisoners went through here yesterday morning   about one half of them were barefooted   some of the gard went around through Camp and picked up old Shoes for them but I guess they was not near all supplied   it was rather hard   I would have given them a pair if I had them for humanity sake not that I fancy the looks or quality of a reb   it rained here last monday till evening when it began to snow   tuesday morning the snow was a few inches deep   it has about all gone of now and very muddy. . . . I am here and you are thare and here I am bound to be until my term of enlistment is out   bear with what ever comes the best you can and do not give up until you have to   it done me a good deal of good to get the letter like the last one although your condition is bad enough   it showed that you would not give up till the very last. . . . Yours in love

Abe. McLellan

To his wife   Margaret McLellan[1]

1. Mss. 26, 21 January 1864.

Headquarters Department of the Ohio, Knoxville, Tenn., January 24, 1864.

Brigadier-General Ammen:

There will be a train of 2,000 horses and mules, with as many wagons as the mules can draw, leave here in three or four days for Camp Nelson via Chitwood's.[1] The horses and mules are sent to the rear on account of not having forage for them. The train will take with it some 200 or 300 poor people from this place who would have to be supported by the Government during the winter, should they remain here. You will send a proper amount of forage for this train to Chitwood's, also 2,000 rations for the poor who are with this train.

J.G. Foster, Major-General, Commanding.[2]

1. Chitwood's probably refers to "Big Chitwood Gap, 10 miles north of Huntsville," Tennessee, which was known as one of four gaps besides Cumberland through which East Tennessee could be invaded. It was on a "good road, easily crossed by an army." *OR,* 1, 10, pt. 2, 315.
2. Foster to Jacob Ammen, 24 Jan. 1864, *OR,* 1, 32, pt. 2, 194.

Headquarters District of the Clinch, Cumberland Gap, Tenn., January 27, 1864.

Brig. Gen. Edward E. Potter, Chief of Staff: * * * *

I consider it my duty to mention that articles of subsistence are decidedly scarce here at this time, the commissary department being nearly exhausted and no commissary stores having left Camp Nelson by the 25th instant for this post, although repeated applications had been made by the commissary of this post to the commissary at Camp Nelson for rations, which applications have not been replied to until after my arrival.

I believe 100 head of cattle will be here in two days from Camp Nelson.

The country around here is so entirely eaten out of everything that I had to send forage train (with guard of infantry and cavalry) 22 miles from here, in the direction of Jackson, to try to get forage and meal, flour, and bacon for the troops at this post. * * * * [*Two paragraphs.*]

T.T. Garrard, Brigadier-General,
Commanding District of the Clinch.[1]

1. Garrard to. Potter, 27 Jan. 1864, *OR,* 1, 32, pt. 2, 233.

Headquarters Department of the Ohio, Knoxville, January 31, 1864.

Brig. Gen. T.T. Garrard, Commanding District of the Clinch:

General: I have the honor to acknowledge the receipt of your dispatch of the 27th instant. It will be necessary for you to send an officer to Camp Nelson to see that your requisitions for subsistence stores are filled and to attend personally to their transportation to the gap. You should endeavor to accumulate a considerable supply, in order to guard against all possibles contigencies.

There are now at Camp Nelson large numbers of pack-mules, originally intended for transporting supplies to this place, but the difficulty of procuring forage along the road and here has induced the commanding general to countermand the order sending them down. A portion of these mules could be used in carrying stores to Cumberland Gap. * * * * [*One paragraph.*]

Edward E. Potter, Chief of Staff[1]

1. Potter to Garrard, 31 Jan. 1864, *OR*, 1, 32, pt. 2, 272.

Point Isabelle[1] Ky 75 miles from Camp Nelson   Feb 2d. 1864

Dear wife   since I wrote last we have moved to this place   I wrote to you before I started from Camp Nelson and was expecting an answer when we started from thare but did not get any   I am anxious to hear from home   thare is no post office here but the mail is left with any Segt that is stoping here   we started from Camp Nelson on monday the 25th day January and got to this place the 31st   was six days on the road and the worst road that evr I saw in my life   I was along with the team   I did not have to carry my knapsack or gun so I had pretty good times until we got of the pike which run forty miles out this way   but when we come on the mud road we had hard work   we were in the mud up to our Knees some times   we have small tents to sleep in   I never felt better in my life   it agrees with me well to travel and always did   some of the boys give out and had to have their loads halled but they all got through very well   we have six companies of our regt along with us   we started for Noxvill but don know whether we can get any farther on account of the bad roads for they get worse the further we go. . . . thare is some talk the teams going back to Camp Nelson after rashions   It may be I get to go a long   I would rather go to Noxvill as we have started than to stay here   thare is nothing here   the country more wild and unsettled than most of the country west   it is 125 miles to Noxvill from here.

. . . . In love
A. McLellan[2]

1. Point Isabel was just south of Somerset, on the banks of the Cumberland River and its South Fork. Located on a corduroy road built and used by the Union troops, it became a headquarters for Gen. Ambrose E. Burnside on his route to Knoxville. Point Isabel was renamed Camp Burnside in his honor, but Civil War records also call it Point Burnside and its original name, too. Burnside State Park has been established nearby. *Encyclopedia of Kentucky* (a volume of *Encyclopedia of the United States*) (New York: Somerset Publishers, 1987), p. 213.
2. Mss. 26, 2 February 1864.

Lexington, February 6, 1864. (Received 8th.)

General Potter, Chief of Staff:
General Fry left Camp Nelson on the 24th. He has only got as far as Point

Burnside. His animals are eating up all the forage in the country. He seized every pretext in his reach to delay his march since he first received his orders to report with his command at Knoxville.

W.P. Anderson, Assistant Adjutant-General.[1]

1. Anderson to Potter, *OR*, 1, 32, pt. 2, 338.

Headquarters U.S. Forces, Camp Burnside, Ky., February 8, 1864.

[Brig. Gen. E.E. Potter, Chief of Staff:]

General: I have the honor to state that my command reached here several days since, and is now detained on account of scarcity of rations and forage at the post. I expected on my arrival here to replenish my trains with the necessary forage and rations, but finding none of either here was compelled to send back to Hall's Gap for them. The train has not yet returned. As soon as it returns I will move directly on unless otherwise ordered.

I deem it proper to state that I have examined the roads for some distance beyond this toward Knoxville and find them in a most dreadful condition; indeed, I may say impassable for loaded trains. I am satisfied it will take me nearly one week to get my train to the top of the mountain from this place, only 8 miles. The most of my teams are young and unbroken mules, and many of them have already given out and been sent back to Camp Nelson.

I have seen and conversed with General Carter and others, and all express the opinion that I cannot possibly get through with my train.

I learn also that all horses and mules have been ordered back to Kentucky on account of the scarcity of forage in the region of the army. This being true, I was at some loss to know whether the general commanding desired me to bring with me any cavalry. I have with me the Tenth Michigan Cavalry, and was compelled when I sent my train back to Hall's Gap to send that with it in order to procure forage until the train returned.

If the general desires, under all the circumstances, for my command to remain here until the roads are in a better condition, I can use them to a great advantage in repairing the roads. There are but few hands at work on them near the point where the work is greatly needed, and their progress is necessarily very slow. I can subsist my men here now, as the boats are beginning to arrive, two reaching here this morning. Several others will be up as soon as they can be lighted so as to enable them to get over the shoals some 40 miles below.

I make this suggestion, believing from what I have seen and from what I have heard from others who have just passed over the road that it will be utterly impossible for me to get through with my train. I will do, however, as I am directed. *

Speed S. Fry, Brigadier-General.[1]

1. Fry to Potter, 8 Feb. 1864, *OR*, 1, 32, pt. 2, 351.

Hdqrs. District of Kentucky, Camp Nelson, February 15, 1864.
General Orders, No. 18.

General Orders, No. 2, current series, from these headquarters, providing for the exemption from impressment for public labor of the negroes of those persons engaged in feeding public stock, are hereby revoked. Hereafter no exemptions of this character will be granted until persons desiring them shall forward their applications to these headquarters, accompanied with a statement of the number of negroes they have subject to the impressment under the provision of General Orders, No. 43, series 1863, from these headquarters, also the number of Government horses and mules they are feeding. The statement must be made in writing and sworn to and subscribed before a justice of the peace or notary public.

By command of Brig. Gen. E.H. Hobson:[1]
A.C. Semple,[2] Captain and Assistant Adjutant-General.[3]

1. Edward Henry Hobson (1825–1901), a native of Kentucky, was colonel of the Thirteenth Kentucky Cavalry. From the June 1–26, 1863, his command pursued John Hunt Morgan for nine hundred miles though Kentucky, Ohio, and Indiana. They pursued him again at Cynthiana, Kentucky, on June 11, 1864, when he was wounded and captured. Promoted to brigadier general, Hobson commanded in many different divisions and departments of the Twenty-third Army Corps. *CWD; Dyer, 1:74; GIB; HR, 1:533.*
2. Alexander C. Semple, born in Pennsylvania, served in a Kentucky regiment and was captain and assistant adjutant-general at Camp Nelson in January and February of 1864; he resigned from the army in March. *HR, 1:874.*
3. General Orders No. 18, 15 Feb. 1864, *OR,* 1, 32, pt. 2, 401.

[*Excerpt from*]REPORTS OF MR. BUTLER. CARE OF THE SANITARY COMMISSION FOR WHITE REFUGEES AT CAMP NELSON.

Until February, 1864, the Sanitary Commission was not called upon to do more than furnish some comforts for sick women and children, and to co-operate with Post Quartermasters in the general care of refugees. The Soldiers' Home was, however, by this time erected, and the number of refugees arriving being too large to find shelter in the few houses appropriated to them in camp, I admitted several members of one family, numbering forty persons, coming in by wagon train, and within three days procured their removal to Cincinnati. After their departure others came, and from the scarcity of accommodations in the camp I adopted a rule to admit to the Home such persons as were willing and able to go North. To such were furnished meals, lodgings, clothing, Government transportation, all necessary information, and a man to attend them to the cars and render such assistance as was required. To these people—almost invariably without means—we furnished food for the journey and small sums of money, without which delays and suffering by the way would have invariably happened. In nearly every case a letter was furnished to aid them in reaching their destination, and other assistance, if needed. The larger proportion of the persons so aided were women and children, either sick, destitute, or so situated as to be utterly unable to proceed further without help.

After February, 1864, the Post Commandant and the heads of other departments sent all such cases to us, and it became no small part of our work to make the necessary provision for their relief. A series of rooms and cabins, which once comprised the homestead of a large Kentucky plantation, was first appropriated to the use of the refugees; and up to the close of the Agency, by means of constant appeals to the successive Post Commandants, the same buildings were retained for their accommodation. Some families established themselves in their own way, but the authorities refused to issue rations or other favors unless through the Sanitary Commission—consequently the whole of the work of their care, in all its complicated details, devolved upon us. We drew rations for them every ten days, and, when practicable, fuel also. When necessary, and not otherwise procurable, we sent fuel from the Soldiers' Home, and in numerous cases sent our employés to perform acts of labor in their behalf. Our commissary sergeant regularly took their rations to their doors, and delivered them to the refugees scattered through the camp, and for six and eight miles beyond. During the winter months the delivery of their fuel required five or six days per month, and was attended with much labor.

During most of the time the refugees occupied any portion of the camp. We found the Commandant ready to authorize all necessary facilities for their proper care. We have scarcely ever appealed without receiving full and satisfactory responses, and expressions of the great relief which our labors afforded the Post Headquarters in assuming the care and supplying the wants of these indigent people. General J.S. [should be S.S. Fry] Fry, while Commandant, deserves special notice for his valuable aid and encouragement. There was nothing within his power that was not readily done; and the full authority of his office was exercised in a humane and exemplary manner.

From the moment the refugees realized that the Sanitary Commission, as represented at Camp Nelson, would spend time and labor in efforts to secure their comfort and happiness, they became as dependent and troublesome as children, and still more unmanageable. They made daily calls on us for labor which, in many instances, they were quite as well able to perform themselves. A general want of economy and regard for the needs of to-morrow, produced by the listless and unambitious lives they led, made it necessary that the assistance rendered to-day be repeated on all succeeding days. As human beings, they were almost imbecile. A few were thrifty and cleanly, but, as might be expected, their moral character was in an undeveloped state.

Very naturally, such a class of people was involved in constant broils and disturbances among themselves. When a party comprising various families remained together, acquaintance and intercourse engendered petty sectional issues, and they resembled overgrown children, full of sinister mischief, whose sole employment and enjoyment were found in strifes and hostilities, frequently unreasonable and violent. Scarcely a week elapsed without one or more demands being made upon us to adjust these contentions; and nothing in all our work was so depressing and discouraging as the violence and irritation which characterized their intercourse with one another. Repeatedly they engaged in pitched battles, when the violence and obscenity of their tongues failed to produce the desired effect. These quarrels not infrequently constituted the entire intercourse of several families under the same roof, and were found susceptible of no other termination than by wide separation of the contending parties. This was effected by sending some North, or by removing them to a safe distance in the camp. It was very sad to find these poor people thus disgracing their inevitable poverty and helplessness, and converting the solicitude of friends into comparative disgust.

One of the most formidable obstacles in the way of our efforts to help these people was found in their unwillingness to separate from each other and to go among strangers, although, from the want of labor, a career of honorable independence was opened to all who were willing to work in almost any part of the North. Like all such people, ignorant and helpless, with little self-reliance and no enterprise, they herded together like sheep or savages, and were distrustful of strangers even to hostility.[1]

1. Newberry, 531–33.

Head Quarters   Camp Nelson Ky   Office of Post Commandant   March 8th 1864

Lieutenant   You will immediately send a sufficient number of the mounted Patrol to the house occupied by the Bird family (refugees) and cause said family to immediately remove outside the lines and also arrest and confine in the Military Prison all parties found there and at the camps of the negros without a sufficient reason. The guard is also ordered to report to these H[d] Qr[s] forth with for further instruction

By order of Maj. H P. Lamson[1]   Comdg Post
W.C.E. Stevenson[2]   Lt & Post Adjt[3]

1. Major Horace P. Lamson served in the Fourth Indiana Cavalry. In addition, he commanded the Second Brigade, First Division, Cavalry Corps of the Army of the Cumberland, but neither of these affiliations explains his title "Comdg Post" at Camp Nelson. He was mustered out of service at Edgefield, Tennessee, on June 29, 1865. Dyer, 1:79; *HR*, 2:120; *Report of the Adj. General of the State of Indiana (1865–6)* in Civil War Archive at www.ancestry.com.
2. Sometimes Stevenson's initials appear to be W.C.G.L., sometimes W.G.G.L, sometimes W.C.E.; in any case, he was first lieutenant in Company M of the Second Illinois Light Artillery, and he served as Lamson's post adjutant.
3. Stevenson to Lieutenant ?, 8 Mar. 1864; Vol. 237/578 District of Kentucky, p. 94; Register of Letters Received and Endorsements Sent, Nov. 1863-Nov. 1865, Entry 1661; Camp Nelson, Ky., 1863–65, Part 4; RG 393.

Hdqrs. Military Division of the Mississippi, Nashville, Tenn., March 15, 1864.

Brig. Gen. J.A. Rawlings,[1] Chief of Staff, Military Division of the Mississippi: * * * * [*One paragraph.*]

The exposed point in the District of Kentucky is Camp Nelson. The troops are not located either to control or prevent the approach of an enemy through Stone or Pound Gaps, via Whitesburg, Proctor, Irvine, Richmond, to this point, the most direct route and best road, and, in fact, there is not a man stationed along this line, and the enemy could reach Camp Nelson without the least intimation of danger. The disposition of the troops proper of the District of Kentucky is not equal to a successful resistance of a raid; they are disposed around Louisville, Lexington, and north and south of this latter point along the rail, with but about 300 men at Camp Nelson, where the largest amount of public property is collected. Camp Nelson should be immediately strengthened and an officer sent there in command, with rank to appreciate its importance, as well as to cultivate a possible resistance to any approach of the enemy. The end of foraging and equipping the cavalry under the command of Brigadier-General Sturgis would have been subserved as readily at Camp Nelson, if not better, than at Mount Sterling. Having exhausted the slight amount of forage within hauling distance, this command is now receiving its forage and supplies by rail to Paris and thence by wagon, 22 miles, to Mount Sterling. There is no reason why this command should not have been ordered to Camp Nelson, with an advance at Richmond, 14 miles, and another at Irvine and Proctor, still closer to the mountain, as a protection to Camp Nelson, with the advantage of a better knowledge of the movements of the enemy.

The supplies necessary, with what is already on hand at this post (they have about 600,000 rations of corn), would sustain this command readily while in position of reorganizing. Camp Nelson as a post is an anomaly, an irregularity of very great proportions. Located on the Kentucky River, about 7 miles from Nicholasville, the terminus of the rail, the camp is formed by the Kentucky River on the south and west sides and Hickman Creek on the east, leaving an exposed front on the north side of about 1 1/2 miles, protected by three lunettes for artillery, connected by rifle-pits. The area of the camp is about 4,000 acres, and in my estimation would require 10,000 men to defend it properly. Yet within this very slight defense there is being carried out an expensive outline of making this point a great depot for storing, manufacturing, and repairing, with all the conveniences of shops, stores, houses, &c. They have nearly completed waterworks, costing from $15,000 to $20,000, raising the water from the river to a reservoir on the hill, and thence distributing by iron pipes through the camp, and this with the river on two sides of the camp and a large spring about the center.

The garrison at this post, that is, the command, is about 300 undisciplined men. The camps of the different companies intended to man the pieces of artillery in battle are located so far from the batteries that any sudden attack must gain possession of these batteries before the men could possibly gain their posts.

At the present time exposed by this slight defense, there is not less than $5,000,000 of public property there, with a growing expenditure constantly going on. If considered as necessary as an advance post to supply the Army of the Ohio at Cumberland Gap and Knoxville, I must state that all supplies sent from this post are packed on mules, requiring from 5,000 to 6,000 for this end, and that from a careful inquiry I am satisfied that every pound of Government stores sent forward in this manner by this channel costs all of $1 per pound. I do not know the urgency that may have originally suggested this line as a military necessity, but I am confident to continue it is an unwarranted expense; it would be cheaper for the Government to finish the contemplated line of railroad through Danville to Knoxville, and open thereby a direct road to East Tennessee. The present mode is unequal to the necessities and attended by great destruction of property.

So soon as it is possible to supply Cumberland Gap and Knoxville by the Cumberland River via Burnside Point, or by the Tennessee River via Chattanooga, the quartermaster's material at Camp Nelson should be forwarded to Knoxville; the shops, store-houses, &c., located there, and all the means of transportation at or near Camp Nelson, and between that point and Burnside Point or the gap, gathered up and directed to the front. In the mean time an officer of the Quartermaster's Department should be sent to Camp Nelson with power to draw from thence all cavalry horses, means of transportation, transfer wagons, &c., that may not be directly required for present post purposes and made available for the Army of the Cumberland. All means of transportation between Camp Nelson and Cumberland Gap, and also Burnside Point, and at that point not required for present use should be ordered back to Camp Nelson, and thence forwarded to this point via Lebanon.

The twelve months' men raised in Kentucky on the call for 20,000 are a disorganized, unavailable band of soldiers strongly in sympathy with a growing class of open and avowed resistants to any enrollment of the colored men. These twelve months' men are partially mounted — that is, one or two or more companies in a regiment, making in the aggregate about 3,000 horses. The nature of the service in connection with their location along the line of the railroad does not require this expensive outfit. The horses are used for pleasure and display, and are fast being destroyed by neglect and bad usage. I would respectfully suggest that these twelve months' men be all dismounted and the horses made available for mounting active cavalry for military purposes.

I have also to state that I spent nearly four days at Camp Nelson examining accounts of Capt. T.E. Hall, assistant quartermaster, at that post. In order more readily to investigate the character of the expenditures and also the integrity with which his duties have been performed, I took with me Captain Grant, acting assistant inspector-general of the District of Kentucky, who had made a report to these headquarters, implying a want of purity in the administration of Captain Hall, giving Captain Grant a full opportunity of bringing before me any person who could make my investigation easy by pointing to facts and directing my research. After a careful and close examination, bring Captain Hall's accounts down to the 10th March, I can only report that so far as investigation could satisfy me, with my very limited powers of commanding testimony, I could see nothing but exact rectitude. Parties that Captain Grant instanced as knowing circumstances impeaching Captain Hall's honesty were examined by me and sworn, and they were some of the most loyal, influential men in the country, but they all to a man assured me that no man had worked more earnestly for the good and economy of the Government than Captain Hall in the execution of his varied duties.

That expenses unnecessary, outrageous, without judgment, without a military purpose, short-sighted, and without the evidence of experience, have been incurred at Camp Nelson cannot be disguised, but in my judgment they are all traceable to the officer in command, who assumed to direct, and is therefore amenable for the unnecessary outlay at this point. *

Jas. H. Stokes,[2] Lieut. Col. and Inspector Mil. Div. of the Mississippi.[3]

1. John Aaron Rawlins, a native of Illinois, eventually became chief of the staff of the United States Army as a whole and secretary of war. *HR,* 1:817.

2. James Hughes Stokes (1814–1890), a Union general from Maryland, was a lieutenant colonel and inspector of the Quartermaster Department for the Military Division of the Mississippi. *CWD; GIB; HR,* 1:928.

3. Stokes to Rawlins, *OR,* 1, 32, pt. 3, 77–79.

Camp Nelson, Ky., March 15, 1864

Dr. J.S. Newberry,[1] Secretary Western Department Sanitary Commission:
Dear Sir—I have the honor to submit to you the following brief report of the erection and present condition of the Soldiers' Home at Camp Nelson:

In pursuance of the purpose of the Chief Quartermaster of this post, Captain T.E. Hall, to make Camp Nelson, as far as possible, replete with all the resources and facilities of a self-sustaining camp, the conception of a Soldiers' Home, its utility and advantages, presented itself to the mind of that energetic officer.

Captain Hall, during his career in the Quartermaster's Department, had already erected three Soldiers' Homes for the use of the Army of the Potomac; the fourth he proposed to build at this post, for the use of the "*soldiers' organized friends,*" the United States Sanitary Commission.

Knowing the great demand for such an asylum, to feed well and comfortably lodge the hundreds that daily passed through the camps—also the great desire and anxiety of the Commission to do all within its legitimate sphere for the comfort and welfare of the soldiers—I at once accepted the proposition in behalf of the Commission. A few days afterward I started for Knoxville. On my return to Camp Nelson, about the 6th of January, I found the Home was in progress.

Captain Hall submitted the plan in detail, when I made several suggestions for alterations, which he readily and cordially endorsed, indicating his desire to render the Home convenient, and in every respect adapted to its object.

After intimating the variety and extent of the furnishings required for such an institution, I immediately reported the whole business, in person, to your office, accompanying which was a plan of the proposed Soldiers' Home.

The following four or five weeks were occupied in collecting and preparing the furniture, also by occasional visits to Camp Nelson in pursuance of the same object.

On the 20th of February the buildings were so far advanced that I was enabled to shelter about forty refugees from East Tennessee, who, after two or three days spent in preparation for entering the world at Cincinnati, went on their way thither rejoicing.

The Home is now nearly completed in every particular. The principal structure is in the form of three sides of a hollow square, comprising two parallel wards; the first one hundred and ten by twenty feet, and the second ninety by twenty feet, while the center building, uniting the wards, is eighty-five by twenty feet, and is designed for the dining hall—capacity about three hundred.

The wards are economically fitted up with substantial bunks—easy of ventilation, and constructed with a view to the most effectual cleanliness. The two wards will accommodate about five hundred.

As the buildings are erected on sloping grounds, the front of each ward has two stories, thus affording two suits of rooms of much value, and indeed indispensable to the Home. Beneath the first ward there is—first, the office, with a porch; second, sleeping room; third, Sanitary store room; fourth, store room for the Home. Beneath the second ward there is—first, a bathing room, with a porch, containing four private bath tubs, supplied by double pipes, with hot and cold water; second, a capacious baggage room. About twenty feet in the rear of the dining hall is a range of buildings, running parallel to it, and consisting of—first, a large laundry; second, wash house, capacity one hundred men; third, kitchen, with cooking power for five hundred; fourth, commissary. There is also a large pantry contiguous to the dining hall, and communicating with the kitchen.

Every roof is overlaid with patent roofing, and every floor is double planked, with an insertion of water-proof paper. Ample arrangements have been made for the supply of any amount of hot and cold water in every portion of the buildings.

In the center of the yard, between the two wards, it is designed to place a fountain, and also a hydrant. The ground surrounding these and in front of the buildings will be sodded, and walks with trees will be laid out. A substantial cedar post and plank fence, commencing fifty feet in front of the porches, encloses the entire buildings of the Home, which, in harmony with the purpose of the architect, constitute the most unique, and, I trust, serviceable and philanthropical institution of Camp Nelson.

The necessity for a Soldiers' Home here has been severely felt for many months past; and now that one has been erected, with ample and superior accommodations, much comfort and benefit may be presumed to be in store for all who come under its care. *

Thomas Butler.[2]

1. Dr. John Strong Newberry (1822–1892) was a founder of the United States Sanitary Commission. *ANB.*
2. Butler to Newberry, in Newberry, 380–82.

Nashville, March 17, 1864.

General Schofield:[1]

I have had an inspection made of Camp Nelson and Mount Sterling. It shows a wasteful extravagance there and also that the points are badly selected. It seems to me that Camp Nelson should be broken up entirely and the public property issued where it will be of service. I would suggest that Brigadier-General Cox or some other intelligent officer be sent into that part of Kentucky, with authority to make such changes as public good may seem to demand. The troops should watch closely an advance of the enemy from Western Virginia. As soon as I return from the East I will try to get up an expedition from Western Virginia to move onto the railroad to the rear of Breckinridge.[2] I have ordered the new cavalry to Mount Sterling, as you request. Cannot Cumberland Gap be supplied from Knoxville better than as now supplied?

U.S. Grant, Lieutenant-General.[3]

1. Major General John McAlister Schofield of New York commanded the Department of the Ohio from February 9, 1864, to November 8. *CWD;* Dyer, 1:97, 524; *GIB; HR,* 1:865.
2. John Cabell Breckinridge (born near Lexington, Kentucky, in 1821; died in Lexington in 1875), major general in the Confederate Army, had defended Vicksburg against Grant's attack and distinguished himself in the Rebel victory at Chickamauga. At the time of Grant's letter Breckinridge was commanding the Department of Southwest Virginia. Late in the war, he was appointed the Confederate secretary of war. *GIG.*
3. Grant to Schofield, 17 Mar. 1864, *OR,* 1, 32, pt. 3, 83–84.

Hdqrs. Military Division of the Mississippi, Nashville, March 24, 1864.

Brig. Gen. Robert Allen,[1] Chief Quartermaster, Louisville:

General: General Potter comes to me from Knoxville, sent by General Schofield, at the instance of General Grant, to inspect the depot at Camp Nelson. General Schofield thinks the depot should not be absolutely discontinued, and it may be well to reduce dimensions gradually, taking from it such wagons and property as are no longer needed. Knoxville will be naturally supplied from Chattanooga, as its railroad is better than the long road from Camp Nelson. I will go to Knoxville in a few days, and then will consult with General Schofield, whose personal experience may qualify my own opinion. You will therefore confer freely with General Potter, and he can examine the depot, and on his return to Louisville, in concert you will be able on my return to supply me with accurate data and information, which will enable me to act according to my general plan.

Of course, I believe in as few depots as possible, and those on a large scale, well guarded. These depots, I think, should be at Nashville, Chattanooga, Huntsville, and Decatur, the two former course the principal. I am not yet clear as to the line of operations from East Kentucky, but if anywhere it should not be far from Prestonburg, drawing from the mouth of the Big Sandy.

We are on the offensive, and should not think of any defensive measure. I wish you to use General Potter to examine the question as to East Kentucky, and be prepared for active removal of the depot or diminution of its capacity, according to the facts elicited.

W.T. Sherman,[2] Major-General, Commanding.[3]

1. Robert Allen (1811–1886), an Ohioan, was chief quartermaster of the Mississippi Valley from November 1863 to 1866. He began his military service in an Indiana regiment. *CWD; GIB; HR,* 1:159.
2. William Tecumseh Sherman (1820–1891) had assumed command of the entire Western theater after Grant's promotion to chief commander of the armies of the United States. *GIB.*
3. Sherman to Allen, 24 Mar. 1864, *OR,* 1, 32, pt. 3, 141–42.

Hdqrs. Cavalry Corps, Department of the Ohio, Paris, Ky., March 29, 1864. Chief of Staff, Knoxville, or Major-General Schofield:

General: I regret to have to inform you that the mounting and equipping of my command does not progress as rapidly as I could wish nor as you have probably been expecting.

The circumlocution which is necessary to be gone through with is extremely trying on the nerves of an impatient man, but there is no such thing as avoiding it.

We met with great delay everywhere, and I sometimes feel as though the great end the staff departments have in view now-a-days is "how not to do it."

When a requisition goes forward the chances are nine out of ten that it will be sent back not conforming, in some trifling particular, with some "form" which has probably been gotten up within the last few days, and which is known only to the authors themselves. This is especially and peculiarly the case with the ordnance department, though the others are bad enough.

In one case I was receiving wagons from Camp Nelson, and directed my quartermaster to request the quartermaster at that place, rather than send the wagons empty and thus lose valuable time, to load them with forage; instead of doing so, however, and at once, and thus putting his shoulder to the common wheel, he telegraphed to know "whether we wanted the forage for animals or for men."

Again, I made requisition for seventy-five or one hundred wagons, and was informed that the wagons were at Camp Nelson, but that General Allen had directed that we receive no more. The result was that we could not supply our animals without falling back to this place.

Again, I made an estimate for funds on the chief quartermaster, Cincinnati, sent my quartermaster for them, but instead of getting them and done with it, he was referred to Captain Hall at Camp Nelson, and Captain Hall said he had no funds for this command.

Again, I made a requisition for 3,500 horses to complete the mounting of my men; the requisition goes to the chief quartermaster at Cincinnati (just where it ought to have gone), and in the course of time he (my quartermaster) is informed that by a new arrangement requisition for horses will have to be made on the Cavalry Bureau at Washington.

Then is it possible to accomplish anything in this way? Longstreet will not be apt to wait for all this circumlocution, but will rather be disposed to take advantage of it himself. When the departments knew this force was coming here, had they placed the proper stores at my disposal we should have been ready for service now, and there would have been no trouble at all about getting their receipts.

You are sending two more regiments and a battalion to be equipped. Now, the necessary stores should start for this place when the troops do. Just see what valuable time might be saved. Instead, however, nothing can be done until the troops arrive; then requisitions will be made out and forwarded, and (if some new form should be adopted in the mean time) will probably be returned for informality, &c., and there is no telling when they may be ready for the field. I do not write this with any hope that it will be in your power to remedy these evils, but simply that you may be enabled to appreciate the embarrassments under which I am compelled to labor, and the reason why we are not now ready for effective service. If the enemy enter Kentucky in force (and I fear he has done so already) he will not probably have less than 6,000 or 7,000 infantry, mounted, and artillery. To meet this force I have but about 3,000 mounted men and 2,000 foot men, all in course of equipping, and not one piece of artillery. To be sure, I am not charged with the defense of Kentucky, and it might be said, therefore, that it is no affair of mine. That would all be true, yet I am anxious about it, and propose to do what I can to keep him out or worst him when he appears. . . . *

S.D. Sturgis, Brigadier-General.[1]

1. Sturgis to Chief of Staff, Knoxville or Schofield, 29 Mar. 1864, *OR,* 1, 32, pt. 3, 182–83. Samuel Davis Sturgis (1822–1889), a native of Pennsylvania, commanded the Cavalry Corps of the Department of the Ohio from July 8, 1863, until April 15, 1864. He had served as commander of the District of Central Kentucky for the month of June 1863, with Camp Nelson as his headquarters. *CWD;* Dyer 1:104, 528; *GIB; HR,* 1:935.

Chapter Two

Black Recruitment

War Dept., Adjt. General's Office, Washington, April 6, 1864.
Special Orders, No. 140.

18. In addition to his duties as commander of the District of Kentucky, Brig. Gen. S.G. Burbridge, U.S. Volunteers, is charged, under the direction of the proper bureaus of this Department, with a general superintendence of the execution of the acts of Congress for raising troops in Kentucky by voluntary enlistment and by drafting. The assistant to the provost-marshal-general of the State will continue in the performance of the duties heretofore assigned him, but will receive from General Burbridge such orders as the latter may deem necessary to secure the most prompt and faithful execution of the laws in questions. * * * *

By order of the Secretary of War:
E.D. Townsend,[1] Assistant Adjutant-General.[2]

1. Edward Davis Townsend began his military service in Massachusetts in 1837; during the Civil War, he served in the Adjutant-General Department, rising to the rank of major general. *HR*, 1:967.
2. Special Orders No. 140, 6 Apr. 1864, *OR*, 3, 4, 218.

Headquarters District   Kentucky   Louisville, Ky., April 8, 1864.

Respectfully returned with the recommendation that the Acting Assistant Provost Marshal General be authorized to receive as recruits into the U.S. Service colored persons offered as such by their owners, according to the terms of the law. That the camps of instruction be established in the District of Kentucky, but that the colored recruits as soon as enlisted and mustered be sent to Gallatin, Nashville, Clarksville, or some other point out of the State, and calls attention to the accompanying letters.

S.G. Burbridge   Major-General Commanding   District   Kentucky.[1]

1. An endorsement by Burbridge, 8 Apr. 1864, *NIMSUS*, 4:2436.

Head Quarters Camp Nelson Ky.   April 30, 1864.
Circular No 3.

In accordance with instructions from Head Quarters 1st Div. Dist. of Ky. Any officer of the Post having one or more negroes in his employ will at once forward to these Head Quarters a correct Roll of such negro or negroes sitting forth first, the name of negro, masters name, residence, how long in Camp and by what authority they are here

The muster will be complete and embrace not only those in Government Employ but all in the employ of individuals as servants or otherwise.

The Provost Marshal will be entrusted with the execution of this order, so far as referrs to negroes who are not employed by any one in Camp and forward his roll as above described, as soon as, possible

By order of Colonel A H Clark   Comdg Post

[*Signed*] Geo A Hanaford[1]   Lieut and Post Adjt[2]

1. George A. Hanaford enlisted January 8, 1864, at Paris, Kentucky, and was mustered in as adjutant in the Forty-seventh Kentucky Mounted Infantry. In July 1864 he was reported as missing from the Forty-seventh, but by January of the next year he was a lieutenant colonel commanding the 124th U.S. Colored Infantry (Invalid) at Camp Nelson. He was temporarily in command of the post. *HR,* 2:108; *OAR,* 4:1292, 8:305; *RAGK.*

2. Circular No. 3, 30 Apr. 1864; Vol. 111/256, p. 39; General Orders, Nov. 1863-May 1865, Entry 905; Camp Nelson, Ky., 1863–66, Part 4; RG 393. (Hereafter abbreviated as "Vol. 111/256, [page number], General Orders, RG 393.")

HDQRS. FIRST DIVISION, DISTRICT OF KENTUCKY, *Lexington, Ky., May 5, 1864.*
Col. C.S. HANSON, *Commanding Third Brigade*

Instruct your brigade commissary and quartermaster to procure all necessary supplies from Camp Nelson. Captain Hall, quartermaster at Camp Nelson, has been instructed to furnish sufficient transportation from that point for all stores going to Irvine. As it is very difficult to procure horses, you will instruct your brigade quartermaster to recruit all broken-down horses of your command. This can be done by renting pasturage and stabling, and dismounting men detailed to feed and care for them. From the disposition of the forces now being made in East Tennessee, it will devolve upon us to prevent raids and invasions through Eastern Kentucky. We will also have to protect the flank of the East Tennessee army, and to do this, will have to make frequent raids into Western Virginia and threaten rebel force in the vicinity of Abingdon and Barboursville, Va. Hence the necessity of us taking care of our stock. I will send you a battery or section of battery as soon as possible, and will exert myself to have your command fully mounted. Keep me advised. *

E.H. HOBSON, *Brigadier-General*[1]

1. Hobson to Charles S. Hanson, 5 May 1864, *OR,* 1, 39, pt. 2, 16.

Head Quarters   Camp Nelson Ky.   Office of Post Commandant   May 6, 1864.
Lieut John McQueen¹   Provost Marshal   Camp Nelson Ky.

Lieutenant: The Colonel Commanding directs that you will at once institute a thorough investigation regarding Lewd Women in Camp and within two (2) miles of the lines.

All women of a loose character will be immediately expelled at least five (5) miles beyond the limits of this Post, and where they are found living in houses which are in condition to be of any use to the Government, the buildings will be turned over to Captain T.E. Hall Chief A.Q.M. for such use as he may direct * * * *

By Command of Colonel A.H Clark   Commanding Post
(Signed) George A Hanaford   Lieut and Post Adjutant²

1. John McQueen enlisted as a private on September 5, 1863, in Lexington. He was promoted to first lieutenant on January 13, 1864, and later promoted to captain in Company K, Forty-seventh Kentucky Mounted Infantry. He became post adjutant and provost marshal at Camp Nelson, but he died of disease on November 29 or 30, 1864. *OAR,* 4:1292; *RAGK,* 1:473.
2. Hanaford to McQueen, 6 May 1864; Vol. 237/577, p. 101; Register of Letters and Endorsements Sent, Nov. 1863-Nov. 1865, Entry 1661; Camp Nelson, 1863–65, Part 4; RG 393.

Berea, Madison Co. Ky.   May 11 /64

Dear Bro. Jocelyn, * * * * [*Five paragraphs.*]

We are near the great road leading into eastern Tennessee through Cumberland Gap. Along this road armies have repeatedly gone & along it government trains continually go, occassionally guerrilla bands.

The little that the people had is taken from them. If corn is taken to them, it is at such price as is beyond the reach of many. Flocks of women and children in most destitute condition on their way to some other part of the state or to the free states pass along this road. The war acts heavily upon the poor in slave states. The slaveholder has the fertile parts of the state — he stays at home with his slave — threatens to carry Ky into rebeldom if his slave is touched. The recruiting officer must get his quota somewhere. He goes to the border & mountain counties. The poor men are most patriotic, leave their homes, and often the little left behind is taken. Perhaps this will react and the people yet see that slavery has been and is their great enemy. War is a great "eye opener."

Our school [*at Berea*] is again started and the people have regular preaching. I have frequent opportunities of visiting camps of soldiers from this and other states & addressing them and distributing among them suitable reading matter. (no break) [*Fee's own note.*]

Some slaves are being enlisted such as have masters willing to take them to the Provost Marshall and get a claim on the government for three hundred dollars. The authorities do not let the slave come and enlist at their own option; if they did, as a Marshall said to me "all the county would come" all slave men in the county would come   Poor white men must be drafted but slaves of rich and rebel masters cannot come even when they desire to. Tell Uncle Abe! Consistency is a jewel but I am afraid he never will wear it.

John G Fee[1]

1. Fee to Simeon S. Jocelyn, 11 May 1864, AMAA 43996. The letter was intended for possible publication in the *American Missionary.*

LEXINGTON, KY., *May 18, 1864.*

Capt. T.E. HALL, *Assistant Quartermaster, Camp Nelson, Ky.:*
    Pay owners of negroes impressed for labor on fortifications without requiring the oath of allegiance.

By order of Brigadier-General Burbridge:
J. BATES DICKSON, *Captain and Assistant Adjutant-General*[1]

1. Dickson to Hall, 18 May 1864, *OR,* 1, 39, pt 2, 36.

May 21st [186]4.
Lieut John McQueen   Provost Marshal   Camp Nelson Ky.

Lieutenant. Information has reached these Head Quarters that the Soldiers of this Post are in some instances disobeying Circulars No. 4 and 5. from these Head Quarters by selling spiritous Liquors and Alc. without discretion and in quantities not authorized by the orders.
    You are hereby directed to look closely after the matter, and notify them that if found violating these orders their goods will be subject to confiscation and their Stores closed.
    You will notify each Sutler that he will know what to expect if they disobey the rules laid down for their guidance.   By command of
Colonel A.H. Clark. Comd. Post.
    [*Signature in different handwriting and ink*] G.A. Hannaford   Lieut & A.A. Adjt.[1]

1. Hanaford to McQueen, 21 May 1864; Vol. 107, p. 7; Press Copies of Letters Sent, May-July 1864, Entry 902; Camp Nelson, 1863–65, Part 4; RG 393. (Hereafter abbreviated "Vol. 107, [page number]; Press Copies; RG 393.")

May 23d[1860]
Maj H C Edgerly   Post Inspector. Camp Nelson, Ky.

Major. The Colonel Commanding directs that you will notify the Proprietors of the Owens House[1] and the Sutlers on the west side of the Pike and in the vicinity of the Owens House. that they must at once Police the grounds in rear of thier buildings.
    The filth will be removed and covered in Earth so as not to Endanger the health of the camp. By Command of
Colonel A H Clark   Comdg Post
    [*Signed*] George A. Hanaford   Lieut and Post Adjt[2]

1. The Owens House had belonged to David Owens since 1847; he no longer lived there in 1864, but his name stuck to the property when it became part of Camp Nelson. See McBride and Sharp, "Archaeological Investigations at Camp Nelson," 18.
2. Hanaford to Edgerly, 23 May 1864; Vol. 107, p. 8; Press Copies; RG 393.

[*Excerpt from*] **REPORTS OF MR. BUTLER.** WHAT THE SANITARY COMMISSION DID FOR COLORED RECRUITS AT CAMP NELSON, KY.

On the 23rd of May, 1864, about two hundred and fifty able-bodied and fine-looking men assembled from Boyle county, Ky., at the office of the Deputy Provost Marshal, all thirsting for freedom. When this body of colored recruits started from Danville for Camp Nelson, some of the citizens and students of that educational and moral center assailed them with stones and the contents of revolvers. On their arrival at Camp Nelson, they created great excitement, for they were the first body of colored recruits that had yet come forward. Reporting to Colonel A.H. Clarke, Commandant of the Post, he refused to accept them, stating that he had no authority for so doing.

There was, at this early stage of the question, great indecision and incompetency shown by those directed to manage the enlistment of colored men. Recruits were hurrying to the army, but no officer was appointed to receive them. These two hundred and fifty men left their homes in the morning, suffering great violence, while the Provost Marshal offered no protection and promised no redress. They arrived in this camp in the afternoon, in obedience to the call of Congress, the President and General Burbridge; yet no order had been sent to the Post Commandant concerning their acceptance, and no provision had been made as to rations or quarters, or to protect them against the efforts of their late masters to recover them. Night was rapidly approaching. They were hungry and tired, and the dust of sixteen miles of travel covered them thickly from head to foot. In these circumstances the men were grievously dispirited. They had suffered all manner of indignities for their patriotism at the hands of their enemies, and now they were punished for their loyalty by delinquent agents of the Government.

Shortly after the Post Commandant had refused to accept them, the Provost Marshal of Camp Nelson, in an unofficial manner, as if to avoid responsibility, sent them to me, expecting them to be accommodated at the Soldiers' Home, although there was a commodious camp of vacant hospital tents, which would have shielded fifteen hundred men.

When they reported to me, I took them to our spacious wash house, and with the assistance of several employés, dressed their wounds and bruises to the best of our ability. I then threw the entire buildings open for their use, otherwise making the best possible arrangement for the accommodation of the white soldiers who needed them.

From May 23, 1864, recruits arrived every day from the counties lying about Camp Nelson, so that early in June I had over fifteen hundred colored men ready for enlistment. The labor necessary for the care of such numbers kept our kitchen busy day and night, and our dining hall filled from before sunrise till long after sunset. With this was the ceaseless retinue of outside wants night and day. Hundreds of letters were written by Mr. Radcliffe,[1] Mr. [Rev. A.L.] Payson (the Hospital Visitor) and myself. Stories of trouble at home, wrongs committed on their wives, children and aged parents, had to be related, in hope of procuring redress. Discouragements pressed heavily upon them, which we sought to dissipate by all means in our power. Several of the officers of the camp came on pleasant evenings, and for curiosity's sake, reviewed the men in line; but when any responsibility was involved they were careful not to be found. Non-commissioned officers took pride in drilling them, and the camp, throughout the day, was alive with squads on drill. They were not distinguished for superior dexterity or aptitude, yet the heartiness of their purpose incited them to untiring practice, which resulted in improvement surprisingly rapid. Their morality was highly commendable, and their subordination to their self-appointed officers, even of their own color, was a salutary example for soldiers of another caste.[2]

1. Thomas Butler's assistant at the Sanitary Commission may have been Samuel Jacobs Radcliffe of Maryland, who was an assistant surgeon of volunteers on February 1, 1864, and a surgeon by May 1865. *HR,* [no page reference].
2. Newberry, 519–21.

May 24 — [186]4
Lt. John McQueen   Prov Mars   Camp Nelson Ky

Lieut.   Furnish this Head Quarters with information of where instructions emanated from directing search to be instituted for Thornton Williams colored man belonging to Offutt of Scott Co Ky   We have no recollection or record of the case in this office.   *

Geo A Hanaford   Lt & Post Adt[1]

1. Hanaford to McQueen, 24 May 1864; Vol. 107, p. 10; Press Copies; RG 393.

May 24th [186]4
Capt T.E. Hall   Chief Quartermaster   Camp Nelson Ky.

Capt. Capt J.B. Dickson has ordered the negroe troops here to be detained until further orders, as the Provost Marshal at Lexington Ky is not prepared to receive them. I suppose they have no "Soldiers home" at Lex —
        In consideration of the above the recruits will remain at the "Home," and you will not proceed to Lexington as directed until you hear from me again.   *

Geo A Hanaford   Lieut and Post Adjt[1]

1. Hanaford to Hall, 24 May 1864; Vol. 107, p. 18; Press Copies; RG 393.

May 24ᵗʰ [186]4.
Major T.C. Barnes[1]   Comdg 47ᵗʰ Ky. Vols.   Camp Nelson Ky

Major. you will furnish one (1) Captain. one (1) Lieut. and Eighty (80) Enlisted men from your Command fully armed & Equipped. with three (3) days rations. to report as soon as possible. At these Hᵈ Qᵗˢ to go to Nashville, Tenn. as cattle guard.

Transport wagons. will be here to convey them to Danville, Ky tonight to report to Capt Aiken.[2] C.S. at that place. By command of

Colonel A.H. Clark   Commanding Post.
[*Signed*] Geo. A Hanaford   Lieut and Post Adj[3]

1. Thomas H. Barnes enlisted as a private in Company E, Forty-seventh Kentucky Mounted Infantry on August 25, 1863, in Paris, Kentucky. By January 5, 1864, he was enrolled and mustered in as major of the Forty-seventh. *OAR*, 4:1292; *RAGK*.
2. Dwight A. Aiken, commissary of subsistence at Danville, was born in New York, but began his military service as a lieutenant and regimental commissary of subsistence in the Fifth Michigan Cavalry on September 8, 1862; he was promoted to captain the following November. *HR*, 1:154.
3. Hanaford to Barnes, 24 May 1864; Vol. 107, p. 15; Press Copies; RG 393.

May 26ᵗʰ [186]4
Lieut John McQueen   Provost Marshal   Camp Nelson Ky

Lieut. The Col Comdg directs that you administer Ten (10) lashes upon the back of each woman now in Military Prison and then send them under guard beyond Bryantsville Ky   *

Geo A. Hanaford   Lieut and Post Adjt[1]

1. Hanaford to McQueen, 26 May 1864; Vol. 107, p. 25; Press Copies; RG 393.

May 27ᵗʰ [186]4
Col. F.A. Alexander[1]   Comdg. 30th Ky Vols.   Camp Nelson

Colonel. You are directed to order the Asst Surgeon. of your Regiment. to report immediately to Capt W.C. Goodloe.[2] of these Head Quarters to Examine the Colored Recruits, at this Post. as they are about to be Enlisted in the service of the United States.

By command of Col. A H Clark   Commanding Post.
[*Signed*] Geo. A Hanaford   Lieut and Post. Adj[3]

1. Francis N. Alexander of Monticello, Kentucky, enlisted first with the rank of captain on July 1, 1861, at Camp Dick Robinson and then as captain on October 1, 1863. He was promoted to colonel of the Thirtieth Kentucky Infantry on April 19, 1864, and served as commander of the 2nd Brigade, 1st Division, District of Kentucky, 23rd Army Corps, Department of the Ohio. Dyer, 1:46; *HR*, 2:74; *RAGK*.
2. William Cassius Goodloe (born 1841 in Kentucky; died in 1889), provost marshal of

Boyle County, was a captain and assistant adjutant-general from June 1, 1863, to January 31, 1864. Goodloe's interesting Civil War scrapbooks (two volumes) are in the Special Collections and Archives, University of Kentucky Libraries; *HR,* 1:463.

3. Hanaford to Alexander, 27 May 1864; Vol. 107, p. 36; Press Copies; RG 393.

May 27th [*1864*]
Lieut John McQueen   Provost Marshal   Camp Nelson Ky

Lieutenant   You are directed to place beyond Bryantsville Ky. under guard, the following named Refugee women said to be of bad characters.

Mrs Asslinger.
" Bird & two (2) children.
" Lydia Epps

They can be found at the Refugee Camp.
It will be necessary to send a cart or team to transport their luggage.
                    By Command of Colonel A.H. Clark   Commanding Post.
                    [*Signed*] Geo A Hanaford   Lieut and Post Adj[t1]

1. Hanaford to McQueen, 27 May 1864; Vol. 107, p. 35; Press Copies; RG 393.

Head Quarters, Camp Nelson, Ky.   May 27th 1864.
[*Addressee illegible; presumably Capt. T.E. Hall*]

Captain. I am not posted in regard to the object or condition under which negroes are to be Enlisted.

There has been about four hundred (400) negroes fed at this Post. nearly a week and not one of them has been Enlisted.

If it is the object of the Government to Encourage the Enlistment of Negroes. Four hundred (400) could have been Enlisted at this Post in the last three days. A great many are now going home, through the different influences which has been brought to bear, & the great delay caused by postponing their enlistment

Unless this Recruiting business is better managed it will cost the Government a great deal of money and very few Negroes will be Recruited.
                    [*Signatures mostly illegible*] A H Clark[1]

1. Clark to [Hall?], 27 May 1864; Vol. 107, pp. 42, 43; Press Copies; RG 393.

May 28th [*186*]4
Captain W.C. Goodloe. Pro. Mar. Boyle County   Camp Nelson, Ky.

Captain, The Colonel Commanding directs that when the Surgeon Examines one of the Colored Recruits and finds him unfit for the service by reason of disability.

that the Surgeon furnish the man with a Certificate which when presented at these Head Quarters will Entitle him to a pass through the lines and at the same time will be a safeguard against the Draft. *

Geo A Hanaford   Lieut and Post Adjutant[1]

1. Hanaford to Goodloe, 28 May 1864; Vol. 107, p. 44; Press Copies; RG 393.

May 29th [186]4

Quarter Masters Department will furnish transportation from Nicholasville, Ky to Covington, Ky. for Mr Jonathan Mills, wife and six (6) children — destitute Tenn. Refugees.

By order of Colonel A.H. Clark. Commanding Post.
[Signed] Geo. A. Hanaford   Lieut and Post Adjutant[1]

1. Hanaford to Quartermaster's Department, 29 May 1864; Vol. 107, p. 44; Press Copies; RG 393.

[No date; 29, 30 or 31 May 1864]
Dr. C.C. Radmore[1]   Asst Surgeon U.S.V.   Camp Nelson, Ky.

Doctor   The Colonel Commanding desires that you report to Capt. T.E. Hall on Monday morning to Examine the Colored recruits at that Post.

Dr^s Rankin[2] and Mitchell[3] will report at the same hour to assist you in the Examinations. *

Geo A. Hanaford. Lieut. and Post. Adjutant.[4]

1. Dr. Charles C. Radmore, a resident of Wenona, Illinois, served as assistant surgeon in two Illinois regiments—the 44th and the 107th Infantries. On July 5, 1864, he was mustered in at Camp Nelson as surgeon for the 114th U.S. Colored Infantry. *Illinois: Roster of Officers and Enlisted Men (1900)* in the Civil War Archive at www.ancestry.com; *OAR,* 8:295; *RAGK.*
2. Dr. Andrew C. Rankin, a resident of Loda, Illinois, enlisted on August 27, 1862, as assistant surgeon of the Eighty-eighth Illinois Infantry. He came to Camp Nelson as a physician at the Hospital of the Refugee Home, and he was in charge of the post hospital in the fall of 1865. *Illinois: Roster of Officers and Enlisted Men (1900)* in Civil War Archive at www.ancestry.com.
3. Dr. Robert S. Mitchell of Richmond, Indiana, served as assistant surgeon in the Fifty-seventh Indiana Infantry for almost two years before resigning for disability in September, 1863. He then served as assistant surgeon for the Thirty-eighth Indiana, resigning on October 3, 1864. While serving with various regiments, he was also chief surgeon at Camp Nelson, and was finally appointed Surgeon of Colored Refugees. *Report of the Adjutant General of the State of Indiana (1865–66)* in Civil War Archive at www.ancestry.com.
4. Hanaford to Radmore, 29, 30, or 31 May 1864; Vol. 107, p. 46; Press Copies; RG 393.

June 1st [186]4

Quarter Masters Department will furnish transportation from Nicholasville

Ky. to Covington Ky for Mrs. Martha Smith and family of four (4) Destitute Refugees.

By order of Colonel A.H Clark   Commanding Post.
[*Signed*] Geo A Hanaford   Lieut and Post Adjutant.[1]

1. Hanaford to Quartermaster's Department, 1 June 1864; Vol. 107, p. 78; Press Copies; RG 393.

Hdqrs. Dist. of Kentucky, and Fifth Division, 23d Army Corps, Lexington, June 2, 1864.
General Orders, No. 45.

By General Orders, No. 42, of May 14, 1864, provost-marshals and deputy-provost-marshals throughout this district are directed to arrest and prefer charges against any persons who may discourage volunteer enlistments, and to forward them to these headquarters for trial by court-martial. The said order is so extended as to make it the duty of all military officers under the orders of the commanding general of the District of Kentucky to pursue the same course. Complaints having been made to the commanding general that slaves who had presented themselves for enlistment and were, on examination, rejected have been subjected to harsh treatment in punishment for the attempt, it is hereby declared that any persons so offending are discouraging enlistments and are to be included in the class referred to in General Orders, No. 42. Return passes shall be given to all negroes so rejected which shall secure their immunity from harsh treatment or punishment on account of their attempt to enlist.

By command of Brigadier-General Burbridge:
J. Bates Dickson, Captain and Assistant Adjutant-General.[1]

1. General Orders No. 45, 2 June 1864, *OR*, 1, 39, pt. 2, 77.

SLAVE-HUNTING IN KENTUCKY.
Washington, June 3.

Senator [*Henry*] Wilson[1] [*of Massachusetts*] received a letter today from Kentucky, which says:

"I don't care how loud-mouthed may be the protestations of loyalty here, the negro stands first and foremost. It seems to be the policy to keep Kentucky officers and troops in the State, and the result is that it is a hunting-ground for fugitives, and the hunters are men employed and paid by the United States as soldiers. Since I have been stationed here, now something more than eleven months, it has been an almost daily occurrence for a squad of men to be employed in hunting slaves, and returning them to their masters.

"I have seen a Colonel of a regiment riding at the rear of a slave gang composed of men, women, and children, tied together, and guarded by men in the uniform of U.S. soldiers. Let me give you an instance. Last Saturday, the Commandant of this post gave an order to the Provost-Marshal to seize and deliver outside of the lines, to her master, a slave girl who was employed as cook at the Convalescent Camp. This girl had been away from her master, who is and always has been a noted rebel, for more than six months. She ran away on account of his cruelty.

"The owner of the girl, with the guard, went to the camp, seized the girl, and, amid her cries and frantic appeals for protection, were taking her away. She fell upon her knees and begged the guard to shoot her upon the spot, saying her master would whip her to death if he got her away. This was too much for the endurance of some of the inmates of the camp, and they interfered, and took the girl away from the guard, dressed her in boy's clothes, and secreted her.

"In a few minutes an officer came with a mounted patrol and exhibited an order from the commanding officer to search the camp for the girl, and return her to her owner. Thanks to the soldiers in the hospital, she was not be found. It makes my blood boil to read the high-sounding speeches and campaign orders published in the papers, and then witness these things daily."

The writer then, speaking with loathing of the degradation of United States troops to the brutal business of whipping women, incloses to Senator Wilson this monstrous order:

> HEADQUARTERS, CAMP NELSON, KY.,
> Office Post Commandant, May 23, 1864.
> LIEUTENANT: Information has reached these headquarters that three of the women which you placed beyond the lines yesterday are back again in camp, and the Colonel commanding directs that you send out your patrol and arrest them, and confine them in the Military Prison until they are all collected by themselves, when you will tie them up and give them a few lashes, and expel them beyond the lines the distance heretofore ordered. Also, any negro woman here without authority wil be arrested and sent beyond the lines, and informed that if they return, the lash awaits them.
> By command of:
> Col. A.H. CLARK, Commanding Post.
> GEO. A. HARRAFORD [HANAFORD], Lieut. and Post Adjt.
> To Lieut. JOHN McQUEEN, Provost-Marshal, Camp Nelson, Kentucky.

Adjt. Gen. [Lorenzo] Thomas will be in Kentucky next week, and two silver eagles will take an unusually high flight, and then the slaves of Kentucky will be gathered in by this great recruiter with a rake that will not leave a County unvisited. The epoch of pro-slavery bluster, Border-State sneaking, and military slave-driving, is at an end.

The negroes of Kentucky have got to fight for the Union. Gen. Thomas goes down with plenary powers, and carries in his pocket, to start with, the organization of three regiments, the names of qualified officers who have passed Casey's Board. Sixteen regiments of Kentucky blacks will swell our ranks in a few weeks.[2]

1. Henry Wilson (1812–1875), U.S. senator from Massachusetts from 1855 to 1872, became vice president under Grant. He was a very outspoken abolitionist and a leading Radical Republican, and his three-volume *History of the Rise and Fall of Slave Power in America* (1871–1877) was the first major history of the coming of the Civil War. *ANB; Columbia Encyclopedia,* 6th ed., s.v. "Wilson, Henry."
2. Article dated 3 June in *National Anti-Slavery Standard*, 18 June 1864.

Headquarters District of Kentucky, June 6, 1864.

Brig. Gen. S.G. Burbridge, Commanding District of Kentucky:
General: . . . The principal want of troops just now in addition to a suitable guard for the Louisville and Nashville Railroad is to provide guards for the different provost-marshals and their deputies. It has become generally known amongst the negroes throughout the district that their masters' consent is not necessary to their enlistment. They are flocking in by hundreds — far beyond the ability of the provost-marshal to attend to them — to enlist. This matter is one that has created considerable excitement in many districts. As yet I have no information of any violence, but it would not surprise me to learn at any moment that owners have banded together to resist the enlistment of their slaves. . . . I think there is little danger of an invasion of the State. . . .
J. Bates Dickson, Captain and Assistant Adjutant-General.[1]

1. Dickson to Burbridge, 6 June 1864, *OR,* 1, 39, pt. 2, 81.

Richmond Ky   June 6 /64

Dear Bro Jocelyn   I came to this place this morning to cash a draft you sent me some time since   But especially to enquire of the Provost Marshall (whom I know familiarly) what is being done toward the enlistment of colored men
The latter are enlisting very fast   about one hundred enlisted this fornoon   I have talked with quite a number of colored men. They are anxious to go if they were asshured that they will be cared for and that they shall have freedom & pay   The evidence of this is going to them. The Provost Marshall asshured me that already many thousands have gone to Louisville.
Hundreds of these colored men know me & would have confidence in what I would say to them.
They need encouragement & instruction — I have felt that perhaps I ought to go to Louisville and preach to them, tell them what are their duties & prospects — thus do a good to them & to the government   The sprightliest go and quite a number can read
The Marshall says some ten thousand have gone. I will go & look after them, preach & distribute some good tracts if you shall deem this wise & best.

I desire much to be quietly at the work of building up the school & congregation at Berea & bringing in men into the colony at Berea but perhaps I ought to go to the camp at Louisville see the conditions of these men & try to get suitable chaplains for them & report to you.

If you shall deem this best you will send me another check & I will go unless some event shall show it was not wise to go now —

The slaves will go & Kentucky will be free — God be praised.

I will write more when I shall be at home

You will answer soon

If I shall find the number there I expect I shall not be able to distribute tracts to all who can read without an assistant   Yours

John G Fee[1]

1. Fee to Jocelyn, 6 June 1864, AMAA 44001–2.

[Letterhead][1] *American Missionary Association, No. 61 John Street, New York*
June 6th 1864
Rev John G. Fee   Berea Ky

Dear Brot * * * * [*Two paragraphs.*]

We have now considered the matter in Relation to your visiting the Camps of Colored Soldiers and laboring for their good securing rights to chaplains &c. &c. and instruction, and in view of the former statement and accumulating facts we have decided that you would do well to undertake, at once, the enterprise. We are called upon at various points for schools and missy work at the important posts for Colored troops & where they are drilled after enlistment, and you will Report at once whether there is a call for teaching and whether "Rations & shelter" will be supplied to any teachers and to you or others as missionaries. If the right Chaplains are received as at other points, they can do much to give and secure instruction in letters for the soldiers as well as to do work which missionaries would have to do. In that case the Govt would pay of course their chaplains. We will send a quantity of Books for the teaching of the soldiers to read cipher write &c if you will Report to us and you may order of C. Hudson Cincinnati: their 1st & 2nd books viz <u>Primary Lessons</u>, & <u>First Readers</u> what may be necessary to commence school or class instruction among the soldiers. The Cincinnati Tract society by Bro C. Hudson, will undoubtedly supply tracts for circulation as far as you may require for colored soldiers. * * * * [*One paragraph.*]

S.S. Jocelyn   A m Sec[2]

1. This letterhead has a message at the top: "All money letters, and letters concerning packages of clothing, &c, should be addressed to W.E. Whiting, 61 John Street, New York." In the left-hand corner is a list of the officers of the AMA: Rev. Geo. Whipple, Rev. M.E. Strieby, Secs.; Lewis Tappan, Esq., Treas.; W.E. Whiting, Asst. Treas.

2. Jocelyn to Fee, 6 June 1864, BCA.

Adjt. Generals Office   June 7th, 1864.
Hon. E.M. Stanton   Secretary of War.

Sir: In view of the cruelties practiced in the state of Kentucky by owners of slaves toward recruits rejected by recruiting officers for physical disability, it is respectfully recommended that Brig. Genl. L. Thomas, Adjt. Genl. U.S. Army, be instructed, in effect, as follows, viz:

You will please instruct the Superintendent Volunteer Recruiting Service for the State of Kentucky, to accept and enlist any slave who may present himself for enlistment provided such slave is fit for any military service or duty, in the Engineer, Quarter Masters or Commissary Departments. Such men will be assigned to any Invalid colored regiments in process of organization at the time of their enlistment.

These instructions will not be construed as authorizing the enlistment of free colored men, or of slaves physically disqualified who may be presented by their owners, for enlistment. *

C.W. Foster[1]   Asst. Adjt. Genl. Vols.
Approved: Edwin M. Stanton   Secretary of War[2]

1. A native of Massachusetts, Charles Warren Foster began his military career in a New Hampshire regiment; he was major and assistant adjutant-general from August 24, 1863. *HR,* 1:431.
2. Foster to Stanton, 7 June 1864, *NIMSUS,* 4:2604; and in *OR,* 3, 4, 422.

Nicholasville, Ky., June 9, 1864

Gen. S.G. Burbridge, Commander, Department of Kentucky:
Sir—There is a slave in the county jail here, confined for no civil crime, but because his master feared he would run off. The boy has told me he wishes to volunteer as a soldier. Have I right to take him from the county jail and let him come into the army in the state? *

J.C. Randolph,[1] Deputy Marshal and Superintendent
of Colored Enlistment at Camp Nelson[2]

1. Capt. J.C. Randolph was deputy provost marshal for Jessamine County. According to Young, cited below, "Rev. John C. Randolph was the first native Kentuckian who enlisted negro soldiers in Jessamine County" (185).
2. Randolph to Burbridge, 9 June 1864, quoted in Bennett H. Young, *A History of Jessamine County, Kentucky, from its Earliest Settlement to 1898* (Louisville: Courier-Journal Job Printing, 1898), 185–86.

Head Quarters Camp Nelson Ky.   June 11, 1864.
General Order No. 2.

The Barracks in this Camp will hereafter be known as follows viz:
The Barracks near Fort Nelson as Halls Barracks after Capt. T.E. Hall Chief Quarter Master at Camp Nelson since its organization

The Barracks nearby opposite Military Prison near the north line of Fortifications as Barracks No. 1.

By order of Col. A.H Clark   Comdg Post

[*Signed*] Geo A Hanaford   Lieut and Post Adjt[1]

1. General Order No. 2, 11 June 1864; Vol. 111/256, p. 42; General Orders; Camp Nelson, 1863–66, Part 4; RG 393.

June 12th [*1864*]
Maj. H C Edgerly   Comdg Camp of Distribution   Camp Nelson Ky

Major, You are hereby directed to send a detail of three (3) soldiers, good & reliable ones, to take charge of the negroes at the Soldiers Home and conduct them to the fortifications each morning at six o'clock precisely. The detail will be permanent and will remain in charge of the negroes until the days work is finished.

You will also send the negroes of your camp to the fortifications in squads of (100) one hundred men, each, under charge of a good soldier. They will report to Mr. J.R. Gillis each morning at six o'clock.

By order of Col Clark

[*Signed*] Geo A Hanaford   Lieut & Post Adjt[1]

1. Hanaford to Edgerly, 12 June 1864, p. 185; Entry 902; Part 4; RG 393.

June 14th [*1864*]
Mr Fred Diehler[1]   Leader of the Post Band   Camp Nelson Ky

Sir: The Col Commanding directs that you assemble your Band at these Head Quarters every night at half past six o'clock — provided the weather will admit — to play. *

Geo A Hanaford   Lt and Post Adjt[2]

1. His name is also given as Diehl or Deal.
2. Hanaford to Diehler, 14 June 1864, p. 221; Entry 902; Part 4; RG 393.

Louisville, Ky., June 14, 1864.
Orders No. 21

The incorporation into the Army of the United States, of Colored Troops, renders it necessary that they should be brought as speedily as possible to the highest state of discipline. Accordingly this practice which has hitherto prevailed, no doubt from necessity, of requiring these troops to perform most of the labor on fortifications and the labor and fatigue duties of permanent stations and camps, will cease, and they will only be required to take their fair share of fatigue duty with the white troops. This is necessary to prepare them for the higher duties of conflicts with the enemy.

Commanders of Colored Troops, in cases where the troops under their commands are required to perform an excess of labor above white troops in the same command, will represent the case to the common superior, through the regular channels.

By order of the Secretary of War

L. Thomas   Adjutant General[1]

1. Orders No. 21, 14 June 1864, *NIMSUS,* 4:2620.

Telegram   Lexington, Ky.   June 15, 1864.

Adjutant General:

Owing to the great number of negroes in this State desiring to enlist, the system adopted of having them enlisted by Deputy Pro. Marshals and sent in squads to be mustered by district Pro. Marshals and then sent, via Louisville, to Tennessee for organization proves inadequate. I would respectfully suggest that Major Sidell,[1] Acting Asst Provost Marshal General, Be authorized to appoint Recruiting Agents, and that a camp of rendezvous be established at Jeffersonville, Ind, where Regts may be organized, and also desire authority to use a few Regts. of colored troops for garrison duty at remote points in this District, such as Louisville and Camp Burnside.

S.G. Burbridge   Brigdr. General.[2]

1. William Henry Sidell (born 1810 in New York City; died 1873) organized the Kentucky Volunteers and served as mustering and disbursing officer in the field until July 1863; he served as acting assistant adjutant general of the Department of the Cumberland until March 1863 and returned to Kentucky in administrative posts for the rest of the war. He became a brigadier general, honored for his "meritorious and faithful service" in the recruitment of the armies of the United States. *CWD; DAB; HR,* 1:886.

2. Burbridge to Adjutant General, 15 June 1864, *NIMSUS,* 4:2630.

June 15th [*1864*]

Maj H C Edgerly   Comdg Camp of Distribution   Camp Nelson Ky

Major   Please select thirty (3) negroes to report here to-morrow morning to work on the grounds around these Head Quarters, build a fountain &c. and oblige your obdt. servt and   Sincerely your Friend

Geo A Hanaford   Lieut and Post Adjt[1]

1. Hanaford to Edgerly, 15 June 1864, p. 220; Entry 902; Part 4; RG 393.

June 17th [*1864*]

Lt Jno McQueen   Provost Marshal   Camp Nelson Ky

Lieut.   Information has reached these Head Quarters that a bevy of women and children are quartered near the Commissary Warehouses, the women (colered) are engaged in lewd business annoying every thing and every body in the vicinity. You are directed to place the whole kit beyond the lines for five (5) miles, with a parting injunction to not return on pain of being imprisoned.

By command of Col A.H. Clark

[*Signed*] Geo A Hanaford   Lt and Post Adjt[1]

1. Hanaford to McQueen, 17 June 1864; Vol. 107, p. 234; Press Copies; RG 393.

June 17th [*1864*]
Capt J H Johnson[1]   Post Commissary   Camp Nelson Ky

Captain: The Col Commanding authorizes you to raze the shanties near the commissary warehouses now occupied by negroes. Orders have been issued to the Provost Marshal to place the occupants beyond the lines. *

Geo A Hanaford   Lt and Post Adjt[2]

1. Jasper H. Johnson, a native of Vermont, performed his military service for Kentucky as captain of commissary of subsistence volunteers. *HR,* 1:576.
2. Hanaford to Johnson, 17 June 1864; Vol. 107, p. 235; Press Copies; RG 393.

U.S. Mil. Tel.   June 18 1864   By Tel. from Somerset
To Post Comdg

A report circulated here by Rebel sympathizers that all negroes recruits are branded U.S. at Camp Nelson. It discourages enlistments of negroes very much   Please contradict it over your signature

(Sgd) Thos[s] L.W. Sawyer   Dept. Pro. Mar   Pulaski Co.[1]

1. Sawyer to Post Comdg., 18 June 1864; Vol. 112/258, p. 18; Telegrams Sent and Received, June 1864-Feb. 1865, Entry 904; Camp Nelson, Ky., 1863–66, Part 4; RG 393. (Hereafter abbreviated "Vol. 112/258, [page number]; Telegrams; RG 393.")

June 18" [*1864*]
Captain J H Johnson   Post   C.S.

Captain. I regret to say that everyone of the "pets" are at work upon the Fortifications. If possible I will retain ten (10) of them to morrow for you   *

Geo A Hanaford   Lt and Post Adjt[1]

1. Hanaford to Johnson, 18 June 1864; Vol. 107, p. 246; Press Copies; RG 393.

June 18" [*1864*]
Superintendent of Public Stables   Camp Nelson, Ky

Sir: J.R. Wilmore Citizen of Jessamine Co. Ky. represents that he has a black boy in your stables who is only (12) twelve years of age. And will at once deliver him /the boy/ to Mr. Wilmore.

By command of Col. A.H Clark
[*Signed*] Geo A. Hanaford   Lt & Post Adjt.[1]

1. Hanaford to Superintendent of Public Stables, 18 June 1864; Vol. 107, p. 247; Press Copies; RG 393.

Officer Commandant of Post   Camp Nelson, Ky   June 18, 1864
Tho[s] L.W. Sawyer   Dep. Pro. Mar   Pulaski Co. Ky.   Somerset Ky.

It is a false report that negroes are branded "U.S." upon enlistment into the service and any one who circulates such a report should be arrested immediately

(Sgd) A H Clark   Col Comdg Post[1]

1. Clark to Sawyer, 18 June 1864; Vol. 112/258, p. 129; Telegrams; RG 393.

June 18th [*1864*]
Capt J Bates Dickson   A.A.G. Dist. of Ky.   Lexington, Ky.

Captain   I have the honor to respectfully invite your attention to an act of Congress approved March 13 /62 and made an Art. of War from the date of its passage and published on page 529 Rev. Refutations of the Army Ed. of 1863

I would also invite your attention to the fact that standing orders are on file in this office issued from Head Quarters in D. Ky and H[d] Q[rs] 1st Office of Provost Marshal General directing all negroes that are found in camp without authority from their owners to be placed beyond the lines.

Will you please instruct me what action I shall take in such cases of negroes being here without the consent of their owners. *

A.H Clark   Col 47th Ky Vols   Comd. Post[1]

1. Clark to Dickson, 18 June 1864; Vol. 107, p. 253; Press Copies; RG 393.

June 19th [*1864*]
Brig Genl Lorenzo Thomas   Adjutant General   U S Army   Louisville, Ky

General   I have the honor to respectfully inform you that at the present there are nearly one thousand (1000) negroes in this camp. I suppose about one half of them have been enlisted and in my opinion with the proper facilities in consideration of the surrounding countryside a very much larger number could be congregated at this post for Enlistment.

I am sorry to inform you that those desirous of promoting the Enlistment of negroes have labored very much under disadvantages and I would most respectfully request, if consistent with the view of the Government, that measures be as speedily adapted as possible to regulate the matter in this section

[*Col. A.H. Clark*][1]

1. [Clark] to Thomas, 19 June 1864; Vol. 107, pp. 256, 257; Press Copies; RG 393. The remainder of this document is illegible, but the letter is in Col. A.H. Clarke's handwriting.

Camp Nelson   June 20th 64
Lt. Col. J H Simpson   Corps Engrs.

Col.   Tomorrow the effective negro working force will be 1400 — I will commence a new camp of 300 under Trench to work in the rifle pits in corral back of Gen Frys and mil. road to Bramlette — By the time these are completed the road to Pollys Bend will be ready and the same force moved there

Col. Sedgwick who is to command these negroes arrived yesterday. He & Capt Hall as well as every one else is very glad that I will take care of and work the men until they are ready for them —

I would therefore suggest taking advantage of this opportunity to strengthen these works in every possible manner and to take such additional ones as come up to 1500 —

The only expense is that of overseers — * * * * [*Three paragraphs.*]

John R Gilliss   Asst U.S. Eng[l]

1. Gilliss to Simpson, 20 June 1864, Entry 3541, Box 2; Part 1; RG 393.

U.S. Mil. Tel   June 20, 1864   By Tel. from Camp London
To Col. A.H. Clark   47th Ky. Vols   Comdg Post

The Rebels under Gittens captured your father at Boonsville on the evening of the Sixteenth (16) and murdered him on Red Bird Thursday evening. It was cold blooded murder — we must retaliate. Can you come and see your mother and family? answer

(Sgd) Jas D Foster[1]

1. Foster to Clark, 20 June 1864; Vol. 112/258, p. 19; Telegrams; RG 393.

Lexington Ky   June 20 [*1864*]
To Capt T.E. Hall, A Q M   Camp Nelson Ky

Establish a contraband camp at Camp Nelson. The women and children cannot be left to starve. So soon as Adjutant General Thomas arrives the matter will be referred to him and regulations in regard to such camp published

By order of Brig Genl Burbridge
J Bates Dickson   Capt and A. General[1]

1. Dickson to Hall, 20 June 1864; Vol. 62/117, 119, p. 74; Telegrams Sent, Jan. 1864-Feb. 1865, Entry 2168; District of Kentucky, Part 1; RG 393. (Hereafter abbreviated as "Vol. 62/117, 199, [page number]; Telegrams Sent; RG 393.")

June 20th [*1864*]
Col Thos D Sedgwick A.S.R.S. and M & D.O.   6 & 7" C.D. and A.A.Q.M.

Col.   If possible will you please be so kind as to send me twelve (12) negroes for light work this P.M. I am desirous of completing the fountain in the yard before this office. By sending them at once you will greatly oblige   *

Geo A Hanaford   Lt and Post Adjt[1]

1. Hanaford to Sedgwick, 20 June 1864; Vol. 107, p. 260; Press Copies; RG 393.

June 20th [*1864*]
To J. [*Blot*] Foster   Surg. Mil. Board   London, Ky

Please see my mother. I will come to her assistance as soon as possible.
As soon as possible organize a party for vengence Vengence

A H. Clark   Col   Comg Post[1]

1. Clark to Foster, 20 June 1864; Vol. 107, p. 265; Press Copies; RG 393.

U.S. Mil. Tel.   June 21, 1864.   By Tel. from Crab Orchard to Comg Officer

Have the negroes who were brought from London left Camp Nelson — Please answer immediately

(Sgd) John Blevins[1]

1. Blevins to Commanding Officer, 21 June 1864; Vol. 112/258, p. 19; Telegrams; RG 393.

June 21st [*1864*]
Capt. J. Bates Dickson, A.A.G.   Head Quarters   Dist of Ky.   Lexington, Ky.

The Rebels captured my Father on the 16th inst who was Provost Marshal of Owsley county Ky.[1] After Keeping him a prisoner for some time they murdered him in the most brutal manner — will you allow me to take my Regiment and go to the mountains to avenge the blood of my Father.

A. H Clark   Col 47th Ky Vols   Comdg Post.[2]

1. According to a report sent to Brig. Gen. James S. Fry, provost marshal of the United States, by W.H. Sidell, acting assistant provost marshal general for Kentucky: "No less than seven officers of the Bureau were slain, viz: Capt. Geo. W. Berry, Pro. Mar. 6th District, wounded in fight with Morgan's force and died June 17, 1864, W.M. Brinkley, Depy. Pro. Mar. Calloway County, 1st District, shot in Nov. 1863, W. Hood, Depy. Pro.

Mar. Graves Co. 1st District, Shot January 15th 1864, W.W. Tyree, Depy. Pro. Mar. Carter Co., 9th District, killed in November 1864. A.V. Carlisle, Depy. Pro. Mar. Carroll County, 6th District, shot in February 1865, Wm. Clark, Depy. Pro. Mar. Owsley Co. 9th District, killed June 5, 1865, and F. Simmons, Enrolling Officer in Ballard Co., 1st District, murdered in his own house in April 1864. Besides these thus slain at their respective posts, others were assailed at divers times and places and more or less injured." Being a provost marshal who participated in black recruitment in Kentucky was apparently one of the most dangerous assignments a man could have during the Civil War. General Report of the Actg. Asst. Pro. Mar. General for Kentucky, [1865; no date given], *NIMSUS,* 6:3675.

2. Clark to Dickson, 21 June 1864; Vol. 107, p. 270; Press Copies; RG 393. This letter was published in *OR,* 1, 39, pt. 2, 136–37. On the same day, Col. Clark wrote to Lt. Col. Wilson of the Forty-seventh Kentucky Volunteers, commanding the post at Paris, to say that his father had been "murdered in cold blood in Red bird Clay county, Ky." Clark to Wilson, 21 June 1864; Vol. 107, p. 271; Press Copies; RG 393.

Lexington Ky   June 21st 1864
Col. A.H. Clark   Camp Nelson Ky

General Burbridge will return tomorrow from Louisville when your dispatch asking that your regiment may be allowed to go to the mountains will be answered.

If you desire to go at once to visit your mother come here and I will arrange it for you

J Bates Dickson   Capt and Act. Genl.[1]

1. Dickson to Clark, 21 June 1864; Vol. 62/117, 119, p. 76; Telegrams Sent; RG 393.

Lexington Ky   June 22d [*1864*]
To Col. A.H. Clark

Your regiment cannot be moved away from its present position just now
[*No signature*]   Brig Genl Comdg.[1]

1. Burbridge to Clark, 22 June 1864; Vol. 62/117,119, p. 80; Telegrams Sent; RG 393.

Washington City, June 23, 1864
Compton, Major C.E.
47 U S. Colored Troops.

Report of Inspection of Q.M. Dept. at Camp Nelson, Ky. under Contol of Capt. T.E. Hall, A.Q.M.
[*Written on the file cover:* Memo   Copy furnished for the information. Brig Genl M C. Meigs Q.M. Genl.   one enclosure   Recd W.D.I.G.[1] June 25 "64]

Col. Jas. A. Hardie Inspector General. U. S Army.
Colonel. I have the honor to submit the following report of an inspection

of the Quartermasters Depot at Camp Nelson Ky. in charge of Capt. T.E. Hall, A.Q. M: made in obedience to your instructions, received on the 30th day of May 1864. Location [*All headings appear in the document, but in the left margin.*]

This Depot is located in a bend formed by the junction of the Kentucky River and Hickman Creek, and as a defensible position, is one of the best — if not the best — which can be found in the State of Kentucky. The cliffs, between which these streams flow, nearly surround the Depot, and range from three hundred — 300 — to four hundred and fifty — 450' — in height, forming impassable barriers to the enemy's forces, except in one or two places which can be held by a small force against a host. On the north side, a line of fortifications are being constructed from a point on Hickman Creek to the Kentucky River, the distance between these two points is about nine thousand, two hundred feet (9200'). The area enclosed is about four and a half (4 1/2) square miles. The Depot was built by the direction of Major General Burnside, as a base of supplies for the Army of the Ohio, and intended as the fortified camp in the State of Kentucky. It is now used as the Depot of supplies for the Army in Kentucky, and also the forces at Cumberland Gap; and in some instances for the Army now operating in Alabama.

Duties of Capt Hall

In the month of June 1863 Capt T.E. Hall, AQ.M assumed charge of the Quartermaster's Depot at Camp Nelson Ky. by orders from Department Head Quarters, and was directed by Maj Gen'l Burnside, to erect buildings for Quarter Master's Stores, to build corrals, and feeding sheds, sufficient to feed and care for the necessary number of animals of the Army of the Ohio; to construct buildings for commissary stores capable of containing two millions (2,000,000) of rations, and to put up work-shops and all needful buildings; therefore Under these orders he was assigned to duty as Chief Quartermaster there, and Supervising Quartermaster of the different depots in Central Kentucky and Chief disbursing Officer for the district. A List of Quarter Masters &c with their stations &c who are under his direction is appended to this report and marked "A"[2]

The depot has been constructed under the direction of Capt. Hall and the number, for what purposes used, and the dimensions of the buildings already erected, are set forth in a schedule, appended to this report and marked "B"[3]

Assistants

There are stationed at the Depot at Camp Nelson Ky as his assistants, the following officers. Capt. L.C. Noble, A.Q.M. in charge of Transportation and means of transportation and work shops. Capt. John S. Davis, Jr. A.G.M. in charge of Clothing, Camp Garrison Equipage and Quartermaster's stores, other than transportation and means of transportation. Capt Jos P Santmeyer 7" Ohio Cavalry A.A.Q.M. in charge of unserviceable stock and the recruiting of the same.

Transportation

From this depot, transportation is furnished to haul supplies to and from Nicholasville — the terminus of the rail road communication with the North — and from the surrounding country: to haul supplies to Crab Orchard, London, Cumberland Gap, Burnside Point, Irving &c and until March 1864 to Knoxville. A report of the means of transportation, in the Depot on the 8th day of June 1864 is attached to this report and marked "C"[4]

The stock noted as unserviceable on this report are all fit for light service in and about the depot, for the moving of supplies to points on, or contiguous to, the turnpike roads, and are so used. They are not in a condition to perform the work required in the trains, to points distant from the depot, on the rough and rocky roads, beyond the constructed turnpikes, but the light service for which they are used, and the care and treatment which they receive, soon fits them for service in the regular trains, and they are so used.

Workshops.

This depot is necessarily the receptacle of all the unserviceable means of transportation viz Wagons, Ambulances, Harness and everything pertaining thereto, from the forces scattered through the district, from the Army in Tennessee, and from the Army now operating in Alabama. Commands passing through the district, turn in their unserviceable, and are furnished with serviceable means of transportation.

The timber for repairs is cut within the limits of the Camp, sawed at the mill, and manufactured in every required manner at the shops at the depot.

Harness is thoroughly examined, the parts fit for use retained, and all deficiencies supplied, and made in every respect equally serviceable as when purchased. After full repairs, it is then carefully washing and oiled and stored ready for reissue. Grain sacks are preserved, baled, returned to Cincinatti where they are refilled & reused. Wagon Covers are examined and preserved, the damaged portions, supplied with sound canvas, and reissued. The Shoeing for all the Cavalry, Artillery and Team Horses & Mules for the camp and for Commands going to and from the Camp, and expeditions going to the front, is done at this depot. The articles fabricated during the month of May 1864 and the Articles repaired during the same time are shown in schedule appended to this report and marked D.[5]

The character of these articles are fully equal in all respects and in many, superior to those purchased in the market or by contract and with a view to economy, to say nothing of the facility for the work. It is greatly to the interest of the service to keep these shops in operation.

Unserviceable Stock.

All the unserviceable stock of the district of Central Kentucky are turned into this depot for the purpose of being recruited and rendered again fit for service, and the admirable means that have been adopted — respecting the horses — has insured to the Government a greater return of serviceable animals and a great saving pecuniarily, than when the animals were let out as has heretofore been the practice.

Horses.

The Horses are placed in comfortable stables, and thoroughly groomed twice per day. The feed consists of ground corn and cut wheat or hay, thoroughly mixed and steamed, and after being thoroughly cooked, is allowed to cool and then fed to the stock. A sufficient quantity of hay is fed daily, and clear fresh water furnished twice per day. The horses are turned into the enclosure surrounded by the stables, for two or more hours each day for exercise. Under this mode of treatment, the broken down stock recuperates with remarkable rapidity and good sound serviceable horses are returned to the service, which would in many instances, be entirely lost. When the stock becomes diseased or disabled from other causes, they are sent to the veterinary hospital and there treated by an experienced veterinary surgeon.

Mules.

The unserviceable mules are fed by contract, by parties residing and owning grazing land in the district. The terms of the contract requires that the pasturage be good and sufficient, and that each head of stock be furnished with nine (9) pounds of corn per day, said pasturage to have an ample supply of fresh water, salt and ashes to be kept in the troughs, and straw in sufficient quantities in the racks for the mules, for which there is paid the sum of six (6) dollars per head per month.

A detective is continually moving around the district visiting the different feeders, seeing that the interests of the government are attended to in a proper manner and compelling the parties to fill all the requirements of their contracts.

Inspectors frequently visit the different droves and the animals fit for service are selected, returned to the depot at Camp Nelson, and transferred to the officer having the control of the means of transportation.

The number of animals now being recruited at Camp Nelson, Ky is set forth in the appended schedule and marked "E"[6]

Contracts

The only Contracts now existing, which have been awarded to Capt. T.E. Hall, or his assistants are those, before mentioned, for the feeding of Government Stock. [*In the margin:* List of Contractors who are feeding Stock is appended. Marked F.G.[7]]

Since the 1st day of June 1864, all parties employed in feeding Government stock are required to furnish evidences of loyalty to the U. States or to have such fact endorsed by the Provost Marshal of the district in which they reside. A majority of these endorsements have been furnished on the part of the Contractors and from parties whose knowledge in the cases was undoubted, and who are represented as loyal. I am informed that all the parties now holding contracts will furnish the required endorsements, and also that these endorsements would have been already furnished, had not the recent raid through the district prevented the parties from gaining access to the camp for the period of week or more. No payments are made for the feeding of Government stock until the contractors are properly endorsed by the Provost Marshals of their district.

During the recent raid through the State of Kentucky by the band of thieves under the command of John Morgan, not one head of Government Stock fed by Contractors, has been lost or captured! The parties receiving the Government patronage, residing near the points threatened, on the line of the enemy's march, timely removed the stock to Camp Nelson or to other places of safety.

Finances

There was on the 8th of June, a reported cash balance on the books in the office [of] Capt. L.C. Noble A.Q.M. amounting to three thousand, nine hundred and forty six, 58/100 dollars ($3,946.58/100).

The cash on hand as shown per the accounts of Capt. Jno. S. Davis, Jr A.Q.M. amounted to Two thousand, four hundred and fifty-four 37/100 ($2,454.37/100) dollars.

The Cash account in the office of Capt Jos P Santmeyer A.A.A.M. sets forth a balance in the hands of that officer: four hundred and forty eight 89/100 ($448.89/100) dollars.

The cash records in the office of Capt T.E. Hall A.Q.M. and Chief Quartermaster show a balance due the United States, amounting to Nineteen thousand, two hundred and fifty 10/100 ($19,250.10/100) dollars

These several balances were verfied by me and found correct.

As disbursing officer for the district of Central Kentucky Capt. T.E. Hall furnishes the funds to the different Quartermasters in the district for the payment of their employés, but not for supplies. These when necessary being purchased by him. In small amounts, for cash, and when over One thousand dollars ($1000) by certificates of Indebtedness

Payments

There is not unusual delay in the payment of the employés of this depot, except that which sometimes arises from an insufficiency of funds in the hands of the Quartermaster. When such is the case, and an employé is discharged, certified accounts are given to the party rendering the service, which are paid upon presentation as soon as funds are received. This practice should be obviated if possible, as it generally entails a loss to the party originally receiving the same; as they are for the most part men in indigent circumstances who are obliged to sell the accounts at a sacrifice to obtain the money in hand.

Q.M. Hospital

The Government is at no expense, except for medicines for the Hospital, for the employés of this Camp. The said Hospital being sustained by a voluntary subscription of twenty five (25¢) cents per month from each employé in the department. The Surgical and Medical attendance being paid for from this fund. The surplus on hand on the 8th day of June 1864, amounted to nine hundred and fifty–25/100 (950 25/100) dollars.

Methods of Time accounts

The method of keeping the accounts of time of the employés at this depot is as follows. Each foremen of laborers is required to make a daily report to the General Superintendent of Laborers of the time made by the men under his charge. Foremen of Wagon Makers, Blacksmiths, Harness Makers make similar reports to the Supt of Work Shops. Foremen of Carpenters and Saw Mills to the Superintendent of Construction, all tri-weekly. The time of each employé thus becomes recorded in the books of one of three Superintendents, who hand in their record to the Quartermaster's Office every Saturday night, when it is transferred to the alphabeted office books, two are kept, one for white, the other for colored employés

Purchases of Stock.

In addition to other duties of Capt. T.E. Hall A.Q.M. he is now engaged in purchasing horses & mules, on account of the Government.

System

The Clerk at the Corral on the morning after the purchase of the animals returns a full list to Capt. Hall, descriptive of kind and character. These lists are entered in the book in the office prepared for the purpose, and the voucher for the amount of purchase made and given therefore. Every day's work is footed up. The animals are transferred to the officers having charge of the Means of transportation. The clerk marking said transfer returning his receipts from said officer to Capt. Halls office. who sees that no discrepancies exist between the number purchased, and the number transferred.

Loyalty of Employés.

It has been charged against Capt. T E Hall A.Q.M. at Camp Nelson Ky, by certain Civilians — see Letter appended to this report and marked "H"[8] — that every employé and Contractor, nearly, are rebels or rebel sympathizers. I would here state, to say the least, the report referred to above, is in my opinion, founded upon a mistaken information and a biased judgement on the part of the persons whose names are appended to the letter marked "H." I conferred personally with each of these gentlemen, and learned that the complaint was not made from any personal knowledge of the facts, but merely based upon hearsay evidence.

During my inspection of the depot at Camp Nelson Ky. the Post was threatened by a large force of the enemy under the command of John Morgan. The Military force stationed there, was entirely inadequate to its defense, and it became necessary for the better safety and security of the immense quantities of Government Stores in the Depot, to call for volunteers for this purpose. This was accordingly done, and without a single exception, all the employés came forward and offered their services for the defense of the place. Six hundred men armed — there being only this number of arms in the depot — and placed upon the line of fortifications before mentioned in this report. These men performed duty upon this line, for six consecutive nights, and it is in a measure due to them, that the depot was saved from capture and destruction.

Water Works and Security against Fire.

Owing to the difficulties which arose from an insufficient supply of water to the Camp — all the water being hauled in wagons from the Kentucky River — Capt. T.E. Hall A.Q.M. was ordered per Special Orders Nº 58" Hd Qrs Camp Nelson Ky. dated Sept 21" 1863, issued by Brig Genl S S Fry — then commanding the Post — and approved by Maj Genl Burnside, Comdg Department, to construct waterworks for the depot These works have been completed and are now in successful operation: whether they will prove a benefit to the Government, commensurate with their cost is a matter which can only be determined by actual experiment, and sufficient time for trial. The work was commenced in the early part of October 1863 and has been much delayed by the rocky character of the ground, a good portion of the trenches for the distributing pipes having to be blasted out. The height from the bottom of the pump well, at the foot of the cliff, Kentucky River to the top of the supply pipe in the reservoir is four hundred and seventy (470') feet perpendicular heighth, and the supply pipe, through which the water passes from the pump to the reservoir is twenty three hundred and forty (2340') feet in length. When pump is working at its ordinary rate, this pipe — 8" in diameter will discharge from one hundred and twenty five (125) to one hundred and fifty (150) gallons of water per minute into the reservoir.

The reservoir is an earthwork structure, and will hold about five hundred thousand gallons of water.

The quality of water now being distributed is good. There are now laid about seventeen thousand (17000') feet of distributing pipes conveying the water to almost every Government building within the limits of the camp, where either the use to which it is put, or the value of the goods contained therein render the water a necessity as a protection and a security against fire.

At or near each building in which stores and government property is kept there is a fire plug, and each warehouse is supplied with one section of fire hose — fifty (50') feet in length, with attachment screws at each end. — This hose is kept for the extinguishment of fire, should it occur, and for no other purpose. These buildings are under the care of watchmen specially employed for the purpose.

Hospitals

Each ward in the General Hospital is supplied with water from the reservoir and contains bathing rooms for the patients and I would respectfully recommend that the hospital at this post be enlarged, and the patients in others scattered through the district be removed to this point and if it were deemed advisable they might be broken up.

The cost of these works has been as follows: [*In the margin:* Cost of Water Works]

Engine, Boiler and Pumping Machinery	$4100.
Supply and distributing Pipes	15 754.71
Plumbing work.	8551.32
	$28406.03

Warehouse

The warehouses are placed in the hollows and depressions of the surface of the camp and in case of attack are out of range of the enemy's fire.

They are well adapted for the use for which they were constructed and in them I found the different articles of property systematically stored. Care seems to be exercised to insure its preservation. I would respectfully recommend that these buildings — with a view to their better preservation — be white washed. Lime in abundant quantities can be manufactured at the depot and the work performed by the laborers.necessarily employed about the camp.

Were this to be done to the Stables in my opinion it would greatly promote the health of the stock, have a tendency to prevent disease, and prove in many respects to the interest of the service more than commensurate with the cost of manufacturing the material and performing the labor.

Employés [*In the margin:* Abstract of Employés is appended and marked "I"⁹]

The Employés of the different branches of this depot were on the 8th day of June 1864 mustered by me and lists of persons so employed were carefully compared with the parties themselves

The business of the different quartermasters of the district all passing through the office of Capt. T.E. Hall Chief Quartermaster requires for the proper transaction of the same fully the number of clerks that are now already employed. The only reduction in his force which can be made or rather which it is to the interest of the service to make is to dispense with the services of the Master of Transportation and six (6) of the persons noted on his rolls as laborers.

On the rolls of Capt. L.C. Noble A.Q.M. who has charge of the transportation and means of transportation the number of names of persons employed, is constantly changing owing to the sudden exigency which frequently arises, requiring the hurried departure of trains and the transfer of trains &c from one district and department to another, and the difficulty of procuring teamsters is one argument in favor of keeping them in employ. They might, when not otherwise, engaged, attend to the policing of the grounds, building and repairing roads, necessary for the business in the depot, and thus a large force of laborers now employed could be dispensed with at least 60 Men Owing to the breaking up of several posts distant from and which were formerly supplied from this depot the necessity for the fifteen (15) clerks will be removed, and as soon as the former business and papers are "brought up" which should be at the farthest by the 1st of July 1864: one half this number of clerks can attend to all the business incident to this branch of the service.

It is to the interest of the service to keep the Government Shops in operation and I do not think it advisable to reduce the force employed in them. The Assistant Foreman in the shops can be dispensed with. One of the Messengers and one of the Office boys should be discharged and at least two (2) foremen and forty laborers can be dispensed with.

It has been the practice heretofore to allow the Wagon Masters to hire teamsters, whenever in their judgement they should deem such employment necessary. This is wrong, and should not be permitted, more responsible parties and those who care more for the interests of the service, should have the charge of this duty.

Assistant Wagon Masters should not be allowed unless the trains number twenty four or more wagons.

There has not been the necessary system and regularity in the conduct of this branch of the depot, but this results in the main from the multifariousness of the duties devolving upon the office in charge and not from any culpable inattention to the interests. The officer formerly in charge of his branch has resigned and it is contemplated to place it under the control of an Acting Assistant Quartermaster. This I do not deem advisable   The amount of property continually on hand creates a responsibility altogether too great to be borne by any but regular Assistant Quarter Masters who are compelled to give bonds for the faithful performance of his official duties.

On the rolls of Capt. Davis A.Q.M. in charge of clothing &c &c &c I find there is employed for various purposes in and about the depot about one hundred and fifty laborers. This is in excess of the number required fully seventy five of these can be discharged, with the foremen having charge of them.

The buildings now erected at this depot are amply sufficient for its present business wants and I would respectfully recommend that the construction of any more buildings on account the United States, at this place, be prohibited, and that this prohibition should continue in force until the demands of the service should actually and absolutely require their erection. Should this be done, a large force of carpenters with their necessary foremen and superintendents can be discharged.

In the branch under the control of Capt Santmeyer I do not deem it best to recommend a reduction of the force now employed. They are not in excess of the number actually required for the proper care of the unserviceable stock and the recruitment of the same. Mode of Life.

The mode of life and habits of Capt. T E Hall A.Q.M. are, as far as I can learn from observation and from inquiry of officers and parties qualified to speak, are good, his management of the affairs of the district are creditable, and the energy he has displayed in carrying out the orders for the construction of this depot are apparent to the observer and worthy of note and example.

The interests of the Government are kept in view and watched over with care.

Funds required for the disbursement in the district are procured by proper estimates and requisitions made upon Colonel ———— Swords, Cincinatti Ohio. From funds so obtained, the other Quartermasters on duty in the district are supplied by Capt. Hall.

The system adopted at this depot for the recruitment of Government Stock, particularly at horses, is respectfully and earnestly recommended, to be put in practice elsewhere.

No horses are condemned and sold: the fact that the government can recruit its stock as cheaply as the farmers, grazers and stock speculators of the country, has been tested by actual experiment and the result is, a better class of animals with less expense, are returned to the service, and the loss to the government in the repurchase of animals which have been formerly condemned and sold as worthless or nearly so is avoided, which has too frequently occurred heretofore — I do not refer especially to this district or state — is avoided   The sheds built and used for the purpose of storing grain & hay are well adapted to the end in view but not enough care is exercised in the placement of the lower tiers of sacks of grain or bales of hay to prevent dampness from injuring the forage, a ditch at least eighteen inches (18") wide at the top and twelve (12") inches deep should be dug around the sides and ends of these sheds. This should be done immediately.

The character of the other officers acting as assistants in the administration of the affairs of this depot is unapproachable and so far as I have been able to learn in a careful inspection of their departments nothing reprehensible can be charged against them. *

C.E. Compton   Maj 47" U.S. Col Troops.
Washington City June 23rd 1864.[10]

1. Washington Department Inspector General.

2. This appendix lists twelve officers, mostly A.Q.M.s, under Hall's supervision: the three at Camp Nelson itself, plus two at Camp Burnside, and one each at Paris, London, Cumberland Gap, Nicholasville, Frankfort, Lexington, and Crab Orchard.

3. Appendix "B" is, as might be expected, huge. Compton lists 103 buildings, but that number is misleading, since many numbered entries are for more than one structure. For example, #22 is "5 Buildings at the Hospitals"; #24 is "5 Buildings for Nurses at Hospitals"; #29 "2. Cook Houses at Hospital"; #36 "10 Forage Sheds"; #56 "3 Mess Houses"; #69 "3 Buildings at Hollon's Corral"; #71 "2 Soldiers Barracks"; #85 "10 Quarter Master Warehouses"; #86 "10 Commissary"; #91 "3 Buildings for Refugees"; #102 "3 Mules Stables."

4. Appendix "C" details the numbers of horses and mules, both serviceable and unserviceable, and the numbers of conveyances, such as army wagons and ambulances. At this point, the camp had 396 serviceable horses and 1,060 unserviceable; 2,031 serviceable mules and 50 unserviceable. It also had on hand 7,417 single sets of mule harness (serviceable).

5. This list includes 1,100 Army wagons repaired, plus bridles, harness, and water buckets. Items manufactured at the camp included all the pieces for harness, tools (such as sledge hammers and chisels), ropes, and straps.

6. This appendix is a list of horses and mules being "recruited," with an explanation: "In whose hands and what place."

7. "F" and "G" are lists of local people who were contracted to feed government stock. After almost every name is a notation: "Loyalty endorsed." Many of the families represented and some of the individual names on the list are quite recognizable: Cassius M. Clay, for example, had a contract to feed nineteen horses for Camp Nelson.

8. The letter marked "H," dated May 12, 1864, and signed by five men, consisted of one paragraph addressed to an unidentified general: "Cannot Capt. Hall, A.Q.M. at Camp Nelson, be sent out of Kentucky ? Every employee and Contractor, nearly, are rebels or rebel sympathizers; and the loyal men, and Gen'ls Burbridge and Hobson want him out of the State. You, Randal and Anderson write in a joint note to the Secretary of War, suggesting it to be done. It is indispensable to the ascendancy of the Union party in this quarter of the State." All the contractors, most of whom are marked "Loyalty endorsed," might have been surprised to discover they were "rebels or rebel sympathizers." Cassius M. Clay would surely have been surprised!

9. Appendix "I" lists the numbers of employees supervised by each member of the quartermaster team: Hall, Noble, Davis, and Santmyer. Capt. Noble, in charge of transportation, supervised an astounding 742 workers, including 62 blacksmiths, 27 harness makers, 24 watchmen, 415 teamsters, and 2 office boys. Capt. Davis, overseeing construction, supervised 224 workmen, including carpenters, stone masons, and sawyers—plus 10 watchmen and 1 (unexpected) sexton. Santmyer, in charge of horses and mules, had 181 workers in his department, mostly laborers for "grooming horses, caring for stock &c," but also a veterinary surgeon and a detective. Capt. Hall had direct oversight of the other A.Q.M.s, of course, but he supervised only 36 other people, mostly clerks, and the water works engineers, the plumber, the inspector of stock, and the forage master.

10. Report of Maj. Charles E. Compton to James A. Hardie, 23 June 1864; June 1864 Inspection, Box 2, File C–10 (1864), Entry 15; Inspector General's Records, RG 159.

[Excerpt from] REPORTS OF MR. BUTLER. WHAT THE SANITARY COMMISSION DID FOR COLORED RECRUITS AT CAMP NELSON, KY.

Soon after the introduction of colored recruits into the camp, their old owners came in carriages and on horseback every day to allure them by all kinds of promises and threats, and in many cases to kidnap them back into bondage. On the 26th of June two citizens murdered a colored recruit near camp, and many other outrages were perpetrated in the immediate vicinity. In a neighboring county the ears of two recruits were cut off, and two others were fastened to trees in the woods and flayed alive.

I have said the slaveholders attempted to kidnap and re-enslave those they had once owned. A single example will suffice for proof of the truth of the statement:

A boy had been sent on an errand within the camp limits by myself. I was surprised at his delay; but finally he returned, and stated that, within hearing distance of the Home, he was seized by two men, forced into a buggy, and driven off. When the buggy reached the pickets he told them he wanted to remain in camp, and they compelled his captors to release him. He felt like a man delivered from the jaws of death. Similar examples of violence were of every-day occurrence.

The slaveholders frequently sent their wives, who brought with them the wives of the would-be soldiers, and through them they attempted to bring back the servant and husband to slavery.

From the first day that the slaveholders commenced their visits to the Soldiers' Home to effect the recovery of the recruits, I found it necessary to make a requisition on the Post Commandant for a squad of soldiers to perform guard duty around the entire buildings, and to enforce the restriction that recruits from within and citizens from without should not cross their beat. None were allowed to cross the line except with a proper pass.

The whole care, in fact everything which pertained to the management, protection and employment of the colored recruits, devolved upon us, and we were left to ourselves to devise and prosecute plans to keep them as intact as possible in the service of the Government. The labor imposed upon us was incessant, night and day; and the utmost vigilance was demanded, in order that no event or incident within our field of operation should escape us.

The schemes for the re-enslavement of recruits were numerous, and almost invariably resulted in the discomfiture of their promoters. Here is one of many incidents:

I had heard that about twenty men had been induced by the Provost Marshal of Boyle county to return to their allegiance as slaves. The nature of the inducement held out to them I know not, but do know that passes were furnished them by that officer. I immediately communicated the fact to the Post Commandant, and requested that he would send an order to the pickets, countermanding the passes issued by the Provost Marshal. This was promptly done by Colonel Clarke. Meanwhile, our office orderly, a Michigan soldier, and a shrewd, dashing fellow, desired permission to take a squad of recruits, hasten in pursuit of the men who were returning to slavery, and prevail upon them to come back. Fully recognizing that all I had done to encourage the enlistment of negroes and defeat the machinations of their enemies was unofficial, and having no support from any officer of the Government, I refrained from giving any positive instructions in answer to the request of the orderly. I simply told him that I would spare him for the afternoon. Shortly afterward we saw him at the head of a hundred of the recruits, marching in military style, at double-quick, in the right direction. On the return of the orderly, an hour after, he reported that the Post Commandant's order was delivered, and the twenty men detained by the pickets.

On their return to the Home, the orderly and his command met a cavalcade of carriages, containing the Provost Marshal of Boyle county and a number of slave owners. The vehicles were instantly drawn up to barricade the road, when the orderly commanded them peremptorily to make a way, or he would force one. The Provost Marshal alighted, and inquiring by what authority he had done this thing. The orderly, turning to the men, asked them, "Is there a man here who desires to become a slave again?" Every one responded with vehemence, "No!"—except a poor, weak fellow, whose master's eye was upon him. He stepped from the ranks of freemen, and entered one of the carriages with his master. The orderly then ordered the obstructions removed from the road, and duly arrived at the Home with nineteen of the recruits who had been illegally ordered away.

One bright morning in June the Provost Marshal mustered nearly three hundred recruits into line, and marched them to a grove, distant half a mile from the Home. I had watched the proceedings, and having observed a number of citizens accompanying the Marshal, my suspicions were aroused. I very soon rode over to the grove, and found the men drawn up in single line, apparently under inspection. I saw the Marshal select a number of recruits, whom I recognized as the healthiest and smartest of all he had contributed, and heard him direct them to start at once toward Boyle county. I immediately turned to the men thus illegally rejected, and asked them if they were still willing to enter the service as soldiers. They all replied, "Yes." "Then," said I, "there is no man here who has the authority to order you back to your masters; and while you have the liberty to return at your pleasure before you are enlisted, you have also the liberty to remain here until a proper medical officer examines you." The Marshal was very much enraged, and asked, "By what authority do you interfere with my business?" "Very much better," I rejoined, "than that by which you presume to order these men back to their masters on the plea of physical disability, when most of them say they have never been sick a day in their lives. Moreover, you are not an officer authorized to examine these men, with power to decide upon their fitness or unfitness for service." He threatened me with arrest—a threat I felt safe in disregarding, surrounded as I was by my sable friends and guards. I took the men with me back to the Home, and carefully prevented others from being enticed away.

During a part of June the colored recruits under my care exceeded fifteen hundred; and finding it altogether impossible to provide quarters for all, I requested Major ———, commanding the large, vacant "Camp of Distribution," to receive some or all of them under his care. The Major, though a Northern man and an officer in the army, with ample facilities for doing what I regarded his duty in the matter, was averse to the emancipation movement, and positively refused to have anything to do with them. I then, as advised by Captain Hall, by giving my personal receipt, obtained sixty-five tents, and, taking one hundred men, pitched them in Major ———'s camp, and reported to the Major one thousand recruits; whereupon he very considerately reported them back to me. I however succeeded in transferring to him all the men who had been examined and accepted. I repeatedly endeavored to procure the Major's receipt for the tents, but he steadily refused to give it. Thus the whole labor and responsibility of the work was thrown by the Government agents upon myself and those associated with me.

About this time fears were entertained that John Morgan, the notorious rebel leader, would attack Camp Nelson, as he was then at Lexington, eighteen miles distant. All the recruits, therefore, were employed to strengthen the defenses; and to their immense labor the camp is indebted for its present almost perfect impregnability. The enlisted men were worked very hard and, to somebody's disgrace, very poorly fed, receiving nothing but what could be taken with their bare hands, and not more than half rations at that. Five thousand pounds of new straw had been donated for their benefit, but an order was issued to burn it, and that order executed after it had been slept on but two nights. The men came to me every hour with complaints of abuse and hard treatment; so I concluded, if possible, I would remove them elsewhere. On a representation of the matter to Captain Gillis, the engineer officer under whose superintendence they were working on the defenses of the camp, he readily consented to quarter them among his own employés. The same day I procured wagons, and, with the aid of a detail, removed all the tents and one thousand enlisted men from the camp of Major ——— to that of Captain Gillis, who I knew would deal justly and kindly with them.

Before the close of June, Colonel T.D. Sedgwick was appointed superintendent, and charged with the work of organizing colored troops at Camp Nelson. A few days after the Colonel's arrival he said to me, "Mr. Butler, I am very much gratified by the reports made to me of what you and your assistants have done. Had it not been for the Soldier's Home here, I am persuaded that I should not have found a recruit where now I find five thousand to begin with"; and more to the same effect, not necessary to repeat.[1]

1. Newberry, 520–25.

June 27ᵗʰ [*1864*]
To J. Bates Dickson   A. A G   Dist of Ky.   Lexington, Ky

My scouts have returned from Crab Orchard having accomplished nothing   I have definite information that there are thirty (30) or forty (40) guerillas about Boonsville Ky and as I desire very much to go home for a short time can I have the scouts to accompany me? It will not take but some seven (7) or eight (8) days. It is unsafe to go alone.

A. H Clark   Col 47ᵗʰ Ky Inf.   Comdg Post[1]

1. Clark to Dickson, 25 June 1864; Vol. 107, p. 304; Press Copies; RG 393.

[No place designated] June /64   Rec^d June 27 /64 *[In a different hand]*

Bro. Jocelyn —   * * * * *[One paragraph.]*
    I am glad to live   I bless God for this day — I was seriously anxious & troubled at the time of our expulsion & loss of my son four years since —
    My health is now good — I feel that a glorious door is opening.
    I have this day official information from our prov. Marshall that the colored men of this district will not be sent to Louisville but to Camp Nelson little more than half a days ride from my house   I have yet no answer from you in reference to going to look after the colored people — I shall look next Saturday — I go that day to Jackson co
    I have kept myself for this field — ready — I believed it would come. I am here<u>ready</u> — God is in it * * * * *[One paragraph.]*

Yours in haste

J G Fee[1]

1. Fee to Jocelyn, before 27 June 1864, AMAA 44005.

Louisville, Ky., June 29, 1864

Hon. E.M. Stanton, Secretary of War: . . . I leave to-morrow for Lexington to see General Burbridge and shall proceed to Camp Nelson, where the negroes are coming in rapidly. As soon as I can station detachments at the places indicated in my order to protect the negroes and afford them facilities for coming to these camps recruiting will go forward rapidly. . . . Some 1,500 men are said to be at Camp Nelson. I wish to have at this place a school for field music. Am I authorized to employ a suitable teacher for the drum, fife, and bugle, to be paid from the appropriation for collecting, organizing, and drilling recruits? Such music is very necessary.

L. Thomas, Adjutant-General[1]

1. Thomas to Stanton, 29 June 1864, *OR,* 3, 4, 459–60.

Lexington Ky   June 30" *[1864]*
To Col T.D. Sedgwick   Camp Nelson Ky

General Thomas' instructions are to discourage as far as possible negro women and children coming into Camp. Such as come however must be provided for

By order of Brig Genl Burbridge

J Bates Dickson   Capt and A.A Genl[1]

1. Dickson to Sedgwick, 30 June 1864; Vol. 62/117,119, p. 99; Telegrams Sent; RG 393.

Berea Madison Co Ky   June 30 /64

Dear Bro Jocelyn   I have written two letters asking instructions about going to labor with and arrange for the ex slaves the colored men of this state now enlisted and in Camp

Last week near three thousand were in camp at Camp Nelson about 35 miles from my house   I feel that I ought to go and preach to them — distribute tracts & get suitable chaplains for or missionaries with them

What do you say — * * * * [*One paragraph.*]

Shall I arrange for other laborers there

I desire instructions

There will be a rendesvous for this county then a general one at Camp Nelson & one at Louisville   Yours in haste

John G Fee

* * * * [*Two paragraphs.*]

No one cares for these colored men as I suppose   I want to go & see.[1]

1. Fee to Jocelyn, 30 Jun. 1864, AMAA 44004.

July 1"[*1864*]
Col Thos D. Sedgwick

Col. Is it necessary for owners to have an order to get their slave women and children out of camp and shall I give such orders when applied for   I desire definite instructions in regard to this   *

Geo A Hanaford   Lt and AAAG[1]

1. Hanaford to Sedgwick, 1 July 1864; Vol. 107, p. 322; Press Copies; RG 393.

Telegram   July 2 [*1864*]
Brig Gen S.S. Fry   Care Capt J Bate Dickson   Lexington, Ky

Mr M D Halls wife from Harrodsburg is here & desires to obtain a negro boy belonging to her.   he is only (13) thirteen years old and is quite deaf. Please instruct me what action to take. *

Geo A Hanaford   Lt. & A.A.A.G.[1]

1. Hanaford to Fry, 2 July 1864; Vol. 107, p. 329; Press Copies; RG 393.

July 2 [*1864*]
Capt T.E. Hall   Asst Q.M

Capt.   Mr Caldwell of Bourbon co Ky informs me that he has a wagon and two horses, a saddle and two bridles in your private stable yard, which were stolen from him. I respectfully refer him to you with the request that you will deliver up the property   His credentials are good

By Command of Brig Gen Fry

[*Signed*] Geo A Hanaford   Lieut and A.A.A.G.[1]

1. Hanaford to Hall, 2 July 1864; Vol. 107, p. 316; Press Copies; RG 393.

July 2 [*1864*]
Capt J M Hewitt[1]   Chief of Artillery   Camp Nelson

Captain. You are hereby ordered to fire a national salute on the 4th of July 1864 consisting of Thirteen (13) guns at sunrise and thirty six (36) guns at 12 o'clock M.

You will draw the ammunition necessary from Lieut J.H. Merrill actg Depot Ord officer

By Command of Brig Gen S.S. Fry

[*Signed*] Geo A Hanaford   Lt. and A.A.A.G.[2]

1. John M. Hewitt enlisted on October 4, 1861, at Muldraugh's Hill, Kentucky, as an adjutant in the Second Kentucky Cavalry; promoted to captain on April 30, 1864, he served as chief of artillery at Camp Nelson. *RAGK*.

2. Hanaford to Hewitt, 2 July 1864; Vol. 107, p. 334; Press Copies; RG 393.

Lexington, Ky., July 3, 1864

Hon. Edwin M. Stanton, Secretary of War: There are at Camp Nelson 3,000 negroes, and they will be organized as soon as I can get officers, which is now my great want. I obtained officers for about three regiments from my offices, but these will be required at Louisville. Candidates are being examined here, and General Burbridge expects to give me officers for six other regiments. General Schofield has ordered several regiments of white troops to the front, and the employment of colored troops in this State will thus become a necessity. Indeed, General Burbridge desires to use them. As soon as I get officers recruiting will go on rapidly. The people of the State seem to realize the fact that slavery has almost entirely ceased to exist, and the true Union men are perfectly satisfied that the able-bodied men should be enlisted; and whilst the Southern sympathizers see the same fact, and know that they cannot prevent their enlistment, they keep quiet on the subject. Taking the negroes just now will interfere with saving the crops, but I have stated that the women and children shall be required to remain at home and be cared for by their owners. They can be made useful in securing the grain. It will not answer to take this class of slaves, as employment could not be obtained for them, and they would only be an expense to the Government. In this State, where slavery exists, I conceive I have only to do with those who can be put into the army. The railroad terminus is at Nicholasville, six miles from Camp Nelson. From the former point to the camp all supplies—and they are very numerous—have to be transported by wagons. If this large intrenched camp of 4,000 acres is to be continued—and I suppose such will be the case, as it is a good central point, and important as a base of supplies for Tennessee—it would be economy to construct a railroad over these six miles. It could be mainly constructed by the troops at comparatively little cost. General Burbridge gives me every assistance, and is fully impressed with the necessity of arming the negroes. He makes a good commander, and I hope will be continued in his present position. My presence will be necessary here to-morrow and perhaps the next day. I will return to Louisville.

L. Thomas, Adjutant-General[1]

1. Thomas to Stanton, 3 July 1864, *OR,* 3, 4, 467–68.

July 3ᵈ [*1864*]
Lt Jno McQueen   Provost Marshal

Confine Speech (a colored boy) in Military Prison for stealing a horse.
By Command of Brig General Fry
[*Signed*] Geo A Hanaford   Lt & AAAG[1]

1. Hanaford to McQueen, 3 July 1864; Vol. 107, p. 341; Press Copies; RG 393.

Head Quarters   Camp Nelson Ky   July 3, 1864

Non commissioned officers in command of Picket posts are hereby charged with the prompt execution of the following Order in regard to Colored persons wishing to come into the lines of this Camp.

"Only able bodied Negroes of lawful age who express a desire to enter the U.S. service shall hereafter be permitted to enter this Camp, and any old men, women or children shall under no pretense whatever be allowed to pass the line of Pickets at this Post."

The above Order does not refer to Negroes in Government employ and Negro servants of travelers, who shall be permitted to pass.

By command of Brig Genl S. S Fry
[*Signed*] Geo A Hanaford Lt. and A.A.A.G.[1]

1. Hanaford, Order from Fry, 3 July 1864; Vol. 107, p. 354; Press Copies; RG 393.

[*Excerpt from William Pratt's diary*]
July 4, 1864

Today went in morning to Camp Nelson to obtain information respecting Ed & Haggie two negroes of estate of J.A. Boseby on which I am administering — found these slaves with roll of enlisted & Col Sedgewick offers to send me certificates. Some 4 or 5000 negroes are congregated there, & are being equipped for the service.

I found the road lined with them going, while I was returning. It is now the time of Harvest & negroes are leaving home & I fear the grain will not be harvested.[1]

1. William Pratt Diary, 4 Jul. 1864, Special Collections and Archives, University of Kentucky Libraries. William Moody Pratt (1817–1897) was the slaveholding minister of the First Baptist Church in Lexington from 1845 to 1863. While there he served as school commissioner, operated a private school, and had charge of the Sunday School and book division of the Baptist Church. His diaries span 1838 to 1891.

U.S. Mil. Tel.   July 4 1864   By Telegraph from Danville Ky

Are you turning out the negroes over and under the ages. If so will you send Pa's boys Orange and Mack and T.B. Younger boys Jim on the stage or direct how to get them?
[*No signature*][1]

1. Telegram from Danville, Kentucky, 4 July 1864; Vol. 112/258, pp. 22, 23; Telegrams; RG 393.

Eng. Office   Camp Nelson   July 4th 1864
Lt. Col. J H Simpson   Corps Engineers

Col. I have the honor to make the following report of operations for the month of June —
. . . At my request on the 8th [*of June*] Gen Burbridge ordered the negroes enlisting at this Camp to be set to work on these fortifications — The same day the excitement about Morgans raid commenced and continued for two weeks —
Since the 8th our force has averaged 1200 a day — During the coming months it will be 1500 — more could be had but this is as many as can be worked to advantage. [*Followed by details of forts, batteries, rifle pits, etc.*]
John R. Gilliss   Asst U.S. Eng.[1]

1. Gilliss to Simpson, 4 July 1864; Entry 3541; Part 1; RG 393.

U.S. Mil. Tel   July 5 1864.   By Telegraph from Lexington
To Genl S.S. Fry

My yellow man Joe is at camp. If he wishes to enlist let him do so. If he does let me know
J.C. Hall[1]

1. Hall to Fry, 5 July 1864; Vol. 112/258, p. 23; Telegrams; RG 393.

Head Quarters Camp Nelson Ky   Jessamine Co. Ky   July 5, 1864.
Circular.

The General commanding finding it impossible to give audience to all that visit him in regard to negro women and children, respectfully advises all concerned to remain at home until such time as the authorities provide some way to return all colored persons to their homes that are not fit subjects for the Army.

By Command of Brig Genl S S. Fry

[*Signed*] Geo A Hanaford   Lt and A.A.A.G.[1]

1. Hanaford, Circular dated 5 July 1864; Vol. 111/256, p. 51; General Orders; RG 393.

Telegram   July 5 [*1864*]
Capt J Bates Dickson, A.A.G.   Head Qus, Lexington, Ky

A young man G W Coyte, a rebel, was wounded, accidentally, in the late raid, is about to die. His friends are here, desire to take him home, willing to give bonds to any amount. he is willing to take the oath. Please telegraph me instructions to release him & upon what conditions I may do so.

Speed S Fry   Brig Gen Comdg[1]

1. Fry to Dickson, 5 July 1864; Vol. 107, p. 360; Press Copies; RG 393.

July 5" [*1864*]
Dr C C Radmore   Ast. Surg 107th Ill Vols   In Chg Mil Prison Hosp

Doctor, The General commanding directs that you examine C.W. Coyt, Confederate Prisoner and report your opinion to these Head Quarters whether he can live or not.

By Command of Brig General Fry

[*Signed*] Geo A. Hanaford   Lieut and A.A.A.G.[1]

1. Hanaford to Radmore, 5 July 1864; Vol. 107, p. 361; Press Copies; RG 393.

July 6th [*1864*]
Col J M Brown[1]   Comdg 4th Brigade   Lexington Ky

Dear Colonel. I have the honor to very respectfully inform you that Col A.H. Clark 47th Ky Vols has been relieved from the command of this Post and is now awaiting instructions. having returned from the mountains where he was ordered with a scouting party some two days ago by General Burbridge. Will you please direct him what to do. I am Very

Respectfully

Geo A Hanaford   Lieut and A.A.A.G.

P S

Brig Gen S.S. Fry is now commanding here.

Geo A H.   AAAG [2]

1. John Mason Brown was a major in the Tenth Kentucky Cavalry and a colonel in the Forty-fifth Kentucky Infantry. *HR,* 2:84.
2. Hanaford to Brown, 6 July 1864; Vol. 107, p. 379; Press Copies; RG 393.

U.S. Mil Tel.   July 6" 1864. By Telegraph from Lexington
To Lt Geo A. Hanaford

Issue an order[1] that all negro women and children & men in camp unfit for the service will be delivered to their owners, the delivery to commence on Monday next and continue from day to day until all are sent off. Also issue an order requiring all officers or other persons having negro men fit for service in their employ to report them forthwith to Col Sedgewick, all unfit for service who have come into the camp since the issue of War Dept orders no matter at what engaged must be reported. These are General Thomas instructions to me & directs me to carry them out fully — Frame the order so as to let all know that it is made under instructions from Genl Thomas — Get the men out of prison who stole the wagon & horses from Mr. R.P. Gregory in Boyle Co. send them with women & all the children to Danville ask Agt at Danville to notify Mr. G. when they will arrive — Mr G. will pay for it.

S.S. Fry   B.G.[2]

1. Orders No. 24 was issued later that day; see below.
2. Fry to Hanaford, 6 July 1864; Vol. 112/258, p. 24; Telegrams; RG 393.

Office Provost Marshal   Camp Nelson, Ky, July 6th 1864
Lieut Geo A. Hanaford, A.A.A.Gen'l.

Lieut. I do not exactly understand your meaning as expressed in your last communication. Thompson a wagon master is only man who has been <u>arrested</u> by your order this P.M. I was not aware that you had sent any one here this afternoon to be confined.

P. Bevins, one of my Mounted Patrol was brought here, under guard, a short time ago, but I understand from the guards that brought him that he was sent here by Capt. Hall. A.Q. M and that was all they knew of the matter.

If this is the man you mean he is now here; as near as I can learn, he was arrested for striking a nigger with the butt of his pistol, for calling him a "son of a b——h.

He is now here — and I do not think he has left his Quarters since I ordered him there. If this is the man you mean please send me instructions. *

Jno McQueen   1st Lt. & Provost - Marshall.[1]

1. McQueen to Hanaford, 6 July 1864, Part 4, Entry 1660, pp. 153, 154; RG 393.

Headquarters, Camp Nelson, Jessamine Co., Ky., July 6, 1864
Circular

I In pursuance with instructions from Brig Gen. L. Thomas, Adjutant General U.S.A. owners of slaves are hereby notified that on and after Monday July 10th 1864, all colored men in camp unfit for service in the Army, and all women and children will be delivered up to their owners upon application to these Head Quarters.

II All officers or other persons, having in their employ negro men fit for service in the army are hereby directed to report them forthwith to Col. Thos. D. Sedgewick comdg U.S. Colored Troops at this Post. All men fit for service, as above, who have come into camp since the issue of War Department Orders must be reported, no matter at what engaged.

A prompt compliance with this circular is expected.

By Command of Brig. Gen S.S. Fry
[*Signed*] Geo A Hanaford   Lt and A.A.A.G.[1]

1. Hanaford, Circular dated 6 July 1864; Vol. 111/256, p. 52; General Orders; RG 393. Also quoted in *Military History of Kentucky*, 212, 213.

Telegram   July 6th [*1864*]
Capt J Bates Dickson   A.A.G.   D.K.

General Fry went to Louisville to-day and before leaving, instructed me to have all colored women & children brot here, and to give passes to all that desired to return home   There is not one among two hundred (200) that want to go. A great many are willing to go outside the lines. There to shift for themselves. Shall I keep them in camp or not.

They are laboring under the impression that they will be killed by their masters if they return and can not be assured to the contrary. Please reply giving me definite instructions *

Geo A Hanaford   Lieut and A.A.A.G.[1]

1. Hanaford to Dickson, 6 July 1864; Vol. 107, p. 370; Press Copies; RG 393.

July 6th [*1864*]
Lt Jno McQueen   Provost Marshal   Camp Nelson Ky

Lieut. In pursuance of a dispatch from Brevt Major General Burbridge commanding Dist of Ky dated July 5th 1864 you are hereby directed to release G.W. Coit, Confederate prisoner from custody, upon his giving well secured bonds in the sum of one thousand /$1,000/ dollars and taking the oath. The bond is required to hold his securities responsible for a violation of his oath.

By Command of Brig General Fry
[*Signed*] Geo A Hanaford   Lt. and A.A.A.G.[1]

1. Hanaford to McQueen, 6 July 1864; Vol. 107, p. 373; Press Copies; RG 393.

Copy
July 7" 1864
By Telegraph from   Camp Nelson,

To Capt Dickson, Genl. Hobson issued an order during the last rain that all negroes enlisted or otherwise should work on fortifications here. The order is still in force. It seriously Embarrasses my operations. Can't I have it revoked until I get all mustered and organized. I have one regiment and six companies organized.

(Sd) Thos. D. Sedgwick. Col. &c.[1]

1. Sedgwick to Dickson, 7 July 1864; Entry 1030; Part 2; RG 393.

July 8" [*1864*]
Lt Jno McQueen   Provost Marshal   Camp Nelson Ky

Lieut   The General commanding directs that you release the negros now that stole a wagon and some horses from Mr. R.P. Gregory in Boyle co. If they have any women or children get tham all to gether and send them to Danville this P.M. on the stage. Mr Gregory will pay their fares   The men must not be released until time for the stage when they must be sent to D — as directed without fail   *

Geo A Hanaford   Lieut and A.A.A.G.[1]

1. Hanaford to McQueen, 8 July 1864; Vol. 107, p. 387; Press Copies; RG 393.

U.S. Mil Tel   July 8th 1864   By Telegraph from Lexington
To Brig Gen Fry

The order for negroes to work on fortifications from Brig Gen Hobson is revoked   the negroes will be at once organized by Col Sedgewick

By order of Brig. Gen. McLean
J S Butler A.A.G.[1]

1. Butler to Fry, 8 July 1864; Vol. 112/258, p. 25; Telegrams; RG 393.

Telegram   July 8" [*1864*]
Mr R P. Gregory   Danville, Ky

I have ordered the men that stole your wagon, and horses, to be released and sent with their women & children to Danville this P.M. upon the stage making you subject to pay fares. Unless you devise some other way more satisfactory to yourself, they will arrive to-night

By Command of Brig Gen Fry
[*Signed*] Geo A Hanaford   Lt & AAAG[1]

1. Hanaford to Gregory, 8 July 1864; Vol. 107, p. 388; Press Copies; RG 393.

Telegram   July 8" [*1864*]
Mr R.P. Gregory   Danville Ky

Since I telegraphed you this morning I have learned that your men have en-listed and the women can not be found

Geo A Hanaford   Lt & AAAG[1]

1. Ibid., but a different telegram.

U S Mil Tel   July 11th 1864   By Telegraph from Lexington
To Brig Gen S S Fry

Adjt Gen L Thomas order No. 24 says — None but able bodied men will be received at the various camps, all others will be encouraged to remain at their re-spective homes where under the state law their respective masters are bound to take care of them and those who may have been received at Camp Nelson will be sent to their homes   Owners are not obliged to take the oath of allegiance

J Bates Dickson   Capt A A G[1]

1. Dickson to Fry, 11 July 1864; Vol. 112/258, p. 27; Telegrams; RG 393.

Chapter Three

Soldiers, Missionaries, Refugees

Camp Nelson Jessamine Co Ky.   Postmarked July 12, 1864 [*Written at the bottom of the letter in a different hand.*]

Bro Jocelyn   I will write for the Missionary tomorrow

I have written you almost every week for five weeks past concerning this colored people and no answer

I have felt that I must act. Here are five thousand men — ex slaves more coming — <u>hopeful</u> — I was here several days last week — preached every night — Many of them know me — hundreds from Madison Co — most all have heard of me as their <u>friend</u>. They <u>crowd</u> to hear me — a thousand at a time — many good & promising men here.

In the Providence of God there is a man here from Mass — Capt Hall with a humane heart — he is chief quartermaster — a personal friend of Elnathan Davis[1] — has written for Davis to come out here   So have I —

This man Hall took responsibility when higher officers would not — now has the prestige — he is very energetic

Soon as I came he said you are just the man I wanted to see[2] — I want three things — Religious instruction for this people, schools, and clothing for our barracks for these people for the interim of their coming and uniforms from the government

I agreed to meet the demands for all. I felt I must — for reasons apparent to you at once   What will you say to me   Hall wants all the non-Commissioned officers taught to read & write soon as possible

I set up two tents this day to begin the school — my son is here to work until I get better help. . . .

I must go forward — no [*one*] else here to meet this vast want. Berea at present is small compared with this   Both must go [*on*]. * * * * [*One paragraph.*]

Now I felt I must act for this people and for the society. I waited until I felt Christs Kingdom was suffering and that the interests of the Am Miss Association required I should act. I knew your mails had been interrupted.

I have written to John Drew[3] of Jackson co. to come & help me

My own family wants — I have to pay ten dollars per barrel for flour — 15 miles from home — 25 cts for shugar per pound &c

I have to buy a cow — cannot get one for less than fifty dollars   Please write to me also at this place — I <u>need</u> money.

I have to send by carrier — no time to correct

J G Fee[4]

1. Rev. Elnathan Davis (born 1807 Holden, Mass.; died 1881) was a hometown friend of Capt. Hall.

2. Capt. Hall evidently knew Fee already. On a fund-raising trip for Berea College in 1859, Fee had been in Worcester, Massachusetts, Hall's hometown, to speak on anti-slavery issues. Elnathan Davis, a minister in Worcester, also was acquainted with Fee. (In a letter dated 2 Jan. 1865, Fee mentions having been Worcester in 1859. AMAA 44066.)

3. John Drew was one of Fee's disciples from eastern Kentucky; in 1863 he had been minister of South Fork Church, which Fee had founded in Jackson County. Because Drew was a mulatto, Fee considered him a very appropriate helper at Camp Nelson; he worked there briefly in August 1864, and much later he became minister of the Camp Nelson Church after Gabriel Burdett left for Kansas.

4. Fee to Jocelyn, 12 Jul. 1864, AMAA 44007.

Hd Qrs Camp Nelson Ky   July 12 1864
General Orders Nº 4.

I   The General commanding, for the information of all concerned published the following paragraph of Order Nº 24, promulgated from the War Department:

I   The law authorizing the enlistment of colored troops has only reference to the able bodied negroes capable of bearing arms, and not to old men, the infirm, or women and children. Accordingly none but able bodied men will be received at the various camps designated for their reception, all others will be encouraged to remain at their respective homes, where, under the state laws, their masters are bound to take care of them, and those who may have been received at Camp Nelson will be sent to their homes. This letter is necessary as many cases of disease have made their appearance among both sexes, of such a nature as to require their removal beyond the limits of the camp. Furthermore all of this class of persons are required to assist in securing the crops now suffering in many cases for the want of labor,

II   All officers or other persons having in their charge any old or infirm negro men unfit for service or any women and children will at once report them to these Head Quarters so that they may be disposed of in accordance with the above instructions.

III   The Quartermaster and Commissaries will be allowed to retain in their employ the women they may have hired as cooks and washwomen and they will be allowed to hire as many others, from their owners, as may be necessary to supply the deficiency created by the removal of any now in their employ

By Command of Brig Gen S.S. Fry

[*No signature*]   Lt. & A.A.A.G[1]

1. General Orders No. 4, 12 July 1864; Vol. 111/256, p. 54; General Orders; RG 393. Section I of Fry's order is a verbatim quote of Lorenzo Thomas's Orders No. 24, which was issued

from Louisville on July 6. Later, Thomas's order was filed as an enclosure with a letter written by Brig. Gen. Speed S. Fry on December 15, 1864, defending his conduct in expelling women and children from Camp Nelson in November. Orders No. 24, 6 July 1864; Box 720; RG 92.

Head Quarters Camp Nelson   Jessamine C° Ky   July 13th 1864.
General Orders N° 5.

It is hereby ordered that no colored soldier shall receive a pass from any one to pass the line of sentinels, except when detailed for some duty

Officers in charge of colored troops are forbidden to give any such soldier a pass except in cases of extreme necessity and in all such cases the pass must state the place to which the soldier is allowed to go. The length of time he is to be absent together with the reason for giving the pass.

All such passes will be sent to these Head Quarters for approval.

By command of Brig Gen S S Fry
[*No signature*]   Lt & A.A.A.G[1]

1. General Orders No. 5, 13 July 1864; Vol. 111/256, p. 55; General Orders; RG 393.

Hd Qrs Camp Nelson Ky   July 15th 1864.
Orders for picket guards

The officers of the day will instruct all pickets that when colored persons present themselves for admission into camp they will take all able bodied negro men and report them to Col T.D. Sedgeweick, Comdg U.S.C.T. for examination and enlistment. If he is rejected then he will be conducted together with all women, children and old men to these Head Quarters.

These instructions will be turned over each day to the new by the old officer of the Day.

By command of Brig Gen S.S. Fry
[*No signature*]   Lt. & A.A.A.G[1]

1. Orders for picket guards, 15 July 1864; Vol. 111/256, p. 56; General Orders; RG 393.

Louisville, Ky., July 16, 1864.

Hon. Edwin M. Stanton, Secretary of War: * * * *

I found at this place, as at Camp Nelson, a number of old men, women, and children, which I decided should be sent to their homes, as in this State, where slavery exists, I am only authorized under to law to take able-bodied men for soldiers. They, too, are needed to secure the crops, which we shall certainly require for the army. . . .

L. Thomas, Adjutant-General.[1]

1. Thomas to Stanton, 16 July 1864, *OR,* 3, 4, 501–2.

LEXINGTON, KY., July 18, 1864

Brig. Gen. S.S. FRY, Camp Nelson, Ky.:

Rebels are believed to be about making a formidable raid in the eastern part of Kentucky, and may have already entered the State, though of this we have no positive information. Troops at Boonesborough, Winchester, and Mount Sterling, with scouts well out. Have the camp well guarded and your forces kept well in hand ready for any emergency.

By order of Brevet Major-General Burbridge:
J. Bates Dickson, Captain and Assistant Adjutant-General.[1]

1. Dickson to Fry, 18 July 1864, *OR*, 1, 39, pt. 2, 179. This "formidable raid" evidently did not materialize.

Hd Qrs Camp Nelson Ky   July 18th 1864.
Instructions for guards

The General commanding orders that in future all bathing in the river above the water works will be prohibited. All persons wishing to indulge in this luxury must find some point on the river below the water works.

Any one found guilty of a violation of this order will at once be arrested and placed in confinement in the Military Prison for such a length of time as the General commanding atones for the offense.

By command of Brig Gen S S Fry
[*No signature.*]   Lt. & A.A.A.G[1]

1. Instructions for guards, 18 July 1864; Vol. 111/256, p. 59; General Orders; RG 393.

Hd Qrs Camp Nelson Ky   July 18" 1864
Orders.

The Provost Guard stationed at the spring below the Owens Home is hereby relieved from duty at that place and until further orders that spring will be guarded by colored troops. The officer in charge will instruct his guard not to allow any horses, either public or private to be watered at said spring. Until further orders all stock will be watered in the River or Ponds.

He will see that no difficulty occurs at or around the spring and will arrest any one who creates any disturbance.

By command of Brig Gen S. S Fry
[*No signature.*]   Lt and A.A.A.G[1]

1. Orders, 18 July 1864; Vol. 111/256, p. 61; General Orders; RG 393.

[*Letterhead.*]¹ *United States Sanitary Commission*   **Camp Nelson, Ky.**   **July 18 /64**

Dear Bro. Jocelyn   I have been here some two weeks

Here are some four ~~or five~~² thousand slaves   These are being enrolled, uniformed & drilled as fast as possible And if there be a class of men ~~in this nation~~ which promises great good to this nation, in that class will be found these Kentucky colored soldiers. One of the surgeons who examined them has said to me, "Sometimes we actually stood still in admiration of the wonderfully developed chests and muscles of some of these men." The officers did not begin organizing until some three or four thousand were in camp. Then they "sized" the companies. The companies are very uniform in heighth, some of them are in full uniform with their muskets.

Between three and four hundred of this first colored regiment here raised, are from Madison Co, the county in which I live. These men know me, and many others in adjoining counties know me as their friend. These people crowd to hear me — from five hundred to a thousand at a time — sometimes more.

I have undertaken to teach the non commissioned officers to read and write. Most of these knew their letters; quite a number could spell a little, and some few could read. — I had no help at first, — now I have the help of one ex slave — tomorrow one more. The pupils are making astonishing progress, considering the small facilities they have had. — Perhaps no slaves in the nation are superior in intellectual development to these Kentucky ex slaves — few their equal.

There is one chaplain in the hospital. I am here a voluntary missionary in the camp. My hearers are not those of one regiment but several. — If life and health shall be continued, I shall reach many thousands. In my work I have the written approval of the principal commandants of the place. I have no embarrassment in this most promising work of my life, but the want of colaborers and books. — For the latter I think I shall not wait long. We have tents now as places for instruction; we shall soon have good schoolrooms in permanent government buildings, — also a fixed place for preaching.

I rode out through the camp (six miles in circumference) — to look for two men. I saw several companies resting from drill. Quite a number were pouring over their primers or first readers, and not a card was seen in the companies. — I spoke of my delight in this, as I rode up to them. They spoke freely and contrasted the present with the past to each of us — In the four thousand colored men here I have not seen one intoxicated although I have seen white men drunk. At nights the camps of these colored men are scenes of continual prayer & praise with frequent preaching. It would do your soul good to witness these scenes   Yours in <u>hope</u>

John G. Fee

Private

Your letter was indeed welcome   I had waited 7 weeks no answer   I saw the rising wants of these colored men   no one to instruct them in camp save such preachers as were among them   These could not give facts as I could   I felt I must act upon my own responsibility & my faith in what the society would do

. . . Thro Cincinnati I shall get some clothing for women   Most of the women children & boys & old men are being sent out of the lines — Their masters take them   This is a terror to many but the camp is not a good place for them   outside the camp the land belongs not to government but to individuals

The schools are likely to be permanent   Capt Hall thinks they will continue here after the war is over   This is the rendesvous for two congressional districts — may yet be for the state.

Four good teachers ought now to be here beside myself & these secure the help of such as they could find in the regiments * * * * [*One paragraph.*]³

1. At this point, the letterhead for the Sanitary Commission displayed the motto "Rally Round the Flag, Boys!" above a flying eagle with an American flag in its beak.
2. The word deletions in this letter seem to have been the work of the *American Missionary* rather than Fee himself. All the crossouts appear to be in the ink of the editor who has written "From Rev John G. Fee" at the top of the letter.
3. Fee to Jocelyn, 18 Jul. 1864, AMAA 44008–9; also the public section of the letter appears in *AM* 8, no. 9 (Sept. 1864): 222–23.

U S Mil Tel   July 19" 1864
By Telegraph from Hᵈ Qs Lexington Ky
To Brig Gen S S Fry

Allow no Citizen to visit Camp Nelson on business with Negroes and put a stop to the practice which has obtained there of giving passes to recruits or colored men not yet enlisted but intending to

By Order of Brt Maj Gen Burbridge
J Bates Dickson   Capt   A A G¹

1. Dickson to Fry, 19 July 1864; Vol. 112/258, p. 32; Telegrams; RG 393.

Hd Qrs Camp Nelson   Jessamine Co Ky   July 20ᵗʰ 1864.
General orders Nº 7.

In pursuance with instructions from Dist. Head Quarters no citizen will in future be permitted to visit Camp for the purpose of seeing after negroes.

All orders heretofore issued in regard to the removal from camp of negroes not subject to enlistment will be enforced.

By command of Brig Gen S S Fry
[*No signature.*]   Lt. & A.A.A.G¹

1. General Orders No. 7, 20 July 1864; Vol. 111/256, p. 62; General Orders; RG 393.

Hd Qrs Camp Nelson   Jessamine Co Ky July 23ᵈ 1864
General Orders Nᵒ 10.

Information having reached these Head Quarters that colored soldiers and employees from this Camp, were in the habit of going to their old homes, and in many instances, were guilty of conduct in variance with the Rules and Articles of War, and also, in violation of the laws of the State:

I   It is therefore ordered, that hereafter no colored Soldier or employee shall be permitted to leave Camp, under any pretext whatever, except when ordered out on some special duty.

II   That it shall be the duty of any officer, in command of Troops; and of the Provost Marshals, in the counties from which negroes have been enlisted at this Camp, to arrest any colored soldier or employee found in said counties without permit approved or ordered at these Head Quarters, and the soldier or employee, so arrested, shall be sent, under guard if one can be had, to Camp, if no guard can be obtained, then he shall be confined in jail, notice of which in writing, shall at once be sent to the Post Adjutant or to Col. T.D. Sedgewick in Command of Colored Troops, by the officer making the arrest.

III   Any colored soldier or employee, either with or without a proper permit, who is detected in the commission of any act, in violation either of the civil or military law, shall be arrested, and the officer making such arrest, shall make out, in writing, and forward to these Head Quarters, a statement of the offense, its nature and extent, together with the names of the witnesses to same.

IV   Any colored soldier or employee, found with deadly weapons upon his person, either in or out of the Camp, except such as are furnished by the Government, will be arrested, and such arms taken from him, and no soldier, except when on duty, will be permitted to take his arms and accoutrements beyond the limits of the camp.

V   All officers will be required to see that the last provision of this order is strictly enforced

This order will be read to each Colored Regiment, on Dress Parade.

By Command of Brig Gen S S. Fry
[*No signature.*]   Lt. & A.A.A.G[1]

1. General Orders No. 10, 23 July 1864; Vol. 111/256, pp. 66, 67; General Orders; RG 393.

Lexington, Ky., July 24, 1864.

Hon. E.M. Stanton, Secretary of War:

Colonel Brisbin,[1] appointed for a colored regiment, has reported to General Burbridge. I am forbidden to organize any colored cavalry regiments, but General Burbridge desires to have two such regiments, to be placed under the command of Colonel Brisbin. His plans to mount such regiments are, to take horses in the country, and give certificates stating that if the owners of the animals continue to be perfectly loyal to the end of the war they may receive compensation, provided the Government so determines. Am I authorized to raise these two regiments, as desired by General Burbridge? I leave for Louisvile the 26th instant.

L. Thomas.[2]

1. James Sanks Brisbin (1837–1892), well known as an anti-slavery orator, he became captain of the Sixth U.S. Cavalry in 1861. On March 1, 1864, he was named colonel of the Fifth U.S. Colored Cavalry, after which he served on recruiting duty in Kentucky and acted as General Burbridge's chief of staff. He was promoted to the rank of brigadier-general on May 1, 1865. *ANB; CWD; GIB; HR,* 1:246; *OAR,* 8:145–46.
2. Thomas to Stanton, 24 July 1864, *OR,* 3, 4, 542.

[*Excerpt from the memoirs of Peter Bruner.*]

. . . The next morning about five o'clock I got up and started for Camp Nelson, which was forty-one miles from Irvin[e]. And at eleven o'clock I had gone twenty-one miles and had arrived at Richmond. After I had left Richmond I came upon sixteen colored fellows who were on their way to Camp Nelson and of course I did not get lonesome. I had plenty of company. Just a half hour before sun down we arrived at Camp Nelson and had come forty-one miles in that day. The officers asked me what I wanted there and I told them that I came there to fight the rebels and that I wanted a gun. . . . After I had been there about a week they made up a regiment and called it the Twelfth U.S. Heavy Artillery.

I was enrolled on the twenty-fifth day of July in 1864 to serve three years or during the war, but I only remained two years and a half.

We started from Camp Nelson and marched eighteen miles that day and the dust was about four inches and my readers well know what nice walking it is when the dust is so very deep. When we got into the camp two or three dozen men fell out with the blind staggers, and I was in the midst of these unfortunate men.[1]

1. Bruner, 42, 43. Bruner had tried unsuccessfully to run away from slavery many times before he finally succeeded. He had run away to Camp Nelson once before, but the first time he arrived there he was told "they did not want any darkies, that this was a white man's war"; the second time, when he was nineteen, he was luckier, as narrated above.

Washington, D.C., July 26, 1864.

General L. Thomas:
    The Secretary of War and General Grant both disapprove the raising of any more cavalry regiments. If General Burbridge levies horses in Kentucky they should be used for the cavalry we now have.

H.W. Halleck, Major-General and Chief of Staff.

(Copy to General S.G. Burbridge.)[1]

1. Halleck to Thomas, 26 July 1864, *OR,* 3, 4, 549.

Louisville, Ky., July 28, 1864. (Received 12 p.m.)

Hon. E.M. Stanton:

General Burbridge has earnestly asked for authority to mount two colored regiments, the horses to be seized from citizens of known disloyalty. General Thomas has reported to you fully, favorably on the application. It is most important that this authority should be given, and promptly. These regiments, composed of men almost raised, as it were, on horseback, of uncompromising loyalty, and having an intimate knowledge of the topography of the country, would prove a powerful instrumentality in ridding the State of those guerrilla bands of robbers and murderers which now infest and oppress almost every part of it. Besides, their presence in the different counties engaged in this popular service would exert the happiest influence in favor of the Government policy of employing colored troops.

J. Holt.[1]

1. Holt to Stanton, 28 July 1846, *OR*, 1, 39, pt. 2, 208. Joseph Holt (1807–1894), a native of Kentucky, had been secretary of war from January 18 to March 5, 1861. In 1862 he was appointed Judge Advocate General, and in 1864 he was promoted to brigadier general and appointed first head of the new Bureau of Military Justice; *CWD; GIB; HR,* 1:539; *KE,* 438.

War Department, Washington City, July 28, 1864.

Major-General Burbridge, Lexington, Ky.:

You are authorized to raise two regiments of colored cavalry, to be mounted if you can mount them from horses procured in Kentucky by seizure, giving certificates of payment, payable at the end of the war, to all loyal persons who shall continue to remain loyal during the war. The price not to exceed that paid for horses by the purchasing officers of the Government in Kentucky.

E.M. Stanton, Secretary of War.[1]

1. Stanton to Burbridge, 28 July 1864, *OR,* 3, 4, 557.

**U S. Mil. Tel.   July 30ᵗʰ 1864   By Telegraph from Camp Burnside
To Lt G.A. Hanaford**

Some negroes in Govt employ here on last friday night got some arms & went out of Camp to rescue a negroe woman from her owner. They did not find the woman or her owner & came back   What shall I do with them. Answer

John G Eve[1]   Col Comdg.[2]

1. John G. Eve was enrolled and mustered in as colonel of the Forty-Ninth Kentucky Infantry on December 22, 1863, at Camp Burnside. *OAR,* 4:1294; *RAGK.*
2. Eve to Hanaford, 30 July 1864; Vol. 112/258, p. 40; Telegrams; RG 393. This incident was not an isolated one; a couple of weeks earlier a man named William Abbart had been arrested for taking "a girl to Camp . . . in boys cloths." B.J. Livingston (A.A.C. Chief, U.S. Police) to Hanaford, 12 July 1864; Vol. 112/258, p. 27; Telegrams; RG 393.

Camp Nelson   July 30 1864
Col. J G Eve   Camp Burnsides

If you have any balls and chains put them on the negroes and make work with them on the Severest labor you can put them at. I do not know but it would be a good idea to [*have*] one of them court martialed and Shot. as an example to others

By Order of Brig Gen S S Fry

[*Signed.*] Geo A Hanaford   Lt & A A A G[1]

1. Hanaford to Eve, 30 July 1864; Vol. 112/258, p. 139; Telegrams; RG 393.

Saint Louis, July 31, 1864
Hon. E.M. Stanton, Secretary of War

Dear Sir, * * * *

The recruiting of colored troops in Kentucky is proceeding most satisfactorily. About 10,000 have already been enlisted, and this number, it is believed, will be doubled in sixty days. They have for some time been coming in at the rate of about 100 per day. When we consider the perils and menaces which these down trodden men have to brave in making their way to the recruiting stations we cannot but regard the example of their courage, and loyalty, and zeal as among the noblest and most cheering signs of the times. The commencement of the recruiting of colored troops in Kentucky was signalized by disgraceful outrages perpetrated in the twin and, it would seem, inseparable interests of treason and slavery. Slaves escaping from their masters with a view of entering the military service were waylaid, beaten, maimed, and often murdered. This shameful condition of things, however, has disappeared under an improved public sentiment, and from the vigor and success with which the Government has continued to press its policy. The popular opinion is rapidly reaching the conclusion that the policy of recruiting colored troops is too firmly established to be resisted, and that it is the interest, as it is certainly the duty, of Kentucky to acquiesce in it. The feeble opposition which still remains is fostered mainly by unscrupulous politicians who hope to make out of this popular irritation a certain amount of political capital to be invested in the approaching Presidential election. Upon the whole, the recruiting of colored troops in Kentucky must be held to be a decided success thus far, and to be full of encouragment for the future. . . . *

J. Holt.[1]

1. Holt to Stanton, 31 July 1864, *OR*, 1, 39, pt. 2, 212, 213, 214.

Camp Nelson Ky   Aug 1st /64

Dear Bro Jocelyn
* * * * [*One paragraph.*]
Sixteen hundred men have gone from here — more than that now here.

1. What do you mean by "books enough to start the school   form classes"   Did you mean only enough for one class to recite in? I suppose not. I suppose every one who will attend the school ought to have a copy of the primer & then when sufficiently advanced give him a reader. Is this your mind?

I have from Louisville 52 slates copy books in abundance for this regiment — envelopes & some paper

I have one box of clothing from Cincinnati   Most of it for men winter clothing at that

We need undergarments for women & children   not many of them now in camp — most have gone home

I have much encouragement from the officials here so far as consent approbation & orders are concerned. Their presence I do not expect — Capt Hall proposes to attend the night school

There has been much interruption in the instruction of the regiment that has gone off — by extra duty.

I commence this morning with the 116 Regiment.

Bro Vetters came last evening from Oberlin   He proposes to go as chaplain to the regiment.

I think he is a good man is quite fast, would be considered by some as self consequential * * * * [Six paragraphs.]

Last evening I spoke in the convalescent Camp, set forth reasons for laboring with these colored men, great interest manifested. Thirteen men came forward and offered their services on detailed duty — The meeting was a great success — Their were two principal surgeons present. They came forward and gave their cooperation. With Bro Vitters at one end of the building & I at the other with our assistants we shall be able to have a very effective school — I shall strive for another principal. I cannot teach preach superintend correspond & write articles.

I expect another teacher

I am now enrolling grading & arranging — When convalescents are detailed and do work of this kind they expect some pay additional

I have had one man a citizen helping me   I promised him some pay — This was necessary in order to get anything like adequate instruction to that regiment that was going off.

And this arrangement of securing detailed men is the cheapest way by which to impart the same amt of instruction — The work here is flourishing. These helps we can dismiss at any time — when not needed

Shall I have privilege to so employ help   Tis best can see   The officers offer half of their non commisioned officers forenoon & half afternoon — We hope to make a nice success this week. There are some other small expenses. If you approve you will send me a Draft to be <u>thus</u> expended & I will report all

We have a new good room 80 feet by 30 for a school room   Such facilities in central Ky — the best camp in the state I feel ought to be improved[1]

John G Fee[2]

1. By "to be improved," Fee means "to be employed"; such usage of the word *improve* is now considered archaic.
2. Fee to Jocelyn, 1 Aug. 1864, AMAA 44013–4.

Head Qr^s Camp Nelson Ky   Jessamine Co Ky   August 2^d 1864
General Orders N° 12

The President of the United States by a public Proclamation having appointed the 4th day of August 1864 as a day of humiliation and prayer, and having earnestly invited and requested the heads of Executive Departments of the Government, together with all the Legislators, all Judges and Magistrates; and all other persons exercising authority in the land, whether Civil, military or naval, and all soldiers, seamen and marines in the national service, and all other loyal and law abiding people to assemble in their preferred places of worship on that day and there to render to the Almighty and merciful Ruler of the Universe such homage and such confessions as the Congress of the United States have so earnestly and reverently recommended.

It is therefore earnestly recommended by the Genl Comdg that all places of business within the limits of this Camp be closed on that day; and that all persons, Officers, Soldiers and Civillians in any way connected with the Same, in accordance with Same Proclamation: assemble at such place as may be designated by the chaplain and there render to the Almighty God such homage and such confessions of their Sins as are due from the creature to the Creator and to implore his blessing upon our beloved Country in its day of darkness and peril, that its integrity and Union may be preserved that its armies may be shielded and protected, that success may crown their labors, that its ennemies may be convinced of their error, and that the banner of peace may soon spread over the land.

By command of Brig. Genl S.S. Fry
(Sgd) Geo A Hanaford   Lt and A.A.A.G[1]

1. General Orders No. 12, 2 Aug. 1864; Vol. 111/256, p. 70; General Orders; RG 393.

2 Aug 1864
General Orders N° 13
Discharge of firearms again since an earlier order has been ignored

It is therefore ordered, that hereafter firearms wether in the possession of an officer, soldier, Govt employee or citizen, shall be discharged only between the hours of 2 and 3 o'clock P.M. each day, and at no other time.

A target will be erected by Lieut. James F. Merrill,[1] Actg. Ordn. Officer, in the vicinity of his Depot and any person desirous of practicing, will confine himself to the grounds so designated.[2]

1. Lt. James Flint Merrill claimed Boston as his residence, but served in the Rhode Island Seventh Infantry. Civil War Archive at Ancestry.com.
2. General Orders No. 13, 2 Aug. 1864; Vol. 111/256, p. 71; General Orders; RG 393.

U S. Mil. Tel.   Aug 8th /64 —
By Tel. from Camp Burnside
To Lt. Geo A Hanaford A.A.A.G

Will you please inform me to whom rations at this Post can be issued. There are a large number of destitute and starving families of soldiers & Refugees from East Tenn — who have no money — provisions or friends. They will certainly starve unless assisted by the Govt.

A J. Hogan[1]   Major   Comdg Post[2]

1. Andrew J. Hogan, major of 114th U.S.C.I., was mustered in at Camp Nelson on July 6, 1864; by August 1864 he was commanding the post at Camp (or Point) Burnside. *OAR,* 8:295; *RAGK.*
2. Hogan to Hanaford, 8 Aug. 1864; Vol. 112/258, p. 45; Telegrams; RG 393.

U.S. Mil. Tel.   Aug. 8, 1864
By Tel from Lexington to Brig Gen. S S. Fry.

Your letter is rec[d]. Put all suitable negroes in Camp Nelson except Mechanics into the service.

S.G. Burbridge   Brt. Maj. Gen[1]

1. Burbridge to Fry, 8 Aug. 1864; Vol. 112/258, p. 458; Telegrams; RG 393.

Hd. Qrs. Camp Nelson Ky.   Aug 8th 1864
Capt J S Butler[1]   Asst. Adjt Gen   Lexington, Ky.

A lady is here from Tazwell Tenn. Refugee.   Desires transportation there — family able to support her   Can transportation be furnished by way Chattanooga?

Speed S. Fry   B.G.[2]

1. John S. Butler had been a sergeant major in the Thirteenth Kentucky Infantry. *HR,* 1:269.
2. Fry to Butler, 8 Aug. 1864; Vol. 112/258, p. 144; Telegrams; RG 393.

[*Letterhead.*][1] *U.S. Sanitary Commission*   Camp Nelson Ky   Aug 8, 1864

Dear Bro Jocelyn   I am now in my sixth week of missionary labor among the freedmen in this Camp. Some sixteen hundred armed colored men have been sent out of this camp to other places. The arrivals of new recruits are not so numerous as at first   Masters hold on to their slaves as Pharaoh did to his bondsmen   The masters now threaten their slaves with what the rebels will do when they come into Ky as now into Maryland   Some masters use personal violence; and others offer bribes
    Perhaps recruiting companies of armed men, will be the only means of releas-

ing these slaves   There are yet in the state, this day, from twenty to thirty thousand able bodied men, who would now gladly rush to the help of the government was it not for the restraints of slavery.

How plainly was, and now is it necessary for a proclamation of freedom throughout all the land.

We are now bestowing more labor upon one regiment now here — endeavoring, if possible, to have every non commissioned officer able to read and write intelligibly

We shall instruct many of the privates. We did the same for a previous regiment — far as possible

We have a very excellent school room — a good supply of slates books &c   Some eight days since at evening I preached in the convalescent camp — In the discourse gave reasons why I was laboring to instruct these colored men. I called for helpers. Thirteen men came forward volunteered their help. The same evening Bro Vetters came from Oberlin This supplied the school at once with teachers — we found a majority of them good teachers.

Never have I been so intensely interested[2]   Here are thousands of noble men, made in the image of God, just emerging from the ~~ignorance~~ restraints of slavery into the liberties and responsibilities of free men, and of soldiers. I find them manifesting an almost universal desire to learn; and that they do make rapid progress.

On last Saturday evening, whilst addressing the non commissioned officers present, I asked the professing christians present, to raise their right hands. Little more than half were of that class   I again briefly addressed all present. After this Bro Vitters asked how many are there present who are not christians, and who wish the prayers of Gods people. Twelve raised the right hand.

When we consider that this people have great physical strength, are manifestly capable of rapid intellectual developement, that they are humble, grateful, trusting, religiously inclined — that they are destined to occupy an important place in the army and agriculture of this nation, I feel that it is blessed to labor with such a people. The Lord help

Last Thursday was, as you know, the day set apart for National humiliation and prayer. The commandant here ordered all business stopped, and that the day to be observed. By arrangement of others I preached the sermon. The audience was large, composed of white and black — soldiers and citizens all quiet and attentive

God by his word and his providence is working glorious changes   "The morning light is breaking" May the christian world be ready for the rapid developements   Yours in Christ

John G Fee

Private

I [*have*] no answer from you as to the paying of these helpers — the cheapest we can get — they are good helpers — their hearts in it — no expense of trav-

eling — here at any hour — rations & shelter already prepared — say pay two dollars per week * * * * [*One paragraph.*]
Private   Aug 9
    P S
    I had the misfortune to have twenty dollars stolen from me last Monday — and just yesterday while my mind was much engrossed in writing two letters concerning Military officers here, and in changing pantaloons I left my pockett book in the pantaloon. Whilst I was at the school room this money was taken   At the school room I thought of the pocket book came to my room examined & found the money gone — First I have ever had stolen

J G Fee

* * * * [*Three paragraphs.*]
    I have labored very hard here in six weeks no rest — not a single day   The work I regard as very important. These ex slaves are the brightest of this nation. There is one man[3] here of wonderful preaching talent — meek gentle, childlike — I had him detailed for our school room. I teach him[4]

1. Plain letterhead stationery with no motto, only the title of the organization.
2. In nineteenth-century usage, "interested" means religiously stimulated or moved spiritually.
3. The man Fee refers to is Gabriel Burdett.
4. Fee to Jocelyn, 8 Aug. 1864, AMAA 44016–9.

Head Qr⁵ Camp Nelson   August 9th 1864
General Orders N° 19

    The General Commanding orders that all negro women and children, old and infirm, negro men unfit for any military duty who have voluntarily come into Camp, be at once sent beyond the lines with instructions not to return.
    The officer of the day is ordered to see that none of the above named class of negroes are permitted to pass thro' the lines into Camp and will so instruct the guards each morning when posted at their respective stations. He is also directed to remove all who may in future get into Camp.
    Col. T.D. Sedgewick is charged with the execution of this order so far as it relates to the removal of those now in Camp, and he will see that it is strictly enforced.

By Command of Brig Genl S.S. Fry
(Sgd) Geo A Hanaford   Lt and A.A.A.G[1]

1. General Orders No. 14, 9 Aug. 1864; Vol. 111/256, p. 73; General Orders; RG 393.

U S. Mil. Tel.   Aug. 13, 1864   By Tel. from Lexington
To Brig. Gen. S.S. Fry

    Maj. Gen. Burbridge directs under the acts of Congress and orders from the

War Dept that all women children & men unemployed in Camp Nelson be expelled   No citizen under any circumstances will be allowed to leave the main road or go through the Camp to look for negroes or on any pretext —

by order of Maj Gen Burbridge
J.H. Hamilton A.A.G.[1]

1. Hamilton to Fry, 13 Aug. 1864; Vol. 112/258, p. 46; Telegrams; RG 393.

Head Quarters Camp Nelson, Ky. August 13th 1864
General Orders No. 17

The General Commanding orders that no citizens will be permitted under any pretext to pass through the camp for the purpose of hunting their slaves who have escaped.

Those having slaves in the camp desirous to know their condition or the position they occupy in camp will make their request in writing through the Post Office

By Command of Brig Gen[l] Fry
[No signature.]   Lt. & A.A.A.G[1]

1. General Orders No. 17, 13 Aug. 1864; Vol. 111/256, p. 76; General Orders; RG 393.

Head Quarters   Camp Nelson Ky   Aug 15" 1864

Lieut   In order to enforce the orders relative to expelling women from Camp &c it will be necessary to Employ a Squad of Cavarly and would request the Provost Guard to the number of Twenty (20) be sent immediately to these Hd Qurs also that you send one (1) led horse Eqiped with the Squad. *

Thos D. Sedgewick   Col. Suppt. U S C Troops[1]

1. Sedgewick to Lieutenant ?, 15 Aug. 1864; Vol. 237/577, p. 147; Register of Letters Received and Endorsements Sent, Nov. 1863-Nov. 1865, Entry 1662; Camp Nelson, Ky., 1863–65, Part 4; RG 393.

[Letterhead.][1] U.S. Sanitary Commission Camp Nelson, Ky   Aug 16 1864

Dear Bro Strieby[2]
      * * * * [One paragraph.]
      I do not know what it is to take vacation have worked to exhaustion all this hot season and rejoice to do so & will do so God being my helper — nothing shall stop me * * * * [Three paragraphs.]
      I am shure this is a good work here — the best camp in Ky — more here — central & official favorable to our efforts. Perhaps few exslaves equal to these in every respect for good [The] men instructed have made astonishing progress
      This place may become a permanent school of instruction for the state even

when the war is over   if not I purpose to gather more sympathy & young men for our school at Berea

Friends abroad manifest great interest in this movement here   I believe it will be influential. I wish to do what I can to have it such   The Aid Society at Cincinnati have offered to take over, organize here & sustain a corpse of teachers   I have told them what is true and what I purposed to do That the school is <u>already</u> organized & many teachers employed * * * * [*Two paragraphs.*]

. . . When regiments are liable to go within two or three weeks time, it is very desirable to act <u>immediately</u> — organize a school in the regiment — grade at least the non commissioned officers & place these at once under teachers & teach these to help others in the regiment * * * * [*One paragraph.*]

Many doors are opening for me to preach in the camp & around   This I suppose I must now do   I have done what I proposed to do organize and start the school   Tell Bro Whipple[3] this has been before my mind for more than a year and tell him this was the reason why I did not wish to engage elsewhere   I felt God had a work here for me and I desired to step into the first open door and to keep myself <u>where</u> I could watch for this first open door * * * * [*Nine paragraphs.*]

John G Fee[4]

1. Now the words "Camp Nelson" are part of the printed letterhead.
2. Michael E. Strieby was an officer in the AMA.
3. Rev. George Whipple (1805–1867) was born and died in New York, but he received his education at Lane Theological Seminary and Oberlin College, where he was one of the founding students. He served as secretary of the AMA from 1847 through 1876, and he was editor of the *American Missionary.* Sears, *Berea Connections,* 157; Swint, 169.
3. Fee to Strieby, 16 Aug. 1864, AMAA 44021–2.

Head Quarters   U.S. Col'd Cavalry   Lexington Ky   Aug. 20 1864
To Capt J. Bates Dickson   Col and Sup't Organizing Col'd Cavalry

Captain   I have the honor to inform you that the mustering officer of Camp Nelson says he has no official knowledge of any Colored Cavalry Organization in this state and that he must have an order from you to muster into cavalry   I have two full companies at Camp Nelson waiting muster and I respectfully request you will Telegraph him the required order. Please instruct him in future to muster in Cavalry Companies I present for muster and officially inform him that I am charged with the duty of organizing Colored Cavalry Reg'ts to be designated hereafter. In the case of the Company transferred from the 108th U.S. Colored Infantry to Cavalry, the Mustering Officer requests a copy of the authority of transfer *

[*Unsigned.*][1]

1. Unsigned letter to Dickson, 20 Aug. 1864; [Bound] Vol. 5, Book 88, p. 7; Letters and Telegrams Sent and Received, Organization of U.S.C.T., Entry 2246; Department of Kentucky, Part 1; RG 393.

U.S. Mil. Tel.   Aug. 21. 1864   By Tel. from Hd. Qrs. Lexington
To Brig Gen S.S. Fry

Mr. Alex Brand has a black boy named Cook Scott in the employment of Capt. Black at Camp Nelson   He wishes to enlist him — Have the Pro. Mar. put him in the service at once together with all other stragglers   furnish him a guard to hunt them up

(Sgd) S.G. Burbridge   Bvt. Maj. Gen Comdg[1]

1. Burbridge to Fry, 21 Aug. 1864; Vol. 112/258, p. 49; Telegrams; RG 393.

Camp Nelson, Ky. Aug. 21, 1864
Capt J Bates Dickson   Lexington Ky

I have no H. A [*Heavy Artillery*] ready recruits have almost stopped coming in and I had to depend on the camp I gathered up all, and out of over 500 examined last week more than one half were rejected. I formed one Co. Cavalry (100 men) and have 136 mustered for H.A. I can get no more men in Camp. Will have to wait on recruits. Am disappointed but will keep doing my utmost

(Sgd) Thos. D Sedgewick   Col &c.
(Sgd) Speed S. Fry   B.G.[1]

1. Fry & Sedgewick to Dickson, 21 Aug. 1864; Vol. 112/258, p. 149; Telegrams; RG 393.

[Peter Bruner, former slave, described some of the experiences of his black regiment, sent out on a recruiting trip:]

One day while about eighteen miles from home recruiting we came to two or three large plantations. There were a great many colored people on them and as soon as they saw us they ran. We started after them and succeeded in capturing about 15 of the men. We started with our men and camped out at the foot of a hill and commenced to get supper when we were fired on by the rebels. This scared the recruits so bad we had gotten that they ran again. After this skirmish with the rebels, we coming out victorious, we caught our recruits and took them to camp. They cried, some of them, like babies and we had to let them go. "They had no time for war."

Their masters when they found out where they were, came after them. Instead of giving them up we would keep them as prisoners and make them carry water. We have often had as high as twenty masters' prisoners, who came after their slaves (who came to us for protection). At one time we sent away five hundred men, women and children to Camp Nelson.[1]

1. Bruner, 45–46.

Head Quarters, Camp Nelson, Ky. Jessamine Co. Ky. Aug. 23" 1864
General Orders No. 19.

All negro women in this Camp except those from Tennessee and other States South of Kentucky will at once be expelled from Camp.

All Officers having any negro women in their Employment, will deliver them up to the Patrol to be brought to these Head Quarters

This order will be rigidly enforced and any one attempting to evade it, will be arrested and punished for violation of orders.

By Command of Brig Gen. S.S. Fry

[*No signature.*]   Lt. and A.A.A.G[1]

1. General Orders No. 19, 23 Aug. 1864; Vol. 111/256, p. 78; General Orders; RG 393.

Head Qrs. Camp Nelson, Ky.   Jessamine Co.   Aug. 24, 1864
Orders

Information having reached these Head Quarters that the guard at the Bridge and other points around were in the habit of receiving bribes from negro women to permit them to come into Camp It is therefore ordered that any sentinel found guilty of so gross a violation of orders in future shall be severely dealt with

The Officer of the Day is especially charged to instruct his sentinels each morning when posting them not to allow women and children to enter the camp and he will be held responsible for the faithful execution of this order.

By Command of Brig Gen S.S. Fry

[*No signature.*]   Lieut. and A.A.A.G[1]

1. Orders, 24 Aug. 1864; Vol. 111/256, p. 79; General Orders; RG 393.

Camp Nelson Ky Aug. 27th /64

Rev. George Whipple Dear Bro., After numerous delays we [*William L. Lowrey and his brother John B.*] arrived at Camp Nelson Aug 19th. We missed our connections almost all the way through to Nicholasville from Pittsburg. We were obliged to wait 11 hours before we could get our seats in the cars. after starting the train the car ahead of us ran off the track and were obliged to wait 3 hours more. At Cincinnatti we stayed all night. You readily see that we had not only a tedious but expensive ride considering the distance we travled. Since we came I have busied myself teaching in the school attending meetings evenings & Sabbath. Last Sunday evening I preached to the Colored Soldiers in the school room. We had a large and attentive congregation. Tuesday evening I preaching to White soldiers at the Soldiers home, similar and improving, we intend however to concentrate our labors upon the colored troops. There seems to be a healthy religious influence pervading the bodies of colored troops quartered here. They hold their prayer and praise meetings almost every evening under the immediate direction of their own preachers. But few men attend our school now on account of having to drill several hours extra each day.

We expect large numbers of new recruits at the Camp soon which will give us all the employment we desire. As it is, we find this a good field for labor, as the men enlisted here will probably be sent to distant places in the south. Pray for us.

W^m L Lowrey

* * * * [List of Lowrey's travel expenses.]
We do not draw rations yet as our quarters are not quite ready yet so we have to board at the soldiers home for the present. . . .[1]

1. Lowrey to Whipple, 27 Aug. 1864, AMAA 44025.

[From an article by Rev. John A.R. Rogers.]

I have just returned from a visit to Camp Nelson and Berea, greatly cheered by what I saw. At Camp Nelson I found Brothers Fee and Vetter, and their thirteen volunteer assistants, teaching the colored troops. The teachableness of the colored soldiers, their eagerness to learn, and their rapid progress, were alike surprising and gratifying. I have never seen more rapid progress made by anyone than by them. From what I saw and learned of the white and colored population of Kentucky, I was led to feel that the future progress of Christianity and all that is good depended in this State as much upon the black race as the white. I have been tardily led to this conclusion, for which, if I had time, I should be glad to give you my reasons. "The last shall be first, and the first last." God often chooses the weak things of the world to confound the mighty. I can but think that the black men to whom Brother Fee preaches there—and he preaches to not a few of either the black or white race—are destined to exert a great influence. Colored soldiers will be leaders among colored men.[1]

1. Excerpt from a letter from Rogers to the Secretaries of the AMA, 27 Aug. 1864, AMAA 111091, which is also printed in *AM* 8, no. 11 (Nov. 1864): 263. An early coworker with Fee at Berea, Rogers was in exile from Kentucky at the time of this visit, writing from Decatur, Ohio. All the founders of Berea had been banned from the state by irate local slaveholders in December 1859.

[Letterhead.] United States Sanitary Commission   Camp Nelson Ky Aug 29 /64

Dear Bro Strieby
* * * * [Expense account.]
We had sent us from Cincinnati at my request a magnificent Bell for church & school purposes. The friends their paid for it — $115.00   I paid the freight — 4.60 * * * * [One paragraph.]

We expect large accessions of troops next week — Time has nearly come for me to go home to attend to the interests of the school and church at Berea. I do not see that I can leave here   Doors are opening all over the Camp for me to preach — This is opening for me a door over the state where these soldiers (white & black) shall go. I greatly rejoice in this & thank god for being. Yours in haste

John G Fee[1]

1. Fee to Strieby, 29 Aug. 1864, AMAA 44030.

Aug. 31, 1864   By Tel. from Lexington
To Brig Gen. Fry

The Rail-Road has been instructed to pass persons on your authority in the case of negroes from other States. You will mention the fact that they are Refugees and entitled to the benefit of the Presidents Emancipation Proclamation   the other matter of impressing negroes will be looked into and reported

By order of the Genl R Vane P.M.G.[1]

1. Vane to Fry, 31 Aug. 1864; Vol. 112/258, p. 54; Telegrams; RG 393.

Head Quarters Camp Nelson, Ky. Sept 1" 1864
General Orders No 21

In accordance with recent instructions from Head Quarters Dist of Ky. all negro men from other states than Kentucky, including Tennessee who are or may come within the limits of this Camp are subject to enlistment in the U.S. military service and

It is therefore ordered that all Officers and Chiefs of Departments of this Post at once report to Col Tho⁵ D. Sedgewick C.O. U.S.C.T. all of the above class of negroes in their employ that they may be examined and, if able bodied, enlisted in the service of the United States.

By Command of Brig Genl. S.S. Fry
[*No signature.*]   Lieut. and A.A.A.G[1]

1. General Orders No. 21, 1 Sept. 1864; Vol. 111/256, p. 83; General Orders; RG 393.

Head Quarters Camp Nelson Ky.   Sept. 3" 1864
Orders.

A sufficient number of men will be detached to guard all the inlets to the Camp and the officer of the day will see that they are properly stationed.

Guards will be stationed at all the openings in the fortifications, at the old road leading down to the hill on Hickman creek and instructions will be given to the Sentinels not to allow negro women and children or lewd white women to enter the Camp.

Soldiers will not be permitted to pass outside the lines at any other points than at the bridge and on the road leading to Nicholasville, except when sent out on duty, or by special permit. Any soldier whilst on duty as a sentinel, who shall permit any of the persons above mentioned to enter the Camp without authority to do so will, at once, be arrested and punished.

By Command of Brig. Gen. S.S. Fry

[*No signature.*]   Lieut. and A.A.A.G[1]

1. Orders, 3 Sept. 1864; Vol. 111/256, p. 84; General Orders; RG 393.

Head Quarters U.S.C. Cav   Lexington Ky   Sept 6" 1864
To Capt Thos H Moore   P.M.   7th Dist Ky

Captain   I have the honor to request that you will have the recruits in Barracks No. 1. ready to go to Camp Nelson to morrow at 11 a.m. I will send an officer to take charge of them.

Lieut Becraft turned in ten recruits at Barracks No 1 yesterday and I would not if I were you enlist any more at this place but send them all to Camp Nelson where Col. Sedgewick is charged with that duty and has but little to do. *

[*Unsigned.*] Col and Supt Orgn U.S.C. Cav[1]

1. Unsigned to Moore, 6 Sept. 1864; [Bound] Vol. 5, Book 88, p. 27; Letters and Telegrams Sent & Received, Organization of U.S.C.T., Entry 2246; Department of Ky., Part 1; RG 393.

[*Letterhead.*] *Head-Quarters District of Kentucky, Lexington.* Sept. 13, *1864*.
Capt. J.S. Butler   A.A.G.

Captain — I would respectfully suggest that as fast as the different command draw their horses they should be ordered to Camp Nelson to have them shod. My facilities for blacksmithing are very limited indeed — having barely force enough to keep in condition my post teams and wagons.

At Camp Nelson there are extensive shops, and plenty of workmen and if sent there no delay will be caused to the intended expedition for want of having the horses shod. *

Thomas D. Fitch, Capt. & A.Q.M.[1]

1. Fitch to Butler, 13 Sept. 1864; Entry 1030; Part 2; RG 393.

Hd Quarters Camp Nelson Ky   September 16" 1864
General Orders No 23

All negro women and children, except those who have written permits from these Head Qurs, to remain within the limits of this Camp, will be expelled from Camp on Monday Sept. 19 "64

Lieut Walter Thorn, comdg Patrol Guard is charged with the prompt execution of this Order, and Officers who have any of the above class of persons in their

Employ, are directed to deliver them up to the Patrol Guard, to be brought to these Hd Quarters.

By Order of Col Thos D Sedgewick   Commanding

[*No signature.*]   Lt & A A A Genl[1]

1. General Orders No. 23, 16 Sept. 1864; Vol. 111/256, p. 87; General Orders; RG 393.

Camp Nelson Ky   Sept 22 /64

Dear Bro Strieby

* * * * [*Six paragraphs.*]

A Government Camp for Wives of Soldiers & other refugees

I feel that such a camp is needed. For months the officials here have tried the experiment of sending the women out of camp   Like flies they soon come back — many do

1 Tis hard to see the wife of a soldier driven back to a cruel master

2 Colored women like white women are sometimes vile — dissolute — If we should find many of them so twould not be strange   These if in camp having no other shelter when night comes on they seek the tents karalls — places where they are annoyed exposed & where the vile corrupt others

3 These women could be made useful in doing work for the government and soldiers.

Capt Hall could now give them 150,000 such to renovate &c

I went yesterday to see Capt Hall   He heartily concurs in the plan of having a department within this camp — 11 square miles — so I am informed —

He asked me to prepare a letter for Sect Stanton and he would endorse it   I propose to send it thro Sect Chase   I wish Bro Whipple to at once write me on this subject — give me his opinion — any suggestions he may deem wise

N B Shall I pledge the Am Miss Association to the support of the needed aid of instructors — clothing &c — May be the government will furnish all — may be we will have to furnish a matron

We might have here a field where the reform societies of Cincinnati & Boston would like to cooperate

We propose to have all who shall come as refugees go into that department & not be allowed to come out only at certain hours & then only by permits & for specific purposes. We have not had from you any books as yet —

John G. Fee[1]

1. Fee to Strieby, 22 Sept. 1864, AMAA 44038.

Cincinnati O. Sept 28th 1864.

Transmits memorial of Rev. J.G. Fee and associates. commission of American Missionary society at Camp Nelson, Ky requesting the establishment of a special department for the benefit of female refugees.

Oct 17th [*1864*]   Chase, Hon S.P.[1] (47) [*Number of file.*]   (From Off. Insp. Genl)   Ret'd to Adj't Genl.[2]

1. Salmon Portland Chase (1808–1873), best-known as Lincoln's Secretary of the Treasury, had an extreme anti-slavery viewpoint that made him very sympathetic to reformers like Fee. Known as the "attorney-general for runaway slaves," Chase actively supported many benevolent associations, such as the AMA, and he himself was president of one—the American Freedmen's Union Commission. *CWD;* Swint, 148.

2. Record of receipt and transmission of Fee's request for a Refugee Home, 28 Sept. 1864; Vol. 28, p. 55; Register of Letters Received, Jan. 1864-Mar. 1869, Entry 2172 [Part 9 of 9]; General Records, Department of Kentucky, Part 1; RG 393.

Camp Nelson, Oct. 1st, 1864

D[r] Sir, There are a number of Colored persons, probably from 50 to 100, in and around Camp Nelson, without the consent or approval of their Masters who live in Madison County Ky, and it is the desire of their owners (expressed in a Public Meeting held in Richmond, Ky.) That said persons be enlisted as soldiers in the United States Service, that the County have the proper credit.

My object is to get your assistance, Capt., in having all such persons properly enlisted as above intimated. *

John Bennett

P.S. I understand that there are a number of s[d] persons, in one Capt. Day[s] Employ preparatory to starting South with stock or a train. And there are some employed by other persons.

Jno. Bennett, Agt.[1]

1. John Bennett, agent for Madison County, Kentucky, slaveholders to the mustering officer at Camp Nelson, Kentucky, in *The Destruction of Slavery*, 607.

Camp Nelson Ky   Oct 1st 1864

Dear brother Strieby   I have now been here about a week. I was delayed some two days by the loss of my trunk at Cincinnatti. This also delayed aded a little to my expenses in coming here.

I found brother Fee absent   I am occupying his room. He will be back again next week   What is to be my particular work here I cannot tell till he returns   In the meantime I am employing my time, preaching in the camp and teaching in the School. This School I think is of great importance. The freed-men, children and women too are eager to learn. I have large attentive audiences to preach to, they seem impressable and we can but hope that the seed sown will bring forth good fruit   I find a number of ministers here seeking place and pay from the government. As to the labor of preaching they seem quite willing I should do <u>that</u>.

When I am more settled I will give you further account of this place and the work here. The work here might, and <u>ought</u> to be made to exert a saving moral influence upon the whole State of Kentucky. This I hope we shall all deeply feel. One thing however we must not forget. If McClellan is elected in Nov. our cause is lost in this State, anarchy will reign here and we shall have to pack and leave. I tell you, brother, Slavery here is hoping for a resurrection in Nov. May God in mercy disappoint them * * * * [*Expense account.*]

If you wish a minute description of this place, topography, geography &c. I will give it —

Any line or word of direction will always be gratefully received   My regards to your colaborers   *

A. Scofield[1]

1. Scofield to Strieby, 1 Oct. 1864, AMAA 44040. Rev. Abisha Scofield, born October 27, 1805, in Greenwich, Connecticut, the son of David Scofield and Clara Newman. He married Ann Janet [Jeanette] Marvin on April 3, 1844, in Colchester, Connecticut, and became father of Frank Marvin, Elizabeth, Laura, Gerrit Smith (born 1847), Harriet ("Hattie") (born 1849), and Mary Scofield (born 1851). From 1850 to 1860 he lived in New York, where he became a friend of the famous abolitionist Gerrit Smith. Eventually, his three youngest children and his wife joined him at Camp Nelson, and all of them, even his youngest daughter—small, only fifteen at the time, and quite deaf—taught in the soldiers' school. The family tried to continue teaching at Camp Nelson after all other workers had departed, but a band of vigilantes drove them away late in 1866. Abisha Scofield died in 1898 in Spencerport, New York. Genealogical details from IGI at www.familysearch.org.

U.S. Mil Tel   October 3rd 1864   By Telegraph from Danville
To Genl Fry

Please keep my boys Giles Thomas and Pendliton Gray there until tomorrow   I will come after them

Minerva Gray   colored woman[1]

1. Gray to Fry, 3 Oct. 1864; Vol. 112/258, p. 75; Telegrams; RG 393.

U.S. Mil. Tel   Oct 4th 1864   By Telegraph from Lebanon to Col T.D. Sedgewick

Negro boy Bob stole a grey horse and left for Camp Nelson last night   Please get horse

J.B. True   Lt & . A.A.A.G[1]

1. True to Sedgewick, 4 Oct. 1864; ibid.

Camp Nelson Oct 4th /64

Bro Geo Whipple Dear Sir We have been laboring hard in this camp among the soldiers, and find this an interesting field of labor. Our school is well attended. The schollars manifest a great desire to learn   for numbers please refer to report for this month.

The meetings are quite interesting   we have had several conversions. I have made an application for a chaplaincy in the 116 regiment colored troops. The application is quite favorably received but an appointment cannot be made just now neither would I like to get an appointment just now as my family affairs have become complicated and I expect to be called home suddenly in a few days. My fatherinlaws health is failing fast. He has a disease which is slow, though surely wasting him away. Last winter he was confined to his bed for three months   he partially recovered, but has been taken again and doctors think that he can not recover. This time I wish to stay as long as I can as I like the place, labor, & the people and will try and stay this month and then I will have to go home & settle (if I do not have to go before) the property as there is some considerable to look after. Then if I get my appointment I will have things straightened & ready to accept the position. I have a favor to ask and that is that my brother Robt O Lowrey[1] be appointed to fill my place which I believe will suit all around. At the end of the month we will settle this agreement. Please inform me if this is satisfactory & oblige

W^m L Lowrey[2]

1. The third Lowrey brother never appeared.
2. Lowrey to Whipple, 4 Oct. 1864, AMAA 44041.

U.S. Mil Tel   Oct 8th 1864   By Telegraph from Lexington
Col. T.D. Sedgewick Comdg

Col. The stage from Nicholasville to Harrodsburg yesterday was attacked by nine (9) Guerrillas 3 miles beyond Shakertown — who robbed the mails express and passengers, and carried off a soldier — The Col comdg directs that you at once send about twenty mounted men to that vicinity in charge of a good officer; and if possible capture the scoundrels who are committing these depredations. Advise these Hd Qrs of your action

By Comd of Col James Keigurn
J W Thompson   Capt & A.A.A.G[1]

1. Thompson to Sedgewick, 8 Oct. 1864; Vol. 112/258, p. 78; Telegrams; RG 393.

[Excerpt from the memoirs of Elijah P. Marrs.]
[Approximately October 10–12, 1864.]

We were in camp at Taylor Barracks three weeks, when we received orders to report at Camp Nelson. Some rejoiced, whilst others wept, the latter thinking we were going on a fighting tour. We went by way of Lexington, and arrived at Camp Nelson without the loss of a man. The barracks being crowded, we were assigned to tents, mine being pitched beside the bull-pen.

Whilst passing through Lexington I became acquainted with a young lady named Emma ———. Our love was mutual. She followed me to Camp Nelson, in the neighborhood of which she found employment. She invited me to see her; but it should be at night, after her daily duties were done. One night I called, and not seeing her, presumed her to be in some other portion of the house, and walked in without announcement. My entrance alarmed some one in the adjacent room, whose cries of "murder" hurried me back to camp, with the resolution of never seeing Emma again. The last I heard of poor Emma was that she was dead. Her last thoughts were of me, and her last request was to her kind lady employer to send me her only portrait. She was my first love, and was too early called away.[1]

1. Marrs, 25, 26. Elijah P. Marrs enlisted on September 26, 1864, in Louisville, and rose to the rank of sergeant in Company L, Twelfth U.S. Heavy Artillery (Colored). He spent three weeks at Taylor Barracks in Louisville before being sent to Camp Nelson. It is perhaps fair to say that his account of his "first love" may owe more to nineteenth-century melodrama than to his actual experience. Born a slave in January 1840 in Shelby County, Kentucky, Marrs had a very active life as an educator, Baptist minister, and "an early advocate of civil rights." His memoir, the full title of which is *Life and History of the Reverend Elijah P. Marrs, First Pastor of Beargrass Baptist Church, and Author,* details the feelings of a slave-soldier and narrates a unique account of escorting a large band of slaves (women and children) to Camp Nelson. He died August 30, 1910. *RAGK.*

From Rev. John G. Fee, Camp Nelson, Ky., Oct. 10, 1864.

Since I last wrote you, several thousands of soldiers, white and colored, have been called from this place of drill, to various fields of battle. Though numbers diminish, interest increases: increases in the development of principles and policies, which, we hope, will help mould society in the immediate future.

For months there has not only been regular instruction in the school, organized at first for the instruction of the non-commissioned officers, in colored regiments, but also regular preaching to white and colored. In these meetings, engaged in by all the ministerial brethren here, there were frequent instances of persons awakened and converted; and some of them were baptized. We all felt that it would be for our mutual good to have a recognized association, a church in which there should be mutual watch, care, and discipline. Here were Baptists, Methodists, Presbyterians, and Congregationalists. The question was, How shall we be united? for divided, with four or five different creeds and organizations, we should accomplish but little, and be an occasion of stumbling.

After much conversation, a little preaching and comparing of notes, it was agreed that we ought, "in camp, at least," fellowship all who confessedly "wear the image of Jesus"—who "believe on him with all the heart." All, of course, were ready to acknowledge the Bible as the rule of faith and practice, and that it, like its Author, is no respecter of persons. The next Sabbath, after the "forenoon" sermon, a double invitation was made, including inquirers, and those who, trusting in the Lord Jesus Christ with all their heart, and taking the Scriptures of the Old and New Testaments as their rule of faith and practice, were willing to enter into covenant to walk together in Christian fellowship. Two made profession of their faith, were that day baptized, and entered into fellowship.

Last Sabbath the position was more fully explained, and on profession of their faith in Christ with all the heart, thirty-five persons were "added to the church." These were previously members of different denominations. The scene was one of intense interest to me, almost Pentecostal. In the midst of this slaveholding State was a crowded assembly, listening to ministers from the North and the South, white and black. In the congregation, as in the church, newly formed, were persons from the East, the West, the North, the South.

There were male and female, soldier and citizen, and every grade of complexion, from the fairest Caucasian to the darkest African—all blended together on the one common basis of manifested faith in Christ. Therein, the person of every freedman was a practical demolition of that hated monster, slavery; and there, in the blended association, was a practical crucifixion of that great and virulent enemy of the Gospel—caste. I thank God that I have lived to see this day. Oh! how much cause we have to thank God for his Spirit and his provisions! He makes the very wrath of men to praise Him.

In this State there are lands level, beautiful, and uniform. In other parts of the State, there are great upheavals; and treasures, which long lay imbedded in the depths beneath, have been thrown to the surface—brought into practical utility. So in our country. For a time, we had a surface peace and uniformity, but in the providence of God the earthquake of war has come, the pent-up fires have been let loose, great upheavals have ensued, and principles which, in Kentucky at least, have been long and deeply imbedded, have been thrown to the surface and brought into practical requisition.

God can work and no man can hinder. And he will speedily open in this State a wide and effectual door which no man can shut. Let us pray for grace and length of days that we may see more of his salvation. I go to Berea to remain there a few days—the place where these principles were avowed years since. God will take care of his own truth, and the "bread cast upon the waters shall be seen many days hence."

John G Fee[1]

---

1. *AM* 8, no. 12 (December 1864): 294. a manuscript copy of this report, consisting of one long page—with the first page, constituting the first three paragraphs of the published version, missing—is filed (apparently misfiled) as Fee to the AMA, [no receiver named and no date given], AMAA 44058A. AMAA 44058, a letter written by A. Scofield, is dated November 30, 1864, but Fee's report was written in October. The punctuation and paragraphing of Fee's original is altered slightly in the published version, but no wording is changed or omitted in the existing manuscript page.

Headquarters, Camp Nelson, Ky., October 14, 1864.

Colonel Capron, Comdg. Brigade of Cavalry, Nicholasville, Ky.:

COLONEL: Information has been received that this post is in danger of an attack by guerrillas, who are at Shakertown and other places near camp. Please send here without delay what men you can spare, as we have only a very small force (about 100 armed men) for the protection of a vast amount of Government property. *

Speed S. Fry, Brigadier-General, Commanding.
C.M. Holt, Lieutenant and Aide-de-Camp. (The general being absent.)[1]

1. Fry to Horace Capron, 14 Oct. 1864, *OR,* 1, 39, pt. 3, 283. Corwin M. Holt of the 103rd Ohio Volunteers, was assistant aide-de-camp and post inspector at Camp Nelson by July 1864, lieutenant and aide-de-camp by October.

[*Excerpt from Elijah Marrs's memoirs:*]
[*October 1864*]

Our stay at Camp Nelson was not altogether devoid of excitement, and this event being my first actual experience in the science of war, is now more vivid to my memory, as I presume it is to my comrades who were with me, than subsequent events of the war. One night news reached the camp that the rebels were in Danville, Ky., and in about forty minutes afterwards Gen. S.S. Fry, accompanied by about fifty men, came galloping into the camp with all speed. The alarm was at once given, the long roll of the drum was beaten, and every man roused and ordered to prepare for battle.

We were at once marched to the various forts surrounding the camp, and though up to that time we had only been drilled in infantry tactics, we were commanded to man the cannons. It is true we belonged to the Heavy Artillery, but had never been drilled in the tactics thereof. Nos. 1, 2, 3, and 5, however, soon learned their positions at the cannon, and while apparently paying attention to their work, could not keep their eyes from peering into the darkness beyond the river, from which direction they thought they heard the clang of swords and the clattering of horses coming upon us.

Day broke, however, and no enemy was in sight, so we marched back to camp in great glee, as much so as if we had met the enemy and gained a great victory.[1]

1. Marrs, 27, 28.

Lexington, October 14, 1864.

Col. T.D. Sedgewick, Camp Nelson, Ky.:
Hold all your available men in readiness to repel any attack. Keep scouting parties, under picked officers, out a few miles on the different approaches to the camp. Cannot send you any more cavalry.

By order of Brevet Major-General Burbridge:
J. Bates Dickson, Captain and Assistant Adjutant-General[1]

1. Dickson to Sedgewick, 14 Oct. 1864, *OR,* 1, 39, pt. 3, 283.

[Letterhead.] Head-Quarters Military District of Kentucky   **Lexington,** Oct 17. *1864.*
Special Orders   No 36.

IV. The Employees of the Quarter Master's, Commissary, Ordnance and Engineer Departments at Camp Nelson will be organized by Companies as Infantry and held in readiness in case of any emergency requiring their Services in the defence of the Camp. Each Company will elect its officers, non Commissioned Officers will be appointed by the Captains of Companies. The Post Commandant at Camp Nelson, thro' the different Chiefs of departments, will exercise general Supervision and Control over the force, each Company will be required to drill one hour daily and none will be excused from drilling unless by written permission of their Captain approved by the head of their respective departments. A Consolidated return of the several Companies organized under this order will be made on the 1st 10th and last days of each month.[1]

1. Special Orders No. 36, 17 Oct. 1864; Entry 103; Part 2; RG 393.

Report of Col. James S. Brisbin, Fifth U.S. Colored Cavalry, of the part taken by a detachment of the Fifth U.S. Colored Cavalry, under the command of Col. James F. Wade,[1] Sixth U.S. Colored Cavalry, at Saltville.
Lexington, Ky., Oct. 20, /64

General, I have the honor to forward herewith a report of the operations of a detachment of the 5th U.S. Colored Cavalry during the late operations in Western Virginia against the Salt Works.

After the main body of the forces had moved, Gen'l. Burbridge, Comdg. District, was informed I had some mounted recruits belonging to the 5th U.S. Colored Cavalry, then organizing at Camp Nelson and he at once directed me to send them forward.

They were mounted on horses that had been only partly recruited and that had been drawn with the intention of using them only for the purpose of drilling. Six hundred of the best horses were picked out, mounted and Col Jas. F. Wade 6th. U.S.C. Cav'y was ordered to take command of the Detachment.

The Detachment came up with the main body at Prestonburg, Ky., and was assigned to the Brigade Commanded by Colonel R.W. Ratliff,[2] 12th O.V. [*Ohio Volunteer*] Cav.

On the march the Colored Soldiers as well as their white Officers were made the subject of much ridicule and many insulting remarks by the White Troops and in some instances petty outrages such as the pulling off the Caps of Colored Soldiers, stealing their horses etc was practiced by the White Soldiers. Their insults as well as the jeers and taunts that they would not fight were borne by the Colored Soldiers patiently or punished with dignity by their Officers but in no instance did I hear Colored soldiers make any reply to insulting language used toward [them] by the White Troops.

On the 2d of October the forces reached the vicinity of the Salt Works and finding the enemy in force preparations were made for battle. Col Ratliffs Brigade was assigned to the left of the line and the Brigade dismounted was disposed as follows. 5th U.S.C. Cav. on the left, 12th O.V.C. in the centre and 11th Mich. Cav. on the right. The point to be attacked was the side of a high mountain, the Rebels being posted about half way up behind rifle pits made of logs and stones to the height of three feet. All being in readiness the Brigade moved to the attack. The Rebels opened upon them a terrific fire but the line pressed steadily forward up the steep side of the mountain until they found themselves within fifty yards of the Enemy. Here Col. Wade ordered his force to charge and the Negroes rushed upon the works with a yell and after a desperate struggle carried the entire line killing and wounding a large number of the enemy and capturing some prisoners   There were four hundred black soldiers engaged in the battle, one hundred having been left behind sick and with broken down horses on the march, and one hundred having been left in the Valley to hold horses. Out of the four hundred engaged, one hundred and fourteen men and four officers fell killed or wounded. Of this fight I can only say that men could not have behaved more bravely. I have seen white troops fight in twenty-seven battles and I never saw any fight better. At dusk the Colored Troops were withdrawn from the enemies works, which they had held for over two hours, with scarcely a round of ammunition in their Cartridge Boxes.

On the return of the forces those who had scoffed at the Colored Troops on the march out were silent.

Nearly all the wounded were brought off though we had not an Ambulance in the command. The negro soldiers preferred present suffering to being murdered at the hands of a cruel enemy. I saw one man riding with his arm off another shot through the lungs and another shot through both hips.

Such of the Colored Soldiers as fell into the hands of the Enemy during the battle were brutally murdered. The Negroes did not retaliate but treated the Rebel wounded with great kindness, carrying them water in their canteens and doing all they could to alleviate the sufferings of those whom the fortunes of war had placed in their hands.

Col. Wade handled his command with skill bravery and good judgement, evincing his capacity to command a much larger force. *

James S. Brisbin   Colonel and Supt. Organization U.S. Colored Troops.[3]

1. James Franklin Wade, Union officer from Ohio, became lieutenant colonel in command of the Sixth U.S. Colored Cavalry on May 1, 1864. He was promoted and honored for his meritorious service in eastern Tennessee and southwestern Virginia, finally becoming a brigadier general. *CWD; HR,* 1:991; *OAR,* 8:146.

2. Robert Wilson Ratliff, born in Ohio, commanded the Fourth Brigade, First District of Kentucky, Twenty-third Army Corps, Department of the Ohio. He had been colonel of both the Second Ohio Cavalry and the Twelfth. He was promoted to the rank of brevet brigadier general for his service in expeditions under Generals Burbridge and Stoneman in southwestern Virginia. *HR,* 1:817; *OAR,* 5:19.

3. Report of Brisbin, 20 Oct. 1864, *OR,* 1, 39, pt. 1, 556–57. Also appears, with original spelling, punctuation, and paragraphing, in Berlin et al., series 2, *The Black Military Experience,* 557–58. (Hereafter abbreviated as "*The Black Military Experience.*")

Itinerary of the First Division, District of Kentucky, commanded by Brig. Gen. Nathaniel C. McLean, U.S. Army

The mounted portion of this division moved through Mount Sterling to Prestonburg, Ky., on September 15, and from thence up Louisa Fork to Saltville, Va., skirmishing continually on the route with bushwhackers and rebel force.

October 2.—We attacked the fortified position at the Saltville works with 4,200 effective men, consisting of cavalry and mounted infantry, and three sections of mountain howitzers, manned by detailed men from infantry regiments. The fight lasted until about 5 p.m., when we withdrew from the place, after considerable loss, and marched all night toward Kentucky. The Eleventh Kentucky Cavalry and Fifth U.S. Colored Cavalry joined this expedition with General Burbridge for temporary service, but did not belong to this division; they both fought well. The colored cavalry regiment was dismounted and behaved well for new troops, and repeatedly charged the earth works with their guidons flying, but suffered considerable loss.

An official report has been made of the murdering of our colored soldiers who were wounded and made prisoners by the enemy; also of the murder of Lieutenant Smith,[1] Thirteenth Kentucky Cavalry, by the guerilla Champ Ferguson, while on his bed wounded; at Emory General Hospital, Va.[2]

1. E.C. Smith of the Thirteenth Kentucky Cavalry. He is named in the following letter.
2. Itinerary of the First Division, *OR,* 1, 39, pt. 1, 555, 556.

Report of Surg. William H. Gardner, Thirtieth Kentucky Infantry, of the shooting of Union prisoners.
Lexington, Ky., October 26, 1864.
Capt. J.S. Butler, Assistant Adjutant-General

SIR: I have the honor to report that I was with the command of Brevet Major-General Burbridge in the attack on Saltville, Va., October 2, 1864, and that I was left with the wounded and was captured October 3, and paroled by Major-General Breckinridge.[1]

I would state that on Monday morning, October 3, there came to our field hospital several armed men, as I believe soldiers in the Confederate service, and took 5 men, privates, wounded (negroes), and shot them.

I would also further state that on Friday evening, October 7, at Emory and Henry College Hospital, Washington County, Va., to which place our wounded had been removed, several armed men entered the said hospital about 10 p.m. and went up into the rooms occupied by the Federal wounded prisoners, and shot 2 of them (negroes) dead in their beds.

I would further state that on Saturday, October 8, at Emory and Henry College Hospital, several armed men wearing the Confederate uniform, and, as I believe, soldiers in the Confederate service, entered the same hospital about 4 p.m., overpowered the guard that had been placed by the surgeon in charge, and went up into the rooms occupied by Federal wounded prisoners, and shot Lieut. E.C. Smith, Thirteenth Regiment Kentucky Cavalry, dead in his bed, where he lay severely wounded. They at the same time called out for the other Federal officers confined there, particularly Colonel Hanson, Thirty-seventh Regeiment Kentucky Volunteers, and Captain Degenfeld, Twelfth Ohio Cavalry, swearing that they intended to kill all of them; and I believe that they were only prevented doing so by the exertions of Surgeon Murfree, the surgeon in charge, the steward, Mr. Acres, and the other attendants of the hospital. I would also further state that Surgeon Murfree, the other surgeons, and the hospital attendants did all in their power, even to the risk of their lives, to prevent the perpetration of these outrages; and that they assisted in removing Colonel Hanson and Captain Degenfeld, as well as myself, to a place of safety.

I would further state that we left about 70 of our wounded prisoners in the said hospital, and that I have been informed that these outrages have been perpetrated on them since we left them. *

WM. H. Gardner, Surgeon, Thirtieth Regiment Kentucky Volunteer Infantry.[2]

1. Confederate Maj. Gen. John Cabell Breckinridge, a 1860 Democratic candidate for president and former vice president under James Buchanan, commanded the Department of Southwest Virginia through part of 1864. *GIG.*
2. Report of Surgeon William H. Gardner, 26 Oct. 1864, *OR,* 1, 39, pt. 1, 554–55.

U.S. Mil Tel.   Oct 21ˢᵗ 1864   By Telegraph from Lexington
to Col T.D. Sedgewick

Genl Burbridge and Senator Wade[1] will review all the Colored Uniformed men in your Camp at two o'clock this P.M. . . . Have a good turn out with Band. Have five horses saddled

J.S. Brisbin   Col. U.S.C.T. & A.D.C.[2]

1. Senator Benjamin Franklin Wade (1800–1878), born in Massachusetts, was a Radical Republican senator from Ohio, staunchly anti-slavery.
2. Brisbin to Sedgewick, 21 Oct. 1864; Vol. 112/258, p. 87; Telegrams; RG 393.

Head Quarters Camp Nelson Ky   Oct 21ˢᵗ 1864
Capt J S Butler   A.A.G.   Lexington

The camp of Distribution at this place is now about depopulated. I do not think it is needed   The Officer in charge is ordered away and I have no one to relieve him. Can I break it up and order the property turned over to the Q. M Dept

(Sgd) Thoˢ D Sedgewick   Col Commanding[1]

1. Sedgewick to Butler, 21 Oct. 1864; Vol. 112/258, p. 184; Telegrams; RG 393.

Camp Nelson Ky   Oct 29th 64
Major A.J. Hogan   Commanding   Point Burnside

Preparatory to the Regiments moving you will turn out of Camp all Negro women and children

Thomas D Sedgewick   Col Commanding[1]

1. Sedgewick to Hogan, 29 Oct. 1864; Vol. 112/258, p. 191; Telegrams; RG 393.

[*October 1864*]

Dear Bro. Whipple   Our school during the month of Oct has been quite uniform in attendance but not as large as it was during the preceding month   This is owing partially to the fact that a large portion of the troops have been summoned from this place and more to the fact that our school room has been destitute of stoves.

We expect stoves from government tomorrow but may be disappointed, however. We have had no school so far this week & will have no more until stoves are put up. I took cold & was ill for a few days   During this time Mr Vetters again is in teaching   Bro Schofield comes into school occasionally & has done us good service. We have suffered for want of teachers all through the month   Mr Woodruff[1] taught his 1 week and 1 day. Our school is composed chiefly of women, girls, & boys   Average attendance of boys under 16 35 & girls 5. Average number of women 20. I expect my wife in the course of 1 or two weeks. What will you allow her a week provided she will take charge of the female department in our school   The quarter master refuses to give rations to us this month. *

J.B. Lowrey

[*Followed by a postscript and*] October Report for the Camp Nelson School[2]

1. Maybe Frederick C. Woodruff, who was mustered in as captain of Company I, 119th U.S.C.I. at Louisville, on June 14, 1865; *OAR*, 8:300.
2. Lowrey to Whipple, Monthly school report for Oct. 1864, AMAA 44051.

Camp Nelson Ky   Nov 1st 1864
M.E. Strieby Sec of A.M. Ass.

Dear brother   As directed, I send you herewith my report of labor in this place of Labor

As to expenses I have little to report. In food, I hope we shall be able to live within the rations received from the government. I think we ought. We have more of meat coffee and flour than we can use, which we sell and procure butter and vegitables not included in rations   Of that matter brother Fee will report for our keep. In stationery I have incured a small expense, but will not report till I know whether that is an item you intend to furnish. Allow me here to say that if you think best to furnish me with books tracts testaments &c   I could use them in this camp for lasting good.

As to labor I would say that brother Fee assigns to me as my chief work visiting and preaching the Gospel in this camp. But as the chief Teacher has been sick, I have during the past month spent considerable time in the school   still I have devoted myself mainly to preaching, attending this service from two to four times a week besides frequent prayer meetings. These services have been held mainly among the Freed Men. Occasionly I have preached to Congregations mostly white   The congregations have been full very attentive and often tender[1] The Freed Men I find to be a peculiar class of people to preach to. The qualities in preaching suited to them are earnestness, directness and simplicity. If you speak to them in a round about Rhetorical Method they will not hear you. They believe firmly in the great fundamental truths of religion and of a saving religion. I doubt if there is a colored infidel or free thinker in all the South. No! they are soundly orthodox. They believe in God and the Bible. Of the great facts of Christ's redemption, God Heaven and hell you may preach to them for hours together and they will listen to you, never seeming to tire; they will drink in the truth much as the thirsty earth drinks in a shower of rain! About three weeks since I went out into their camp among their tents one sabbath afternoon, when they came out arranged themselves around me in rows siting upon the ground, while I stood in the center upon a box and preached unto them from the text "turn ye turn ye for why will ye die?" They listened attentively and some wept. When they rose to sing five young soldiers, of their own accord, came forward to the stand to enlist as soldiers of the cross; they knelt at my feet and wept like children. I could not help weeping with them. When we had commended them to God in prayer, they rose and some three or four of them seemed to turn fully to the Lord! On Sunday we have preaching the school room twice also on Wednsday evening. At these meetings we almost invariably call for decisions. from five to fifteen come forward at each time, take the seat in appearent deep concern. Some thirty or forty of these have thus come forward during the past month. Some of them are strangers who come into camp to tarry but for a night. They hear of the meeting come in and hearing the truth become overwhelmed with a sense of guilt and cry out for mercy. Some of them doubtless go away, and forget what manner of persons they are; and what solemn vows they have made   But some of them we have opportunity to observe, and those generally appear well. During the past month some five white men soldiers have come forward and really seemed to dedicate themselves to the Lord. One evening when they were coming forward as we sang, I observed one white soldier pushing his way through the crowd with tearful eye and weatherbeaten visage. I went toward him, gave him my hand and led him along to welcome him to Jesus. When we came to the seat he knelt down and began to confess his sins and to pray. While they all knelt and some bretheren led in prayer I knelt by the side of this man and puting my head close down to his, I listened to the breaking of his heart. Oh my dear brother you would have wept as I did, had you listen to his sad tale of sorrow, and his earnest cries for "mercy"   I learned that he was a German; had been in Georgia, was in the stoneman raid, taken prisoner and put into that dreadful death pen near Atlanta, where he saw hundreds of men rot and die in the hot sun litterally eaten up of worms! But earnest hearts wrestled in prayer for his salvation and I trust were heard. When the meeting closed he went away apparently happy and trusting in the Lord. When I took his hand and gave him a parting shake and saw and heard his gratitude for our efforts in his behalf I felt amply paid for all my travel from New York to Kentucky, to bring the glad tidings of salvation to this needy soul.

    The school is prosperous as could be expected   all attend that can be accomodated in the room. The school I am sorry to say receives little favor from the officials here. We have been promised stoves but have not yet obtained them. The quartermaster Cap Hall has lately been relieved and the man who has come in his stead "knows not Joseph" To day we have been denied Rations, and tomorrow I fear we shall be denied stoves. But the Lord reigns let the Earth rejoice. . . . Nov 2nd . . . . We have formed a church or rather gathered one in this camp of some twenty members, which I trust will by the blessing of God grow to be much larger. We also ordained, a colored brother who is an able preacher of the Gospel and will we think be greatly useful to his suffering fellow freed men. His name is <u>Gabriel</u>, and I can assure you that he blows the Gospel trump with rare eloquence and power * * * * [*Three paragraphs.*]

A. Scofield[2]

1. In nineteenth-century religious parlance, this phrase meant that the congregations were sensitive to the message being brought to them.
    2. Scofield to Strieby, 1 Nov. 1864, AMAA 44052.

[*Excerpt from Marrs's memoirs*]
[*November 24, 1864*]

    After a stay of some weeks at Camp Nelson, we were ordered to Russellville, Ky. It was thought now that we were on our way to the front. Many of us would have preferred to remain at Camp Nelson, but the command was to march. We began to pack up on the morning of November 24, 1864, and we were marched on foot to Lexington, there being no railroad. I shall never forget that day. It was my first long march, and I had to carry my knapsack, my gun, my sword, and army equipments. Though late in the year, the sun seemed to shine with equal force as in the hottest days of July, and the heat was oppressive and overpowering. The roads were inches deep in dust, and it filled my eyes, mouth, and ears. Our thirst was intolerable, and no water was to be had save the stagnated water we would find along the line of our march. To this we would drive the horses, and of it fill our canteens. The use of this water so weakened me that I became completely prostrated and had to cry for help. Lieut. Bossworth, who was an old soldier, and who took pride in aiding and assisting his men, came to my relief, took my equipments, transferred them to his own back, and resumed his march with as light a foot as he had started in the morning.

By sunset we arrived at Lexington, tired and fagged out, having marched a distance of nineteen miles. We expected to get our usual rations of bread, and meat, and coffee, but we did not get it. No provision had been made for our arrival, and nothing could be had but hard tack and water, off of which we made our supper.

After supper I retired. My sleeping apartment was an old hog car, but I was so stiff and so worn out from the effects of the march that day that I was soon asleep and dreaming of home and friends . . . .[1]

1. Marrs, 28, 29.

Chapter Four

The Expulsion

[Excerpt from Capt. Theron E. Hall's report.]
[November 23–26, 1864]

On the morning of the 23" of November last [*1864*] while in Lexington I was informed by Lieut. G.A. Hanaford 41" Ky. Inft. and Assistant Superintendent for the organization of Colored troops, that Brig. Genl. Fry Commanding at Camp Nelson had given orders for the expulsion of all Colored women and children in Camp, and that the order was being executed. As I had taken a very active part in the enlistment of colored troops here, knowing that such a course would operate most unfavorably upon such enlistments, remembering that these people had followed their husbands and fathers to Camp who were then in the Army fighting for that freedom of which it was by this act proposed to deprive their families and firmly believing that the wife and children of the colored soldier were entitled to protection from that government for the perpetuation of which he was imperiling his life, I felt it my duty to interfere, and if possible prevent the accomplishment of the contemplated outrage. The weather at the time was intensely cold, summarily expulsion and exposure to the inclement atmosphere would occasion untold suffering: and knowing this, my efforts were prompted by the instincts of that common humanity to which every heart, not already hardened by familiarity with acts of cruelty, lays claim. I came to Camp on the evening of the 25" and found that the order had been executed indiscriminately. I found that large numbers were congregated at Nicholasville; some had found their way to Lexington, some were sitting by the road-side and all were suffering from cold and hunger. I addressed, at once, to Capt J. Bates Dickson, A.A.G. a telegram as follows

> Camp Nelson Ky Nov 26" 1864
> Capt J. Bates Dickson A.A.G.   Lexington
>
> Can nothing be done for the poor women and children sent from this Camp by order of Genl Fry? They are literally starving to death. I have the affidavit of one soldier whose family was sent out of Camp last

Wednesday, that one of his children was frozen to death after being put out of the lines.

(Signed) T.E. Hall   Capt and A.Q.M. [1]

1. Hall to Restieaux, 16 Dec. 1864; Camp Nelson, Box 720; RG 92. Document hereafter cited as "Hall's report." A clipping of Hall's "Humanitas" letter to the *New York Tribune* (28 Nov. 1864; reproduced below) was evidently enclosed with this voluminous report. Virtually all the telegrams that Hall copied into this report are missing from the regular series of telegrams copied into the records, which appear in Telegrams; Camp Nelson, Ky., Part 4, RG 393.

Camp Nelson Ky   November 26, 1864

Personally appeared before me E B W Restieaux Capt and Asst Quartermaster Joseph Miller a man of color who being duly sworn upon oath says   I was a slave of George Miller of Lincoln County, Ky. I have always resided in Kentucky and am now a Soldier in the service of the United States. I belong to Company I 124 U.S.C. Inft now Stationed at Camp Nelson Ky. When I came to Camp for the purpose of enlisting about the middle of October 1864 my wife and children came with me because my master said that if I enlisted he would not maintain them and I knew they would be abused by him when I left. I had then four children, ages respectively ten nine seven and four years. On my presenting myself as a recruit I was told by the Lieut. in command to take my family into a tent within the limits of the Camp. My wife and family occupied this tent by the express permission of the aforementioned Officer and never received any notice to leave until Tuesday November 22" when a mounted guard gave my wife notice that she and her children must leave Camp before early morning. This was about six O'clock at night. My little boy about seven years of age had been very sick and was slowly recovering. My wife had no place to go and so remained until morning. About eight O'clock Wednesday morning November 25" a mounted guard came to my tent and ordered my wife and children out of Camp. The morning was bitter cold. It was freezing hard. I was certain that it would Kill my sick child to take him out in the cold. I told the man in charge of the guard that it would be the death of my boy   I told him that my wife and children had no place to go and I told him that I was a Soldier of the United States. He told me that it did not make any difference   he had orders to take all out of Camp. He told my wife and family that if they did not get up into the wagon which he had he would shoot the last one of them. On being thus threatened my wife and children went into the wagon. My wife carried her sick child in her arms. When they left the tent the wind was blowing hard and cold and having had to leave much of our clothing when we left our master, my wife with her little ones was poorly clad. I followed them as far as the lines. I had no Knowledge where they were taking them. At night I went in search of my family. I found them at Nicholasville about six miles from Camp. They were in an old meeting house belonging to the colored people. The building was very cold having only one fire. My wife and children could not get near the fire, because of the number of colored people huddled together by the soldiers. I found my wife and children shivering with cold and famished with hunger. They had not recieved a morsel of food during the whole day. My boy was dead. He died directly after getting down from the wagon. I know he was killed by exposure to the inclement weather. I had to return to Camp that night, so I left my family in the meeting house and walked back. I had walked there. I travelled in all twelve miles. Next morning I walked to Nicholasville. I dug a grave myself and buried my own child. I left my family in the Meeting house — where they still remain. And further this deponent saith not.

his
Joseph Miller
mark[1]

1. Affidavit of Joseph Miller, 26 Nov. 1864; M999:Roll 7, Frames 682–84; BRFAL, RG 105. (Hereafter, the words "Roll," "Frames," and "BRFAL" will be omitted from M999 references; e.g., M999:7:682–84; RG105.) Apparently, this affidavit was one of the collection sent to the Freedmen's Bureau by Capt. T.E. Hall, mentioned in and accompanying his letter of June 22, 1865. Also reproduced in *The Black Military Experience*, 269–71. In an affidavit by the sexton of Camp Nelson, filed June 26, 1865 (see chapter 5, below), the deaths of all Miller's remaining children, his wife, and himself are all reported.

[Excerpt from Capt. Hall's report.]
Camp Nelson Ky.   Nov. 26" 1864
Capt J. Bates Dickson A.A.G.   Lexington

The colored women and children are still being put out of the Camp. It is done by the order of Genl Fry. Many of them are lying about the Depot in Lexington and are in a suffering condition. It is reported that one child was frozen to death the day they were sent out.

(Signed) T.E. Hall   Capt and A.Q.M.

On the 27" finding that the helpless outcasts were actually starving, I purchased of the Commissary 200 rations of meat, bread, coffee and sugar which I caused to be distributed among them, and on the same day I sent the following to the Genl Commanding the District of Kentucky, who was then absent with his troops in the field.

Camp Nelson, Ky   Nov. 27" 1864
Col. J.S. Brisbine   Chief of Staff   Cumberland Gap.

More than four hundred poor women and children families of Colored soldiers have been sent from Camp the past week. Some have died and all are in a starving condition. They are sitting by the roadside and wandering about the fields. Can you not induce the General to interfere on their behalf. No more potent weapon could be placed in the hands of the rebels to prevent enlistments than this. The whole community are loud in denouncing the outrage. Please answer

(Signed) T.E. Hall   Capt. and A.Q.M.[1]

1. Hall's report.

Lexington   Nov. 27" [*1864*]
To Bvt Maj. Genl S.G. Burbridge   Cumberland Gap

I understand Gen'l Fry has turned out of Camp Nelson the Colored women and Children. They are coming here where there is no shelter for them. They are suffering and should be taken care of at Camp Nelson. Please telegraph Gen'l Fry to take care of them at Camp Nelson

J Bates Dickson   Capt and A.A. Gen'l[1]

1. Dickson to Burbridge, 27 Nov. 1864; Vol. 62/117,119, p. 351; Telegrams Sent; RG 393.

U. S Mil Tel   [*No date; evidently November 27, 1864*] By Telegraph from Cumb Gap
To Brig Genl S S Fry

You will not expell any Negro women or children from Camp Nelson but give them quarters and if necessary erect buildings for them and allow back all who have been turned out

By order of Brig Maj Genl Burbridge[1]

1. Burbridge to Fry; Vol. 112/258, p. 97; Telegrams; RG 393.

[*Excerpt from Capt. Hall's report*]
By Telegraph from Cumberland Gap   Nov. 27
To Capt T.E. Hall   A.Q.M.

The General Commanding has given orders to give quarters to every woman and child and if need be to erect buildings for them. Have them all gathered into Camp. Comunicate with Capt Dickson

(Signed) Charles M. Keyser   Capt and A.A.A.G[1]

1. Hall's report.

Lexington,   Nov. 28" [*1864*]
To Brig. Genl S.S. Fry   Camp Nelson, Ky.

The General Comd'g directs that the Colored women and children who seek refuge at Camp Nelson be sheltered and fed there. So far as practicable they will be employed by the Government at such labor as they are fitted to perform. Capt. T.E. Hall A.Q.M. has been placed temporarily in charge of arrangements for the care of these people and the Gen'l Comd'g directs that you afford him every facility in carrying out this instruction   *

J Bates Dickson   Capt. and A.A. Gen'l[1]

1. Dickson to Fry, 28 Nov. 1864; Vol. 62/117,119, p. 353; Telegrams Sent; RG 393.

Lexington   Nov. 28" [*1864*]
To Capt. T.E. Hall A.Q.M.   Camp Nelson, Ky.

While awaiting other orders at Camp Nelson the ·Genl. Comd'g directs that you superintend the arrangements for the care of Contraband women and children at Camp Nelson. If other shelter cannot be provided have buildings erected for them in a suitable place and have them profitably employed. See that none are turned out until the General's return. Gen'l Fry has been notified of these instructions and directed to afford you every facility for carrying them out.

J Bates Dickson   Capt. and A.A. Gen'l[1]

1. Dickson to Hall, 28 Nov. 1864; Vol. 62/117,119, p. 353; Telegrams Sent; RG 393.

CRUEL TREATMENT OF THE WIVES AND CHILDREN OF U.S. COLORED SOLDIERS
(Correspondence of the N.Y. Tribune.)
CAMP NELSON, KY., Nov. 28, 1864.

This camp has recently been the scene of a system of deliberate cruelty, which in ferocity of design and brutality of execution, suggests painful misgivings as to whether we, indeed, live in an enlightened age and a Christian land. At this moment, over *four hundred* helpless human beings—frail women and delicate children—having been driven from their homes by *United States soldiers*, are now lying in barns and mule sheds, wandering through woods, languishing on the highway, and literally starving, for no other crime than their husbands and fathers having thrown aside the manacles of slavery to shoulder Union muskets. These deluded creatures innocently supposed that freedom was better than bondage, and were presumptuous enough to believe that the plighted protection of the Government would be preserved inviolate.

Since June last, Camp Nelson has been a recruiting rendezvous for slaves. During this period, over nine thousand colored soldiers have entered the army from this post. When these men left their masters, they assumed the responsibility of their acts. Most of them left without their masters' permission, and knowing the nature of Southern chivalry, they had clear perceptions of the torture to which their families would be subjected at the hands of their indignant masters. Indeed, in some instances, the wife and children were turned out of doors when the husband enlisted. Hence the recruit was frequently accompanied with his family, and received assurance that, on his entering the army, his wife and children would be provided with shelter, and allowed an opportunity to earn a livelihood by cooking, washing, &c., within the limits of the camp. Assured that his family was relieved from the vengeance of an exasperated master, and provided with a home, however humble, he entered with a cheerful heart upon his new career; and thus the ranks of our army were replenished by men whose subsequent achievements reflected honor on their race. This arrangement, at once just and expedient, entailed little or no expense upon the Government, for these people lived in huts built by themselves from materials unserviceable for other purposes.

Yet that these Kentucky slaves should thus falsify the predictions of their former masters, who delighted to dilate with horrifying amplitude upon the miseries which would inevitably overtake the families of enlisted slaves—this was an act of unpardonable impoliteness in the eyes of certain officers who commanded the camp, and who had a kindly regard for the Southern Moloch. These gentlemen, therefore, put forth persistent efforts to justify the prophetic wisdom of their slaveholding friends, by driving the women and children from camp, and leaving them no alternative but starvation or fetters. Through the influence of some parties who had not the fear of the Slave Oligarchy before their eyes, these benignant designs were frustrated for a time. But the furious wrath thus delayed acquired new intensity, and only awaited a favorable opportunity to burst with increased violence upon the heads of the devoted victims. This opportunity was presented last Wednesday. Diabolical malignity could have desired no better day on which to perpetrate atrocious cruelty. The air was intensely chilly: the thermometer was below the freezing point all day, and strong men wrapped their overcoats close around them, when the provost guard turned four hundred women and children from their dwellings to face the wintry blast, with light and tattered garments, no food, and no home! Here, indeed, is a picture for an American Macaulay to incorporate in his next volume of his "History of the Rebellion." Armed soldiers attack humble huts inhabited by poor negroes—helpless women and sick children—order the inmates on pain of instant death, and complete their valorous achievements by demolishing dilapidated dwellings. The men who did all this were United States soldiers, and not Sepoys,[1] and they acted under instructions from a Union General, and not Nena Sahib.[2]

These are stern truths, amply corroborated by affidavits similar to the one which I have the honor to inclose. To-day these children of misery are exposed to the pitiless storm. Four are already in their graves; one was frozen to death. Others will undoubtedly find speedy shelter in the tomb, and God only knows what will become of the rest! Slavery is bad; but here is an act which transcends, in deliberate depravity and cool malignity, the darkest associations of the slave mart. I pass unnoticed the mental anguish, the social sufferings and the domestic sorrows—nor will I attempt to portray an amount of suffering which no language can depict, but which these people now endure. Their condition must be seen to be very approximately realized. No more efficacious plan could be devised for arresting the progress of negro enlistments than that which visits upon their families a merciless prosecution, compared with which Slavery or even death itself, would be a positive blessing. And it is no wonder that slaveholders in this State loudly applaud the course thus adopted, and point their slaves to the sad spectacle as an illustration of what the families of negro soldiers may expect. The heart revolts at the thought that such unparalleled atrocities should be perpetrated with any prospect of impunity; and my design in writing you is to arouse the Christian and patriotic people of the North to a sense of the duty which they owe these innocent sufferers. Let the potent, irresistible voice of a just and humane public demand of the authorities at Washington, that immediate steps be taken to arrest these barbarities, and to bring the responsible agents to stern account.

HUMANITAS.[3]

[*The article continues with a copy of Joseph Miller's affidavit of November 26 (see above)*]

1. The Sepoys were Indian soldiers who rebelled against British rule in India in 1857–1858. The rebellion was notorious for the atrocities committed by both sides, but "Humanitas" is clearly referring to the barbaric war crimes of the Indian soldiers. See *Columbia Encyclopedia,* 6th ed., s.v. "Indian Mutiny."

2. Nana Sahib was the leader in the Indian Mutiny undertaken by the Sepoys. Under his command his men massacred the British garrison and colony at Kanpur in June 1857. See ibid., s.v. "Sahib, Nana."

3. *The Liberator,* 9 Dec. 1864. The *N.Y. Tribune* story, which also contained the affidavit, was reprinted by William Lloyd Garrison's *Liberator.*

Camp Nelson Ky.   November 28" 1864

Personally appeared before me Edward B.W. Restieaux Captain and Assistant Quartermaster, John Higgins, a man of color who being duly sworn, upon oath says.

I am a soldier in the service of the United States, I belong to Company "I" 124" Regt. U.S.C. Infty. When I [*went*] to Camp for the purpose of enlisting my wife and two children came with me. This was in the last part of October 1864. My family had been driven out of doors by their master Moses Robbins of Lincoln County Kentucky. I was told by the officer who enlisted me that my family would be provided for in some way within the Camp. In company with another man I built a small hut wher[e] I resided with my family.

We were never notified to move until the evening of Thursday Nov 24" when the provost guard told my wife that she and her children must move out of the Camp on the following morning. On Friday afternoon Nov 25" 1864, the guard came with a wagon into which they ordered my family   My wife was sick and begged that she might not be driven out into the cold, when the guard told her "that be damned, if you do get out we will burn the house over your heads" or words to that effect.

Thus threatened, my family went into the wagon and were driven outside the lines.

On sunday Nov 27" I went in search of my family, I found them in Nicholasville, about six miles from Camp. They were in an old building through which the rain fell. It had rained hard while they were. My wife, in consequence, of the exposure was very sick   While my family were in Camp they never eat a mouthful off the Government. My wife earned money by washing. And further this deponent saith not

his
John x Higgins
mark[1]

1. Affidavit of John Higgins, 28 Nov. 1864; Box 720; Records of the Office of the Quartermaster General, RG 92.

[*Excerpt from Hall's report.*]
Camp Nelson   Nov. 28" 1864
Brig Genl. Fry   Commanding Camp Nelson

General   I have the honor to transmit copies of telegrams received from Cumberland Gap also from Capt Dickson A.A.G. Capt Restieaux informed me that the barracks on the east side of the Pike can be used temporarily for this people until others can be erected. I have the honor to request that you will give such orders as shall enable me to carry out the instructions of the General Commanding. *

To this Genl Fry replied

Hd Qrts Camp Nelson   Nov 28" 1864
Capt T.E. Hall   A.Q.M.

Capt   I will confer with Capt Restieaux in regard to Barracks and will then issue such orders as may be necessary *

(Signed) Speed S. Fry   Brig. Genl

And

Head Quarters Camp Nelson   Nov 28" 1864
Capt T.E. Hall   A.Q.M.

Capt.   I have my instructions from Capt Dickson in regard to negro women and children and all orders on that subject will eminate from these Head Quarters. *

(Signed) Speed S. Fry   Brig Genl

Finding that the poor people were still excluded from Camp as you will perceive by referring to the affidavits of Messrs Sears, Sinen [Linen?], Larter [Sarter?],[1] Schofield and Vetter, I sent the following despatch to Cap Dickson A.A.G.

Camp Nelson Ky   Nov 29" 1864
Capt Dickson A.A.G.   Lexington

I have furnished Genl. Fry with copies of my orders. He does not seem disposed to recognize me at all except to notify me that all orders will eminate from his Head Quarters. He has ordered Capt Restieaux to furnish quarters for such women with their children as are employed by the Government. He says further that he has telegraphed General Burbridge concerning the others. I can do nothing unless Genl Fry is directed not to interfere with me — Answer.

(Signed) T.E. Hall   Capt and A.Q.M.[2]

---

1. William A. Sears (for certain), Sinen (or Linen), and Larter (or Sarter) were clerks at

Camp Nelson. The given names of the last two are unknown and their surnames are always written indecipherably.

2. Hall's report.

Lexington, Nov. 29" [*1864*]
To Brig Genl S.S. Fry   Camp Nelson, Ky.

Capt. T.E. Hall A.Q.M. has been ordered temporarily to take charge of and superintend matters connected with the colored women and children seeking refuge at Camp Nelson. Those in Camp as well as those who have been turned out and may return there are to be cared for in such manner as Capt Hall may see best. You will afford him every facility in carrying out his plans on the subject.

By Command of Bvt Maj. Gen. Burbridge
J Bates Dickson   Capt. and A.A. Gen'l[1]

1. Dickson to Fry, 29 Nov. 1864; Vol. 62/117,119, 356; Telegrams Sent; RG 393.

[*Excerpt from Hall's report.*]

Learning that Adjutant General Thomas was in Lexington I went there to present the case to him and while there I received the following from Lt. Col. Whitfield[1] 123" Regt U.S.C.T.

By telegraph from Camp Nelson   Nov 29" 1864
To Capt T.E. Hall

The guards have positive orders not to admit the colored women into Camp. They are turned back at all points along the fortifications." [*Evidently end of telegram.*] I then had the honor of a personal interview with General Thomas who at once sent a despatch to Genl. Fry ordering him in the most peremptory manner to revoke his order turning the poor people from Camp, and directing that all who sought refuge there should be received and cared for.[2]

1. Smith A. Whitfield was a captain, commanding Camp Nelson's camp of distribution in February 1864. On October 15, 1864, he was mustered in as colonel of the 123rd U.S. Colored Infantry, organized at Louisville. *HR*, 2:160; *OAR*, 8:304.

2. Hall's report.

U. S Mil. Tel   November 29" 1864   By Telegraph from Lexington
To Genl S S Fry

I understand that you have sent helpless women and children without your lines and that you refuse to receive those who present themselves. It is ordered that you receive all who come and that you take back all you have sent out.

L Thomas   Agt Genl[1]

1. Thomas to Fry, 29 Nov. 1864; Vol. 112/258, p. 103; Telegrams; RG 393.

Cumberland Gap, November 29, 1864

Hon. E.M. Stanton: A large number of colored women and children have accumulated at Camp Nelson. Many of them are the wives and children of our colored soldiers. There will be much suffering among them this winter, unless shelters are built and rations issued to them. For the sake of humanity, I hope you will issue the proper order in this case as soon as possible.

S.G. Burbridge,
Brevet Major-General.[1]

1. Burbridge to Stanton, 29 Nov. 1864, *OR,* 1, 45, pt. 1, 1165.

Lexington,   Nov 30" [*1864*]
To Adjt Genl L. Thomas   Camp Nelson, Ky.

Orders relieving Gen'l Fry from Command at Camp Nelson will be sent from this office by mail in accordance with directions received by telegraph from Brv't Maj Gen'l Burbridge   *

J Bates Dickson   Capt and A.A. Gen'l[1]

1. Dickson to Thomas, 30 Nov. 1864; Vol. 62/117,119, p. 356; Telegrams Sent; RG 393.

Camp Nelson   Nov. 30th 1864

Dear brother Gooddell[1]   There is a dispute arisen here about the rights of the slave under the law of considerable importance. A few days ago Gen. Fry commanding this post drove out of the camp 400 women and children wives and children of soldiers, most of them. Gen Burbridge was telegraphed to, and promptly rescinded the order, and ordered them brought in again. Now the question is raised whether these persons are free by the enlistment of their husbands and Fathers. Now I suppose you are well posted in these matters. Will you give us light? When a Slave in Kentucky enlists how does it affect his family? Are they free? You will at once see the bearing of this question.

Please answer immediately. *

A. Scofield[2]

1. Rev. William P. Goodell (1792–1878) was a prominent antislavery reformer, author, lecturer, and editor, associated with William Lloyd Garrison. Among many other publications, he authored *Views of American Constitutional Law in Its Bearing Upon American Society* (1844) and *The American Slave Code in Theory and Practice* (1853), two works which eminently qualified him to answer Scofield's question. Goodell, a thinker whose views influenced Fee throughout his anti-slavery career, is mentioned repeatedly in Fee's letters, and the two conducted a correspondence before the war. See my *Berea Connections,* 64, 65.
2. Scofield to William Goodell, 30 Nov. 1864, AMAA 44058.

Lexington, Dec 1" /64
To Brig Gen'l S.S. Fry   Camp Nelson, Ky.

The orders relieving you from duty as Commandant at Camp Nelson and appointing Lt. Col. Carpenter[1] to command, are hereby temporarily suspended

                    J Bates Dickson   Capt. and A.A. Gen'l[2]

   1. Louis Henry Carpenter, a native of New Jersey, eventually became Camp Nelson's
commandant (at least by April 1865). He had served in various military capacities since 1861
and had fought in the Battle of Gettysburg. By October 1, 1864, he was lieutenant colonel in
the Fifth U.S. Colored Cavalry. *HR,* 1:284; *OAR,* 8:145.
   2. Dickson to Fry, 1 Dec. 1864; Vol. 62/117,119, p. 357; Telegrams Sent; RG 393.

[*Letterhead.*][1] *The U.S. CHRISTIAN COMMISSION*   Camp Nelson   Dec. 1ˢᵗ 1864

Dear brother Strieby, * * * * [*One paragraph.*]
   . . . This mission needs a more permanent and deffinite form. The room we
have occupied for the School, we could not control. The officers and soldiers had
access to it without any regard to our rights there. In warm weather we got along
tolerably well. But when it was cold we were destitute of stoves and wood — we
were faintly promised both, but after an effort of two weeks could obtain neither.
We then picked up an old condemned stove bought some stove pipe and put it
up   Then taking our axes went into the woods cut and drew in wood for the
room. But a few days ago, a great rush of soldiers came into camp. We went down on
Monday morn to the room — we found our benches out doors, the stove broken,
and the wood nearly gone — our room had been converted into barracks — for
this the officers seemed not to care   In short our rights were not respected   Under
such circumstances I thought best to close the school.
   So during the last month the school has been about 2 Weeks with about 40
pupils. In the meantime 200 could be obtained if we had a suitable place for them.
Since the relief of quartermaster Hall from duty here our enterprise meets with little
favor. And then, one week ago last tuesday, the Women and children were driven out
of camp by order of Gen Fry   we felt quite discouraged. But God taketh the wise in
their own craftiness. Just at that time God so ordered that Capt. Hall should come
back to camp. He at once gave us a helping hand. He telegraphed to Gen. Burbridge
at Cumberland Gap who ordered these people into Camp again and provided for.
Some of them have come in. Some have died on the road from exposure — some
have gone to Ohio, and some have gone we cannot tell where. Slave holders have been
thick around camp for a few days — for what reason — perhaps Gen. Fry can tell.
   P.S. [*Written vertically on this page, not at end of letter*] We are gathering the
Freedmen together in little compound here and there teaching them. A.S.
   The order now is, confirmed I am told by Gen. Thomas, that Capt Hall shall
put up at Government expense suitable buildings for these people, a permanent
Home, where they can be educated and furnished with work. That is just the thing

here needed, and will at once greatly enlarge the usefulness of your mission. Two or three hundred women and children would thus be brought permanently into the school — and Camp Nelson will become the most important place in the State of Kentucky. We had a meeting of the friends at Cap. Hall's two days ago — tomorrow we have another   I sent for brother Fee; we expect him to day.

As to myself I have I believe fulfilled my weekly appointments during the past month — excepting last sabbath when brother Vetter and myself took a load of provisions to Nicholasville and spent the day in dealing bread to the hungry — they were some of those who had been driven out of Camp. I came home tired and sick. I fear I shall not throw off the disease without a little respite. I have the jaundice. I want to go home in about two weeks and stay till New Years. Can I go? And what can you do to help me? Please answer *

A. Scofield[2]

1. The printed message on this letterhead reads "The U.S. CHRISTIAN COMMISSION sends this sheet as a messenger between the soldier and his home. Let it hasten to those who wait for tidings." The image is a flying pigeon with a letter tied around its neck.
2. Scofield to Strieby, 1 Dec. 1864, AMAA 44059.

Lexington,   Dec. 2" [*1864*]
To Brig Gen'l S.S. Fry   Camp Nelson, Ky.

Upon what charges is Capt Hall, A.Q.M. placed under arrest. Please inform me. *
J Bates Dickson   Capt. and A.A. Gen'l[1]

1. Dickson to Fry, 2 Dec. 1864; Vol. 62/117,119, p. 357; Telegrams Sent; RG 393.

Camp Nelson, December 2, 1864

Capt. J.S. Butler, Assistant Adjutant-General: I have just received a letter from a most reliable Union man in Washington County, giving an account of the most horrid outrages committed by a gang of guerrillas upon the people in that county. They have killed in a few days past some fourteen quiet, inoffensive citizens, among them one discharged soldier. I have now 150 of the Thirteenth Kentucky Cavalry, sent back by General Burbridge. If there [are] no orders for them to move, I respectfully request that I be allowed to send a portion of them in that region to catch these scoundrels, and then afford these people (the most of whom I know to be loyal) some relief.
S.S. Fry, Brigadier-General[1]

1. Fry to Butler, 2 Dec. 1864, *OR*, 1, 45, pt. 2, 28.

War Department   Adjutant General's Office   Washington   Dec. 2. 1864
To   The Quartermaster General U.S. Army   Washington. D.C.

Sir: On the representation of Brevet Major General Burbridge, U.S. Volunteers, that a large number of colored women and children have accumulated at Camp Nelson Kentucky, many of whom are the wives and children of our colored soldiers, and that there will much suffering among them this winter unless shelters are built and rations issued to them, the Secretary of War directs you to supply the wants of these persons with means under the control of the Quartermaster's Department   *

E D Townsend   Assistant Adjutant General[1]

1. Edward D. Townsend to Quartermaster General, 2 Dec. 1864; Box 720; RG 92.

Lexington, Dec 2" [*1864*] 4.45 P.M.
Brig Gen'l S. S Fry   Camp Nelson Ky.

Release Capt. Hall A.Q.M. from arrest and permit him to visit Lexington to see Adj't Gen'l L. Thomas. Send the charges against Capt Hall to Gen'l Thomas at once.

By order of Brv't Maj. Gen'l Burbridge
J Bates Dickson   Capt. and A.A. Gen'l[1]

1. Dickson to Fry, 2 Dec. 1864; Vol. 62/117,119, p. 358; Telegrams Sent; RG 393.

Lexington,   Dec. 4" [*1864*]
To Brig. Gen'l S. S Fry   Camp Nelson, Ky.

The orders relieving you and appointing Lt. Col. Carpenter to command have been suspended not revoked. You will retain Command until further notice. *

J Bates Dickson   Capt. and A.A.G.[1]

1. Dickson to Fry, 4 Dec. 1864; Vol. 62/117,119, p. 359; Telegrams Sent; RG 393.

Louisville, Ky., December 7, 1864
Hon. E.M. Stanton, Secretary of War, Washington, D.C.:

II.—TEMPER OF THE PEOPLE

Kentucky remained in the Union to preserve slavery and avoid becoming the theater of war, although strongly in sympathy with the rebellious States. Being humored and favored for the first two years, many people avowed their devotion to the Union; but the moment that Government attempted to draft men or enlist negroes, the true feeling of these people was evinced. They resisted our officers, and became more violent in their denunciations of the administration than the original rebels. A large majority of Kentuckians are today undoubtedly disloyal. * * * *

E.H. Ludington,[1] Assistant Inspector-General[2]

1. Elisha Harrison Ludington. *HR*, 1:646.
2. Elisha H. Ludington to Stanton, 7 Dec. 1864, *OR*, 1, 45, pt. 2, 93.

Lexington, Dec. 12" 1864
To Brv't Maj. Gen'l S.G. Burbridge   Bean's Station   Via Cumberland Gap

An energetic Post Commander, who will stay at his post and attend to his duties is needed at Camp Nelson. I would suggest that Gen'l Fry be permanently relieved and Col. Carpenter appointed. The report of Captain Saunders, A.A.I.G. [acting assistant inspector-general[1]] shows a condition of affairs there that demands an immediate change. General Thomas left this morning for Louisville. He will, if possible, stay in the State until you return. Guerrillas are becoming very bold, and I fear may do serious injury if the command remains absent much longer. I know nothing officially of Forrest's[1] movements, and hear nothing further of Lyon.[2] All well.

J. Bates Dickson, Captain and Assistant Adjutant-General[3]

1. The explanation of the abbreviation occurs in the *Official Records*.
2. Hylan Benton Lyon (1836–1907), a Confederate general from Kentucky, led a brigade under Forrest in Tennessee. Stewart Sifakis, *Who was Who in the Civil War* (Facts on File Publications: New York, 1988), 400–401; *CWD*.
3. Dickson to Burbridge, 12 Dec. 1864; Vol. 62/117,119, p. 365; Telegrams Sent; RG 393; also reproduced, with corrections and identification of A.A.I.G., in *OR*, 1, 45, pt. 2, 165, 166.

Camp Nelson, Ken.   Dec 14 /64

My Dear Friend Davis — I am truly sorry that you did not come out here. We have had the great fight of the struggle since my return and thanks be to God have won a signal victory. The struggle is over and the question settled forever in Kentucky. I have not time to write all the manouvres of the enemy. Now the devil put it into the hearts of the slave oligarchy to put into my hands the most potent weapon I could use. . . . * * * * [*One paragraph.*][1]

I have been appointed Superintendant to organize a home for them, and the buildings are already commenced. I design building wards for them in a section of the camp retired from the troops, with school room, work shop, and all the necessary buildings for a completed home.

I design having this all enclosed with a fence and have but one point of ingress or egress and that through the office of the Superintendent. Here they will be cared for and prepared for freedom.

I have now arrived at a point where I must have aid from abroad. I have thus far fought this battle in Kentucky almost alone. Now I must call for help. I want a man for superintendant, one who will devote himself to the work for the love of it. I want clothing, books, cooking utensils, teachers. Infine, I want everything. This must be a success. It is the death blow to slavery in Kentucky.

Already are the conservative men urging upon the legislature to take steps to emancipate the slaves, and they use the same argument I suggested to you, viz., that the labor is unprofitable. I propose to receive at the Home only the families of colored soldiers or those dependant upon them for support. In this way we shall get

the last man into the army and the last slave of any value into the camp — Truly
has God made the "Wrath of man to praise Him"   Had it not been for the
inhuman treatment of these poor people we should have had a longer struggle, but
great good resulted from the evil — I have them all back in camp again in temporary shelter, until there quarters can be prepared for them. Now you ask me how I
have got along personally in the fight. Well I have of course subjected myself to
much abuse. No open violence has been offered, altough much has been threatened.
Once in order to stop me, General Fry commanding here put me in arrest and
ordered me to stay in my quarters and not to communicate with any Head Quarters
but his own — A dispatch to Brig Genl Thomas secured my release in less than
eight hours. Now I propose to play a game of shoulder strap with him   If I am
not mistaken he will lose his ere many months. Already has an order been issued
relieving him from command here — Let me hear from you at once   What can
you do for the poor in this camp? Remember they come here destitute of everything. If anything is done it should be done at once   I will await your reply before
looking elsewhere   *

T E Hall, Capt & aqm.[2]

1. In the omitted passage, Hall again describes the events of the expulsion, and goes on
the say that he had sent a "statement accompanied by the affidavits of some of the sufferers to
the leading news papers in the country." This statement was the "Humanitas" letter included
above.
2. Hall to Elnathan Davis, 14 Dec. 1864, AMAA 44061; also excerpted in *AM* 9, no. 2
(February 1865): 30, 31.

Louisville, Ky., December 15", 1864

General: I observe today, (15" Decbr.) in the correspondence of the Louisville Union
Press a letter dated Camp Nelson; 7" Decbr., 1864, which discusses the policy by
which the families of enlisted negroes were deprived of U.S. protection. I do not
propose to discuss that policy, but merely to call your attention to a passage in the
letter which states that the masters of men who have enlisted turn away their families to shift for themselves and that they thereby become paupers and take refuge at
U.S. posts. The letter writer says further, that masters deter the men from enlisting
by making a threat to treat their families thus.

I add to this statement an extract from the tri monthly report of the Pro. Mar.
of 4th District: viz. "Colored Men are willing to enlist and, if possible, a thousand
men in this District would go to the army — Attend to their wives and families
and they would immediately rush to arms."

This matter involves consideration of large importance and the case merits
the attention of the highest authority, and there may be partial remedies within the
power of the Commanding General.

In cases known to be like those stated above, the masters might be either
required to keep the female and young members of the families of enlisted men and
treat them well, or in case they did not, might be assessed for their support—and in

case of threats of the kind made to deter men from enlisting there is already an adequate military remedy.

All women and children thus turned out by their masters and compelled to be supported by the U.S. should be thereby made free.

An incidental difficulty is that all thus seeking to be supported by the U.S. are not the wives and children of enlisted men but are often simple runaways, or castaways, or are the families of runaways or of unenlisted employees of U.S. officers, &c, &c.

It may thus be seen that though the whole subject is complicated and from its importance worthy of adjustment by the highest authority, yet that a partial remedy in regard to some points may be applied by the Military Commander, so far at least as regards the families of undoubted enlisted men, and of those desiring to enlist and therefore I make this communication. *

W.H. Sidell[1]

1. William H. Sidell, assistant provost marshal general for Kentucky, to the commander of the District of Kentucky, 15 Dec. 1864, in *The Destruction of Slavery*, 610.

Louisville, Ky.   Dec. 15, 1864.
Orders No. 29.

Having ascertained that in many cases the families of Colored Soldiers are suffering for the want of proper shelter at the Camps of Rendezvous, causing many of the soldiers to complain that their families are not provided for, and preventing the enlistment of others, fearing that their wives and children will not be cared for during the winter, Major General Burbridge will see that the humane intention of the General Government respecting these people, as far as possible, may be carried out. Accordingly, at Camp Nelson, and such other points where this class of negroes are received, he will cause the erection of suitable buildings on an economical scale, for their quarters, and otherwise provide for their comfort. He will assign suitable officers to have them specially in charge.

L. Thomas   Adjutant General[1]

1. Orders No. 29, 15 Dec. 1864, *NIMSUS*, 4:2844.

Camp Nelson Ky.   Dec [15] 1864

Personally appeared before me Capt E.B.W. Restieaux John Burnsides[1] a man of color who being sworn upon oath says: I am a Soldier in Company K, 124 Regt U.S.C.T. I am a married man   My wife and children belonged to William Royster of Garrard Co, Ky. Royster had a son John who was with Morgan during his raid into Kentucky in June 1863. He got separated from Morgan's command and went home. The Provost Marshal instituted a search for him at two different times. He was not found. My family were charged with giving information which led to the measures of the Provost Marshal. William Royster told me that my wife had been trying to ruin him for the last two years and if he found that this (meaning the information) went out through the black family meaning my family he would scatter them to the four winds of heaven. This was said about the last of September 1864. In consequence of this threat my family were in constant dread and desired to find protection and employment from the Government. At that time I had been employed at Camp Nelson and was not enlisted. A few days afterward I was sick at my mothers. I sent my sister to see Col. Sedgwick and inquire if my family might come to Camp and if they might would they be protected. She returned the same night and informed me that Col Sedgwick said tell him (me) to bring them in and I (Col Sedgwick) will protect them. Before I was unwilling that they should come but on receiving the promised protection of Col Sedgwick, I told them to come. While my wife and family were in Camp they never received any money or provision from the Government but earned their living with hard work. On Friday afternoon Nov 28" 1864 the Provost Guard ordered my wife and family out of Camp. The guard had a wagon which my wife and family were forced to go and were then driven out the line. They were driven to a wood belonging to Mr. Simpson about seven miles from Camp and there thrown out without any protection or any home. While they were in the woods it rained hard and my family were exposed to the storm. My eldest daughter had been sick for some time and was then slowly recovering.

(Signed) John Burnsides[2]

1. John Burnsides was a slave-soldier who remained in Camp Nelson after the war was over. His troubles were far from over at the time of this affidavit: he was wounded and left for dead by vigilantes who drove Rev. Abisha Scofield out of Camp Nelson in November 1866.

2. Affidavit of John Burnside, 15 Dec. 1864; M999:7:678–79; RG 105. Apparently, this affidavit was one of the collection sent to the Freedmen's Bureau by Capt. T.E. Hall, mentioned in and accompanying his letter of June 22, 1865. Also filed in Box 720; Records of the Office of the Quartermaster General, RG 92.

Head Quarters   Camp Nelson Ky   Dec. 15th 1864.
Capt E.B.W. Restieaux   A.Q.M.

Capt.   Having been informed that a communication had reached you from Washington City making some inquires in regard to the expulsion of negro women and children from this Camp, and also calling for the order under which they were expelled, in order to save you time and labor, I herewith enclose the order and the only one which has been issued upon that subject, with the request that you forward it on with any report you may make upon the matter. This order has never to my knowledge been countermanded, and I hope will prove entirely satisfactory.

If any other information however is called for I think I shall be able to furnish all that is necessary.

I had a conversation with Adgt. Genl. Thomas on this subject, in which I think I satisfied him that no violation of orders had occured and that the act was under the circumstances one of necessity. I also had a conversation wtih Brvt

Maj Genl Burbridge Comg Dist of Ky. in which he told me to execute the order at once.

It is not necessary I suppose to make any further statement at this time, but hold myself in readiness at any time, to give any information that may be required, and should you wish anything further by communicating with me I will cheerfully give it. *

(Signed) Speed S. Fry   Brig. Genl.

True Copy
E.B.W. Restieaux   Capt and A.Q.M.[1]

1. Fry to Restieaux, 15 Dec. 1864; Box 720; Records of the Office of the Quartermaster General, RG 92. The order to which Fry refers is Orders No. 24, July 6, 1864, issued by Lorenzo Thomas; all old men, infirm, and women and children who had already been received in Camp Nelson were ordered to be removed "beyond the limits of the Camp."

[Letterhead.] Office of Chief Quartermaster, Camp Nelson, Ky.   Dec 16" 1864.
Maj Genl M.C. Meigs   Quartermaster Genl.

Genl: I have the honor to acknowledge the receipt of your communication of the 7" Inst in regard to the alleged inhuman treatment of "helpless women" the wives and children of colored soldiers," at this Post, and instructing me to furnish a full and detailed report of the circumstances connected with the affair so far, at least, as regards the Quartermaster's Department"

In compliance with your instructions, I immediately on the receipt of your letter sought, and obtained an interview with Captain Y.Y. Smith,[1] Provost Marshal of the Camp under whose directions the alleged inhuman treatment took place, and who informed me that his actions were in accordance with orders received from Brig Genl S.S. Fry commanding the Post. What those orders were I have been unable to ascertain; but Capt Smith voluntarily informed me that they were verbal, and declined to disclose their nature stating at the same time that he delayed their execution in the hope that they would be modified. Genl Fry, however, on being informed that under instructions from Washington," I had instituted inquiries into the affair, favored me with a copy of "order" upon which he acted: a copy of which with accompanying communication I have the honor to enclose [Speed S. Fry's letter of 15 December 1864 and Orders No. 24, 6 July 1864.]

From the information which I have received and the testimony which I have the honor to enclose there is no doubt but what the women and children were expelled from Camp under circumstances of peculiar hardship; and I respectfully refer you for fuller particulars to the affidavits embodied in the enclosed communications of Capt T E Hall A Q M at whose instance they were taken and in which privates Miller, Burnside and Higgins testify to what their families endured; Messrs Sears, Linen and Larter — clerks in this department — testify to the condition of the exiles on the highway; and the Reverend Messrs. Schofield and Vetter testify to the [two or three indecipherable words] of the unfortunates.

I am happy in having the honor to inform you that as regards the execution of the aforementioned "order" the officers of the Quartermaster's Department are in no way responsible. Indeed it was enforced at a time when this department was busily engaged in equiping an expedition under Genl Burbridge; nor was I aware of the measure until it had been sometime in force. The wagons used by the Provost Marshal were ordered to proceed to Nicholasville, and the officer in charge on his own responsibility, furnished transportation, as an act of mercy, to such women and children as were ordered in that direction   So far as I know, the only officer of the Quartermaster's Department who interfered in the affair was Capt T E. Hall, A.Q.M. who while awaiting orders on being apprized of the condition to which the women and children were reduced promptly interposed in their behalf procured them temporary sustenance, and relief at his own expense, and by the direction of Bvt Major General Burbridge, superintended their return to Camp. Knowing the active interest he had manifested in the affair, I addressed him a communication upon the subject a copy of which with his response thereto, I have the honor to enclose and to which I invite special attention. I may be permitted to state that I have recently received orders from the Hon. Secretary of War through Brig Genl Robt Allen Chf Q.M. Louisville Ky to provide food and shelter for the wives and children of colored soldiers at this Camp. Hoping that I have satisfactorily answered the questions which you did me the honor to propound   *

E.B.W. Restieaux   Capt. and Asst. Qr. Mr.[2]

1. It may be V.V. Smith; in any case, he also is mentioned as supervisor of the provost marshal's office and prison at Camp Nelson.
2. Restieaux to Meigs, 16 Dec. 1864; Box 720; Records of the Office of the Quartermaster General, RG 92. The enclosures accompanying this cover letter included Fry's letter, with its enclosure of Thomas's order, and Hall's enormous report, with its enclosure of a long newspaper clipping; the various documents amounted to a package of reporting on Restieaux's part.

Camp Nelson Ky.   Dec 16" 1864
Captain E.B.W. Restieaux   Chief Quartermaster   Camp Nelson Ky.

Captain   In response to your communication of this date requesting that I furnish you, without delay with any information which may be in my possession relating to the late expulsion of colored women and children from this camp, I have the honor to reply that the importance of the subject seems to demand from me a report which must of necessity be voluminous and detailed. * * * * [*Most of the omitted portions of this letter, which is many pages long, are presented above as excerpts from Capt. Hall's report; the following paragraph is the last portion of that report.*]

Since that time [*November* 29] none has been turned out to my knowledge but many who were sent away have returned. Some Alas! have gone where the cruelty to which they were subjected here and which disgrace manhood, cannot reach them. One who wandered from place to place until driven by starvation to her forrmer master, was, if the statement of her husband is to be believed so cruelly beaten that she <u>died</u> in consequence. Some four hundred are now in Camp and owing to the fact that their former humble homes were ruthlessly destroyed by the military authorities they are now sheltered in Barracks built by the government. In accordance with order from the Major General Commanding buildings are in process of erection for them where it is proposed to care for them in a more systematic manner than can be done in their present condition. Their present condition however loudly calls for immediate action on the part of the Government. Many of them are destitute of shoes and all are indifferently clad. Sincerely thanking you in your hearty cooperation and sympathy in my efforts to ameliorate the condition of these poor people and your politeness in receiving the affidavits when other officers had refused. *

T E Hall   Supt in Charge[1]

1. Hall to Restieaux, 16 Dec. 1864; Box 720; RG 92. A newspaper clipping of Hall's "Humanitas" letter was evidently enclosed with this voluminous report. Virtually all the telegrams that Hall copied into this report are missing from the regular series of telegrams copied into the records.

Camp Nelson Ky.   Dec. 16, 1864

Personally appeared before me E B W Restieaux Capt and A.Q.M., Abisha Scofield who being duly sworn upon oath, says   I am a clergyman of the congregational denomination and have been laboring among the Freedmen at Camp Nelson Ky. under the auspices of the American Missionary association since the 20th of Sept 1864. The families of the colored soldiers who were in Camp lived in cabins and huts erected by the colored soldiers or at the expense of the women. During my labors among them I have witnessed about fifty of these huts and cabins erected, and the material of which they were constructed was unserviceable to the Government. I have had extensive dealing with these people and from my observation I believe that they supported themselves by washing cooking and &c.

Until the 22nd of last November I never heard any objection made by the military authorities of the Post to the women and children of colored soldiers residing within the limits of the Camp. On Tuesday the 22nd of November last the huts and cabins in which the families of the colored soldiers lived were torn down and the inhabitants were placed in Government wagons and driven outside the lines. The weather at the time was the coldest of the season. The wind was blowing quite sharp and the women and children were thinly clad and mostly without shoes. They were not all driven out on one day but their expulsion occupied about three days.

When they were driven out I did not know where they were to be taken and on the following Sabbath Nov 27" I went in search of the exiles. I found them in Nicholasville about six miles from Camp scattered in various places. Some were in an old Store house, some were straying along and lying down in the highway and all appeared to be suffering from exposure to the weather. I gave them some food. I received the provisions from Capt T.E. Hall A.Q.M.

The food was absolutely needed. On Monday Nov. 28 I saw and conversed with about sixteen woman and children who had walked from Nicholasville in the hopes of getting into the Camp. The guard refused them admittance. I told the guard that the order by which the women and children were expelled had been countermanded. The guard told me that he had strict orders not to admit them. They were not admitted. Among the number was a young woman who was quite sick and while I was conversing with the guard she lay on the ground. A day or two after this they were allowed to return to Camp. They were then very destitute most all complaining of being unwell. Children trembling with cold and wearied with fatigue. Since that time they have been crowded in a school room in Camp and their condition has been most abject and miserable, whereas they were pretty comfortable before they were driven out. While out of Camp they incurred disease and are now suffering from the effects of this exposure. As a clergyman I have no hesitation in pronouncing the treatment to which these poor people have been subjected as exceedingly demoralizing in its effects in addition to the physical suffering it entailed. And further this deponent saith not

(Signed) Abisha Scofield[1]

1. Affidavit of Scofield, 16 Dec 1864; M999:7:670–72; RG 105. Apparently, this affidavit was one of the collection sent to the Freedmen's Bureau by Capt. T.E. Hall, mentioned in and accompanying his letter of June 22, 1865. On file also in Box 720; RG 92; and reproduced in *The Black Military Experience*, 715, 716.

Camp Nelson Ky   Dec 16 1864

Personally appeared before me E B W Restieaux Capt. and A.Q.M. John Vetter who being duly sworn upon oath, says   I am a clergyman of the congregational church and have been laboring among the Freedmen of Camp Nelson Ky under the auspices of the American Missionary association since the 1ˢᵗ day of August 1864. I have heard and read the testimony of Rev. Abisha Schofield regarding the huts cabins &c. in which the wives and children of the colored soldiers lived, also regarding their means of living and I fully corroborate said testimony in every particular. I was in Camp Nelson on the 22' day of last Nov. It was a bitter cold day the wind was blowing quite hard and many of the women and children were driven from the Camp. I counted six or eight wagon loads of these women & children being driven away on Thursday or Friday. When they were expelled their huts were destroyed and in some instances before the inmates got out. The work of destruction commenced on Saturday Nov 26". I went to Nicholasville to inquire into the condition of the outcasts. I found that one hundred or more had taken shelter in the woods, having been driven from a meeting house in which they had taken refuge. I saw some in the town in a very destitute condition and the Provost Marshal of that place, Capt Randolph told me that those in the woods were entirely destitute of shelter or food. I returned to Camp on that night and stated the facts to Capt T.E. Hall who on the following morning supplied Rev. Mr. Schofield and myself with rations for distribution among the sufferers. On reaching Nicholasville on Sunday Nov. 27" I found that those who had gone to the woods had been scattered by the storm of the previous night and those we found were without food. I helped distribute the rations and saw that they were entirely destitute, some were sick. I learned that several had died. On Saturday Dec. 3" I went to Lexington to ascertain the condition of some of the women and children who having been driven from the Camp had taken refuge there. I found fourteen in an old shed, doorless and floorless sitting around a stick of burning wood with no food or bedding. One woman was apparently over come by exposure and another had given birth to a child in that place. Among those around the fire was a boy evidently near death whom on the following morning I found dead. I believe he died through exposure and want. In another old building I found about half a dozen sick without even the necessaries of life. And upon evidence which I believe, I was assured that one woman had been so pressed with hunger as to offer her child for sale in the City to obtain bread. I brought a number of the sick with me to Camp in an Ambulance. As a Clergyman I believe the tendency of the measure was very demoralizing and highly prejudicial to the interest of enlistments of Colored troops. And further this deponent saith not

(Signed) John Vetter[1]

1. Affidavit of John Vetter, 16 Dec. 1864; M999:7:673–75; RG 105. Apparently, this affidavit was one of the collection sent to the Freedmen's Bureau by Capt. T.E. Hall, mentioned in and accompanying his letter of June 22, 1865. It is also filed in Box 720; RG 92.

Camp Nelson Ky. Dec. 16. 1864.

Personally appeared before me E.B.W. Restieaux Capt and A.Q.M. William A. Sears who being duly sworn upon oath says.

I am a Clerk in the Quartermaster Dept. at Camp Nelson Ky. — and reside about two miles from Camp. On or about the 29th of Nov. 1864 when going home about five o'clock, in the afternoon, I met some colored women and children who had been driven out of Camp. I think, there were in all about a dozen. They had applied for readmission to Camp and had been refused. When I saw them they were in a lonely condition and were wandering about the highway having no place to go. I rode up to them and asked if they could get in Camp, and one of the number (a woman with a child in her arms told me that they had walked from Nicholasville and on applying for admission they were driven away by the guards who told them that if they did not go away they would be put in the "Bull Pen," meaning thereby the Camp Prison. When I left they were in the condition of poor houseless wanderers. And further this deponent saith not —

Wm A. Sears[1]

1. Affidavit of William A. Sears, 16 Dec. 1864; Box 720; RG 92. Another affidavit dated the same day (Box 720; RG 92) contains Sinen and Larter's testimony that Sears's affidavit was "true in every particular."

Lexington   Dec 17ᵗʰ [*1864*]
To Capt. T.E. Hall   A.Q.M.   Camp Nelson, Ky.

The Quarter masters Department will furnish transportation from Camp Nelson Ky. to Syracuse New York and return for Mr. Schofield, Agent of the American Missionary Ass'n. who visits Syracuse to obtain clothing for Colored refugees at Camp Nelson.

By command of Brv't Maj Gen'l Burbridge
J Bates Dickson   Capt. and A.A. Gen'l[1]

1. Dickson to Hall, 17 Dec. 1864; Vol. 62/117,119, p. 368; Telegrams Sent; RG 393.

Camp Nelson, Ky.   Dec. 26, 1864

Dear Bro. Scofield   I wish you a merry Christmas, though you may think it is already too late for any such congratulations. I am in Bro. Fee's room. We are crowded out. Butler took possession of our rooms, while absent to Cincinnati. I expected war in the Camp as soon as I went out the gate. I am sorry that it is so. But then my grief is not very harrowing. I have building near the Quarter masters that will be handier and more convenient to our work. The old Quarters of Col. Whitfield are occupied by the field staff of the 119 Reg. Co. I., who came last week. There are eight or ten officers — in our quarters. They stopped our commissary operations too. I lived on hard-tack on Saturday. To day I will draw something if I can. I clothed women & children yesterday. I found one child entirely naked. It is about two years old. It had not one thread of clothing and her mother could not get out of bed for want of clothing. I was glad I could help these poor people. I asked to start an Industrial Concern to make up a lot of stuff.

The Cincinnati Freedman's Aid Soc. wishes to be represented here in their work. It seems to me it would be multiplying agents here very much. Capt. Restieaux thinks I had better represent them, as I am already acquainted with the ground. I would do so, if I were not connected with the Association. But then this can be adjusted I presume. I write you this simply to give an idea how matters are progressing &c. I am as ever in God's will, Your brother,

John Vetters[1]

1. Vetters to Scofield, 26 Dec 1864, AMAA 44062.

Lexington, Ky., Dec. 27, 1864

Hon. Edwin M. Stanton, Secretary of War:
      * * * * [*Two paragraphs and a list of "Colored Troops in Kentucky."*]
      Recruiting continues dull. Most of the able bodied negroes in the Cities and large towns and the country adjacent thereto, have been enlisted, but we require mounted troops to penetrate the interior counties which abound with Southern

sympathizers, and who adopt every means possible to prevent the negroes from proceeding to the Camps of Reception. When General Burbridge returns from his expedition, the mounted Colored force with him can be used for this purpose. The incomplete Regiments will then soon be filled. I do not propose to organize any additional Regiments in Kentucky, but take the recruits to keep up the standard of those already organized. * * * * [One paragraph.]

I found it necessary to order shelter for the helpless women and children at Camp Nelson, where there is quite a number, and that number constantly increasing. On Christmas day a large number arrived, stating they were driven from their homes, and in some instances they stated their masters had their cabins pulled down over their heads. I have no reason to suppose that the thorough Union men treat their helpless slaves with any inhumanity, but it is the Southern sympathizers, who are opposed to the policy of arming the Blacks. Such of them as have lost their able-bodied men are anxious to get rid of those who are an expense to them, and in many cases drive them off to seek shelter where they best can. I feel bound to take charge of all such, and afford them food and shelter until other provision can be made for them. I learn that a number of women can be profitably employed at Camp Nelson. * * * * [Two paragraphs.]

L. Thomas, Adjutant-General[1]

1. Thomas to Stanton, 27 Dec. 1864, in *NIMSUS*, 4:2853–55; and in *OR*, 3, 4, 1017–18.

Report of the commissioners of investigation of colored refugees in Kentucky, Tennessee, and Alabama.
Washington, D.C., December 28, 1864.
[*To Edwin M. Stanton, Secretary of War.*]

Sir: The undersigned special commissioners, appointed by your order of June 2, 1864, to investigate and report upon the condition and treatment of colored refugees at Nashville, Tennessee, and Louisville and Camp Nelson, Kentucky, submit the following report and recommendations: * * * * [*Huge report; seventeen pages omitted here.*]
Of Kentucky.

We made a brief visit to Louisville, Lexington, and Camp Nelson, Kentucky. There is no organized camp for the reception and care of colored refugees within this State. That at Camp Nelson had been broken up and abandoned, by order of Brigadier General L. Thomas, Adjutant General; the propriety of which order we think may be seriously questioned. It not only encouraged the hopes of secession sympathizers in Kentucky, but, in like ration, discouraged enlistments of colored men, who will not leave their families to the tender mercies of Kentucky hospitality, humanity, or Christianity. Owing to the great numbers of colored men who have enlisted in the federal service, in many cases their wives and children are left in a suffering condition on account of being driven from their homes by their Union-hating masters. In addition to women and children residing in the State, hundreds of refugees from other States are congregating here for safety and protections, and unless something is done for them by the general government there will be of necessity great suffering among them. We would therefore recommend that a general camp of reception be at once instituted for them, both white and colored, at Camp Nelson; and that provision be made by the government for their support and maintenance, using their labor in such way as may be most useful; this would certainly be not only humane but just, as their husbands, fathers, and brothers are doing the country service in the field, and are, consequently, unable to care for and protect them. We would recommend that the quartermaster at Camp Nelson be authorized and instructed to make whatever preparations may be proper for their accommodation and care. We found General Burbridge, commander of the district, a gentleman whose sympathies are largely with these distressed people; and the recommendations we here make are strictly in accordance with his views and wishes, and which we sincerely hope may meet with your approval.

.   The policy, or rather purpose, of the government in attempting to provide for the wants and ameliorate the condition of these unfortunate refugees, is a wise and philanthropic one, growing out of individual necessities on the one hand, and the highest possible public duty on the other. The manner of doing this great service through the agency of these camps is, we understand, to some extent an experiment. We have endeavored to present the results of this experiment in the summary of the evidence collected by us, containing a partial history of what has transpired at the camps of Nashville, Huntsville, Gallatin, and Clarksville. While there has been much carelessness, indifference, and criminal neglect at some of these points by the officers intrusted with the interests and well-being of these refugees, resulting in pecuniary losses to the government, as well as great losses and suffering to the refugees themselves, we think the experiment, so far as it has been fairly made, has not proved a failure. It is an enterprise entirely novel in its character, for which there has never before been either occasion or precedent. In the most devoted hands, in many things, at first, it might not prosper so greatly as is to be desired. In the hands of weak, unsympathizing, and dishonest men it could not prosper at all. The experiment thus far shows more what *might* be accomplished under judicious management than what *has been* accomplished. In its very failures it is full of suggestions and instruction as to what might be done for the present comfort and ultimate welfare of the refugees under well-devised and well-regulated agencies of this kind. As in all other great enterprises, success must depend upon the good sense and good faith of those intrusted with the execution of such a work. These camps could be not only made a success in themselves in relieving and educating the thousands who may flock to them, but may also be made common centres from which relief and education will radiate, reaching multitudes far beyond the immediate neighborhoods of the camps. Some carefully devised system ought at once to be adopted, under which every camp should be organized, and by the rules of which the business and duties of every camp should be conducted or performed. A few plain, practical rules defining the authority of those having charge of the system, and defining the duties of subordinates having charge of the camps, would be sufficient. These suggestions are, of course, made upon the supposition that sound judging, sagacious, energetic, and philanthropic men are chosen permanently for the work. Men selected to gratify favorites, or through mere political influence, or through temporary expediency, because there is no other use for them, or speculators, or men having more sympathy with slaveholders than for the wasting humanity around them, ought never to be selected for so grave and important duties. After a well-considered system is determined upon and the means provide, the next and only force needed to warrant the most complete success is to be found in men fit for the service. The condition of these refugees is peculiar, differing in every respect from the condition of any people ever found in a civilized country before. They not only need relief in the way of food and clothing, but in everything besides. Those who find their way to the camps, and the untold thousands who do not find their way there, are peculiarly helpless. They differ, however, materially, in character. While all are helpless in some degree, some are more helpless and require more assistance than others. In very many cases the strong, able, and brave men have either gone or may go to the army, leaving their families entirely unprovided, and too feeble, both physically and mentally, to support themselves, and with only a glimmering hope of sustenance from the charity of citizens, or in the lavishly squandered or stintily doled supplies furnished by the government by the hands of heartless or indifferent public officials. There is a common obligation, in every possible way consistent with the public necessities and the public means, to relieve all who suffer under the common misfortune of this strange war. The obligation in this case is not a common one; it is peculiar and specific, growing out of the anomalous condition in which they lived before the war began; upon the now singular condition into which they have unresistingly and ignorantly drifted, either through the action of slave masters or through the exigencies of a fearful military struggle. They owned nothing while slaves; they own nothing now. They owned neither themselves nor the means of subsistence before. While they own themselves, they have no means of subsistence now. They never have learned to be self-reliant, and are not so. They never had any care for the future, and therefore never learned to be provident for the future. They never took care of each other, in either sickness or health, before, and are not capable of doing so now. As they were entitled to the world's sympathy before, they are entitled to its sympathy, and its most liberal charities, now. They were degraded, and they suffered through a nation's weakness: they have a right to be lifted up by a nation's wonderfully developing strength. That the condition of multitudes of these refugees is worse now than before the war began, and before they were refugees, is not adduced here as an argument in favor of their condition while they were slaves; it is a stronger argument against the continuance of a subjection that has so degraded them as that they have lost, through centuries of oppression, almost all the elements of manhood. A very large number of these refugees have claims upon the government for another reason: the strong, hardy men have been induced to turn from peaceful labor to become soldiers. They had a right to expect that their families would not be permitted by the government to suffer while they were perilling all in defence and support of that government; the government, on this account, has become doubly indebted to them. They go now to aid in the defence of a government that has never done anything for them. It has never protected them in the enjoyment of their rights of person or of property; they go to aid in sustaining it, notwithstanding all this. White loyal soldiers know that as they leave family and home behind, there are always relatives and friends and bounty-paying States to support them. Not so here. They are amidst suffering, and want, and odious oppression. They leave parents, and children, and wives, with no reliance but promises of public authorities — promises well intended, but too idly made, or promises made in fraud, and broken with little hesitation, and less shame. To cheat a negro by a private citizen or by a public officer is too much a pastime. To plunder him of all he has seems little of a crime, because he has so little. To cheat or starve his family, while he fights to maintain a government which supports the plunderers, is the ostensible business of too many who wear the nation's livery.

While these people have cause to complain, they quietly, in ignorance, simplicity, and squalid woe, drag on, wondering at the changes in their own condition and the condition of all around them, knowing only that they suffer, and that there is no prospect of relief, so far as by any experience they have been taught. They have the right to some kind of assistance, and the government alone has the means and ability to furnish it. If we take colored soldiers into our armies, knowing the condition of the families they leave behind, we must take them under the obligation to take care of the families that would be otherwise left in want. When the enlisting colored soldiers are assured that the care of their families shall be the care of the government, that assurance must be made good. If we exact good faith from them, we must keep good faith with them. If the "promise made by lips is broken to the hope" hereafter, as heretofore it has been, in too many cases, enlistments not only will stop, but those already enlisted will become hopeless as the treatment of their families has been heartless, and their service become an unwilling drudgery, instead of a cheerfully performed duty.

S.W. Bostwick   Thomas Hood.[1]

1. Published report of S.W. Bostwick and Thomas Hood to Edwin M. Stanton, Secretary of War, 28 Dec. 1864, in Letter of the Secretary of War, Senate Documents 1864–65, Serial 1209, pp. 1, 18–20, 23. Bostwick and Hood, special commissioners appointed by the secretary of war, have not otherwise been identified. S.W. Bostwick had once before been a special commissioner for the secretary of war, appointed on November 9, 1863 "to hear and determine the case of state prisoners" at the military prison in Alton, Illinois. *OR*, 2, 6, 492.

[December, 1864]

End of year report to the U.S. Sanitary Commission from Thomas Butler

We review our efforts for the relief of the suffering in the District of Central Kentucky with much pride and pleasure. Scores have blessed the Sanitary Commission, through us, for its seasonable and abundant aid, and have thus crowned its work with a satisfactory proof of success. . . .

Although justice seemed occasionally to demand it, yet never, through our agency, has a soldier been committed to the guardhouse or prison. A deep regard for his liberty and reputation, and a profound commiseration for those whom I have seen suffer long and bitterly for some trivial offense, have prevented me from inflicting pain upon some soldiers guilty of serious misdemeanors, even while the guards were at the door ready to take them in custody. . . .

It would be evident from the reports made to you during the past month, that we have been exceedingly busy. The raid of Breckenridge through Eastern Tennessee has drawn into this District a large number of troops to resist him. Detachments and regiments, from Knoxville and elsewhere, have come to this camp for supplies, and all have combined to fill up the measure of our work. During the month we have furnished forty thousand three hundred and thirty-three meals and fourteen thousand seven hundred and twenty-two lodgings.

The refugee women and children from the South still come here for protection and assistance. Occasionally we forward a family northward, generally to Cincinnati; while several families, having gone for months through a series of diseases, still remain on our hands.

The prison which, when we commenced our labors in the spring in behalf of incarcerated soldiers, contained several hundred, now contains but forty, and these principally old and sentenced offenders.

The Soldiers' Home, by universal consent, has performed a good work by providing comfortable quarters and well-cooked meals for quite an army. For the past ten months the number of men received has been seventy-nine thousand eight hundred and eighty-three; lodgings furnished, two hundred and forty-seven thousand three hundred and forty-nine.[1]

1. Newberry, 384, 385.

[Letterhead.] The U.S. CHRISTIAN COMMISSION   **Camp Nelson Ky**   **Jan 2 /65**

Dear Bro Whipple   I have been kept at home — by soar throat hoarsness, and an affliction that hindered riding

I came here last sabbath — There has been much suffering

There is a good thing now going on here in way of provision for women and a school for children

I saw the condition of the women who came into the camp — tempted corrupted — many had been put out They would return soldiers wives and children abused at home came in — often thrown out   This injured the faith of the soldiers

I went to Capt Hall then Quarter Master here told him there ought to be a place for the women and children with grounds for culture in the spring rooms in which to do work with superintendents & guard of faithful colored men "Elders" taken from the invalid Corpse.

I went to Capt Hall with the plan   He asked me to draw up a paper directed to Sect of War and he would sign it But that he could not move directly in this matter because what he did would have to pass through the hands of officials here not friendly

I did so — set forth four reasons for such request — propriety & utility of such   Capt Hall also signed it with others

.I forwarded the petition to Sect [*Salmon P.*] Chase & Sen [*Henry*] Wilson — Both responded saying they had given such recommendation as would likely secure action   The thing requested is here   Capt. Hall is absent   I will see him soon as he shall return

Provision will be made for a magnificent school — the sight is a high beautiful one — fifty acres   The building thus far the finest in the Camp.

Now I wish to know how you friends feel in reference to the enterprise here   I have thought that perhaps you regarded the matter as an irregular small thing

Our remittances for expenses were delayed   This I think has arisen from other pressures * * * * [*Five paragraphs.*]

Now your many calls at other & older places may make it impossible for you to do much here   If so we wish to know it   The door will soon open for an immense work in the state

The Aid Society of Cincinnati are here [*represented*] by one agent — another this week have been here once before. I was here then in the providence of God here now am not ready yet to be transferred unless <u>necessity</u> demands & propriety demands

Bro Vetter is half inclined to become the agent of Cincinnati   I have asked him to hold on   They have three times soliced my cooperation — as their agent   I declined   They are now trying him * * * * [*Four paragraphs.*]

Cincinnati is close by and in time of emergency as in last month they can send clothing books &c quickly   Perhaps if you think best we had better have clothing through Cincinn and all religious teachers through you. Cincinnati wants to get <u>teachers</u> into the <u>school</u>. The school will be <u>the</u> thing of the state as I believe

If we have to have aid in support of teachers I would rather have from Chicago & clothing from Cincinn   what do you say * * * * [*Seven paragraphs.*]

John G Fee

Bro Vetter has done good among these sufferers who were thrown out of camp   Others would do the same good & not offend by his manner — yet those others are not plenty as black birds — nor are all men perfect — . . . . * * * * [*Three paragraphs.*][1]

1. Fee to Whipple, 2 Jan. 1865, AMAA 44064–6.

Lexington, Ky., January 2, 1865.

Hon. E.M. Stanton, Secretary of War:

Major-General Burbridge, with his command, has just returned from a most successful expedition. Five hundred negroes accompanied his command and Gillem.[1] A battalion of the Sixth U.S. Colored Cavalry, 300 strong, attacked and whipped Duke's brigade, of 350—the last remnant of Morgan's force. The rebels were driven half a mile, with a loss on their side of thirty men killed and wounded. They were on the crest of a hill at Marion,[2] and the negroes charged over open ground, and did not fire a gun until within thirty yards of the rebels. This is the first time that any of these men were under fire. Three full regiments of colored troops will leave for the Army of the James about the end of the week. Can I be authorized to send recruiting officers to Cincinnati, where there are a large number of Kentucky negroes, any of whom will, no doubt, enlist? At the request of many influential men of Kentucky, I will attend the convention at Frankfort, the 4th instant. They say my presence there will do much good.

L. Thomas, Adjutant-General[3]

1. Union general Alvin Cullem Gillem (1830–1875) was brigadier quartermaster in Kentucky early in his military career. By January 1865 he was commander of the Fourth Division, Cavalry Corps, Army of the Cumberland. He led an expedition to East Tennessee from August 1864 to March 1865, during which John H. Morgan was killed at Greeneville. *CWD*.
2. Marion, Virginia, is the county seat of Smyth County, where Saltville is also located.
3. Thomas to Stanton, 2 Jan. 1865, *OR*, 1, 45, pt. 2, 494–95.

Head Quarters Camp Nelson   January 5th 1865
General Orders No 30

The repeated complaints made by citizens to these Head Quarters of the loss of Horses and mules stolen from them by white men and negroes, has induced the belief that a regular system of thieving has been established by hangers on about this camp who have their agents out through the country from the purpose of stealing and taking away horses and mules from their proper owners.

It is therefore ordered that no person within this Camp will be permitted to purchas from any white man or negro any Horse or mule where their is the slightest reason to suspect that the animal has been stolen.

It shall be the duty of officers Corrill Keepers Stable Keepers wagon masters and Detectives to seize and report to their Head Quarters all white men and negroes who may came to Camp with any species of property which they cannot account for together with the property in their possession.

Any white man or negro hereafter found in or around this Camp with property in the possession which he cannot account for will be arrested and turned over to the Civil Authorities to be delt with according to the laws of the State.

It is made the duty of all officers besides those already mentioned to execute the provisions of this Order and any Officer Soldier Corrill Keeper Stable Keeper Wagon master or any other person who may violate its provisions will be held to a strict accountability   By Order of

Brig Genl S S Fry

[*No signature.*] Lt. & A.A.A.G[1]

1. General Orders No. 30, 5 Jan. 1865; Vol. 111/256 District of Ky., pp. 100, 101; General Orders; RG 393.

Camp Nelson   Jan 9th 1864 [*1865*][1]
Rev Geo. Whipple   Sec of A.M.A.

My Dear Sir — I have yours of the 31st ult. making inquiries concerning the wants of the colored women & children in this camp — You are already aware of the severe struggle we have had here and of its triumphant result. I am now constructing buildings for these people with a design to their moral and intellectual improvement   The plan contemplates a school, a work shop, laundry, &c. — I have found in the person of Rev. L. Williams formerly of Holden Mass a man I think will make a good Superintendent & as the work progresses we will want teachers and books — At the present we need clothing for the women especially — their cut off garments can be made over for the children — We now have in camp more than six hundred of these people and they are coming in every day — Anything you can do or suggest will be thankfully received — I think M[r.] [*Elnathan*] Davis could be sent here to look the matter over. I shall be in N York in a few days and will if possible call and see you —   *

T E Hall   Late Capt & a q m[2]

1. Hall missed the change in the year and continued writing 1864.
2. Hall to Whipple, 9 Jan 1864 [1865], AMAA 43987.

[*Letterhead.*] *U.S. CHRISTIAN COMMISSION*   Berea Madison Co
Ky   Jan. 10 /65
(Private)

Dear Bro Whipple — As I returned from Frankfort Gen Burbridge sought a conversation — told me the paper which I sent to Sec. of War was sent back to him for approval — that he approved with all his heart — had directed Capt. Hall to select a spot and erect buildings for the women & children   He offered me facilities — God opens the way.

I went on to Camp — Capt Hall asked an interview. He proposed Rev Williams as superintendent — an acquaintance of his. I proposed Bro. Scofield, previously — Capt H objected — thought Williams a good man — a lawyer previously had some experience in Tenn — had been an anti slavery lecturer — pastor of a church in Mass for years — had the most "organizing mind"

On hearing the man speak and seeing more of him, we agreed to put Williams in on trial — if he does well he continues as superintendent

The Capt desires that I be one of the board of Directors — He requested that two more men (Kentuckians) be the board — that Geo D Blakey[1] be one of the three — until we agree upon the third Capt Hall will act — Bro Scofield may be that third.

These will be subject to appointment by Gen Burbridge.

Capt Hall will probably call on you soon & submit this arrangment — * * * *
[*Four paragraphs.*]

J G Fee[2]

1. Fee writes "Blakey" in this letter, but the man's name was Blakeman. In later letters, Fee gets it right. George D. Blakeman was Camp Nelson's official "Farmer" after Willard W. Wheeler left for Berea, and he was one of the founding trustees of Ariel Academy.
2. Fee to Whipple, 10 Jan 1865, AMAA 44070.

Camp Nelson Ky   Jan. 20th 1865

Dear Brother Fee.   I would like verry much to see you and here your advice on matters at this time. I myself have no room to complain for I am well and doin well, but som things do not please me for I love peace and union and I have lived longenough to know that if men do not love each other they do not love God and if they do not love God they will not werke for him.

Though they may worke yet is not for him for if the love of the world be in a man the love of the Father is not thare. and if we love not our brother whom we have seen how can we love God whom we have not see.

but how vane it seames to me to see men strive one against another as thoug they knew not that thare was a God who ruls the Heavens and the earth. but enough of this now but I would like for you to come and See yourself how things are going on. and rite up matters as soon as you can   I would be glad to have time to studdy but cannt at this time. please come soon for I would like to See you very much and brother Scofield would like to see you please come with out delay for if you do not come soon he will resine. Thare has been much sickness and many deaths here. since Dec. 24th /64. thare has been 43 deaths and still they die. but we cannot complain for death is abroad in the land. I remain your brother in Christe

Gabriel Burdett[1]

1. Burdett to Fee, 20 Jan 1865, AMAA 44071. An endorsement on the letter, dated January 20, 1865, states that Fee had sent the letter to the AMA "to show the progress of the writer and the feeling of the Colored people."

[*Excerpt from*] **REPORTS OF MR. BUTLER.** CARE OF THE SANITARY COMMISSION FOR WHITE REFUGEES AT CAMP NELSON.

On a wintry night in January, 1865, a poor woman with six children applied at the Home for food and shelter. She told us that, three months before, the rebels had driven her and her children from their home, and destroyed their property; that her husband, who was a discharged Union soldier, in attempting to bring her to this camp, was captured, and taken toward Virginia; that for many weeks she and her children had wandered, homeless, hungry and sick, through the cold and stormy weather, to reach Camp Nelson. We cared for them through the night, and, on the morrow, procured a building, into which we removed them, supplying them with food and fuel.

Toward the evening of the same day, a sickly and dejected man came into our office, and requested food and lodging for the night. In answer to our usual questions, he stated that he had been discharged from the service, at Knoxville, six months before. Being overburdened with a great sorrow, he sought relief by telling us his troubles, from which we inferred that he was the missing protector of the woman and children who had come to us twenty-four hours earlier. He said that he had been captured by the rebels three months before, while trying to reach this camp with his wife and six children; that, after a long march with his captors, he had effected his escape, and returned in search of his family. The name of both parties, together with their residence, fully proving their relationship, I felt safe in telling him where he could find his family. He sprang up with a cry of joy—would not wait an instant for food—but, with a guide, started off for wife and children at a double-quick. There was joy in that poor, mean dwelling, that night, which few can realize.

On the morrow, disease entered this re-united family, and, for many weeks, the poor man nursed wife and children with assiduous and untiring watchfulness. Yet death followed apace; and when, weeks after, with a bowed form and broken spirit he left our camp, three children were his only companions.[1]

1. Newberry, 535–36.

[*Excerpt from*] REPORTS OF MR. BUTLER. CARE OF THE SANITARY COMMISSION FOR WHITE REFUGEEES AT CAMP NELSON.

They [the Appalachian refugees] were even more wretched and more pitiable than the "contrabands." After the removal of General Fry from this post, they received less than one-third of the amount of food furnished *per capita* to the colored refugees. From the 1st of February, 1865, a large ration was issued to colored women and children, while the white received the substance of only one meal per day. Fuel was continued to the colored, but discontinued to the sickly white people. Good buildings were erected for the negroes, while the white refugees remained in old log huts and miserable, dilapidated places. These were troubles arising from the caprice of the Quartermaster and Commissary of the camp, and were justly felt and mourned over when the children cried for bread and they had nothing with which to satisfy their hunger. The fault was not with the Government, which made suitable provision for the poor and unfortunate without regard to race or color, but from a narrow and unreasoning sympathy with an oppressed race on the part of those who, absorbed in the great work of freeing that race from bondage, seemed to forget, or even disbelieve, that there were any loyal men at the South. Thus many persons, in their devotion to the interests of the colored race, allowed themselves to be unfeeling and unjust to the women and children of their own color, at the extreme of human endurance from hunger, cold, bereavement, hardship and sorrow of every form, and these often the wives and children of men who had never been slaveholders, but had laid down their lives in the struggle of freedom against slavery.

While ourselves doing and risking far more for the freedmen than for the white refugees, we can hardly be accused of partiality in behalf of the latter, and yet, during all the term of our administration of the affairs of the Sanitary Commission at Camp Nelson, we felt impelled to do all in our power for those whose circumstances we have sketched; and it has only been matter of regret with us that so large a part of the evils they endured were beyond the ability, not only of our hands, but of any other human hands to relieve.

Many efforts were made on our part to have the aid rendered by Government to fugitives at Camp Nelson equalized to the white and black; yet, though the subject was regarded in its true light by General Palmer, Commandant of the Department of Kentucky, and orders were issued by him, distinctly forbidding the discrimination to which I have referred, the officers having local authority at Camp Nelson united to render these orders inoperative, and they were never enforced.

During the last months of our occupation of Camp Nelson we had ever before our eyes an illustration of official partiality and injustice in a discrimination between two groups of our protegés, equally deserving and equally destitute and wretched, by which one received three times the amount of assistance from the Government that was rendered the other. Previous to the removal of General Fry, kindness and even-handed justice were awarded to all over whom he had supervision; but after the day he ceased to command there, white and colored refugees alike had cause to mourn his absence, and the entire aggregate of Christian sympathy and effort for the unfortunate failed to fill the void thus made.

At Camp Nelson, as elsewhere, diseases in many forms was added to the afflictions of the refugees. Small pox and measles were specially prevalent among them, and caused many deaths, and not a few were prostrated by them before they reached the camp; hence every unoccupied house and miserable hut for miles outside the lines was taken possession of by these unfortunates. Our services were frequently required to procure for them medical attention, as well as food and other comforts, and to care for the varied wants of those who were in such utter helplessness and distress. Within camp limits it soon became necessary to establish a hospital for all cases of eruptive disease, and the number of inmates was, for months, large. Dr. R.S. Mitchell, the surgeon on charge, labored untiringly and tenderly among them, and saved very many to begin life in a new field or to return to their old homes in the South. Though Sanitary relief and medical skill were unsparingly bestowed upon the sick, death made many seizures among them, as one group of about sixty graves, and others located according to family inclination, plainly indicate.[1]

1. Ibid., 533–35.

[*Letterhead.*] *The United States Christian Commission.* **Camp Nelson Ky.**   Feb 4th **1865**

<u>Dear brethren</u>   The first month of the New Year has expired and you will expect from me the usual report.

I called at Cincinnati on my way out and obtained a stove, and Box of Blankets and several boxes of clothing which were sent on and distributed during my abscence. These I obtained the usual report.

During the past month my time and strength have been devoted mainly to clothing the naked. When we had moved the suffering and dying women and children from the crowded school Room into the more roomy Barracks, it was thought best that I should make a journey North for the purpose of obtaining clothing.

To this end I received an order from Gen. Burbridge and free transportation to Syracuse N.Y. I went into Madison Co. and obtained six boxes of clothing one from Lebanon two boxes from Georgetown two from Hamilton and one from Peterboro. Worth in all $250. Some few persons unasked handed me a little money. I received from Lebanon in cash $6.00 from Peterboro the same, in all $12.00 — from the "<u>Freedmens Aid Commission</u>" —

A few days ago I was ordered by Gen. Fry Com. of this Post to go to Cincinnati and obtain more clothing from the same source. I have just returned. I obtained a box of blankets and four boxes of clothing, which have not yet come to hand. The work of clothing these naked ones is for the present assigned to me. Probably I shall finish up this work in about two weeks more, Though it is not quite the labor I came here to do, yet the way will thus be prepared for instruction and brother Fee also thinks all things considered I had better attend to it till it is done or at least till the present supply is exhausted.

The new buildings are going up but the quartermaster I am sorry to say appears to have little regard for the work of instruction. I would recommend that you apply at once to the War department for the use of the school room and for lands and shelter for Teachers for the purpose of instruction   The school then would be under our charge and would afford instruction to 6 or 8 hundred people. Now is the time to move. * * * * [*Expense account and two paragraphs.*]

A. Scofield[1]

1. Scofield to the brethren, 4 Feb. 1865, AMAA 44075.

Camp Nelson   Feb 7th 65

Dear bretheren   I have waited a day or two before sending in my Report to see what were to be the developements here in relation to my field of labor in this Camp. So far as I am able to see it is about closed. Capt Hall and friends so far as I can learn have taken the entire possession of the contrabands in camp. They are puting them into the new buildings, and claim supreme control. They are it is said appointed of the government with large salaries and what surprises me I hear that you have also put them into service as your agents, but with what additional pay I have not learned. One thing I think is certain they are likely to make a rich thing out of it.

Well, where shall I labor? I have borne the heat and burden of the day — I have stood by the cause. When no man stood with me — But while I was away, the whole matter was changed and no field of labor in this new movement has been alloted to me. The school Room remains still unoccupied, and several hundred soldiers are in camp near it. Brother Fee thinks I had for the present better open School there. Probably in a few weeks these soldiers will be gone and then the present appearances are that my work in Camp Nelson will be done.

From the first dear bretheren, I have been opposed to having the government undertake this work any further than to shelter protect and possibly feed. No man in this work should receive high government pay mischief will come of it. But enough — Will you not assign to me another field of labor? I love this work. I have a wife and two daughters who could be Teachers. We can work for such wages as you are accustomed to give. Let me have a School to manage and see if I can do anything to purpose. Write me immediately   Affectionately

A. Scofield[1]

1. Scofield to the brethren, 7 Feb. 1865, AMAA 44078.

War Department, Washington City, February 8, 1865

Maj. Gen. John M. Palmer:[1]

General: The President has assigned you to the command of the Department of the Ohio, comprising the state of Kentucky, and constituting a part of the division east of the Mississippi now commanded by Major-General Thomas . . . .

. . . Major-General Burbridge, your predecessor in the District of Kentucky, will be relieved from command and ordered to report to Major-General Thomas for duty in the field. . . .

Second. The enlistment of colored troops is an important part of the service, to which you will not fail to direct your immediate attention. Camps have already been established, which you will promptly inspect in person, and cause to be placed under proper police and discipline. The President is grieved to be informed that much hostility still exists in the minds of some evil-disposed persons in the State of Kentucky against the enlistment of colored soldiers, and that, in order to discourage their enlistment, many cases have occurred of their cruel and barbarous treatment and murder. Your hand should be laid heavily upon all outrages of this nature. The Government stands pledged, and will expect its military commanders, of every rank and degree, to fulfill that pledge, to give protection and encouragement to colored persons desiring to enlist in the armies of the United States. Whatever resistance or obstacle is thrown in the way of such enlistments constitutes a hostile act against the Government, and should be dealt with accordingly. To the destitute women and children of soldiers in the service of the United States, without regard to color, protection and support should be given, so far as their necessities may require. You will therefore, under proper regulations, be authorized to issue rations of food, also clothing, and afford fuel and shelter to helpless women and children of persons in the service of the United States, whose necessities may require such assistance, causing a separate account to be kept by the proper staff officers of all such issues, in order that the expense may be distinguished from other war expenditures. Large numbers of refugees from territory held by the rebels are reported as coming within your department in very distressed and necessitous circumstances. To this class of persons you will also be authorized to furnish adequate supplies, under similar regulations as above expressed, as well as transportation, to enable them to go into the Northern States, where they may find homes and employment for their support. A strict accountability on the part of all officers engaged in these duties should be enforced and a proper system of accounts required.

Third. The State of Kentucky is reported to be infested with bands of guerrilla parties, consisting of rebels, who have been some time or other in the military force of the rebellion, and of their sympathizers at home. These parties, it is said, are accustomed to making raids in different portions of the State, plundering and murdering peaceable citizens who are obnoxious to them. All such persons are to be treated as enemies of the human race, and no effort spared to root out and destroy them in the most prompt and effectual manner. . . . * * * *

Fifth. By order of the President, the State of Kentucky is under martial law. . . . * * * *

Edwin M. Stanton, Secretary of War.
War Department, Washington City, February 8, 1865 [2]

1. John McAuley Palmer (born 1817 in Scott County, Kentucky; died 1900) began his military service as colonel of the Fourteenth Illinois Infantry. He quickly became a brigadier-general, assigned as commander in the Army of the Mississippi and the Army of the Cumberland. He returned to Kentucky late in his military career, commanding the Department of Kentucky from February 10, 1865, until April 1, 1866, when he resigned from the army. His "reign" in Kentucky was marked by his determination to free as many slaves as possible and by the immense hostility he aroused through his emancipation policies. After the war, he became governor of Illinois on the Republican ticket; eventually, he won a Senate seat and ran for president of the United States. *ANB; CWD;* Dyer, 1:91–92; *GIB; HR,* 2:767; *KE,* 708–9.

2. Stanton to Palmer, 8 Feb. 1865, *OR,* 1, 49, pt. 1, 670, 671.

[*Letterhead.*] *The United States Christian Commission*   Camp Nelson Ky   Feb 8 /65

Dear Bro Whipple   The interest in this camp, so far as the colored people are concerned, continues to increase.

There are here parts of three regiments of colored soldiers.

Within a few days our school room for soldiers will again be ready for their reception and instruction   Bro Scofield will probably have the care or them for the present.

There are near eight hundred women and children now in camp; and yet they come. Seventy seven came yesterday. Bro. L. Williams, of Mass, has the care of these for the present.

As you are aware, the government has set apart a tract of land for wards, school rooms, workshops and extensive gardens. Buildings being put up. Within two wards are some three hundred women children. Many of these are in a condition truly destitute.

I know one of our representatives in congress said a few days since that "slavery in Ky was not that horrible thing which northern abolitionists describe" — Slavery is essentially the same everywhere — it is a system of force and violence   As counted a few days since, there were within this Camp, seven hundred and fifty three women and children. Of this number, one hundred and fifty say they were cruelly treated on account of their husbands enlisting, and three hundred and ten say they were driven off "from home"   Three were so horribly lacerated that the military authorities after examinations by surgeons sent them to Cincinnati. These persons were [*turned over*] to the care of the Freedman's Aid Society.

Of the first three thousand colored men examined in this camp for military service, three out of five bore on their bodies marks of cruelty. This is to me the personal statement of both the surgeons who examined them.

Many of these women and children have not enough of one poor dirty suit to cover them well — no changes of raiment

The government offers to these people rations and shelter. We must depend upon the benevolent public for clothing for these people, at least for a time.

It is the purpose of the government here to erect speedily cottages for other fugitives that may yet come — also a large school room & chapel. "We" shall very soon need assistant teachers & matrons — not novices, but sober, industrious women who are willing, by sacrifice and toil, to do this poor, oppressed people good.

No class of people on this earth are to me more hopeful, so far as moral good is concerned, than these exslaves of Kentucky — receptive obedient trusting.

We ought to praise God for this free access to these humble trusting millions. Tis a privilege to give and be coworkers with Christ in the redemption of suffering humanity.

John G Fee[1]

* * * * [*Thirteen paragraphs.*]

I have seen the principal carpenter   find we can have cottages for 8 or 10 built quicker & cheaper than huge wards in which to pile in 125 or 150 — noise feuds disease and disgust is engendered in such — my mind is decided in favor of Cottages   I have submitted the thing to Capt. Hall. I think he will adopt the plan in farther construction.

Conclusion

There are many doors now opening to me in this state.

Thank God for the privelege.

But apparently the best thing for my health & progress in knowledge and good of my sons is to settle down in some one place as Berea or here & build up <u>one</u> thing well. I have great sympathy for these colored people tis meat & drink to me to help them & in God's providence I know the antislavery enterprise & habits of this people better than I do science — How do you see duty to me

J G Fee[2]

    1. Fee to Whipple, 8 Feb. 1865, AMAA 44079–82.
    2. Fee to Whipple, 9 Feb. 1865, AMAA 44083–86. This section is a postscript to the preceding letter.

[Letterhead.] Head-Quarters U.S. Colored Troops, Lexington, Ky.   **Feb 15th** *1865.*
John G Fee

Dear Sr   Your letter of the 13th dated at Berea, is recd. and in reply I have to inform you that Capt Hall is appointed the Superintendent of the Colored Home at Camp Nelson but that as yet his authority does not extend over other parts of the state. In my Judgement it will be wisest for one of the several Benevolent Associations to appoint a proper person and send him out to look after the Colored Home and that the person so designated be appointed and confirmed by Military appointment. No more homes can at present be erected and it is not best to encourage women & children to come in. Only those who are ill treated and indigent should be received. The Home is not intended as an Alms house but as an Assylum for the unfortunate and oppressed. There will be more abused and ill treated unfortunates than can be well cared for and therefore only the worst cases should be recd

    I wish you would inform me what Society has done the most for the Institution as far as it has gone   *

Jas. S. Brisbin B Brig Gen[l] & Supt of U S Col[d] Troops[1]

    1. Brisbin to Fee, 15 Feb. 1865, AMAA 44090.

[Elijah P. Marrs; after the last of January, 1865, when Marrs was marched to Bowling Green.]

My efficiency as a sergeant had proven to the officers that I was capable, and as a consequence I was ordered to report to headquarters for assignment to more important duties. At this time hundreds of women and children, the wives and families of men who had gone into war, had flocked into Bowling Green for protection, their former masters having driven them from their homes. They sought that protection at our headquarters, and I was detailed to collect them together and look after their needs. I made my headquarters in the old colored Methodist Church on the hill, my duties requiring that I should see that their rations were duly distributed among them, and power was conferred upon me to punish the unruly. Unfor-

Hickman's Bridge*

General Hospital

Magazine

*All of the photographs were taken at Camp Nelson, Kentucky in 1864. The first ten are reproduced courtesy of the National Archives and Records Administration, Still Picture Branch. Originally, these pictures were accompanied by an official quartermaster's report describing the whole of Camp Nelson in great detail. The remainder of the photographs, taken by G.W. Foster & Co., appeared first in a book of plates titled *Photographic Views of Camp Nelson and Vicinity*, published in 1864 by the Government Office, Print, on Main Street of Lexington, Kentucky.

Post Headquarters

Mule chutes and pens

U.S. Bakery

Workshops

Ambulance yard

United States Colored Troop barracks

Cliff below Camp Nelson with water pump in the Kentucky River

The White House, the only building at Camp Nelson remaining from the Civil War period. It has recently been restored.

Soldier's Home

Quartermaster's Office

Unidentified building

Convalescent Camp

Variety of housing: barracks, tents, and huts

Class of refugee children with their female teacher and her male supervisor

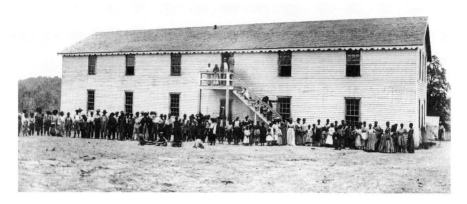

Refugees lined up outside their barrack-style dwelling

Street scene in the Refugee Camp

tunately, the General Government did not provide them with clothing, and as some of these poor people were driven from their homes without even a second garment, their condition was pitable in the extreme, as in four weeks' time many of them were unable to hide their nakedness. They looked to me as if I were their Saviour. Whatever happened in camp to disturb or annoy them, the story was at once detailed to me, and I was expected to remedy every evil. Sometimes fifteen or twenty would engage in a broil, and the weaker party would invariably come to me for protection. On these occasions I would call a court-martial, sit as judge, examine witnesses, and condemn the guilty to such punishment as in my judgment the offense deserved; as a rule, that was the last of it. There were in camp two or three old women who were always in some row. These I would talk to, and tell them they ought to act as mothers to the younger women, in which they would coincide, but before long would again be in trouble. They used to say to me:

"God knows dat's a good child! God mu' be wid him, kase he couldn't act as he do wid dese niggers."

They were in camp in Bowling Green for six months when orders were received to transfer them to Camp Nelson, and I was directed to canvass the town and ascertain who among them would go. I set out one morning betimes, with my little book in my hand, to take down the names of those willing to go. Many of them had a grave misapprehension of my object and fled at my approach, but after considerable trouble I gathered together about 750, the majority of those having no place of shelter. They embraced all ages, from the child six months to the woman eighty years. Among them were some of the prettiest girls I ever saw, and every shade of color was represented in the multitude.

Captain [*Cyrus*] Palmer, myself, and ten men were detailed to go with them, and leaving Bowling Green at 7 o'clock at night we arrived in Louisville the next morning at the same hour. But one accident marred the pleasure of the journey, and that was when, awaking in the night, I found three women piled on my head. Arriving in the city, we found it full of soldiers, and had great difficulty in making our way through the streets. At 5 P. M. we were off for Lexington and arrived there in due time. Late in the night Captain Palmer had passed through the city without leaving orders for me. We had no provisions, our supplies having been left on the L. & N. Road. The women and children were almost famished for want of food, and the children even eating dirt. I spent all the means I had for the poor sufferers, and then called upon the commander of the post General Burbridge. He agreed to furnish us with one ration apiece, and at one o'clock I received orders to march the women around to Morgan's old negro pen, where we found everything heart could desire. It was astonishing how the colored ladies of Lexington stole these little children in order to take care of them. Some of the women gave their children away in order to get rid of them. * * * *

At 5 o'clock P.M. we were off for camp [*Camp Nelson*], where we arrived about 11 o'clock. I was angry, for we were compelled to walk nearly all the way from Nicholasville to the camp. On arriving, the guard ordered me to halt, which I refused to do at the risk of my life. How often I have been frightened about it since!

Marching my people around to the headquarters, I there met Captain Palmer for the first time since leaving Louisville. Down through the streets of the City of Refuge we went, the scene presented being a beautiful one. Every door was open, and in each of them stood some one with a torch in hand to light us on our way. There was no room for us in the neat little cottages, but abundant shelter had been provided in tents for my troop of females, two families being assigned to each tent. It was late in the night, and I was compelled to leave them in the hands of the Lord and under the care of the commanding officer. Mounting a stump, I delivered to them a neat little speech, wishing them well, which called forth such expressions as they would make to a father. With many tears I bade them adieu, telling them to trust in God, who was able to do more for them than I could. They clung to my coat-tail, and I remembered the scripture that says, "The time will come when seven women will take hold of one man." I did not know but what that time had come, but I was not prepared to stand it.

I formed my men in line and marched to the Soldier's Home, where we demanded our supper. The cook soon served us a supper in fine style, which made me feel happy temporarily. I had the first happy night's rest I had enjoyed since leaving Bowling Green, as the case of those poor women and children were off my mind.

The next morning I met Captain Palmer, and he instructed me to give passes to those who desired to visit the ladies. I did so, and that was the last I seen of the Captain until I arrived in Bowling Green.

I gave one of the men a pass to go home and see his mother, who lived about five miles from Camp Nelson. While there the rebels made a raid on the place, and he moved back to camp on double-quick time.

Camp Nelson was overrun with troops at that time, and the place looked gay. Thousands of people were coming in from all directions, seeking their freedom. It was equal to the forum at Rome. All they had to do was to get there and they were free.[1]

1. Marrs, 60–65.

Head Quarters Camp Nelson Ky   February 17th 1865
Genl Orders No. 34

For the better regulation of the Home for Colored Refugees at this Post the following Rules and Regulations will be observed

I   All Colord Refugees arriving at this Post will at once report to Supt of Soldiers Home to be sent to Camp of Reception where they will be vaxinated by the Surgeon in charge for the purpose of preventing the Spread of Smallpox before being admitted to the Home

II   After admission to the Home the women and Children will not be permitted to Straggle over Camp or leave their quarters except by permission in writing from the Superintendent and then only on business that will be attended to at once and return without delay

III   Permission to Visit the Home of Colored Refugees by Strangers will only be granted from these Hd Quarters and the Superintendent of the Home except they be accompanied by an Officer or one of the Superintendents   By Order of

Brig. Genl. S.S. Fry

[*No signature.*]   Lieut & A.A.A.G[1]

1. General Orders No. 34, 17 Feb. 1865; Vol. 111/256, p. 105; General Orders; RG 393.

[*Letterhead.*] *The United States Christian Commission*   **Camp Nelson Ky   Feb. 21 /65**

Dear Bro Tappan * * * * [*Two paragraphs.*]

There was at the time of your gift cold, wet, snowy weather — very cold. Many had not shoes or stockings — others had not a change of under garments, nor enough to keep them warm. The money was used by purchases to meet such wants.

The first benefaction was to an aged colored woman who had in the army <u>five</u> sons — her husband a few years since was whipped to death in Fayette co. Ky. — The Mother is feeble with neuralgia — is very neat in person; and previous to the cruel exposure, in throwing them out of camp, was paying her rent — sustaining herself by washing, & had by washing and sewing, laid up some seven dollars — This was all expended, when your favor came.

There is yet much distress & mortality. Out of 400 cast out about 250 came back into camp. Of this number just one hundred and two have died in consequence of being exposed to cold & then herded together in Barracks, until better buildings could be prepared! The buildings now prepared. though somewhat artistic & well <u>meant</u>, are not suitable for women and children. — With 150 persons in one building, — noise, disease & death rage. — Oh the suffering incident to Slavery! To day as I looked upon the sick and dead — little ones — I was completely overcome & wept for the poor sufferers.

Bro. Williams of Mass is local superintendent   Capt Hall is appointed superintendent — He is not often there — is a business man with much business in iron & oil — away from here — Bro Williams means well I think but is not much with the suffering ones — Bro Scofield does more than both —

The poor creatures need someone who will mingle among them, — "bear their infirmities." Yours in Christ

John G Fee

I have been laboring to abolish the ward system — have these cut up into rooms & then build cottages for others — When pneumonia attacks the colored people if they are left to inhale pestilential atmosphere & dust, they die quickly — no help.

Cottages are cheaper in erection than wards; — It is cheaper to buy additional fire wood than coffins and graves. The habits of this people must also be considered. They have been <u>accustomed</u> to the fireplace & cabin. What scope for thought, labor — <u>benevolent action</u> — how blessed the gospel of Christ that teaches us to bear one another's burdens

    Yours in haste

    I now expect to spend days & perhaps weeks here in helping to relieve suffering & trying to make <u>freedom a success</u>   If the effort <u>here</u> fails this will hinder the cause of freedom all over the State —

    I shall displace no one willingly, but volunteer help.

    Go learn what that meaneth, I will have mercy not sacrifice   Yours

                                John G Fee

Love to sister Tappan[1]

    1. Fee to Lewis Tappan, 21 Feb. 1865, AMAA 44091–2; also, better punctuated, in *AM* 9, no. 4 (April 1865): 85. Tappan had sent "$152 for the relief of destitute women and children in camp."

**Head Quarters   Mil Dist of Kentucky   Lexington Ky   Feb 21" 1865.
Brig Genl S. S Fry   Camp Nelson, Ky.**

General   The General comdg directs that you relieve two companies of the 123[d] Regiment U.S.C. Infantry from their present duties and order them to report to T.E. Hall Supertendent of the home for colored refugees for permanent duty at the home.

    General Brisbin has received instructions to replace companies with other troops. *

             J Bates Dickson   Capt and A A Genl[1]

    1. Dickson to Fry, 21 Feb. 1865; Vol. 25/107, p. 224; Letters Sent, May-Sept. 1863 and Sept. 1864-Mar. 1869, Entry 2164 [Part 2 of 4]; General Records, Department of Kentucky, Part 1; RG 393.

[Letterhead.] *The United States Christian Commission*   **Camp Nelson Ky**   **Feb 21 / 65**

Dear Bro Whipple — * * * * *[Eleven paragraphs.]*

    Capt Hall recommends his Sisterin law Miss Mann[1] & Mrs Daimon[2] — a widow — both about 32 years of age — They are acquaintances of Mrs Williams and their experience as teachers & age will be commendations — we shall <u>need</u> person of age and experience   I should favor their appointment as teachers   We are not yet ready for their reception — superintendents house not up yet

    The mortality here among the children is greater than ought to be — much larger than with those who are out in their little cottages   I am working hard for cottages instead of wards — four deaths last night — four night before — I fear great complaint will go out — I know there is now, and not without ground. The ward system is horrible — noise, disease, infection, dust — to those afflicted with pneumonia pestilential atmosphere is very destructive.

I am working hard to get the wards cut up into rooms and cottages made hereafter

Also I have volunteered daily work in fixing bunks, getting the place of each person & getting better bread & fruit — a change of diet, with some bathing — "Mercy is better than sacrifice" — .... * * * * [*Five paragraphs.*]

My son Burritt is with me here   He is near 16 years old   Bro. Scofield desires his help in teaching the soldiers — the male & female school will be separate   I shall leave Burritt to help one month — pay as you do other such teachers — he is very faithful & has had some experience in teaching — at Berea * * * * [*Five paragraphs.*]

John G Fee[3]

1. Jennie Mann was the sister-in-law of Theron E. Hall, who had married Jemima W. Mann on May 8, 1844, in Holden, Massachusetts. It is unclear from the record whether Jennie Mann actually taught at Camp Nelson or only considered it. Genealogical details from www.ancestry.com.

2. Caroline Damon (Fee invariably misspells her last name), widow of A.C. Damon, came from Holden, Massachusetts, where she had known T.E. Hall before the war. She taught at Camp Nelson, under the auspices of the AMA, from mid-April to about October 20, 1865, when the schools at Camp Nelson were closed by the Freedmen's Bureau.

3. Fee to Whipple, 21 Feb. 1865, AMAA 44093–4A.

[*Letterhead.*] *The United States Christian Commission*   **Camp Nelson Ky**   Feb 25 /65

Dear Bro Whipple   This is a turning point — a crisis in our history here, and your action.—Therefore I had better write frequent — one day may determine your action.

I went again to Capt Hall yesterday morning — we talked over the cottage arrangement — He consented — said to me go and see the soldiers, ask them if they are willing to pay for the <u>erection</u> of the cottage the government furnish the lumber & have the house — soldiers family have the use of the house during good behaviour — have, for his money, the asshurance of a secure place — then he could furnish beds & fixtures that would be his own   But we may ask If Government has ordered shelter why not the government give to him the <u>cottage</u> without any cost of erection? — The two answers are "white soldiers support their own families"

2. This tax will lessen expense of government — perhaps do the col soldiers no real injury — give his family a sort of claim to the house after the war is over — a home for widows and orphans

If you have a word of suggestion to Capt Hall write to him — if to me write to me care of Rev A Scofield   My son is quite sick and I may have to take him home   This is quite a disappointment to me — ....

We had a case yesterday that was a sort of test question   A slaveholder, "a good union man" wife a New York woman called to get a slave girl — Capt Hall said "Yes" — "I know Mr Barnes" — "She will be better off there than here"   Bro Williams said No!

I said <u>No</u>! The Capt gave me a private chat. I said "No"! — "not for a moment!!

1 Her <u>father</u> is here a soldier — natural guardian

2 We must do for her <u>morally</u> what Mr. Barnes as <u>Chattel</u> owner will not do — this is more than "hog & hominy"

3 I said we have the <u>right</u> on our side, with it the letter of the law — war department on our side this time, and we will use the opportunity to "knock the starch" out of slavery far as we can. — tis slavery that stands between Ky and loyalty — tis these respectable slaveholders that makes the institution tolerable — The Capt winced & retired — We know not what he will do — he is superintendent but I do not believe he will farther aid Mr Barnes — we shall see   Bro Williams showed unflinching devotion to principle — raised himself in my estimation as a quiet cool sort of Puritan. * * * * [*Twenty-five paragraphs.*]

J G Fee[1]

1. Fee to Whipple, 25 Feb. 1865, AMAA 44097–101.

[*Letterhead.*] *The United States Christian Commission*   **Camp Nelson Ky   Feb 27/ 65**

Dear Bro Whipple — This day Gen. Fry asked me to start a school for the children of surgeons officers & other persons within this camp — that would be a <u>white</u> school   I told him I would find the teachers, he the house. He agreed —

Now we think we can make the school self sustaining and that the school through its <u>teachers</u> will naturally assimilate with the colored school and the field of usefulness be enlarged. * * * * [*Five paragraphs.*]

John G. Fee[1]

1. Fee to Whipple, 27 Feb. 1865, AMAA 44102. Nothing came of this plan; no body of white students ever "assimilated" with the colored school at Camp Nelson, through its teachers, or any other impetus. In fact, no one seems to have mentioned this proposal ever again.

Head Quarters   U.S.C. Troops   Lexington, Ky.   February 28th 1865. Lt. Col. L.H. Carpenter   Commdg. 5th U.S.C. Cav.   Camp Nelson Ky.

General Palmer will arrive here to-morrow morning and visit Camp Nelson to morrow or next day in company with General Burbridge and myself. Have the 5th and 6th ready to parade, if the General should so desire. Inform Genl. Fry, Hall, Santymire[1] and Restieaux of our coming. When you will be paid? Answer.

[*Unsigned.*] Brevt. Brig. Genl and Supt.   Organization U.S.C. Troops[2]

1. Capt. Joseph P. Santmyer [or Santmyre] enlisted, at the age of thirty-seven, on October 1, 1862, as a first lieutenant; he was promoted to captain on April 2, 1864, in the Seventh Ohio Cavalry. At Camp Nelson he was acting assistant quartermaster in charge of unserviceable stock, according to C.E. Compton's inspection report. *OAR,* 5:13; *Official Roster of the Soldiers of the State of Ohio (1886)* in Civil War Archive at www.ancestry.com.

2. Unsigned to Louis H. Carpenter, 28 Feb. 1865; [Bound] Vol. 5, Book 98A, p. 61; Letters and Telegrams Sent and Received, Organization of U.S.C.T., Entry 2251; Department of Ky., Part 1; RG 393.

[*U.S. Sanitary Commission report.*]

On the 1st of March, 1865, Mr. [*Thomas*] Butler [*of the U.S. Sanitary Commission*] reports a marked falling off in the number of soldiers received at the Home, but great activity in the care of refugees and freedmen. For this time our work gradually declined. The subjugation of the principal armies of the rebellion materially lessened our legitimate work for the soldier; although the Home, the regimental hospitals in the field, the sole care of all the white refugees, and an important share of the business pertaining to the colored refugees, gave, for some months, constant employment to our agents.[1]

1. Newberry, 385–86.

[*Excerpt from*] **REPORTS OF MR. BUTLER.** WORK FOR COLORED REFUGEES.

An attempt to describe the crowd of colored refugees who flocked to Camp Nelson, their numbers, their sufferings, and the efforts made for their relief, would extend the report of the Sanitary Commission relief work at Camp Nelson beyond reasonable limits. Suffice it to say that there were for months from five to fifteen hundred colored women and children in Camp Nelson, who were not only otherwise homeless, but who, in their destitution and misery, constituted the most pitiable class of refugees. Nowhere in the whole range of my observation of misfortune and misery occasioned by the war, have I seen any cases which appealed so strongly to the sympathies of the benevolent as those congregated in the contraband camp at Camp Nelson. Fortunately they were not solely dependent for relief upon the efforts we could make in their behalf; for, aside from the interest taken in their fate by Captain Hall, Camp Quartermaster, and Mr. E.D. Kennedy,[1] a worthy man, who was appointed their superintendent, Rev. John G. Fee and Elder A. Scofield, representatives of the American Missionary Association, with their colored assistant, Gabriel Burdett, a noble and extraordinary man, with tender and indefatigible efforts, labored for their welfare night and day.

The Sanitary Commission was prominent in all measures for the amelioration of their condition, and heartily co-operated with the good men I have mentioned in the care and assistance of the contrabands, so materially needed. In common with all others who came to Camp Nelson to do good to the unfortunate, Messrs. Fee, Scofield and Burdett made their homes with us at the Soldiers' Home, and received all the assistance and co-operation we could render them in their work. Dr. R.S. Mitchell, who was appointed surgeon of colored refugees, also labored faithfully in connection with Messrs. Fee and Scofield. There were others who were nominally engaged in the work of relief among the contrabands at Camp Nelson, but, I am sorry to say, with little benefit to those for whom their time was professedly spent and little credit to themselves.

Great difficulties and discouragements were encountered in our efforts in behalf of those so utterly helpless and friendless as the contrabands proved to be. And—what was most disheartening—much of our difficulty and much of their suffering was plainly the result of incompetence on the part of those who had been constituted their special guardians. . . .

In addition to all other causes of suffering among the colored refugees, disease was always specially rife among them. In the month of February, 1865, the population of the colored refugee camp was about eight hundred women and children, of whom four hundred were sick. Their hospital was always crowded, and the condition of the inmates may be gathered from the testimony of Mrs. John Christopher, of Louisville, a lady who spent much of her time in good works at Camp Nelson.

After visiting the refugee hospital, Mrs. Christopher says: "I found the poor people huddled together in rags and dirt. The wards were full of human wretchedness. I found poor women dying, amidst filth and suffering, for the simplest food, within twenty steps of the superintendent's office," (we are glad to say that the superintendent mentioned here was not M. Kennedy.)[2]

1. Evan D. Kennedy enlisted at the age of thirty-four in 1861 in New York City. He served in Company H, 79th New York Infantry, and was mustered out on May 31, 1864. He was a superintendent of colored refugees and then became captain of Company H, 119th U.S. Colored Troops, mustered in June 8, 1865. *OAR*, 8:300l; *New York: Report of the Adjutant General* in Civil War Archive at www.ancestry.com; *RAGK*.
2. Newberry, 527–29.

[*Letterhead.*] *The United States Christian Commission* Camp Nelson Ky   ~~Feb~~ Mch 2 /65

Dear Bro Strieby * * * * [*Two paragraphs.*]
The cottage system is now being adopted — this will work a great change — in health & accession — many more now will come — I have obtained clothing — cleansings — also soda crackers Black boy syrups &c. for sick — the weather is also more favorable — for some reason fewer deaths — The crowd is being thinned by removals into other wards —

At close of Feb Capt Resteaux informed Capt Hall that he could not have so many on his pay Roll — this he also had done previously — Capt Hall proposed (as before) that Bro Williams be commissioned by the Am Miss Association — and that he not doing all the work of a Superintendent would make up to Mr. Williams a chaplains salary 118 dollars per month.

Mr Williams did not like pay from two sources — talked crossly about being "nosed about" and that he "did not care whether he stayed or not" He could do as well at other places. The capt was displeased at this — said he was sorry to hear Mr Williams say so — thought he ought to care

The capt said as for his part he took hold <u>only for a</u> <u>time</u> — because he thought he could do more with Burbridge & Resteaux than any other

So thus Capt Hall expects (at present) to vacate for some other. You will therefore be on the look out   You may see it wise to confer with Capt Hall — He did expect to go to Washington — start this night   Yours in haste,

J Ġ Fee[1]

1. Fee to Strieby, 2 Mar. 1865, AMAA 44103.

War Department, Washington City, March 3, 1865.

His Excellency Abraham Lincoln, President of the United States:

Sir: I have considered the joint resolution entitled "A resolution to encourage enlistments and to promote the efficiency of the military service," referred to me for my opinion upon the point whether the proposed measure would materially encourage enlistments and promote the efficiency of the military service.

The resolution proposes to give freedom to the wife and children of persons who have enlisted or may enlist in the military or navy service of the United States.

I have the honor to report:

First. That, in my opinion, giving freedom to the wife and children of persons who have been or may be mustered into the military or naval service of the United States would be a strong inducement to enlist in that service, and would therefore greatly encourage enlistments.

Second. That the liberation of the wife and children from slavery and placing them under the protection of law as free persons would relieve persons enlisting from great anxiety in respect to the condition of those whom they love and desire to protect, and would afford a strong inducement to encounter cheerfully every species of toil and danger to secure them the boon of freedom, and therefore that such measure would promote the efficiency of the service.

Third. For the foregoing reasons the joint resolution is, in my opinion, of great value to the military service and may be regarded as a military measure of the highest importance by adding to the numerical and efficient strength of the Army. *

Edwin M. Stanton, Secretary of War.[1]

1. Stanton to Lincoln, 3 Mar. 1865, *OR*, 3, 4, 1219.

Chapter Five

The Refugee Home

Head Quarters   Dept. of Kentucky   Louisville, Ky.   March 3" 1865.
Brig General S S. Fry   Comd'g Post at Camp Nelson Ky
Throg 1st. Div   Dept of Ky

General   I have the honor to inform you that the Maj. General Comd'g the Dept. has approved special order no. 4. from your office, and directs that, in accordance therewith, "rations in kind" be issued "to commissioned officers of U.S. Colored Troops who have received no pay and are destitute of means to purchase them." *
            J P Watson   Capt. and A.A.A.G[1]

1. Watson to Fry, 3 Mar. 1865; Vol. 1, p. 9; Letters Sent, May–Sept. 1863 and Sept. 1864–Mar. 1869, Entry 2164 [Part 3 of 4]; General Records, Department of Kentucky, Part 1; RG 393. (Hereafter abbreviated "Vol. 1, [page number]; Letters Sent, RG 393.")

[*Letterhead.*] *U.S. Sanitary Commission*   *Camp Nelson, Ky*   Mch 7 1865

Dear Bro Strieby
    * * * * [*Four paragraphs.*]
    I have spent here three sabbaths — have aided in the encouragement of the Fugitive home, attended to the wants of many of the sick — have aided in refitting the school Room for males — soldiers — We have in this the best field as I believe in the state. There are here large parts of three Regiments of colored troops — two of the three are cavalry men, young, bright — I preach to them with great interest.
    I also preach in the "Freedmans Home" — the new quarters for women & children — Last sabbath I made a call for enquirers — 24 came forward — we had a season of prayer — have meetings for their instruction — I am also ~~assist=~~ ~~ing~~ instructing Bro Gabriel Burdett in such work. Bro Vetter seldom preaches. Bro Williams as I believe has preached but once — that to the white clerks   They have their time now much occupied with other things   Bro Scofield has been sick. He and Burritt (my son) & Bro Burdett are in the school (col soldiers) as teachers   Bro. Scofield superintends
    Now I wish to say a word about Bro Scofield. He is a good preacher — our

best — He has had a large experience — his age gives confidence — he ought to <u>preach</u> — <u>give himself wholy to the gospel</u> — and let this dabbling a little in every thing alone. He has been teacher, farmer, Mechanic, Merchant, asher, lumber man & I do not know what else until he has formed the <u>habit</u> of looking to almost every thing with the enquiry "Could I not that way make a support for my family"

Bro Whipple gave an exhortation last year in one line which greatly impressed me. I think of it almost continually — it was this "give yourself to the work of preaching the gospel with all your heart" I too have had too many things in life not as a means of making a support, but way of spending my support   I have had schools, colporters,[1] then reports — church building, constitutional questions, ie whether I could speak against slavery without violating its letter & spirit, and now schools for these soldiers their wives & children and difficult is it for me to get rid of it. I came here first — the officers know me, had the habit of hearing me & looking to me & they do not like to know but one head. How shall I get out of it — This was the reason why I did not at first say I will take the superintendency of Freedmans Home. I thought I should have my time so engrossed with "serving tables" rations, rooms, beds, &c that I would not do the work I ought — "preach the word" and now if I were to consent to assume the name it would be simply to hold power for supposed good — give direction to the institution — have power to controll   I should have to have some man attend to the never ending detail   A Post Chaplaincy would come nearer the position here I should desire. I would then have oversight over all religious interests together with schools. I have a wide field now but not authority to enforce. * * * * [*Three paragraphs.*]

John G Fee[2]

1. Fee is referring to colporteurs, distributors of religious tracts, books, and Bibles, who worked for the AMA and other missionary societies. During his earlier career as an AMA abolitionist missionary, Fee had supervised the hiring and deploying of colporteurs in Kentucky.
2. Fee to Strieby, 7 Mar. 1865, AMAA 44106–8.

Hdqrs. Department of Kentucky, Louisville, Ky., March 12, 1865
General Orders No. 10.

The General commanding announces to the colored men of Kentucky that by an act of Congress passed on the 3d day of March, 1865, the wives and children of all colored men who have heretofore enlisted, or may hereafter enlist, in the military service of the Government, are made free.

This act of justice to the soldiers claims from them renewed efforts, by courage, fortitude, and discipline, to win a good name, to be shared by a free wife and free children. To colored men not in the army it offers an opportunity to coin freedom for themselves and posterity.

The rights secured to colored soldiers under this law will, if necessary, be enforced by the military authorities of this department, and it is expected that the loyal men and women of Kentucky will encourage colored men to enlist in the army; and, after they have done so, recognize them as upholders of their Government and defenders of their homes, and exercise toward the helpless women and children made free by law that benevolence and charity which has always characterized the people of the State.

By command of Major-General Palmer:

J.P. Watson, Captain and Acting Assistant Adjutant-General.[1]

1. General Orders No. 10, 12 March 1865, Printed leaflet in *NIMSUS,* 6:3597 and also transcribed in *OR,* 1, 49, pt 1, 904.

[*Letterhead.*] *Head-Quarters* 124th *U.S. Colored Infantry, Camp Nelson, Ky.*   Mar 17th *1865.*
Lieut. G.E. Goodyear   A.A.A.G.   U.S.C.T.   Louisville Ky

Lieut   I again beg leave to submit the subject heretofor presented too frequently perhaps, of the neccesity of providing suitable quarters for the officers of this Regiment. They are now occupying old rotten, and condemned hospital tents which the high wind of the past few weeks have torn almost in shreds and the canvass is so very rotten that the guy ropes will not hold   In Weather the [*two indecipherable words*] no protection whatever being very thin and full of holes. The duties of the officers are such that they cannot perform them in Shelter tents and it seems to me that it would economical to the Government if quarters for officers and Barracks for the men were erected at this post   I must respectfully urge that this suggestion be submitted to the proper authority with the recommendation of the supt. that it receive early attention and action   *

Geo A. Hanaford   Lieut Col Comdg 124th U.S.C.T.

[*Endorsement.*] **Head Qrs Dept of Ky   Office Organization U.S.T.   Louisville Ky   Apl 3 /65**

[*Military code.*] Respectfully referred to Maj Genl Palmer with recommendations that the quartermasters Department at Camp Nelson be directed to furnish proper quarters for the Officers and men of the 124th U.S. Col'd Infy, that Regt being on duty in the Q.M. Dept at Camp Nelson

Jas. S. Brisbin   Bvt Brig Gen'l and Supt of U.S. Troops [1]

1. Hanaford to Goodyear, 17 Mar. 1865; Camp Nelson, Box 720; RG 92.

Camp Nelson   March 24 /65

Rev. M.E. Strieby,
My Dear Sir, I wrote you on the tenth of last month fully in relation to the home for colored refugees here, giving you diagrams of the buildings, copies of notes, &c and

asking for some definite information as to what the A.M.A. would do for us here. I have had no reply to that communication and am wholly at fault as to the intentions of the society. In the mean time the people are [landing?] upon us. The late law of Congress freeing the families of colored soldiers will throw at least 20,000 people upon the charities of the benevolent. I do not understand that the "Freedmans Bureau" affects us in Ky. one way or the other. This is not an insurgent state and the law is inoperative here. Genl Palmer, commanding this department informs me that he shall make this camp a general rendezvous for all these people in Ky — Now the question arises, what can be of use   What will the American Missionary Association do

I am putting up the hundred cottages in addition to the larger frame buildings — but we must have more <u>help</u>. We want teachers — and some one or two good men. We particularly want a <u>farmer</u> to take charge of that branch of business. Now please write me at once and let me know just what you can do. Can you not send a man here or come yourself and look this matter over   I can give you good reasons why this is the most important field of operations in the whole country. I would write you more at length if I had time —

Yours for the slave —

T.E. Hall, Supt of Refugees Home Camp Nelson, Ky — ¹

1. Hall to Strieby, 24 Mar. 1865, AMAA 44114–5.

[*Letterhead.*] *The United States Christian Commission*   **Camp Nelson Ky**   **Mch 24 /65**
Private

Dear Bro Whipple   After filling the app. at Berea I returned here one week from last Tuesday — held Meetings every evening that week — some twenty four enquirers — six professed peace in trusting Christ — preached twice on sabbath following — baptised three of the Co that evening   Bro Burdett — colored — former slave) baptised the other three[1] — he had not baptised before — was ordained after coming into Camp. It was estimated that there were two thousand persons present — The Commandant of the post was present — gave his personal influence for good order he is personally friendly   I addressed the multitude on the duty of Repentance & baptism.

Bro Williams had been to Cincinnati — returned Saturday with his wife[2] — neither present — he came to preaching in the forenoon, was weary. Capt Hall never has attended worship since I have been in Camp save on one occasion when he had for other purposes come to the ward. He returned that day from Lexington   He is in sympathy with the colored people I believe. He is active, executive — does not mature plans well I think — often changes

He has made an offer to his oil company to become the business agent. — if so he will quit this work — says he thinks it will fall upon me.

I think I acted with an eye single to the glory of God — I may have erred in judgment. But think not. He has obtained more from the Q M here than I probably would. I suppose a common money, probably oil, interest has bound them together.

I suppose I ought to preach rather than build houses — yet I should have builded more favorably for health than he has

He has an immense workshop erected without tools or occupants when there are not cottages to give requisite space for those dying in the crowded wards

I told Capt Hall you said you would furnish teachers   Our committee assented to two he proposed & I said to him you would pay them — also hire of a farmer. I much desire that you keep your hold on this state and this place will probably be the key to it so far as colored people are concerned. * * * * [*Two paragraphs.*]

I expect to return here next week if health of my wife will admit   She will be confined in May — is more complaining this time than formerly.

I am greatly interested in the work here   yet the majority are women and children — soldiers enough now to preach to — know not how long they will stay

The school for men is doing well   Burritt my son is doing most labor   he has two assistants   Bro Scofield is now gone   I am frequently in   Pay for teachers needed next week — Send check for $100

John G Fee[3]

1. Despite the peculiar punctuation, Fee clearly means that he baptized three of the converts himself, while Burdett baptized the other three.
2. Ann E.W. Williams.
3. Fee to Whipple, 24 Mar. 1865, AMAA 44116.

Camp Nelson Ky   March 24 1865

Personally appeared before me J M Kelley Notary Public in and for the County of Jessamine state of Ky Martha Cooley a woman of color who being duly sworn according to law doth depose and say

I am a widow woman. My husband Simon Cooley was a Soldier in the 5th U.S.C. Cavalry and was killed at the Salt Works during Genl Burbridge's last raid. My master's name is John Nave and lives in Garrard County Ky. I have four children who belong to said Nave. About three weeks ago I told my master that I wanted to go to Camp Nelson. He said, "I will give you Camp" and immediately took a large hickory stick with which he commenced beating me. He gave me more than thirty blows striking me on my head and shoulders and breaking one of the bones of my left arm. I have not the right use of it now. I told him I wanted my children. He said I could neither have my children nor my clothes. My master beat me for this request. I watched my chance and ran away. I had to leave my children with my master. I have been in Camp about two weeks and am very anxious to get my children and further deponent saith not

Signed Martha Cooley[1]

1. Affidavit of Martha Cooley, 24 March 1865; M999:7:676; RG 105. Apparently, this affidavit was one of the collection sent to the Freedmen's Bureau by Capt. T.E. Hall, mentioned in and accompanying his letter of June 22, 1865.

Camp Nelson Ky   March 24" 1865

Personally appeared before me J M Kelley Notary Public in and for the County of Jessamine State of Ky., John G. Fee Clergyman and T.E. Hall Supt. of Refugee Home at Camp Nelson Ky who being severally and duly sworn according to law, do depose and say

We have seen the arm mentioned in the affidavit of Martha Cooley and find that the <u>Ulna</u> <u>bone</u> of the left arm has been broken. The muscle of the arm is much bruised displaying every evidence of recent and severe injury from the consequence of which the arm is at present powerless. From what we have seen we believe the injury to have been inflicted by the means set forth in her statement

(Signed) John G Fee   T.E. Hall[1]

1. Affidavit of Fee and Hall, 24 Mar. 1865; M999:7:677; RG 105. Apparently, this affidavit was one of the collection sent to the Freedmen's Bureau by Capt. T.E. Hall, mentioned in and accompanying his letter of June 22, 1865.

Head Quarters   Dept of Kentucky.   Louisville Ky.   March 25" 1865.
Capt T.E. Hall.   Camp Nelson Kentucky

Dear Sir: — The lands inside the fortifications of Camp Nelson are for our purposes to be assumed to be the property of the Government. This is only the repetition of what I said to you when here. Make the rule operate as lightly as possible upon the present occupants.

I am more and more convinced of the urgent necessity of pressing your farming and gardening operations at the camp. We must have so many homes and separate plats of ground for the people as possible. I wish we had one hundred cabins with suitable lots of ground for the use of families all ready for immediate occupation. *

John M. Palmer   Maj. Gen. Comdg.[1]

1. Palmer to Hall, 25 Mar. 1865; Vol. 1, p. 24; Letters Sent; RG 393.

Camp Nelson Ky   March 25 1865

Personally appeared before me J M Kelley Notary Public in and for the County of Jessamine State of Kentucky Patsey Leach a woman of color who being duly sworn according to law, doth depose and say —

I am a widow and belonged to Warren Wiley of Woodford County Ky. My husband Julius Leach was a member of Co D. 5" U.S.C. Cavalry and was killed at the Salt Works, Va. about six months ago. When he enlisted sometime in the fall of 1864 he belonged to Sarah Martin Scott County Ky. He had only been about a month in the service when he was killed. I was living with aforesaid Wiley when he died. He knew of my husbands enlisting before I did but never said any thing to me about it. From that time he treated me more cruelly than ever whipping me frequently without any cause and insulting me on every occasion. About three weeks after my husband enlisted a Company of Colored Soldiers passed our house and I was then in the garden and looked at them as they passed. My master had been watching me and when the soldiers had gone I went into the kitchen. My master followed me and knocked me to the floor senseless saying as he did so, "You have been looking at them damed Nigger Soldiers" When I recovered my senses he beat me with a cowhide   When my husband was killed my master whipped me severely saying my husband had gone into the army to fight against white folks as he my master would let me know that I was foolish to let my husband go he would "take it out of my back" he would "kill me by pi[e]cemeal" and he hoped "that the last one of the nigger soldiers would be killed"   He whipped me twice after that, using similar expressions. The last whipping he gave me he took me into the kitchen tied my hands tore all my clothes off until I was entirely naked, bent me down, placed my head between his knees, then whipped me most unmercifully until my back was lacerated all over, the blood oozing out in several places so that I could not wear my underclothes without their becoming saturated with blood. The marks are still visible on my back. On this and other occasions my master whipped me for no other cause than my husband having enlisted. When he had whipped me he said "never mind God damn you when I am done with you tomorrow you never will live no more." I knew he would carry out his threats so that night about 10 o'clock I took my babe and travelled to Arnolds Depot, where I took the Cars to Lexington. I have five children   I left them all with my master except the youngest and I want to get them but I dare not go near my master knowing he would whip me again. My master is a Rebel Sympathizer and often sends Boxes of Goods to Rebel prisoners. And further Deponent saith not

Her
Signed   Patsey Leach
mark[1]

1. Affidavit of Patsey Leach, 25 Mar. 1865; M999:7:668–69; RG 105. Apparently, this affidavit was one of the collection sent to the Freedmen's Bureau by Capt. T.E. Hall, mentioned in and accompanying his letter of June 22, 1865. Also reproduced in *The Black Military Experience*, 268, 269.

Camp Nelson Ky   March [25] 1865

Personally appeared before me J M Kelley Notary Public in and for the County of Jessamine State of Kentucky Frances Johnson a woman of color who being duly sworn according to law doth depose and say —

I am the wife of Nathan Johnson a soldier in Company F. 116th U.S.C. Infty. I have three children and with them I belonged to Matthias Outon Fayette County Ky. My husband who belonged to Mary Outon Woodford Co, Ky. enlisted in the United States service at Camp Nelson Ky. in May 1864. The day after my husband enlisted my master knew it and said that he (my husband) and all the "niggers" did mighty wrong in joining the Army. Subsequent to May 1864 I remained with my master until forced to leave on account of the cruel treatment to which I was subjected. On Wednesday March 8th 1865 my master's son Thomas Outon whipped me severely on my refusing to do some work which I was not in a condition to perform. He beat me in the presence of his father who told him (Thoˢ Outon) to "buck me and give me a thousand," meaning thereby a thousand lashes. While beating me he threw me on the floor and as I was in this prostrate and helpless condition he continued to whip me endeavoring at one time to tie my hands and at another time to make an indecent exposure of my person before those present. I resisted as much as I could and to some extent thwarted his malignant designs. In consequence of this whipping, [I] suffered much pain in my head and sides. The scar now visible on my neck was inflicted at that time. After such treatment I determined to leave my master and early on the following morning — Thursday March 9" 1865 I stealthily started for Lexington about seven miles distant where my sister resided. On my arrival there, I was confined on account of sickness produced by the abuse I had received from my masters son as aforementioned.

During Friday March 10" 1865 I sought a lodging for myself and children — Towards evening I found one and about 7 O'clock at night I left for my masters, intending to take my children away. About 9. O'clock I arrived there, much fatigued, went to the Cabin where my children were, no one but the colored folks knowing that I was present, got my children, with the exception of one that was too sick to move, and about 10 o'clock P.M. started for a neighboring Cabin where we remained during the night. At day break next morning I started for Lexington. My youngest child was in my arms, the other walked by my side. When on the Pike about a mile from home I was accosted by Theophilus Bracey my masters son-in-law, who told me that if I did not go back with him he would shoot me. He drew a pistol on me as he mad[e] this threat. I could offer no resistance as he constantly kept the pistol pointed at me. I returned with him to his (Bracys) house, carrying my children as before. I remained at Bracys all day. My sick child was moved there during the day. I tried to find some chance of running away but Bracey was watching me. He took my eldest child (about seven years of age) and kept her as an Hostage. I found I could not get away from Braceys with my children, and determined to get away myself hoping by this means to obtain possession of them afterwards. I knew Bracey would not give me my children or allow me to go away myself so at daybreak on the following morning Sunday March 12" I secretly left Braceys, took to the woods in order to elude pursuit, reached Lexington and subsequently arrived at Camp Nelson. My children are still held by Bracey. I am anxious to have them but I am afraid to go near them knowing that Bracey would not let me have them and fearing lest he would carry out his threat to shoot me. And further the deponent saith not

her

(Signed)   Frances   X   Johnson

mark[1]

1. Affidavit of Frances Johnson, 25 Mar. 1865; M999:7:662–65; RG 105. Also reproduced in *The Destruction of Slavery*, 694, 695.

Lexington, March 27, 1865.

Major-General Palmer, Headquarters:

If you have sent to Camp Nelson immediately 500 horse equipments, I will furnish sufficient force to protect Louisville and Nashville Railroad; also clean out Metcalfe and Monroe Counties. I have no mounted force that can be sent without exposing other points. I will do all I can to organize force for purposes named in your dispatch. If I had been supplied with equipments for First Kentucky, I would have had men there now.

E.H. Hobson, Brigadier-General.[1]

1. Hobson to Palmer, 27 Mar. 1865, *OR,* 1, 49, pt. 2, 102.

Camp Nelson Ky   March 27 1865

Personally appeared before me J M Kelley Notary Public in and for the County of Jessamine State of Kentucky Clarissa Burdett[1] a woman of color who being duly sworn according to law doth depose and say

I am a married woman and have four children. My husband Elijah Burdett is a soldier in the 12" U.S.C.H. Arty. I and my children belonged to Smith Alford Garrard County, Ky. When my husband enlisted my master beat me over the head with an axe handle, saying as he did so that he beat me for letting Ely Burdett go off. He bruised my head so that I could not lay it against a pillow without the greatest pain. Last week my niece who lived with me went to Camp Nelson. This made my master very angry and last Monday March 20" 1865 he asked me where the girl had gone. I could not tell him. He then whipped me over the head and said he would give me two hundred lashes if I did not get the girl back before the next day. On Wednesday last March 22" he said that he had not time to beat me on Tuesday but now he had time and he would give it to me. He then tied my hands threw the rope over a joist stripped me entirely naked and gave me about three hundred lashes. I cried out. He then caught me by the throat and almost choked me then continued to lash me with switches until my back was all cut up. The marks of the switches are now very visible and my back is still very sore. My master was a very cruel man and strongly sympathizes with the rebels. He went with the Rebel General Bragg when the latter retreated from the State. He took me and my children to Beans Station and sent the parents and two sisters of my niece to Knoxville where he sold them. After he whipped me on Wednesday last he said he would give me until next morning to bring the girl back, and if I did not get her back by that time he would give me as much more. I knew that I would be whipped so I ran away. My master frequently said that he would be jailed before one of his niggers would go to Camp. I therefore knew he would not permit any of my children to come with me. So when I ran away I had to leave my children with my master. I have four children there at present and I want to get them but I cannot go there for them knowing that master who would whip me would not let any of my children go nor would he suffer me to get away

her

(Signed) Clarissa Burdett

mark[2]

1. Clarissa was Rev. Gabriel Burdett's sister-in-law, married to his brother Elijah.
2. Clarissa Burdett, 27 Mar. 1865; M999:7:685–87; RG 105. Apparently, this affidavit was one of the collection sent to the Freedmen's Bureau by Capt. T.E. Hall, mentioned in and accompanying his letter of June 22, 1865. Also reproduced in *The Destruction of Slavery*, 615, 616.

Headquarters Department of Kentucky, Louisville, Ky., March 28, 1865. Circular, No. 1

Under authority granted from the War Department you are authorized to issue subsistence to the wives and families of soldiers of the United States when the conditions of the supplies at your station will justify such issue and the circumstances of applicants seem to render it necessary for the Government to give them assistance.

First. Each ration to be issued under this authority shall consist of 4 ounces of pork or bacon, 4 ounces of flour, soft bread, or corn meal, 2 ounces of beans, pease, or hominy, 2 ounces of brown sugar, and 5 ounces of tea to every 30 rations. In authorizing this issue it is not intended to do more than help sustain the families of those who are absent.

Second. So far as practicable, applications will be filed on the 1st of each month, and an officer will be charged with the special duty of investigating and reporting upon the claims of the applicants.

Third. The commanding officer will countersign the returns and will be held responsible for the justness and propriety of the issue, which for convenience should generally embrace the entire month and be made from the 3d to the 8th.

Fourth. The commissary of subsistence making the issue will keep a separate abstract for the same.

By command of Major-General Palmer:

E.B. Harlan, Captain and Assistant Adjutant-General.[1]

1. Emory B. Harlan, Circular No. 1, 28 Mar. 1865, *OR*, 1, 49, pt. 2, 112–13.

Camp Nelson Ky   March 29 1865

Personally appeared before me J M Kelley Notary Public in and for the County of Jessamine State of Kentucky William Jones a man of color who being duly sworn according to law doth depose and say —

I am a soldier in the 124th U.S.C Infty. Before enlisting I belonged to Newton Craig Scott County Ky   My wife [*Marilda*] belonged to the same man. Desiring to enlist and thus free my wife and serve the Government during the balance of my days I ran away from my master in company with my wife on Saturday March 11th between nine and ten O'clock at night. Our clothes were packed up and some money we had saved from our earnings we carried with us. On our way to Camp Nelson we arrived at Lexington about Three O'clock next morning, Sunday March 12" 1865 where we were accosted by the Capt of the night watch James Cannon who asked us where we were going. I told him I was going to see my daughter. He said I was a damned liar, that I was going to Camp Nelson. I then told him that I was going to Camp whereupon he arrested us, took us to the Watch House where he searched us and took our money from us, taking Fifty Eight (58) dollars from me and Eight (8) dollars from my wife. I told him that the money was my own that I desired to have it. He told me that he would send it with the man who would take us back to our master and when we got there we should have it. I said I would rather die than go back to master who said he would kill any of his niggers who went to Camp. Cannon made no reply but locked us up in the Watch house where he kept us all that day and night, and on Monday morning March 13" 1865 he sent us back to our master in charge of an armed watchman whose name I believe was Harry Smith. When we arrived at my masters, master was away from home and Smith delivered us to our mistress. I asked Smith to give me my money. He said Cannon had given him none but had kept the whole to himself. I ran away from home that day before master came home. I have never received a cent of the money which Cannon took from me. I have three Sons and one Son-in-law in the service of the United States. I want to get my money back. And further the Deponent Saith not

his

(Signed) William Jones

mark[1]

1. Affidavit of William Jones, 29 Mar. 1865; M999:7:666–67; RG 105. Apparently, this affidavit was one of the collection sent to the Freedmen's Bureau by Capt. T.E. Hall, mentioned in and accompanying his letter of June 22, 1865. Also reproduced in *The Black Military Experience*, 276, 277.

[*Excerpt from William Pratt's diary.*]
April 2, 1865

Last night our servant woman left while we were asleep — & we found the kitchen in the morning swept, garnished, & Empty — & wife Mary & myself went about to work to get breakfast — About two weeks before, our cook Lucinda rec^d a letter from Camp Nelson, written by some white man for her husband, Henry, & telling [her] that she was free, & to Either price herself to me, or to somebody Else in town, or to come there, when provision was made for them — she sent the letter for me to read. I went into the kitchen to talk to her upon the subject, & told her she could leave or stay just as she pleased. I offered to give her $2 per week if she would stay, & that she might have four days in the week to work for herself — She said she had rather stay with us, that we had always used her well, & that she was satisfied she could not do as well any where else as with us. I told her, I would be glad for her to stay if she felt contented & would do as she always had & not to be running about to consult with the free negroes — I suppose, however, She was persuaded to leave — I found the kitchen cleaned up — the bread raised & put ready for baking & kindling at hand to make a fire — I hope she & her daughter will do well — they have been faithful servants & I believe it would have been for their interest to have stayed with us.[1]

1. Pratt Diary, Special Collections and Archives, University of Kentucky Libraries.

Head Quarters   Dept. of Kentucky   Louisville, Ky.   April 5, 1865.
Post Commandant   Camp Nelson, Ky.
Through Head Qrs. 1 Div. D.K.

Sir: The Commanding General directs that you arrest and hold subject to orders from these Head Quarters. Smith Alfred, who is charged with inhumanly beating Clarissa Burdett a colored woman. You will also prepare a list of witnesses in the case and forward them at once. *

E B Harlan   Capt. and A.A. Genl.[1]

1. Harlan to Post Commandant, 5 Apr. 1865; Vol. 1, p. 37; Letters Sent; RG 393.

Head Quarters. Dept. of Kentucky.   Louisville. Ky. April 6, 1865.
Capt. E.P. Ransom[1]   Camp Nelson, Ky.

Captain: The General Commanding directs me to answer the questions contained in yours of 1st inst. as follows. viz. "Is the ration therein prescribed to govern issues to the colored women and children in the camp of contrabands at this post?" It is not! Special instructions from the War Department govern in this case.

Is said ration the whole allowance of Southern refugees sent North?" It is! *

E B Harlan   Capt. and A.A. Gen'l.[2]

1. Ransom, an Ohioan, first lieutenant and regimental quartermaster of the Seventy-first Ohio Infantry, promoted to captain and commissary of subsistence; apparently he worked at Camp Nelson on special assignment, since his regiment was never there. *OAR,* 5:163.
2. Harlan to Edward P. Ransom, 6 Apr. 1865; Vol. 1, p. 43; Letters Sent; RG 393.

Camp Nelson Ky   Apr 12, 1865

Dear Bro. Strieby . . . I have looked at Camp Nelson, especially the part of it appropriated to the use of the colored refugees, as well as the rain and mud would allow. . . .[1] If
"Uncle Sam is rich enough to give us all a farm", he may be able to provide for these
poor families till tough experience shall compel the demented oligarchy of the state
to throw open the gates of "freedom for all" — for their <u>own</u>, as well as for the
good of the long oppressed poor! I am deeply impressed with the solemn importance of our work — that of <u>christian</u> instruction — to the race that is, as it were,
being "born in a day", in the prime but <u>ignorant</u> State of Kentucky — I
think, by the way, the surrender of Lee has had a stunning effect on the slaveholders
of Kentucky. I trust it may, as the colored soldier said of his comrade struck by a
shell — "Knock 'em <u>sensible</u>". . . .

E Davis[2]

1. Although this letter is all one paragraph, the omitted passage is quite long, but its major
points appear in Davis's later report of April 28.
2. Elnathan Davis to Strieby, 12 Apr. 1865, AMAA 44121.

Head Quarters   Dept. of Ky.   Louisville Ky.   April 13" 1865.
T.E. Hall, Esq.   Camp Nelson Ky.

Dear Sir: Lt. Col. L.H. Carpenter, Commandant at Camp Nelson, writes to the General Comdg for instructions relative to colored women and children arriving at Camp
"whose husbands are not in the army and who cannot properly be received by you"

The General Comdg directs that you receive and care for all destitute colored
women and children who seek refuge at Camp Nelson. The class above refered to as
well as those freed under the recent act of Congress. *

J Bates Dickson   Capt and A A. Genl.[1]

1. Dickson to Hall, 13 Apr. 1865; Vol. 1, p. 52; Letters Sent; RG 393.

Head Quarters Camp Nelson Ky   April 15th 1865
General Orders No 42.

In consequence of the official intelligence of the death of the President of the
U.S. and in obedience to orders from Head Quarters District of Kentucky, a gun
will be fired every half hour beginning at sunrise April 16th and ending at sunset   the
Commanding officer of Battery E 1st Ky Light Artilery is charged with the execution of the above Order
     II   It is in addition directed that all flags will be displayed at half mast and all
places of business closed at this Post upon the day indicated as above, April 16tth 1865[1]

1. General Orders No. 42, 15 Apr. 1865; Vol. 111/256, p. 116; General Orders; RG 393.

Headquarters Department of Kentucky, Louisville, Ky., April 18, 1865.

Hon. E.M. Stanton, Secretary of War:

The provost marshals refuse to muster in the recruits raised for colored regiments now organizing. Please allow me to recruit them to the maximum. It would be well to continue enlisting blacks at least until May 15, when the State Legislature meets and will probably pass the amendment,[1] if colored recruiting is kept up till that time. We are recruiting as an argument forcible.

John M. Palmer, Major-General, Commanding.[2]

1. The Thirteenth Amendment, abolishing slavery, was passed by Congress on January 31, 1865, and ratified on December 6, 1865.
2. Palmer to Stanton, 18 Apr. 1865, *OR,* 3, 4, 1271.

Washington, April 18th, 1865.

Major-General Palmer: — The Provost Marshals in Kentucky are hereby authorized and directed to continue mustering in colored recruits to fill up the colored regiments to the maximum, any previous order to the contrary notwithstanding. A copy of this, to be certified by you, will serve as a formal order for that purpose, which on notification from you they will obey accordingly.

Edwin M. Stanton   Secretary of War.[1]

1. Stanton to Palmer, 18 Apr. 1865, *NIMSUS,* 6:3622.

Head Quarters   Camp Nelson   April 18th 1865
General Orders No 43

In obedience to instructions from Head Quarters Dept of Ky. all labor will be suspended at this Post and places of business closed on Wednesday the 19th Inst. the day of the funeral of the late President of the United States. Flags will be lowered and left at half mast and it is recommended that the Comdg Officers of Regiments and Independent Companies will make any arrangements that may be necessary to have religious observed during the day

II   At 12 o.clock meridian April 19th Twenty one (21) guns will be fired at intervals of one minute

[*Unsigned.*][1]

1. General Orders No. 43, 18 Apr. 1865; Vol. 111/256, p. 117; General Orders; RG 393.

[*An excerpt from Collins,* **Historical Sketches:**]

April 24 — Maj. Gen. Burbridge [was] presented, at Camp Nelson, with a $1,000 sword, belt and spurs by the colored cavalry in brigades 5th and 6th U.S.C.C.

of Ky. Gen. Brisbin made the presentation speech, in which he spoke of Gen. Burbridge as "the pioneer of freedom to the slaves of Ky." Gen. Burbridge said "the war is over with the rebels, and he expected and hoped soon to see our colored troops sent to Mexico.[1]

1. Collins, 1:159. The only Kentuckians disposed to honor Gen. Stephen Burbridge, despite his rather illustrious military record, were former slaves and anti-slavery advocates. In 1867 he wrote that he was not "able to live in safety or do business in Kentucky" (*DAB*). The people of his own class (he had been a plantation owner and extensive slaveholder) simply ostracized him, partly because of his guerrilla reprisal policy (among other provisions, it ordered that four guerrilla prisoners, one for each unarmed Union citizen who had been murdered, were to be "publicly shot to death in the most convenient place near the scene of the outrage" [*OR*, 1, 32, 42–43]). According to De Falaise, "The list of executions [was] a long one" (112). Burbridge also was hated for his part in recruiting Kentucky's slaves and in fomenting the strange episode called the Great Hog Swindle of 1864. See De Falaise, 101–27.

[*April 28, 1865*]
To the Ex. Com. Am. Miss. Assoc.

Brethren — Having within the last three weeks, at the request of the Sec[t] of the Asso. visited Camp Nelson, Ky. for the purpose of inspecting the condition and wants of the freed people there, and also of conferring with Gov[t] officials, and other friends of these poor people, on the ground, in respect to their christian elevation — I submit the following report: —

1. Camp Nelson — built in 1863, under direction of Maj. Gen. Burnside, as the base of supplies for the Army of the Cumberland — is finely located in a sharp bend of the Kentucky river — in the extreme south part of Jessamine Co., and is about 115 almost due south from Cincinnati. It is defended by magnificent limestone bluffs on the East, South, and West, and by strong earthworks and forts on the North extending from Little Hickman Creek to Kentucky river. Its defenses include, at least, 4,500 acres of excellent land — well watered by springs, and by steam water works capable of forcing, I am told, 140 galls. per minute from the bed of the Kentucky to large central reservoir <u>470</u> feet above it. The Camp is therefore on high land — is "beautiful for situation", and must be, I think, healthy.

2. A portion of this Camp — the best of the whole as it seems to me — is appropriated by the Gov[t] as a Home for the destitute col[d] refugees — mostly the families of soldiers — seeking the protection of the government within its defenses. This portion is so extensive that Capt. T.E. Hall, gov[t] Supt. of the Home, informs me 2000 acres, if necessary, may be put under the plow. Between 3 & 400 acres are already in process of cultivation for the present season. It is expected that the labor upon this land will be mainly performed by the women and boys congregated in the Home. Seven large buildings . . . have been erected. One more is to be added. Sanitary considerations, however, have led to the plan of building cottages 32 X 16 feet, around in the center, making two rooms 16 X 16 in each cottage,

designed to accommodate 10 persons, possibly 12, or 20 to 24 persons in each cottage. These cottages are now being built by the government at the rate of three per day, and thus far making shelter for 60 newcomers daily. The building of these cottages it is supposed will relieve the necessity of crowding the people into wards, and leave the large barrack buildings free to a great extent for hospital, mechanical & school purposes.

3. These refugees are fast congregating at Camp Nelson. On 1st of April there were 1266 persons, nearly all of them women and children, in the Home. From 1st to 11th of Apr. 354 were recd. On sabbath Apr. 16th, 54. The number today Apr. 28 congregated there cannot be less than 2000. The condition of these poor people — driven out of the old places by their former masters in the very Spirit of their predecessors of Christ's time, who before they relinquished their grasp upon a victim "rent him sore" — is often wretched in the extreme, but they came to the city of refuge hopeful and as a general thing earnest for improvement — for religious culture, for mental training. This wide field, now opening so rapidly, appears to me as promising as it is large and needy. * * * * [Two paragraphs.]

In conclusion, I take the liberty to recommend for your considerations and adoption the following actions —

1. To pay Mr. J.C. Chapin,[1] now acting as clerk &c. at the Home, or some other suitable person in his stead should he not remain, a salary of $50 per month, from May 1st prox for one year — and the salary of a farm supt., the same salary on the same conditions.

2. To pay Mrs. Knight[2] now at Camp Nelson — as matron of the teachers home, or some other suitable person in her stead — Mrs. L. Williams Jr. Mrs. A.C. Damon,[3] and Miss Jennie Mann (if she decides to go) a salary, as teachers, not exceeding 15 per month, in addition to board & quarters. Also to commission and sustain additional teachers, as accommodations may be provided & the refugees may need their services, for the year ensuing — I suggest that Mrs. L. Williams, Jr. be requested to take charge of the organization of the schools at the home, and take the general oversight of them till some one else may be designated to fill this position.

3. To request Rev. Jno. G. Fee to take charge of the religious interests of the Home. And since this work is opening so rapidly, and he will be liable, from his wide acquaintance in Kentucky, to calls for labor outside of Camp Nelson, that he be requested — from considerations connected with his own health and wider usefulness to confine himself to this department of labor in the Home and in the Camp. *

E. Davis[4]

1. Joseph C. Chapin, who attended Oberlin Academy from 1855 to 1856, was secretary and clerk at the Soldiers' Home and Rev. Lester Williams's chief assistant. Fee called him an "usher & disposer of clothing." [Oberlin] Alumni Register Graduates and Former Students, Teaching and Administrative Staff 1833–1960 (Oberlin, 1960), 337 (hereafter abbreviated "Oberlin Register").

2. The wife of E.P. Knight, she and her husband were from Worcester, Massachusetts, the same region as Capt. Hall and many others. As matron, one of her duties was to cater.

3. Caroline Damon, a widow from Massachusetts, was hired to teach at the Refugee Home at Camp Nelson on the basis of her acquaintance with Capt. Hall. This reference is the only clue to her husband's name, since "A.C." are apparently his initials; he may have died as a soldier in the war.

4. Davis to Executive Committee of the AMA, 28 Apr. 1865, AMAA 44124–5.

War Dept., Provost-Marshal-General's Bureau, Washington, D.C., April 29, 1865.

Maj. Gen. L. Thomas, Adjutant-General, Louisville, Ky.:

The Secretary of War having directed that the recruiting of men in the loyal States for the volunteer forces be stopped, now directs that the recruitment for the volunteer forces of all persons, including colored men, in all States be embraced in the order, and their enlistment be discontinued.

James B. Fry, Provost-Marshal-General.[1]

1. Fry to Thomas, 29 Apr. 1865, *OR,* 3, 4, 1282.

[*Letterhead.*] *U.S. Sanitary Commission*   Camp Nelson Ky   May 2 1865.

Dear Bro Strieby —
 * * * * [*Two paragraphs.*]
 I will speak this once   The men and women who will be appropriate help-ers for this people must be those [*who*] can mingle amongst them & treat them <u>kindly</u> gain their confidence then we can get hold of them.

But if a superintendent or teacher is reserved & cross if when one trembling fugitive comes into his presence and begins to enquire and he gruffly says "Who are you" I am Milly. They tell me there is a letter here for me — "They tell many stories about letters"   The woman retires   this [*is*] all. * * * * [*Two paragraphs.*]

Bro Davis & Capt Hall think we need "Massachusetts precision" here in Ky — no doubt But these poor babes need not starch and fastidiousness but Christ like sim-plicity . . . . * * * * [*Four paragraphs.*]

Yours in Christ
John G Fee[1]

1. Fee to Strieby, 2 May 1865, AMAA 44126. When Fee wrote this letter, he was prepar-ing to hurry back to Berea, where his wife had given birth in his absence. Elizabeth ("Bessie") Fee, born April 30, 1865, was the last of Fee's six children.

Office of Supt of Refugees — Camp Nelson   May 8th 1865
Rev M.E. Strieby

Dear Sir * * * * [*One paragraph.*]
 . . . . Bear in mind that the most of these people are field hands and know comparatively nothing of cooking or sewing — there should be several persons to cover this branch of the home — It is not sufficient that these people are taught to

read. They must be taught to <u>take care of themselves</u>. I respectfully and earnestly recommend that you send three or four good earnest laborers for this field — . . . . One other and important subject. <u>Clothing</u>. These people come here <u>almost naked</u>. The government will not issue clothing. What can be done? Permit me to suggest that your society issue a circular setting forth the wants of these people and call upon the churches at the North for contributions of clothing for them. It is not too soon to begin to prepare for the winter. God grant I may never witness a repetition of the suffering of last winter. . . .

T.E. Hall[1]

1. Hall to Strieby, 8 May 1865, AMAA 44128–30. The quoted passage is part of a very long paragraph with sizable omissions at the beginning and the end.

Camp Nelson Ky   May 8th 1865.
Rev. M.E. Strieby

Dear Sir, I have received and read the circular of the Am. Miss. Society calling for a brief statement from applicants wishing to engage as teachers in the service of the Asso. and in reply will submit the following. I am a Widow with no family. Have enjoyed good educational and religious advantages. I came here knowing well, what sacrifices I must make. I am willing to stay as long as my services are needed. For a certificate of my fitness for this particular work, I will refer you to Capt. Hall. *

Caroline Damon[1]

1. Damon to Strieby, 8 May 1865, AMAA 44131.

[*Letterhead.*] *War Department   Inspector General's Office, Washington, D.C.   May 13. 1865.*
Bvt. Brig. Gen. Jas. A. Hardie   Inspector General, US Army.

I have the honor to submit the following report of an Inspection made pursuant to Special Orders. No 173. War Department. Adjutant General's Office April 17th 1865.
<u>1. Camp Nelson, Kentucky.</u>
[*In the margin:*] <u>Location.</u>
This camp is located on the Kentucky River, 6 miles from Nicholasville, the terminous of the Ky. Central R.R. 110 miles NorthWest from Cumberland Gap, and 112 from Cincinnati. As a defencible position it has probably no equal in the state, surrounded as it is upon two sides (South and West) by the Ky. River whose banks are high and precipitous, and inaccessible by Artillery; and upon the East bounded by Hickman Creek, a tributary of the last named river, with almost equally formidable natural defences upon the Western bank.
The defences consist of three Forts, ("Taylor", "Jackson" and "Nelson.") each

mounting six 12 pounder Napoleon guns and one 30 pdr. Parrott. The forts are connected by rifle pits and are well constructed and effectually command the approaches. If properly manned, the works are susceptible of defence against almost any force. I found however, that with the exception of a Battery of Light Artillery (Battery "E." 1st Ky. Lt. Artl'y) numbering 77 men, not a man of the garrison had any training or experience in working the guns, and they are practically useless in case of attack. Capt. Brush, in charge of the defences had entered but one of the magazines, and half an hour was required to find the Keys. The ammunition had not been inspected or aired within the memory of the oldest inhabitant, and was damp, and much of it useless. The Magazines are not provided with any means of ventilation or sub-surface drainage. They need sodding also. The heavy rains this spring have washed deep gulleys in them, and will soon destroy them. If this Camp is to be maintained, a battalion of Heavy Artillery is much needed to take proper care of guns and ammunition and form an adequate force for defence.

In addition to the defences extending across the neck of the peninsula, there is a small battery at the southern outlet of the Camp, commanding the bridge over the river, and a Fort, ("Bramlette") upon a commanding point of land between the river and Hickman Creek, and separated by the latter stream from the Camp. No guns are mounted in either of these works. For Bramlette is garrisoned by one company of Infantry. A macadamized turnpike runs through the Camp, being the main public highway between Nicholasville, and Danville. Tolls to the amount of $4.000 per month are paid by the Qr. Masters Dept. for the use of this road. Of this sum, about $1.000 per month is paid for that portion of the road from Nicholasville to Camp Nelson. The monthly cost has been much larger until the past winter. The completion of the Rail Road from Nicholasville would have been an economical expenditure, and if Camp N. is to be maintained for any length of time, this work should be done now. The distance is but six miles, the grading would not be heavy, and no bridges of importance would be required. Sixty (60) wagons are now in constant use in the transportation of stores over this six miles of road.

The Camp at the time of my visit (April 26) was commanded by Lieut. Col. Geo. A Hannaford. 124th U.S.C. Inft'y. Lt. Col. L.H. Carpenter, 5th U.S. Col. Cav'y was relieved on the preceding day, and upon the 28th a third commandant arrived, Lt Col. Albert Coates[1] 6th US Col'd. Cavy. Lt. Col. Hannaford is, I think, an energetic and efficient officer, but had been in command too short a time to introduce any thing like order or discipline into the Camp. Most of the evils and irregularities which were conspicuous everywhere, are attributable to this continual change of commandants and no suggestions can be made which will lead to any practicable results until an efficient officer is assigned to the permanent command.

To an officer who assumed command yesterday and expects to resign it tomorrow, no suggestions from an Inspector, or orders from a superior will have much force or lead to permanent amendment. The only basis of reform at Camp Nelson is the immediate assignment of an efficient commandant. The records of the Post are in a miserably confused and imperfect condition. No Morning reports are required by Post Head Quarters, and Provision Returns are approved without any means of verifying their correctness.

[*In the margin:*] Post Fund.

There has been a Post fund arising from a tax upon Sutlers, of the amount of this fund there is no record and no exhibit of expenditures. No returns have ever been made. Within the limit of the [*In the margin:* Sutlers] Camp there are no less than thirteen (13) persons selling sutlers goods. All under authority from Maj Gen. Burbridge. They were all expelled from Camp by Brig. Gen. Fry, when in command, but returned within a short time with written authority to resume their sales. They are allowed to sell Ale and beer but no other liquors. I recommend that they be all expelled and one sutler regularly appointed for the post. An application was made for such an appointment in May 1864, and declined by the War Department.

[*In the margin:*] Garrison.

The troops at this Camp consist of one Company, 2nd Battalion V.R.C. (on duty at Gen. Hosp.) Detachment of 123rd & 124th U.S. Col'd Inf., Battery "E" 1st Ky. Lt. Artillery, and a number of recruits now being organized into the 119th U.S.C.I., in all, 894 officers and men present. Of this number, but 180 are armed. The 124th U.S.C.I. is an "Invalid Regiment," enlisted for duty in the Q.M. & Engineer Depts. They present a very creditable appearance. The expediency of enlisting men for this kind of service, without arms has been, it is presumed, fully discussed and favorably determined & is not now open to suggestions. About 300 of this Regiment are detailed as teamsters and employees of the Q.M. Dept.

[*In the margin:*] Colored Recruiting service

Lt. Col. Hannaford is also the Superintendent of Colored Recruiting service at this Depot. As I have before remarked, he seems an active and intelligent officer. Since March 20th 1865, when this rendezvous was established, four hundred and eighty three (483) men have been mustered in. The records are much better kept than those of the post, the barracks in good condition and a better state of police and discipline apparent than in other portions of the Camp.

[*In the margin:*] Colored Refugee's Home.

Under authority from Maj. Gen. Palmer, a Camp has been established for contraband women and children, the families of soldiers enlisting in the Army. About 1700 of these people are now provided for, furnished with quarters, rations and fuel. They are coming into Camp very rapidly. 907 were received during the month of April, and the Q.M.D. is taxed to the utmost to erect barracks with sufficient despatch to provide for them. Mr T.E. Hall, formerly A.Q.M. at this post is the Superintendent. He was absent at the time of my visit, is represented as an energetic & efficient man; when A.Q.M. he was deemed an honest and active Officer, but somewhat extravagant & injudicious in his expenditures. The buildings erected, consist of the superintendent's house (75 X 30 feet, and two stories in height) rather a munificent provision for this officer and his assistants) — a Dining room and Kitchen, (100 X 30 feet with two wings each 50 X 30 feet) a work

Shop of about the same dimensions and of two stories which is now occupied by women and children as barracks, four buildings also used as barracks — 25 X 75 each and containing 120 refugees, and (30) thirty "Cottages" 32 X 16 feet, divided into two compartments and intended to contain 20 or 30 inmates. As many more are in process of erection. The cost of these "Cottages" is $400. each. I could get no accurate estimate of the cost of the larger buildings. The lumber is sawed almost entirely by the Machinery in charge of the Post Qr Master and the doors shingles &c are made here. The cottages are to be paid for (theoretically) by the soldiers whose families occupy them, at the rate of $25. each. as a gross rental during the whole time occupied, but no contracts are made, and there is no practical system established for carrying out this design. 200 acres of arable land have been plowed and are to be devoted to gardening and raising broom corn this summer — from which brooms will be manufactured by the women during the Winter. This experiment is just being initiated and no data as to its economy or practical workings can be furnished.

The establishment is in excellent condition, the barracks clean, the general health of the people good, and the drainage and police of the grounds fair. This bids fair to become a large and expensive experiment, and without careful supervision by the Department Commander, extravagant outlays are to be apprehended. There are a number of buildings now unused, or not needed in Camp Nelson, the material of which is good and perfectly available for the erection of barracks for thse people. I would suggest that the erection of New buildings be suspended until at least, this surplus material is used.

A "soldier's home" is among the needless appurtenances of Camp Nelson. The buildings belong to the Government and should be at once used for contrabands. The "Convalescent Camp" (of which I shall have occasion to speak further) has in use (8) eight buildings which are not needed. The reduction which it is presumed will soon take place in the business of the Q.M. Dept. will vacate many more, and I believe it will not be necessary to erect any more barracks from new materials for the purposes of this Refugee Home. The laws of Kentucky provide, I think, that the Master shall care for the aged, infirm and helpless among his servants. It is not clear that the emancipation of slaves relieves him from this duty. Even if it does have this effect, he is still legally responsible for the care of women and children not freed by the enlistment of the head of the family, and many of those at Camp Nelson are of this class, and have been driven from home, oftentimes with the most malicious cruelty, because no longer useful. In view of the burdens of the General Government present and prospective, and the requirements of simple justice, the Masters of Kentucky should be compelled to provide for these people, or if cared for by the Government, the expences should be assessed upon the owner. The charitable societies of the North have supplied a great deal of clothing for these people. What is most needed is some systematic and organized effort throughout the North West whose object shall be to secure for these people labor and wages and thus relieve the Government as soon as may be of their support, and at the same time constitute the most practical and needed charity to the refugees themselves.

[*In the margin:*] <u>Nelson U.S.A. Gen'l. Hospl.</u>]
   The Nelson U.S. General Hospital under charge of Surgeon <u>H.L.W. Burritt</u>, U.S. Vols. is a well conducted and highly creditable establishment. Seven Acting Assistant Surgeons are employed.

No. of Wards	10
No. of Beds	700
No. of Sick	517
No. of Attendants	50

Since January 1ˢᵗ 1865. 1590 cases have been treated, of whom, 229 have died. This large proportion of deaths is owing in great measure to the large number of Colored inmates, among whom diseases are said to be more generally fatal, and to the lack of regimental Surgeons with the Colored Regiments to treat and arrest disease in its early stages. Many are past recovery before being sent to Genl. Hospitals. The internal cleanliness and order of the Wards is noticeable. The policing of the grounds is not so well attended to. The drains are not clean. Refuse matter is allowed to collect in them and under the buildings. Surgeon <u>Burritt</u>, has been but a brief time in charge, and I am satisfied will remedy these irregularities, to which his attention was called. The Hospital fund in March amounted to $5.677.39. of which $4.343.45 were expended judiciously — leaving a balance of $1.333.94.

[*In the margin:*] <u>Convalescent Camp.</u>
   A Convalescent Camp is another of the excrescences of this Post. This establishment is in charge of Acting Ass't Surgeon, <u>A.C. Rankin</u>, with whom is associated Act. Asst. Surg. <u>W.W. Hoover</u>, assisted by 25 attendants besides a number of laundresses. This formidable corps is in charge of 199 convalescents, of whom about (50) fifty require some little treatment, and occupy (76) seventy six Hospital tents & (8) eight buildings.
   The Surgeons live in rather an elegant mansion, with highly ornamented landscape gardens in front of their quarters, and a fountain playing in the centre. Although a change would be by no means pleasant or desirable to the parties, I would recommend that the "Convalescent Camp" be at once broken up, the sick sent to the General Hospital where there is abundant provision for them, the remainder to their regiments, and the Surgeons ordered to a more laborious field of duty or dispensed with entirely.[2]
   Camp Nelson is supplied with water from the Kentucky River by means of machinery driven by a steam Engine which pumps the water into a Reservoir 475 feet above the river. The supply is generally abundant. Fourteen men are constantly employed in the management of these water works. Much has been said in regard to the extravagance of this expenditure. The original cost was a little more than $50.000. as will appear by the report of John B. Earnshaw, "annexed and marked" (A).
   Camp Nelson has been a costly experiment altogether, but when it was determined to establish it, a supply of water was a necessary and unavoidable adjunct,

and the items of expenditure are not apparently unreasonable. The Machinery is in good condition and can be now disposed of, I am assured, for a much larger sum than its original cost. There is a sufficient number of fire plugs near the workshop and storehouses to secure safety against fire, with proper precaution, but there is a deficiency of small hose, and no fire buckets or axes are provided. As in almost all of our permanent camps there is great danger of fire and but little thought, or care, in regard to the matter. I have called special attention to this danger at all camps, and am satisfied that ample provision against it, will be the wisest economy in the world.

The Provost Marshal, Capt. F.A. Tencate, of the camp, has in charge 44 Prisoners, of whom, 27 are under sentence of Gen. Court Martial, 14 awaiting trial, and two citizens arrested for stealing. The Prison is internally in good condition, but the drainage and policing, especially about the Kitchen, very bad. One Prisoner, B.F. Livingston, formerly a Colonel in the State service and serving as Chief of Police (whatever that may be) of Kentucky, had been convicted of embezzlement and frauds of various Kinds, and sentenced to confinement for a term of years. Upon the certificate of Acting Ass't Surgeon Henry Percy, in charge of Prison Hospital, that he was too sick to be moved, he has been kept in barracks outside of the Prison Enclosure. This fact was disclosed to me as I was leaving the Camp, and the further fact that during the preceding night he had effected his escape. I send word to the Commandant of the Post that the Surgeon should be at once arrested and an investigation held. Without the complicity of this Surgeon, such an imposition would seem impossible, and the Provost Marshal deserves the severest censure for carelessness, and for concealing the fact that the prisoner was thus confined. Actg Ass't Surg. Percy has charge of five or six patients, such as are sick from time to time among 44 prisoners, and his services can be dispensed with without serious disadvantage. I failed to see Maj. Genl. Palmer in Louisville, as he and staff were absent at Indianapolis. I recommend that the subject of the escape of the man Livingston be at once referred to him for special investigation. The other Prisoners confined at Camp Nelson were guarded by recruits from the Camp of organization, many of them placed on duty at the prison for the first time and receiving their first and only instruction in the manual of arms and the duties of a sentinel at guard Mounting.

The Qr. Master's Department is in charge of Capt. E.B.W. Restieaux, who appears to be an accurate business man — active and competent.

Learning that Colonel J.D. Bingham,[3] Inspector Q.M. Dept. had completed, a few days previous to my visit, a minute Inspection of Capt. Restieaux's accounts and vouchers, I deemed it unnecessary to examine them critically. To give a general idea of the extent of the business of this depot a list of public buildings and machinery is appended, to-gether with a list of employees. Of the latter, 1218 appear upon the rolls, and this number does not include nearly 300 enlisted men detailed as teamsters, woodchoppers &c from the 124th U.S.C. Inf. So long as the present amount of transportation and machinery is maintained at this depot, this formidable roll of employees may be necessary — a recruiting depot for worn out horses is a part of the establishment, requiring a large number of men — 437 are teamsters, and a large proportion of the remainder are employed in repairing wagons and harness, and in the Steam Saw Mill and Machine Shops which have been established.

The present wants of the service it is presumed will not require the maintenance of so extensive a depot, and its immediate reduction is advisable.

The recent Orders from the Q.M.G.O.[4] will lead to such a result. A charge was preferred by Lieut. Charles Harkins, 124 U.S.C.I. that a number of the detailed men from his reg't in the Q.M. Dept. performed no duty except menial service for clerks employed by Capt. R. He failed however to point out the men or to produce any evidence of the fact. The charge is denied by Capt. R. and it was not practicable to muster the men, many being absent in charge of supplies sent to Cumberland Gap, woodchopping etc. This is however an abuse likely to occur where so many unarmed colored soldiers are detailed, where no reports are made of the duty performed, and there is no accountability for a proper use of enlisted labor. I suggest that the attention of the Major General Commanding the Department be called to this subject.

The Commissary Department, in charge of Capt. Edward P. Ransom, is in good condition, records and returns promptly and neatly Kept, and stores in good order. Thirty six (36) employees are on the rolls of the office. Accounts of Hospital and Contraband funds and purchases made therefrom accurately Kept. A Post Bakery is in operation. The savings from flour are taken up regularly upon the Returns. They have never formed a part of the Post fund at this Camp.

Camp Nelson is apparently an extravagant experiment and the necessity for its maintenance is not clear. The large depots of Government supplies and Q.M. property there, are kept up now solely for the use of the few troops in the Camp and the small garrison at Cumberland Gap. The distance from the latter point to Knoxville is but 68 miles and it would seem more economical and perfectly practicable to supply the garrison from that depot. * * * *

[*This report, part of a collection of reports detailing inspections of camps in Davenport, Iowa, Johnson's Island, among other places, was referred to Lieut. Gen. U.S. Grant by order of the secretary of war on May 26, 1865. The referral, basically a long summary of the foregoing, was signed by C.A. Dana, associate secretary of war, who was not the writer of the report.*]

Murray Davis   Major A.A.G. Vols.[5]

1. Lt. Col. Albert Coates (born in Ohio) of the Sixth U.S. Colored Cavalry, occasional commander of Camp Nelson, resigned from the army on January 25, 1866. *HR,* 1:312; *OAR,* 8:146.

2. The section of this report concerning the convalescent camp was relayed to the medical director of the District of Kentucky, Col. A.J. Phelps, with an endorsement directing him to "break up the Convalescent Camp at Camp Nelson Ky., and to discharge the Acting Assistant Surgeons" by order of the Surgeon General. On May 3, 1865, Acting Assistant Surgeon A.C. Rankin, "In charge Convalescent Camp Hospital Camp Nelson Ky," was ordered "to take immediate measures to discontinue the same transferring the patients to the Nelson Gen. Hospital." Rankin was further directed to turn over all medical and hospital property to the "Med. Storekeeper" and all quartermaster's stores to the assistant quartermaster of Camp Nelson. File S49, Box 10 (1865); RG 159.

3. Judson David Bingham, a native of New York, began his military service in Indiana, became an assistant quartermaster in 1861, and continued in the Quartermaster Department for over twenty years. *HR,* 1:218.

4. Quartermaster General's office.

5. Davis to Hardie, 13 May 1865, F6 D–17 (1865), Box 7; Entry 15; RG 159.

Frankfort Ky   May 18 /65

Dear Bro Strieby

* * * * [*Two paragraphs.*]

. . . The Association gave to Gabriel Burdett a commission — at the time I stated to the society there was a claim on him as a soldier detailed here had not been mustered in — his regiment going to front

He worked in here as an evangelist doing good   Recently he has been mustered in   He is in need of a stove — cooking stove — will you send him thirty five dollars on the past — let him pay   He will do extra work the work of preaching teaching writing &c for colored people —

Bro Davis will tell you that Burdett is a valuable man. * * * * [*Four paragraphs.*]

J G Fee[1]

1. Fee to Strieby, 18 May 1865, AMAA 44134.

Camp Nelson, Ky   May 22^d 1865.
Rev. M.E. Strieby

My Dear Sir, . . . I have already organized and set in operation two schools, one for boys and one for girls between the ages of five and ten years. Each numbers from ninety to ninety five scholars. I found on an examination that ten of the boys could read and twenty could say their letters. Of the girls, twenty could read and forty say their letters. As a whole, they look bright, animated, and intent to learn.

Thus far the enterprise shows a face of very pleasant encouragement. I find my time largely occupied, aside from other duties, with writing letters for these poor oppressed women to their husbands & sons that are in the army — defenders of the union. * * * * [*One paragraph.*]

Ann E.W. Williams[1]

1. Williams to Strieby, 22 May 1865, AMAA 44136. Her maiden name was Ann Eliza Warren, thus her frequent signature: A.E.W. Williams.

(Private)
Camp Nelson Ky   May 30 65

Dear Bro Strieby   we ought to have here some colored teachers

1. That these people may <u>see</u> what they <u>can</u> be

2. That by <u>example</u> we may help put down the spirit of cast
Tis not as I believe best to move the colored people from this state   some favor this

    1 They ought for highest good to have homes of their own — better than to be floating hirelings better for their children also <u>parents</u> can watch over them

    2 Lands here are cheaper than free states

    3 The presence of free people of color will help continue the weakness of slavery — until <u>all</u> hope is gone of its recuperation

    4 Climate here suits these colored people.

<u>Danger</u>
If life in colonies by themselves they will perpetuate the negro habits & superstitions

    1 Education will help correct this —

    2 Have there the white teachers missionary medicine merchant &c

    . . . . Capt Hall is in favor of having these people go to the free states — thinks that will help kill slavery — My decision is no — this is just what slave owners want — absence of "free nigger" — then what they have are more quiet & secure

    I have a discussion going on in my mind.

    Camp Nelson cannot be the receptacle for <u>all</u>   How then shall we get education to the great mass who stay scattered over the country   What we have here is only a drop in the buckett

    Outside of military posts the people will not yet be favorable to schools where colored children can be taught   We think we can do this at Berea soon as we can get ready for the children — next Spring   Get house up this fall and winter
<u>Decision</u>

    After your observation — is it best to get colored children & whites into the same towns and schools or will that be all the while a forced effort and small and we be compelled to get the colored people together in groups for a generation and there educate and then by the force of example in persons already educated & cultivated break down the spirit of cast

    Is this your decision? What?

    We are needing teachers here very much   school room ready for five hundred pupils

    Mrs Daimon is in the room with fifty boys forenoon fifty girls afternoon — You ask, what does Mrs Williams do? I answer help "organize" — thats all   Writes letters, better teach letters — but enough — You have had an inspector here and he did the best he could in a short stay seeing the sunny side.[1]

    The work is the source of some good, yet radically defective and you are not at fault — perhaps I am most to blame

    I expected you would have the power of appointing a superintendent. You will have now, as I suppose, one more opportunity through the Bureau at Washington   Gnl Howard — and Col Fisk for the district of Kentucky & Tennesse

Let me then again suggest

1 Let the management be in the hands of christian men men who will administer in the name of Christ — and in the spirit of [*Christ*] — in field & house — not one who merely assents to the theory of christianity without the practice.

That christianity ought to be . . . a christianity that can take such to his table, <u>work</u> with them and show by example — in marked patience & kindness bear their infirmities.

2 The man who conducts this should make this a <u>speciality</u> — not divided with other interests —

His assistant should not be a finely dressed gentleman with his hands in his pockets only to give orders, but one in simplicity of dress & with willing hands <u>take</u> <u>hold</u> and show — say come aunty woman or "we come to <u>help</u> you" — "we come to work, too"

The sub assistants should not be fashionable young men on horseback to drive women & children after the "plantation" order * * * * [*Three paragraphs.*]

I gathered the children together last sabbath — 527 between age of five & 20 for a <u>beginning</u> — some six said they could read. we will see about this next sabbath — I give to them Bible stories with their connection with redemption — Had no one to help me but Mrs Daimon — Bro Burdett (colored) is called to his regiment — will probably be sent with Regiment to Texas[2]

Bro Williams thinks his labors are enough without preaching — declines. I have more than two thousand people here to care for without any helper at all now —

If you had a good principal of the school, instead of Mrs Williams he could take the labor of the sabbath school & greatly aid me otherwise * * * * [*Five paragraphs.*]

John G. Fee[3]

1. Fee is referring to the sanguine views expressed by Rev. Elnathan Davis in his report to the Executive Committee of the AMA, 28 Apr. 1865 (see above).
2. Gabriel Burdett's regiment, the 114th Colored Infantry, was sent to Texas in June and July 1865; it had duty in Brownsville and other points on the Rio Grande until April 1867, when it was mustered out of service. Dyer, 2:1739.
3. Fee to Strieby, 30 May 1865, AMAA 44139–41.

[*Letterhead.*] *War Department   Washington City*   June 2 1865
Major Gen Howard

General   I beg to call your attention to the condition of the Freedmen at Camp Nelson in Kentucky which is represented from authentic sources to be very bad. A man named Hall who is said to be very unsuitable appears to be in charge probably by some order of Adjutant General Thomas. He should be promptly removed. Judge Goodloe[1] of Kentucky who will hand you this note and may be relied upon will give you details. *

Edwin M Stanton   Sec of War[2]

1. Danville Judge William Cassius Goodloe became Freedmen's Bureau superintendent for Boyle, Lincoln, and Mercer Counties.
2. Stanton to Howard, 2 June 1865; M999:7:635; RG 105.

Resolution of the General Assembly of Kentucky.

Resolution requesting the President to withdraw Negro Troops from the State of Kentucky.

Whereas, Negro soldiers that have been recruited in the State of Kentucky, have been quartered in different parts of the State, much to the detriment of the citizens thereof, said troops committing many outrages upon the lives and property of many citizens; and whereas Kentucky is one of the loyal States of the Union, and therefore entitled to the privileges and immunities of other loyal States; and there exists no necessity for the presence of said troops within the State, in fact their presence is a source of great irritation to their former owners and the citizens generally, therefore,
   Resolve,
   That the Governor be requested to respectfully request and earnestly urge the immediate removal of all negro troops from the State by the President of the United States; and that for the necessary protection of the people, a sufficient number of white soldiers may be assigned for duty to this Commonwealth.

Approved June 3, 1865 (Acts of the General Assembly of Kentucky 1865. p. 166)[1]

1. Resolution of the General Assembly of Kentucky, 3 June 1865, *NIMSUS,* 6:3661.

Camp Nelson Ky   Jun 6 /65
Hon Chs Sumner[1]

I have just seen Genl. J M Palmer — at his request. He is deeply interested for humanity is working efficiently in this state — He will do still more or be relieved
   I wish you would try and see him whilst he is in Washington   He started yesterday to see President Johnson at Washington
   In order to [*insure*] success in this camp of eleven <u>square miles</u>, I believe it is all important that hundreds of acres, within the camp, belonging to Rebels, that we know have helped raise rebel companies & fight the Union army, be confiscated and the lands be sold for benefit of a school for humanity. Perhaps tis not best to say for a school for <u>Colored</u> people — tis not best to draw the lines ourselves & make a kind of Liberia here for "niggers" — that will only perpetuate the spirit of cast. I suppose the union of both white & colored is best. We made this start at Berea Madison Co Ky where my home is and family are now some six years since. * * * *
[*One paragraph.*]
   Two thousand woman and children here have claims on me   I have asked for their freedom, now some one ought to care for them when others cast them off   The school here will probably number 5 to 6 hundred children soon as more teachers come in. I preach to all on sabbath.

I am leaving my own family for a time — must return to them or bring them here to me.

If it shall be deemed best to keep this merely as a camp of refuge for negro women & children wives & children of soldiers and then have a place for the higher school in grade of education for whites & blacks together thus we can go to Berea Madison co — 32 miles — for that school. We have now a hundred lots for sale there.

You are the friend of education and Gods poor. Will you not see Genl Palmer and confer with him — lay plans for great good in this state? I know not any of the Bureau at Washington. Yours in haste

John G Fee[2]

1. An uncompromising and vehement supporter of abolition and equal rights for African-Americans, Senator Charles Sumner (1811–1874) of Massachusetts was one of the most radical of Republicans. *CWD.*

2. Fee to Sumner, 6 June 1865; M999:7:624–25; RG 105.

Camp Nelson Ky   June 9 /65

Dear Bro Whipple . . . . I have recently learned the appointment of a Bureau — That may overlook everything here

Capt Hall thinks he cannot offer to put me up a little house here because of uncertainty — There is not room in superintendent's house for my family. . . . * * * * [*One paragraph.*]

The war is now over — guerrillas are gone and slavery is nominal in law — the habit of slavery lives yet. But there is not a necessity that women run here for protection as heretofore.

Now we should arrange for a more natural and efficient system. We need now to remove fast as possible all unnatural appliances and restore those of compensation and natural affection — we need to get these people in cottages attached to small plots of ground or some mechanical labor, from either or both of which they can earn something. They will work for themselves as they will not for Uncle Sam or any other than self. In so doing so they will govern themselves, thus far, and avoid the driving of overseers. I have within the last two days visited more than one hundred families — and registered the name and condition of each member — about one thousand. By this have the domestic social and religious state of each one — I so mark each one. I have worked very hard to get this — shall go on again this day. Now I find many sleeping, lounging & dodging who would otherwise be out at work — This must be overcome by the natural stimulus before a success can be attained.

Now we must either introduce machinery or scatter these cottages (now in straight rows (three) and each house about 18 feet apart) out onto little plots of ground which plots shall be worked, not by government compelling some of these to work the ground, but by letting each family work themselves & have the entire profit of their own work; and thus sustain themselves — "pump or drowned" — no true success here without something like this.

To this we must we must either, through government, get title to lands here — . . . or machinery introduced so as to have remunerative labor here & so as to have a class, not continually coming in, so as to merit & change their status, & then going, but a class of permanent laborers here, on whom we can make some lasting impression.

Let government give title & protection & then hands off. Let the remainder be done by benevolent instruction and individual effort. * * * * [*One paragraph.*]

If I could see some asshured plan for this place for this remunerative labor and self supporting plan I could gather by solicitation tens of thousands for this people — for their education intellectual & moral or religious

I want quickly to commit myself for some such definite work here, or at Berea in Madison co — 32 miles distant from here. . . .

With adequate effort, timely effort, we can have a very efficient work in this state for the redemption of this people

There is a danger just here — that after all we are attempting to treat the black man as a "Nigger" not as a man — To get the right use of his bones and muscles he must stand as other men — not too much nursing   Also we should avoid making a "nigger" school — avoid the idea that there must be separation   I believe we ought to make this a school for humanity — make efforts to have in here a due measure of white faces   I fear we shall not be able to get this here   Already the impression with all classes is that this camp is for black people   We may have to make the true model at Berea — possibly try at both *

John G Fee

* * * * [*One paragraph.*]

Please give me your opinion as to the probability of our success in a school for colored & white together — Will we have to yield to pressure of prejudice for a generation & have practically schools separate   or does the gospel & war so fast overcome this prejudice that by the time we shall be really ready we can have practically a school or schools for humanity

2 Shall we encourage this people to come together in towns of their own — in places where we can buy a thousand or two — or 5 thousand acres for them and there let them have homes of their own small lots with their school and church — missionary, teachers & mechanic, merchant &c or shall we say to them suffer no isolation stay all over the country — then battle along even for a generation — get what of instruction & land in that way you can and do not let the Irishman root you out

Genl Palmer inclines to the latter idea — so do I if we can carry it out — if we can get access to these colored people all over the state — get schools also to them   I told him that in order to have this access it will be necessary that the government through its military see that we have protection in so doing — prestige thus far in the work.

I have presented not personalities but principles — principles of action. They

are distinct and worthy perhaps of mature reply. I should like to hear from you. * * * *
[*One paragraph.*]

Shall <u>we try to reach them all over the state in their scattered condition</u> &
teach society thus to reach <u>them</u>, or <u>shall we</u> arrange villages & <u>schools</u> for them

I would rather be shure I am right than have the backing of a Bureau

Mrs Williams is sick — Does not <u>teach</u> when well — we have but one
teacher — the delay is apparently a great detriment — boys & girls are daily scattering — going to the country — Am I to hire Mrs Colton & daughter &
friend — with a male principal — or wait — J G F

I purpose to go out to Madison co next week — absent 7 or 8 days — preach there[1]

1. Fee to Whipple, 9 Jun. 1865, AMAA 44145–7.

**Head Quarters   Dept of Ky   Asst Inspector Gen's Office   Louisville
Ky   June 10th 1865
Capt E.B. Harlan   A.A.G. Dept of Ky**

Captain   I have the honor to report the result of an inspection made at Camp
Nelson Ky in accordance with Special Orders No. 82 dated May 16th 1865.

I. Adjutant's General's Department.

I found on my first inspection of this office it was under the control of 1st
Lieut W[m] C. Root 1st Ky Cav. a young officer who appears desirous of doing his
duty, but from want of experience, and, it would seem, proper instruction, he had
the office in a very poor condition. Papers could not be produced without searching
for them a long time. The books not neatly kept, not even a Morning Report received or kept of the forces. Since the 1st inst Col F.H. Bierbower[1] 124th U.S.C.T.
Comd'g has procured the services of R. Vance[2] 26th Ky. Inf as A.A.A.G and has
opened a new sett of books. Morning reports rec[d] regularly, guard details made
properly, and the business of the office is conducted in the right way.

II. Inspector General's Department

I found that 1st Lieut S. A Miller Bat'y "E" 1st Ky Lt Art'y A A.I.G. on the staff
of the Comd'g Officer absent on leave. He returned before I left, and upon examination of his books and papers, am satisfied that he is a thorough business man, and
a young officer of much promise.

III. Provost Marshall and Mil'ty Prison.

Lieut Harkins 124th U.S.C.I. in charge of the office and prison deserves credit
for the good condition of both, and the manner in which he discharges his
duties   There are now in the prison fifty four (54) prisoners, 34 of whom are
undergoing sentence, 12 awaiting trial and 8 confined for minor offences. By an
order of Lt Col. Coates 6th U.S.C.C. late in command of the camp, the Pro. Mar.
was directed not to work the prisoners outside the yard. I directed the order to be
revoked, and a sufficient guard furnished to work those that had been sentenced for
various times of hard labor.

IV. Ordnance Department.

This Department is in charge of Capt F F Perdue who has everything connected with his establishment in excellent order.

V. Commissary of Subsistence Dept.

This Department conducted by Capt E.P. Ransom who has his Warehouses, Bakery, Ration Cooks and papers in good order

Please find appended, marked ('A') a communication giving the statement of funds and Subsistence stores on hand from June 3ᵈ 1865. Also one marked ("B") giving balances of savings due different Hospitals and Refugee Home   In regard to the latter I do not know by what authority the fund is created; if the Supt of the "Home" can save such an amount I think the ration should be reduced.

VI. Quartermasters Department.

This department under the control of Capt E.B. Restieaux as chief, and Capt Jos. P. Santmyer 7ᵗʰ O.V. Cav and A.A.Q.M. in charge of transportation. Capt Restieaux' office, work shops &c are conducted well. Herewith you will find Lists of Q.M. stores Camp and Garrison Equipage Public buildings & Machinery. Unserviceable property, Reports of persons and articles hired — Lists of persons who have been discharged since April 1ˢᵗ 1865. It will be seen from these papers that the establishment is by far too great for any purpose at present; and I would respectfully suggest the reduction of it one half. I cannot see the necessity for any further use of the Saw Mill and Machine shop, as all buildings have been stopped and there is sufficient quantity of lumber on hand for repairs, and should my suggestion be carried into effect I think the buildings that will not used, such as shops, stables, warehouses, foragehouses &c. should be taken down, and the lumber preserved; for if they should be left standing, it would be an expense to the Government of $50 to $100 per month for each building, to pay watchmen and repairs — Balance of funds on hand May 31ˢᵗ $80246.87. Report of persons and Articles hired by Captain Jos P Santmyer for the month of May, shows an aggregate of 685 persons during the month, 177 were discharged, leaving the number on the 31ˢᵗ of May 508. A still greater number can be discharged as the Comd'g Officer has ordered 5 companies of the 124ᵗʰ U.S.C.I. (Invalid) to report for duty to Capt Restieaux. Also Daily reports of means of transportation and acct. current for May showing a balance due the U.S $1538.75.

VII. Nelson General Hospital.

This Department is in charge of Surgeon Meeker, assisted by one surgeon and four acting Assistants   The Assistants are on duty at the General Hospital, — the Hospital for Qr Ms employees, — Hospital at Military Prison, — Small Pox Hospital and Refugee Home. On the 4ᵗʰ of June the morning Report showed 579 patients and 50 attendants. The Surgeon's books and papers are all made up for May, and everything in and about the establishment, was in the very best condition. This is in my opinion also too large for the present wants of Camp Nelson.

VIII. Draft Rendezvous.

Under charge of Lt. Col. Hanaford presents a neat appearance — books and papers in good order. There are but a few married recruits left, and the Lt. Col. is busy closing up the Rendezvous as recruiting has been stopped.

IX. Refugee Home.

On the 31st of May I visited this place and made a thorough investigation of the books and papers, and found that all records prior to the 1st of January 1865 in a very unsatisfactory condition. Since then under the superintendence of Captain T.E. Hall, and Asst Mr Williams a complete record of all the transactions are in good order. I found the book to consist 1st Record of arrival, showing name, age, whether married or unmarried; Regiment and Co of Husband, Date, name of Master or mistress and remarks. 2nd — Daily record of arrivals, showing the number each day entitled to full refugee or half rations. 3[d] — Record of deaths; showing name, date and age. 4th Clothing books, showing date, name to whom issued and articles. 5th Rations drawn from Commissary of Subsistence. May 26th for six days the record shows rations for 1043 women 1174 children making a total of 2217 for 6 days, or 6258 whole refugee rations, and 3522 ½ ditto. 6th Records of Discharges showing those that leave temporarily, those that leave permanently — to whom hired, rate of hire, Post office addresses of parties hiring. This last book has a check in the form of a contract signed by the parties hiring binding themselves to pay the amts to the refugees personally, to be returned to the home when required by the Supt & to be suitably clothed & fed by the hiring party. It is proper to mention that the clothing is received from benevolent societies, and not any expense to the Government. I find a permanent detail of five enlisted colored soldiers, in the General Kitchen, and the "Home" Hospital. The Hospital is well supplied with medicines, but the medical attendance is not sufficient. Acting Surgeon Rectanus and Medical Cadet Mays, both detailed by Surgeon Burrett[3] in charge of Nelson General Hospital. They both informed me that it was impossible to give proper attention to the sick, the number of whom is very large, they cannot get through them more than twice a week — They keep no books and the weekly sick report is made out by guess. This requires correction and the Supt informs me that it is impossible for him to correct the abuse unless he can have some control over the Hospital Dept   The Home at present has three hundred acres under cultivation, and in the course of a few months will produce enough to reduce considerably the amount required from the Government for their support.

The cost and number of buildings are as follows:

One building for offices & teachers two stories30 X 100 ft. — cost	$2484.50
Four wards 1 story high 25 X 75 ft cost $724 each	$2896.50
One schoolroom 30 X 100 ft 2 stories	$2000.00
One Dining room 30 X 100 fitted for Laundry	$2475.50
97 Cottages 16 X 32 cost $306 ea.	$29,482.00
Total cost of buildings	$39,537.50

Of the number of employees, I find the Government pays monthly,

1 Supt $125 — 1 Acct do $100 — 1 clerk $75
1 clerk $50 and 2 foremen $50 each, making a total of $450   Other persons consisting of 1 chaplain, 1 Farmer and three Lady teachers, are supported by the American Missionary Association of New York.

At present the force of teachers is inadequate, but they are expecting an additional supply soon from the same source.

I visited nearly all the cottages and found their occupants apparently contented, — great neatness and order prevail everywhere and in conversation with some I find their great source of trouble to be a fear that the Govt intend breaking up the establishment and turn them out on the charity of the world. Accompanying this please find report of the Superintendent, marked "C"

X. Troops and General Condition of Camp.

On the 2nd inst. I made an inspection of the troops commencing with the 74th Co 2nd Batt V.R. Corps, under command of Capt R M Voorhees,[4] on duty as guards, nurses and attendants at the Nelson Genl Hospital — They presented a very neat and cleanly appearance, in arms, equipment and Clothing. They are armed with the Starr revolvers and non-com officers swords   Capt Voorhees' papers are all made up for May. Accompanying this please find acct of Co. fund, marked "D"

124th U.S. C Inf.

This is an invalid regiment under command of Lt. Col Haniford — presented a fair appearance, they are not armed, and the clothing, police of Quarters and Camp was excellent. There were 8 companies present, Cos "E" and "I" presented a particularly neat appearance. The books and papers of the regiment & company officers as a general thing complete.

Detachment 123d U.S.C.I. (Invalid)

This detachment composed of Co. "G" & "H", under the command of Lts. Clark & Renfroe, are on Guard duty at the Military Prison. They require much — arms, accoutrements and Clothing very bad and dirty   Their drill very indifferent, and I doubt much if either the Lieuts competent as company commanders   Lieut Renfro Comd'g Co "G" has his books and papers complete. Lieut Clark has his also excepting the Description book, which he is at work on. Police of quarters and camp very good, — The day I inspected, but upon another occasion which I visited the camp, unexpectedly, I found them in a very dirty condition — The men also require much instruction in their duties as Guards and sentinels.

119th U.S.C.I.

Under the command of Col. Chas G. Bartlett[5] presented a very neat appearance   Only five companies of the Regiment are armed, and the arms and accoutrements are in excellent order. The regimental and company books and papers are incomplete, from the fact that all of the Officers have been absent until yesterday, recruiting. Col. Bartlett and his Officers deserve much credit for the advanced state of efficiency; this new regiment possesses and would even now in point of discipline shame many of the older organizations. The regt. is filled to the maximum. Police of Camp & Quarters excellent.

6ᵗʰ U.S.C. Cav.

Under the command of Major J.B. Day.[6] I cannot say much of this regt. as a whole   They are armed with the Enfield rifle an arm unfit for Cav service, and lack much of a uniformity of drill, every company commander appears to have a system of his own. The arms, accoutrements & clothing of Cos. "A" "B" "C" "D" "E" "H" & "I" are very dirty, but the police of camp & Quarters good. Cos. "F" & "G" if possible are worse than the others. The non-com officers of Co "F" were the dirtiest in the Co. I recommended the officers [*indecipherable*] to have them reduced, as an example   The police of the Camps of these two companies and condition of kitchens very poor. The men of this regiment are indifferently taught Their duties as guards, and sentinels. Books and papers of the regiment and companies are generally incomplete, from the fact that they have been all absent recruiting.

Battery "E" 1ˢᵗ Ky. Art'y

Under the command of Capt L.E.P. Bush,[7] is in a very poor condition. The officers not properly uniformed. — The men not properly clothed & dirty, belts, sabres, and pistols dirty — poorly disciplined, — poorly drilled, ammunition good but not packed in Caissons for want of tow. In order to have the Battery drill, I had to have the ammunition all taken out. Neither the Capt or 2ⁿᵈ Lieut knew much of their duties as Lt. Art. Officers. The 1ˢᵗ Lt. (Miller) now A.A.I.G. of the post is the only one that appears to know anything of his duties and should be in command of the Battery.

Upon the night I visited the pickets I found all the sentinels on the alert, but they are not properly taught thier duties. The guard at the magazines are from Bat'y "E" 1ˢᵗ Ky Lt Art'y, at one post the whole picket guard had but an old Sabre without a scabbard, at the other but one revolver. I recommended the Comd'g Officer to have the Capt draw a few muskets or rifles for guard duty.

The fortifications & Magazines are all in good order, but dismantled, I believe by an order of Lt Col Coates 6 U.S.C.C.   Where he got his authority I am unable to tell.

At the Camp there are too many sutlers all claiming appointments from different sources   One at the Refugee Home — one at the Genl. Hospital — one at the Convalescent Camp and about twelve or fifteen claiming to be Post Sutlers; all of the above exclusive of Regimental Sutlers, I would respectfully suggest the appointment of one Post Sutler under the provision of an act of Congress on Mar 19" 1862.   *

LaFayette Hammond[8]   Major 2ⁿᵈ O.H.Art   A.A.I.G.[9]

1. Frederick Huber Bierbower (born 1833 in Maysville, Kentucky) was inducted as a captain, but became major of the 40ᵗʰ Kentucky Infantry and then colonel of the 124ᵗʰ U.S. Colored Infantry, mustered in May 15, 1865, at Lexington. In July 1865 he replaced Capt. T.E. Hall as superintendent of Camp Nelson Refugee Home, serving under the Freedmen's Bureau. *HR,* 2:80; *OAR,* 8:305; *RAGK.*

2. Richard Vance joined the Twenty-sixth Kentucky Infantry as a hospital steward on October 1, 1861; he was promoted to the rank of first lieutenant by 1863. Vance evidently served as Bierbower's assistant adjutant-general for only one month as he was mustered out on July 10, 1865. *HR,* 1:981.

3. Henry Le W. Burritt of Connecticut, who became an assistant surgeon in the volunteers on September 2, 1862, and a captain and commissary of subsistence in June 1864. *HR,* 1:266.

4. Richard M. Voorhees.

5. Charles Gratiot Bartlett began his military career as a sergeant in the 7th New York State Militia in 1861; served as colonel of the 119th U.S. Colored Infantry by May 10, 1865; and occasionally commanded the post at Camp Nelson in 1866. *CWD; OAR,* 8:300; *HR,* 1:196; *RAGK.*

6. James B. Day was a major in the Sixth U.S. Colored Cavalry. *HR,* 2:94.

7. Llewellyn E.P. Bush enlisted as a sergeant on October 2, 1861, in Smithland, Kentucky; he served in Company 1, Twentieth Kentucky Infantry, and was discharged for promotion on December 31, 1863, after which he was captain of Battery E, First Kentucky Artillery. *RAGK.*

8. Lafayette Hammond, a native of Pennsylvania, was a lieutenant in the First California Infantry. After attaining the rank of captain and resigning from his first service, he reenlisted as a major in the Second Ohio Artillery. He was inspecting Camp Nelson as an A.A.I.G, acting assistant inspector-general. *HR,* 1:495.

9. Hammond to Harlan, 10 June 1865; Reports of Inspections [unarranged], Entry 2217; Inspector, Department of Kentucky, Part 1; RG 393. The portion of this report that deals with the Refugee Home was also filed earlier (June 3) with Capt. J. Bates Dickson in Lexington; Report to Capt. J. Bates Dickson on the Refugee Home at Camp Nelson, 3 June 1865; M999:7:636–39; RG 105. The last portion of this report (one page or more) is missing from the series in the National Archives records.

[*Letterhead.*] *The United States Christian Commission*   **Camp Nelson   June 15**[th] **1865**

Dear brother Strieby * * * * [*Three paragraphs.*]

I find brother Fee very much dissatisfied with the management of the Refugee Home — and I think justly — It is altogether too stiff and Warlike for such an enterprise — this is probably unlike any other case in the land

1. We are not a camp of men but of women and children

2. We are not in a state of War but of peace

3. Women and children cannot live on soldiers rations and fare — these particulars seem to be entirely forgotten, and guards and whips and bullets too are made fearfully imposing. If you want facts you can have them. The mortality also is fearful — From one sixth to one seventh of the whole number die every month! They come and die! Come and die! This results from two causes 1st bad plan 2nd bad management — It is a bad plan — to crowd so many of these poor people together: It makes a great show, but there is "death in the pot" It will never do!

2nd It is bad to have a dozen men and Women to care for these poor ones who rarely mingle with them — never know their wants — till they are dead —bad to feed sick children on ham — bad to let sick women lie on bare boards — when the straw lies unused under the shed!

Besides the School is doing very little. Mrs Williams is feeble and unable to go forward with such heavy work — Brother Fee and brother Scofield offer to go forward with the schools But we are told it is none of our business — The missionary society have organized the school, put Mrs W at the head and we must not disturb it — But enough   your brother

A. Scofield[1]

1. Scofield to Strieby, 15 Jun. 1865, AMAA 44148.

FROM A LADY IN KENTUCKY.

The following letter is from an anti-slavery lady[1] in Kentucky, whose husband is or was a slaveholder. Her occasional letters for several years past have afforded us much gratification. She is loyal and discriminating, and her statements are entitled to attention. In the midst of slavery she has contributed to the anti-slavery cause, well knowing the pernicious influence of slavery in her surroundings and in her State.

JESSAMINE COUNTY, June 16, 1865 * * * *

Camp Nelson is increasing rapidly. Numbers of blacks are getting in. Mr. Fee told my husband the other day that the mortality was fearful. So we may safely assume from these facts that slavery in Kentucky is not worth contending for. It is an awful way, however, of getting rid of it. One of our boys was in town yesterday, and says he saw a poor woman from the Camp die in a stable. Then we hear of them again dying in waggons and on the road side. The poor creatures get tired of Camp life and leave without having places, and, when sick, both white and black seem afraid to take them in. We had some little boys that went to the Camp because they saw others go, but their father went of his own accord and brought them back. Their brothers that were old enough went into the army as soldiers, and we thought it right that the government should have their services, though it deprives us of much the greater part of our income, and leaves those at home that have to be supported.[2]

1. Her name, withheld from the *American Missionary* introduction, was Evelyn Woodson. At this Victorian stage of American history, the names of ladies were generally not published, and the editors of the *Missionary* were very scrupulous about removing them from published correspondence.
2. *AM* 9, no. 8 (August 1865): 186, 187.

Camp Nelson Ky   June 20" 1865
Hon. E.M. Stanton Secy. of War

Sir   I have just learned that Maj. Genl. Palmer has been ordered by the War Dept. to relieve me from my position as Superintendent of the "Refugee Home" in this Camp. As far as being relieved is concerned, I am glad if the time has come when I can leave this vexatious and trying position. I had long ago solicited of Genl. Palmer that I might be relieved as soon as he could do so consistently with the interests and success of the institution. The order, however, seems to imply that the duties have not been discharged in a satisfactory manner to the Dept. Permit me one word of explanation[1] . . . . Without boasting, I assert without fear of successful contradiction that I inaugurated the system of negro recruiting in the State which was so successful; that I, unaided and alone, amid the scoffs and jeers of those who have since claimed some of the credit, received into the Camp, protected and cared for, over Five thousand colored men, And had them ready for the recruiting officer, so soon as one could be obtained; that I sheltered and cared for the families of these men when the fury of the Slave master was poured out upon their defenceless heads. No wonder that I brought upon me the ire of the slave drivers. No wonder that they should insist upon my removal. I have been in their way. But thank God, the work I have inaugurated cannot stop! Borne upward by the resistless current of events, it must triumph.

It matters very little to me whether I have any credit or not. I will live in the hearts of the poor and lowly and this is enough.

I respectfully ask an investigation into my administration here as Superintendent and demand to know what are the charges brought against me. *

T.E. Hall[2]

1. It is quite ironic that Hall asks permission to write "one word of explanation," since the ellipses in the text represent several hundred words in which he details once again the story of the November 1864 expulsion and reiterates the part he played in it and the subsequent work of the Refugee Home. His reply is all in the nature of a defense of his own alleged extravagance.
2. Hall to Stanton, 20 June 1865; M999:7:653–55; RG 105.

Camp Nelson   June 22nd 1865

Major Genl Howard Commissioner in Charge of Freedmens Bureau Washington D.C. * * * * [*Two paragraphs, the last a brief history of Refugee Home.*]

This, General, was the origin of the "Home". I have been in charge of it from that day to the present   I am aware that I have aroused the ire of the slaveholder. For this I care not. I am well aware that they have boasted that they would have me sent out of the State. This I have laughed at. The time, I apprehend has gone by for a man to be tried, convicted, and condemned unheard. I am aware that they have boasted that you would break up this Home. This I did not believe until you have at least listened to the other side of the question. I pledge myself to show that this Home is almost the only protection the poor colored woman has. Not a day passes during which free colored women are not imprisoned and whipped by the slave power of Kentucky. Not a day passes during which I am not entreated by some poor defenceless wife or child to interfere for their protection against the fury of their master. I beg you to examine this subject carefully ere you decide to discontinue this "Home," this "City of refuge" to which they can flee and be safe. For myself I ask nothing. I have no desire to remain one hour as Superintendent of this institution. But I do ask, in the name of the plighted faith of the government that there shall be some protection for these poor, defenceless creatures. Protection from the present prejudice growing out of the fact that these colored men for once in their lives dared to act for themselves; and offered themselves as a shield for the protection of the institutions of the country. As an illustration of this prejudice let me say that the wife and the child of a colored soldier cannot have a burial in some places in Ky. Only this day a colored woman walked from Nicholasville six miles, bringing in her arms the <u>body</u> of <u>her</u> <u>dead child</u> because the Chivalry in Nicholasville, through prejiduce, refused it burial! The child was brought to me and I had it buried. Remember, I beseech you that this was the child of a soldier, and that soldier away from his family, in the field fighting for that Government that did not or could not protect the body of his own child from insult. I beg your candid and careful perusal of the accompanying affidavits, particularly those of Joseph Miller and Albert A. Livermore * * * * [*One paragraph.*]

T.E. Hall Superintendent of "Refugee Home" Camp Nelson Ky. [1]

1. Hall to Howard, 22 Jun. 1865; M999:7:640–643; RG 105; also quoted in *The Black Military Experience,* 717, 718.

June 25 [*1865*]
Captain Fred A Tenants Comdg 12" U S C Inf.   Camp Nelson Ky.

Captain, I have the honor to forward this day in compliance with you communication of 23[d] inst. one hundred blank certificates of freedom

You will please sign these officially and give to the colored soldiers who apply, keeping a record of the names of the soldiers and, when possible, that of his wife. *

A R Mills[1] Capt and A A A G[2]

1. Augustus R. Mills was captain of the 124th U.S. Colored Infantry in 1865. *OAR,* 8:305.
2. Mills to Tenants, 25 June 1865; [Bound] Vol. 57, Book 90, p. 292; Press Copies of Letters Sent, Mar.–Sept. 1865, Entry 2247; Subordinate Offices; Organization of U.S. Colored Troops, Department of Kentucky, Part 1; RG 393.

State of Kentucky County of Jessamine   June 26, 1865

Personally appeared before the undersigned, a Notary Public within and for said State and County. Albert A. Livermore[1] who being duly sworn according to law on his oath says:

"I am engaged as Sexton at Camp Nelson Ky and have served in that capacity since October 1864. I remember the time when the colored women and children were driven out of Camp Nelson Ky in Nov 1864. I knew Joseph Miller.[2] My attention was called to the fact of his child dying by cold at that time. He told me that his wife and children had contracted disease in consequence of their exposure at that time.

From the record of interments kept at my office I take the following statements, viz.:

Joseph Miller, Jr. (son of Joseph Miller, Sr.) died December 17th 1864.
Isabella Miller (Wife of Joseph Miller) died December 17th, 1864.
Maria Miller (daughter of Joseph Miller) died December 27th 1864.
Calvin Miller (son of Joseph Miller) died January 2[d] 1865.
Joseph Miller, Private, 124th U.S.C.I., died January 6th 1865.

A.A. Livermore

Sworn and subscribed to before me this 26th day of June 1865. C.W. Norwood
Notary Public[3]

1. Albert Augustus Livermore, the sexton at Camp Nelson from October 1864, was the
nephew of Theron E. Hall, a son of Hall's sister Electa, born July 18, 1830, in Sutton,
Massachusetts. In a capacity far removed from grave digging, Livermore offended Fee greatly
by dancing with some of the young female teachers from Cincinnati. Genealogical details
from IGI at www.familysearch.org.

2. In his affidavit of November 26, 1864, which appears in chapter 4 above, Private
Joseph Miller asserted that he had four children, one of whom had just died as a result of the
expulsion from Camp Nelson. It is clear from the sexton's record that all three of Miller's
surviving children and his wife died within little more than a month of the expulsion, and
then Miller died himself.

3. Affidavit of Albert A. Livermore, 26 June 1865; M999:7:680–81; RG 105. This affidavit was one of the collection sent to the Freedmen's Bureau by Capt. T.E. Hall, mentioned in
and accompanying his letter of June 22, 1865. Apparently, Livermore swore to his affidavit
before Norwood after he shared it with Hall.

Camp Nelson Ky   Jun 27 /65

Dear Bro Whipple
      * * * [*Ten paragraphs.*]
      The people continue to die in a ratio terrible, at rate of 190 per month out of a
population of near twenty five hundred — 12 [*months*] would waste all at that ratio
      Most of the cottages were erected without stoves or fire places — from 8 to
12 persons in a room — 16 feet square — one door in the room. I asked Capt
Hall in the beginning to have a door on the opposite side with place for a shed in
back part — rejected — not artistic —
      The whole thing must be radically changed or broken up — if it is not
changed I shall (if as now) consider it my duty to go home — link myself with a
growing enterprise rather than a dying one — Now some twelve persons here have
professed peace in Christ and stand propounded for baptism next Sabbath — We
have another meeting of enquiry this night — had an immense crowd last night as
a preliminary meeting — preparation for the 4 of July — such as Ky never witnessed — we shall expect from five to ten thousand colored people   They are
arranging to come from the county twenty miles distant   We shall have cannon
drums, fifes — speeches — dinner — amusements. Yours in haste
                                                                John G Fee[1]

1. Fee to Whipple, 27 Jun. 1865, AMAA 44149.

Nashville   June 27th 1865
General Fisk   Bureau Refugees &c

      Dear Sir   I desire, most respectfully, to tender to you, my Services, to aid
you in prosecuting the objects of your important mission. My Regt 73d Ill. Vol. Inf.

has been mustered out of service. I have been detained a few days on special duty, and therefore have not yet been mustered out. I much prefer retaining my present rank as colonel — provided it can be so, if not I am ready to enter upon any duty you may assign me: Feeding the hungry, clothing the destitute, superintending the education of the people under your care or any such work (will be prosecuted by me faithfully) as a citizen. *

James F. Jaquess   Col 73ᵈ Ill. Vol. Inf.

(Care Col. James J. Davidson)   Refugee Home   Nashville Tenn [1]

   1. Jaquess to Fisk, 27 June 1865; M999:7:1393; RG 105.

Camp Nelson   June 28ᵗʰ 1865

My Dear Brother. . . . If you will look in your files you will find an important letter written May 8ᵗʰ & still unanswered. I do not complain, but if you will transfer yourself into the meanest part of the meanest state of this union, I mean so far as the slavery question is concerned, and attempt to carry upon your own back a load like this Refugee Home against all the predjudice and opposition of Kentucky, you would sometimes feel a little tired. . . . In haste. *

T.E. Hall[1]

   1. Hall to an AMA officer, 28 Jun. 1865, AMAA 44150.

[U.S. Sanitary Commission report.]

   On the 1ˢᵗ of July, 1865, the last of that corps of faithful men who, through-out the history of the Home, had aided so faithfully and efficiently in performing the great work accomplished there—the detailed assistants—was mustered out of the service, and returned home, to resume again the duties of citizenship. Camp Nelson, like other exclusively military posts, had dwindled into comparative unimportance; and though, had the Home and depot been continued for months later, there would have been work to do, still in magnitude it scarcely justified the attendant expense.[1]

   1. Newberry, 386.

Camp Nelson Ky   July 1ˢ /65

Dear Bro Whipple I have yours of 26 ᵘˡᵗ· I have had a very violent attack of diar-rhea — cannot now write but a line

   I suppose it is useless for me to write about teachers   Capt hall has some week or two since telegraphed to Cincinnati for ten teachers (as though they could come on next train)   They are not here — are as yours scattered over the country   Levi Coffin has just gone from here   He says there is an understanding between the societies that each are to furnish some. They expect to send out some soon. . . . * * * * [*One paragraph.*]

There ought to be some Matrons here paid by some society — whose business it should be to go to each room & aid in nursing sick and instructing young mothers. I have Engaged two colored women to work for a time   I have paid small charges on books —

I have not anything by which to pay these with $6 assessment on my board here for this month — above our rations * * * * [*Three paragraphs.*]

John G Fee[1]

1. Fee to Whipple, 1 July 1865, AMAA 44151.

No. 7. Shearman House, Chicago, Il., July 6th, 1865.

My dear Friends, J.H. Tuke, and F. Seebohm,[1]

In my last letter[2] from Cincinnati, I mentioned that whilst at Camp Nelson, Levi Coffin and I had attended a meeting of freedmen. This meeting was, to me at least, a very interesting one. . . .

. . . The meeting had been called together without our knowledge, by John G. Fee, the zealous and earnest missionary who represents, in this camp, the American Missionary Society. This gentleman has, I suppose, done more for the good cause than any many, or any half-dozen men, in Kentucky; and the simple narration of his hair-breadth escapes from the hands of outraged slaveowners would of itself make a most interesting and exciting book. Mr. Fee is held in the highest esteem by the colored people in Camp Nelson; and with good reason, for he has been a true friend to them all.

At about 7 P.M., then, we entered the large wooden building in which these poor people take their meals. It is a one-storied erection, 100 feet by 30 feet, lighted only by a few candles, and well-fitted with forms. We did not expect to find more than 100 or 200 people there, at the outside; but instead of this, we could just discern, by the dim light, not less than 600 black and brown faces, all waiting the arrival of our party.

The men (soldiers chiefly) were seated on one side, and the women on the other. As the forms would not accommodate all, many sat upon the floor, whilst others stood during the three hours, or three and a half hours, the meeting lasted; and better order could not have prevailed, I am sure, in any assembly, white or black.

I shall not soon forget that interesting spectacle, when the whole assembly rose, and joined with true negro harmony in that glorious hymn, "Blow, trumpets, blow." How those large, black, lustrous eyes glistened, and how rich those deep, bass voices sounded in the still night air, is something to remember for a lifetime.

After a short and simple prayer, during which all knelt down, Mr. Fee introduced Levi Coffin to the meeting, as an old friend of the slave, of over thirty years' standing; an Abolitionist in days when to be so was to be a marked and despised man, both North and South.

Levi Coffin narrated some of his old experiences as a director of the "Underground Railway," and his more recent experiences in England. When he told of England's sympathy for the freedmen, and of the money England had sent, and was still sending, to aid in their clothing and education there went up a cheer which did my heart good. The poor people had not heard of this before; and one or two of them came to me after the meeting was over, to say, "how glad they were to hear dat dey know 'bout us some t'other side de 'Lantic." They seemed to think that it behoved them, in the matter of gratitude to England, to make up for lost time; and I must say, that if a hearty shake of the hand is any test of such feelings, my hand could bear full testimony thereto. As Levi Coffin was suffering from exhaustion (the heat was great), he called upon me to read to the assembly the address from Bishophill girls to their "coloured sisters in America." This had been previously read at the girls' school in camp that morning, much to the delight of the sixty or seventy children then present. The address was greatly applauded, especially that part of it which stated, that the English girls were busy making up clothing for the freedmen's children. The practical force of this seemed to take hold of the minds of all; the more so, when I stated to the meeting, that in school that afternoon I had seen one of the children wearing a dress which I felt sure had belonged to a little sister of mine in England. "It was," I said, "a thin muslin, with a small sprig on it." Rarely have I witnessed such cheering and laughing as this little incident produced. It seemed to take the fancy of the women entirely, and they literally shrieked with delight.

. . . I was followed by an old coloured man, known as "Uncle Davie." His curly hair had become grey with years and care, but energy and humble piety were evident in all that the good man said and did.

I fear it is impossible to give you any idea of the earnestness and ease with which these men spoke. When giving us the account of their life "behind" (i.e., in slavery); of their escape; of the tales told them by their former masters, to deter them from trusting themselves to "Yankee nigger-whippers;" and of the much prized liberty they now enjoyed with "Uncle Sam," they poured out their whole souls in such a flow of language as perfectly astonished me. "Ah," said Uncle Davie, "you know, my bredren, how dey try to keep us from gittin' to Camp Nelson. Some o' you hev only jist got from behind; where Massa ask you, 'Would you like to be free, David?' O' course I should; but den, if I say so, dey jist cross my hands, tie 'em up, strip me; den whip me wid the cowhide, till I tell a lie, and say 'No.'"

And then Davie went to counsel them, now that they had got away from bondage, "to earn your own bread by honesty; shew dem dat de col'd people will work, if dey are let try; and date we rader pay for our cahn and clodin' ourselves, dan ask oder people to pay." He spoke to them, also, as to being "mighty civil to white folks," "for day say dat now we are free we become too proud."

When Davie sat down, he was loudly cheered; and so was a fine looking youth, who said he "only jist wished to say how thankful I feel in my heart, for all dis young gen'man say to us; and all de kindness of de people in England to us coloured people. I thank de Lord very much indeed; I do indeed." Poor fellow! he seemed quite overcome with his feelings.

A middle-aged serjeant-major was the next speaker. His language and action were even more energetic than others; especially when he told us how his master used to fance he was flattering him, by calling him "a very smart nigger."

"Yes, my friends, a very smart *nigger.* A nigger! where d'you find that word in the Bible? Nowhere! And does not de Bible say that 'God made of one blood all nations of de earth,' and that 'He is no respecter of persons?' Yes; He says thus, and we must now make ourselves a people. I want us to be a people. See how much better off we are now dan we was four years ago. It used to be five hundred miles to git to Canada from Lexington, but now it's only eighteen miles! *Camp Nelson* is now *our* Canada. Why, four years ago, if dis young gen'man from England had said in Kentuck what he said jist now, dey would have hung him up as high as Haman."

These were a few of the sentences which I took down at the time. . . .

Before the meeting separated, Captain Hall, the Quartermaster and Chief Superintendent, addressed the meeting, lamenting that America had not set her slaves free as England did; and stating his conviction that in all these great changes God's omnipotent hand was evident. "Till the North shewed herself in earnest in putting down slavery, our arms were never victorious. Look at Bull's Run! Had we succeeded there, slavery would still have been rampant. Look at our other battles! We were never victorious till we were in earnest in this sacred cause. I know that I speak the truth about these battles; for I was there, and saw for myself."

The people then collected a subscription among themselves to purchase eat-ables; wherewith to have a grand celebration of the 4th of July — the first of the kind to them — and soon after ten p.m. they all went quietly to their huts. It would not be right, however, to omit saying that I was charged by many of them (of both sexes) to express their gratitude to the English people for thinking of them, and especially for helping them so liberally, just at this hour of their necessity.

On the whole, though I was much shocked and distressed at the great mortal-ity and physical misery of so many of these poor people at Camp Nelson, I was more than satisfied that the institution of such a camp as this, in the very heart of Kentucky, is of the utmost importance to the cause we have at heart. By its aid, and by reason of the insecurity it causes to the Kentuckian slave-holders, the holding of slaves at all, though still legal in this state, has been a very risky and unpopular business; and it must in time be rendered practically impossible, to any large extent. Even now, every Kentuckian slave becomes free if he crosses the Ohio, gets into Camp Nelson, or is the wife or child of a U.S. soldier. Of the six hundred persons at the meeting referred to, only *four* were free before the war broke out, and nearly all were from Kentucky. * * * * [*Four paragraphs.*]

Joseph Simpson.[3]

1. James H. Tuke and Frederick Seebohm were finance secretaries of the Friends' Central Committee in London.

2. Unfortunately, Joseph Simpson's "last letter from Cincinnati," which would have contained a number of his observations of Camp Nelson life, was lost by the Friends' Central Committee for the Relief of the Emancipated Negroes, "through some oversight." In an earlier letter, written in Cincinnati and dated June 28, 1865, Simpson stated that he planned to set off for Camp Nelson in Kentucky, possibly accompanied by Levi Coffin, the next day. Simpson, 20, 25.

3. Simpson to Tuke and Seebohm, 1 July 1865, 20–25.

[*Letterhead.*] *U.S. Sanitary Commission*   **Camp Nelson Ky**   **July 6 1865**

Dear Bro. Whipple

* * * * [*20 paragraphs.*]

Bro. Whipple, I stayed here at great sacrifice of feeling & family interest — instruction of my sons — I did it all for this people — <u>for the sake of turning all into your society</u> — for good reasons — and for the Kingdom of Christ. Now I think the matter is likely to slip through your fingers. I did consent after the delay, in answers & supplies, to have Cincinnati have a share, but only a share & less than half as I supposed (so as to have a share of their clothing). But now Cinci. has four teachers here — two more commissioned — will occupy the ground I guess —

Well, this may all be for the highest good, but I "cant see it" — yet —

Cincinnati has commissioned Mrs Colton[1] & friend. I have asked for some good elderly lady or ladies to be appointed as matrons   I asked for a principal for the school — If best I will be still — do only one thing: preach & visit — But if I have ungodly helpers if the managers — "white folks" — "head ones" — be ungodly I shall be hindered.

We could do a good thing here by continuing the school for men — soldiers — colored.

J G Fee[2]

1. Mary Ann Thome Smith Colton, sister of famed abolitionist Rev. James A. Thome, had attended Oberlin Academy from 1834 to 1835. She first married Dalzell Smith, by whom she was the mother of Anna Smith, who accompanied her to Camp Nelson. Mary Ann's second husband was a Colton. She died December 1, 1873, in Independence, Iowa. *Oberlin Register*, 384.

2. Fee to Whipple, 6 Jul. 1865, AMAA 44153.

[*Letter from William A. Warfield[1] published in the* Weekly **Anglo-African** *on 22 July 1865.*]

This is an age of wonders, and not the least among them is the celebration of the Fourth of July at Camp Nelson, Ky., by the colored people. To see so many thousands, who a year ago were slaves, congregate in the heart of a slave State and celebrate the day sacred to the cause of freedom, "with none to molest or make afraid," was a grand spectacle. It was the first time we have ever been permitted to celebrate the Nation's Day.

The celebration was under the management of Capt. [T.E.] Hall, and Rev. J.G. Fee. These men deserve much credit for their zeal and untiring activity in the cause of our race.

The people gathered in from far and near. With several regiments of colored soldiers, with the thousands at the Refugee Home, and with the many from different parts of the country, the numbers swelled to many thousands. Such an assemblage of colored people on the "sacred soil of Kentucky" was never before beheld.

The exercises consisted in martial music, songs, speeches, and declamations, with an interlude of a good dinner. The first part of the exercises were performed by the colored people themselves. The school-girls took an active part in the singing and recitations. Speeches, pointed and witty, were made by several colored speakers. In the afternoon, toasts were given and responded to in well-timed and effective remarks. Almost boundless enthusiasm prevailed throughout.

In the forenoon, a review of the troops in this camp was held. Of all the regiments on review, ours seemed to take the banner for its soldier-like appearance.[2]

1. Warfield was a sergeant in Company D, 119th USCI.
2. William Warfield letter, 7 July 1865, published 22 July 1865 in *Weekly Anglo-African;* quoted in Redkey, 187–88.

Head Quarters   Dept of Kentucky. Louisville Kentucky. July 12, 1865.
Col. F.H. Bierbower   Camp Nelson Ky.

Colonel, I have been informed to day . . . that there are now well-founded complaints that Negroes and others steal horses and perhaps mules from the country around Camp Nelson and then sell them.

That the (a) Quarter Master on duty at Camp Nelson sent on Tuesday one week ago a large number of horses from that place to the city of Cincinnatti on private acount (his own) for sale and that others amongst them a Lieutenant have horse at the Camp in numbers and also send from there for sale at Cincinnatti. He reports unlawful and fraudulent combinations at the sales of Government horses much to the prejudice of the Govt. Please enquire vigorously into these reports   spare no efforts to arrive at the facts and report at once. *

John M Palmer   Maj. Genl. Comdg.[1]

1. Palmer to Bierbower, 12 July 1865; Vol. 1, p. 158; Letters Sent; RG 393.

Camp Nelson Ky   July 12 /65

[*P.S. only.*][1] Col Fisk has not yet arrived

The order of General Palmer issued yesterday will probably open the gates here and let evry person here go free who desires to seek employment

J G F[2]

1. The main portion of this letter is no longer than the postscript.
2. Fee to Whiting, 12 Jul. 1865, AMAA 44156. On July 10, 1865, in General Orders No. 49, General Palmer had extended the provisions of his General Orders No. 32, dated May 11, 1865, and applicable only in the city of Louisville, to all points in Kentucky where federal troops were stationed, urging "'colored people congregated about posts' to obtain military passes to allow them to travel freely in search of employment." The crucial provision of the original order was as follows: ". . . It is ordered that the Provost Marshal of the Post of Louisville, upon the application of any colored person who may report him or herself as unable to find sufficient employment in the city of Louisville, will issue a pass to such colored person and for his or her family, specifying the number of persons to be passed, and their names, and the point to which they wish to go, to engage in or in search of employment." General Orders No. 32, 11 May 1865, Head-Quarters Department of Kentucky, Orders and Circulars, Entry 44, RG 94 and General Orders No. 49, 10 July 1865, ibid.; as quoted in *The Destruction of Slavery*, 620–21.

REPORT [*Camp Nelson, 1865*][1]

DATE	No who drew rations on last return		No who have arrived since last return		No who have been discharged since last return		No died since last return		No who are entitled to draw rations on present return	
	Women	Chil	Women	Chil	Women	Chil	Women	Chil	Women	Chil
April 11	728	813								
" 16	744	844	39	45	14	4	9	11	744	848
" 21	744	848	79	85	7	2	5	22	811	909
" 26	811	909	57	95	3	1	4	26	868	969
May 1	868	969	79	128	6	8	5	29	953	1102
" 6	953	1102	50	54	7	0	8	29	978	1137
" 11	978	1137	27	40	6	3	2	24	997	1150
" 16	997	1150	36	14	10	8	4	26	1019	1130
" 21	1019	1130	35	55	15	4	10	21	1029	1160
" 26	1029	1160	32	38	14	11	4	13	1043	1174
June 1	1043	1174	58	31	6	13	13	23	1082	1169
" 6	1083	1169	32	33	10	1	3	23	1101	1178
" 11	1101	1178	76	82	20	1	3	17	1154	1242
" 16	1154	1242	71	56	7	2	8	15	1210	1281
" 21	1210	1281	59	39	19	4	1	25	1249	1291
" 26	1249	1291	39	26	8	1	3	32	1277	1284
July 1	1277	1284	33	45	15	4	7	28	1288	1297
" 6	1288	1297	54	59	7	4	6	21	1329	1331
" 11	1329	1331	89	80	5	21	5	17	1408	1392
" 16	1408	1392	24	25	17	13	3	7	1412	1397

1. M999:6:1040; RG 105. The compiler of this report is not named and the letter that probably accompanied it is missing. However, Lester Williams completed the report (with a ten-day hiatus) in his letter of July 31, 1865 (see chapter 6, below).

Chapter Six

Administrative Troubles and the Belle Mitchell Incident

Camp Nelson   July 15th 1865

Dear brother Strieby
* * * * [*One paragraph.*]

There are some three thousand colored soldiers now in camp — The opportunity is too good to be lost. They are calling for instructive teaching and preaching. I am doing what I can — brother Fee is helping me as he can be spared from the "Home". We could employ several teachers if we had them. Could you do anything for us in that direction? If so let us know. Gen Fisk is here and will make <u>some change</u> in the Home. We shall know in a day or two. Death and confusion we hope will come to an end there — you will hear from me again in a few days. In the meantime please let me know what you can do as to teachers if we should conclude to send for them — *

A. Scofield[1]

1. Scofield to Strieby, 15 Jul. 1865, AMAA 44157.

Private Letter
Camp Nelson Ky Monday morning — July 17 /65
Genl Fisk

Dear Bro   The announcement yesterday of your order requiring all able bodied persons to go out and get work — employment, created some stir among the people here. We spoke of the necessity of each one doing all they could to relieve the government & help themselves.

The end proposed is right and we will give it our <u>vigorous support.</u>

We see some difficulties

1 Here are 3,000 persons — the surplus of all parts of the state here — 228 came saturday night from Bowling Green —

Now suppose we cast these out or so many of all as can go; will <u>this surrounding country</u> absorb all that ought to be distributed over the whole state?

They have not money — are strangers to the region around — this region hates Camp Nelson & all that come from it — will employ any other rather than one from this Camp.

I believe this — If you deplete this camp you will need to employ an agent • to go over this state and find locations for these refugees, then report to this Home & the inmate go at once.

Many of these mothers insist that they shall be allowed to take their children with them — this will greatly weaken our school.

If we have a permanent success we must have permanent homes for those who desire to educate their children — we must confiscate these lands or go elsewhere — * * * * [*Three paragraphs.*]

I hasten to the school room — we are not cast down — full of quiet hope.

May the Lord God be with & guide you in all your ways. Yours in Christ

John G Fee[1]

1. Fee to Fisk, 17 July 1865; M999:7:51–53; RG 105.

Camp Nelson Ky   July 18 /65

Dear Bro Whipple   Genl Fisk has been here — we like him very much indeed

He will relieve Mr Williams & Capt Hall & put in a Military Comm, a Superintendent — dismiss several others — urge the able bodied to scatter & hunt work. Genl Palmer has ordered that free passes to go & return at will — when & where they will — freedom to all who shall be found within camp — military ports — & who wish to go & get employment. This is virtual freedom to Ky — all can have freedom who will come within a military post[1]

Gen Fisk will retain Bro Chapin — asks me to stay by all means — has asked me to give him my suggestions as to the conduct of the home in writing — I have done so — He has given the military control, for the present, into hands of Col Bierbower with instructions to have the cooperation of myself & Bro. Williams in the internal management.

I told him I could not stay unless there is a prospect of having here a continued school in which to <u>train youth</u>. He desires to have a school somewhere in the state where he can have several hundreds male & female educated.

Until a military man shall be appointed for the state he has given the superintending of this school into my own hands. This was unsought by me — . . . . * * * * [*Four paragraphs.*]

Will a military camp with military control be the most favorable circumstances under which to have our school — perhaps the school of the state — I can collect thousands for such a school —

Here is a central place — protected — where government has large accommodations for shelter — where there are even now from four to six hundred children — about four now in school. Some one must help controll it & I must have my children here or go to them. Genl Fisk told me to go and take possession of a piece of land & put a house on it if I can   He says the Association ought to furnish me one — Maybe I can do so myself   If I can I should prefer —

It may be that Berea will be found to be the best place for this school. This one cannot be removed for the present and I think it will continue here

Col Bierbower who is comm. of this post & has here the present controll — is my personal friend & commits all the conduct here to my decision — This may not be long — yet he is likely to stay. He ask that I consent to be the Post Chaplain of this camp & thereby increase my power & have control of all the schools. This would not now be true as I suppose under the existance of the Bureau. I doubt the success of obtaining a chaplaincy <u>now</u>, even if I were persuaded that the acceptance were best. He is sanguine of success. * * * * [*One paragraph.*]

J G Fee[2]

1. Gen. Palmer's Orders No. 49 urged all black people who were unable to find employment the right to apply to provost marshals or commanders of troops for "passes authorizing them to pass at will in search of employment, upon any railroad, steamboat, ferryboat, or other means of travel in the state of Ky. or plying out of it from any point in it." These were called "free papers." Collins, 162.

2. Fee to Whipple, 18 Jul. 1865, AMAA 44160–2.

[*Letter from George Thomas*[1] *published in the* Weekly Anglo-African *on 12 August 1865.*]

. . . I enlisted in the 12th U.S. Colored Heavy Artillery in the Fall of 1864, and my only sorrow is that I did not enlist sooner. I left a home such as would have made a slave happy, as long as there was a grain of happiness to be found in slavery. While living in Nelson county I indeed thought that it was right that all colored people should be slaves, and I was far from being the only one having the same opinion; but, oh, how different now! There were five or six colored people in the county who could read, and they were disliked very much by the white people on that account; so you see, although we were capable of being taught, the fear of our masters and mistresses kept us bound in the frontiers of ignorance. A man could not visit his wife, living a mile from him, scarcely once a week, and the infringement of any rule was followed by at least a hundred lashes; but, thanks be to God, those terrible days have passed away forever. At that time those cruel practices were not strange to me, neither did I think the masters cruel until I was, by the providence of God, partly released from ignorance by learning to read; then I saw that slavery was contrary to the laws of God and debasing to man. Things like this caused me to look forward, hoping and praying for the time at which these things must end — and behold, the time has come, and I see, as it were, a nation born in a day — men and women coming forth from slavery's dark dungeons to the noonday sunshine of the greatest of God's gifts — liberty.

Our wives are now cared for by our government, homes for them being already prepared at Camp Nelson, and we fell like men, and are determined to be men, and do our duty to our government honestly and faithfully, as good soldiers ought to do. . . .[2]

1. Thomas was a corporal in Battery L, 12th USCHA, Fort Smith, Bowling Green, Kentucky.

2. George Thomas letter, dated 18 July 1865, published 12 Aug. 1865 in *Weekly Anglo-African*; quoted in Redkey, 188–90.

Asst Comr Ky & Tenn   July 20ᵗʰ [*1865*]
Maj Genrl Howard   Comr &c   Washington D.C.

General   . . . I have just returned from a personal inspection of the "Colored Refugee Home" at Camp Nelson, Ky.

Of Camp Nelson it may be truthfully and emphatically said "<u>Magna res est</u>" — The Government's money has been most lavishly expended in the erection of buildings — construction of water works road &c.&c. It does seem to me that hundreds of thousands of dollars might have been <u>saved</u> and then furnished us with new and better accommodations for the "Home" than we now have.

I found the Home full — to overflowing — with Colored women and Children and the numbers increasing daily. There has not been proper effort to find homes and employment for these [freedmen?]. The Supt, teachers & others have I conclude rather been inclined to keep up a <u>big</u> establishment. I at once inaugurated radical changes in the conduct of the entire institution and shall diligently labor to keep the family small, although it <u>will be</u> quite large in spite of all we can do to keep the number reduced.

Kentucky is just now stirred to its bitter depths on the slavery question. A hotly contested political canvass is agitating the entire state. The only issue before the people is the ratification of the constitutional amendment forever prohibiting slavery in this Country. The leaders of the barbarians cling to its putrid carcass with clutching tenacity. Kentucky I fear will refuse to become one of the twenty seven (27) pall bearers required to bear the remains of the Great Abomination to its final resting place. Maj Genl Palmer Comdg the Dept of Kentucky has by General Order stricken the shackles from all slaves who will leave the state of Ky[1]   Post Commandants throughout the State are now granting passes to all colored persons making application   Rail Roads, steamboats and ferryboats are required to transport all who present the Military pass and pay their fares. This order was issued on the 10th inst and the result has been that Droves have crossed the Ohio and are now crowding the towns and cities of the State.

I am daily looking for a message from Indianapolis or other Northern City that may lift up its voice against the Continuance of the <u>black military</u>   The Emancipation and deportation by Genl Order and the agitation caused by the political canvass has aroused every colored individual in Kentucky to the importance of striking for freedom, and now. The consequence is that the more [——]ative these women and children are generally on the move for some place beyond the reach of masters. In many localities the most cruel & fiendish atrocities are being visited upon the Slaves by their maddened and despairing Masters — especially is this true as relates to the wives and children of the colored men who have enrolled in the army from Kentucky and the latter does push for military posts. Genl Palmer has directed his Post Commandants to forward all such to Camp Nelson. "Receive all that come" is the General's order. Five hundred (500) of this class were sent to Camp Nelson during last week alone — I give you these facts that you may fully understand the difficulties in the way of an early breaking up of the home there at Camp Nelson.

I have relieved Capt T.E. Hall from the Superintendency of the Home. I thought it best. He is not the man for the place. He is a good friend to the colored man: of this there is no doubt. . . . I have not as yet appointed a permanent successor from the [mere?] fact that I can not easily find the proper man. My chief difficulty throughout the District is the scarcity of the right kind of officers & men for duty in the Bureau. I have ordered that houses and employment must be found for every man woman and youth who has ability to labor. It is almost impossible to procure employment for a woman who has five or more children depending immediately upon her for care   I have therefore directed that the younger children who can not take care of themselves be for the present retained in the cottages at the "Home" in charge of the aged and infirm women and be kept in the [camp?].   The farms and gardens attached to the Home can be worked by the larger boys. I assure you that every thing that can be done consistent with my duty to the freedmen shall be done to relieve the numbers at Camp Nelson but the Home there or elsewhere in Kentucky will be a necessity for some time to come.

Very many of the good union anti-slavery men of Kentucky have become prejudiced against the institution because of a want of confidence in Capt Hall. His removal will stop much of the just Clamor that has been raised against the Home.

The schools at Camp Nelson are in excellent hands. I made many changes during my stay there and trust my visit will result in good.

I am pushing my District to organization as rapidly as possible — I find much to do but am daily overcoming difficulties and bringing the people to a better understanding of their duties. *

Clinton B Fisk   Brvt Genl   Asst Comr[2]

---

1. Gen. John M. Palmer himself claimed much more for his General Orders Nos. 32 and 49, since he believed the War Department's General Orders No. 129 on July 25, which extended the right to travel freely in search of employment to every black person in the United States, was issued "as a consequence" of his own orders (Palmer, 242). The last sentence of his memoirs advances his claim of "driving the last nail into the coffin of slavery in Kentucky" (622).

2. Fisk to Howard, 20 July 1865; M999:1:374–78; RG 105.

Fee Jno. G. **Camp Nelson Ky**

Applies for the detail of Private Gabriel Burdett 114th Regt U S C Inf to minister to the spiritual wants of the people of Camp Nelson. Recommends him highly
July 21 1865   Respy for^d to Maj Gen Howard Chf of Bureau with an earnest recommendation that Private Gabriel Burdett 114th USCI may be detailed to report to me for duty and consider him capable of doing more good than any white soldier whom I could use the detail of.

                                                Sgd Clinton B. Fisk BG & Ast C[1]

   1. Fisk to Fee, 21 July 1865; M999:4:696; RG 105.

July 23^d [1865]
Major Bannister   Chief Pay Master   Cincinnati Ohio

   Dr Major   I have a tellegram from the war Dept and also one from the Pay Dept saying in reply to my application for pay of the troops (col^d) now serving in the Dept that they shall be paid before the election.
   Please inform me what you have heard from the Dept on the subject and if no instructions have been recd please find out as soon as possible when the payment will be made   It is likely the troops will be scattered three or four days before the election and it is important if possible the payment should be made while they are all massed — Five thousand are now at Camp Nelson alone. The Claims for pay increase daily. Officers are ragged and soldiers families starving. Please write me by return of mail and let me know all you can about this matter   *

                                                Jas S Brisbin   Brig Genl[1]

   1. Brisbin to Major Bannister, 23 July 1865; [Bound] Vol. 57, Book 90, pp. 341, 342; Letters Sent, Organization of U.S.C.T., Entry 2247; Dept. of Ky., Part 1; RG 393.

[U.S. Sanitary Commission report.]

   . . . On the 25th of July the [Soldiers'] Home was closed, having entertained ninety-five thousand three hundred and thirty-seven soldiers, and furnished them two hundred and eighty-six thousand six hundred and fifty-six meals, and one hundred and two thousand five hundred and twenty-one lodgings. These figures do not include the large numbers of soldiers' families and other objects of charitable labor who shared, to a greater or lesser degree, the hospitalities of the Home and the ministration of our agents. All stores on hand, and the entire equipment of the Home, excepting the range and some more expensive articles of furniture, were turned over to the inmates of the camp of colored refugees—a most munificent donation, and one that was of priceless value to several hundred women and children, all destitute, and many sick, who at that time occupied it.[1]

   1. Newberry, 386.

War Department, Adjutant-General's Office, Washington, July 25, 1865.
General Order No. 129.

To secure equal justice and the same personal liberty to the freedmen as to other citizens and inhabitants, all orders issued by post, district or other commanders, adopting any system of passes for them, or subjecting them to any restraints or punishments not imposed on other classes, are declared void.

Neither white nor black will be restrained from seeking employment elsewhere when they cannot obtain it at a just compensation at their homes and when not bound by voluntary agreement, nor will they be hindered from traveling from place to place on proper and legitimate business.

By command of the secretary of war.
E.D. Townsend, Assistant Adjutant-General.[1]

1. This order is quoted by Gen. John M. Palmer in his autobiography, 242–43.

Camp Nelson   July 31, 1865
Gen. C.B. Fiske Asst. Com.

The present report which I have the honor to make includes six days, so as to complete the month.[1] The record stands as follows.

	Women	Children
Total July 26th.	1474	1495
Arrivals to Aug[t]. 1st	59	48
Discharged " "	71	55
Cut off from drawing Rations	4	6
Died during the six days	5	16
Total Aug[t]. 1st	1453	1466

There are ten schools in successful operation, having a total of 653 scholars. Of these 276 are girls, 247 are boys, 50 are women, 80 are soldiers, composing our guard. Other teachers are expected very soon when other schools will be opened.

In a conversation had with you while here, remarks were made concerning having all teachers commissioned by one benevolent organization. I have written to the Western Freedman's A. Com. at Cin., & the idea was welcomed & acceded to there, provided the A.M.A. consented to the transfer. I then wrote to the Sec. of the Am. Miss. Ass°., who declined, with much ardor of language, to yield the interest they held in the schools here. *

Lester Williams Jr[2]

1. This letter completes the chart of information (presented above in chapter 5) concerning women and children in the Refugee Home.
2. Williams to Fisk, 31 July 1865; M999:9:119–20; RG 105.

Camp Nelson Ky   Aug 2 /65

Dear Bro. Strieby

  * * * [*Twenty-one paragraphs.*]

I have been urged by the Commandant here to become Post Chaplain so that I would have controll of all schools, be able to receipt for properties & be able to demand aid in many ways   Possibly the Kingdom of Christ does not need this authority & I not to be in any respect tied by Military power however small. I will not be trammeled in anything I thought duty   I would not suffer this

  You gave no answer in reference to our agent to secure places for these people now thrown out of homes by angry masters   Thousands are receiving passes to go and get employment "at will" — under Genl Palmers order No 49

  * * * * [*Three paragraphs.*]

                                                                J G Fee[1]

1. Fee to Strieby, 2 Aug. 1865, AMAA 44171–2.

War Department   Bureau Refugees Freedmen and Abandoned Lands   Nashville, Tenn   Aug. 4th 1865
Rev. John G. Fee   Chaplain   Camp Nelson Ky. * * * * [*Two paragraphs.*]

  My positive instructions from Washington are "to break up the Refugee Home at Camp Nelson at the earliest possible day consistent with humanity &c" This cannot be done immediately but we must not make any moves with a view to permanency there. Yourself and friends ought to carry out your old scheme of a permanent industrial school at your old home. Private enterprise and benevolence must look to the elevation of the race. The Govt will cooperate but cannot run a Governmental Institute. I cannot be at Camp Nelson before September at the earliest. I am overwhelmed with my duties & especially pertaining to organization. I am unable to find good men for my subordinates. I wish I had a hundred John G. Fees. I am waiting for more definite instructions from Washington as to what to do in Ky. I am glad to hear from you always. I trust yourself the Col & Supt Williams are moving on with harmonious vigor. *

                                        Clinton B. Fisk   Maj Genl. Apt. Com.[1]

1. Fisk to Fee, 4 Aug. 1865, AMAA 44174–5. A press copy of this letter is in the Freedmen's Bureau records as well (M999:1:475–77; RG 105).

August 5th [*1865*]
Mr. L. Williams Jr.   Supt. Col Refugee Home   Camp Nelson Ky.

Dear Sir: I am directed by Brig Gen. C.B. Fisk Asst. Com'r for Ky Tenn. and Northern Ala. to acknowledge the receipt of your communication of the 1st inst. and in reply to say that the General cannot see the necessity for having a Sutler at a "Charity Institute" What use can he be please explain. The General also directs me to inform you that he still must insist on having all the teachers at Camp Nelson under the auspices of one Association and thinks that your Camp being so near Cincinnati that the Western Freedmens Aid Commission are the proper parties to supervise and furnish the requisite teachers &c for Camp Nelson. It will not be understood from this that the General is hostile to the American Mission for on the Contrary he has plenty of work laid out for that Society. There will now be Established within this District a large number of Plantation Schools and the American Mission will be called on for all the aid they can render.

It is not deemed advisable to have two Societies in charge of any one Camp as it is liable to cause a conflict of authority. *

Jno. H. Cochrane Major 101ˢᵗ USCI and A.A.A.G.[1]

1. John H. Cochrane to Williams, 5 Aug. 1865; M999:1:480–81; RG 105.

Camp Nelson Ky   Aug. 9 [*1865*]
(Private)
Brig. Genl Fisk

Dear Brother
        * * * *

John G Fee[1]

Col Bierbower told me last evening that he was waiting your reply in reference to Mr Vincent[2] — Now you expect from me more than intimation.

1 Mr Butler, agent of Sanitary Comm, and Mr Kennedy Capt in 119 Ky Col Troops, told me Mr Vincent was regarded as fraudulent

Mr. Kennedy as clerk in same camp professed to know   Mr Kennedy said Mr V was notoriously licentious   Mr Butler bore the same testimony — even at his own laundry at the Soldiers Home

2 Mrs Vincent is a very imbecile inefficient woman seldom doing anything but mere presiding at the Table.

Her daughter, a young lady here, is still more worthless — boarded somehow.

3 Mrs Colton is here — the lady whose letter I shewed to you — she is about fifty years of age — has much of physical & mental vigor with active piety.

Col Bierbower knowing these things ought not to leave you with the trouble of deciding but ought with his own judgment to at once decide and let not affairs drift

J G F[3]

1. This is a long letter of several pages from which only the second postscript is presented.
2. Mr. Vincent and his wife were in charge of the mess at the Refugee Home.
3. Fee to Fisk, 9 Aug. 1865; M999:7:133; RG 105.

Camp Nelson Ky   Augᵗ 11, 1865
Rev. M.E. Strieby

My Dear Bro   I am compelled to say that the representative which the Am. Miss. Asso. has here in the person of Mr. Fee, Chaplain of the Ref. Home is a singularly unfortunate one.

He has not the respect & confidence of any one employed here who has been here a [*indecipherable*]. [It is] given to him at first, naturally, from his [position, but?] he soon loses it, & has no power or capacity to regain it. Whatever he once was, he now is a most restless, uneasy man. He interferes & interposes himself unwarrantably in other people's business. By his under-working he causes trouble & disturbances among those with whom he associates. I unhesitatingly assert that he is a double-minded, double-tongued, double-dealing man.

What is the matter with him? Is he insane? He is certainly unfit to represent here the organization with which we stand connected.

It is not pleasant to me to write the foregoing, nor am I in the habit of doing the like. I am

Yours, Very Truly & Fraternally,
Lester Williams Jr   Civ. Apᵗ Col. Ref. Home[1]

1. Williams to Strieby, 11 Aug. 1865, AMAA 44178.

Camp Nelson Ky   Aug. 11 /65

Dear Brother Strieby, I have a letter from Genl Fisk, very flattering — as to my labor here &c. He asks me to nominate man for the superintendency that man must be a military man   He also asks me to find an agent to secure homes for these people

He says this Home must be broken up soon as humanity will allow.

He suggests that we go on with our school at Berea — by all means

He says that benevolent societies must do this work of educating

My opinion is that though there is here much more sickness than at Berea yet in despite of Genl Fisks purpose it will be hard to break up here — here I think will be a town perhaps a town of Colored people — mostly

I have two invitations to go and address these colored people now being freed at Lexington and Danville — also organise schools for them and get for them aid for a time   I expect to go next week.

Now what will you say to me — shall I pledge a teacher at each place as principal — or if only one teacher, pay as part of salary?

Or will you give up Kentucky to Western Freedman's Aid?

The invitation to go to these places was unsought & unexpected to me. Reason assigned was "they know you & have confidence in you, & think you will not tell them any thing but what is for their good"

I go ("Deo volente" [*God willing*])   shall I promise aid or leave this field in part or all to Western Freed Aid

Bro Oyler[1] who is here as principal in the school here will leave last of this month — he is a good man   have you someone to send in his stead * * * * [*One paragraph.*]

Shall I promise teachers for these places

John G Fee[2]

1. Charles P. Oyler, briefly principal of the school at the Refugee Home, was apparently captain of the 124th U.S. Colored Infantry. Later, he became Freedmen's Bureau superintendent at Covington, Kentucky. *OAR*, 8:305.
2. Fee to Strieby, 11 Aug. 1865, AMAA 44179.

Aug. 15th [*1865*]
Col D.C. Jaquess[1]   Supt. Lexington Sub-District   Camp Nelson Ky

Sir   You have been assigned as Superintendent of the Lexington Sub-District with Head Qrs at Camp Nelson — and are specially charged with the supervision and entire Control of the Colored Refugee Home at Camp Nelson. For its proper management you will be held formally responsible.

I am directed by my superiors to close out the Camp at the earliest practicable day and to its early and complete <u>abolition</u> your energies are to be devoted. You will therefore not receive into the Home another individual old or young except humanity evidently demands it. It will require your best energies and superior management to get rid of the families there now — before the winter sets in. It will not be practicable to maintain any Camp or Home at that point after Cold weather comes on as fuel can not be obtained except at an immense cost to the Government. And even were it practicable as to location and cost it is not best to encourage the establishment of permanent camps.

You will at once select good parties citizens if officers can not be found, who will travel and secure homes and employment for the families. There are many Soldiers families <u>there</u> who can now be removed by the Soldiers themselves as the Government has recently paid off all colored troops. There will be some few old and infirm people. You will ascertain from where they come and send them into the Counties from which they have been sent to us and require their old Masters to provide for them. Many of the Colored people at the Home may desire to go north of the Ohio River. No objection is made to such a journey — <u>Everything</u> to break up the camp and not entail <u>suffering</u>. There will be some suffering do the best we can. I am satisfied that the demoralization now at the Home will more than overcome all the good we are doing. You will be opposed in the breaking up of the Camp by almost all the Attaches of the Institution — And <u>I</u> <u>fear</u> <u>you</u> will look upon its discontinuance as an impossibility. You must look to the <u>greater</u> <u>good</u> and relieve the Government of the burthens these Camps are bringing upon it.

The Chaplain John G. Fee the Ass't Superintendent Mr Williams and all the

School teachers will make every possible effort to continue a <u>big</u> establishment — as the larger it is kept the more flourishing the schools congregations hospitals &c.

You will find Chaplain Fee a most excellent man. He would break every shackle on every slave to day if he had the power. He is not practical in his views now that the slave is upon us. He is almost a monomaniac on the subject of human liberty and it is excusable for he has been through the fiery trial in <u>Kentucky</u> at that. You must listen to him kindly but <u>do</u> what <u>you</u> think is right.

Mr Williams is a good man but rather <u>slow</u>. I should think he would do well as a travelling agent to find homes & employment. He has been at the Home a long time, and it may be well to change his duties. A Mr Vincent & family can be spared at once   Reduce expenses <u>rapidly</u>. I was much pleased with a young gentleman who acts as Clerk. The Surgeon in Charge is a good man.

You will make regular reports <u>every</u> <u>five</u> <u>days</u>. So that I may know how you are progressing in getting rid of the families. I shall <u>hope</u> for <u>much</u> <u>good</u> to result of your well directed efforts at Camp Nelson. Remember that Slavery yet breathes out its threatenings and Slaughter in Kentucky   *

Clinton B Fisk   Brig Genl   Ass^t Comr²

1. Fisk addressed this letter to D.C. rather than J.F. Jaquess, but was simply mistaken about the new superintendent's initials. And apparently no one else knew how to spell the man's surname! In his own signature, it was Jaquess. James Frazier Jaquess (1819–1898) was a Methodist clergyman and soldier, whose life was full of incident before he saw Camp Nelson. He had been president of two colleges, and colonel of the Seventy-third Illinois Volunteers, known as the "preacher's regiment" because so many of its officers were ministers. In the summer of 1863 he was convinced that he personally might bring the war to a peaceful conclusion through religious persuasion; the intensity of his convictions impressed Abraham Lincoln, among others, and Jaquess was given permission to enter Confederate territory and seek a personal interview with Jefferson Davis. He reached Petersburg, Virginia, but was not allowed to confront the Confederate president. A subsequent attempt, discussed below, was successful. *DAB,* 615–16.

2. Fisk to Jaquess, 15 Aug. 1865; M999:1:547–50; RG 105.

Camp Nelson Ky Aug 16 /65

Dear Bro Strieby

* * * * [*Four paragraphs.*]

We are suffering now, as heretofore, for the want of a religious head here. Capt Hall you know is gone — Col Bierbower has done well in efforts toward freeing "niggers". But does not realise the necessity of having spiritually minded teachers — loves women wine, & music — late hours — was here with violin last Wednesday night at late hour —

A man here, as undertaker, proposed to one of the teachers sent by Freedman Aid, to walse — they did so — I had retired, so had sister Colton (sister to Rev Jas A Thome¹) & others before the music began — Sister Colton hearing the dancing supposed the colored people had possession of the room below — annoyed got up to ask them to go away — seeing "whites" she turned in disgust came to my room knocked & asked if such things were to be allowed here. I was in bed — cried out not if I were superintendent — Next day she talked at breakfast table then to Mrs. Daimon in a manner abrupt & severe — said there were other young ladies who wished to come & who were "exemplary" also made impression in Sister Daimon's mind that she was writing a report of proceedings here — this is the worst offense to sister Daimon — Mrs Colton asked pardon for severe manner. Other young ladies who were reflected upon were not reconciled   Col Bierbower was called — lugged into it — got up his shivalry for the young ladies and at suggestion of Mr Williams sanctioned an order which Mrs Williams got up and sent the woman by positive order out of camp. This was to me a great trial

Whilst I regret the manner & spirit of sister Colton in some respects yet I feel she was badly treated.

I opposed the Colonel strongly. This he regretted & felt for I had been his councellor —

So you see I have to struggle on a while longer before I have this work ready to leave it. I believe these men here are a hindrance to the good of Christs poor and interests of Christs Kingdom — as such I intend under God to root them out — effect yet a radical change. Sad it is to have these poor creatures (ex slaves) turn away in disgust from their professed friends.

I have acquainted Genl Fisk with your wish to hold on to at least half of the enterprise here. I send you a copy of one of his recent letters that you may see what is his purpose in reference to Camp Nelson & what is his estimate of our enterprise out at Berea. I was at Berea last sabbath, baptised four persons whom I have recd 3 weeks previously — am now gathering there white & colored. I wish to have that place in harmony with this   this with that

Then if I can start schools at Lexington & Danville I shall possibly feel that I can retire — The Lord direct

I do not think Genl Fisk can break up this refugee home soon   wives and children of absent soldiers are here

I think very probable that some benevolent society as yours or that at Cincinnati will propose to take the government houses here lease lands at low figures from the government and hold a school here. The place is central well watered has facility of building material but not of firewood

I think Bro Wheeler[2] will make you a better agent than Bro Elnathan Davis — in judgment of men — Perhaps Bro S. better than either   Yours in Christ,

John G Fee[3]

---

1. Rev. James Armstrong Thome appears in Camp Nelson records only because he was Mrs. Mary Ann Colton's brother, but he was a very famous evangelical abolitionist in his day. Both he and his sister were from Augusta, Kentucky, John G. Fee's hometown; so Fee knew them well.

2. Rev. Willard Watson Wheeler (born 1837 or 1838 in New York; died in 1898) had been a student at Oberlin when he joined the Union Army, enlisting in Company C of the Seventh Ohio Volunteer Infantry. He was wounded and taken prisoner, but after his discharge he went to Camp Nelson as a missionary and became the first official "Farmer" spon-

sored by the AMA. Very soon, Fee persuaded him to go work at Berea instead, where Wheeler and his wife were among the first teachers at the newly integrated school. Sears, *Berea Connections*, 156–57.

3. Fee to Strieby, 16 Aug. 1865, AMAA 44180–1.

(Private)
Camp Nelson Ky Aug 18 /65
Brig Gen Fisk   Nashville Tenn.

Dear Bro   Does the power of Col Bierbower extend to the <u>moral qualifications</u> of teachers of the school here? He has by order and by threat of force sent away Mrs Colton, not for violation of military rule — not proven immorality — but as stated yesterday —

Now if I am Superintendent of school — have I not right to say who are worthy & not worthy? — as teachers?

Also I have requested the teachers here to refrain from late hours & rollicking at that time with young men.

The Col with others have been here almost every night during the week past until late hours — night before last again last night rollicking playing, laughing tussling with one of the teachers until after midnight last night. I ask that I may in some way have power to stop this — For the honor of Christ & well being of these poor give me or someone power to stop this thing * * * * [*2 paragraphs.*]

Do as you shall feel God would like to have you & I will try to help you   But if I stay here as I do from my family & at continual cross bearing I wish opportunity to do good & correct all evil I can   I have offered all I can offer   yours,

John G Fee

I have talked with Mr Williams about the course of some of these young ladies   He takes sides with them

So I did with the Colonel[1]

1. Fee to Fisk, 18 Aug 1865; M999:7:153–54; RG 105.

Camp Nelson   Aug 18ᵗʰ 1865
M.E. Strieby, Sec. A.M.A.

Dear brother   I am yet in Camp Nelson. For the last month have been teaching and preaching with the soldiers. There are here some two thousand soldiers with whom I have been laboring — teacher and preaching. We hope our labor has not been altogether vain in the Lord. We have seen some four or five soldiers of the 124ᵗʰ converted unhurt unto Christ. Our meetings on the sabbath are well attended   I preach two or three times on the sabbath once generally in the open air. During the week I teach — I have about one hundred and fifty soldiers under instruction — and about forty childen — but could have twice that number if I had the proper teachers — I am now using the soldiers Home for a chapel and schools — there has been no such opportunity before for giving instruction to the soldiers — the officers also join with me in the work.

I have a son now 18 years of age ("Gerrit Smith Scofield") he would be good help for me here in these schools — He is now at Lebanon, N. York, and earning about $20. per month and board. Could you not afford him that to help me in this good work   It would also be a good to him as well as a comfort to me. Can you not send him along? —   * * * * [*Expense account and one paragraph.*]

Rev. A. Scofield[1]

1. Scofield to Strieby, 18 Aug. 1865, AMAA 44182.

Private
Aug 22 /65

Dear Bro Strieby   Genl Fisk & Col Jacquess (superintendent here) encourage the idea — both protruded the suggestion that we carry out our scheme of a school at Berea. A school here will do good. There ought to be a normal school somewhere in the state where we could educate several hundred of these children for teaching   The district schools will not probably do this

That school must be at Berea or at this place   I do not think the people of Danville or Lexington will allow the idea of a concentration of negroes at either place

These colored children will need the facilities of a High School soon as we can have such ready for them

I must now leave here — leave things in Bro Scofields hands and go to Berea and direct attention there or go to work here try to get hold of the rebel lands here — ie get congress to confiscate & let Trustees sell to colored & white persons — also get hold of these government houses

I could have some influence with [*Sen. Charles*] Sumner & [*Sen. Henry*] Wilson — Col Jacquess is a Methodist   unless I & Bro Scofield take hold of this land & property the sects will.

I could leave Bro Scofield here and I go to Berea   These soldiers are now being paid off & ought now to be locating — They cannot buy here until congress shall confiscate * * * * [*Two paragraphs.*]

John G Fee[1]

1. Fee to Strieby, 22 Aug. 1865, AMAA 44184.

Camp Nelson Ky   Aug 23rd 1865
Brig Gen C.B. Fisk   Freedmen's Bureau

Dear Sir   I have come, and seen, and hope to conquer. Have met all the opposition and objections you anticipated — It will require the prudence and sagacity of an angel of light — the kindness and gentleness of a woman, and the <u>firmness</u> and <u>stability</u> of the everlasting hills to succeed.

The work you have assigned me <u>shall be accomplished</u> <u>in the shortest possible time</u>. . . .

James F. Jaquess, Col. & Supt Lexington Sub Dist Freedmen's Bureau

P.S. In many instances it will be absolutely necessary to furnish transportation — to get the people away from here — how shall I enact that? No one here is willing to give it — unless I am authorized to do so — I can close the thing out in short order, if I can give transportation — many will not require it — [1]

1. Jaquess to Fisk, 23 Aug. 1865; M999:7:1405–6; RG 105.

Camp Nelson Ky   Aug 23 /65

Dear Bro Strieby   Col Jacquess is here to take the superintendency of affairs   Col Bierbower & Bro Williams are relieved   Col Jacquess takes their place — I will probably retain the schools — Bro Scofield may remain   The Commandant of the post is against him for council not to regard a command given to Mrs Colton — May all pass on & new conflict —

Mr Scofield desires some of his family to come   I think they could do good & hesitate not to employ his wife & oldest daughter because they are christians. I said to him as for commissions & expense of others I would leave that with you

Bro Scofield is collecting claims for the wives of soldiers   If successful he will get money. Some person who is reliable ought to do this work for these poor people but <u>preachers</u> good as he ought not to serve tables — He is anxious not only to get up a school for soldiers but of children also   I hope he may not make division — perhaps will not

J G Fee[1]

1. Fee to Strieby, 23 Aug. 1865, AMAA 44185.

August 24th [1865]
Col. James F. Jacques. Supt. Camp Nelson Kentucky.

I have the honor to state that I am in receipt of your telegram asking if you could give transportation to Freedmen going to homes. I replied by telegram "Yes letter by mail"   General Fisk has authorized the issue of transportation to Freedmen going to homes or places of Employment from Camps to Refugees when they can produce satisfactory Evidence that on arriving at their destination they will not become a charge upon the Government. * * * * [*One paragraph.*]

Jno. H. Cochrane   Major 101st U.S.C.I. and A.A.A.Genl[1]

1. Cochrane to Jaquess, 24 Aug. 1865; M999:1:585; RG 105.

**Head Qu⁵ Lexington Sub Dist   Freedmen's Bureau   Camp Nelson Ky
Aug 29 /65**

General: This work goes bravely on. I start for various destinations in the A.M. over a hundred persons. I find that I must preceed them this P.M. to Lexington and perhaps to Louisville to <u>bridge</u> a <u>pass</u> way beyond. I <u>am getting</u> things in shape, and you will see a large decrease soon. I have found it necessary to admit a few persons, none but soldiers families — of those who are in Texas[1] — and whose families are homeless — You may depend upon my pushing this work with constant vigor — The School here is a <u>humbug</u>, amounts to nothing. Mr Fee and the teachers are in a constant quarrel. I will regulate them soon   Mr Fee has many perfectly impractical views[2] — I hope I shall be able to dispense with the services of several here soon — *

James F Jaquess Col & Supt. &c [3]

1. The 114th and 116th Colored Infantries, both organized at Camp Nelson, were sent to Texas. Dyer, 2:1739.
2. Given the accounts of Jaquess's own views, it seems extremely ironic that he should make such a comment about Fee's ideas.
3. Jaquess to Fisk, 29 Aug. 1865; M999:7:1420–21; RG 105.

**Camp Nelson   Aug 30th 1865
Mrs Bucks Tel. operator**

The number of colored refugees fed in Camp Nelson July 1ˢᵗ was 2585. The number fed to day is 2656. If the telegram recᵈ asks for the number also of <u>white</u> refugees fed in Camp at the above dates I have not the information & have no means of knowing. Possibly Capᵗ. Ransom Com. of Sub. may know something of it.

L. Williams Jr

For Col. J.F. Jaquess, absent
I have no answer to your telegram so I send this[1]

1. Williams to Bucks, 30 Aug. 1865; M999:15:1603; RG 105.

[*No date*] Colᵈ Ref Home.

Rev J.G. Fee, Your introduction into this house & to the table of a woman of color, without the consent of the occupants of it, & of those who conduct the mess, excites much comment & just repugnance to the act. There lies before me a written request signed by all the members of the mess with but two exceptions, that I hereby signify to you the above fact, & their united request that you withdraw from the table, & the house at once the above mentioned person.

A speedy compliance with the above will oblige. *

L. Williams Jr.[1]

1. Williams to Fee, [no date], AMAA 45339; also reproduced in Willard W. Wheeler's copy in AMAA 44187–8.

Colord Refugee Home   Camp Nelson Ky   Aug 31ˢᵗ 65
Rev. Geo. Whipple, New York

Dear Bro   I have been here a little more than one month, most of which time I have spent at Superintending the farming. I found this a much larger work than I had anticipated. I found it not only very difficult to get the people out to work, but almost impossible to get much done after they reached the field. At length the corn and potatoes became large enough to eat and I then began giving them out to those who worked. I then had no difficulty in getting hands. Every hoe was in use and hands to spare. That taught me that with a proper reward the colored people will work. It is true that they have been supported here for a long time by Govt. and ought to do a little something to pay back. But they could not see why they should not have some of the potatoes, which their own hands helped raise, and if they could have some they were willing to work for them. My experiences with the Freedmen tells me that they will work, only give them an inducement and who would without?

Besides the work done I think much good has been accomplished, in several ways. More just views of labor and their duty in this respect, have been instilled, and in some cases _enforced_ so that they could see _the point_ — I have noticed with pleasure that the disposition to quarrel which was so prevalent when I first came, has nearly disappeared. Evil speaking is now seldom heard compared with what it was one month ago. The general deportment of the girls is softening down very much. There seems less of the roughness of the soldiers about them. It was once perfectly shocking. . . . Bro F was out at Danville and, hearing of a young colored woman who had prepared herself at Xenia Ohio for a teacher, and learning of her correct christian deportment and unexceptionable personal habits, and moreover being in great need of help, hired her. I might mention here (though I know it would make no difference with you) that her features are good European her complexion but little darker than yours or mine and her hair of "the most straightest sect." So that I think Bro Fee was fortunate in chancing on one so faultless in all these respects. A few days before she was expected here Bro Fee told the Superintendent Col Jacquess that he had hired a young colored lady and she would be along soon. He also asked the man who had charge of our "mess," to prepare a room and seat at the table for her, telling him that she was slightly colored. He remarked that he had no prejudice and would as soon eat with a black person as a white. Bro Fee supposed the coast was clear. The lady came and sat down at a small table where Bro Fee sat. It was easy to see that her appearance created a sensation. The lady teachers soon began to absent themselves & Bro Williams seemed greatly ruffled. Col. Jacquess (who is also a Methodist minister) immediately fell to compromising as is their wont. He was afraid Bro Fee had committed a great blunder, suggested that the young lady be sent down to the "Soldiers Home" till the storm was overpast. Bro F refused. He [*Jaquess*] said the Societies will not sustain you. Well then, I will stand alone [*Fee replied*] But Bro Fee I am Supt of this home. Very well, I will risk all on the issue. Then he [*Jaquess*] flew right around and said I will have nothing to do with it. I will leave it with the mess. Thus washing his hands as Pilate did, of old and with about as much effect in clearing his skirts of guilt. Henceforth, Mr Williams is the champion of the faction and the Col went to Louisville on business. Now the disaffected in the mess prepare to besiege the camp of the uncircumcised. We daily went to our meals at the ringing of the bell, and they remained away till after we were through, meanwhile circulating a petition for the girls removal from the house & table.

I give you a copy of the communication addressed to Bro F. by Bro. Williams * * * *[1]

You will notice the crime which is charged upon your agent of "introducing into the mess a <u>woman</u> of —   — <u>Color</u>," and also the "just repugnance" manifested at such atrocious conduct. Ought you not immediately recall this man Fee? for you must know that this is not the first time he has excited the just repugnance of sensitive, Christian people — even often of holy ministers of the gospel. He is a pestilent fellow and I firmly believe he seeks to turn this part of the world upside down. He has often been rebuked and sometimes the good people of these parts have found it necessary to whip him and in diverse other ways to express their "just repugnance" of his actions.

But to return to the communication. Bro Fee asked for the petition that he might reply to it, but was informed that "The petition is addressed to myself." Any communication which you may have to the signers can be presented through me. At least this is the substance. Bro Fee then sat down and answered the request that he should remove the woman of color. He utterly refused and demanded for her the common civilities of the house. This house was set apart by the Bureau for the use of the teachers officers and employees of the Refugee Home. The mess was formed for the same and now we claim a right in all good faith to bring in any <u>competent teacher</u> of good moral & christian deportment and we claim that charges of a more serious nature than being a woman of color are necessary to eject her from the house. That persons professing christianity should act so unchristian is a wonder to me. Inded all admit that were Christ himself here he would act differently. "But then I am not Christ." . . . .

. . . I also think that Bro Fees action in all respects has not been wisest but I do feel that his motives have been <u>good</u>. He is <u>suffering very great persecution.</u> The spirit manifested by the other party is cruel vindictive & spiteful. Indeed the whole work here is degenerating below the dignity of christians and equals the most petty personal spite I have ever seen. Bro Fee I think keeps himself from this spirit —

But I must close   May God have mercy and appear and deliver his beloved cause from the hands of the enemy   Affectionately

W. W. Wheeler[2]

---

1. Here Wheeler supplies a word-for-word copy of Williams's undated letter to Fee, presented above.
2. Wheeler to Whipple, 31 Aug. 1865, AMAA 44187–8.

[Letterhead.] *U.S. Sanitary Commission*   **Camp Nelson Ky**   **Sept 1ˢᵗ 1865**

Dear Brother Strieby
* * * * [*One paragraph.*]

 The work of teaching the soldiers is rapidly increasing in extent and interest. I have a school in the Soldiers Home or rather two schools one during the day and one at night. The attendance is large; and every day increasing. The day school is devoted chiefly to children and women connected with the Regiments — <u>some who will not</u> go to the Refugee School, there are about 60, and can be 100. In the night school strictly for the Soldiers I have an average attendance of about 120. Our Room will seat 200, but we cannot teach them without more help. In the day school I am entirely alone — I have had a small boy at 2 per week but he is not such help as I need. In the night school such help as I can pick up for the occasion sometimes good sometimes poor. I have also started two schools in the 124ᵗʰ Reg. nearly a mile away from the Home, but you will see that I cannot give them much attention.

 Well, I have with the advice and consent of brother Fee concluded to send for my wife and two daughters. They will be here next week. My wife is an experienced teacher. My daughters too can teach — and there is work enough for them Brother Fees son has left and gone to School — there is room here for my boy to teach these soldiers. Could he be sent I think the Soldiers would pay his wages for teaching — I hope our plans will meet the approval of the committee

 Dear brother Fee has his heart and hands full with the Refugee Home on the hill. The machinery will not run smooth up there — never! no never! till there are important changes

 It is astonishing to see what small pebbles block the wheels of that institution. Two days ago brother Fee hired an accomplished teacher from Danville to go in there to teach, but alas! the poor girl had a face <u>slightly</u> tinged! — and will you believe it There was a general uproar among the teachers and superintendents because of it — the high bloods really refuse to eat in the same Hall with her though they can sit at another Table! — And that too when they have employed half a dozen <u>black faces</u> to wait on them at the table and brush off the flies! <u>Shame</u>![1]

 Some colorphobia there "I reckin" — Seriously I ask shall such a wrong be sustained?

 The matter is not yet settled. A word of comfort from your committee to brother Fee would not be amiss.

 Hoping that your committee will see fit to help on my school with teachers, I remain as ever, yours for the poor,

        A. Scofield, Missionary[2]

1. Scofield pressed so hard here with his pen that his handwriting resembles bold font.
2. Scofield to Strieby, 1 Sept. 1865, AMAA 44189.

Head Quarters   Camp Nelson Ky.   Sept. 2^d 1865
Lt. Chas. Harkins[1]   Pro. Marshal

Lt: Information has been received at these Head Quarters, that the buildings and sheds of the Ordnance Department of the Command are occupied by negroes without any authority.

The Col. Comdg. directs that you inform these negroes to find other quarters immediately — and if none can be found, the Supt'd of the Col^d. Refugee Home will provide for them temporarily. You are directed to see that these houses are cleared as soon as possible reporting your action at these Head Quarters *

O.A. DeLeuw[2]   Lt. & A.A.A.G[3]

1. Charles Harkins, a native of Ireland, saw his first military service in Nevada, then joined the 2nd Massachusetts Cavalry, only to end up as 1st lieutenant in the 124th U.S. Colored Infantry and provost marshal at Camp Nelson. *HR,* 1:501

2. Oscar A. DeLeuw enlisted on February 19, 1864, as a private, but became 1st lieutenant in the 122nd Illinois Infantry. *Illinois: Roster of Officers and Enlisted Men (1900)* in Civil War Archive at www.ancestry.com.

3. DeLeuw to Harkins, 2 Sept. 1865, Part 4, Entry 1661, p. 237; RG 393.

Sept 3^d [*1865*]
Maj General Howard   Comr &c   Washington D.C.

General   I am reducing Camp Nelson though not so rapidly as I could wish — It is a difficult matter to conduct a Bureau for Freedmen in a Slave State. Yet there is no reason for discouragement. The right will prevail. During the last six days I have been able to reduce the numbers in Camp Two hundred and twenty four (224) — and during August Three Hundred and forty two (442)

In the Camp Sept 1st	Women	1208
" "	Children	1269
		2477

I shall make every reasonable effort to close out the entire camp before cold weather   *

Clinton B. Fisk   Brig Genl   Asst Comr[1]

1. Fisk to Howard, 3 Sept. 1865; M999:3:1264; RG 105.

Lexington Ky   Sept 4 /65

Dear Bro Fisk   I learn from Col Bierbower that Col Jacquess has gone to Nashville. My writing to you may therefore, in time of his <u>presence</u>, be same in writing as addressing you <u>through</u> him.

But lest he be not there when this shall come allow me now to say to you — I employed Miss Bell Mitchell — a lady <u>slightly</u> colored

1 Several of our teachers were sick — some had gone home — we <u>then</u> <u>needed</u> help.

2 I was empowered by Am Miss Assoc to employ teachers.

3 Miss Mitchell was of a very exemplary family in Danville Ky — she had been educated in Ohio for teaching had testimonials from her teacher of qualifications &c — is a member of the Methodist church in <u>good</u> standing.

4 I felt it was right to encourage such & that the precedent would be stimulating to others.

This was before Col Jacquess had arrived. Soon after he came I told him I had employed such a teacher & the reasons   He did not then dissent   I construed silence into consent & felt reproved for offering to a member of the Freedmans Bureau such an intimation that the incident of blood might be a matter of rejection when <u>merit</u> was there

I then went to Mr Vincent, the man who had the care of the ("mess") table, and told him I had employed a teacher & desired a place & that "she is slightly colored." He replied "I am not like some people" & then pointing to colored woman darker than Miss Mitchell said 'I could eat with that woman as readily as with anybody'. He went & prepared a place for her

She came in that evening & some feeling was manifested.

My opinion is that if there had not been some ungodly young men boarding at the table & Bro Williams had not "sided" with them, there would have been little or no opposition — you ask Bro Jacquess if he does not think so. * * * * [*One paragraph.*]

Bro Fisk that woman is <u>in the house & in the school.</u> She is efficient & exemplary. For me to consent to withdraw that young lady is to disgrace her because of the tinge of blood — to exclude <u>Christ</u> in the person of his humble ones — No! Bro Fisk this I cannot do. If done the sin will be on some others   There are 6 of the mess opposed to the actions of Mr Williams & others   Better far for the cause of Christ that you have the school conducted by them, than yield to the ungodly demand — so I feel

May God direct you & all concerned. * * * * [*One paragraph.*]

John G Fee[1]

[*Accompanying this letter in the Freedmen's Bureau file is a summary, presumably written by the secretary who filed it.*]

Lexington Ky.   Sept 4th 1865

Informs Bro. Fisk that Col. Jacques is in Nashville. That he (Fee) employed Miss Bell Williams[2] who is "slightly Colored" as a teacher in consequence of which some of the "ungodly & perverse of heart" refuse to admit her on terms of Equal right &c. Wants General Fisk to sustain him &c &c &c &c[3]

1. Fee to Fisk, 4 Sept 1865; M999:7:187–89; RG 105.
2. The Freedmen's Bureau Clerk gave Belle the wrong surname; he means Mitchell, not Williams.
3. File summary; M999:7:186; RG 105.

September 5th [*1865*]
Captain E.B.W. Restiaux   Asst Quarter Master   Camp Nelson Ky.

Captain. I have the honor to authorize you to issue upon the order of Colonel J.F. Jacques Supt Sub Dist Lexington Bureau Refugees Freedmen &c transportation for Freedmen and Refugees on all Rail Roads north and south of the Ohio River   *

Clinton B. Fisk   Brig Genl and Asst Com^{r.1}

1. Fisk to Restieaux, 5 Sept. 1865; M999:1:638; RG 105.

Camp Nelson Ky   Sept 5 /65
Brig Genl C.B. Fisk

Dear Brother
      * * * * [*One paragraph.*]
      As to the case of Miss Mitchell — teacher slightly colored — I claim the house and its appurtenances was set apart by the Freedman's Bureau for the reception & accomodation of Teachers missionaries & employees in the Refugee Home — As such, Miss Mitchell being properly called & worthy, has a <u>common right</u> to the the house & the table.
      Now should she be compelled to leave because of the prejudice of others. Because of prejudice unchristlike may they expel her from her <u>rights</u>
      If the mess choose to take part of the dining hall & part of the table ware and organise a separate "mess" that is their right and we of course cannot complain of invasion of our <u>rights</u>. We might complain (religiously) of the unchristian spirit.*
[*Fee's asterisk; see below.*]
      Now I am quite content to take our share of the house and of the table furniture and with Mrs Colton & Miss Smith Miss Mitchell Mrs Scofield (Mis French is the corner) and Mr. Blakeman (was here, as before) and the new principal of the school soon as he shall come, and with these constitute a "mess" or let them leave us as a "mess"
      I know a house divided against itself cannot stand and they of the opposite party will die away   Col Jaquess I think has seen enough of their spirit to satisfy him that this is true   The providence of God will be against them. These colored people will be against them — there was here a demonstration since Col Jacquess left during my absence and uninstigated by any save themselves — The march of enlightened christian conscience will be against them. Faith can wait   Yours in kind regards

John G Fee

*Already they have two of the three tables — and ours is separate, but they demand also that the young lady be put out withdrawn from the house also.¹
[*Accompanying this letter in the Freedmen's Bureau file is a summary, once again, presumably written by the secretary who filed it.*]

Enlarges upon the case of Miss Mitchell ("Slightly colored") <u>Fee</u> likes to eat at the same table with her. Others — Teachers and Missionaries do not — A small family quarrell over the <u>victuals</u> whereon Fee expends much rhetoric — and is finally of the opinion that "Faith can wait.[2]

1. Fee to Fisk, 5 Sept 1865; M999:7:191–92; RG 105.
2. File summary; M999:7:190; RG 105.

Head Quarters Lexington Sub Dist Refugee Freedmen &c Bureau Camp Nelson Sept 9th 1865
To Brig Gen Fisk, Freedmens Bureau Nashville Tenn.

General   On my arrival I presented your Order to Capt Restieaux, A.Q.M., directing him to furnish transportation to my order. At the time he made no objection, but signified a willingness to do so. This A.M. I received a line from him calling my attention to the following order which he said he had just received from Q.M. Gen. at Washington

"Officers of the Quartermasters Department will furnish Supplies of Quartermasters Stores, Means of Transportation, Buildings, Storage &c to officers of the Bureau of Refugees Freedmen &c only on requisitions which have been approved by the commissioner of the Bureau, and then submitted to the Sec. of War for his approval orders them on"

This document — Gen Order 49 — which I presume you have seen, bears date Aug 21st Signed by Q.M. Gen Meigs &c — This order Capt R. claims cuts him off from doing anything more for us without papers bearing the approval of the Sec of War. I have telegraphed Gen Palmer to direct him to furnish us with wood &c till I can get this <u>kink</u> out of this piece of red tape. Capt. R does not refuse to furnish transportation according to your order but wishes the question of transportation settled with the other points in the order — , and is hesitating and reluctant enough to lock the wheels of my machinery here. I now have some four, or five hundred persons ready to leave, but I must delay till I hear from you. I can clear out this camp on the double quick — if I can have what you have intended me to have "Transportation for all". It has occurred to me that you might get the Sec of War to put this matter at rest by an order covering the case —

Among other changes since my return I have found it necessary to remove Mr. Fee from all connection with the day school. The other changes are such as you indicated.

You will understand that Capt. Restieaux Q.M. Camp Nelson, on the authority of the order referred to (No 49) declines doing anything for us, in his department till the Sec of War approves. He does not seem unkind about it — but thinks this necessary for his protection *

J.F. Jaquess, Col & Supt Lext Sub Dist. Freedmens Bureau[1]

Freedmens Home Camp Nelson   Sept 11th 65

P.S.

General I have this moment word from home, to the effect that my interest in money matters, to the amount of several thousand dollars — in mortgage in my favor — requires my immediate attention and presence. I have concluded to go at once instead of waiting till the 20ᵗʰ as I spoke of to you. I can attend to this item of business, and my Committees too and be absent only some three or four days — will be here in time to receive your reply. *

J.F. Jaquess Freedmens Home &c ²

1. Jaquess to Fisk, 9 Sept. 1865; M999:7:1449–51; RG 105.
2. Jaquess to Fisk, 11 Sept. 1865; M999:7:1453; RG 105. Although a clerk filed the postscript as a separate letter, it is an addition to that of 9 Sept.

Camp Nelson Ky   Sept 10 1865
Rev Geo Whipple

Dear Bro   You see from the date of my letter that I am here in this supposed home for the oppressed. I came here because I would have my daughter, my little son with me & because bro Fee was an old acquaintance of my childhood.

But bro Whipple I must tell you how pained I have been & still am at the unchristian, ungentlemanlike treatment which not only I but bro Fee receives every day from a man said to be a baptist minister in Holden Mass, Rev Lester Williams. All he can do he has done to injure Bro Fee in the estimation of this poor people & the teachers also, & I am sorry to say some of the teachers were pretty apt scholars, & speak of him as "old Fee" Their great hostility to me is owing avowedly to my friendship for Bro Fee. * * * *¹ [*Two paragraphs.*]

. . . [*Fee*] paid a visit last week to his family living in Berea, & during his absence Mr Williams wife came. She tried to influence Belle to leave stating it must be very unpleasant to be here when there was such a feeling & under such treatment. Belle told her that Mrs Colton & Miss Smith treated her well, but none of the others spoke to her, that if she could not board in this house she would rather go home as she knew her mother would not wish her to board out among the freed people as Mrs Williams had proposed.

Mrs Vincent told Col Jacques that several times the colored girls had told Belle to wait but she would not. I told him I had heard those messages delivered & always as coming from Mrs. Vincent, & once with the threat if she came to breakfast she would have Col Jacques order her out of the room. I am thus full & explicit for I feel she was deeply wronged. At last they told her in a note that she was not needed, when one of the teachers was sick, one going to leave, & scholars in the camp sufficient to employ six or eight teachers. Belle asked to stay until Mr Fee returned but Mrs Williams told her that he would have nothing more to do with the schools as she was Superintendent. So they made her leave offering to pay her fare in the stage Williams giving her the money. Dʳ Mitchell a surgeon here & Rev Mr Scofield wanted her to remain until a committee from Cincinnati should come

& examine into such arbitrary proceedings, but the poor girl was afraid   Mrs Williams claimes to have been sent out by your society, & is acting very perversely refusing to let Mrs Scofield or I teach (because we are friends of bro Fee) but she says because we don't acknowledge her authority — Bro Fee has his commission from Gen Fisk, while she has one from Col Jacques. I told her I did not think a Col had power to supercede one appointed by his Gen. She threatened to send for the negro guard to put me out of the school room if I did not leave. * * * * [*Two paragraphs.*]

Belle Mitchell left Monday yet Tuesday night they accepted invitations to eat supper with the colored people in their hall, & sat down with blacks on one side & the white on the other, to an excellent supper furnished by the blacks, & gave them permission to dance, which they did until almost if not quite midnight, & this in the hall where the Sabbath school & preaching is conducted.

I could say more & tell you how I have been treated, but I forbeare. I often think of our Oberlin life, & think of the strange changes in this lapse of years. I have had the great pleasure of seeing my soldier son at St. Louis on my way here. *

Mary Colton[2]

1. In the omitted passage, Mrs. Colton gives an account of the Belle Mitchell incident, very similar to both Fee's and Williams's.
2. Colton to Whipple, 10 Sept. 1865, AMAA 44196–9.

Camp Nelson Ky   Sept 15 /65

Dear Bro Strieby   I have yours of Sept 2[d]   I returned yesterday from Berea absent one week   I had two children very sick — had an appointment there to preach to the church   Marriage ceremony [for] my daughter[1] — came soon as apparent health of my child would admit

On arrival found Col Jacques had returned and by order had sent off Miss Bell Mitchell. . . . others had been sent off — Mrs. Colton . . . she took with her her daughter, Miss Smith[2] — We then needed teachers — Miss Mitchell, as I have told you, is slightly colored — features not African ("I speak as a fool") she was very exemplary in conduct. This lady, during my absence, Col Jacquess sent home — When she was advised by Mrs Williams to go, she declined.

When advised by Mrs Colton "to stay until Bro. Fee should come" Miss Mitchell replied "I must go   Col Jacques told me I must — to day (Saturday) or tomorrow" She told him she could not go saturday — clothing out to wash & that Sabbath she did not wish to use as a day of traveling!

On Monday Bell went home — This was not because her help was not needed as teacher * * * * [*Four paragraphs.*]

Miss Mitchell at time said to Mrs Williams there are scores of children yet in camp who could be gathered into school if we had teachers

During my absence Mrs Williams returned here and Col Jacques placed her as superintendent of the schools and this morning I have a note from his clerk saying Mrs Williams is placed as superintendent of the schools and you are therefore relieved from all further duty as superintendent of the schools" By order of Col Jas F Jacquess.

1 This "relief" can be for no offence but my refusal to remove that young lady after employed and already in the school & boarding house   No reason is given to me — My Commission or appointment is from Genl Fisk. I suppose Jacquess has instructions from Fisk   Jacquess has been to Nashville — is now gone again to Ill[inois]. He has left Mr Williams in command & this after telling me he believed the interests here required the removal of all & the putting in of other officers   Pilate & Herod made friends over the slain body of Jesus — Miss Mitchell

Since the removal of Miss Mitchell, the next night, Williams & wife, Mrs Daimon Bro Chapin, Cort,[3] all save Mrs Colton went into the common dining Hall for the colored people and there sat down white folks on one side & colored women on the other side & ate of the supper prepared   All right so far as eating with Colored people is concerned but why be so fastidious about entering in the same room with a nice tidy educated, christian young lady & then go into a greasy common dining Hall & eat with the uncouth.

It was a condescention to "niggers"

2 It was, after all drawing a line of whites on one side & niggers on the "tother" an invidious uniting that the poor creatures had not strength to resent.

There has been an invitation by one colored family to Mr Williams & Vincent & wife to go to a supper   The intention of this party was not to extend it to the caste feelers but to all the white folks including Mrs Colton with Bell Mitchell   But Bell was sent off before the party came off   It was the intention to have had Bell Mitchell in it   But I will stop this   I would not thus have written but the Western Freedmans Aid Society is likely to split over it so Bro Wheeler told me — he went to Cincinnati — Your society will be called upon — now is — to decide   Do you approve the act of your teacher & clerk in demanding the removal of the young lady from the table & the house

Do you approve the action of Col Jacquess in her removal and mine

Do you endorse the action of Mrs Williams

Is she sent back by your society to supersede me as superintendent of the schools   I say no until further informed   But an expression of your society is now needed   I learn by a line from Cincinnati that action of that society has been had with an exhortation to me to firmly maintain the position I have assumed under God. I intend so to do God helping me.

I cannot endorse such a school — its moral effect is now only a curse — a baptism of the spirit of cast — the lesson daily taught to each child — "after all, you are only niggers" My preaching cannot become a Tacit consent to this   I must therefore be in conflict with Jacquess — one or the other will probably leave   I must probably return to Berea shaking the dust off my feet against this conduct & thus teach the colored people to do the same or I must stand here and appeal to Genl Fisk & then to Genl Howard.

The work of superintendent of schools is one I do not desire for the <u>works</u>

<u>sake</u> — only as a means of doing good   would gladly have some one else have the place if that one was <u>morally</u> <u>right.</u>

If Jaquess is sustained I shall probably go to Berea   I have there a home for my family — none here — I proposed to come soon as requested by Bro Whipple   Capt Hall thought then he could not put up any more houses   Soon my wife was confined then we had to wait for growth of infant & adequate strength of mother for camp life. Then word came "break up the Refugee Home" Berea offers permanent growth for future & education for my sons with prospect for better health to myself & family

At present most children & parents here and I have the confidence of these people — so of those in Madison co — 5,000 there

I had an encouraging visit to Lexington spoke there three times — open door now in almost every direction   The highest success of the Berea School requires my effort for it — perhaps Bro Rogers may do the work   I hope to go where I can do most for Christs kingdom. *

John G Fee

Mrs. Colton will be removed from here. She doubted Jacquess right to place Mrs Williams in as superintendent. Mrs Colton & Mrs Williams were in the school room. Mrs Colton drew a stick — a turned pointer over Mrs Williams & told Mrs W she felt like "laming" her — that she "deserved it" Mrs Colton says this was after Mrs W threatened to put her first out with a Negro guard — Mrs Williams says it was before

It was unfortunate for Mrs Colton to have drawn the stick   I think she regrets it now   Tis constitutional to the family to be quick in resentment — <u>severe</u> in condemnation . . . .[4]

1. Fee's oldest child, his daughter Laura Ann, was married to William Norris Embree on September 12, 1865, at her parents' home in Berea. Of course, Fee performed the ceremony himself. One of Fee's sick children was his eldest son Burritt, who had been forced to stop teaching at Camp Nelson and return to Berea. He would die of tuberculosis in a few years.
2. Mrs. Colton's daughter and fellow teacher, Anna Smith, returned to Camp Nelson and married a white officer of a colored regiment, 1st Lt. William H.H. Musick of Company H, 119th U.S. Colored Infantry. *OAR,* 8:300, 305; *RAGK.*
3. G.W. Cort was a clerk at the Refugee Home.
4. Fee to Strieby, 15 Sept. 1865, AMAA 44202–3.

Colored Refugee Home Camp Nelson Ky.   Sept. 15 1865.
Rev. M.E. Strieby

Dear Sir, After an absence of some weeks, with recruited health, I have returned to this place and engaged again on duty. I was, last week, reinstated by Col. J.F. Jaquess Supt. of Lexington subdistrict Freedman's Bureau, as Supt. of schools at this Home. As such, do you wish from me any report of the schools? If so, will you state what? — Mrs. Caroline Damon, a teacher here, under appointment by the Am. Miss. Ass. informs me that she now receives twenty dollars per month, as do other young ladies here, commissioned by the W.F.A. of Cincinnati. This being true, my own pay, I take it for granted, will be, at least, as much. If so, be pleased to inform me. *

A.E.W. Williams[1]

1. Williams to Strieby, 15 Sept. 1865, AMAA 44205.

Camp Nelson Ky   Sept 20 /65

Dear Bro Whipple   I have as yet no answer from your society on the cast question   I do not expect to change my position —

I shall expect to be in moral antagonism with Col Jaquess the military Superintendent, also with Rev L Williams who demanded of me that I withdraw the young lady from the table & the house & also with Mrs Williams, now placed as superintendent of schools in lieu of myself — also with such teachers as they will sustain —

The society at Cincinnati may refuse to furnish them teachers — (no report yet).

Of the teachers then here employed by your society, Mrs Daimon & Bro Chapin (clerk) lent their names to the paper asking that the young lady be withdrawn from the table & the house   I do not think either of them would have done so but for the influence of Col Jaques & Rev L Williams. * * * * [One paragraph.]

Burritt H Fee was here teaching for a few weeks. He did not yield to the cast spirit — Bro Wheeler was here — not stout enough for the farm — was for the school — did great good as principal — taught also regularly — the full time — 6 hours — only four taught now — in 24   Bro Wheeler did not yield — did good.

The world needs to be converted, not to Methodism or Presbyterianism or Baptistism, but to principle — to Christ the personification of all principle; and the man or society that [elevates?] hold[s] up the right principle — a correct standard by which the world shall be converted does an infinite good to the world. * * * * [Three paragraphs.]

And is it best to have the proposed normal school for the state — (colored children) — in connection with the Freedmans bureau — or independent of the government authorities? Are we not liable continually to be trameled by "state"

What do you say — you can answer very briefly — you have as yet no secretary at Cincinnati and time for action is here — the camp is to be broken up — so says paper command & winter is close at hand —

J G Fee

You asked me last spring to come here. I did so. Capt Hall could not then furnish me a house — soon my wife was to be confined — she could not then come until hot weather over   then order to break up — I must go to my sons — my family or they to me —

I mean I must act thus soon — soon as interests to Christs Kingdom will allow — I want to settle what that is   *

J G Fee

Is the Bureau such that we can trust it? We cannot Id guess.[1]

1. Fee to Whipple, 20 Sept. 1865, AMAA 44207.

Camp Nelson Ky   Sept 23 1865.
Rev. M.E. Strieby

Dear Sir, I have learned to day, that there has been statements made in regard to affairs at the Refugee Home, Camp Nelson, that are utterly false, and as a teacher employed here by the Am. Miss. Association I deem it my duty to defend myself, as best I can. I will simply state the facts in regard to the charges made without the slightest tinge of coloring.

1st. Dancing is spoken of. I came here upon the opening of the Home, have remained here without the absence of a single day, until the present time.

I do not dance myself, and have never seen any dancing since I came.

One evening a gentleman who is an amateur performer upon the violin was playing a Waltz and one of the young ladies in the most innocent manner skipped upon the Hall floor with one of the boarders. Some minds "strain at a gnat & swallow a camel."

2d. Refusing to sustain & encourage Miss Belle Mitchell, in her efforts here to improve and educate her race. As far as I am concerned, I told Mr. Fee before she came that there could not possibly be the slightest objection to her coming, and told him also, I would teach her out of my school hours — if she would come to my room — as I had been teaching a Mrs. Taylor in the same manner, who was superior in many respects to the colored people here. I had none other than the purest sympathy for her, but for reasons which seemed best at the time I did place my name upon a petition to have her board with her friends in Camp. I still think as I always have that Miss Belle Mitchell ought to be assisted and encouraged in every possible way in her efforts to rise above the mass of the Colored people. If you doubt my interest in the people here, and in my school particularly, I do not know how I could convince you otherwise. If I knew how to do it I certainly would try, for I am grieved and pained after spending so much strength and affection, even upon my scholars, and many others with whom I come in contact, that I should be so grossly misrepresented. I have had, almost every discipline as I supposed that I could have, but I can truly say the 5 months I have spent in Camp Nelson have been one constant discipline, and such an one as I never had before. I hope I may profit by it. *

Carrie Damon.[1]

1. Damon to Strieby, 23 Sept. 1865, AMAA 44209.

Letterhead.] *U.S. Sanitary Commission, Soldier's Home. Camp Nelson, Ky.,* **Sept 26 1865**

Dear Bro Strieby   Last evening a letter came from some one of your association saying teachers who had had complicity in the matter of expelling Miss Bell Mitchell would not retain commission from your Assoc. This is substantially what Mrs Daimon told me.

Also that there was a complaint from some one connected with this Home that there were "regular dancing parties here" — that she supposed I had given such information.

I think I did not make the impression that there were "regular dancing parties here."

I think I spoke of Miss Jones having danced or waltzed across the Hall with Mr Livermore. Probably also that Miss Hager[1] had danced — so informed by one of the servants.

This I narrated (if I am the informant) in reference to Mrs Colton's rebuke of the young ladies for their late frolicking. Perhaps I ought to have retained a copy but to literally rewrite is labor & time. Perhaps Bro Wheeler is the informant. Will you ask a clerk to send to me so much of my letter as appertains to the dancing? — if I wrote about dancing.

Mrs Williams came into Mrs Daimons room last evening whilst we were talking and in a very excited manner asked if I thought she had taken any part in having Miss Mitchell removed   I told her from what I had been informed, I was constrained to believe she had — that she had urged Mitchell to go out into the cottages to board — then to go home   Mrs Williams claims that Bell came to her for council & she sympathised with her and advised her to go out into the cottages — Mrs Williams asked me to state this in writing to you. I gave her the note she will send

Now if Mrs Williams has no objections to sitting in the same dining hall where a colored lady sits, she has this from a conviction to do so is right. She should then have sought to have the other young ladies do right & not have Bell Mitchell yield to an indignity & disgrace; for so far as their conduct is concerned Bell is disgraced in all this country and it is understood that Mr & Mrs Williams were active in trying to get her away and yet needing help and did on the next Monday solicit help   I have written to Miss Mitchell to give her statement. If Mrs Williams did not try to get her away I shall rejoice   Mrs. Colton who was here says she did

Mrs Williams with much feeling (and repeatedly) said to me, "You brought the young lady" (Miss Mitchell) "into this trouble" So did Moses some of his friends — Christ his — Paul his — or rather was the occasion — It was the enemies of right that made the trouble.

I think Mrs Daimon is more kind in spirit than Mrs Williams.

Mrs. Daimon has been very exemplary usually — is our best teacher in her school room — is not active in prayer meetings — not demonstrative as many but is faithful in her school room. I told her kindly, in the conversation, which she sought, that I thought she did wrong in three respects

1 In not making an advance to speak to and encourage the embarrassed stranger

2 In staying away from the dining room until after Miss Mitchell was done eating

3 In joining in the petition requesting Miss Mitchell to be withdrawn from the house & the table

I told her I did not think she would have done so had she not been influenced by others   she will have a chance to repent & restore if she is willing.

Last evening Louisville Press brought the published account of the arrest of our Superintendent Coll Jaquess for complicity in a case of abortion & consequent death in 8 hours of his paramour or "mistress" a "Georgia woman." He left here on pretence of going to his family in Ill[inois] went to Louisvill wrote back he was sick there — He was arrested by the police in the work of procuring abortion[2]

God will defend his poor yet — We only need to stand still & see the salvation of God

A carrier is waiting

J G Fee

This Coll Jaquess is the Coll who went with Gillman to see Jeff Davis[3] — is a Methodist Preacher preached here

I send you a copy of the petition which the others sent to me   Miss Smith says she did not sign it   I did not   Miss Mitchell did not   Bro Wheeler did not   Bro Blakeman did not[4]

1. Annie Hager, resident of Springfield, Ohio, was an unmarried Swiss-American woman who arrived at Camp Nelson as a teacher for the WFAC. She was hired by the Freedmen's Bureau to clear out Camp Nelson and other establishments where freed people had assembled, such as Walnut Hill Home, a WFAC post in Cincinnati. After her work at Camp Nelson she taught in a freedmen's school in Shelbyville, Tennessee. In her letters, she frequently called herself "Hagar in the Wilderness of Camp Nelson."

2. Jaquess wrote to General Fisk on September 30 to protest his innocence. It was a tragedy, he stated, in which he was "by accident involved." The woman in question was Mrs. Lou C. Williams, whom Jaquess had met at Nashville, where she was a refugee (she was "very poor and drawing rations"). According to his account—extremely long and muddled—Jaquess happened to be in Mrs. Williams's hotel room when she died, and that was the reason he was arrested. He concluded by begging Clinton B. Fisk to come to his trial, perhaps to testify in his behalf (Jaquess to Fisk, 30 Sept. 1865; M999:7:1465–69; RG 105). Fisk replied that his engagements were such that he could not go to Louisville. "I hope you will be able to demonstrate your innocence <u>so clearly</u>," Fisk wrote, "that all the world will be compeled to acknowledge that you have been wrongly charged." He concluded (ironically?) by sending his regards to Jaquess's wife (Fisk to Jaquess, 3 Oct. 1865; M999:2:24; RG 105). The case was postponed, still pending on December 15, when Jaquess wrote to Fisk again, to ask if he would consider giving a position to "Rev. L Williams formerly of Camp Nelson—one of my witnesses, and an important one" (Jaquess to Fisk, 15 Dec. 1865; M999:7:1517–19; RG 105). I have made no effort to learn either the outcome of Jaquess's trial or of his plea for the employment of Rev. Lester Williams.

3. In the summer of 1865, Col. Jaquess and James R. Gilmore (Fee has his name wrong) had gone to Richmond, Virginia, on a peace mission, the second such mission for Jaquess; they intended to speak with President Jefferson Davis and call him to repentance, exhorting him to return immediately to allegiance to God and his country. The interview took place on July 17; Davis informed his pious visitors that "the South was fighting for freedom or annihilation." Jaquess, who publicized his interview with Davis as part of the presidential campaign of 1864, was something of a celebrity. *DAB,* 616.

4. Fee to Strieby, 26 Sept. 1865, AMAA 44210–1.

Col. Ref. Home Camp Nelson Ky   Sept 27ᵗʰ 1865
Rev. M.E. Strieby, Cor. Sec A.M. Ass.

My Dear Bro   I propose to write to you with entire frank[ness] though what I may say shall prove as unplea[sant] for you to read, as it will be for me to [present?] [*indecipherable*] him   I ought to have written before; & to re[frain] from doing so any longer will be a ma[jor] injustice to parties concerned. I refer to [the course] that has been pursued for months past by Mr [Fee.]

What I write, I write fearlessly, without fear [of con]sequences, for I shall <u>say</u> nothing but what [I can] easily prove. Mr Fee is a <u>falsifier, an [unmiti]gated falsifier</u>. There are young ladies here [who pla]ced the fullest confidence in him when they [came] who have now so found out his character, [as I] have stated, to my certain knowledge, they [can]not possibly believe his unsupported word. [He is in] the habit of dealing with falsehood as if it [were] on equality with the truth. This is only the simple [truth, surpris]ing as it may sound. In July four young ladies [came] here as teachers under the auspices of the Western [Freed. Aid] Com. Two reached here on Thursday, & two on Friday   [On the] first Sunday after, in the morning, before [meeting?] he went to the rooms of two & made, very [confi]dentially, false & slanderous statements in re[ference] to three other persons here, to whom they [were] strangers, yet with whom they must nec[essa]rily associate, & succeeded in prejudicing; & [poiso]ning their minds against the three, so that [after] he left, believing that he spoke the truth, [tal]king it over, they concluded they never should [get] to know them. From that room he went to [that of] the other two & went through the same ma[licio]us work. In the lapse of time eyes were [grad]ually opened to the real character of all parties. [They] began to see for themselves, & put different things side by side, & compare them. They at length found [they] had been deceived; & not merely so in that one respect, but in various ways at other times. Finally, after weeks had passed the truth was revealed. When Mr Fee was confronted with his mis[state]ments he denied them. When he was brought before [the p]arties to whom he had made them, he denied them again, until they were so clearly arraye[d against] him that he could do it no longer; when [he sud]denly shifted, & took the ground that what [he had] said was all true! Other histories of [like] character with this might be related when he [has told] <u>absolute falsehoods, wholly fabricated</u>

Mr Fee is a treacherous & hypocritical man [who pro]fesses friendship to the face & maligns behind [the] back. He has gone from one person to ano[ther in] this spirit, with insinuating words he has s[tabbed the] hearts of his neighbors here, broken their peace [*indecipherable*]rassed [embarrassed? harrassed?] their minds. Last winter when Bro [Vet]ter was associated with me in connection with [freed?] people & Home, Mr Fee was anxious to displace [him.] He conceived this plan. A Mr Butler was in charge of the Soldiers Home at that time. He would oust Mr Butler from his place & remove Bro V. into it. His [method?] was to talk with Capt [Hall] about it. He then [told?] Bro. V. about it, saying he had talked with Capt. Hall concerning it. Bro. Vetter told him he had not [been told] of the plan, & did not care for it. All the [time] he was the <u>professed friend of both</u>! At the same time he was talking against the Soldiers Home, & its [admin]istration to Bro. V. & others, & associating familiarly with Mr Butler & was invited to his table!

[He wi]ll propose an interest in you, & make you [thin]k he is a fond friend to you to your face, [and a]t the very same time he will stab you under [the short?] rib, or is proposing to do so. There are those [tha]t dread to come in contact with the man [lest?] some smart should follow somewhere at [some] time. The household has been, & is in the [unha]ppy condition of anticipating some unknown [pre-scribed?] disturbance & trouble arising from his course of conduct, yet not known, from what [mat]ter, or how, or when it will come.

[Al]l that I have narrated I have only given for [*indecipherable*] instances of what he has done, to tell the [whole] of which would occupy hours.

[After] all this, you may exclaim, "I cannot believe it. [I do] not believe it." Nevertheless, that does not change [the] fact. You have known him for years, & he has [been] your agent, & you had never learned anything [about] this before. Very well. The <u>whole, & more</u> [can be] proved. I would rejoice in the thorough proving [of the] whole matter, & it would be well if a [*indecipherable*] & suitable person was commissioned to do it. [The] man ought to be known as he is; & that he is a [*indecipherable*] liar I have not the shadow of a doubt. *

Lester Williams Jr.[1]

1. Williams to Strieby, 27 Sept. 1865, AMAA 44212. This letter has a large blot running the vertical length of one side of every page, which accounts for the unusual number of readings supplied in brackets.

Nashville   Sept 28th [*186*]5
Bvt. Brig Genl W W Barrett[1]   Supt at Camp Nelson Ky.

General: You have been ordered to assume the supervision of the Colored Refugee Home at Camp Nelson Ky and will at once enter upon the discharge of your duties.

The Home <u>must</u> <u>be</u> <u>closed</u> <u>out</u> and your energies will be directed to this end.

On and after the 15th proximo the issue of rations except to the few who may then be in Hospital will <u>entirely</u> <u>cease</u>.

Neither Refugees nor Freedmen will be admitted to the Home after this date.

You will make every practicable effort to find good homes and employers for the inmates either within or beyond the limits of the state of ky.

The Post Quarter Master at Camp Nelson will be authorized to honor your requisitions for transportation.

The Western Freedmens Aid Commission in Cincinnati will give good aid in securing homes.

You will at once make any changes in the force of workers at the home that good order and [*indecipherable*] efficiency may demand.

Proceed with vigor economy & humanity.

Let the requirements & pleadings of no man woman or child deter you from the necessary work.

Let <u>daily</u> reports of the operations of removal be made here at my office   *

Clinton B Fisk   Brig Genl   Asst Comr

Official Copy respectfully provided Capt R E Farwell Supt &c for his information
Jno. H. Cochrane   Maj 101ˢᵗ U.S.C.I.[2]

1. Wallace W. Barrett, Union officer from New York, began his military service in Michigan, but became a captain in the Forty-fourth Illinois. He was breveted as a brigadier-general for his war services at Stones River, Chickamauga, and Peach Tree Creek. After serving for a brief time as superintendent of the Refugee Home at Camp Nelson, he left to work for the Freedmen's Bureau elsewhere. *CWD; HR,* 1:194.

2. Cochrane to Barrett, 28 Sept. 1865; M999:2:79–81; RG 105.

Colored Refugee Home   Camp Nelson Ky   Sept 28ᵗʰ 1865.
Rev. George Whipple   Cor. Sec.

Dear Sir, Your letter of the 20ᵗʰ Inst is received. I read it, I must confess, with much supprise & not a little indignation. I will note the various points of your letter.

You say you cannot find any report of my labors either as Supt. or as a teacher. In answer, I will say I made two reports in full of what I had done here with all needful statements concerning the schools sending them to Mr. Strieby. These reports were for May & June. * * * * [*Three paragraphs.*]

I was appointed, as early as Feb. by a letter to Capt Hall, as mistress of the household & Supt. of schools. With this appointment, I left home the 13ᵗʰ of March, to enter upon the work. During March, I occupied much of my time in writing letters for this people, visiting them in the wards &c. At the same time I boarded a mile from this Home, & continued there till April 24ᵗʰ as the family house was not ready to enter till then. I never made any charge for service during March, nor yet for board till Apr 24ᵗʰ though paying five dolls. per week for it.

When Rev. E. Davis was here in Apr. it was thought by him & Capt. Hall that to be matron of the household & have charge of the schools would be too much for one person, & the duty was divided & I retained the latter.

You say that Mr. Fee has been appointed to the oversight of schools. I will say that the courtesy has never yet been accorded to me of informing me before of the fact or that I was relieved of that duty.

You arraign me for mistreatment & injury done to Miss Mitchell, a colored teacher employed here. I scorn the implication, Sir. I arrived here on Thursday P.M. Miss M. left here the first Monday after. During those three or four days, I defy anyone to prove that I treated Miss M. otherwise than with entire respect. My whole bearing toward her & conversation with her, was such as I would give a sister or ask for a sister. Furthermore I will add that I am probably as rabid and consistent an abolitionist as yourself. Further, I feel that I have been grossly and shamefully misrepresented by some person or persons, & I request to know by whom & what.

Now, Sir, in conclusion, I hereby lay down all connection with the Am. Miss. Asso. *

A.E.W. Williams[1]

1. Williams to Whipple, 28 Sept 1865, AMAA 44213.

Freedman's School located at Camp Nelson, Ky.
Taught by Caroline Damon

Report for the month ending Sept. 30, 1865

No. Enrolled	66
Average attendance	
Under 6 years age	12
In A.B.C. Class	18
In Reading & Spelling	48
Mental Arithmetic	15

1. Number of days taught during month   20
2. Number of days lost during month   0
3. Number of hours engaged in school daily   usually   5
4. Number of hours instructed in sewing during month
6. Is singing taught in school?   It is.
7. In what branches do the advanced scholars show greatest proficiency?   In Reading & Spelling
8. Do mulattoes manifest more capacity than Blacks?   My experience thus far, is, that mulattoes manifest more capacity than Blacks.

My school is constantly changing. People go from Camp & take their children just as they are learning rapidly, which makes it exceedingly discouraging for a teacher. The average attendance however is very commendable. Often being for the week 62 — 58 — 59 &c. *

Carrie Damon.[1]

1. Damon's monthly school report, 30 Sept. 1865, AMAA 44214. This report is written out by hand in imitation of the regular printed form.

[*Letterhead.*] *U.S. Sanitary Commission*   **Camp Nelson Ky**   **Sept 30 1865**

Bro. Strieby   Genl Fisk has been here — is very kind — expressed great confidence in me personally — wished me to go on with the idea of a normal school for Ky — He was more favorable to Berea than this place — That is not central as this — to colored people   He was anxious to break up this camp within 17 days — advised that I say nothing about Miss Bell Mitchell case — "let it go now." I do not know how he feels about the question of "caste" . . . . Miss Bell Mitchell came here yesterday   She went to the dinner table with Anna Smith — daughter of Mrs Colton

Genl Barret the new Superintendent called for her, Anna Smith & myself after dinner — said to Miss Mitchell "You cannot come to the table when I am here" Other things were said. I think we have evidence that our schools, as suggested before, must be free from Government officials.

If we have a school here as well as at Berea I must go out and raise ten or twenty thousand dollars & buy lands here & resell to friends — take proceeds for the school, or let Bro Scofield go along with a small school & work its way along and I retire to Berea & let these buildings go   The schools will be cut short here now.

Your society has acted promptly & decisively in reference to treatment of Miss Mitchell all right. Mrs. Daimon, our teacher, is hopeful. Day before yesterday a committee was out here from Cincinnati (Coffin & Sawyer) and required their teachers to sign a paper declaring they would not make complexion a condition of association among teachers. This was wormed out after a long time of working.

Mrs Daimon your teacher here came forward and <u>volunteered</u> her name   I regard her as hopeful a most estimable lady an excellent teacher — In teaching she surpasses any we have here

Let me here remind you that I did not send for Bro Scofields two daughters who are now here . . . . * * * * [*Three paragraphs.*]

Hattie is a good sort of girl not a professed christian but quite serious & kind — is small — Mary is quite young & hearing not good   Hattie will do very well with her mother present to govern   The three will make two perhaps

Bro. Scofield has his time now very much engrossed as claim agent. He will soon have paper made out for 100 persons. The law allows him $10 on each. He now takes 50 cents & if they succeed he will probably take 5 dollars — He is doing good. Might do more if he were preaching during the week — he preaches every sabbath — is industrious.

J G Fee[1]

1. Fee to Strieby, 30 Sept. 1865, AMAA 44216–7.

Camp Nelson Ky   Oct 1st, 1865.
Rev. Geo. Whipple

Dear Sir, Yours of Sept. 23 has been received. I will admit I was surprised. I am thirty years of age, and in all the Boarding Schools that I have attended, and Schools that I have taught, I never had such a reprimand before. I have tried to faithfully do my duty since I came here, not, with John G. Fee's help, but with the help of God. Gen. Fiske has been here, together with two of the officers of the board of the Western Freedmen's Aid Commission. A thorough investigation of affairs was the result of their coming. I have permission to refer to the officers of the board in writing to you. But it seems you have lost confidence in my uprightness and therefore I shall ask you to correspond with them in regard to the matter, in order that the Board may obtain satisfactory information in regard to Miss Belle Mitchell. Other information you have had too, touching my character. It is more than I can bear patiently. Gen. Fiske, Mr. Levi Coffin & Mr. Sawyer understand me fully, and my motives for doing as I have done.

I feel that an expression of thanks is due you, for the promptness with which you have replied to my bills for services.

From the date of this letter, I withdraw from any further connection with the American Missionary Association. *

Mrs. Caroline Damon[1]

1. Damon to Whipple, 1 Oct. 1865, AMAA 44220.

Gen. Fisk   Levi Coffin suggests to Genl Barrett a change and in view of that change in present superintendence of schools, what do you expect me to do — even if the schools shall continue but one week they may two — Do you expect me to assume former response & care of the schools Yr

J G Fee

I shall, in good faith help break this camp   J G F[1]

1. Fee to Fisk, 2 Oct. 1865; M999:7:235; RG 105. No date or place appears on this letter itself, but the date of receipt was October 2, 1865, from Camp Nelson. It was very uncharacteristic for Fee to omit the date and place, but this whole letter is unusual because it was written in a huge, scrawling handwriting in pencil on a sheet of paper that might have been ripped from a child's tablet. Given the appearance of this little sheet of correspondence, Fee must have been very nearly out of control at this point.

Camp Nelson, Ky., Oct. 2, 1865
Rev. George Whipple New York

Dear Sir, Yours of 23 Inst. came duly to hand, but as investigation of the object of your inquiries was at hand by Gentlemen representing the Western Freedmen's Aid Society, I waited at reply until the result of this investigation was made known.

It is closed and the gentlemen (Levi Coffin & Bro. Sawyer) have gone to lay the investigation before the board.

We think they left perfectly satisfied that the actions of all that signed the request for the removal of Miss Mitchell were not only justified but that the circumstances were such that it was demanded of them —

My own object in signing the request was that peace might be restored in this household. I saw at once that the presence of the table caused unpleasant feelings. Many of the boarders refused to come to the table at all — I therefore entreated Mr. Fee to allow Miss Mitchell to board in one of the Cottages occupied by Miss Mary Turner, a Lady far superior to Miss M. in general appearance and natural abilities, but my entreaties were vain. He seemed determined after thrusting her into the mess to keep her there, let the result be what it may. Not one of the others was counciled in regard to the matter, except Col. Jaquess & Mr. Vincent. It was Natural that, under such circumstances, some should refuse to come to the table.

Her Color was no objection to any one, so far as I can learn. Her conduct, which was exemplary so far as I know, was no objection, simply the manner in which she was thrust into the family, that and that alone, was the objection with all, I believe, except myself.

The whole subject has been thoroughly investigated by our Ohio friends and I presume you will soon hear from them the facts in the case. There are other matters that need investigation at this Home and I wish it might be had. *

J.C. Chapin[1]

1. Joseph C. Chapin to Whipple, 2 Oct. 1865, AMAA 44221. This letter is so faint that it is impossible to see whether punctuation marks are present or not.

For the Am. Missionary[1]
[Letterhead.] U.S. Sanitary Commission <xthru>~~Soldier's~~</xthru> *Refugee Home   Camp Nelson, Ky.,* Oct. 2[d], 1865

Dear Bro Whipple — Fifteen months since I came to this camp. I came to encourage & help the soldiers, especially the colored men of our state, who were then enlisting and needed an instructor and a comforter.

At the suggestion of Capt T E Hall I organised schools for the instruction of non commissioned officers in the various colored regiments. We soon had a large school — some thirteen teachers at one period. The schools were ultimately extended to privates and to children — Hundreds of these soldiers were instructed. A considerable number learned not only to read, but also to write, and now, from the army in Texas, send letters to their families and friends in this Camp.

A church was organized — "Church of Christ at Camp Nelson Ky". Some eighty one names have been enrolled of those who here have professed faith in Christ, and received as such. Thousands have attended the regular sabbath preaching.

Many sermons and addresses have been delivered by Bro Scofield and myself in the different regiments during the week — between sabbaths.

Many copies of the the New Testament have been distributed to such soldiers and children as could read — Tracts & papers without number.

At the solicitation of friends a Refugee Home was prepared in part of this camp, separate from the soldiery. Here were erected four large wards, dining hall, school building containing seven rooms, ninety seven cottages, two rooms in each, sixty government tents and fifty cabins erected by the colored people. Into these tenements many thousands of women and children came — at one time there were here 3060 colored persons. To these thousands the gospel has been regularly preached every sabbath, and many times during the week. Many persons male and female have been instructed as to their duty to government and as to what government is doing for them ~~would likely do for them~~. Many souls have been ~~instructed and~~ made to stir with new hope, and renewed efforts for good.

Within this Refuge Home there has been a school organized chiefly for the education of the children within this Refugee Home. In this school more than six hundred children have been regularly taught & quite a number are now reading — able to read the New Testament, copies of which have put into the hands of such.

Much of this time of instruction I have had a daily watch care over these children in the school rooms. I do not believe any class of children learn ~~more~~ faster than these — few schools of white children so good in behaviour. Submission has been the habit of their lives. When kind sympathizing teachers ask this submission it is readily yielded.

Just at this time, when much apparent good is being done, an order comes from the War Department requiring this Refugee Home to be broken up. But the labor of love will not be lost. These children will carry their books and a knowledge of letters wherever they shall go. These parents will carry sentiments and truths which shall comfort their hearts and mould their lives, wherever they shall be cast. Yours

John G Fee

[*All of the foregoing was included in the* American Missionary's *publication of this letter, but none of what follows:*]

One thing has chilled the hopes of many of these people and some of their friends here. A teacher slightly colored qualified, and of exemplary character, was employed, but was constrained to leave by the action of a part of the teachers, and the superintendent. This action has been reaffirmed by a second superintendent one in place of the former. Whether such action will be approved by Genl Fisk and Genl Howard we cannot now tell. If they do then benevolent societies who purpose to treat all persons civilly must keep free from the Freedmans Bureau

J G Fee

(Private)

Bro Whipple if you think it wise to draw out the Freedmans Bureau <u>over me</u> you append to my article that which I have briefly written concerning Miss Mitchell — colored teacher. If you prefer not to do so omit what I have sent on that different sheet. Mrs Colton may send you a similar statement.

You may prefer to write to Genl Fisk or Genl Howard yourself & thus feel them privately. I think the Bureau ought to express itself clearly some way

John G Fee

The article I send is a general outline of work here   I thought you & your readers might desire such so as to know what has been done — J G F[2]

1. This directive appears in Fee's own handwriting at the top of this manuscript.
2. Fee to Whipple, 2 Oct. 1865, AMAA 44223–7; the shortened version is in *AM* 9, no. 11 (November 1865): 246, 247.

Camp Nelson Ky.   Oct. 3, 1865.
Rev. Geo. Whipple

Dear Sir, Yours of the 29th is just received, in which you ask me "to take an early opportunity to reply to your enquiries." In a letter from you dated Sept 23, you say "our rules require that we should not sustain teachers who refuse proper respect to others." I felt at once I was censured by you for an act that I did not consider very heinous at the time. I will here say I had no ill feelings towards Miss Belle Mitchell on account of her color or position as teacher. I will confess, any person could have spoken kindly to me and I should not have thought of placing my name upon any petition.

Compulsion in acknowledging Miss Mitchell as an equal, was the only reason I did <u>as</u> I did. I do not say I did right, or, that I should do the same again. It will be very difficult for you to understand the thing in all its bearing. I sincerely wish you could have been present at the investigation by the W.F. Aid Commission *

Caroline Damon.[1]

1. Damon to Whipple, 3 Oct. 1865, AMAA 44228.

Camp Nelson Ky   Oct 4 1865
Rev. M.E. Strieby, Sect., A.M.A.

My dear Sir, I left Cin[ti] yesterday P.M. hoping to come thro' to Nicholasville last night & ride over early this mor[n]g — but the train came only to Lexington. This mor[n]g I spent in prospecting <u>that</u> town as a possible field for Missy labor. There are five <u>pay</u> schools already in the town $1.25 per mo. tuition — about 275 or 300 pupils in all — leaving a large number of children out of school who are not able to pay — especially soldiers children. A large number of soldiers families have moved into the town. The col[d] people had a "mass convention", as a Baptist preacher told me, a few days ago & appointed a com[ee] to take measures to open a free school for these poor children — He says they will find a room for the school if a teacher can be procured — Wants a col[d] teacher on acc[t] of the noise that might be raised if a white teacher sh[d] come.

On coming here I have heard no little of Belle Mitchell — the teacher secured by Mr. Fee for this Camp & sent off by the negrophobic combination of officers & teachers, among which latter I am sorry to find here some in our employ — Belle lives in Danville, 16 miles — I have arranged with Mrs. Colton, one of the teachers here (without employment for a few days) to go over to Danville & see if B. will go to Lexington & if she consents, to go to L. & make the necessary arrangements for her to go at once & open her school.[1]

The field in L. is an attractive one & when affairs are less mixed in Ky. — that will be an important point to make I think. The five teachers there are of the crudest sort &, if the little fellers were not bent on learning <u>whether or no</u>, would amᵗ to <u>nothing at all.</u> Rev James Monroe's school, which I visited this May, has 60 pupils — They had each a story & Spelling book & were all spelling out their words aloud. They were too busy to think of play in school & must make some progress spite of a very illiterate teacher.

I have ventured on this matter because it seemed to me feasible <u>now</u> & more easily accomplished in the way I have suggested than any other. I have spent the P.M. in looking over this Camp with Mr. Schofield — Mr. Fee is at his home in Berea —

A peremptory order has been recᵈ — to break this camp in 15 days — 30 at the longest — It will not be done, I think, for the reason that it cannot be done without creating scenes of suffering & positive cruelty, which I do not believe our govt. will be guilty of

The camp can & will be greatly reduced, probably down to 500 in the course of two months.

Mr. Schofield has fallen legatee to the "Sanitary" effects remaining at their breaking up & has quite a comfortable home for himself & family. Just now his wife is quite sick. His daughter is teaching a school at the Soldiers Home — an important school as Camp affairs are now — In the breaking process it may become unnecessary — Mr. S. has his hands & heart full with these poor things & is doing a good work — I give it as my judgement that it is not worth while for Mr Fee & Mr Schofield to be both employed at this camp, even if the camp continues at a considerable number — I shᵈ advise that Mr F's connection with the camp cease — That Mr. S. be left to work his way as best he can & accomplish what can be done amid these personal conflicts —

I have not seen Mr & Mrs Williams. They are out of town for a few days — My impression is that Mrs. W. ought not to be continued in the employ of the Assoⁿ — Her treatment of Belle Mitchell & her open opposition — both to Mr. Schofield & Mr. Fee are sufficient cause for dropping her.

Mrs. Damon has, I understand, sent in her resignation — to yr. office to day — If she has not I shᵈ advise that she be let go also —

This Camp has been a grand field for work, & I believe a grand work has been done, but Bro. Fee has managed to [brush?] every stump in the clearing — A man in charge with half his Zeal & double his discretion would have brought ten times the result. So it seems to me after listening to the history of Camp N. for the year past.

I think Mr. Fee's course of bringing Belle Mitchell unwise & the opposition to it <u>Shameful</u>.

Does not Mr Fs work at Berea come more in the line of the Home Missy than yours?

I sh^d think that after a little while more might be done in Lexington & something in Frankfort & perhaps other towns, especially if you can find competent Col^d teachers who can work their way without attracting much attention — But I do not think that either Mr. F. or Mr. S. is the man to open the work or superintend it — * * * * [Six paragraphs.]

Rev. Edwd P.Smith[2]

1. Belle Mitchell taught at one of the first Freedmen's Schools in Lexington under the auspices of the AMA.
2. Smith to Strieby, 4 Oct. 1865, AMAA 44229–32. Rev. Edward P. Smith, secretary of the AMA, had been a student at Oberlin Academy from 1852 to 1854. *Oberlin Register*, 384.

Camp Nelson Ky   Oct 9 1865.
Rev. G. Whipple

Dear Sir, Yours dated Oct 6th is received. I felt badly upon reading it. I might as well overcome my pride and confess that I am fully aware that I have done wrong & have felt so, since the moment I placed my name upon that petition for the removal of Miss Mitchell. You do not know, however, all I have had to contend with.

My proud spirit was broken too when I read "Those who refuse proper respect to others will not be commissioned by us."

I expected a dismissal from the Field. My pride rose again & I sent in my resignation. I supposed I was through at Camp Nelson, but the idea of giving up my pupils was exceedingly painful to me.

Therefore I am still teaching. If the Board of the A.M.A. will give their consent I would like to come under the W.F. Aid Association.

If not I shall teach without recompense. *

Carrie Damon.[1]

1. Damon to Whipple, 9 Oct. 1865, AMAA 44233.

Camp Nelson Ky   Oct 10th 1865

Rev. Geo. Whipple,

Acting under instructions from your Agt, a Mr Smith who recently visited this Camp, I have been to Danville &, after some persuasion gained the consent of the parents of Miss Belle Mitchell to allow her to remain under your auspices, & have taken her to Lexington to take charge of a free school for the children of col'd soldiers. I secured her board in the family of Mrs. Mitchell,[1] who also boarded the Methodist minister, at $16. per month. This is not high for Lexington. . . . Mrs Britton is willing to afford Belle every facility to do her own washing, & remarked she was willing to accommodate her for the good of their race. Mrs B is almost white, has a little girl[2] 12 years old, who is the most remarkable performer on the piano, & melodian I ever saw.

God speed the day when all <u>must</u> admit their capacity for development. Mrs B. said there would be a concert in Lex, (by the col'd people to build a room for a free school — this week. I hope they will be successful in the good work. *

Mary Colton

Mr Williams & Lady were in Louisville last week   Did not see bro Smith. He seemed surprised to find she still remained at the hed of the schools   Said the communication she re'cd was a virtual dismissal. The Gen Barrett who fills Jacquess place, is not much more of a friend to these poor people than he was   Williams is still here. I think Gen Fisk winked at a great wrong when he did not reinstate Bro Fee. But then Miss Mitchell would have been brought back & that would not suit these lady teachers.

They talk of sending us to Louisville.[3]

1. Mrs. Colton has "misspoken"; she means Mrs. Britton, not Mrs. Mitchell.
2. The little girl mentioned here was Julia Britton, who would attend Berea College, become its first African American teacher, and go on to become a founding member of the N.A.A.C.P. and the grandmother of Benjamin Hooks.
3. Colton to Whipple, 10 Oct. 1865, AMAA 44234.

Camp Nelson Ky.   Oct 11: 1865.
Rev. George Whipple

Dear Sir, Your last note is received. You say you supposed I was fully informed that Mr. Fee had occupied the position of Supt. of schools. I was informed that Mr. Fee had an appointment from Gen. Fiske, to take charge of the schools here at the Home during my absence, but I did not know, till I received your letter of Sept. 20th that the A.M.A. had appointed him to that work.

I left Mass. the 2nd of Sept. and have been engaged in duty since. My resignation bears date Sept 28th or 9th, therefore I enclose a report of the schools and bill for service during that month. Also a statement made by Miss Mitchell in the Office of the Home before witnesses, in reference to my conduct and language toward her while at this place.

I hope to labor among the Freed people here for the present, & with the consent of the A.M.A. would like to connect myself with another organization. Will you oblige by signifying your consent, as it is a matter of comity between Asso. that such should be done. *

A.E.W. Williams

Rev. George Whipple,

I hereby send you a report of the schools at this Refugee Home for the month of Sept.

Teachers	Whole no. enrolled for the month	Average attendance for the month
Caroline Damon	256	238 $^2/_5$
Ella M. Reed	262	186 $^2/_5$
Maria Balentine	181	165 $^4/_5$
Emma Jones	242	187 $^1/_5$
Anna Smith	263	201

Miss Balentine was in school only three weeks of the month on account of sickness. I had a class of 110 scholars from which I kept the schools filled to their maximum. The Home is being diminished and there is more or less change in the schools every day. *

A.E.W. Williams[1]

1. Williams to Whipple, 11 Oct. 1865, AMAA 44235–6.

Col[d] Ref. Home, Ky   Oct 13 1865

I hereby certify that I was present when a conversation was held between Mrs. Williams and Miss Mitchell. And Miss M. stated clearly and substantially as follows: Miss M. says that Mrs. W. told her that she was willing she should have a school and she would assist her all she could. That I had just as good right in the Parlor as any one else. Miss M. also asserted that Mrs. Williams always treated her with respect and always came to the table.

J.C. Chapin[1]

1. Joseph C. Chapin to whom it might concern, 13 Oct. 1865, AMAA 44238.

Chapter Seven

Closing The Camp

Camp Nelson Ky   Oct. 13th 1865
Genl C.B. Fisk

Dear Sir: I arrived here last evening. Have been engaged taking a <u>diagnosis</u> of this Case; hope I may be able to finish tomorrow

Mr Williams assures me that the patient is very low and has no doubt a <u>little</u> purging would do good but thinks my method of treatment will kill instead of cure   He says it is inhuman to break up the camp entirely & he would not do it ordor or no ordor.

I informed him that I had the ordor to close the concern and that the ordor and my own judgment & sense of duty were in perfect harmony and there would be a storm soon and advised him if he had any preparation to make not to <u>imitate men of Noah's day.</u>

I think he can be spared next week.

Will you be kind enough to send me an ordor for transportation like the one I took to Clarksville? In Ordor 138 there is this clause, "provided such transportation be confined by Ass^t Com's within the limits of their jurisdiction"   The Q.M. here wishes me to call your attention to the clause and ask how you construe it and for this reason <u>viz</u> many colored people who by the law of this state can be held as slaves wish to go north and he does not feel at liberty to send them beyond Covington   Capt Ransom wishes me to call your attention to the Freedom Camp fund which now amounts to $5600. dollars   Said he mentioned it to you, but perhaps you might have let it slip from your memory

It would be very handy to have some portion of it to use here

I know well it will take some funds to break this camp

The military men here believe it ought to be closed up but there have been so many attempts they have no faith now

I hope to be able to report progress by the <u>first of Nov</u>^l * * * * [*Two paragraphs.*]

You must not expect much the first week   There is a regular clique here at the camp who wish me back at Nashville and they are bound to play the dog in the manger   Williams does not know yet that I am here or rather does not appear to   I think he will find it out next week   This week I <u>diagnose</u> & <u>preach</u>. Next week I will have the rails laid and will off coat *

R.E. Farwell[2]

1. Farwell was mistaken. His report for November 1 (below) begins "I assure you the work of reducing this camp is not progressing. . . ."
2. Farwell to Fisk, 13 Oct 1865; M999:7:264–66; RG 105.

Camp Nelson Ky   Oct 14th 1865
Gen[l] Clinton B. Fisk   Asst Com R Frd Ab Lds[1]

I have the honor to forward a Telegram received by me this moment with request accompanying it that I would furnish transportation to Cin[ti] for the persons named. Please to instruct me as to duty in such cases

Kentucky is in a <u>perfect ferment</u> and if such cases are <u>to be</u> refered to me you will have to instruct me and clothe me with all necessary power but till I hear from you I shall act according to my best judgment under my appointment as Special Agt of the Bureau   I hardly know now which course to pursue whether it is best to retain the people where they are with a view to having their cause righted or whether it is best to send them on to Cin   I have not had any chance to consult any one and it is a new case

Now Martial law is not in force I expect a lively time and cases will continualy come up affecting the breaking up of this Camp   *

R E Farwell Spec Agt Bur R F & Ab Lds and
Supt Freedm Home Camp Nelson Ky.[2]

1. Assistant Commissioner of Refugees, Freedmen, and Abandoned Lands.
2. Farwell to Fisk, 14 Oct. 1865; M999:7:258–59; RG 105.

Camp Nelson Ky   Oct 14th 1865.
By Telegram from Nicholasville Ky   To Mr Frank Whiting

About fifty colored men women & children came here last night under the following circumstances   Their Master living in Casey County freed them and then rented a portion of his farm to them   They raised a crop and had just gathered it when one night last week they were ordered to leave in a hurry   The Cabins were then burned and they were ordered to leave in some wagons furnished for them   They are here without money and wish to go to Cincinnati   Can you not send an order for transportation?[1]

1. Telegram [sender unknown] to Whiting, 14 Oct. 1865; M999:7:260–61; RG 105.

[*Letterhead.*] *U.S. Sanitary Commission, Soldier's Home, Camp Nelson, Ky.,* Oct 14ᵗʰ 1865

Facts for the People
The Rights of the families of Colored Soldiers are not regarded in Kentucky.
Case No. 1.
Martha wife of Isaac Stephenson private of 124ᵗʰ U. Col Troops could not get her children from her master Lewis H Bryant of Crab Orchard. Her husband went with eight United States soldiers and took them by force
No. 2.
Matilda wife of John Brunson pri. of 6ᵗʰ U.S.Col. Cavalry after her husband enlisted, worked in the field all summer for her master Esq Brunson of Richmond Ky who then sent her off and her four young children without pay. He carried her within 20 miles of Camp Nelson and set them down on the road to shirk for themselves
No. 3.
Elias Ball of Danville sent up 3 of his slaves to Camp Nelson for the "Yankees to take care of" [*In a different hand someone has written in the margins:* Send these people back to Elias Ball] — The mother is old and lame — one boy was sick, unable to stand or walk and body reduced to a skeleton. They are here now in the Home, without clothing or comforts except as supplied by the hand of charity.
        These cases can be greatly extended and names and dates can be given.
                        A. Scofield Agent of A.M. Asscn. No 61, Whist, N.Y.[1]

Oct. 14ᵗʰ 1865
Facts for the People
1st. Civil Officers refuse to aid the wives of Colored Soldiers in securing their claims.
Case No. 1.
Sarah White, wife of Phillip White deceased Private 124ᵗʰ U.S. Col. Q, from Bath Co. went with her witnesses to certify to her claims before the Judge of the Court and Justice of the Peace. She says that they threattened to shut her up in Jail if she did not leave the county immediately. She left without getting her papers certified. It cost her some $10. to go and return. Under the law she is entitled to Bounty back pay and Pension. She has four dependent children and must have help or suffer
Case No. 2.
Ellen Woodson wife of David Woodson deceased private of 12ᵗʰ U.S. Col. H. Art., entitled to Bounty Back pay and Pension, went with the necessary papers and witnesses to Scott Co. The officers sent her away and would not swear her witnesses
Case No. 3.
        Lydia Weathers wife of Willis Weathers deceased Private 124ᵗʰ   Went to the County seat of Lincoln Co. to get her papers certified, the Judge executed the claim paper for pension, but the papers for arreas of pay and Bounty, the Justice refused to have any thing to do with. She returned with her papers unfinished and was compelled to go some fifty miles into another Co. to get her papers certified.

Fact. No. 4
Many of the Widows of Soldiers, and some fathers of deceased Soldiers, and some discharged soldiers when they learn that they must go to their old houses in order to perfect their claims, refuse to do anything about it, saying they rather lose their money than their lives.

These cases are quite frequent. These families are needy and will have to be aided in support unless their just dues can be obtained.

A. Scofield, Missionary[2]

Oct 18th
[*Accompanying the Scofield reports:*]
[*In one handwriting, scrawled on the side:*] Lawrence,

What can be done for poor old Kentucky? [*Followed by an initial, indecipherable*]

[*In a different hand:*] Oct 18th Gen   Would write a strong letter to his Excellency, Gov. Bramlette, asking him to give a Proclamation calling upon the civil officers to give such aid as the law requires them to give, and apprising them that neglect of their official duties, and outrages upon the widows of colored soldiers, such as are detailed in this paper, will be punished. If the Gov. will not take the matter in hand report it to <u>Congress</u> and the <u>People</u>.

Lawrence[3]

1. Scofield's "Facts for the People," 14 Oct. 1865; M999:8:1133–34; RG 105.
2. Ibid.; M999:8:1135–36; RG 105. The problem about claims was even greater than Scofield's letter reveals. According to a United States Sanitary Commission report, "A very large percentage of the people in the colored refugee camp had claims against the Government. Their husbands, sons and brothers had died or become disabled in the service; so, among the many demands for assistance which they honestly made upon us, were claims for back pay, bounty and pensions. For several months prior to the close of the Sanitary business at Camp Nelson this feature of our work assumed great importance and labor. . . . At least two hundred claims against the Government exist in the colored refugee camp, while from every section of the District the families of colored soldiers still come into camp to commence application for such dues" (Newberry, 529).
3. John Lawrence to General ?, 18 Oct. 1865; M999:8:1137; RG 105. Maj. John Lawrence was a Freedmen's Bureau agent who was eventually sent to "reconstruct" Scofield and inspect Camp Nelson.

Freedman's Home   Camp Nelson Ky.   Oct. 16th 1865

Gen. C.B. Fisk:
Sir: This Monday morning I began in earnest the work of closing out this camp, and have hoped all day that I would be able to make a very large reduction this week. I addressed the people yesterday, stated your wishes, and desires, and assured them that you have their best interests at heart, and tried to make them feel that while I would carry out your order with all the <u>energy at my command</u>, and <u>insist</u> that <u>all my assistants should contribute</u> their <u>full share</u> toward the same object, at the same time I would not forget to temper my action with <u>justice and mercy</u>

I told them that I would not forget to deal <u>kindly</u> and <u>gently</u> as possible with the old infirm and sick   The case was a peculiar one   I wish you had been here to see for yourself that great audience, and the way in which they received and responded to my message. Here they fled from bondage worse than death. There before me were tender women whose scared and mutilated backs attested the _infernal_ and <u>hellish spirit</u> of their masters, and as I beheld those <u>terrible badges</u> of slavery I felt that liberty was a priceless boon and cheap at any sacrifise

They were willing and ready to strike their tents and move on, but the blinding tears that filled their eyes and coursed down their cheeks showed was no light thing, and well they might think so, for some of them knowing that the camp must soon be closed had previously sought the old home in order if <u>possible</u> to bring away some dear child they had left behind, hoping that when the hour for closing the camp should come they might be ready to cross the Ohio and be forever beyond the lash of the tyrant: but what a reception! They were hunted & driven from the old home like savage beasts   Their masters were firing at them with their rifles.

Wives of Soldiers who have been freed by act of Congress cannot get their children and even their own freedom is contested at every step.

If I find a soldiers wife employment the old master claims the wages and men who are humane and kind dare not hire them for fear of litigation

All day since early morning I have been at work making up a company to send to Ohio and everything seemed favorable the people themselves doing everything they could to help the enterprise along, and as I have before said I was expecting to report great progress this week but I have just learned that the colored people free & bond are refused passage on the railroads.

I think there is no mistake about this but in the morning I shall send four or five to Nicholasville to test the thing & probably before this reaches you you will receive a telegram in regard to this matter

The conduct of the colored people is worthy of all praise: but <u>how can</u> I break up this camp under such circumstances   There is no such thing as enforcing your ordor by calling the military to my aid for Martial law has gone off as you know. The job is a hard one at the best and as matters <u>have been</u> [_Farwell left the sentence unfinished._]

I will keep at work, but I cannot think you would justify me if I should drive <u>free women & children</u> into <u>cruel bondage</u> while the <u>husband and father</u> is serving his country in arms   This state of things can't last. I hope you will not tire reading this long letter   I thought you would like these details   The company about which I wrote you got transportation left their own horses tied to the fence & went on to Ohio before I got to them   *

R.E. Farwell Supt Refugee Home Camp Nelson [1]

1. Farwell to Fisk, 16 Oct. 1865; M999:7:282–85; RG 105.

Camp Nelson   Oct. 16ᵗʰ 1865.
Rev. Geo. Whipple

Dear Sir, I left my home in Mass. for Camp Nelson the 17ᵗⁿ of Apr. I taught under the auspices of the A.M. Asso: until the 1st Oct. which would be about 6 months. Then according to your Circular I am entitled to a free transportation home. Camp is being rapidly broken up. My school will not be in operation many days longer when I suppose I will be obliged to go home. Will you please favor me with an early answer? *

Caroline Damon.[1]

1. Damon to Whipple, 16 Oct. 1865, AMAA 44239. After leaving Camp Nelson, Caroline Damon apparently found employment in other Freedmen's Schools in Augusta and Atlanta, Georgia. Swint, 181.

Oct 17th [*1865*]

Capt. R.E. Farwell   Supt. Camp Nelson Refugee Home

Dear Sir. In acknowledgement and reply to your communication of the 13th inst. would say that I trust the <u>diagnosis</u> is ere this taken and the patient receiving vigorous treatment.

I want no inhumanity visited upon any body — not even upon the Government — There may be some cases at Camp Nelson that will require aid — in some way — for a longer period than the Refugee Home can possibly survive — under my orders — The Home as a Government Institution <u>will</u> <u>be</u> <u>closed</u> and that speedily.

You will not require the farther services of Mr Williams. You will therefore relieve him immediately upon the receipt of this communication

Chaplain John G. Fee can render you good service in selecting homes and forwarding the people to them — but do not retain him about the Home a single day unless he heartily cooperates with you in the execution of my orders. Let this rule apply to every employee and teacher on the premises.

The Schools will be closed <u>at once</u>. Teachers will report by letter to their associations for assignment elsewhere   Mr Ogden[1] Superintendent of Schools will direct where they can be best employed — but it is better that the Schools continue no longer at the Home — as they doubtless have a tendency to lead the people to a belief that we are not in earnest about breaking the institution up —

There is no time to be lost. Cold weather is already upon us. The Home is not comfortable these damp days. The people will get sick by hundreds — as there are but few stoves and floors in the Cottages.

Captains Restiaux A.Q.M. and Ransom A.C.S. you will find to be first class gentlemen and very obliging officers   They will aid you to the extent of their duty   Say to Capt Ransom that I have requested the Secy of War to turn over the Savings fund to myself. I have no reply from the application.

Captain Restiaux I think is justified in issuing transportation into the States of Ohio, Indiana and Illinois. You will see that the Secy of War directs in the letter herewith returned that I send a woman to Knox County Ohio   Tell the Captain to go ahead and if he has any doubts about it I will procure a special order from the War Department to cover lines.

I am of the opinion that the major portion of the families at Camp Nelson will desire to remain in the state of Kentucky and I doubt not they can do so at or near their old homes among acquaintances. The families of colored soldiers must look to the soldier for support the same as the family of a white soldier does. If the woman is a widow she is entitled to pension, back pay & bounty. We will aid her in securing it. You and I have had too much experience within the last three months to be made to believe easily that my action is to produce suffering to any alarming extent — better — far better that there be some suffering than to continue Camp Nelson Refugee Home —

Bro Scofield Missionary is a good kind hearted man — we will make no objection to the exercise of the largest benevolence & Christian Charity through private enterprise — but no more Government poor houses will be run by my advice & consent —

I shall visit Gov Bramlette within a few days and endeavor to make an arrangement with him & Genl Palmer that will protect all the freed people of Ky — It is not easy to conduct a Freedman's Bureau for slaves. I shall move immediately upon Kentucky's works when I can go over there and say there are no more Camps for idlers — Pitch in — Do nothing inhumane — but move the column.

You can draw on me for all the funds necessary to care for the positively destitute &c — as heretofore — If you should need money Capts Restiaux or Ransom will loan you. Telegraph me and I will forward am^t by Express —

Send the best kind of a woman to the friend of the Secy of War in Knox County —   *

Clinton B. Fisk   Brg Genl   Ass^t Comr[2]

1. Prof. John Ogden was Superintendent of Education and Freedmen's Schools for the Bureau.

2. Fisk to Farwell, 17 Oct. 1865; M999:2:121–25; RG 105.

Nashville   Oct 18th [186]5
Capt R.E. Farwell   Supt Ref Home   Camp Nelson. Ky —

Devote your energies to the breaking up of the Refugee Establishment   at Camp admit none — refer all outside cases to the Civil Authorities until further orders —

Clinton B. Fisk   Brig Gen Ast Comr[1]

1. Fisk to Farwell, 18 Oct. 1865; M999:4:539; RG 105.

Col^d Ref. Home   Camp Nelson Ky   Oct. 18, 1865
Rev. Geo. Whipple, Cor. Sec.

Dear Sir   Yours of the 2nd Inst. is at hand. In brief I have simply to say that I have not the slightest objection to your sending my letter to Mr Strieby to Mr Fee; but I shall append this requirement, that you send to me all letters, or copies of letters of Mr Fee's containing any statements detrimental to myself, or Mrs. W.

You say you hardly know how to reconcile my note to Mr Fee in relation to Miss Mitchell, with a letter rec^d today (Oct. 2) from Mrs Williams. You greatly misunderstand when you say that "Mrs W. probably united in the request for the removal of Miss Mitchell." Mrs W. was a 1000 miles from here when the request was made. As to the Miss Mitchell affair, whatever of indignation was felt on the part of any was directed against Mr Fee. The steps taken were by the advice of Col. Jaquess, who was as much opposed to Mr. Fee's course as any. It was not the girl that aroused hostile feeling. If your neighbor should introduce a black man into your house & invite him to sit down at your table, you would be very apt to think you should have something to say about it. *

L. Williams Jr   C. Supt. Col^d Ref. Home.[1]

1. Williams to Whipple, 18 Oct. 1865, AMAA 44241.

Camp Nelson   Oct 18 1865
Genl C.B. Fisk

Dear Sir   This morning went to Nicholasville to see whether I could get a company of about one hundred through to Ohio   The Agt. of the road backed down from the position he took three days since and concluded to send my company through   If the weather will permit will send them in the morning

On my way back overtook a company that I sent to Lexington yesterday   They were rather a poor crowd <u>not very desirable</u>, and were literaly driven back

The Commander of this post returned from L this morning. He tells the same story as the Colored people & says they are thrown in jail and persecuted in every possible way

I have a classe here that do not give me much trouble yet for the reason that I have not reached their case, but I wish you would give me your views in regard to my best plan of procedure.

I refer to the <u>blind Old crazy & fools</u>   If I send them to the counties where they belong they will come back

I shall leave such and the sick of whom there is a large number till the last.

If <u>I finish this camp by the first of Dec</u> I <u>think Congress ought to vote me a Sword</u>   *

R E Farwell <u>Capt Spec Agt & Supt of Refugee Home Camp Nelson</u>[1]

1. Farwell to Fisk, 18 Oct. 1865; M999:7:355–56; RG 105.

[*Letterhead.*][1] *United States Sanitary Commission*   **Camp Nelson**   [October 18, 1865]

Messers Strieby and Jocelyn, Sec A. M Ass

Dear brethern,

    * * * * [*Three paragraphs.*]

    The last of August I sent for my wife and two daughters to aid me in teaching. My wife was to be employed by brother Fee in the Refugee Home to teach there, but during his absence Mrs Williams would not allow her to teach un[less] she would report to herself as supreme. This she could not do. We then set to the enlarging of the school at the Soldiers Home. The School is now large and furnishes full employ for my wife and one daughter, the other daughter being quite unwell.

    The School Roll numbers 130, but average is about 70, still increasing. Bro. Smith your agent has just been here and wishes us to keep on our work for the winter. He advises that I give my time mainly to looking after the general interest of this people during the winter, as it seems likely that many of them will remain and some one will be needed to look after their rights as well as their comforts. We are every day hoping to be relieved of the presence of Mr and Mrs Williams and think there will be a little more of both peace and freedom when they are gone. The hypocrisy and falsehood they have practiced toward brother Fee and Bell Mitchell ought to be exposed. The motive to all of which seems to have been malice toward J. G Fee. The Lord I trust will stand by the right and bring down high looks * * * * [*Expense account.*]

    I am doing something in looking after the claims of the widows and soldiers, which just now occupies considerable of my time — many of them suffer great wrong from their white oppressors. Officers and citizens together conspire to cheat and plunder them

    On the Sabbath I preach to them in several places over the Camp. There are yet some three thousand people in Camp and much work to be done * * * * [*One paragraph.*]

                           A. Scofield[2]

---

    1. This letterhead includes the motto "OUR COUNTRY — ONE AND INDIVISIBLE" above an image of an eagle flying with an American flag in its beak; underneath the bird adds " NO MORE DISUNION — NO MORE SECESSION — NO MORE SLAVERY."

    2. Scofield to Strieby and Jocelyn, 18 Oct. 1865, AMAA 44242.

Cin. Ohio   Oct. 19th 65

General Fisk. Nashville, Tenn. Supt. Lester Williams. Capt. Ransom. Col. Bierbower. Gen Barett & Col Jacques before a friendly destiny plunged him into misery[1] to give him better texts & through words & appearance more powerful sermons — these men told me to make out my bill of expense & send it to you & they would see that I should be reimbursed. They told me they told you of me when you was in Camp Nelson & that you know & would know all about me and my work. First I brought out of the land of Egypt, I mean Camp Nelson 47

    next 75
    next 63
    & now 103
    in all 288

not reckoned little babes of whom there were so many. My travelling expenses fares & telegraph &c expenses are $235.

Capt. Restieau gave us free transportation for two Companies but the commanding officer that came in his place gave me only free transportation to Cin & directed me there to Capt. Hunt. but Capt Hunt asked for this Ordre and that Ordre but Miss Hager had no Ordre. she had only 63 Negroes cold & hungry at little Miami Depot Cin. She took the shortest way. She gave security to Conductor & Ticket Agent & started at 10 O'clock P.M. for Springfield, O. The fare was $3.00 per person 3 [x] 63 — $189.

All what we ate, remember we always were a 1 1/2 day on the Road & had to be a night in Cin. or Xenia — amounted to $117   no doubt a little cheaper than when you or other big folks travel, but also were we but dirty insignificant Negroes. I had 22 mothers widows & soldiers' wives, who had 6 & 7 children. The oldest I hired out, the youngest I left with their mothers & provided for them. Beddings stoves & c. Rents & c. & c. till these poor persons can help themselves a little — paid out already, on my name down to pay for them yet $113

They tell me you'll send the Ordre to Supt. Williams on Capt. Ransoms Camp Nelson. I suppose you know better about that yourself. All I can say is only: what you do, do it quickly for I & my Negroes need money.

Shame on your lunatic Officers in Camp Nelson who during summer did all they could to fill Camp Nelson & to encourage them to make their home there & now they are cold & shivering & without home. If I had my way Mr Fee would have to provide for every one of them. That I could have Jacques to work with me there. This terrible interruption. The Negroes I took with few exceptions are doing well & the time will come when we will exclaim: & through all dificulties & hardships yet these Negroes have it better in soul & body than they had it before.

Have no mercy on Camp Nelson. Strike, break it up but quickly before colder weather destroys them by force. May God & not public opinion & tattling help us & may we finally hear that still small voice, surpassing all understanding: I gave to the homeless a home. Address

Miss Annie Hager   Springfield Ohio[2]

1. Apparently, Hager is referring to Jaquess's abortion trial, but what she means by her remark is anybody's guess.
2. Hager to Fisk, 19 Oct. 1865; M999:7:1076–78; RG 105.

Camp Nelson Ky   Oct 19th 1865
Brig Genl C.B. Fisk, Asst Com R F & Ab Lds

Dear Sir   This morning I received a Telegram from Nicholasville saying "You need not send your people as I cannot transport them today"   I at once telegraphed Mr Blackburn the agent, as follows "Can you send them tomorrow? And if not why?" Soon I received a dispatch in reply saying — "I am ordered by the President of the Kentucky Central R R not to take any more <u>Freedmen</u>"

Note the language: not <u>slaves</u> not <u>colored</u> people but <u>Freedmen</u>

My back was up & I concluded to "move on their works" and so I Telegraphed as follows To the Agent of the Ky C R R at Nicholasville

"I shall send twenty <u>free Colored</u> people to Nich[l] with a Gov order for transportation to Covington"

"I demand transportation over your road for them in accordance with the laws of Ky & your Charter as common carriers"

I have not received any reply nor do I expect any.

I shall send twenty Soldiers wives & children — persons who are as free as you or me, and who will have papers certifying the fact   If the roads will not transport such people I hope you will not wait till I get this camp closed before you "move on Kentucky" One of the women will be a woman I have selected to go to Knox County Ohio   I shall go myself or send some good white man with them to Nicholasville

There have been a crowd of men here all day some of them claiming that they have Slaves in the Camp and they want us to go in & take them <u>willing or not</u>

I believe I have been able to preserve a calm exterior but I do asure you I have not felt very amiable, and have not been in any mood for turning this Camp into a hunting ground

I told them that I would send for such persons & have them come to the Office and if on investigation I felt convinced that the people would be kindly treated I would press them to go home: but I <u>could not</u> permit any man to go into the camp & <u>force</u> a person away on the ground that he or she was or is <u>a slave</u>

Have I done right? I do not think it would look well for me to do such a thing

I would rather turn the people outside, and let them have an <u>even thing</u>, and I think it would be better for the reputation of the Br R F & Ab Ld[s], and it may be that before this reaches you my course of action may result in just this last state of things, and if so it cannot be said that I kept a <u>slave pen here</u> in your name only that I broke up the camp and left the responsibility of all subsequent matters with the people of Ky and the Gov   I never did get hold of anything where there were so many things to <u>annoy torment</u> and <u>impede</u> my progress as in this job: but I shall try to wade through & I mean to do it

In addition to the annoyances before mentioned, the wether has not been propitious   Good wether is very desirable, in this business perhaps as much so as though I had an army to move * * * * [*Two paragraphs.*]

Don't be discouraged because I dont make greater progress for I will get the lever fixed and lift it by & by   I have not had any such before all things considered.

I do not believe you can move on Kentucky too soon

. . . Capt. Ransom says it will immortalize the man who breaks up this Camp   I hope it can be so done that it will not be an immortality of infamy   *

R.E. Farwell Supt Refugee Home Camp Nelson[1]

1. Farwell to Fisk, 19 Oct. 1865; M999:7:291–94; RG 105.

Camp Nelson Ky   Oct 20th 1865.
Brig Gen. C.B. Fiske, Ass^t. Com^r Freedmen's Bureau

I have the honor to report the following numbers in connection with this Home, according to the records of today. Women 840; Children 890; [Total] 1,730. *

L. Williams Jr.[1]

1. Williams to Fisk, 20 Oct. 1865; M999:9:207; RG 105.

Refugee Home Camp Nelson   Oct 20 /65.
"The Situation"
Brig Genl C.B. Fisk   Asst Com

Dear Sir   Your Telegram has just come to hand

Went down to Nicholasville with a company for Ohio. . . . They were Soldiers wives & Children & they did not dare refuse, and I do not believe they will dare refuse any. They asked me if they would all be soldiers families that I would want transported, and said if they were not they could not take them   Told them they were not but by the grace of God and Genl Palmer they were all free and I would bring them down and demand that they be transported wherever they might wish to go

You instructed me to send them to homes in or out of Ky and I take it for granted you think they have a right to go

The Conductor wanted to know whether I would come with a guard to enforce the demand I informed him I would not. "Then he says, What will you do if I refuse to take them"? I replied that I would at once telegraph Genl Palmer and yourself, and in that event it was my opinion Genl P would run the road   I think they will take all persons that I say are free and I <u>presume</u> they are <u>all free</u> The conductor & Agent of the road are both pleasant Gentlemen and I believe the President of the road will cave in if I keep pushing

This has been a splendid day and just suited to the work in hand and the camp is crumbling fast

I know the foundation is giving way   At a meeting last evening I made the colored people choose a committee of five (including two of their ministers) to go through the camp and make a list of persons who ought to be helped by issuing rations to them once more   The people were satisfied with that

I instructed the committee before the people that they must proceed with great caution and report no man woman or child who in their judgment could earn their daily bread and said to them that I wanted them to do just as they would wish they had at the <u>Judgment</u> — that I was not going to bear all the responsibility and they must take their share   The plan succeeded like a charm

They have worked hard all day and are about half through

They report only fifty seven who ought to be fed. They will finish tomorrow

& I expect the whole number to be fed exclusive of those in the regular Hospital will not exceed one hundred & fifty [*In margin*: all old or sick]   I think that will not be a bad weeks work and bear in mind this is the decision of the people themselves

Could you have a fact in regard to the Colored people of more importance?

A people just emerged from bondage and nine out of ten represented by Father Husband Son or Brother in the army (and many of them away in Texas) almost all women & children no home no employment and yet they say that eighteen hundred & fifty people with few exceptions can support themselves and will ask no farther help from the Gov. I think it is wonderful and brands as false the oft repeated story that they are good for nothing & cannot care for themselves   And when you consider the circumstances under which this is done (I need not repeat them) I do not believe you can find a parrallel   The people would be glad to stay here on the soil of Ky if they could stay and not have the life tormented out of them. I met a woman an hour since who has been in this Refugee Home and at Camp Nelson for three years   She has never drawn a ration, but made her own living supported two children & laid by $304. her own earning

Her Husband is a soldier in Texas   I am getting a good opinion of the capacity of the race in fact, it grows upon me the more I have to do with them   I have not relieved Williams yet, for the reason that I sent Mr Vincent to Cincinnati with the company today and want W till he returns   He understands me first rate now and so do all the others

The schools closed to-day and the teachers have all reported to their employees   It is a good idea to stop them   *

R.E. Farwell, Supt. of Camp Nelson Refugee Home[1]

1. Farwell to Fisk, 20 Oct. 1865; M999:7:296–302; RG 105. Caroline Damon wrote to the AMA on the same day to report that the schools were closed and her claim upon the AMA ended. Damon to Whipple, 20 Oct. 1865, AMAA 44243.

Office Refugee Home Camp Nelson   Oct. 21st 1865
Genl C.B. Fisk   Asst Com

I sent out a company to Danville or beyond yesterday   some of the party were free   One woman had free papers and went out to labor for a man who came in here & contracted with her on the 19th

The Gov Team in which I sent them out was stopped just in the suburbs of D[anville] the driver informed that the citizens of D had passed a law that no Colored people should come into or pass through the City   He was threatened with personal violence if sighted and left the people by the road side & returned

The Wagon master reported to me this morning that his men dare not go there any more

There is one family laying by the roadside that were left some five days since in the same vicinity

I have telegraphed the facts to Gen¹ Palmer and asked for assistance & protection in the execution of your ordor.

Have I done right? I think it must be that <u>Satan is loose in Ky</u>   *

R.E. Farwell Supt Refugee Home¹

1. Farwell to Fisk, 21 Oct. 1865; M999:7:344–45; RG 105.

[*Letterhead.*] *Bureau Refugees, Freedmen & Abandoned Lands,*
States of Kentucky, Tennessee and Nor. Alabama
Assistant Commissioner's Office.
Nashville Tenn.   October 23 1865
Captain R.E. Farwell Superintendent &c. Camp Nelson Ky.

Dear Sir, Your respective favors of the 19th & 20th have been received and perused with much satisfaction. I am glad the Kentucky Central Rail Road Company took the proper view. I have received authority to seize and operate the Rail Road myself provided the Railway Officials refused to carry our people in Government transportation.

Your views and action are entirely approved. The Bureau must not be made instrumental in causing a singled individual (colored) to suffer.

I would prefer to be cashiered for maintaining the Home than that <u>one</u> free struggling fugitive should be remanded to <u>slavery</u>. I shall do all I can to protect the freedmen in their freedom and in <u>letting</u> the oppressed go free.

I have commenced the establishment of County Agencies in Kentucky and I shall <u>go on</u> in the good work until restrained by my superiors.

If Civil Authorities refuse to aid me I shall see that colored troops are stationed at each County town in the State. I will fight out the Kentucky conflict on that line or go home. I have not yet heard from Gov Bramlette. I want to get him on paper.

Dont you allow any Slaveholder of Kentucky to take from Camp Nelson Refugee Home a single article of his so-called property. Arrest and send to me under proper guard any Villian who attempts to take a colored person from you under the plea of property. I can not run a Freedmens Bureau for Slaves or Slave-holders.

The facts you give me touching the results of the Committee labors & decisions are indeed wonderful. You will hardly be able to shut off the rations as suddenly as that — see that their baskets are well filled when they leave you.

If you need new goods for clothing and shoes for women and children I will provide them. I shall go to Louisville some day this week, and may visit you at Camp Nelson. I trust that your people will not lodge in the Cincinnati Freedmen's Camp — look out for that. <u>Homes, homes, homes</u> is the word. Kentucky needs every ounce of the manual labor in the State. Why does she give herself over to strong delusion and believe lies and be damned   Let me hear from you frequently. *

(Signed) Clinton B. Fisk, Brig. Genl. & Asst. Com.

[*Clinton B. Fisk's actual signature appears under the words:*] True copy.¹

1. Fisk to Farwell, 23 Oct. 1865; M999:7:358–59; RG 105. A press copy of Fisk's original letter, demonstrating that the letterhead copy was accurate word for word, appears in M999:2:163; RG 105.

Camp Nelson Kentucky   October 24" 1865
General C.B. Fisk   Nashville Tenn.

I have a party at Nicholasville bound for Ohio. the road refuses to take them. what shall I do?

(sgd.) R.E. Farwell

True copy [*Signed by Clinton B. Fisk.*][1]

1. Farwell to Fisk, 24 Oct. 1865; M999:7:360; RG 105.

Nashville   Oct 25 [*186*]5
Capt R.E. Farwell. Supt &c   Camp Nelson Ky —

Refer such cases to the Superintendents of the poor — give the Civil authorities every opportunity to do their duty. If they refuse try and get such refusal in writing —
I shall see Gov Bramlette in a day of two — push on the work — do Rail Roads refuse to transport on your passes

Clinton B. Fisk   Brig Genl   Assᵗ Comr[1]

1. Fisk to Farwell, 25 Oct. 1865; M999:4:536–37; RG 105.

Refugee Home Camp Nelson Ky   Oct. 25ᵗʰ /65
Gen¹ C.B. Fisk   Asst. Com.

Yours of 23ᵈ has just come to hand. I am glad my action as reported is approved
This morning I sent a company down to Nicholasville swelling the number who were obliged to lay there last night to about Seventy   I anticipated your telegram, which I have just received (or its tenor)   I applied to Capt Anderson post Commander for help last evening   He telegraphed to Gen Brisbane & wished me to telegraph the facts to Genl Palmer   I did so but have received no reply up to this hour from Gen¹ P but Capt A received a reply late this morning but just in time as follows from Gen¹ Brisbane
"See that all passes are respected"
The Provost Marshal & myself at once started for Nicholasville & were there just in time. We were obliged to call a guard to enforce the ordor and we will be obliged to send a guard with every company   Now I would respectfully submit that while such action will secure the rights of the people in this home there will be thousands in Ky of colored people whose rights will not be respected at all

Not a single colored person save soldiers wives & chil. get on the cars at Nicholasville unless they come from this home and are backed by Armed Soldiers   I do hope this sore may come to a head now.

The Committee returned two hundred and seven names of persons who would have to be fed   As you anticipated I could not cut the rations down to correspond with their report   I presume I have fed about 700 but the move was a perfect success for it tends to urge the people on to effort and besides makes them perfectly satisfied with any ration   I do put the screws on pretty hard in the cases of single women and where there is the least chance for a person to provide for themselves and the result is there is a genuine effort to make provision for themselves   I do fill their baskets when they leave and send none empty away   I think all the Devils in the Country must have entered into Ky for as you say they need every one of these people but are in a fair way to drive them out

The fact is this camp ought to have been closed up when the people wanted labor   I think if it had been they would have behaved a little better

I have relieved Mr Williams but he is still here   Mr Fee has just come in   I hope you will come to Camp Nelson   You will not find ordor & system just now but you will see that there is some hard work to be done here — a great deal of poverty and a grand chance for the exercise of the largest humanity — and I trust you will be satisfied that I am trying to fill the bill

There are many Soldiers familes here who are waiting anxiously for the mustering out of the regiments to which they belong I cannot cut such off as the husbands are expected every hour and they beg me to delay till they come

I shall put a guard on the train and keep it there as long as the necessity exists or till further orders from you and save myself further trouble   I do not blame the Officers of the R.R   in fact, I know they will be glad & welcome a guard   They fear the State Authorities   *

R E Farwell, Supt Refugee Home Camp Nelson Ky

P S I will examine Hagar Bill[1]

1. Farwell to Fisk, 24 Oct. 1865; M999:7:347–50; RG 105.

[*Letterhead.*] *Bureau Refugees, Freedmen & Abandoned Lands,*
States of Kentucky, Tennessee and Nor. Alabama
Assistant Commissioner's Office.
Nashville, Tenn., October 25", 1865
Captain R.E. Farwell   Superintendent &c Camp Nelson Ky

Call upon the nearest District or Post Commandant for force to aid you in executing my orders.

If the Railway Officials refuse to transport the people who are seeking homes and employment to places where they will not be a charge upon the Government,

place a Military guard upon the trains, and see that the people are promptly transported. Refer Military Commandants to General Order No. one hundred and two
(102) War Department current series.

Clinton B. Fisk, Brig. Genl & Asst. Commissioner, Bureau R.F. and A.L.

True copy [*Signed by Clinton B. Fisk.*][1]

1. Fisk to Farwell, 25 Oct. 1865; M999:7:361; RG 105.

Cold Ref. Home Camp Nelson Ky   Oct. 28, 1865
Statement of Miss Hagar's services in behalf of the Freed people.

First trip from Camp N. Sept. 11. 20 women & 19 children.
2d Trip. Oct 3d.   32 Adults & 21 children.
3d Trip. Oct 12th.   31 women & 20 children.
4th Trip. Oct. 19 – 20   From Springfield Ohio to Cinnati & back   women
& children.

The charge for transportation from Cin. to Sprfd might be adjusted by obtaining the proper papers in accordance with the original order.

The charge for travelling expenses, telegraph, &c a favorable judgment would say
might be correct in the sum of $50.00. The bill of Miss H. includes nothing for her
personal services. She should be well paid for her own labor. It was arduous & difficult.

L. Williams Jr.

[*Included with Williams' report is a slip of paper in Annie Hager's handwriting:*]

My own travelling expenses $285.00
Transportations for 63 $189.00
Provisions on the Road $117.00
Assistance to the weak & feeble $113.00
                                $654.00 [1]

1. Report of Williams, 28 Oct. 1865; M999:7:1079–80; RG 105.

Camp Nelson Ky   Oct 28 /65

Dear Bro. Strieby   We need here a good <u>male</u> principal for our school   Bro.
Scofield has his time wholly occupied in the claim agency   He has a license by the
civil authorities for collecting & his time is so completely occupied that he has no
time for the school

His wife & daughter do not cannot as I believe maintain adequate order

We cannot probably hinder the colored people from settling here   They
will need a school we need to occupy as many places as possible [*before*] others get
hold of the <u>colored people of this state</u>   I have seen Genl Brisbin — comman-

dant under Genl Palmer — Brisbin said to me put your schools where you please   I will protect you   I have no fear of war between the races"   I believe god intends to save this nation   the leaven is working

It is probable that we can have these government buildings as ours for school purposes. . . . We must hold them or let them fall into the hands of others. . . . There is now an open door for me at Lexington Ky for good if I had a house there & adequate means of support   I should then have hold of several social centers — means of extended good

J G Fee[1]

1. Fee to Strieby, 28 Oct. 1865, AMAA 44244.

Refugee Home Camp Nelson Ky   Oct 31 /65
O.O. Howard   Maj. Genl. & Com. R.F. & A.L.

Sir — We, the undersigned, have the honor to request that the buildings of, and all the appurtenances to the Refugee Home in Camp Nelson Ky be conveyed to us, and our successors in office — to be used by us, as we now design, for school purposes; and this on condition that we in paying for the lands (farm) on which the buildings are erected, shall satisfy Mr. Joseph Moss for damages he now claims from the government.

John G Fee   Gabriel Burdett   Geo. Blakeman   A. Scofield[1]

1. Fee et al. to Howard, 31 Oct. 1865; M999:7:312–16; RG 105. The first letter is in Fee's handwriting; each signature is in the handwriting of the person signing, and all the signers are identified by a marginal note as "Trustees." The long letter following the petition, transcribed below, is once again in Fee's hand.

Refugee Home Camp Nelson, Ky., Oct 31 1865 * * * * [*An account for damages claimed by Joseph Moss of Camp Nelson.*][1]

The Refugee Cottages extend across the farm and a short distance onto the adjoining farm. The cottages on the latter we can remove without damage to that farm. Mr Joseph Moss is known to be loyal. He wishes to sell his farm, because now unfitted for agricultural purposes as he wishes. Colored soldiers now being mustered out desire to buy the land, divide it into lots, attach one of the cottages to each lot (from 4 to 5 acres each) — have a home for their families, and a school for their children.

Martial law now repealed, they are unwilling to thrust their families into the country. There, in most places, they would be without schools. Here we shall have facilities for education, with the influence of the gospel

We also propose to intersperse white families, who are true friends, far as possible. The precedent will be good, and the highest good of the colored people promoted.

To such friends as shall thus come in, we shall give the same facilities we do to colored men.

Also, we suppose it is best, and desire to have the lot of ground, buildings, the school and its interests committed to a board of trustees, as requested, rather than have the houses and school under the guidance of an agent of the Bureau or any Aid Society — Reasons

(1) Several of the trustees will be constantly on the ground   This is the present fact and probable future — all are here now —

(2) They will be personally interested in the success of the enterprise

(3) Money must be collected from abroad and expended in improvements, such as plastering the houses, procuring aparatus library &c

4 Several of the trustees (present and anticipated) are known to the friends of humanity abroad.

(5) Capt R E Farwell special agent of the Bureau and Superintendent of this Refugee Home will, as we believe faithfully represent the Government and see that the contracts are just to the Freed men and their friends

Unless some such enterprise shall be sprung & encouraged so that there shall be a demand for the houses upon the ground the houses will sell but for a very small sum, not perhaps one half demanded as damages; so that as a mere business transaction, the offer is a good one to the government, and a prospective good to those who have periled their lives for the government.

To the above we respectfully request an early reply as many are waiting the decision

John G Fee   Gabriel Burdett   A. Scofield[2]

1. Joseph M. Moss, member of a local family in Jessamine County, owned the seven hundred acres on which the Camp Nelson Refugee Home (among other structures) was located; he served briefly as Camp Nelson's official "Farmer." Moss claimed $5,800 in damages, including $500 for a hemp factory used and destroyed, and $700 for twenty thousand rails. The biggest item on the claim is for "Fifteen acres of excellent timber, estimated at 95 cords this estimated at the then usual price, three dollars per cord": $2,750.

2. Ibid.

Office Asst Quartermaster Camp Nelson Ky   Oct. 31" 1865.
Brig. Gen. C.B. Fisk, Asst. Comsr. Freedmens Bureau   Nashville Tenn.

Sir: I have the honor to request that you furnish me with an Order authorizing the issue of transportation to refugees into States not within the limits of your jurisdiction. I have been issuing transportation in compliance with your request since September to various points north of the Ohio River for which I am personally responsible. It is necessary for me to have an order relieving me of the responsibility and covering the transportation issued in September and October by your order. *

E.B.W. Restieaux Capt & A.Q.M. [1]

1. Restieaux to Fisk, 31 Oct 1865; M999:8:757; RG 105.

Camp Nelson, Ky., Oct 31st 1865
Rev M.E. Strieby, S.A.M.A.

Dear brother, * * * * [*Expense account.*]

you see I have charged nothing for the extra help, my 2nd daughter. The labor is heavy, and it requires the help of both much of the time. We have now the only School in Camp. Our large Hall is full, numbering over two hundred. Some are making very commendable progress. We intend to have an exhibition at the close of the term. Much of my time is taken up in looking after the rights and wants of this people, in working out their claims, and devising means for the poor to live. If we continue the School during Winter We shall need some $40 to $50 in Wood. Shall the School go on? There are many who wish to attend. Some of them young men of promise who are discharged Soldiers and desire to devote Six Months to School. They care for themselves but could give nothing for their instruction.

Shall the work proceed? Mr. Williams and co. have left so nothing will be done at present in the way of teaching in the Refugee Home. That institution appears to be gradually dissolving. We have proposed to the discharged colored soldiers to purchase the whole establishment and convert it into a public school — so at last that some little good might come of it. The project meets with great favor. I trust that you will be ready to give any aid & counsel in the matter which the case may demand.

Freedmens Bureau you are aware doubtless is strongly Methodist and seek to turn all things in their peculiar channel. I hope we shall meet all those tendencies kindly but firmly. This work is here the work of the A.M. As. The work was begun by them, the field is theirs. I hope they will maintain their ground till a great and good work is done.

But I must close. If anything in my act or word is amiss, please state faithfully. *

A. Scofield[1]

1. Scofield to Strieby, 31 Oct. 1865, AMAA 44249–50.

Camp Nelson Refugee Home, Nov. 1st, 1865
Brig. Genl C.B. Fisk, Asst Com R F & A L

Dear Sir

* * * * [*One paragraph.*]

I assure you the work of reducing this camp is not progressing as fast as some other jobs I have put through.

I suppose I have about 1620 on hand and have arrangements made to send away about sixty tomorrow.

Last Sunday a woman with three children came in from New Castle Ky

No food had passed the lips of the party for about twenty four hours, and as it was a cold bleak day, the little ones were chilled through

They were literally driven away from home and their only offence was they were the wife and children of a Soldier.

The Soldier was formerly the pastor of the Colored Church.

The Colored people owned the Church building and proposed to let the pastor's wife live in it, but the <u>White</u> Christians would not permit her to do so.

I received fed and warmed the poor woman believing you would endorse my action.

I will send them to Ohio in the morning. I have spent the last two days visiting every family in the Camp Where I have found persons who ought to be selfsupporting. I have started them in the most summary manner.

I have taken a list of every family I have visited, making a careful note of their condition Made a note of all Boys & girls large enough to earn their bread and assured the parent that I would send all such to places, as fast as I can find suitable homes

Most of the people are averse to going out of Ky   The people of Ky have adopted Franklin's Maxim: we "keep no more cats than will catch mice"

They know a Soldiers wife & children can never again be Slaves and they know that a woman with from four to twelve little children will not pay and if they have not got such on their hands they will not take them at this season of the year and if they have them they will get rid of them as soon as possible

Every day I am pressed to take in Slaves who have become unprofitable, and in all such cases, the masters insist that there is no such thing as Slavery

A Dr Jessup of this county came in yesterday and wanted to bring in twelve women & children — said Jacques promised him he might

I said no at once and then he threatened to turn them out to die.

I told him I thought it would be a good idea for everything indicated that the whole slaveholding people of Ky were bound for <u>hell</u> and it would be right fine when <u>he</u> got there to feel conscious he was in the right place

He rode off I hope a wiser & better man

I wish I could see you for I fear you will be disappointed about my breaking of this Camp. I am wearing away on it but slowly   I could knock the bottom out and close it with a rush, but I fear you and I would in that event go to hell with the people of Ky I have made <u>some</u> progress, for Williams and the teachers have left

Now I will just give you a few notes as I took them today.

Cabin No 71 Occupants Sophy Smothers and three little children of her own all less than six years old   Besides her own three motherless children and three more full Orphans and her Old Father & Mother the flour all bolted out of them and nothing but the bran left   The Husband of Sophy and a number of Brothers in the Army & away in Texas   This is a very good specimen.

As fast as the men are mustered out they take their families away but how can a woman leave a large family for days to hunt a home and even if they could, there is no home for them There is no sort of provision made for such poor   Every team that I send out into the country I put on an old crazy woman by the name of

Edie that is if the team is going to her county but like a bad penny she came back every time

I cannot get any <u>one on paper</u> as per your request for none will touch them   Gen[l] this is a queer case indeed   This camp was filled up this last summer   The people were invited in it was part of Gen[l] Palmer's plan for undermining <u>the system</u> in this state.

The husbands were enlisted with a distinct promise that their wives & children would be protected and cared for by the Gov

They were not merely <u>invited</u> in but the master of ceremonies Capt Hall sent out into the highways & hedges and compeled them to come in bringing them in in Gov wagons so <u>the people say</u>

The Husbands are still in the Army   The Bad Masters will not let them return and they do not want to leave the State while the husband is away and even if I did compell them to go to Ohio, there are very few left who could find homes with all their little children

God only knows what will become of them if Gov support is withdrawn at this season of the year   The work might have been pushed through and the Camp closed in the summer <u>months </u>and when Martial law ruled the state   If the 124 Reg. is mustered out it will relieve me of a great many families and I understand it is to be soon

If you have any idea that I am not pushing hard enough, I hope you will say so   I do not like to grind the face of the poor till I cant sleep nights but will do my best to execute your ordor and push the work as fast and hard as I think you would wish or justify me in doing   *

R E Farwell Supt Refugee Home[1]

1. Farwell to Fisk, 1 Nov. 1865; M999:7:318–23; RG 105.

Camp Nelson Ky   Refugee Home Nov 2[d] /65
Brig. Genl. C.B. Fisk, Asst. Com.

Dear Sir, Enclosed please find statements of L Williams in relation to Hagar Miss Annie's bill.

You will see that his figures differ materially in regard to the number taken out of Egypt by Miss H.

This may be accounted for in this way and her figures may be correct, for a company almost always exceeds the transportation order and Williams bases his figures on that

Her charge for transportation of $189.[00] you will see by statement of W might have been covered at the time and probably could be now if Hagar had as much <u>sense</u> as <u>zeal</u>.

The first item we talked over and my opinion is the same as expressed by W $50. ought to cover actual expense   Provision bill may be <u>all right</u> or <u>all wrong</u> that is a matter I cannot decide it all depended on circumstances

I took a company from Louisville to Rockford Ill in Jan last (150 persons) and it did not cost me anything to feed them or to care for the weak & feeble   I was able to draw on the <u>good</u> people along the route by appealing to their sympathies for all I needed in that line   I know it would be a very easy thing to spend a large amount of money in such an enterprise but I do not think it necessary

I think Williams statement is entitled to consideration on this point of expenses (personal), as he & Hagar are <u>chums</u> and he was disposed to make it as favorable to her as possible

Williams and the teachers have left except Mrs Colton who is sick. *

R.E. Farwell Supt. Refugee Home[1]

1. Farwell to Fisk, 2 Nov. 1865; M999:7:333–34; RG 105.

To John G. Fee, Camp Nelson, Ky
Cincinnati, 2[d] Nov., 1865

Dear John, Yours of 31st Ulto. just to hand. I have no time to act as trustee; yet your plan looks feasible. I will loan you $500. — & you can, if you will, use it for the benefit of the home — & <u>your own interest</u>, paying me 6%; & the state & Gov. tax I shall have to pay, which I believe will be 2%, or in other words, have it net me 6%. Of course, you know I can do better, but I desire you to be benefited as well as the home. *

E. Harwood[1]

1. Harwood to Fee, 2 Nov. 1865, BCA.

Camp Nelson Ky   Nov 2 /65

Dear Bro Fisk   Our friend Capt R. E Farwell will bear to you a paper, perhaps unexpected, after the conversations we have had

Events do not always fall out according to our judgment. During my absence soldiers returned — martial law was withdrawn — these mustered out soldiers did not like to thrust out their families — the former talk about buying the farm was revived and money subscribed.

Stay many will — the question is, shall they have a school & the gospel? here we think it wise to avail ourselves of these buildings and <u>multiply</u> schools   This is the way people do in free states   We intend to so manage the lands as to make them pay U.S. damages to Moss — have but little expense upon the benevolent public

We will need to collect a little for plastering, desks &c

We can get coal & wood here cheap as anywhere in <u>interior</u> Ky   This River will furnish both — not as cheap as out at Berea — my other home

Sickness incident to an old camp (as cholera is approaching) is an objection

If you still think it best to make here only a neighborhood school please say so. We have no arrangements yet beyond this   If the war camp shall be broken up much of the miasma of the camp will cease * * * * [*One paragraph.*]

We like Capt R E Farwell very much   He is approachable practical industrious and executive — a good exchange have we — Yours fraternally

John G Fee[1]

1. Fee to Fisk, 2 Nov. 1865; M999:7:329–31; RG 105. At the bottom of this letter someone has written: "Oh: Lord . E E.J.H.C." This particular Fee letter was sent to General Fisk as an enclosure in Farwell's letter of November 3, which follows.

Nashville Tenn   Nov 3ᵈ [*186*]5
Maj Genl Howard   Comr &c.   Washington D.C.

Genl   In order to close out Camp Nelson Ky Colored Refugee Home it has been necessary to transport many of the inmates thereof to points in Ohio and Indiana where they can support themselves — Genl Order No 138 A.G.O. current series authorizes me to transport such persons only within the limits of my District — I have the honor to request your approval of issues of transportation to freedmen-dependents at Camp Nelson to points opposite Kentucky where such transportation may be deemed necessary in order to place the freedmen where they can be made self supporting. Captain Restiaux A.Q.M. at Camp Nelson has already issued transportation to some persons going north of the Ohio River and I desire your approval or that of the Secy of War for such issues. *

Clinton B. Fisk   Brig Genl   Asst Comr[1]

1. Fisk to Howard, 3 Nov. 1865; M999:3:1310; RG 105.

Camp Nelson Refugee Home Nov 3ᵈ 1865
Genˡ C.B. Fisk   Asst Com

Dear Sir   I sent away about fifty yesterday from this camp

The Post Commander informed me that there would be a military conductor on every train and said I need not go to Nicholasville

This morning part of the Company came back

One of the persons who returned is a soldiers wife but she had no free papers and it is somewhat difficult for her to get them as she has no letters from her Husband though she can prove it by persons who have known them in years past

Is this to be the rule in this state? Must a free person forever carry about on their person proof of freedom? When will Kentucky come to her senses?

I cannot get wood from the Q M even for the use of the hospital

He says tell the Genˡ "I would be very glad to do so but fear it will come out of my pay unless he gets an order from the Secy of War to cover me"

I am buying wood for use of office and hospital   It must be had at same rate   I make the people go out on the cliffs and get their own

I have not drawn on you for any money as I have not yet hit on any plan for using it.

Capt Ransom says I can draw the last cent of the fund in <u>kind</u> if I wish to use it and if I could close this camp by so doing I would not for one moment hesitate to draw and use the last dollar of $6000. for I think it would be cheaply done at that   Would it not be well for me to draw all I am entitled to even if there is a large saving and then it will be in the Bureau

I am doing so now and instead of drawing on you for funds to pay my telegraph wood bills &c I have sold three bbls of flour to returned soldiers and others in camp who have means to buy   Gen. ordor says close up as you have elsewhere. I sold savings of rations at Clarksville and will do so here unless you ordor otherwise and thus make one hand wash the other

Now there is another trouble about my work here   all the teams are being turned over and sold and I fear there will not be any means of transportation for such as are ready to leave

I could send away quite a large number in the morning but I cannot get a team

I am on the coals broiling or at least feel as though I am

I will send you request of J G Fee   He was going to send it to Genl Howard, but I advised him to send through you   I think it would be a good thing for the Gov to grant his request and shall so endorse the paper knowing that if it goes through you that if you dont approve you can send it to a <u>pigeon hole</u>   If the request is granted the camp might be closed so far as the Gov is concerned in this way

The surplus rations might be drawn and distributed among the poor and then the whole matter left to private benevolence, and that is the only way I can see to do it in the present condition of things

Gov may not like the idea and there are objections I well know

I have not returned the paper in regard to donation of Soldiers home and will retain it till I hear from you in relation to this request   *

                                                              R E Farwell Supt Refugee Home[1]

1. Farwell to Fisk, 3 Nov. 1865; M999:7:325–28; RG 105.

Camp Nelson   Nov 29th 1865
Genl C.B. Fisk

Dear Sir   I have delayed making any report for some time expecting that you would call on your return from the north

The present number in camp is about 1441

I am issuing only about Seven hundred rations and probably less even than that number There are nearly One hundred Orphan Children here and I would respectfully second that a Guardian be appointed so that their intrests may be secured

Many have back pay & bounties due them

I want to send them all to Ohio where they can find homes

If I send them away before I hear from you I will note all the facts and then whoever is appointed can look after their intrests just as well as though they were here   *

R.E. Farwell

Supt Ref Home Camp Nelson[1]

1. Farwell to Fisk, 29 Nov. 1865; M999:7:309–10; RG 105.

[*Letterhead.*] *U.S. Sanitary Commission*   **Camp Nelson, Ky   Nov 30 1865**

Dear Bro Whipple   I have been absent from this post near three weeks — Burritt my eldest son has been very sick with fever. I nursed him day & night — He is now convalescent * * * * [*Four paragraphs.*][1]
My future

I shall probably go back to Berea, at least for winter quarters

1 Bro. E.P. Smith, your agent when here told Bro Scofield he did not think it wise to have two such men as himself & myself here and advised Bro Scofield to continue his claim agency

2 Capt Farwell wishes to have as little interest here as possible so as the more easily to break up this Refugee Home

3 My son Burritt is now too feeble to move here if I even had a house for my family

4 Bro Rogers & Hanson[2] at Berea desire my help in getting school there on foot   Bro Wheeler thinks Northern friends will be disappointed if Berea is not made a success

This last does not influence me much. If I am doing that which will most please Christ & advance most Christs Kingdom I shall be satisfied

There is a consideration of importance to us all   That is a homestead for the Colored man   In the "Blue Grass" — fertile portion of central Ky men own large farms & to grass cattle & mules. At present they are not disposed to sell to "niggers"   The colored man there must be a hireling, an attachee — Many very many are buying small lots about the towns & putting small houses upon them & then depend upon "days work" — here some will fall into want & steal — then a "hugh & cry" will be against them. They need to be encouraged to go out into the hill country — even to the mountain counties & there spend their four or five hundred dollars (as these soldiers have) in getting a home that will support them.

Let enough get into a neighborhood to sustain a school & church there — not all into one county — scatter into different counties—and as at Berea intersperse with some white friends.

By my position out at the foot of the mountain region I may attract — I can attract many — if I only had a company at my hand who would buy out several farmers & then <u>parcel</u> to colored men as well as whites   Then I would take to them the teacher & missionary through you.

Let me say I believe you will do well to encourage this effort and have a man who is truly honest & a friend to these people go and hunt lands — homes for them — not to feed them & hold them up but as you send agents to look out places for schools for them — open houses & show them where they can get knowledge, so to these who have not traveled & are restrained by copperheads & wicked institutions, show them where they can have ground an axe & a hoe — a home * * * * [*Five paragraphs.*]

John G Fee * * * * [*Twelve paragraphs.*][3]

1. In the omitted passage Fee speaks of Berea, where he had been preaching and looking after the schools. Willard W. Wheeler and his wife, Ellen, were working there; she had become the teacher for the first colored school at Berea, which had twenty students. Fee had just had five applications from black men who "very anxious to get homes there in order to educate their children." Many of the first settlers at Berea had first met Fee at Camp Nelson.
2. John G. Hanson, first cousin of John G. Fee, was one of the co-founders of Berea.
3. Fee to Whipple, 30 Nov. 1865, AMAA 44260–3.

[*Letterhead.*] *U.S. Sanitary Commission   Soldier's Home   Camp Nelson, Ky.,* Dec 1st 1865

To Brothers Strieby & Jocelyn, * * * * [*Expense account.*]
Our school has greatly increased and has amassed something over two hundred. Many more would be glad to come. I fitted up another room for Mary my daughter where she has taught sixty, for which I charge you $15.00 and I board, which of course is small wages. The 119th Regiment have come here to winter and want my family to teach the soldiers, but we must suspend some of our schools here to do it. What do you advise? I have a son at home 18 years of age. If you will pay him $25. per month   I will board and bear all expenses of hand to have him come and teach in the Regiment. . . . Last year I came here and bore the heat and burden of the day — In mud in snow in perils often in sickness, and [*indecipherable*] much — six months for $200. on which my family could not live, and became a public charity. My brother I do not complain. . . . In my judgment there is a great demand for teaching here, and the schools ought to be kept up — you have only to say what you think you can allow for teaching these people — 40 or 50 scholars is all that one teacher can care for, especially in the cold weather — . . . .When Brother Smith was here the widows and soldiers were continually applying to me to attend to their claims. He instructed me to attend to that business, and make thorough work. I have done so, and just now it occupies a large share of my time — more than I expected — I charge them fifty cents a piece to pay for postage & paper blanks &c If the business continues as brisk as it is now I shall if you so advise, put it in the hands of some one and relieve myself from the care — for sometimes I have to sit at the desk sixteen hours in the day. Of course I cannot do this business and live on it at the fee I receive from the people. What they will <u>receive</u> is as yet all uncer-

tain — but not less than one hundred thousand dollars is due from the Government to the dead soldiers in this camp alone. I am trying to save something of it for their poor families. Sharpers and Robbers are all around here <u>helping</u>, also charging enormous prices, in some cases taking <u>all.</u> Should I <u>succeed</u> in getting their claims, they would likely give me something of their own account. I leave that entirely with them.

. . . Is it right for a poor missionary who has sacrificed everything in the anti slavery cause for thirty years to save anything for his family? If we go on with the school I must now lay out $50. for wood — Indeed I have already bought it — but can easily sell it if that is best

Can you send me one hundred dollars <u>and full instructions</u>   As my family are here I should like to have them employed for 2 or 3 months more at some price — But will endeavor to follow instructions — . . . . Your affectionate Missionary

A. Scofield[1]

1. Scofield to Strieby and Jocelyn, 1 Dec. 1865, AMAA 44265–6.

Col^d Ref Home   Camp Nelson   Dec 4" 1865
Rev. George Whipple

Dear Sir

* * * * [*Two paragraphs.*]

The 23^d of March I recd. [*a letter*] from Rev^d LWilliams Ass Supt of this Home requesting my assistance immediately — made arrangements soon as possible, left my home the 24" March, and arrived here the 1st of April. Entered upon my duties at once — so varied were they that I cannot enumerate them all. The most prominent at that time were receiving, recording, and making provisions for the destitute beings as they arrived.

Receiving, invoicing, and opening clothing

Receiving and opening Rations

Receiving, writing, and delivering letters

Receiving and recording Deaths, and ordering Coffins from Mil. Camp

Hiring out inmates, writing bonds

Writing and opening passes in and out of Home

Answering a thousand and one questions which would naturally occur under the circumstances

My pay was to be 50 Dolls pr. month & Rations —

No length of time was specified —

No particular services specified —

<u>No</u> Payment <u>has been made me from another source!</u>

The last, I think a most singular question. I answer it, because it was required and knowing as I do the influences of parties in this camp representing the Am Miss Ass., I do not object to it —

Bro Whipple, the day will come when you will know <u>why</u> success has not attended the Societies labors in this camp. You may not receive the information from one so ignorant as myself, but you surely will be informed. It has been my wish in all the troubles in this Home (and the Lord knows we have had a good share of them this past summer) that you might be represented here — and have often so expressed myself

Perhaps the troubles have been honestly and fairly reported to you, but I doubt it —

So far as reporting to you individually of my labors, I never conceived it my duty to do so; another was the accredited Agent of your Socy and supposed if necessary to report, he would do it and not myself — and I think he has done it, probably to his satisfaction if not to mine, and others employed here —

I think I have answered all your questions. I sent my bill for October and Nov. services just before I recd. your last.

You have thought it best to discharge me just as the inclement season is upon us, a thousand miles from home, retaining what is due me, obliging me to remain here 9 or 10 days, after losing my first months labor of 50 Dollars and expenses of coming and returning 67 Dollars more —

I would like to hear from you as soon as possible — *

J C Chapin[1]

1. Joseph C. Chapin to Whipple, 4 Dec. 1865, AMAA 44273.

Farwell R.E.   Sp Agt.
Dec. 6   1865.

Respectfully returned. Crowd them out as rapidly as possible — consistent with humanity.

(Signed) Jno. H. Cochrane   Maj and A.A.A.G[1]

1. Endorsement to Farwell, 6 Dec. 1865; M999:4:768; RG 105.

Refugee Home Camp Nelson Ky   Dec. 6th 1865
Genl C.B. Fisk

I have the honor to request that some provision be made for stoves for this home.

Doct Mitchell the surgeon in charge of the hospital here has been ordered to turn over and send to Louisville all gov. property now in his hands

This Ordor will include the stoves and beding now in use at the hospital

We have a large number of sick including twenty-five cases of small pox

I am at a loss to know what to do if this ordor is enforced. I would respectfully request that if possible all property now used at this home of the character named be retained

There are many families (wives and children of soldiers who are now in Texas) living in a very destitute condition

Many have no stove or fireplace and are compelled to build their fires on the floor of their Cabin with no protection against fire except flat stone laid on the floor

I understand there are plenty of stoves not in use now in the hands of the Q M here but he cannot furnish them for this people without an Ordor from his superior officer

Can anything be done to relieve our necessities   *

R E Farwell Supt Refugee Camp[1]

1. Farwell to Fisk, 6 Dec. 1865; M999:7:369–71; RG 105.

Camp Nelson Ky   Dec 9th 1865.
Rev Geo Whipple

Dear Bro   I am but just recovering from a severe illness, induced by the violent cold I took going to Danville for Miss Mitchell, in Oct. All the teachers have left, but my daughter & I, & now as winter is setting in & my funds rather low, I dread to turn out to seek some other occupation. I know I could be useful here to these poor creatures & they dislike to hear us talk of leaving.

The 119th Col Reg have taken up their winter quarters in the Hospital near us, & Bro Fee kindly introduced my daughter [*Anna Smith*] to the Chap. & gave her a recommendation as teacher for the soldiers, but today when she went to see about it, the Chap. told her Rev Mr Scofield let his daughter come & teach gratis. I had had no opportunity to see bro. Scofield & ask the reason for thus taking Anna's place when he knew she had applied for it, but I think his object is to get & hold it until his son, 18 years old, can come on here. His daughter is only 16, & another 14, quite deaf, & bro. Fee felt grieved at the great want of order & discipline in the school of children they have. They have near a hundred at their own school & there are I understand five hundred soldiers here. I do hope dear brother you can find us some employment. I hear from some of my lady friends employed in Tenn that they are kept busy day & evening & fear they cannot endure such constant labour.

Here the disappointment among the parents & children was very great. It seems as tho the school might as well have gone on as there are so many running about — learning evil, & a great many go to bro Scofields school if permitted.

Please let us hear from you as soon as convenient. Your friend

Mary Colton.[1]

1. Colton to Whipple, 9 Dec. 1865, AMAA 44278.

Camp Nelson Ky   Dec 16 /65

Dear Bro Whipple   Yesterday buildings here were advertised for sale. I rode previous day in extreme cold here from Berea to retain if possible buildings for school purposes. Genl Fisk had stayed sale of those at Refugee Home — all right until spring   Families are scattering from here and settling around Berea   Lands beyond there are within the reach of colored people — soldiers returned can buy — at from five to ten dollars per acre.

Gabriel Burdett — colored soldier — commissioned by your society was ordered into service (contrary to our expectations) detailed again at my request by Genl Fisk ordered him to help find homes for these refugees

This would enable him to preach & do good over the country — He has been doing so. He had bought a good horse — that took sick & died   He has a wife & two children of his own — his sisterinlaw and nine children in his family — promising children.

In his last tour in Madison co he has had to hire a horse. I think him eminently useful   Also I think it would be right that you send him a draft for twenty five dollars. I know he needs it. He will now be ordered by Capt Farwell to be steward of the Hospital here. That will tie him up for 6 or 8 weeks.

Capt Farwell reports that Genl Fisk is discouraged about the success of the colored people — advises that they be not aggregated in towns or cities.

The 6th Cavalry have killed their Coll — They regarded him as swindling them — great have been the continual outrages upon these colored soldiers   The Coll of the 124th Reg robbed his men here of 12 thousand dollars some of these officials seem to make it their study to to rob & defraud their colored men. They will learn to distrust almost any white face. Complaints here are accumulating against Capt Hall former Q M here.

I think it well for me if I shall have moral influence over these people that I did not consent to superintend nor collect bounties — to receive no payment of them nor from government over them —

Chief Justice Chase said "They know who are their friends" These can influence these colored people   It will be a good thing for these people to have an agent who shall get homes for these people. They have not traveled — have not business habits or knowledge & feel the proscriptions of society. May I employ some safe honest man to meet the wants of these people as they shall wish to settle near Berea? I am here also to inquire how many preachers will come only occasionally to Berea — Berea is not central — but free from dissipation. Lexington is central —

John G Fee[1]

1. Fee to Whipple, 16 Dec. 1865, AMAA 44283.

Camp Nelson, Dec. 21st, 1865
Brig. Gen[l] C.B. Fisk

Dear Sir   Enclosed you will find a copy of a proposition made me by Gen[l] Burbridge

I can get up a company of one to five hundred and I believe it is the best that can be done for the people and in fact the only way I could possibly get off women with a large number of children

I have begun to make up the company.

If you approve, please to give me authority to close the contract so there will be no question on that point and also give me written authority to make contracts in the case of Orphan Children

I have promised to have the company ready to start next week Wednesday counting on your approval and believing myself already authorised to make the contract but I want it so there will be no question in the mind of Gen[l] B

He will take the Orphan Children on terms that you may think fair and just

If you will endorse the plan I can make a very large reduction of the camp

Capt Ransom closes up with this month and after that there will be no post commissary here

He is ordered to turn over all commissary stores and funds now in his hands to L[t] Col. McFerrel at Cincinnati   The camp fund goes into the hand of Col. F

I have tried to arrang so as to still be able to draw on the fund after the chang, but cannot do so

I have about 300 sick and no earthly means with which to provide for them after the change. I have not a pound of flour for the sick and cannot get any more

Capt Ransom proposes to turn over all I will take of such articles as he still has on hand and in view of the necessities of the camp, I shall take all I can get

I know it is right and proper to urge out all who can possibly go but there are many who must be cared for for awhile — I hired Chapin to remain at $50 per month as per your instructions when I was at Nashville

Yesterday Vincent received his discharge from the Q M

I cannot do without him at present

Reynolds who has been in the Doct's Office was also discharged

Doct Mitchell considers his services indispensable at present and will probably write you to that effect but that is a matter about which I have nothing to say with this exception viz he does a very large share of the labor and were it not for the small pox ward could do the whole and I have no idea Mitchell can make a single report himself. [*This paragraph is marked* Private *in the margin.*] I never knew till today how dependent he has been upon Reynolds

(We have today 1,000 in camp)

Reynolds has been on the Q M Books at a salary of $50 per month

I would respectfully recommend that he be retained by the Bureau as I have been informed within a <u>few moments</u> that he will venture to run the small pox ward. [Private; *in margin of this paragraph.*]

Gen[l] Burbridge requests me to write you in regard to transportation

He takes the people beyond your jurisdiction and wishes you to make some provision for their transportation through

Please to instruct <u>me at your earliest convenience</u>

How shall I run the hospital after the fund passes out of Capt. Ransoms hand

How and where shall I have rations for such as I cannot dispose of to Genl B   *

R E Farwell Supt Refugee Home[1]

1. Farwell to Fisk, 21 Dec 1865; M999:7:385–88; RG 105.

Col^d Ref Home Camp Nelson Ky   21st Dec 1865
Capt Farwell, Superintendent &c

Sir   I want and will contract for from one to two Hundred, or more, if they can be furnished, freedmen, to go with me to my plantation in Washington County Mississippi and work for the year 1866, on the following terms, viz

for 1st Class Men for Month	$10 —
2^d " " "	8 —
3" " " "	6 —
Boys according to size	3 to 5
1st Class Women	7
2 "	5
Girls	3 " 4

And in addition to this amount of pay per month, to furnish them food and Clothing and pay their Doctors bills free of charge to them.

In making this proposition I want of course sound and able bodied people, and expect them delivered to me on the plantation.

I will give any guarantee for the proposition that may be required by the Freedmans Bureau or other department of the Government — competent to this contract   *

F A Harrow

I guarantee the above proposition —

F A Harrow and myself being general partners in above business and propositions

S G Burbridge Maj Genl U.S.A.

The plantation is on the Mississippi river.[1]

1. F.A. Harrow and Burbridge to Farwell, 21 Dec. 1865; M999:7:390–91; RG 105. This whole letter is a copy transcribed for Farwell. All of it, including the signatures, is in the same handwriting except the last line, which is in Farwell's own hand.

Camp Nelson Dec 22nd 1865
Brevet Maj Genl C.B. Fisk

Dear Sir   Permit me to congratulate you on your recent promotion. It gives me pleasure to be able to do so

I have been busy getting up a company for Missippi to day and now have one hundred pleged to go

It is not just what I would like for them if I could have my choice but all things considered, I believe it the best that can be done

Gen¹ Burbridge is a very clever gentleman but it is evident he will leave the details of the business to his partner Harrow who is without doubt the owner of the plantation and is a very good specimen of the swell head, whiskey drinking Southern planter

It will be very important to have a straight contract.

If you leave the matter of contracting with me, I will do the best I can to secure the interests of the people

Gen¹ in todays Cin. Gazette I read in a letter from the pen of Justice "that there was a time when you went out from the home of your widowed Mother a barefoot boy and remember well when that mother placed the last mouthfull of food on the table she had in the house"

This morning many a mother in this camp did the same thing for her children and then came to me to have the larder replenished

They are not to blame for being here for they were coaxed and driven and draged into this camp   I have not means at my command with which to supply the wants of the sick and those who cannot by any means help themselves

I have no flour or sugar and both are indispensable among the sick

This Camp was a war measure and was an instrument in the hand of the Hon Secy of War with which he harassed and worried the enemies of the gov.

The innocent women and children ought not to suffer and persist now in the hour of the nations victory after having contributed their full share to secure that victory

It would be well for our Hon Sec of War to recall the memorable words of his predecessor on a certain occasion "This nation cannot afford to do injustice to a single citizen even though he be a black man, for one poor black man with God and justice on his side is mightier than all the hosts of the rebellion"

By the memory of the early days of your own life Gen¹ I pray you to do what you can to enable me to do what humanity and justice so urgently demand

I do not know how I could have done more than I have to disperse this people (for the way has been constantly blocked) and still there are a large number here

To day I have been told by poor women that the thing is turning out just as the rebels of this state predicted viz you will be draged into camp in the summer and turned out to die in the winter

I do not believe in heeding every word these people say but I am a little sore to night

The fact is that in every step in the late strife the nation has been compelled by the providence of God to do justice to the colored race

It has not been free voluntary cheerful but we have been scourged into the right way

In the case of this Missippi party I could not feel justified in getting it up were it not for the confidence I feel that you will follow & protect the people and unless you do so I have no doubt they will curse me and the day they consented to go

Hagar is coming here in a few days   Please to send some certificate so she will stand all right when she goes before the people of Ohio to ask for charity as you proposed

I believe she ought to have <u>some</u> compensation   It is just & fair and ought to be settled satisfactorily, for she has certainly saved the Gov a large expense and done the people good

Gen[l] I must have that fund if it is a possible thing so I can use it to procure wood for the hospital at any rate   it will be a cursed shame if it cant be procured some way   *

R.E. Farwell, Supt Refugee Camp[1]

1. Farwell to Fisk, 22 Dec. 1865; M999:7:373–78; RG 105.

Nashville   Dec 25th [*186*]5
Capt. R.E. Farwell   Supt &c   Camp Nelson Ky

Dear Sir — I have rec[d] yours of the 21st and telegraphed you that the proposition of Genl Burbridge was approved. Transportation would be furnished via Cinti. & Steamers to his plantation on the Miss. River. The children can be apprenticed at Vicksburgh by the Ass[t] Comr <u>there</u> — under the Mississippi Regulations. Close the Camp as rapidly as humanity will permit. The Washington authorities are quite impatient at its continuance into winter — I go to Louisville to night and will make some arrangements for rations — draw all you can — say thirty days supply from Capt Ransom before he leaves — Dr Mitchell remains for the present & you may retain Reynolds — <u>Push Push Push</u>. I want you at Louisville.   *

Clinton B Fisk   Bvt Maj Genl and Asst Comr[1]

1. Fisk to Farwell, 25 Dec. 1865; M999:2:396; RG 105.

New York, Dec. 28th, 1865
Rev. J.G. Fee, Berea, Ky.

Dear Sir, We want definite and accurate information relative to Camp Nelson, Ky., and in addition to the reports asked for in the accompanying blank, I want to get answers to the following inquiries.

1st. How many colored people are there at the camp?

2d. How many are of suitable age, and should be in school?

3d. What accommodations are there for schools?; (a) numbers of buildings; (b) size and kind of buildings?

4th. How many persons rendering any service to the American Missionary Association or looking to us for any compensation? Their names and employment. Ministers, teachers, or family missionaries, or other laborers. If ministers, where and to how many do they preach? If teachers, whether they teach alone or in company, and how many scholars they have to teach?

5th. The number of employees there from other societies and what kind of labor they perform.

Please return an answer as early as possible, and if definite answers cannot be given to any of the inquiries, please give your opinion on the subject and so state. I trust you will reply at once and oblige, Yours &c.,

Geo. Whipple   Cor. Sec.[1]

1. Whipple to Fee, 28 Dec. 1865, BCA.

Louisville, Ky., Dec. 29th, 1865

Bro. Fee, Your letter reached me day before yesterday in Cleveland on my return from New York. I am sorry that any business should transpire between yourself and Bro. Scofield in connection with the property turned over to the Refugees through Bro. Scofield which needs the least reference of the matter to me at this late date.

I am sorry that any proposition to sell property thus turned over has been made, for that would be violating the trust which had been reposed.

I, of course, have no authority in the matter now as the U.S. San Com. has ceased to Exist. I, however, hope that Bro. Scofield will deal with this matter in a manner worthy of my confidence in the future, as I have ever found him in the past. I really cannot see why there should be any difficulty, when in turning the stores over it was distinctly understood that they were for the benefit of the Colored Refugees. * * * *

Thomas D. Butler[1]

1. Butler to Fee, 29 Dec. 1865, BCA.

KENTUCKY.
From Rev. A. Scofield
CAMP NELSON, KY., Dec. 30, 1865.

Our school at "The Home" has been large, but we could not accomodate so many in the cold weather as at other times. The average attendance for the current month has been something over one hundred, taught by my wife and daughter, with what I could aid them. The scholars are making good progress in learning, but there is great need of books, readers and spelling books, which could be sold if we had them. In conjunction with the Chaplain of the 119 Regiment of Colored Troops, we have opened a school in the barracks for the soldiers, where about a hundred are taught with good success. In this school my other daughter is teaching, with usefulness, I trust. The Camp is gradually dissolving, still there are many people here and much call for labor. Brother Fee has left, and my labors are much increased by having the poor and the suffering to look after in the Refugee Home. Slowly, but surely, that institution is passing away. There is much suffering there, and some bitter complaints. I think a Normal School might be started here for the education of colored teachers that would be productive of great good—when the Camp, as a government institution, shall be no more.[1]

1. *AM* 10, no. 2 (February 1865): 32; also in Scofield to Secretaries, AMA, 30 Dec. 1865, AMAA 44287.

Letterhead.] U.S. Sanitary Commission   Soldier's Home Camp Nelson, Ky., **Dec 30ᵗʰ 1865**
Bro. Whiting

* * * * [*Expense account.*]
When brother Fee was here, I lent him all the money I had supposing that the call I made for one hundred dollars would be sent   you sent $50 to my daughter and $75 to me, the amt due here — of course I have been moneyless — I am living on borrowing and <u>have been since</u> I lent that to brother Fee. I hope you will be able to remit me something without delay — for my credit will not hold out much longer. My family at home also (for there are three of them there yet) are needy and will need something more soon.
Hoping you will find this act [*account*] satisfactory *

A. Scofield[1]

1. Scofield to Whiting, 30 Dec. 1865, AMAA 44288.

KENTUCKY.

REV. JOHN G. FEE is anxious to provide some way to make it possible for the colored people of Kentucky to become owners of land. He says that white men there, owning from two hundred to four hundred acres of land, "will not sell a scrap to a nigger." He has proposed to persons in Ohio and elsewhere, to form a company, and buy and sell lands to colored men and others on equitable business principles, securing a moderate but fair profit.
He says lands in some parts of the State are selling at from $50 to $100 per acre, but in the mountain counties they can be bought for from one to five dollars per acre. He advises colored men to locate there, and thinks that by their becoming owners of the soil, and producers of valuable commodities, they will soon rise higher than the condition of mere boot-blacks or day-laborers.[1]

1. *AM* 10. no. 1 (January 1866): 18.

Camp Nelson   Jan 3ᵈ 1866
Brev. Maj Genˡ C B Fisk

Dear Sir   Your favor of Dec 29 and previous telegram and note were duly received
Before receiving yours of the 29 of Dec I had stoped the issue of regular rations, but opened a sort of Soup house for the hardest cases
I think everything is made as disagreeable for the people as you could desire. At any rate, my ingenuity is completely exhausted.
If anything more can be done I think the man has got to grow who can do it
The column is moving tolerably fast and very few now call in question the dispersion of the people at an early date

I sent fifty to Nicholasville yesterday on their way to Miss but Capt Restiaux will not give transportation beyond Covington nor will Capt Baker[1] who relieves him tomorrow

Capt R says you promised to get an ordor to cover him in such cases but he has not seen it   I shall send them to Covington in the morning and have Gen[l] Burbridge to work his way through for I have done all I can   They are out of this home and the emigration idea works like a charm for I push and it creates a panic and ten go other ways while one goes to Miss.

Capt Ransom turned over all stores left on hand to me.

I have after consultation with Capt R made a bill for hospital supplies large enough to cover the ballance or nearly so of the fund

After charging the supplies turned over to me the ballance will probably be about $2000

It is sort of whipping the devil around a stump since I dont know as you will approve but I have acted by advice of those who are interested in the question of the propriety of the act and after revolving the matter in my own mind concluded to take what I can get

If I get the ballance as I expect I will not use any part of it till instructed by you

Miss Hagar is here and would come to Louisville to see you but we expect you here every day   She is in distress, but if she has money to pay the bills contracted on account of our Camp Nelson people she will be all right

I hope you will come up or if not have an interview at Louisville

I will make report for Dec in a few days   *

R E Farwell Supt Ref Home[2]

1. Baker is unidentified.
2. Farwell to Fisk, 3 Jan 1866; M999:7:407–10; RG 105.

Camp Nelson Ky   Jan 8th 1866
Brev. Maj Gen[l] C.B. Fisk

Dear Sir   In accordance with your instructions I took all the rations I could get from Capt E.P. Ransom

You will see that after deducting my issue for the month of Dec from what I received from Capt Ransom I have left on hand a ballance of $5744.26 of that amount $3816.41 is value of rations on hand and the ballance $1927.85 in cash * * * * [*One paragraph.*]

. . . I have no flour meal or bread stuf of any kind and must buy at once   The people are leaving in a hurry   I cannot tell how many I have on hand, for they go without reporting in many cases

If I could get teams, I could send away one hundred & fifty tomorrow

I get all the teams I can of the Q M and hire all I can

From this to the end of this month I shall not be able to give the exact number on hand or the number of rations issued

I think I have from 700 to 800 in camp and issue or use about 300 rations per day   The leading articles of diet are <u>Beans & Split Peas</u>   <u>The people want to leave</u>   *

R.E. Farwell Supt Refugee Home

P S Your favor of Jan. 6ᵗʰ is in hand   The ballance of the fund in Capt Ransoms hands is about $400[1]

1. Farwell to Fisk, 8 Jan. 1866; M999:7:404–5; RG 105.

Camp Nelson, Ky   January 10ᵗʰ 1866.
General: * * * * [*One paragraph.*]

I am entirely idle, having no employment which brings me money, and am, therefore, naturally very willing to undertake anything which will enable me to live comfortably. I am expecially willing to go into the work in which you are engaged, and if you can find something for me to do I will be glad to go at it.

My cousin, Mr. C.E. Bierbower[1], who has been on duty at Camp Nelson as "pass master", is, equally with myself, in want of work. He is an excellent clerk, and is an educated gentleman. I will be very grateful if you can give him employment — either in your own office or as an agent of the Bureau. Genl. Burbridge was only partially successful in getting laborers at the "Home". The Freedmen are greatly prejudiced against going to the South: and it was only on great exertion and after many days that 75 was induced to volunteer. A few were conscripted and driven to the cars, but — I believe many of them deserted in Louisville. However, they are now away from the Home and must shift for themselves. * * * * [*One paragraph.*]

F.H. Bierbower

Brev. Brig. Genl. C.B. Fisk, Asst. Commissioner, &c. Freedmens Bureau[2]

1. Charles E. Bierbower (born 1841 in Baltimore, Maryland), clerk and pass master at Camp Nelson, was a first cousin of Frederick H. Bierbower. Their relationship is confirmed in the IGI at www.familysearch.org.
2. Bierbower to Fisk, 10 Jan. 1866; M999:9:483–84; RG 105.

Camp Nelson Ky   Jan. 12ᵗʰ 66
Brev. Maj. General C.B. Fisk!

Dear Sir, In yours of the 6th inst. to Capt. Farwell you express a desire to know the facts in relation to my labor among the Freedmen.

Col. Jacques, Gen. Barrett, Mr. Williams wished me to labor in connexion with them to close up Camp Nelson Refugee Home. At that time I was receiving $1200 per annum in Springfield Ohio & I said to Col. Jacques that I could not live on air and must return to my School & Seminary. He urged me to remain and said

I should be paid as much as the salary I received for teaching. But the salary is not of as much consequence to me as another matter.

I took from Camp Nelson 350 (directly from Camp Nelson not reckoning the 2 Co.^{ies} which Capt Farwell sent off by Mr Vincent & whom I met in Cin. & took to homes provided for them) I say I took from Camp Nelson 350 poor colored Refugees, some of them very young others quite old — and conducted them to the state of Ohio. Very many of that number would today be in this home & dependent on Gov. had I not taken them away. They were poor & had neither money or friends. I could not take them away hundreds of miles without incurring a large expense.

I paid the expense out of my own purse and after my own means gave out gave my note and became personally responsible. When I could not get transportation from Capt Hunt in Cin., when the[y] laughed of[f] Orders of Gen. Fisk & Freedmens Bureau what did I do? I gave my name to the amount $189. I took my Co. and went & all was well. This expense is not among this bill. What shall I do with it? The expense paid besides the notes I gave amounts am. to $900

I am ashamed to go before the people where I gave my notes, for I have no means to pay them. I enclose with this note an account of my expenses. I cannot think of going to Ohio to beg for I have no gift in that direction. I would much rather as much as I need the money never see a penny than to beg for it. I was engaged in taking away the people from the 14th of Septbr. up to Nov 29 th.

If you can consistently do anything about the matter I should be very glad, but when not I can charge it over to humanity.

Capt. Ransom said to me that you said to him: set aside $500 from the fund for Miss Hager's use, but he could not do it.

Could you not come here & see things & matters & persons   There are yet 580 pers. here. The orphans I take with me to Ohio. Please answer, but far better come visit us. *

                                                                    Annie Hager

[*On the file for this letter someone has written:*] On the rampage. Hagar still lives. [*And, in a different hand, someone adds:*]   — Sweet morsel —[1]

1. Hager to Fisk, 12 Jan. 1866; M999:10:348–50; RG 105.

Camp Nelson Ky   Jan. 15. 66

Gen. Fisk! Capt. <u>Farwell is pretty</u> well posted in things and matters concerning me. Col. Jacques, Gen. Barrett, Mr. Williams hired me for the work. I've take 350 directly from Camp & upward of 100 indirectly through Vincent & others brought to Covington, where I met them. As to the expenses & railroad bill &c to which I signed my name, he also may know most of it, so the matter is in his and your hand. Do you both as ye please and according to your doing be your inward satisfaction. I have no confidence in all of you. They promised and begged untill they had me engaged in the dirty work. you yourself said to Capt. Ransom to appropriate $500 from the fund for Miss Hagers Negroes & now when the work is done & a situation which yielded me $1200 per an. is sacrificed than you can send me to beg before the generously disposed people of Ohio, as if Ohio had not done enough when she received the disordered women of Camp Nelson, the halt and the maimed and the blind & cured them and gave them a home and I taught them neatness and activity — but go on, Gen., may it feel grand to be insulting, give me more, it will not disturb my peace nor my activity among the Negroes. Do as you please. Hagar lived before she saw Camp Nelson & her glorious commanders & she will be able to live yet long after your Missions & Coms. of insult lay moldering in the dust.

Annie Hager.[1]

1. Hager to Fisk, 15 Jan. 1866; M999:10:277–80; RG 105.

Camp Nelson, Ky., Jan 15th, 1866
Rev. W.E. Whiting

* * * * [*One paragraph, followed by an account, but all indecipherable.*]
One of my daughters is teaching class in the 119th regiment. But my wife and second daughter have more than their hands full. The school was steadily 125 and others want to come. I have to day fitted up another room with stove and benches & will [surely?] make some additional expense for wood for the present month.

If on the receipt of this you send check for $50 to my daughter, Elizabeth Scofield, at Willett, Cortland co state of New York it would be gratefully accepted. One half of our family is there and in circumstances of need. With much regard, I am, your brother in the field

A. Scofield[1]

1. Scofield to Whiting, 15 Jan. 1866, AMAA 44292.

[*Letterhead.*] *U.S. Sanitary Commission   Soldier's Home Camp Nelson, Ky.,* **Jan 15th 1866**
Rev Geo. Whipple

Dear brother   Your letter of the 28th ult. should have been answered sooner but better late than never. You ask how many colored people are in the camp. An. [*Answer*] 6 companies of the 119th reg. about 1500 Women and children in every conceivable condition of wretchedness and sorrow. Then some 3 or 4 hundred discharged soldiers, most of the 124th and 175th reg. nearly 5000 in all.

2. How many are of suitable age and should be in school   We have in our school at the Home a steady attendance of 175. Had we teachers could easily have three or four hundred. There are five hundred here in and about camp who ought to be in school this winter. But as the government is literally compelling them to leave the Refugee Home, many of them will soon be gone.

"What accommodation are there — no. of buildings &c." Ans. 1st there are the large Rooms at the Refugee Home, capable of accommodating 7 or 8 hundred pupils, now empty and forsaken and soon to be sold, because of the policy of the Freedmens Bureau to break up all camps of colored men. 2nd, there is the Old Soldiers Home, occupied by us, which with a little outlay could accommodate 4 or 5 hundred. These buildings will be sold in a few weeks probably, unless something is done to stay the sale. $700 dollars will likely buy them, though they cost 3 or 4 thousand. The superintendent of the Refugee Home says the government would give them to your society if you would apply for them.

3ᵈ There are the old Hospital buildings now occupied by 119ᵗʰ, will be vacated in spring four substantial buildings in good condition ten wards 15 feet long and about 40 ft wide just the thing for virtual school. These two will be sold for a song.

4ᵗʰ How many are rendering service to American Miss.   A. Scofield Minister teacher & preacher on the sabbath, sometimes during week writes letters distributes clothing gives counsel draws up contracts and attends to soldiers claims when called on. Mrs Anne J. Scofield his wife teacher in the school at "the Soldiers Home" Miss Harriet Scofield teacher of class in the 119ᵗʰ Reg. Miss Mary Scofield assistant teacher at the Home. No other teachers are here except Mrs. Anna Musick[1] wife of one of the officers in the 119ᵗʰ paid, I believe by the soldiers. Mr Chapin, secretary of the Home keeps the Books gives out paper keeps Record of Rations &c of that dying institution

The chaplain and myself are the only ministers here who look after the spiritual welfare of this wide and wicked camp. As he confines his labors entirely to his Reg., all the rest comes under my pastoral. Camp Nelson as a government institution will probably by 1ˢᵗ of May be numbered among the things that pass. If some of these building here and about 30 acres of this land could be turned into a school great good could be done. Now is the time to move. So confident am I of the success of such an effort that had I the means I would undertake it as an individual enterprise — But I entrust all to your superior wisdom — and will only add that I truly believe the salvation of Kentucky as well as the whole South depends upon a speedy and thorough education of the freedmen   Respectfully your brother

A. Scofield[2]

1. Anna Smith had married William H.H. Musick by this time.
2. Scofield to Whipple, 15 Jan. 1866, AMAA 44293–4.

Berea Madison co Ky   Jan 16 /66

Dear Bro Whipple —
* * * * [*Five paragraphs.*]
3. "What accommodations — [*Fee is answering the same set of questions from the AMA as Scofield above*] (a) Number of buildings — size & kind of buildings" In the Refugee Home there are I believe 97 cottages — each 32 feet long by 16 wide — one partition making two rooms in each. There are four wards, 25 by 75 feet One large Dining Room 30 by 100 feet with two large cells *[*Fee's asterisk; at bottom of sheet: *one school house 2 stories high 7 rooms —] one superinten-

dents house two stories high with 18 rooms in it — some five other buildings, as offices &c — pertaining to the Hospital.

These are separated from the rest of the buildings of the camp   There are ten General Hospital buildings 25 by 100 — these are plastered & white washed — neat buildings. The buildings in the Refuge Home are not plastered, but good frames — The cottages are "box houses" the other buildings are weatherboarded. These buildings are still kept by order of Genl. Fisk   We proposed to the War Department to take the buildings & pay the damages the land holder asked but the refugees could not then be put out and Genl Fisk holds the buildings and will probably continue to do so until March or April. Then he will probably turn them over to some association for a school. Capt Farwell gave me to understand that this would be true & said Genl. Fisk is fixing for the birth of a foreign minister. Farwell had just returned from a visit to Fisk and said to me Fee any arrangement you may make for schools at Camp Nelson or at Lexington Genl Fisk will likely endorse   He wants the people of Ky themselves to take the responsibilities of the schools

Farwell said he would rather we would not then make any move toward schools — he wanted no attractions there then — said he would keep me posted as to movements there   I had expected him here before this date. Genl. Fisk did not encourage the location of a school at Camp Nelson as at Berea. The latter he has not seen & knows not how insignificant it is.

You were not ready to encourage any definite action at Camp Nelson   You advised that I "do not move my family yet" — that was last fall — My son Burritt was soon sick with fever — Berea needed a lift and my sons my presence and so I retired to Berea

We are now getting up another charter & preparing to go before the benevolent public, soon, for aid. * * * * [Two paragraphs.]

The school either at Camp Nelson or at Lexington will be essentially a colored school — perhaps wholly so. Here it will be mixed — probably   The colored are coming fastest and many more will come if we give them a "fair show" This may result in the running away of the "whitefolks"   We think we will make the school so excellent that the whitefolks will stay for the sake of the advantages and after a time outgrow former prejudices. * * * * [Eleven paragraphs.]

J G Fee[1]

1. Fee to Whipple, 16 Jan. 1866, AMAA 44295–7.

Head Qrs. Dept of Kentucky   Louisville   Jan 17, 1866.
C.G. Bartlett   Col. 119. U.S.C. Inf.   Comdg Camp Nelson, Ky.
Thro' Head Qrs.   1st Division, Dept of Ky.

Colonel: The Major General Comdg directs that you extend Captain Farwell Supt Colored Refugees &c every facility in your power to enable him to speedily close out the Refugee Home at Camp Nelson, Ky. *

E B Harlan   A.A. Genl.[1]

1. Emory B. Harlan to Charles G. Bartlett, 17 Jan. 1866; Vol. 25/25 DKy, Letter No. 28 [no pagination]; Letters Sent, May-Sept. 1863 and Sept. 1864-Mar. 1869, Entry 2164 [Part 4 of 4]; General Records, Department of Kentucky, Part 1; RG 393.

[*Letterhead.*] *Office Superintendent*
For Boyle, Lincoln and Mercer Counties, Ky
Bureau R.F. & A.L.
Danville, Ky., **Jany 22ᵈ 1866.**
Bᵗ Maj Genl C.B. Fisk   Asst. Comʳ Ky and Tenn.

I have the honor to state the following facts, that you may know the dificulties we have to encounter here.

The Country is infested with Guerrila bands and the outrages most generally are committed on Colored persons who are precluded from testimony against them.

I am powerless to accomplish anything without Soldiers. The people are generally well enough disposed so far as taking a proper view of the labor question is concerned, but are misled by politicians and seem to think the object of the establishment of the Bureau in Ky, was to oppress them.

I found a great deal of vagrancy here but by the aid of many Loyal Citizens and the efforts of the leaders of the Colored population have to a great extent caused it to disappear.

You are quite aware that I have had to grope my way in the dark, the manual promised will be hailed as an Angel of light. *

William Goodloe   Supt &c[1]

1. Goodloe to Fisk; M999:10:48–50; RG 105.

Camp Nelson   Jan 26ᵗʰ 1866
Brev. Maj Genˡ C B Fisk

Dear Sir   I have fifty seven vacant Cottages

Nothing would expedite the task of closing this Camp like selling and demolishing the buildings

I can constantly decrease the issue of rations but many will not leave till they see that the buildings are to be removed   *

R.E. Farwell[1]

1. Farwell to Fisk, 26 Jan. 1866; M999:9:1432; RG 105.

Camp Nelson Ky   Jany. 27 1866
Genl. C.B. Fisk

Dear Sir   Having learned that the Buildings at this place occupied by the Colored refugees are soon to be vacated and disposed of in some way, I have taken the Liberty of writing you a proposition on behalf of Mr Jos M. Moss on whose Lands said Buildings are Located. It has been intimated to me that the Govt. would probably give up such Buildings in part or full payment of the Claims of parties owning the Land upon which they are erected. I can say for Mr Moss that he has a claim. and I think a very just one against the Govt as he has had nearly everything he was worth in the world, except his land, taken from him and all used for the benefit of the Army. and besides that he has submitted to his losses with a cheerfulness and resignation which but few would have worn.

Mr Moss is a truly Loyal man and has been since the Commencement of the Rebellion.

If therefore it is the purpose to turn these Buildings over provided the owner of the Land will take them, he would like to Know and also Know at what time they will be vacated. Mr Moss is willing to take the Buildings at a fair valuation to be entered as so much received upon his claim against the Govt.

I understand there is some probability that Buildings here on other Lands will probably be turned over to parties owning the Land.

If this meets your approbation I will then make out for Mr. Moss a formal proposition to take the Buildings.

Please answer by return mail. You can write to me at Danville or to Mr. Moss at this place. *

Speed S. Fry[1]

1. Fry to Fisk, 27 Jan. 1866; M999:12:51–53; RG 105. Fry, no longer in the military by this time, was working as a lawyer in the region.

[*Letterhead.*] *Head-Quarters Department of Kentucky, Office Chief Quartermaster, Louisville, Ky.*
Jany 29th **1866.**
Maj. Gen. M.C. Meigs   Qr. Mr. Genl U.S.A.   Washington D.C.

General, I have the honor to report that I have made a personal inspection of the following Qr. Mr. Property remaining on hand at Camp Nelson and not required for the public service and to respectfully recommend that it be sold at public auction at that Post.

One Steam Engine, Boiler, Pipe and Machinery used in supplying the Camp with water, condition, good.

4063 Bushels Coal
380 Cords Wood
20,000 Lbs Horse Shoes unpacked
5,000   "   Mule   "   "

I am General   Very respectfully   Your obt ser't
R.N. Batchelder   Bvt Col & Chf Q.M.[1]

1. Richard N. Batchelder to Meigs, 29 Jan. 1866, Box 720; RG 92.

[*Letterhead.*] *United States Sanitary Commission.* **Camp Nelson Ky**   **Feb 4 66**

General Fisk!   Forget not your Hager & your promise to make a bill, I believe of time or work for Oct. Nov. Jan. & Feb.

Refugee Home leaders have united hands & head & heart to pull now in one direction & I am overjoyed to see it. We do little enough even if we are perfectly agreed. Scofield, Mitchel, Captain all seem to go in perfect harmony.

There are precisely 299 persons in the cottages & 53 in the two hospitals.

The thing shall & will take a quiet peacefull end. We are busy. Trouble not your head about us. We do under such circumstances the best we can. They call me Haene Col. & Gen. When the thing is closed & I can get hold of Gen. Fisk I'll tell him why & he will smile a little. All morality & nobility has not left the Negroes of Camp Nelson. There are still some noble traits to be found.

Do not lose faith in us, I tell you we are working &, more than that, working in harmony. Affectionately your

Hagar in the wilderness of Camp Nelson

My love to your loving Secretary, if you please.[1]

1. Hager to Fisk, 4 Feb. 1866; M999:10:338–39; RG 105.

Camp Nelson, Ky. February 13, 1865 [*actually 1866*].

General: I have the honor to address you in behalf of my cousin, Mr C.E. Bierbower, who, you will no doubt remember, was employed with your sanction to perform such clerical duties at the Post H^d. Qu. as related to the affairs of the Freedmen's Bureau.

When I was assigned to duty at the Refugee Home there were no white soldiers in the camp except a few who belonged to the Veteran Reserve Corps, and who, were by order from the War Dept, placed under the exclusive control of the Surgeon in charge of the Genl. Hospital. None of these men were competent to perform the duties required of my cousin, and even had I found any of their number who were competent the Surgeon in charge would have promptly refused to separate them from their command.

While in command of this Camp I issued free passes to (13322) thirteen thousand three hundred and twentytwo negroes and most of these passes were filled up and recorded by my cousin. His post, as you must be aware, was no sinecure. He was closely confined to his office and diligently and faithfully performed his work. . . . * * * * [*Four paragraphs.*]

F.H. Bierbower

Maj. Genl. C.B. Fisk, Supt. Freedmen's Bureau, Ky. & Tenn.[1]

1. Bierbower to Fisk, 13 Feb. 1866; M999:9:611–13; RG 105. In the omitted para-

graphs, Bierbower protests because his cousin has been denied payment by the Quartermaster's Department on the grounds that he was a civilian working for the Freedmen's Bureau at Camp Nelson.

Copy [*This word appears above address and date.*]
Hillsdale, Michigan   February 18ᵗʰ 1866
Genl Speed S Fry   Camp Nelson Ky

General   your letter of Jany 19ᵗʰ asking for information from me in relation to property of Mrs Scott[1] taken at Camp Nelson Ky by the Quartermasters Department while under my direction in May & June 1863, arrived during my absense in Washington and I embrace the earliest leisure since my return to answer your inquiries. When I arrived at Camp Nelson in May 1863 there were no troops there except a Battery of East Tenn troops commanded by Capt R Clay Crawford   they were encamped near Mrs Scotts house and were guarding the bridge across the Ky River   there was no forage of any kind taken from Mrs Scott by myself or by my orders   of this I am perfectly confident as I brought all the forage used by the public animals from Lexington. what makes me more certain of this is the fact that during the month of Febry 1863 [*two or three indecipherable words*] at Mrs Scotts place while on a march from Lexington to Danville at which time I was acting Quartermaster of the Command & at that time I was obliged to use all the Hay on the place and as there was no Corn or oats I obtained them from other parties in the neighborhood for all of which I gave receits which were all settled & paid by Captain H J Latham A Q M at Lexington. Afterwards in March of the same year our forces were driven back from Danville across the Ky River by the Rebels under Genl Pegram and our forces were encamped on Mrs Scotts place for three or four days and consumed all the forage in the vicinity. if the forage you mention had been on the place at that time it would most certainly have been used. with regard to the wheat growing on the ground, I have to say that I caused one or two roads to be used though the fields for the purpose of hauling timber from the woods. Animals were not allowed in the field except for that purpose and very little damage was done to the growing wheat not to exceed two acres. the wheat was harvested & taken away by Mr John Scott a son of Mrs Scott. I do not recollect about the corn growing on the Scott place. I commenced at Camp Nelson about the middle of May which is I think Corn planting time. I am confident that no corn on the ground was disturbed by my orders while I was on duty in charge of construction. I was relieved of that duty in July by Captain T.E. Hall A Q M after which time I was in charge of property while I remained at Camp Nelson and had no control of the grounds. Captain hall can doubtless give you information of what was done during his administration of Camp Nelson. I believe Genl I have answered all your inquiries in relation to this matter   Mrs Scott may have a good claim for compensation for the use of her land but she certainly has none for forage taken by me or by my direction. I shall send your letter with a copy of this to the Quartermaster General *
J.H. Pratt Late Capt & A Q M[2]

1. Mrs. Mary Scott, who launched a very long claim (in both senses) against the Federal government for damages to her Camp Nelson property, was the widow of Robert Scott (who died of yellow fever in New Orleans before February 1818), mother of Thomas B., Margaret, John, and Frances ("Fannie") Scott; Frances was the wife of Oliver H. Perry (they owned the White House, the recently restored officers' quarters of Camp Nelson). The Scott family had been prominent in Jessamine County, virtually from its inception, but Robert Scott married Mary Sappington on December 3, 1810, in Bourbon County. Several Mary Sappingtons appear in the records, but the one who became Mrs. Mary Scott was probably born about 1785 in Clark County, the daughter of Sylvester Sappington and his wife, Sarah. Information from Jessamine County Deeds and Probate Records, with genealogical details from IGI at www.familysearch.com. For more on the Scott property, see the first note in chapter 8.

2. James H. Pratt to Fry, 18 Feb. 1866, Box 1012; RG 92.

[*Letterhead.*] *United States Sanitary Commission* **Camp Nelson   Feb 26**[th] **1866**
Brev Maj Genl C B Fisk

Dear Sir   The buildings here were turned over by Capt Baker to me and I receipted for them

I shall soon be through — think this week would close up if I could get transportation.

But I cannot get anything I want   Please to instruct me what to do with the buildings when the people are out. If they are left, they will be filled up or burned   *

R E Farwell

P.S. I want to get away as soon as possible[1]

1. Farwell to Fisk, 26 Feb. 1866; M999:9:1470; RG 105.

Camp Nelson Ky   Feb 26 /66

Gen. Fisk!   Things go fast. A few more days & Camp is gone up. Orphans gone, few more sick in the hospitals & people that settled along the line, to our great distress, are fast moving on plantations. things Will take a happy end, thank God. Forget not my purse & your promise. The Secretary may remember it. I only say the more the better. If I put on pants & coat will you not commission me & give me employment?

Your wellknown Hagar in the Wilderness of Camp Nelson[1]

1. Hager to Fisk, 26 Feb. 1866; M999:10:436; RG 105.

Feb 28th **[*186*]6**
Miss Annie Hager   Camp Nelson Ky

Dear Madam — I enclose herewith for your signature vouchers for your services four months @ $100 [00] per month — you will please sign and return them to me. A draft will then be sent you for the amt less tax &c —

I thank you for your good earnest services — and God will reward you for your interest in the cause of the suffering poor. *

Clinton B. Fisk   B^t Maj Genl   Asst Comr[1]

1. Fisk to Hager, 28 Feb. 1866; M999:3:154; RG 105.

[*Letterhead.*] *Bureau Refugees, Freedmen and Abandoned Lands,*
States of Kentucky and Tennessee.
Assistant Commissioner's Office
Nashville, Tenn., **February 28 1866**
To Maj Gen'l J.L. Donaldson   Chief Quarter Master   Mil. Div. Tennessee
Nashville

General   I have the honor to inform you that all the buildings at Camp Nelson Kentucky, (109) one hundred and nine in number and which have been under the control of this Bureau according to authority from the Quarter Master General's Office dated Washington January 4th 1866 are no longer required therefor, and will be ready to be turned over to the Quarter Master's Department by March 10th 1866, for sale or such other disposition as you may deem proper.

I respectfully request that orders be issued to receive them at that date from this Bureau. *

Clinton B. Fisk   Bt. Maj Genl U.S.V. and
Assistant Commissioner States Ky and Tenn.[1]

1. Fisk to Donaldson, 28 Feb. 1866; Box 720; RG 92.

KENTUCKY.
From Rev. A. Scofield.
Laboring at Camp Nelson, Kentucky.
[*February, 1866*]

Tell the good friends in England that we feel grateful for their kind remembrance of our suffering poor. The blankets (one bale) they sent us through your kind ministration, have warmed and comforted at least four hundred needy women and children. I will mention a few cases in particular. One woman called on us for a blanket, and, as she appeared destitute, we gave her one. I followed her a few hundred yards to see how she fared. But, oh me! what a house! Slabs nailed in the form of a pen, about eight feet square, with a rude fire place on one side, one bench and a pail, comprised the whole furniture. On a few loose boards, which served for a floor, lay a pile of rags which served for a bed, a loose board answered for a door, and open cracks and corners supplied the place of windows! And whom do you think I found there? Two women and six children, two of them quite young. There they were, cold and huddled up around their fire, made of boards gathered up here and there around the camp. It was a sad sight, and I trust neither you nor the good friends in England will blame me for sending them a second blanket. Only a moment ago, one of these children was in here begging for bread, on this bitter cold day, and not one pint of food for the whole eight to eat!

A day or two since I saw a ragged blind man passing by, I caught up a blanket, and running up to him threw it over his head. With surprise, he asked what that was for. I replied, "A present to you from the good people of England." I left him pouring out his blessings upon the heads of the donors.

But I cannot multiply cases. Let it be the consolation of our good friends over the waters, that their donations have come to the hands of the poorest of *all creation*. There are none more needy, none more grateful among the suffering poor of this world, than the freedmen of this country.[1]

1. *AM* 10, no. 4 (April 1866): 85, 86; also a dated "copy of a letter from Rev. A. Scofield laboring at Camp Nelson," Feb. 1866, AMAA 44314.

Camp Nelson Ky   3/4 [*March 4*] 1866

Dear General!   Thank you for your excellent letter. It made me think I felt as good as the Dutchman or was perhaps the Dutchman myself whose happiness the king established by granting three wishes. first wish, beer, 2^d as much beer as he could drink, 3^d and a pitcher full besides. And I had money, as much money as I needed to pay my debts & a little besides & I shouted: hurrah for money, hurrah for Hager & hurrah for Gen. Fisk & hurrah I felt happy. I thought so at least.

General! we are done here, really done, we want to drive off a few more that settled close by the lines & thats all we have to do or can do.

You dont need to thank me for what I have done. I did not more than any other Swisswoman would have done had she seen so much lazyness & wickedness as I did. I may leave about the 14th or 15th of this mth. Clear out Cin. Walnut Hill Home. there are only ten more there; ask Coffin how his Gen. Hager went to work to have it done in 7 days & if that wasnt the right way. General, oh Gen I had remarkable success. If you had seen all the disordered women & the brutish me & yet not one blow not even a curse nay, most of them writing letters of love, thanking me for all I did to them, leading all another, leading a better life. Oh Gen. how I feel happy! how I put my head low & low & very low & say: Father I thank thee, it was thy work. I may be back here again in about 2 weeks, but merely to peep in how smallpox hospital & br. Scofield & those that settled around the Camp are getting along, & if in that time they will not be ready to go a little farther away from the soldiers & more into the country. Your bill goes to the end of April — farther than any of us will remain; regret it not; it will make up for the months in which I had no pay. When I see I have nothing more to do in Camp or Cin. then — oh Gen. dont think I am a fool — but I am crazy to take a leap to Chattanooga or Nashville & see the Schools so much spoken of at West. Freed. Aid Com. & here & there & everywhere. I want to see for myself. If I find any place that looks as Camp Nelson in June 65 I stick my self right there & go to work. But heaven preserve me from a

Commission of West. Freed Aid Society or any body else. if I feel it is my place I go to work & if I work noble persons will sustain me as you sustained me as Coffin & others no doubt would sustain me if my work was worthy of it. Confess Gen. thousands work & want to work for the Freedmen not because their heart is bound to bring them nearer humanity & freedome no. just to make a living. We need now women and men such as Pestalazzi, when he gathered his 300 child[ren] ragged, dirty, miserable, from around the Alps and lived with them, worked with them & made of them teachers of the people, men of sense & energie. But I preached to you long enough — By the way, when I paid the fare for my orphans Mr Wright & Coggeswell cancelled the heavy transportation bill I owed $189. so much gained for the Gov. Wish I had it in money. In all my traveling only once had I a free ticket but you know I am a woman. truly your,

A Hager

[*Written upside down across the bottom of two pages:*]Do not think I have fallen out with Coffin or his Society. this letter which you may keep or send back again will teach you better. I only mean a Commission if you do not feel that you are doing good is of no account, no matter how much it brings. But General, good night; kiss your wife for me & be happy & lay up some money & we [*will*] take a trip to Switzerland & there upon the Alps we [*will*] rest from the troubles of the Freedmans Bureau & the lice of Camp Nelson & all is well.[1]

1. Hager to Fisk, 4 Mar. 1866; M999:10:488–90; RG 105.

Berea Madison Co Ky   Mch 9 /66

Bro C B Fisk, I know Gabriel Burdett has not every excellence — needs more energy yet I regard him as a most excellent man — sensible, discreet, pious — one who has not hostile feeling toward the white race — one who will do more to allay <u>such feeling</u> than any other colored man I know.

In this respect he will do <u>much</u> good — also in other respects. In the region around about Camp Nelson he can do much good. I do hope you see it wise to <u>somehow</u> let him remain and have liberty to travel (as agent — in some way) and thus do good

I hope the Lord God will prosper you greatly in every good word & work.

I am ready to cooperate   Yours in Christ,

John G Fee

Capt. Farwell has made us a visit at Berea & done us much good as I believe [*An endorsement on the file for this letter reads:*]Let Burdette go to Camp Nelson with Farwell for duty there   J.[1]

1. Fee to Fisk, 9 Mar. 1866; M999:9:1693–95; RG 105.

Danville Ky   March 10. 1866

Dear Col. [*Bvt. Col. R.N. Batchelder*[1]]   I have the honor to acknowledge the receipt of yours of the 5th Inst. and am induced from the information it contains to answer at once. In regard to the [*two or three indecipherable words*] Q.M. General as to cost of Buildings at Camp Nelson I can only say they did cost a great deal of money and a great deal more than the Govt. will ever realize for them either at public or private sale. Many of the Buildings have already been sold at public outcry and but few if any have brought as much as the owners of the Land would be willing to give for them. There has been an immense sacrifice in the sale of these Buildings and necessarily so because of the waste of Lumber in tearing them down.

If then the Govt can dispose of them privately at an advance upon the public sale and thus pay of[f] a claim either in whole or in part, is it not better than to go to the expence of a public sale? The time and expense in making a private sale of the whole of them would not be as great as that attending the sale of one Building at public outcry. I have attended some of these public sales and know exactly what they amount to. In spite of all the office in charge can do, outside combinations will be formed for the purpose of getting property very cheap. Such things cannot be prevented.

The owners of the Lands upon which these Buildings stand are willing to pay a fair price for them. the amount of their valuation to be credited upon their claims agst the Govt, claims not in the nature of "<u>actual</u> damages," but claims for rent of Lands for wood and rails taken from them by the Quarter Masters and actually used for the benefit of the U.S. Army.

Whilst they have sustained incalculable damage in the distribution of crops growing upon their Land at the time the camp was establishing, by the erection of Fortifications, by running turn pike roads though them, by Quarrying by ditching, by the wasting of the Land by the destruction of the grass, and by cutting down valuable fruit trees, yet they claim nothing for these things, but will be content to get for the articles first above mentioned the Lowest estimate placed upon them, both in quantity and value by Loyal men and men too familiar with all the facts, and men also in every way reliable.

If the Buildings were disposed of there would then be nothing to require the presence of officers and soldiers and the Camp could at once be abandoned.

As I remarked in one of my former letters to you on this subject, these people for whom I ask these Buildings, have been very great sufferers by our Army, not only by the destruction created but by being deprived of the use of their Lands so long. This will make the fourth Season they have been deprived of their Lands. If the Lands were turned over to them to day they Could do but little in the way of crop this Season, because of the impossibility of making the necessary fencing in time.

Now I wish you if you please to Lay these facts before the Genl, and see if he cannot under such circumstances as those given above, grant this one request. I feel fully persuaded that time and money will be saved by it, and besides afford these people a chance to go to work at once to repair their farms.

Timber is very scarce in the region round about Camp Nelson and I do not see how they are to fence in their farms, except at an enormous expense, unless they can procure the Lumber in these old Buildings

In order to satisfy the Genl. that these Buildings will sell very Low at public sale, at a sale of some about a week since I purchased three 32 feet Long 16 feet wide containing, exclusive of the shingles, some 4000 feet of Lumber for the sum of $41.50/100. I mean for all three. The Lumber in these three Buildings just from the saw, with shingles added would to day cost me the neat little sum of $430 —

I shall await with some anxiety a reply to this letter and sincerely hope it may bring me a favorable answer   *

Speed S. Fry

[*Endorsement:*] Respectfully submitted to the Qr. Mr. Genl. U.S. Army and attention invited to my report of April 4th relative to the property at Camp Nelson. The buildings referred to be Gen Fry was having been purchased by him for $41 50/100 were used as a Small Pox Hospital, which will account for the low price at which they sold.

R.N. Batchelder   Bvt Col & Chf. Q.M.   O.C.Q.M.
Dept of Ky   Louisville April 5th 1866[2]

1. Richard Napoleon Batchelder, Union officer from New Hampshire, had risen in the ranks of quartermasters; he had been a captain assigned as quartermaster since February 1865. According to *CWD*, he was breveted as a brigadier-general rather than as colonel.
2. Fry to Batchelder, 10 Mar. 1866; Camp Nelson, Box 720; RG 92.

Camp Nelson Ky   Mar 12th 1866
Brev Maj Gen[l] C.B. Fisk

Dear Sir   I have the honor to report the refugee home closed

Expected to leave for Nashville this morning but received an Order from Gen[l] Ely[1] to arrest and try Henry Thomas   It will require some days. . . . * * * * [*Three paragraphs.*]

R.E. Farwell[2]

1. Gen. Ralph Ely, Union officer from New York, had been a captain in the Eighth Michigan and rose to the command of the First Division, Ninth Army Corps, Army of the Potomac. *CWD;* Dyer, 1:63; *HR,* 1:404.
2. Farwell to Fisk, 12 Mar. 1866; M999:9:1672; RG 105.

Nicholasville Kentucky   March 12th 1866
Hon. S. McKee and others — Members of the U.S. Congress

Hon. Sirs: — Believing it just and right that our Representatives in Congress should possess the facts on both sides of every question presented for their consideration and action — and especially so, where large sums of money are claimed as Damages — we beg permission to present the union side of a few facts bearing upon the case of the claim for Damages by Mrs Mary Scott at Camp Nelson Ky.   J.C. Merritt Esqr. former Post Master at Camp Nelson and for many years a resident and land holder in the immediate neighborhood of Camp Nelson, states that he is thoroughly posted as to the price of land and the value of land in that section of the County — knows of tracts of land sold adjacent to the Scott property both before the war a short time and after its Commencement — and he states that no land in that section of the County either did sell or could be sold for more than twenty eight dollars per acre — that he is confident the Scott farm of 800 or 900 acres — for which Damages have been claimed, of from $100,000 to $140,000. never could have been sold for over $25 per acre — that $25 to $28 per acre would have been a big price for it and he does not believe it ever could have been sold at any time to any one at the highest named figures above. No man acquainted with the facts will state differently.

As to the claim of "Loyalty" set up, either by or for them — any of them — male or female — old or young — claiming Damages in the above case — it is simply monstrous. It would be ludicrous, if it was not a hideous crime. Because every body knows, that has even the most superficial knowledge of them, that they were from first to last most notoriously hostile to the Government of the United States. We do not believe that a loyal feeling or thought ever sought refuge in the heart of one of the name now Claiming Damages in the case alluded to above — from the moment of the outbrake of the late war of Rebellion to its close — Certainly not, if language and action are any index to the feelings of the heart.

One of the chief claimants in that case (tho' his name may not appear as one of the claimants) is Tho⁵ Scott son of Mrs Mary Scott, who after having been arrested for disloyal conduct — and having taken the oath of Allegiance to the United States, violated his oath while Bragg held possession of this part of Ky. made up a company of men for the Rebel Army and left the State with Bragg's Army. And we have every reason to believe that all those now claiming Damages in this case approved of his course. The Government is now asked to pay $140,000 Damages, to such persons upon property which never could have been sold for more than $25,000. This is a notorious fact, and can be established by any number of witnesses.

Lt. S.S. McFaden R.Q.M. 8th Tenn Infy States that this same Mrs Mary Scott, in whose name these large damages are claimed, stated to him and in his hearing more than once "that she hoped the Rebels, her friends, (so designating them) would come and drive the Yankees off and that they would come; and when they came they would stay for good and hold Kentucky". This and much more he is willing to be sworn to as transpiring in his presence and in his hearing. We would not be guilty of the presumption of offering advice to the officials at Washington who have this matter and all similar cases in charge — but we do not think it wrong to make a statement of facts for their consideration in so important a transaction involving such large sums of money, and to such persons. These statements we boldly make and hold ourselves responsible; and are ready to prove all and much more than here stated, whenever called upon to do so. It will be at once apparent to all why this paper is addressed to the "Hon. Mr McKee and others" We wish to place it in the hands of the friends of the government — those who love the Country and hate Rebellion — not those who reserve all their curses for their Government, for the "Heresy of Abolitionism." —

We would state further that by consulting the County Assessor's Books we find this property was never Assessed at more than ($9,500)   If they, year after year, were willing to swear that it was worth no more than ($9,500) cash we do not see the justice of now claiming such Damages as they claim.

J.C. Randolph   Supt Freedmen's Bureau for Jessamine Co.[1]

1. John C. Randolph to McKee and others, 12 Mar. 1866; Box 1012; RG 92. Mrs. Mary Scott did not live to see a settlement of her Camp Nelson claim. An appraisal, dated July 26, 1871, lists "One United States Government claim valued at $87,000.00" as one of the assets of her estate. Jessamine County Will Book L, 173.

Camp Nelson   Mar 14th 1866[1]
Brev Maj Gen[l] C.B. Fisk

Dear Sir   I send you this morning my last report for this Camp   In regard to the issue of rations a part of the rations received in the month of Feb and credited on Feb report have been issued this month

I have arranged with Co[l] Cha[s] Bartlett to adopt the small Box hospital as a post pest house

If Doct Mitchell is relieved Col Bartlett will make all necessary provision so that it need not longer be considered as an appendage of the Bureau.

The case of Charity Smith[2] is all that now detains me here   *

R.E. Farwell[3]

1. Farwell writes the place and the date in a big, expansive hand. The words "Camp Nelson" are especially large and showy.
2. The nature of this case is unknown.
3. Farwell to Fisk, 14 Mar. 1866; M999:9:1674; RG 105.

Chapter Eight

Claiming the Remains

Camp Nelson Ky   March 20" 1866.
To Maj. Genl. M.C. Meigs   Qr. Mr. Genl. U.S.A.   Washington D.C.

General, I hereby agree to take the buildings erected by the United States Government on my land at Camp Nelson Ky. in part payment for damage done to my property by the United States. The valuation of the buildings to be decided by any United States officer you may please designate. I have previously forwarded to you a proposition similar to the above. *

> [*Only the letter's signature is in her handwriting.*] Mary Scott[1]

1. Scott to Meigs, 20 Mar. 1866, Box 1012; RG 92. The Scott property at Camp Nelson had a complicated history. The first member of the Scott family in Jessamine County was a Virginian known as John 2/9 Scott, so called because he had arrived in Kentucky with "only two shillings and nine pence in his pocket." When he died he was one of the largest property owners in southern Jessamine County, and he held much of the land that was to become Camp Nelson. Before 1818, John 2/9's son Robert Scott built a house on the southern end of Camp Nelson on the west side of the turnpike, which was still the residence of his widow, Mary (Sappington) Scott, their son Thomas B. Scott, and his family by the time of the Civil War. Mary Scott owned 875 acres. Thomas B. Scott had over 200 acres of his own, just north of his mother's land, that had also once belonged to John 2/9. "In 1863, the U.S. Army condemned and leased all of Mary and Thomas B. Scott's property and established Camp Nelson. It is uncertain whether Mary continued to live in her house during the federal occupation; her son Thomas B. apparently fought for the South, fled to Canada, and returned at some point. Part of Mary's property was used for the Camp Nelson Hospital and Convalescent Camp. Thomas B.'s northern property contained both the Camp Headquarters and the Machine Shop, as well as numerous other structures." When the war was over, Mary and Thomas B. Scott reclaimed their land and reoccupied the house. McBridge and Sharp, 15.

Berea Ky   Mch 26 /66

Dear Bro. Whipple, * * * * [*Two paragraphs.*]
     Bro. [*Edward P.*] Smith after hearing all I had to say about Camp Nelson Lexington & Berea, thought that for the present I had better work on at Berea   He thinks this the preferable place for a Normal School — teachers' department — better for a seminary for ministers — that those who will come to us will be of a

better class than those we would go to promiscuously. I told him how insignificant a place Berea is — on paper or plan more than on earth —

He has gone on to Camp Nelson but could not now come to Berea, but thought he was satisfied & could now decide   I feel much drawn to labor for these colored people — so humble, grateful, receptive & trusting. * * * * [*Six paragraphs.*]

John G Fee[1]

1. Fee to Whipple, 26 Mar. 1866, AMAA 44322.

March 29th [*186*]6
Maj Genl. O.O. Howard   Commissioner R.F and A.L.   Washington D.C.

General, I have the honor to request that application be made to the War Department for the assignment to this Bureau of the building known as the "Soldiers Home" at Camp Nelson, Kentucky. *

Clinton B Fisk   Brt Maj Genl. U.S.V. and Asst. Com'r Ky and Tenn.[1]

1. Fisk to Howard, 29 Mar. 1866; M999:3:1396; RG 105.

Head Quarters, Dept of Kentucky. Office of Chief Quartermaster   Louisville Ky.   April 4", 1866.
Major Gen'l M.C. Meigs   Quartermaster General U.S.A.   Washington, D.C.

General, I have the honor to acknowledge the receipt of your communication of March 10th calling for a report in relation to the rent of and damages to the property upon which Camp Nelson is located and in reply to submit the following report.

The owners of the land are Mrs. Mary Scott, Mr Joseph M. Morse,[1] Mr John Morse and Mr. N.T. Merritt.

Mrs Scott owns from eight to nine hundred acres of land upon which is located the Camp, Corrals, and all of the Government buildings remaining unsold. This lady is some eighty years of age and has three children, two sons and one daughter, who are said to be the real owners of the property.

One of the sons, Thomas Scott, took the oath of allegiance at the commencement of the war but afterwards violated it, having raised a company and having gone south and joined the Rebel Army where he remained until after the surrender. The other son, John Scott, was a violent sympathizer with the Rebellion throughout the War, as was also the daughter, Mrs Perry, and her husband.

Mrs Scott is also reported to have been an open and avowed rebel; as late as last October she stated that no money could ever tempt her to take the oath of allegiance to the U.S. Government. Her place consists of from eight to nine hundred acres of land which was assessed by the Tax Assessors at $9,500°° for several years before the War and it was probably worth from $20,000 to 25,000; all the manure made upon the place during its occupancy by the Government still remains there and has greatly increased the richness of the soil, so that the only loss sustained by the Scotts consists in the rent of the place, and some three hundred acres of wood that was cut by the troops stationed there.

During the time of Gen Burnside's Command at Camp Nelson in 1863, he appointed a commission of three citizens of Jessamine County to fix the price to be allowed Mrs. Scott for the rent of the place; that commission decided that the Government should pay a rent of One hundred and sixty six & 66/100 ($166 66/100) dollars per month. I understand that Gen Burnside directed that payment should be made at that price, and that under the order Capt. T.E. Hall paid Mrs Scott Five hundred ($500^{00}) dollars, but that upon representations being made of the injustice done to the Government the General forbid any farther payments.

Since that time no money has been paid, but the property has been carried upon the Rolls of the Quartermasters stationed at Camp Nelson at the price fixed by the Commission, and on the 1st of January it amounted to Four thousand six hundred and sixty six and 66/100 ($4666 66/100) dollars as shown by Report (Form No. 2) of Capt E.B.W. Restieaux, for December, 1865.

Some three hundred acres of wood has been cut from the Scott place for the use of the Army. Mr Morse and Mr Perry owners of the land adjoining state that before the war, wood was worth one (1) dollar per cord delivered on the bank of the Kentucky River, and that it cost from fifty (50) to seventy five (75) cents to cut and deliver it there, and that it was worth only from twenty five (25) to fifty (50) cents per cord, standing in the tree. Allowing fifty (50) cents per cord; and reckoning the wood at thirty cords to the acre, which is believed to be a fair average, the wood on three hundred acres would have been worth Four thousand five hundred ($4500^{oo}) dollars. Sales of wood standing in the tree, were made by the Scotts to private parties at fifty (50) cents per cord, after the place was taken possession of by the Government.

Capt. T.E. Hall was the Quartermaster at Camp Nelson at the time the wood was cut from the Scott place, and it is said that it was taken up by him on his Abstract "N."

There are One hundred and ninety six (196) buildings left on the place, which are estimated to contain 1.503.509 feet of lumber, at six ($6^{00}) dollars per thousand feet, which is about the average price received for the buildings sold at auction, they would amount to nine thousand one hundred and fifty one & 5/100 ($9.151. 05/100) dollars.

Attention is invited to the enclosed remonstrance of J.C. Randolph and other citizens of Jessamine County against the payment of the Scott claim.

Mr Joseph M. Morse owns two hundred acres of land within the fortifications all of which has been occupied by the Government, the Freedman's Village having been located thereon. Forty Acres of wood was cut and used by the troops.

Two buildings, 250 X 30 and 350 X 11 respectively, built for a rope walk, have been torn down and taken away by the Government. Mr Morse is reported to be a loyal man.

John Morse, brother of Joseph, owns one hundred acres of land which has been occupied by the Government. The wood cut from this place was paid for by Capt. Hall at the time it was taken. Mr John Morse is also said to be a loyal man.

Mr. N.T. Merritt owns three hundred acres of land on which a Brigade was Camped for a short time, his only being one hundred cords of wood and about six hundred panels of fence. Mr Merritt is a strictly loyal man and has been in the U.S. service.

The above comprises all the property that has been used by the Government within the lines of the fortifications.

I respectfully request that the decision of the Department, relative to the disposition of the Government buildings may be made at an early date. *

R.N. Batchelder   Bvt. Col & A.Q.M.[2]

1. The correct surname for both Joseph and John is Moss.
2. Richard N. Batchelder to Meigs, 4 Apr. 1866, Box 720; RG 92. Another copy of this letter, in a different handwriting, is filed in Box 1012; RG 92; this copy was sent to E.M. Stanton, secretary of war, to accompany the letter dated May 11, 1867.

Office Supt 2ᵈ Dist Lex. Sub. Dist. Nicholasville Ky   April 20 1866
A. Scofield   Claim Agent,

Sir: — I am compelled to send this man back to Camp Nelson to be forwarded if possible and as soon as possible to his own county. Regulations require this. I do not wish any more sent to these Head Quarters who came from other counties. They must be sent Back where they came from, if sent any where.

W.F. Rice,[1] Supt   Lexington Sub Dist[2]

1. William F. Rice, the Nicholasville bureau agent, was the brother of agent James H. Rice, chief superintendent of the Lexington Subdistrict.
2. Rice to Scofield, 20 Apr. 1866; M999:11:1268–69; RG 105.

Camp Nelson, Ky., April 21ˢᵗ 1866
To Gen Fisk

Sir   Please find enclosed a note[1] from Mr Rice, Sup. of the 2ᵈ District of Lexn which I beg you to see.

When Capt Farwell left here there were certain paupers, blind, sick, halt, and lame scattered around among the poor of their own color to whom he gave some provisions to last for a short time only. With me he left 4 bll. of pork, a bushel of peas, and about 20 lbs. of Rice — to distribute as I might see the people need. Now this short allowance is all gone and these people are in a sad condition of suffering. In their distress they run to me, and it seems I must take the bread from my own family and feed them or see them starve!

In this case we have an old worn out slave, who leans upon two staves, going half bent, groaning as he goes. The family who took him to keep for a season, turned him out some two weeks ago to beg or die as best he might. He came to me.

I could not send the poor creature away — I fed and clothed him. But having so many to help and no means, I gave him a note and sent him to Nicholasville to the Bureau Headquts — supposing of course that they were there to attend to such cases. But they returned the man with the note I send you; Telling him Mr. <u>Scofield would press a team and send him to his county!</u> Now this man has lived here in this county over one year and I suppose is a resident here if anywhere. Besides what poor house in any county in Kentucky will receive a Black pauper? Besides what can Mr. Scofield do without authority, and without means? "Regulations require this" says Mr Rice. In the name of humanity what regulations require a poor old man who can scarcely with great effort and pain stumble over 3 miles in twelve hours, to be turned out to go he knows not whither, and live he knows not how! Now to be plain, Gen, this talk sounds to me more like coming out of a <u>gizzard</u> than out of a heart! But enough   something must be done — there are some 10 or twelve cases here who are paupers who must be fed and cared for by somebody who cannot by any possibility care for themselves — I appeal to you because I believe in your humanity and wisdom. I could make suggestions but will wait for any directions you may give   *

A. Scofield, Missionary[2]

1. Scofield refers to the previous letter.
2. Scofield to Fisk, 21 Apr. 1866; M999:11:1270–71; RG 105.

[*Letterhead.*] *U.S. Sanitary Commission* Camp Nelson   April 22 66

<u>Bro. Strieby</u> . . . . I want you or brother Whipple to send me 12 copies of the Freedmans Journal or some such paper for colored families here who have learned to read   send the numbers for M. & april if you can. I will distribute them and send the names to you as permanent subscribers — it will do them "a heap of good"

There are many of the [colored?] people here yet — some of them are doing finely — have bought their little Homes and teams and rented lands — they are the happiest creatures you ever saw. What they need is a good school — I could get one hundred schollars in 6 hours time and good schollars too who in a little time would themselves become teachers.

They need some potatoes corn garden seeds in for plantings which I hope brother Smith will see fit to send me

There are some <u>paupers</u> here in a sad condition. They are sick, and blind and lame no provision is made for them some of them I am supporting from my own scanty means. I applied to some of the sub-sub agents of the Bureau at Nicholasville   he seemed offended with me and said I must send them to the counties where they came from   This of course I cannot do without means or power   so they still lie at my rooms and I cannot see them starve. This young man swore at me profanely and threatened to report me to Gen Fisk for keeping the people in camp and hindering the work of the Beaureaus — as I thought he needed reporting I was not long in sending a letter to Gen Fisk myself —

Can you do anything for these helpless ones — they are slowly melting away — occasionally we get one off somewhere — on to somebody — some of them die and then I have them to bury which costs genally about two or three dollars done of course in a very coarse way. This I have to say — the people run to me for everything, and I am sorry to say they have no other helper. Since my family went home the work is very heavy for me — and then to have the curses of these young gents, who ride around in their carriages is not quite so comfotable. But God looks on — the sweet words I get from these people keep my courage up — The Beaureau must have a different class of agents or it will soon become a hiss and bye word among the people — I have written to Gen Fisk a letter which I hope may work some change   Now if you could furnish say $100. or even $50. for disposing of these twenty paupers — I could at least bury them when dead and could probably dispose of them somehow by the 1st of June Would not our dear Saviour bless us for it?

Please let me hear from you soon   Yours in the bonds of love,

A. Scofield[1]

1. Scofield to Strieby, 22 Apr. 1866, AMAA 44331–2.

Bureau Refugees Freedmen and Abandoned Lands. Head-Quartrs Sub District of Kentucky   Louisville Ky. May 4th 1866
L[t]. Levi F. Burnett,[1] V R.C.   Actg Asst. Adjt General,

Sir: I have the honor to report that in obedience to Paragraph N°. 1 Special Orders N° 18 Bureau Refugees Freedmen and Abandoned Lands, Head Qrs. Sub Dist of Kentucky, Louisville, May 1st. 1866,) I visited Camp Nelson Ky, for the purpose of inspecting and investigating the condition of the freedmen at that place, and found that the statement made by W[m] F. Rice, Supt of the affairs of the Bureau in the 2nd Dist of the Lexington Sub Dist of Ky. in his communication to this office, of April 24th 1866, and the endorsement of Capt. James H. Rice, Chief Supt Lexington Sub Dist, thereon, were correct.

There are at Camp Nelson between five and six hundred freed people, a number of whom claim to have purchased the shanties in which they are living, in a crowded and filthy condition.

About one third of the freedwomen there are prostitutes and have no means of support aside from thier prostitution, and by this means a vast amount of sickness and loathsome diseases are introduced in the Camp. Some thirty, or fourty of the women of this class occupy one of the Government buildings and are there living in a state of filth and misery difficult to describe. I asked a number of these women who gave them permission to occupy said building. they replied that Mr Schofield gave them permission to live there.

The freedmen who are living the Camp are, with a very few exceptions, able bodied and perfectly able to work and earn a comfortable living. When asked why they did not leave the Camp and go to work, they said that they did not care to do so just now, but intended to go to worke after a while" I am satisfied that every one of these freedpeople could have obtained employment and good homes had they been so disposed and the reason for thier choice in remaining is, no doubt, due to Schofields influence and advice. Mr Schofields influence over these people is very strong and it is useless to endeavor to induce one of the freedmen to accept employment outside of Kentucky, unless he give consent to thier going. they have implicit confidence in him and they readily yield to his wishes, and claim that under his supervision they will be protected and allowed to remain in the Camp. So long as Mr Schofield continues to encourage the freedmen in the opinion that it will not be necessary for them to seek employment elsewhere, they will be content to remain at Camp Nelson and nothing but force can drive them from it.

I am at a loss to know how these five or six hundred freedpeople sustain themselves in idleness. Many of them, I know, suffer for food, yet so strong is thier attachment to Camp Nelson that they prefer to remain thier and suffer, rather than except employment at good wages elsewhere.

Lt. Butler,[2] 2nd U.S. Infty. at present comdg at Camp Nelson, informed me that it required the entire strength of his Company to prevent these people from stealing Govt. property under his charge. He also informed me that people residing in the neighborhood frequently came to him with complaints of theafts committed be [by] these people. A number of the freemen are discharged soldiers and while thier money lasts they can, of course, live without work.

I asked Mr Schofield by what authority he occupied a Govt building within the Camp limits, and why he opposed the legitimate workings and authority of the freedmens Bureau? To the first interrogatory he replied that the only authority he had for remaining there was first, by suffrage, and second by the common dictates of humanity. That it was his mission to look after the interests of his Colord friends. To the second interrogatory, he disclaimed any intention to interfere with the working or authority of the bureau. I then asked him why he encouraged the freedmen to remain at Camp Nelson when it was the intention of the bureau that these freedmen should accept lucrative employment, where such was offered, as in the case refered to by Capt Rice. Mr Schofield said that the experiment of sending these people South was very unsafe, and that he did not feel disposed to encourage them to leave Kentucky — I inquired to know how these people could support themselves at Camp Nelson? He informed me that he was endeavoring to have them procure land — plant it and raise a crop. This information lead me to investigate the manner in which the arrangements for carrying out this plan of Mr Schofields were made, and in this investigation I found that there was a very singular and incomprehensible state of affairs at Camp Nelson. In the first place, the Government still has possession of the Camp and holds it, as far as I am informed, as seized property, and the parties claiming to own the property have purchased some of the Government buildings on this land, and now rent said buildings with three acres of land to each room at Nine Dollars ($9) a month to be paid monthly in advance, and it is expected that a family of from two to Ten can support themselves from the products of this land. All the arrangements pertaining to the renting of the said houses and land adjoining are made thr° Mr Schofield and by verbal agreement. The rooms thus rented are small and not large enough for more than two persons to occupy. Yet Mr Schofield admitted that they might, in many cases, be occupied by families of Eight and Ten persons.

Mr Schofield said that he had solicited and received from the American Christian Mission Garden seeds gratuitous distribution among the freedmen and that he had so distributed the seed. After seeing Mr S. I learned from good authority that he sold the seed, and was paid for the same.

The sanitary condition of the freedpeople at Camp Nelson is very bad, and unless they are removed from there before the heat of Summer the amount of sickness and mortality among them must, inevitably be great. It is my candid opinion that if Mr. Schofield were to leave the Camp the freedmen would not be long in leaving also. The present deplorable condition of affairs at Camp Nelson is, no doubt, due to the influence of this Mr. Schofield. Every white person with whom I conversed regarding affairs there was, with but one exception, free to express the opinion that Mr. S. was activated by other motives than Christian sympathy and pure philanthropy for the deluded freed-people over whom he exerts so great an influence. If he is indeed, activated by either, the practical results of his system are anything but desireable and encouraging, and can but continue to place obstacles in the way of the successful operation of the intention and purpose of the Bureau.

The idea that "God has selected the freedpeople at Camp Nelson as His Chosen people" is with Mr Schofield (according to profession) paramount to everything else.

After a careful investigation into the affairs of the freedmen at Camp Nelson I am free to express the opinion that both the interests of the freed-people, and the Bureau, demand that Mr Schofield be removed from there, and that, (after a proper arrangement can be made for providing places for the freed-people who are now there) the Camp be broken up, and the removal of Mr Schofield would, (in the opinion of all with whom I have conversed on the subject) tend more than any other measure I can think of, toward this end.

Prostitution — disease, and suffering must inevitably result to a still grater extent, if the people are permitted to remain there — subject to no sanitary measures — no authority or restraint only such as Mr Schofield exercises.

There are about thirty aged and helpless people now there, and I could learn of no provision for thier care and support other than such as thier fellow freedpeople may from time to time, provide for them. Some of this class said that they were hungry and suffering. In my conversation with Mr Schofield, I called his attention to this class of persons, and was informed by him that they had been provided for out of his private larder. This statement of his I cannot believe.

In connection with my duties as Actg Inspr Gen¹. and in obedience to verbal instructions, I inspected the books and papers relating to the affairs of the Bureau in the office of the 2nd Lexington Sub Dist. at Nicholasville Ky, and found that the present Supt. (Mr. W^m. F Rice) was attending to the affairs of the Bureau with commendable care and industry. I also found that the books of his office were properly kept, and in my opinion, Mr Rice is a very suitable person for the place.

Capt. Randolph, Mr Rices predecessor in the office did not, from what I could learn, keep any books or records of the business of his office. He is however, spoken of as an earnest friend of the freedmen, and as having been (while Superintendent of the affairs of the Bureau) faithful in their interests.

The sanitary condition of the freedmen in the town of Nicholasville is good. *

William H. Merrell   Capt. V.R.C.   Actg Inspt Gen^1   Sub Dist of Ky^3

1. Levi Frank Burnett, a New Yorker, began his military career as a private in the Eighty-fourth New York Infantry, but transferred to the Veteran Reserve Corps and was promoted to the rank of brevet first lieutenant. *HR,* 1:264.

2. James Butler, first lieutenant in the Second U.S. Infantry, commanded the post several times in 1866. In1864 he had been a second lieutenant in the Twelfth Kentucky Cavalry. *OAR,* 4:1234.

3. Merrell to Burnett, 4 May 1866; Volumes 1–9, 1866 L-R, Box No. 5; Kentucky Assistant Commissioner, Letters Received, Entry 1068; RG 105.

[*Letterhead*]^1 *Literary Institution   Berea, Madison Co., Ky.,*   **May 13 1866**

Dear Bro Fisk

＊ ＊ ＊ ＊ [*Two paragraphs.*]

Now I do not need to say any thing to you about our enterprise here. We have had much talk about it, at least frequent talk. We think it best to go forward with the school here — it has some advantages.

I think a school ought also to go on at Camp Nelson.

If you approve the enterprise here and deem it duty to give a short letter of commendations we shall be glad to use it.

One friend says to us "I will be one of ten to raise ten thousand dollars for a good boarding hall"

The Lord direct us all   Yours in haste

John G Fee

I yet feel there ought to be a school at Camp Nelson — we could purchase two of those Genl Hospital building & have a school there

Also I am willing to raise money, East, to aid in putting up a good building in Lexington I hear of no other person thus moving. Your endorsement would be a good   The Lord direct — ^2

1. In the upper left corner of this letterhead is a list of the officers of Berea Literary Institution, headed by Rev. J.G. Fee, pastor, and including Rev. W.W. Wheeler, principal, who had recently made a successful move: from Camp Nelson "Farmer" to Berea principal.

2. Fee to Fisk, 13 May 1866; M999:9:1756–58; RG 105.

[*Letterhead.*] *U.S. Sanitary Commission*   *Soldier's Home*   **Camp Nelson, Ky.,**
May 15th 1866
<u>**Gen Clinton B. Fisk**</u>

<u>Dear Sir</u>   It is with extreme reluctance and sorrow that I feel it my duty to address you again on matters here in Camp. I think I can honestly say that in all my labors here I have not sought Notoriety, but only usefulness. How far I have succeeded in the last mentioned particular I shall of course leave others to judge. And as to the former I would not allow my self to be brought into notice, but justice to myself and the cause I am endeavoring to serve, compel me to speak. It seems, that you listened to my traducers and concluded to recommend Rev E.P. Smith to remove me from Camp Nelson! Did I believe you were fully acquainted with the facts, and <u>all the facts</u> here I should be filled with inexpressible grief at your decision; grief to think you could be so lenient to the faults of my accusers, and deep grief, to think of the undeserved disgrace you would heap upon the heads of myself, and helpless family; But Sir it affords me no small relief to feel that you have but a biased and partial statement of the facts. Now Gen, in all sincerity, I ask what have I done that I should be singled out and accused as I am? Have I violated any law of Camp Nelson? — any order of the War department that I should be driven out as a culprit from the face of the people? If so, I beg of you let the world know what it is — Nay more, I respectfully ask that those who have been reporting me adversely to you meet me face to face and allow me to speak in my own defence. If these accusations are such as Mr. Rice of Nicholasville, has in a very gross, and insulting manner thrown out to me, allow me to say that they <u>are untrue, nor can they be proved against me</u>. He says I advise the people to stay in camp as keep them here to their detriment and in opposition to the wishes of the Beaureau — But <u>it is not true</u> — that I advise the people to stay in Camp — but have constantly advised them to seek homes elsewhere, with the exception of those families who had bought houses or rented lands and were able to manage their affairs anywhere. Indeed I have repeatedly urged Mr. Rice, and others who have been here, to go out with me, and offered to aid them in removing from camp, companies of worthless idlers who were continually corrupting the morals, and living upon the industry of those who were willing, to Work. Especially have I urged that these halt, lame, blind and decrepit ones should be removed, poor creatures, some of whom for several weeks I have been supporting to keep them from starvation. But these men have done nothing. While they could spend <u>hours</u> in accusing and catechizing me, all worn out with incessant labors, they had no time to look after these poor — no! though I have repeatedly, urged it, they, have refused to go into the kitchen of this building even, to see one decrepit old man, who but for my feeding him, for ought that can be seen, would starve, and who for want of a couch, sits upon the hard bench till he falls to the floor, where he would inevitably die if no kind hand was near to raise him up! Is this I ask, is this caring for these poor helpless ones the crime for which I am to be expelled forcibly if need be, out of Camp Nelson? — But Mr. Rice charges

me with interfering with his business, and roughly orders me out of Camp because he says I am doing so   He gives out his public orders concerning me on
this wise "Scofield" — "Scofield"!" Who is he God damn him! Is he interfering
with my business yet? "God damn him!" and such like language. * * * * [*Four huge
paragraphs.*]

A Scofield — [1]

1. Scofield to Fisk, 15 May 1866; M999:11:1379–87; RG 105.

'Copy'   Camp Nelson — May 23. 1866.
<u>Dear Brother Smith</u>

    I write you this morning with a <u>heavy heart.</u> It seems that I have become the
mark of wicked intriguing men & their aim is to <u>crush and destroy me</u>! As you
instructed me, I closed the missionary work here on the 15th inst. & wrote Gen. Fisk
so, telling him that I was here simply as a private citizen, or respectfully asking the
privilege & protection of a citizen especially till I could close up the claims on my
hands which I wished to do with the least possible delay, & denying of course, as I
in truth could, all charges of meddling with the affairs of the Bureau. But the agents
of that institution at Nicholasville and Lexington (two brothers Rice by name) have
continued roughly to assail & threaten me with arrest & imprisonment. They have
gone anywhere among the wicked to pick up evidence against me & most of all to
create a prejudice against me among the freedmen. They have collected witnesses to
prove that I have been selling rations & gardens seeds which were sent here to be
given away! The agt at Nicholasville came to my office on the 15th & ordered me to
leave Camp & then demanded all my papers relating to claims & peremptorily
forbid my doing anything more in that business. I told him I was closing up the
business & wished only to dispose of the cases on hand — but he still demanded
all that I had in that business, & was particular to inquire if any of the claims <u>had
been paid</u>. On Friday we received notice from the post commander to leave the
Soldier's Home. On a little inquiry I learned that the order was from somewhere (I
could not tell where) & that it was to the purport that I must leave Camp. So on
Saturday I packed up & with the tears running down my face fled up into the old
Refugee Hall now owned by Mr Moss, the owner of the lands here — where the
post commander said he thought I had a right to be, & kindly said he could not
drive me out at the point of the bayonet which I had resolved he should do, if I was
called to go, & then came the heaviest stroke of all. Day before yesterday I received
notice from Washington that my name was dropped, or rather "had been struck
from the list of Claim Agents permitted to prosecute claims against the Government" No reasons assigned! Unexpected & sudden the crushing bolt fell upon my
innocent head, & all was still again as the house of death. It was a terrible blow to
me for I saw in it not only the loss of living, but the loss of honor also. Forgive me
dear brother, if I betray weakness in this affliction — But when I consider how

hard I have labored, working at all hours of the night in order to keep this business along with my other labors, how needy my poor family is, how long & patiently I have suffered in the antislavery cause, & how ceaselessly I have been accused & belied, it seems a burden too heavy for me to bear.

I have succeeded in getting acknowledged at Second Auditor's office over 250 claims & have over 100 more nearly completed, the compensation for wich at moderate charges would be over two thousand dollars. This I suppose forms the glittering prize in the eyes of these Bureau men which they are now intent on forcing out of my hands into their own! And alas, seem likely to succeed. Probably at the request of Gen¹ Ely, or possibly Gen Fisk, I have been cut off at Washington — apparently with as much unconcern as the gardener would cut off a weed or a thistle. Now dear brother what am I to do? Must I suffer all this loss & shame without any possibility of relief?

As to the charges of my keeping families here &c. they are almost without foundation, so far as design or effort is concerned they are wholly so — that by kindness my attention to their interests, in short my moral influence over them has a tendency to keep some of them here is doubtless true. But this relates to the good families of them, who are handsomely providing for themselves. For these I have asked they be let alone in the free service of their natural rights as free independent citizens; but have been told by these agents — so full of gushing sympathy for the freedmen, that the good ones must make market for the bad ones! And this is all I have done. Repeatedly have I aided in making up companies to go south and never have opposed, only as indicated above. The truth is brother, I have stood in the way, somewhat, undesignedly to be sure, of speculators in the muscles & labor of the poor freedmen who are doing well entirely above board where they are. This & the money likely to come into my hands are I firmly believe the causes of this relentless persecution now dealt out to me. These agents, & especially the one at Nicholasville are very profane ungodly young men! And to say that such a man has any sincere regard for the well being of these poor people is <u>simply saying nonsense!</u>

But I must close this extended letter — Let me ask in conclusion, that you would if possible relieve me from condemnation at Washington, at least to allow me to collect the claims I have completed.

Will you not think too, seriously about schools The poor children looked sad last Sunday when I told them that the Sabbath School was done — some of them wept with sorrow. *

(Signed) A. Scofield —

P.S. Dr Mitchell says tell brother Smith there are 100 scholars out of the lines wanting a teacher. Schools at different points could be easily started under your patronage at very small cost — ¹

1. Scofield to Smith, 23 May 1866; M999:11:1337–42; RG 105.

[Edward Smith copied and forwarded Scofield's letter to General Fisk, who wrote the following instructions on the file:]
Memphis   May 31 /66

Respectfully referred to Maj John Lawrence who will please proceed without delay to Camp Nelson Kentucky and see "whats the matter" — I am suspicious that Mr Scofield has not been justly dealt with — He may have been an incubus upon the deportations of idlers — It was so thought by Farwell & Ogden & Col Lewis believes it — He certainly <u>ought not</u> to be interfered with in his private business and I exceedingly regret that he has been disturbed in his claim business — Please put him in a new vain & reconstruct his Camp Nelson relations

Clinton B. Fisk   Bv Maj Genl &c [1]

1. Note by Fisk, 31 May 1866; M999:11:1342; RG 105.

[Letterhead.] The American Missionary Association, 93 West Sixth Street, Cincinnati, Rev. Edward P. Smith, Sec'y for the Middle-West[1]   May 26 1866
Clinton B. Fisk, Maj. Gen. &c Asst. Commiss^r R.F. & A.L.

My Dear Genl Enclosed please find copy of a letter just rec^d from Rev. A. Scofield at Camp Nelson Ky. I wish if possible you would give it a reading and a few moments consideration.

Mr. S. is a good & true man — I verily believe the <u>truest</u> friend the col^d people have had at Camp N. — not always the wisest — I know he has worked very hard in extra hours to get these 250 or more claims in proper shape — that very many of them except for his personal interest & incessant labor never would have been acknowledged at Washington — He has in this way saved thousands of dollars to the widows & orphans of Soldiers — He has done this thus far without charge except barely enough to cover postage & often not that. When the returns came in he would, by a moderate charge when the claimant could afford to pay get a fair remuneration for his labor — Now the Bureau ag^t steps in & seizes his papers & gets him cut off at Washington. The ag^t is as ever in position to make any am^t he pleases, from $1,000 to $10,000 or more off the claimants, & they have no redress or very unlikely to ask for any — Mr. S. who has done all the work & done it <u>in love</u> to the Col^d people, as Simple & pure, <u>unselfish love</u> as you can find in the world and pinched his family to poverty while doing rather than take anything out of the poor people in advance, is driven away in disgrace & shame — I am sure you will not allow this to be done — Cannot Mr. Scofield be <u>reinstated</u> as a claim agent at Washington & allowed to <u>finish</u> the work he has in hand? He is not likely to give any more trouble about deportation — He can settle those claims already nearly thro' better than anyone else — Many of them belong to parties that are scattered & in the hands of such persons will never reach the owners because of the difficulty of getting at them. If I were a soldier dying I sh^d rather leave a claim for my boy in Mr. Scofields hands than anywhere else & sh^d ask no voucher — Is not this the kind of man to whom you would prefer to entrust these claims when there is so much difficulty in getting them to the proper persons & when they can be so easily misappropriated —

I write thus earnestly because it is a sort of relief to me to express my feelings & not because I suppose you need any anguish or appeal to deal justly by a poor missionary. *

Edw. P. Smith Sec., A.M.A. [2]

1. Printed above Rev. Smith's name is the following message: "The American Missionary Association has been working twenty years for the good of the African race. Since the Rebellion it has turned special attention to the Freedmen, sending teachers and missionaries, and furnishing clothing to the destitute."
2. Smith to Fisk, 26 May 1866; M999:11:1343–44; RG 105.

[*Letterhead.*] *U.S. Sanitary Commission, Soldier's Home.*   *Camp Nelson, Ky.,*
June 6th 1866
Gen. Clinton B. Fisk

Dear Sir   Capt Farwell sent me a request a few weeks ago to get five boxes of shoes at Nicholasville sent there for the use of this camp   After some little delay in geting the bills properly signed, I obtained the boxes in his order and brought them up to camp for distribution. Just as I was entering upon the work and had a number of needy cases, Mr Rice, the Sup, came here and forbid me doing any thing with them — so the shoes now are doing nobody any good — Please say what shall be done with them?

Maj Lawrence has been here to day. I thank you sincerely for sending us so good a man. His views appear to be just, and his conduct generous. Thank him for me. I am greatful also for your kind and frank letter received a few days ago. Let me assure you that I shall be ever ready to aid you in any way I can, in the good work you are so faithfully prosecuting. *

A. Scofield[1]

1. Scofield to Fisk, 6 June 1866; M999:11:1346; RG 105.

Bureau R.F. & A.L.   Nicholasville Ky   June 6 /66
Lieut. Levi F. Burnett   A.A.A. Gen'l   Sub. Dis't Kentucky   Louisville Ky

Sir, In obedeince to the provisions of Special Orders No 22. Hdg'rs Sub. Dist Kentucky. dated May 8/66, I have the honor to report that the Refugees & Freedmen's Camp at Camp Nelson is broken up. Those Freedmen who still remain are capable of supporting themselves and families. There are none now living in the Gov't buildings and those living within the limits of the Camp owning building which they bought at the Gov't sale, have made arrangements with Mr Scott, the owner of the land, to pay him rent as soon as the property comes into his possession. I had the cordial cooperation of Lt. Butler 2nd U.S. Inf'try Comd'g Post in the execution of the order *

W.F. Rice   Supt Bureau R F & A L   2nd Lex. Sub Dist   Nicholasville[1]

1. Rice to Burnett, 6 June 1866; Volumes 1–9, 1866 L-R, Box No. 5; Kentucky Assistant Commissioner, Letters Received, Entry 1068; RG 105.

B.R.F. and A.L. Nashville, June 8th [18]66
Capt H.S. Brown   A.A.G.

Sir — I have the honor respectfully to inform you that in obedience to your order I proceeded to Camp Nelson, Ky., and beg leave to submit, in a brief report the situation as I found it and left it.

1. The success of the Bureau in ridding the place of its vast supernumerary population has been very remarkable.

2. About fifteen alms house cases have been left at the place (four of them are blind) and the county of Jessamine seems unwilling to make any provision for them; and they are now wholly dependent on such charity as Mr Scofield is able to eke out to them. I think Capt Rice should be directed to issue fifteen rations a day to those poor people until some other provision can be made.

3. I doubt whether the families remaining at the camp, and adjacent to it, could do better at present. They are nearly all of them, the families of soldiers, now in Texas, and expected home during the summer. Quite a number of these families have rented lands of Mr Moss — and are cultivating three acres each. Some colored men, living at the camp, are cultivating fifty, and others a hundred acres of land; and are doing it well.

4. I was greatly astonished to find no School there, and to learn that the American Missionary Association had felt afraid to open one for fear of coming into collision with the Freedmen's Bureau! There are about the camp, between 150 and 200 children, mostly children of Federal soldiers, and a school should be opened at once. I think the place a most desirable one for a permanent School, and Capt Rice, the agent for Jessamine Co., agrees with me. It is a charming locality. I do not know a more inviting locality for a school in the South.

5. The agent of the Bureau, Capt Rice, has not made any report to the 2nd Auditor against Mr Scofield, nor has he, in any way, interfered with his claim business. Mr. S. is a regularly licensed Claim Agent, and can do where he is what no other man could do. It is my opinion, and the opinion of Capt Rice, that he should be encouraged to go on and prosecute the claims.

6. Bad feeling has existed between the agent and Mr Scofield, but it has its origin partly in a misunderstanding, and partly in diversity of disposition. Capt Rice is an honest, outspoken soldier, and a little rough, but a noble man, and a true friend of the blacks; Mr Scofield is an old liner, a little canting in his way, and too indulgent and tender to every thing that has colored blood in it. But he is a good and deserving man, I think and will do more for the poor and sick at the camp than

any other man. He has a good church there, and a very interesting revival in progress. I advised Capt Rice to smooth the old veteran down, and to use him for the benefit of the colored people in the county. I think there will be no further trouble between the Capt and the Missionary.

6. [7.]¹ If Mr Scofield's name has been stricken from the roll of agents at Washington through the interference of any of Capt Rice's superior officers, I think the officer, whoever he is, should place him right again. It is probable, however, that his name was dropped through some latche [lapse?] of his own. He tells me that when he paid his second years tax he omitted to sign his name to some paper, and the who[le] difficulty I think is found there.

Much that is in Mr Scofields letter to Mr Smith is purely imaginary.

I was much pleased Capt Rice and with the appearance of things in Jessamine.

The very devil appears to be in the people about Lexington. The colored people there are apprehensive of a mob. I hope their apprehensions are ground-less. Col Rice thinks they are; but the spirit of rebellion is green in the Blue Grass. *

John Lawrence   Supt &c²

1. The report really has two paragraphs beginning with the number six; they are on two different pages in the original.
2. Lawrence to Brown, 8 June 1866; M999:11:1347–51; RG 105.

Camp Nelson   Sept 10ᵗʰ 1866
<u>Col</u> Johnson¹   **Lexington Ky,**

<u>Dear Sir</u>   I wrote you a few days since enquiring if we could look to you for protection for our School — My Daughter begins her school to day. <u>We are threat-ened</u>. Things look a little serious. A band of 20, or 30 men, go around, <u>at night</u>, among the colored people — robing them of arms and ammunition, <u>pretending to act under authority of the Bureau</u>. Last night they robed several families with[*in*] a mile of this Home. I fear blood will be shed unless something is speedily done. Possibly the civil authorities would attend to this matter if called upon by the mili-tary. Let me venture to hope that you will be able to do something for this poor people. Please let me know immediately what we may hope for   *

A. Scofield   <u>Missionary</u>²

1. Probably Lt. Col. William C. Johnson, commander of the Fifty-third Regi-ment of Kentucky Volunteers. *HR,* 2:116.
2. Scofield to Johnson, 10 Sept. 1866; Mar. 1866-Dec. 1868, Box No. 49; Lexington, Ky. C.S.O.C., Letters Received, Entry 1185; RG 105. Scofield's letter is accompanied by endorsements from Col. Robert E. Johnston, who referred the matter to Bvt. Lt. Col. James H. Rice, who referred the matter to his brother, Agent W.F. Rice, 2nd District at Nicholasville; the latter's report of September 18 is filed with Scofield's letter and reproduced below.

Bureau R.F. & A. Lands   Agents Office   L. Dist. L.S.D.   Nicholasville
Ky   Sept 18ᵗʰ 1866
Bvt Lieut. Col. J.H. Rice   Supt. 2nd Dist   Lexington Ky

Sir   I have the honor to submit the following report of my action in regard to the enclosed paper [*Scofield's letter*]. I proceeded to Camp Nelson and saw the parties who had been robbed, viz Martin Luther Susan Luther William Jackman Hord Ward Lucy Paine. They took from Luther a Gun and Ten dollars — money from Jackman & Gun from Ward Waters a Watch. It is almost impossible to find out the names of the parties but the woman Susan Luther says she can swear that the parties who came into her house were of the following names "Joseph Hicks." Stephen Grant". Lewis Clark. They visited some fifteen of twenty cabins and compelled the occupants of them to open the doors claiming they were acting under the authority of the Bureau. I have applied to the County Attorney but he says he cannot take action in the matter because there are no white witnesses   All the Negroes concur in the statement that there were fifteen or twenty in the party who came to their houses.   *
      W.F. Rice   Agent Jessamine & Garrard Cos. Ky   2ᵈ Dist Lex Sub Dist[1]

1. William F. Rice to James H. Rice, 18 Sept. 1866; Mar. 1866-Dec. 1868, Box No. 49; Lexington, Ky. C.S.O.C., Letters Received, Entry 1185; RG 105.

Danville Kentucky   September 27, 1866
Brevet Major General J.L. Donaldson   Chief Quartermaster Dept of the Tenn.

General: My last communication dated at Lexington, September 23, gave the result of my explorations at that place and on the several [*indecipherable*] of Railroads, and closed with a recommendation in the regards to the disposition to be made of the Union dead.

      The next place visited upon my route was **Camp Nelson** [*emphasis in original*]. The favorable circumstance under which the burials at the place must have been made, naturally led to the expectation that every thing would be found in good order and arranged with system and Care. Although I was not wholly disappointed in my expectations, yet I was much surprised to find that the burials by the Quartermaster had been made originally in four separate localities. I was also informed that a large number of scattered dead had been recently gathered into one of the yards by the agent of Colonel Batchelder, Chief Quartermaster of the District.

      The several yards were all enclosed and new head boards had recently been placed at the graves. The first yard visited contained upwards of an acre of land and was nearly filled, containing soldiers, both white and black, negro women and children and refugees. The soldiers were buried at either end, the negro women, children and refugees between them. This yard is without the limits of the fortifications and is on the land of a Mr. Oliver Perry.

      The second yard is situated in the interior of the Camp and contains about two acres. It is about 1/2 mile East of the public road or pike. I found buried here with considerable regularity and in pretty good order 2,235 bodies, consisting of white and colored soldiers and rebels buried to some extent promiscuously. The new boards had been erected alike to all graves both Union and rebel, and had been numbered consecutively to include all in the order in which they lay. There were in this yard 1530 white soldiers 691 colored and 14 rebels.

All of the ground is not yet fully occupied and it is so located that additional land may be taken if required. The order of the graves is such that they will not require to be reburied: lines can be straightened with little labor and by a few removals suitable walks and roads can be constructed.

About one mile West of this yard are two more, near each other, one containing 20 white soldiers and the other 26 colored and two white — all of whom died from small pox. These four yards, with the exception of three or four scattered graves comprise all that are known to have been buried at Camp Nelson.

The number of burials at this place are so numerous, and those in the larger yard so will made, that it does not seem desirable to remove the bodies to any other locality; but manifestly they should all be collected in one place, and the larger yard is the most suitable for that purpose and by a slight enlargement it will conveniently contain them all.

I would therefore recommend that a tract of land, embracing the larger yard and of sufficient area to contain all that are to be found at the Camp, be taken for the purpose, and that the right of way from the cemetery to the public road or pike should also be secured. The whole number of dead found in all of the yards is 672 white 808 colored and 14 rebel. Total 1,494.

A report signed by Captain Restieaux, A.Q.M now before me dated, November 30, 1865, states that all burials at this place have been made by the Q.M. Dept. and comprise 676 white and 1,52[?] [*last digit indecipherable*] colored soldiers, and 23 rebels; Total 2,176.[1] If that number have been buried there, the localities were not discovered and are not known by any of the inhabitants; — possibly the graves of refugees and the colored women and children before referred to may have been included as soldiers; — otherwise the discrepancy cannot be accounted for. * * * *[2]

1. The arithmetic here does not add up: the 699 white and rebel soldiers subtracted from the total of 2,176 gives 1477, which is definitely not the number of colored soldiers mentioned by Restieaux; however, accurate or inaccurate, the numbers in the report are all very legible, except for one digit. In any case, the total reported by Restieaux far exceeds the number located by the cemetery inspector. A map titled "Showing Location of Remains of Union Soldiers in the Department of Kentucky, June, 1866" assigns 2,176 burials to Camp Nelson (Entry 576; RG 92 [no further information available]).

2. Cemetery inspector to Donaldson, 27 Sept. 1866; General Correspondence and reports relative to national and private cemeteries, 1865–90; RG 92 [no further information available]. The last page of this report, with the reporter's signature, was not included in the researcher's notes.

[*Letterhead.*] *U.S. Christian Commission Rooms.*[1]   Camp Nelson Sept 29th 1866

Dear Brother Smith   As requested, I sent to our agent at Cincinnati my full report, which had in parts been reported before.

The amt. due me Sept 1st 1886, is for labors and expenditures $693.00.

Bro. Fee and myself have just been to Cincinnati and we were both much in need of money and I especially was living upon borrow. We ventured to draw on your treasury for $500. Is it all right?

We went to Cincinnati to confer with brother Cravath[2], and if possible to loan[3] the money for a short time to put us at once in possession of this farm. But brother Cravath was not there and the men we wished to see were also gone from the city so we got only good wishes   Brother Fee and myself concluded to undertake to raise the money if we could get time on it. So I made an offer to purchase — to pay one quarter down — one quarter 1st of April, and the same amt. in one year. Mr Moss has taken the matter into consideration and will let us know in a day or two. But the rebs are using all their power with him to stop the trade, and as to "Old Scofield", he must be driven out of Camp and killed if need be and his Negro School must be stoped! This is the talk — But two Blue Coats with a few gun Caps in their pockets would scatter the whole gang into the bushes.

My daughter is still going forward with her school and the people have a great interest in it — she has an average of about 85 pupils daily — not more than one half could be accommodated — Surely it is a pitty that this golden opportunity should be lost — only a loan of $500 for six months on good security — for one year and the thing could be done — done nobly and the good would be immense. * * * * [*Six paragraphs.*]

A. Scofield[4]

1. The letterhead is crossed out, including the address, 13 Bank Street, Philadelphia. The officers of the U.S. Christian Commission are listed at the top left, including Rev. E.P. Smith, field secretary.
2. A corresponding secretary of the AMA, Rev. Erastus Milo Cravath (born 1833 in Homer, New York; died 1900 in St. Charles, Minnesota), graduated from Oberlin College in 1857 and from Oberlin Seminary in 1860. He earned a Doctor in Divinity from Grinnell in 1886. *DAB; Oberlin Register*, 6.
3. Scofield means "borrow."
4. Scofield to John W. Smith, 29 Sept. 1866, AMAA 44354–5.

For Am. Missionary, [*No date*]

Dear Bro. Strieby,

* * * * [*Six paragraphs.*]

At Camp Nelson there is now an opportunity to buy the farm in which the refugee buildings were erected and with this the buildings we sought to obtain twelve months past.

Ten thousand dollars would now procure to us one hundred and ninety acres of fertile ground, about thirty cottages & one large "Superintendent's building." Most of this farm could be sold out in lots to colored men so as to refund the money to the one who will advance it, with a fair percent in addition. We can reserve a small portion of the land, and the large buildings for recitation rooms. With the cottages many families would at once have homes. Other lands would soon be bought and there would be in the center of Kentucky a nucleus which would be felt for good. Is there not some one of God's stewards who will advance the ten thousand? We think it could be returned in a short time.

Settlements could be made in other localities, if we had a company of men who would buy up large tracts of land and then sell on a small advance to these people. They will be oppressed until they shall get homes. * * * * [*One paragraph.*]

John G. Fee[1]

1. Fee, an undated essay for the *AM, AMAA* 44357–61.

[*Letterhead.*] *U.S. Sanitary Commission, Soldier's Home.*   *Camp Nelson, Ky.,* Oct 4th 1866

<u>Dear</u> Brother Whipple   Your letter of the 29th ult is just Received, and I thank you for it, but it fills me with inexpressible <u>grief and sorrow</u>. Bad as it might have been to [have] had the draft "<u>protested</u>" I should have suffered far less keenly with that, than I do now with this. If there is any pang I feel more excruciating than all others, it is when I am treated with <u>grace</u> for crimes I have never commited! Pardon me if I am a little sharp, for I write under the full gushings of present grief and I am so full of wounds that any spot on me is tender. O sir! if the letter you have sent me could be seen and known in and around this camp, my life would not be secure a <u>single night</u>! Two wicked "<u>Rebs</u>" have just left our home, who threatened to "blow hell out of Old Scofield" — and what had I done, why simply advised or rather directed a poor abused black man to go to the civil authorities and make complaint, for this my life is threatened and our camp and school house is to be burned down, they say. All they need is to know that I am not sustained at home, and my life would not be safe an hour. But let it be known that we are sustained by the great North and I had as lieve face a company of these poor cowards, as so many rats that thieve around at night for a livelyhood. But about my "<u>draft at sight</u>". Well, perhaps it was wrong, but if so I shall ask brother Fee to share it with me. I made it for his accommodation rather than my own. True I needed money, went to Cincinnati on borrowed money, with the full expectation of geting some when I got there, but should not have drawn on you for a <u>single dollar</u>, but for the judgment of brother Fee that <u>all would be right</u>. I suggested that my acct. was not audited, but he thought it would make no difference; and as the man we borrowed the money of was an old line abolitionist I ventured to make the draft, but I made no such draft as was sent. I simply filled up one of your orders, expecting that you would have time for adjustment of acts. — but when the paper had been signed which I made out, Mr Harwood wanted it drawn at sight — <u>quite another thing</u>. I was quite unwilling

to sign it, but we had proceeded too far to stop there, and as they seemed to think it would be all right, I consented — I must say however that I told them unhesitatingly that the society was in debt to me to that amount and more. This is the way it was done, and now for the immediate reasons. Brother Fee and myself had concluded to go to Cincinnati to raise if we could, the money to buy this farm of Moss, to give us time to arrange the lots and raise the money by sales and donations. Mr Moss wants <u>all</u> the cash by the 1st of Jan. To do this, we must make a loan. So as I said we went to confer with your agent there and see what could be done. Brother Fee wanted to borrow of me $300 I <u>wanted</u> to make some purchases for ourselves and for a small supply of groceries for the people in this camp. . . . I also was out of money and could not go longer without it, except on credit, which I had done to the extent of $150. — So these are the reasons — allow me here to say that when I came here I was ordered to report to John G. Fee and as I found him to be a truly wise and good man have relied much upon his judgment and advice. [*Written vertically beside the paragraph:*] We did not find the men we went to see * * * * [*Ten paragraphs and an account, but one of the paragraphs is several pages long.*]

Saturday morning — good morning brother Whipple! The God of David has been round about us and we are unharmed. O praise the Lord! I set the house in order, and at two in the morning laid down my weary limbs in my clothes, ready to start at a moments warning, but no spoiler came. There is a drunken gang of about 40 around here who have made several night raids upon the freedmen families plundering them of money and arms, and now they threaten "Old Scofield." They think I suppose that if they can "smite the shepherd, the sheep will be scattered."

But I am not afraid of their faces: I know that God is stronger than they. I am firmer than ever in the belief that this ground must be held — nay, I feel like saying it <u>shall be</u>, and the decision must be made "<u>right now</u>" What we want as I said is a loan of five thousand dollars for six months or a year. Mr Moss wants his money paid down by 1st of Jan. We can raise one half — provided there is no war, and there will be none — the North wind of the fall elections will blow those dark clouds all away. Now can't you find us the man who can let us have the money on <u>good security and good</u> interest? Depend upon it, this is the point to make a stand for the salvation of the Freedmen of Kentucky, two hundred thousand freedmen are to be affected by this decision. . . . * * * * [*Three paragraphs.*]

A. Scofield[1]

1. Scofield to Whipple, 4 Oct. 1866, AMAA 44362–8.

Cincinnati, O., Oct. 24th, 1866.
Rev. J.G. Fee, Camp Nelson, Ky.

Dear Bro., Two letters from Camp Nelson reached me this morning. As I have before written Bro. Schofield the A.M.A. cannot involve itself [*at*] all in connection with the purchase of that land. We will cooperate in School and religious work. I think it would be an injury to the cause of the Freedmen for any attempt to be made to raise funds by <u>collections</u> for the purchase of land to be sold at Camp Nelson or Berea. I should be unwilling to endorse such a movement for it would embarrass our home work. I will assist all I can by countenancing & approving any effort — to get individual capitalists to assist you. Bro. Gabriel Burdett must send in his apl. in due form before salary can be paid. My answer to your former letter will answer many of the inquiries of the later ones. *

E.M. Cravath[1]

1. Cravath to Fee, 24 Oct. 1866, BCA. Two days after this letter, Fee received another disappointment. Thomas M. Howe, executive director of the Avery Fund "for the Education and Elevation of the colored people," refused to give Fee money to buy "real estate," and disagreed with Fee's argument that the Camp Nelson plan would produce income. Howe to Fee, 26 Oct. 1866, BCA.

Pekin Jassamine Couny Ky   November 7th 1866

Gen [*M.C. Meigs*]   I received a few days since a communication from your office notifying me that my claim for rent of my land could not be allowed on account of disloyalty of myself and family, I cannot understand how or through whom the information as to my disloyalty was communicated to your office and regret exceedingly that I have had no opportunity of meeting by proper proof a charge of so serious a charater as I am satisfied I could successfululy refutied it and at least place myself in a fair atitude before the high officals of my Goverment, the idea that I should be charged with entertaining treasonable sentiments towards the Goverment which had so long protected me and for which my Father made so great a sacrifice in the days of the revolution is well calculated to bring me down to the grave in sorrow   I do not know Gen that I have ever utered a disloyal sentiment in my life and if I have it was done under a moment of exitement when I saw my property taken from me and a large portion of it swept away under such circumstances as these I may have sayed something which might have been construed into disloyalty but if I know myself I can assure you that whatever I may have sayed was not entended to apply to the Goverment or those in authority but only to thoese without proper authority as I though who took possession of my property without previous compansation   my place is situat ed midway betwen Lexingtown and Danville and for two years there was not a day that I was not feeding soldiers and caring for the sick   I devided my last bread and coffee and left my Home leaving the sick without any to care for them, I left my home in great distress not knowing what to do for a shelter   I am the lawful owner of twelve hundred and sixty six acres of land same upon which Camp Nelson was located and at the time of its occupancy by united States military orthorities it was in a most excellent cultivation and enclosed by superior fencing and in addition to all this nearly one half of it was covered with the finest timber in that region of Country, my beautiful fields are lade wast   my fencing all destroyed and every tree valuable for timber or wood cut and used by the Goverment for the benefit of the army   my land has been badly cut up by fortifications erection of water works to convey to different potions of the Camp   for three years it was used for a military post during wich time I had not orthority to cultivate one foot of it or exercise any controle and for this long and wastefull occupancy I received only the small sum of five hundrid Dollars payed me by Capt T E Hall A Q M under order of Brig Gen Boyle then comanding the district of Kentucky

I requested that the publick buildings erected on my land might be turned over to me as part compensation for the great loss I had Sustained but even this was denied me, every building was sold and there is not now standing up on my land one hundred Dollars worth of buildings erected by the Government but such as I have bought and payed for,   after the milatary took possession of my farm I was compelled to buy me a small farm in ordor to secure me a tempory home and for which am still in debt and have relilied upon my claim against the Govermnent for money to meed that debt, my expectations it seems had been diapointed and that no doubt by the false representations of malicioous persons and dsinging [*designing*] persons, I was told last Spring when my claim was made out that I would be called upon to meet the charge of disloyalty but could not beleave that any one with whom I was acquanted with in this section of the Country would have the hardyhood to do such and that in a secret underhanded maner, I leave this mater with you Gen and whatever may be the final result of my claim I hope what I have said will remove all impression from your mind that I am or could be unfaithful or disloyal to my Goverment, I deny the charge denounce it a foul slander — — — I have perhaps intruded on your attention   permit me to say if my Goverment does [*not*] pay me the damage I have sustained and the occupancy of my farm for three years I do not know what will become of me, I shall be compelled to give up my little Home   to whom shall I go   will my Country leave me to starve   I have been a law abiding Citzen and payed a larg tax   I was raised by an indulgent Grandfather in all the luxuries of life   I knew no want but allas he is no more,   reflect Gen on my destitute situation now suffering for Winter clothing   this is hard and no money to buy any   this is the situation of a Daugher of 76   will you be so kind to answer this letter as soon as conveinent that I may know what I may expect from my Goverment — — beleave me Gen I wish you may never know the povrity in which I am involved is truly the wish of — — — — — —

Mary Scott

My address is Pekin Jassamine County Kentucky [1]

1. Scott to Meigs, 7 Nov. 1866, Box 1012; RG 92.

[*Letterhead.*][1] *Camp Nelson,* Ky   Nov. 30, 1866

Dear Bro Strieby   I have been absent from this place near three weeks nursing my son Burritt at home — sick with fever — He is now better — out of danger as we commonly speak — hence delay in answering your note.

Lands in the "bluegrass" — limestone region — fertile and level are worth from fifty to one hundred dollars per acre. Such lands kept up during the war because the copper heads who distrusted greenbacks were anxious to invest in such lands as fast as they got Greenbacks

Lands in the "Hill country" are worth from twenty to forty — more or less improvements

Lands out in counties still more broken — oak lands can be bought for five to ten dollars per acre

And many thousands of acres can in counties known as "Mountain counties" be bought for from one to five dollars per acre

Now it is in these counties & in the third class I referred to that I advise the colored people to go. They to [achieve] highest development must not remain a nation of bootblacks or mere stevedores. They must become owners of land and producers of valuable commodities. Then they will be esteemed in their own eyes and in the eyes of others

I have proposed this now to two persons in Ohio — & two or three here — to form a company buy & sell to these people and good white men on fair business principles — fair profits and thus do these people a good for most white men here who have two & four hundred will not sell a scrap to a "Nigger"

But friends of the colored man will & then so arrange sale of lots as to have them in community, so as to have for them schools & churches.

What do you say? Some one may say, "let the colored man alone — let him find his own way" — why not then dispense with educational efforts for him

I do not propose to feed him but put an axe & land within his reach & let him work out his salvation — help him to a home Yours in haste

J G Fee

I expect to go back to my family in Berea early next week
P.S. I would avoid aggregating in one county or part of the state — have groups all over the state (interspersed with as many good whites as would go in) so as to sustain schools & church — Give lands & education — then prejudice will more readily give way —

I desired to propose this thing to Bro Tappan Lewis Tappan.[2]

1. This unusual letterhead has only the words "Camp Nelson" printed at the top. It must have been quite rare as it is the only stationery of the sort in this entire collection of letters!
2. Fee to Strieby, 30 Nov 1866, AMAA 44378.

Bureau R.F. and A. Lands   2nd Dist   Lex Sub Dist   Nicholasville Ky   Dec 2nd 1866
Bvt Lt Col Jas. H Rice   Supt 2nd Dist &c

Sir   I have the honor to request that you send to Camp Nelson, a detachment of troops to remain there for ten days, until Mr. Schofield can get his business settled up. He has a great deal of business there in an unfinished condition, business pertaining to the claims of colered soldiers their widows &c for pay bounty, pensions &c. and he dare not remain there without the protection of the military. I would suggest that he be protected there until he can get his business straitened out and then withdraw the troops, ordering him to leave. I think it would be much better for the freed men there to have him go, as he inspires them in a great many ways.

I have not seen Susan Luther to obtain any additional evidence in the Hicks & Grant case. I have learned where she is, and have sent you all the information I can get from her.

I think it should be immediately sent to Louisville, as the friends of the prisoners are there trying to get them released on bonds.   *

J.G. Nain   Ag [*Agent*] 2 Dist   L.S.D.   BRF & A.L.[1]

1. Nain to Rice, 2 Dec. 1866; [Bound] Vol. 168; Letters Sent, Agent—Nicholasville Ky from Nov. 23, 1866 to Oct. 8, 1867, Entry 1242, Vol. 1 of 1; RG 105.

[*Letterhead.*] *Literary Institution. Berea, Madison Co., Ky.,* **Dec. 12 1866**

Dear Bro Whipple
    * * * * [*8 paragraphs.*]
    Whilst I was gone to Lewis co a mob rushed upon Bro Scofield at Camp Nelson They broke into the rooms & carried out Bro Scofield & his son & made them promise to leave They have left — gone to Nicholasville   Mr Moss the owner of the land declines to sell or allow the colored people to stay The Military came & made two or three arrests   What the result will be I cannot tell
    Gen Ely does not like Bro Scofield & Genl Fisk did not. The Bureau men were against him partly from jealousy   What he did in the way of securing claims and retaining colored people here detracted from their profits — He had less protection than he would have had had he not been secularly engaged
    There will as I suppose be no possibility of doing anything there unless we can get ten thousand dollars to buy out Mr Moss   His neighbors were opposed to his selling to colored people or for a school of such
    I regret this break up — I have been much interested in that field very much More will now concentrate here. . . . * * * * [*One paragraph.*]
                                                                    John G Fee

You may fear we will be broken up [*at Berea*] as Bro Scofield [*has been at Camp Nelson*]. He had no social protection — not one white family — we have many
    Also the mobs expect us not to yield — if driven we will come again[1]

1. Fee to Whipple, 12 Dec. 1866, AMAA 44387–8.

Nicholasville   Dec. 14th 1866
Revd Strieby and Whipple Secretaries of A.M. Association

<u>Dear bretheren</u>, You have doubtless heard ere this of the calamity which has befallen us at Camp Nelson. And though I have informed one agent quite fully of this matter I thought it might be a matter of interest to you to hear direct from us concerning the troubles we have been, and to some extent are <u>still</u> passing through. On the first of Sept. we started our School in the Old "<u>Refugee Hall</u>", under very favorable aspects   The school was directly under the charge of my daughter. She began with about forty, but during the first month her list ran up to nearly 180, having a daily attendance of about one hundred. The School was large, but our room was commodious, and with what aid I could render, it was a success beyond anything we had seen in Camp Nelson.

We had bargained for the farm of Mr Moss of 190 acres with all the cottages about 30 in number, had divided it into small lots of from 3 to 5 acres each and sold most of the lots to the people reserving about twenty five acres with the dwelling house and two large buildings for the School. On the 1st of Jan 1867 we were to pay five thousand dollars one half the purchase money, and take <u>entire</u> possession. On this farm we had caused to be sown about 50 acres of wheat which stood fine. Every thing looked encouraging. Families were coming in and depositing their money for payment on their lots. My son had opened a small store for the accommodation of the people and shops were to be opened and rope walks built in early spring to give employment to poor families who wished to gain the advantages of the school but were unable to purchase homes   These fair prospects our enemies saw as well as we. Their envy and hate were aroused to a high degree. They swore that "Old Scofield should be hung and that "<u>Niggers nest</u>" should be broken up." At first this was loud talk only but presently they began to act. In the beginning of Oct raids upon the black people near and in camp were frequently made by night. Bands of armed ruffains broke into and plunded their houses taking what arms and money they could find. Every night they would come a little nearer to our home. By the way of a kind of introduction to us, anonymous letters would be thrown into our windows, telling me that my life was in hourly danger and that our buildings would be burned unless we broke up and left. These facts we fully communicated to Agents of the Bureau, who assured us that we should be protected. Time went on, and we kept to our work. On the night of the 20th of Oct — we were aroused from our slumbers about midnight by a loud rap on our front door, and my name was called. As the moon was shining bright I went to the door and asked what was wanted   A man standing on the steps said he wanted to see me. I opened the door, and there stood a man one pistol in hand another in his belt, just behind him fully armed stood ten more in a line of battle. The foreman demanded that I should come out to them, but I refused. He then, after sundry accusations of keeping a gang of Nigger thieves, and puting myself on a level with them — imperitively demanded of me a promise to leave within ten days, but I told him I could make no such promise. he then called for his companions to come up, but I quickly shut the door and turned the bolt. He made a rush for the door, but it was fast. He thrust his pistol in at the window and demanded that I should open the door. I still refused to open or promise. While I was sliping on my clothes, they left saying they would return with a larger number in a few days, drive us out and fire the buildings.

We then felt that something should be done — that protection should be at once given us or our enterprise must be abandoned. We lost no time in communicating our fears and wishes to the agents of the Freedmens Bureau. We sent to Nicholasville to Lexington by word and letter, finally, to Louisville, asking for help. We were again told we should be protected and directed to arm our men and keep a nightly watch till soldiers could come. This we did at considerable expense of time and money. From 12 to 15 men were put under arms every night, <u>indeed we slept upon our arms</u>. But the men after two weeks became quite weary of this. To work all day and watch all night, was a tax they soon became wary of, and as I could not afford to pay them for this night work, after about two weeks, it was given up. <u>No soldiers came.</u> — But we hoped for the best and still went on with our work — new families came in and selected their lots. But the fatal hour at length came. On the night of the 19th of Nov about one O'clock A.M. a loud crash came against our unprotected Home. Thirty armed men while we were all asleep, had noiselessly surrounded the building and by a signal gave a dash at our windows and doors breaking them open and smashing them in. The few arms in our room were seised and my son and myself ordered to be shot if we attempted to move. Their work was short. Several of them guarded us while others rushed out to keep any of our men who might come to our aid. Taken by surprise, the blacks were panickstricken and all but one man fled in terror from their houses, he noble fellow John Burnsides, stood for his family and fought like a tiger. He fatally wounded one seriously another of his assailants. But he was soon overpowered by numbers, pulled out of his house knocked down, and left in his yard for dead — they then fired several shots through the house at the women and children and hastened off with their wounded comrads. This diminished the number who guarded us and probably under God saved our lives and our buildings. They hurried us over the hill to shoot us, but suddenly concluded to Lynch us with whips, but soon concluded to release us on promise that we would break up the School and leave. In the mean time a pack of them went in pursuit of my daughter They lit a candle and sacked the house, and went very near to her, but she kept her self possession squat close, and kept still — so the Lord delivered her out of their wicked hands. They set fire to the buildings, but they had wett the black powder and were in too big a hurry to stay to see them burn. The fire ashamed of its makers and its work turned pale and went out!

In the morning, we lost no time, but applied immediately to the agents of the Bureau, first at Nicholasville then at Lexington. Again we were assured that soldiers should be sent to protect us. We again mustered our men and turned our rooms into barracks of War — for eight days we did not put off our clothes for sleep — At last on saturday night the eighth day of our siege, the soldiers came, greatly to our relief and joy. On Monday morning about 1 A.M., they left us and went in pursuit of some of the Robber Band who were reported to be in the neighborhood. They arrested two young men citizens within a mile of us with equal reason, they might have taken several others had they gone for them. But having taken these two they made a hasty march to Lexington 18 miles leaving us to get away the best we could. In the morning all was confusion and alarm. Bands of mounted Rebels were riding furiously up and down the streets swearing very angrily [at] us for their captured comrades. Nothing remained but to fly. But how to get away was a question not easily solved. There was but one way only and that was thronged with bands of armed men, now maddened with the arrest of their guilty companions. The terri-fied people absolutely refused to help us off, and almost blamed us for being the cause of our trouble. One team was procured and loaded but all were afraid to drive out. For a time it seemed we must either abandon our goods to pillage, cross the River in a skiff, and wander off in the country taking the stars for our guides or stay and be murdered in our Home — that night! We resolved at all hazards to go to Nicholasvill. Our daughter started first, taking an old nag and cart she procured a Black woman to drive and wrapping herself up she passed safely through as a "sick woman" Toward night our ever faithful brother "Gabriel Burdett" came to our re-lief — he found courage to mount the wagon with us and drive us safe to Nicholasville. We went to the Buford House, a large and comfortable Hotel, and called for accommodations. In the morning we were told that we must leave — I asked for board for my daughter for a few days, but the gentleman proprietor told me plainly no, and then by way of explanation, remarked to some of his customers, that if "they chose to associate with niggers, they might go." — So we paid our bill of six dollars for one nights tarry with quite ordinary fare and left

Turned thus again into the street, we found a small office where we thrust in the goods we had saved and made the best of a bad matter, spreading our mats on the floor at night and taking our lunch on the top of our boxes and barrels. Two days after on the day when you good people were giving thanks to God, I ventured back to camp to look after the balance of our goods. But desolation reigned in once quiet and happy home: our rooms had been broken open and plundered of every-thing of value. About one hundred dollars worth was gone beyond the hope of recovery! Some of our people had fled and others were preparing to leave. John Burnsides who fought so nobly and effectually, had recovered from his wounds so as to fly and had left his family in hope of finding for them some place of greater security. But night drew on, I knew I had been watched that day and learned that the evening before suspicious men had been there enquiring for me. There was no house where I could be safe, so bundling up as best I could, with a piece of bread and meat in hand for supper, which a good woman gave me I started for the field. Once out in the lot I felt safe. Hapily the night was dark and dreary. Never did deep darkness feel so welcome to me as there. I knew and felt that none but God was there! O brethren I cannot tell you how much I thought as I lay on the cold wet ground, that long, long, sad night. I thought of my dear family far, far, away, and how sad they would feel if they knew to what extremities I was driven. I thought too of you in your quiet happy homes, rejoicing in the comforts of a thanksgiving day. Then too I realised as I had never done before what solemn work it was to be a missionary of the cross, and what those dear missionaries must have been in holiness and virtue, who in early times devoted themselves unto death for the cause they had espoused. But morning came at last and I emerged from the place of my concealment. When I came to our rooms I found the robbers had been in that night and rummaged through the house, "but him they found not." Gathering what I could of the remnants of our goods, I procured a wagon and hauled them to our little room. But even here we appeared not to be safe. The boys would gather about our room set up a wild yell, and sometimes stone the building — and all this within a dozen rods of the office of the Bureau agent, who has never looked in upon us or enquired after our welfare. I have made my complaints to him till I am ashamed   he seems to take little notice of them; whether from fear — want of sympathy or want of power, I am unable to say. Brother Cravath, hearing of our unpleasant condition, kindly sent to my daughter to go to the Mission Home at Lexington where she is now, not quite contented to spend her time doing so little.

One word about the arrests by the soldiers already mentioned. Well — they took those two young men on to Lexington. On, mad with rage, went a whole company from within and about Camp Nelson, out of hole and corner and bush issued here somebody; some to swear, some to bluster and scold, and some to bale out the boys. When the crowd got there, two others were found among them, siezed, and sent to prison at Louisville to await their trial. But influential friends came to their rescue, and all have been bailed out and all are again at large!

What will be done with Camp Nelson remains yet to be seen. It has been currently reported, that the military intend to make a permanent post there and so afford protection to our enterprise. The citizens about there evidently fearing this and thinking their conduct might be looked into, have had a meeting, which has been reported to us and to Gen. Ely at Louisville to the purport that we might return to our work and no disturbance should come from their neighborhood. But they deny ever having disturbed us! Why then did they have a meeting? They give no promise of protection only that they have not disturbed us and will not. If they lie, in their denial, as almost everybody believes, then we cannot trust them, but they have *not* disturbed, then their promise amounts to nothing.

Of one thing there we feel fully settled, that it will be rashness in us to return without military protection. We are waiting for orders, but cannot wait much longer. Brother Cravath wrote me about one week ago that such protection would likely be given and that he was anxious to see our enterprise carried through   But as we hear nothing, can only prepare to take a final leave. I went down to camp on foot last sabbath to preach to the people again. They listened tenderly while I discoursed to them from the words "there remaineth therefore a rest to the people of God" — In the morning I hope to take my walk again to my disconsolate people and speak to them of that better country where the weary are at rest and the wicked cease from troubling.

But I must close, give my kind regards to dear brother Smith, do you all pray for us & farewell. Your brother in tribulation for the deliverer of the oppressed

A. Scofield, Missionary[1]

1. Scofield to Strieby and Whipple, 14 Dec. 1866, AMAA 44390–2.

Bureau Refugees Freedmen & A Lds   Asst Comr Office   State of Kentucky   Louisville, Ky. Dec 20th 1866
Bt Brig Genl John Ely   Chief Supdt &c State of Ky.   Louisville Kenty.

General: I have the honor to report, — that in obedience to Special Orders N°
105. dated Bureau R. F and A Lands State of Ky. Louisville Ky Dec 13th 1866 — I proceeded to Camp Nelson Ky and investigated the circumstances attending the breaking up of the Freedmens School at that place, and also the condition of the Freedmen in that neighborhood.

The circumstances connected with the breaking up of the school refered to are as nearly as I could ascertain as follows: [1]

About 12 oclock PM Oct 19th 66 ten men armed with shot guns and revolvers visited Camp Nelson. the leader of this party Knocked at the door of the building occupied both as a School and by Mr Schofield. Mr Schofield got out of bed and went to the door in his night clothes and was met at the door by the Leader of this party (the remaining nine men standing near) who pointed a pistol at his head and demanded a promise from him to leave that place by the Saturday night following. this promise Mr Schofield declined to give. that he was simply there in discharge of his duty and that he should remain there as long as he was permitted to do so. that he had wronged no one, and was using every effort in his power to encourage the Colored people to support themselves and to Educate their children. Upon Mr Schofield's refusal to leave the Camp the gang made a rush for him, but he sprang aside locked the door and returned to his room which he had no sooner reached than one of the party appeared at the window of his room with a revolver pointed at Mr Schofield again demanding a promise that he would leave threatening to shoot him if he refused to comply with the demand, at the same time telling the party that as there were troops not many miles from there they had better go. the party then started to go away. but halted long enough to tell Mr Schofield that if he was not away by Saturday night they would come with a party strong enough to Kill him and with torches to burn every building on the place, that they "were not going to have the damned negro educated while we poor white boys must remain in ignorance". They then left Cursing Schofield and his damned negroes. Between this time and the 15th of October the Colored people living in the Camp posted pickets around the Camp every night; during this interval parties of men armed and mounted appeared within a half mile of the Camp but seeing the Colored people armed and on the lookout for them they came no further. The Freedmen getting tired of Picket duty refused to stand guard any longer.

On the night of Novr 20th a party of twenty five or thirty men armed with Shot guns and revolvers continuously approached the Camp and without the least warning broke in the door and windows of the building occupied as a school and by Schofield, rushed in, seized Mr Schofield and his son who were in bed. the Leaders of the party made them get up and put on their clothes, after which he placed a strong guard on them and the rest of the gang visited the cabins occupied by the Freedpeople most of whom had fled from the Camp. John Burnside (Colored) remained in his cabin, defended himself until he was beaten senseless. Burnside fired six shots, two of which took effect and it is believed beyond doubt Killing one of the party and the other severely wounding another. I will add here that Burnside recognized the party that came to his cabin but as he was obliged to leave the Camp the same night I did not see him, but gave to Col R E Johnston Supdt &c at Lexington Ky such information as will enable him to find him in case is testimony is required.

The party meeting with such a repulse at Burnside's Cabin returned to Mr Schofield and took him and his son to a ravine a short distance from the Camp. Mr Schofield daughter was in the house when it was attacked but secreted herself. Some of the party demanded to know where the "gal" was but she was not found. After getting Mr Schofield and his son in the ravine the party held a consultation. Some were in favor of shooting and the rest were in favor of hanging. Immediately after one of their secret consultations Mr Schofield and his son were ordered to stand up, which they did   One of the party then took a position opposite to them and brought his gun to the position of aim. The Leader of the party stepped up and ordered this man not to fire, saying "it is not time yet. let us take them over the hill." they then took Mr Schofield and his son over a hill which [w]as a half mile distant from the ravine just refered to which after reaching they proceeded to arrange their ropes and to cut a lot of twigs which they made into whips. while these preparations were being made the party continued to heap imprecations upon Schofield and his "damned niggers"   about this time Mr Schofield heard a scream and thinking that his daughter had been found and was being outraged by some of the party he reluctantly gave his promise to leave the Camp and that vicinity within ten days. Mr Schofield was then released   the Leader of the party telling him that if he made any complaint or took any steps toward their arrest that they would follow him into any state in the U S that he might go and kill him   that they had five thousand men in the land and would surely find him wherever he went. Mr Schofield thinks he would be able to identify any one of the party wherever he might meet them

There were about 190 scholars in this school and it was in a prospering Condition. and there were about 300 Colored people in the Camp at the time the Camp was broken up. It was Mr Schofield's purpose to form a Colony of Freedmen at Camp Nelson, and had already negotiated for the purchase of land and had obtained funds from the "Freedmen's Christian Aid Society" for that purpose.

The first payment was to have been made by the 1st of Jany 1867.

190 acres of land were to comprise the settlement. Rope walks and other

industrial pursuits were to be inaugurated, School houses and Churches were to have been erected. all this was to have been accomplished by the joint efforts and pecuniary aid of the "Christian Aid Commission" the "Freedmen's Aid Society" and the Freedmen themselves.

The Colored people who were in the Camp on the night it was attacked say that they know the names of a number of the men engaged in the outrage, but their testimony is wild and conflicting and very unreliable, not sufficient to warrant the arrest of any of the persons named by them. There is no doubt but that they do know most of the party, but they freely acknowledge themselve afraid to testify against them. these people are not yet educated up to point where they can see any advantage to themselve by aiding in bringing their tormentors and enemies to justice. John Burnside seems to be the most reliable one among them and he can no doubt identify some of them   Mrs Burnside and Mrs Kennedy (Colored) can swear to the identity of some of the party. Mr Overstreet (white, who lives at the Mill near Camp Nelson says he knows a man who knows the man wounded by Burnside. Ray Moss the boy who was arrested by Col R.E. Johnston and released on bond was identified as one of the party. this boy is very young and a son of a respected Citizen and good Union man, who has frequently confined this boy to keep him away from the vicious men of the neighborhood. Suspicion points strongly toward the following named men, Viz:

Wm B. Brown, Peter Merritt   Ray Moss   Alfred Fame

A man named Bower living near Sulphur Hill, Ore Scott, Alexander Hagan, James W Grant   Steve Grant and Joseph Hicks. the evidence gained thus far does not warrant the arrest of the parties mentioned, but Mr Nain the Agent of the Bureau at Nicholasville and Mr Schofield hope to be able to obtain evidence sufficient to warrant the arrest of the parties named.

If the Colored School at Camp Nelson is to be continued a detail of troops will be required to guard it   The people residing in the vicinity of Camp Nelson will not tolerate a School for Colored children at that place or anywhere else in Jessamine County if taught by white teachers. If the School should be reopened under protection of the Military Authorities the presence of the troops would be required for an indefinite period and ultimately when withdrawn the present manifest hostility towards Colored schools would no doubt be increased and the School, freedmen, and all connected with them would be left to the fury of an unreasonable and prejudiced band of wicked and merciless Regulators.

Mr Schofield says he will cheerfully abide by the decision of the Military Authorities and that his only aim is to do right and if possible to avoid trouble. He would like very much to continue the school but will yeild to the judgment of the Military Authorities.

The Union people residing in the neighborhood of Nicholasville and Camp Nelson all agree that it would be impracticable to reopen the School at the former place, but they feel that Mr Schofield is entitled to some recognition by the Military Authorities for the reason as they allege that, if the manner of Mr Schofield's being driven from Camp Nelson is allowed to pass as a precedent, that should any of the Unionists of the neighborhood become obnoxious to the band of "Regulators" in that County they would be proceeded against in the same manner.

The hostility as manifested in the breaking up of the school was not toward Mr Schofield alone but there appears a settled determination not to have a Colored School with a white teacher in their midst. There are two Schools in Nicholasville (6 miles from Camp Nelson) both of which are taught by Colored teachers. These Schools have not been molested and it is believed that they will not be.

There are a number of Soldier's wives and Children at Camp Nelson, a number of whom are in destitute circumstances, and unless some steps are taken by the Bureau authorities to provide for them there will be a good deal of suffering among them. I would respectfully suggest that Mr Nain Agt &c at Nicholasville be instructed to take such steps as the Asst Commissioner may deem best to ameliorate their condition and as soon as possible to provide homes and employment for these people

As a general thing the Freedmen are employed but there appears to be a disposition on the part of the Employer to defraud them of their just dues. Mr Nain is a faithful Officer and adjudicates all cases growing out of the disposition referred to. Very few cases come to a trial for the reason that the Employer seems to dread the interference of the Bureau and is very anxious to Compromise. From 3 to 5 cases of this kind are compromised and settled each day by Mr Nain. Although Mr Nain has been threatened for the part he has taken in ferreting out and endeavoring to bring to justice the parties engaged in the outrage upon the school and Freedmen at Camp Nelson, he has thus far escaped personal violence

Mr Schofield remains in Nicholasville, and has been subjected to no little annoyance and to numerous insults yet he does not seem inclined to leave there until requested or ordered by more Competent authority than invested in the gang who tried to drive him away from there.

The Citizens of Jessamine Co heald a meeting a few nights since and passed resolutions condemning the Conduct of those engaged in the attack upon M[r] Schofield and the Freedmen school of Camp Nelson. The Union men of this County have but little faith in the resolutions passed at this meeting. in their opinion the meeting was called for the purpose of stopping any further action on part of the Military authorities toward the investigation and arrest of any of the parties composing the band engaged in the breaking up of the Freedmen School. *

William H. Merrell   Act Lt 42 U S I.
Act A Inspr Genrl BRF&AL   State of Ky[2]

1. The following three paragraphs of this report narrating the events of the night of October 19 are substantially in agreement with Scofield's account, but with the addition of many more precise details, some of them quite graphic. The scene in the ravine near the camp is simply blood-curdling.

2. Merrell to Ely, 20 Dec. 1866; Volumes 1–9, 1866 L-R, Box No. 5, Kentucky Assistant Commissioner, Letters Received, Entry 1068; RG 105.

Berea Madison co., Ky.   Jan 13 /67
Bro Geo Whipple & Bro E.M. Cravath & all "to whom it may concern"

Dear Brethren: —
     * * * * [*15 paragraphs*]
     I have for many months been looking to this work of a normal school: — talked with General Fisk about it — corresponded with Bro Whipple about it, sought to be connected with it (simply because it is a <u>position</u> for <u>good</u>) and sought to the know the <u>place</u> for it
     For this I visited Lexington again & again — for this I lingered at Camp Nelson — for this I still let my family stay at Berea. God in his providence has gathered us here and the crowning consideration of a <u>practical recognition of the brotherhood of man</u>, the true exposition of the spirit & practice of the gospel, together with the highest good of society — its harmony, security & efficiency seem to say this [*Berea*] is the place. I think Camp Nelson as the next facility, Lexington the next.
     What is opinion
     Camp Nelson & Lexington are in the midst of a more dense colored population (in this county there are 5,000 colored people) but probably white pupils could not be induced to go to a school in either place at least in Lexington for the present
* * * * [*Two paragraphs.*]
     The time perhaps has come when you must choose some one place   If you shall choose this place we will like to insert the fact in our next circular. Let us hear from you immediately. Yours in Christ,

John G Fee[1]

1. Fee to Whipple and Cravath and all to whom it may concern, 13 Jan. 1867, AMAA 44407–9.

Berea Madison co Ky.   Jan 25, /67

Dear Bro. Whipple   I have your letter in reference to the Pittsburgh fund
     I like your letter — clear & well matured.
     1 You ask me what I will say in reply to the fact that the Avery fund is designed for the education & <u>elevation of the colored</u> race I reply as I did to Mss. Howe & King I believe there is no way in which we can so successfully <u>elevate</u> the colored race as in schools where their true manhood shall be honestly practically & freely recognised
     Not to flatter them — elate them — but accustom them to a practical, moral, & social equality, in the school, in the Lyceum, in the church, in all —
     (along with white pupils —) is part of an important education — or rather an important part of his education. We are likely here to have so many white pupils, male & female, that we can give to the colored youth this <u>practical</u> recognition.
     Also here the number of white pupils will not likely be so overwhelming that the colored pupil will feel that any courtesy to him is a mere matter of condescencion

to him as in a feeble minority. But his number will likely be such that he will feel the stimulus & support of a majority.

If we cannot have the effect of a practical equality here — presence of respectable white pupils I would say, 'let us go at once to Camp Nelson   There we should be in the midst of a large colored population — ease of transportation &c. — a branch of the Rail Road south will probably go near to that place.

I yet regard Camp Nelson with favor — its central position — its elevation — fertile soil, gushing springs, numerous ponds — immediately on the bank of the river as a source of supply of fuel — coal & wood — all these make it a power.

Yet I am here. My presence seems to be needed yet — then the fact that colored men must gravitate to the mountains for homes, & the moral power here of an impartial & practical recognition of the manhood of the colored man, these considerations reconcile me to Berea & cause me to think it a good place for the education & elevation of the colored race.

2 So far as security in the south is concerned. I say (1) That is with God, just as in other missionary fields — the field needs culture we must do it (2) I feel that that providence & union majority that put the rebels through will put Andy [Andrew Johnson] through

I can simply say there is a generation now that needs education — we must work whilst it is called to day. If money is thereby spent, it is in a good cause

Gabriel Burdett is now at my house. He thinks to leave Camp Nelson — put his family here for education & travel as an evangelist. This he tells me is the council of Bro Cravath.

Our pressure is such that our board say I must go abroad & solicit means.

The Lord direct — Yours

John G Fee[1]

1. Fee to Whipple, 25 Jan. 1867, AMAA 44413.

Berea Madison co Ky   Feb. 11 /67

Dear Bro. Whipple, * * * * [8 *paragraphs.*]

I said if we cannot have a school here open to all white & colored — practically, effectively so, then let us go at once to Camp Nelson, where we can have more colored children than here.

You say that may be out of the frying pan into the fire, if Bro Scofields letters be a fair exhibit. I have no doubt but radical as I am regarded I can go to Camp Nelson undisturbed — be welcomed by Mr Moss the owner of the land & be protected there by the white citizens.

Gabriel Burdett has been recently at my house. He lives there. He told me Dr. Evans & other citizens met in convention & passed resolutions condemning the action of that mob, extended to Mr Scofield an invitation to return with asshurances of protection.

I feel that we are almost as secure here as you are in New York City

Bro Scofield did good in Camp Nelson, & I like the man in many respects. But he might have done much more good if he had devoted himself to preaching the gospel instead of getting claims for soldiers & their wives. That was a work others who were not Ministers could have done, and done with as much success & satisfaction as he, for a large portion of the claims forwarded were rejected. — This left the colored applicant dissatisfied. Bro Scofield had his fifty cents and had failed. His business impinged against some of the Bureau agents — they did not like him. Thus he had not from colored & white the sympathy which he might otherwise have had.

A minister of the gospel should do as you counciled me on one occasion, "preach the gospel with your whole heart".

Mr Moss offers yet to sell the land, 190 acres with the houses — about 20 to the colored people & offers to give Gabriel Burdett a home & 3 acres of land. Gabriel will not act without my council & cooperation. I feel that a school ought to be there also. The place has many excellencies, tis central to a large, colored population.

The Lord direct * * * * [3 paragraphs.]

John G Fee[1]

1. Fee to Whipple, 11 Feb. 1867, AMAA 44424.

Bureau Refugees Freedmen & A. Lands   **Nicholasville Ky**   **March 26" 1867**
Bvt Lt Col Jas H Rice   **Supt 2ᵈ Dist**   **Lexington Ky**

* * * *

It will be necessary to rent a Building for the school at Richᵈ [*Richmond*] and for the one at Lancaster. I think we could open a school at Bryantsville, one at Keane and one at Camp Nelson, under colored teachers, the white citizens will not oppose colered teachers, but would make it very unpleasant for a white person attempting to teach a school. I suggested to our colered people to open night schools for the benefit of Adult freedmen who have to work during the day. I think it the only possible plan to extend their knowledge.   *

J.G. Nain   Agt 2ᵈ D.   L.S.D.[1]

1. Nain to Rice, 26 Mar. 1867; [Bound] Vol. 168; Letters Sent, Agent—Nicholasville Ky from Nov. 23, 1866 to Oct. 8, 1867, Entry 1242, Vol. 1 of 1; RG 105.

April 29ᵗʰ 1867
To the President of the United States

Sir, I trust you will not think me assuming to address you this letter written in the language of suffering humanity — I am the owner of the land on which Camp Nelson was located containing twelve hundred 500 and seventy five acres of land   when the Officers of the Goverment sayed I must leave, my plantation was in a high state of cultivation, having three fine apple Orchards on it and various other valuable fruits, my Crop of all discription was soon destroyed. the crop I had

made in 1862 they used for themselves   I made another Crop in 1863 which they
took from me, burned all my rails a vast quantity and ordered me to leave my Home
where I had lived 40 years   my valuable timber 500 and seventy five acres of my
land and built fine Houses for the use of the Government, there is not one tree
standing on my hole tract of land, my timber land was valuable to me timber being
scarce in Jassamine County   I was selling it at a good profit — the army distroyed
a fine Spring they sayed to get more water but failed and the streem was lost

These Sir is but the outlines of my wrongs I have suffered, I am now getting
old and reduced to poverty, I know not what I shall do if the Goverment does not
give me a just compansation for my claim, I had so much confidence in my
Goverment that I purchased a small place which cost me seven thousand Dollars
which is still unpayed; if the Goverment doese not give me just compansation I shall
be compelled to give up my present Home, now in my old day thrown on the cold
charity of an unfreindly World unless the free Masons aid me. I am the Wife and
Daughter of free Masons   my Husband died in 1817 my Father in 1824   my
Father gave me money to buy Camp Nelson and my Grandfather gave me Negroes, to
you Sir I appeal not in vain I trust to do me justice as head of the Goverment — I
heard it has been written to Washington City that the right of Camp Nelson in not
in my name that it belongs to my Son, this can easily be established as false, I have
a deed recorded in Jassamine County Kentucky that the land is mine which can be
proved, another false statement the Goverment made over to me ten thousand Dollars worth of Houses never was a greater falshood, I wish not to intrude on your
time or patience to speake the whole truth my situation is very destitute   I ask for
nothing but what is justly mine   I am not unworthy of your attention   I have
seen better days, in the morning of life — — — may kind Heaven Help you
in all things beleave me is the wish of

Mary <u>Scott</u>

my address is Pekin Jassamine County Kentucky, please write me the prospect of
getting a just compansation[1]

1. Scott to Andrew Johnson, 29 Apr. 1867, Box 1012; RG 92.

[*The following printed letter was sent to all A.M.A. teachers; Gabriel Burdett's reply
is written on the printed form. In the text below the printed portion is in italics and
the handwritten part is in regular type.*]
Rooms of the American Missionary Association
53 John Street,
New York, April 25th, 1867.
Rev. G. Burdett
Camp Nelson, Ky.

*On account of our large expenditures for our 450 teachers and an unexpected
decrease in our receipts caused undoubtedly by the falling off of trade and prices, we are*

constrained to ask the indulgence of our missionaries and teachers. We do not intend that any one shall suffer for want of a prompt receipt of the slight salary promised for self denying labor in the mission fields, but any who are in circumstances to allow their payments to be deferred will help relieve us from anxiety by giving us time.

On sums of $30 and over left standing to the credit of the teachers, on the books of the A.M.A. for three months or more, we propose to pay interest at the rate of seven per cent.

Will you please fill the blanks on the opposite page, complete the letter begun, and return to us by early mail.

Very Truly Yours, EDW'D P. SMITH, Gen'l Field Agent   A.M.A.

Camp Nelson Ky.   May. 21ᵗʰ 1867.
Dear bro Smith   Your favor has been received And it would afford me great pleasure to comply with your request.

But it is not in my power to do so as I am poor and have been a slave all my life until I joined the army And have had to take care of my family which have been much expence to me.

And since I have been discharged from the army I have been laboring to help my poor downtroden people.

And now I am in a place where I can get no help but what you give me   the people are poor and can note pay more than the wrent for the house in which we teach school and have Church   so I cannot tax them But am compelled to look to my friends abroad for help

Though the school that I am now teaching is a district school and the Commissioner of the Schools in the County say I shall have the public money of the district

But if I get that I will not get it until next spring so it would be doing injustice to my famly and my self I to loan any money now at this time   I have borrowed some money and it is now due and I have to pay five dollars wrent per month

And have all my provision to buy and my famly is in want now for clothing. so you see it would be wrong for me at this time to say I could spear any of the small salary that I am now geting.

[*Printed questions; handwritten replies.*]

   1. *How much of the payments now due can be delayed?* none

   2. *How long?*

   3. *How much will the Am. Miss. Ass n owe you the 1st of July next including all amounts now due you?* $. 75

   4. *How much of this can you loan to us at the rate proposed, for three months from the time it falls due?* not any none

   5. *How much for six month?* Cannot tell yet

May 1867.

Rev. Edw'd P. Smith, 53 John St., N.Y.

Dear Sir: Your circular of inquiry as to my ability to assist in retrieving the solicitude of the executive officers of the A.M.A. came duly, and I take an early opportunity to say in reply that I am here in the same place where bro Scofield was and have reorganized the Church and school but the people are poor and unabol to help me any And you must not think hard of me for not complying with your request. Yours in Christ

Gabriel Burdett[1]

1. Smith to Burdett, 25 Apr. 1867, and Burdett to Smith, 21 May 1867, AMAA 44462.

Camp Nelson, Ky   May 24th, 1867.

Dear bro Smith   I prommised [to] give you a small scech of those things that you wrote to me concrning of   I am young and have so much to do at this time I fear I will not be abol to furnish you with as much as I would like to   But if it would be any satisfaction to you to give a small account of sum of the old peoples stories.

We have an old man living here in Camp Nelson who came from the State of Virginia when but a yout. But says he well knew when he was a boy that they had an old man on the farme where he lived   And the white people were quite hard with there slaves And they tried to lick the old man but he would not take it from them But would run away and they would hunt him with the dogs and ketch him and chain him to brake him as they said they had to brake a negro like a horse.

So they put an iron coler on him once and he ran away and broke off and brought it home thro — it down at the door and then went away and made his way of from them.

And thoug he was old he loved liberty and found it in his old age   Then the old man that related this story to [me] was sent away from his mother when he was but a boy and he says when he was sent away from her she had the preacher to come the night before he was brought away and pray for her child that the Lord would be with him where ever he went and bless him and he says the Lord has been with him

For when came to this state he fell into hard hands but he remembered the councl of his mother and how she useto pray for him when he was but a boy and how she wept over him when he was taken away from her and brought to this Country   And when he became a man he be come converted, and now he is an abol minester of the gospel and though he was old when the call was mad for colored soldiers to go into the field he went into the field like a man and filled his post until he was mustered out like a man   And now he is one of our best men here in Camp Nelson in the first free spot of ground in Kentucky and though he is old he is here doing all he can to elevate his race by preaching and living pious and Godly

And there are many other like stories we might tell but we will relate one more of an old man who lives in our Camp by name Philip Banks   he was born in this state but was sold down in the Mississippi and when he wa sent there he wa quite a wicked man

And belonged to a wicked man who allowed them all to dance and be as wicked as they wished to be.

But did not allow them to pray or have meetings But this man was convicted once when on the danceing floor he had prommised the Lord before he left Kentucky that he would serve him but he had become quit wicked and gone far a stray from his prommis But one night when he was on the dancing floor he was struct down under conviction And in a few days he was converted to Christ and then began to preach but he had to go into the cane one mild from the hous to keep his master from hearing him pray or preach but he would go at night into the cane and there he would bow down and pray to God to be with him.

But at that time ther was not a Chritan in all that country But in a short time there was some of the colored ones went out to see what made Philip go into the cane But when they went to the place where he was and heared him pray they become convicted and it went on from one to another until there was some thirty converted to the faith,

But his master learned that he wa preaching and determined to make him give it up, But his attempt to do that only made the matter worse so after talking to him about it and seeing he was determined to have his way he tied him down on the ground and said he would give him three hundred licks but as he raised up his hand to strike the whip fell from his hand.

He said to him go preach pray and sing as much as you please. And then he built a church for his slaves   And he preached on until he left that part of the country and came to Kentucky again a short time before the war   But when the time rolled round that the colorad men of this state were called to go fourth he walked out like a man in the name of the Lord as hundreds of others   And now he is here and is laboring like a man to build up the people in the faith.

And we are here in the first free place in the state And we want to keep it for the Lord as he has done so much for us we want to gloryfy his name — here in the birth place of liberty in this state   And we want the prayers of God's people in our bhalf   But those days of Slavory have passed and gon and now liberty is proclaimed in all the land

But now we have to fight more against the spieriet of cast   But as we have over come in part we will gain the victory at last. *

Gabriel Burdett[1]

1. Burdett to Smith, 24 May 1867, AMAA 44463.

[On the] Steamer Leneliote   June 18 1867

Dear Bro Whipple, As I passed through this place [Cincinnati] some weeks since Bros King and How voted one thousand dollars as certain to Berea & Bro. How said "if there be that much unappropriated we will try to save up four more thousand"

I called to say to them it may be we can make that 4 thousand do more good at Camp Nelson

1 We can throw our present charter over Camp Nelson & render all transactions legal — safe

2 We can then have a good elementary school that will help feed Berea

3 By an outlay of the 4 thousand we can then secure a nucleus, a school & church and by which induce colored men & their friends to invest ten thousand in small tracts around the school and thus give protection and constant support

4 We shall give to these men a chance to get <u>homes</u> — attach themselves to the soil — escape the extortion of the former master.

The 114. Regiment of colored soldiers who were enlisted in that camp are soon to be mustered out. They are saving their money with which to buy homes — I propose that we first know how many will take lots — deposit the money in Bank — Then say we will furnish the nucleus — The school grounds a church & teachers — the Am Miss Association furnish, for the present one teacher. The people here must sustain all others — say, now you can have such & such lots. Thus will we for or with a small sum enlist the investment of two or three times as much by the colored men themselves — arrangement at once a good work

The houses are ready — the land is ready — it is central — easy of access   we will look after it — the Bureau will soon be gone. The planting of these returned soldiers then will give to the place <u>social protection</u>

These will be a good class to begin with — in the midst of a well developed class of colored people — just on the highway from Cincinnati to the South.

Can we find a place where the same amount of money will call forth more prospective good? so <u>soon</u> secure of a good school?

Moss is ready to sell — it may pass into other hands. He has a contract with me to let me have it for ten thousand dollars, if I can raise the money. I think if I can raise 4 thousand from Bro Howe & King, as virtually promised on my way eastward, I can induce the investment of the other 8 thousand — buy that which lies between Moss & the turnpike — lay this off in lots put on these lots some of those cottages yet there, rent them houses & lots, as a perpetual fund to the school — "for the education & elevation of the colored race."

Bro King heartily approves the plan & if Bro Howe shall consent he will vote the money. Mr Howe is absent will be some three days. Mr King said you had made an application for two thousand since I had called for the four thousand — that if you should see that the thing proposed is just in the line of your society & probably as <u>good</u> a work as can now be secured by the money and should say so to Coll. Howe there will be no doubt about our getting the money. I have the belief that the money cannot be applied where it will secure more immediate & prospective good. The house will be lost to us — the school & church now there broken up & lost — Gabriel is there gathering in souls evy sabbath. I have a heart to work there. I believe the Lord called me there   The school was begun by my labors   The house was erected at my suggestion to Capt. T E Hall and my petition to the War department   I feel they were prepared by the Lord for this purpose, and I beg of you to say yes, that we may have them. The houses are there, the children are there, the teacher & preacher is there, the soldiers & patrons will come. Is it not safe to say to the Lord, "This [*is*] a present existing good, put already into our hands. It ought not to be <u>lost</u>, I can trust for the two thousand from some other source"

I do not know but that How could give us 4 thousand & then have two thousand — better to furnish such to you than to build up <u>colored colleges</u> in Ohio & Pa. Of this however he must judge   In reference to Camp Nelson he will be much influenced by your opinion as I suppose

Now is the time to act — There are from two to three thousand dollars worth of wheat on the place — 72 acres of good wheat — soon that 114 Reg of colored troops will be mustered out   They will then have the money — they should have opportunities to invest before they squander.

Will you do a present good and trust. I will help you not only to do the good, but to raise the money. We need to buy now or loose —

Will you write to Mss King & How   If a line is sent to me in care of Mrs. Scott, 28 West 4th St. Cincinnati Ohio I will get it

I believe the Lord has raised me up for this work — I want to do it. I am in much better health than in 59 or 60. I was then exhausted, I felt then almost ready to use the language of Elijah, "Let me lie down & die — I desired not that but I felt the bitterness of death. Ahab & Jezebel have fallen — I am improving in spirit & strength. In the name of the Lord Jesus I want to help take possession of the land. One word from you will give to us the privelege.

The Lord guide Yours in Christ
Rev John G Fee[1]

1. Fee to Whipple, 18 June 1867, AMAA 44473–4.

Jessamine [*County*], Ky.   Sept 14th 67
Rev. M.E. Strieby

Dr Sir, When I saw you in N York last month I spoke to you about the colored school at Camp Nelson. I have just had an interview with Burdett who tells me he has over eighty scholars some of whom come over four miles to the school. He feels the need of assistance, and I think that unless he can have it the school had better stop   He is not competent to teach and he feels this himself. Now can you not send <u>good</u> teachers here? The point is a good one, and the influence of a good school would be felt for miles around here. I promised Burdett I would write you, and get some definite information from you, if possible. In haste

*

T.E. Hall

[Note on the back of Hall's letter in a different hand:]
Cravath   This is from Capt. Hall, the former Q.M. at Camp N. — A good man — I told him I thot you would find Burdete a first class teacher & an asst. on condition that the cold people would raise the support — The Capt. thot they would.

Burdete's establishing a good church (on Fees basis) at Camp N. & teachers would be able to do a per[t] religious work there.

E.P.S.[1]

1. Hall to Strieby, 14 Sept. 1867, AMAA 44491.

B.R.F. & A L.   Nicholasville, Ky   Oct 8" 1867
Capt R.E. Johnston[1]   **Chf SubAst Com   Lexington Ky**

Sir   I have the honor to make application for permission to rent a Building for the use of freedmens school at Camp Nelson Ky   I can get a suitable Building, Eighty by forty feet, containing two (2) Rooms, belonging to Joseph M. Moss, for $10 per month

We have a very large School there (near one hundred pupils and the tuition is so very little that it will not justify a teacher in hiring an assistant and renting a building.

And unless the Building is furnished them they will be compelled to allow the school to go down.   *

J.G. Nain   Agt R.F. & A L Nicholasville[2]

1. Robert E. Johnston, a native of Virginia, entered military service in West Virginia. He rose to the rank of lieutenant colonel in the Veteran Reserve Corps before becoming Captain Johnston, the chief sub-assistant commissioner of the Freedmen's Bureau in Lexington. *HR*, 1:578–79.
2. Nain to Johnston, 8 Oct. 1867; [Bound] Vol. 168; Letters Sent, Agent—Nicholasville Ky from Nov. 23, 1866 to Oct. 8, 1867, Entry 1242, Vol. 1 of 1; RG 105. This letter is the last entry in the volume, which has many blank pages following; the Freedmen's Bureau in Kentucky had simply come to an end.

Camp Nelson Ky   Mch 14 /68

Dear Bro Whiting   a check for $75 is due me this day — My wants are pressing. This is a sufficient reason for asking — sufficient to those who have ever been so ready to respond

I have expended more than one hundred & fifty dollars out of my own pocket in efforts to get hold of this place — trips to Louisville, Cincinnati Lexington & other expenses here. I have done this believing that to get hold of this place would be another power for good in the state. I have for years, as perhaps you know, had my heart set on this as a place for good.

I suppose it is now in my possession — all that is wanting is reply from Cincinnati as to the validity of certificates of deposits now sent forward

I go back to Berea next week, God willing

Please send check to me there. You will hear from me soon. *

John G Fee[1]

1. Fee to Whiting, 14 Mar. 1868, AMAA 44525.

Office Sup't. Nat'l Cemeteries, D.C.   Louisville, Ky., April 2, 1868.
Bv't Major General Tho⁵ Swords,[1] Ass't Quartermaster General, Louisville, Ky.,

General: I have the honor to transmit herewith for the information of the Quartermaster General, as requested . . . : * * * *

VI. . . . [*The cemetery*] at <u>Camp Nelson</u>, it will be seen, will afford ample room
for the dead at the following places: — Frankfort, Ky., 112; Covington, Ky, 441;
Richmond, Ky., 241; London, Ky., 260; Lebanon, Ky, 865; Perryville, Ky., 974.
Totals, 2893.

VII With the facilities at command, I think the dead at <u>Lebanon</u> can be taken
to Camp Nelson in less time and at much less expense than to New Albany; VIII
and those at <u>Covington</u> can also be removed to <u>Camp Nelson</u> and reinterred at a
much less cost than at Cincinnati. The cost of disinterment would be the same in
either case. The cost of transportation per body from Covington to Nicholasville,
by railroads, would be from 20c to 25c. The Gov' has its own teams at Camp
Nelson to take them from the depot, and the cost of land would be much less there
than at Cincinnati. In fact <u>the land has already been taken for the purpose at Camp
Nelson, and is prepared for the reception of the bodies</u>.

IX. The <u>Frankfort dead</u> could be either interred on vacant ground at Lexington or transported to <u>Camp Nelson</u>. If taken to the latter from there would be a
saving of at least one dollar per body in the cost of reburial.[2] * * * *

[*The following may be part of the letter above. It is definitely in the same handwriting.*]
12. Camp Nelson National Cemetery.

This cemetery is situated upon a conspicuous hill within the limits of what
was known as Camp Nelson, Jessamine County, Kentucky. It embraces 3 acres of
land and contains all the dead originally buried within the Camp, those at
Nicholasville, Stanford, and Lancaster, Ky., and some scattering dead in the surrounding country — about 1600 in all.

The original site of one of the graveyards was taken for this purpose. It has
been enlarged and completed during the past winter, by a burial party under my
direction. That portion of the ground occupied by graves is surrounded with a
temporary fence.

The title to this land has not yet been completed, but the land has been surveyed.
The consent of the owner has been obtained, and the price agreed upon. The necessary
papers are being prepared. The work cannot be completed until after the erection of the
permanent wall, as the outside walk lies exterior to the present enclosure. * * * *[3]

---

1. Thomas Swords, a New Yorker by birth, rose to the rank of lieutenant colonel and
deputy quartermaster general in the 1850s; he began his Civil War service as colonel and
assistant quartermaster-general. By 1865 he was breveted as a major-general for "faithful and
efficient service" in the Quartermaster Department during the war. *HR,* 1:941.

2. [E.B. Whitman] to Swords, 2 Apr. 1868, RG 92 [no further information]. The underlining and the Roman numerals in this letter were not part of the original document, but
penciled in (with a very soft, dark pencil) by a different hand. The author of this report, like
the other cemetery reports, was undoubtedly Edmund Burke Whitman, who was in charge

of the new government cemetery at Camp Nelson in 1867. A native of Massachusetts, Whitman had entered the army in Kansas, becoming a captain and assistant quartermaster by 1862. He was breveted a major and lieutenant colonel for "meritorious service" in the Quartermaster's Department during the war. Honorably mustered out on August 20, 1868, he died in 1883. *HR,* 1:1030.

3. The cemetery reports included in this entry were copied by researchers who did not keep an exact record of their dates or of their whereabouts in RG 92.

Apr. 9, 1868

Dear Bro. Smith
* * * *

I have had a protracted and arduous effort at Camp Nelson — 32 miles from this place, trying to get that farm with the buildings, Bro. Scofield was at. I have succeeded. It was not in a safe condition before this time — It is now freed of two claims that neither Bro. Scofield nor I saw. It is now clear at least the part I get — 130 acres. I have turned over to trustees property worth five thousand dollars, the Bureau paying 15 hundred toward this. A good man is there & the school started — one large building, 75 feet long & 30 broad, 2 stories high — 18 rooms. The two wards, 75 by 25 feet each — situated in a fertile region, surrounded by a large colored population. We must multiply schools & put education within their reach.

With the officials & leading men at Nicholasville, the county seat of Jessamine Co., my intercourse is very pleasant. They all treat me with marked respect. I have not had there a single word or act of disrespect. I have preached there to the colored people, several times. I preach to these in Lexington, Danville, Lancaster, Richmond — all around.

Bro. Smith, I regard these colored people as by far the most hopeful class so far as the kingdom of Christ is concerned. They are humble, trusting, receptive — consider it a privilege to hear the word of God, & manifest an intense desire to read it.

God has given me wonderful access & these the evangelizing power of the South. I have very largely their confidence. Now I do not intend to prostitute this influence of mine & this thirst of theirs to sect & denominational strife. The School and Church at Camp Nelson (Ariel is the name of our town and academy there) is, as at Berea, devoted simply to that which is Christian — "Church of Christ at Ariel" in Camp Nelson, Ky. * * * *

John G. Fee[1]

1. Fee to Gerritt Smith, 9 Apr. 1868, Gerritt Smith Miller Collection, Syracuse University, no. 80, copy in BCA.

Bureau of Refugees, Freedmen, and Abandoned Lands, Assistant Commissioner's Office, State of Kentucky, Louisville, Kentuy, April 10, 1868

General [*Oliver Otis*] Howard: I have the honor to submit the following report of the operation of the bureau in Kentucky, for the month of March, 1868:

[*Under the category:* SCHOOLS.]

In obedience to your ordrs I proceeded to Camp Nelson, Kentucky, and purchased Aerial[1] Academy for the sum of $1,520. It will require about $800 to put these buildings in order.

Aerial Academy consists of one large two-story building 75 by 35, containing 12 rooms, to be used as a boarding-house; one wing, five rooms, 75 by 25, to be used as a school-house and one wing, 75 by 25, to be used as a chapel.

This academy is situated in the midst of a fertile and populous district. A large number of freedmen live within the sound of its bell. Many will come from Danville, Nicholasville, and Harrodsburg and the adjoining counties to enjoy its privileges. The buildings could not have cost less than $6,000 when new. Altogether it is an excellent investment. * * * *

Ben P. Runkle[2], Brevet Co., U.S.A., Chief Sup't., &c., State of Kentucky[3]

1. Runkle consistently misspells Ariel.
2. Benjamin Piatt Runkle, a Union officer from Ohio, was named colonel of the Forty-fifth Ohio on August 19, 1862, served in Kentucky, and commanded a brigade in Kentucky and Tennessee. He was mustered out of service in July 1864 and commissioned lieutenant colonel in the Veteran Reserve Corps. For the rest of the war he was on duty with the Memphis Freedmen's Bureau. *CWD.*
3. *Freedmen's Affairs in Kentucky and Tennessee. Letter from the secretary of war. . . .* (Washington, D.C.: GPO, 1868), 14.

Berea, Madison Co., Ky   Apr 14 186[8]

Dear Bro Whiting   As you have probably learned through Bro Whipple my labours during the last five months have been frequently from home and my expenses large

I have succeeded at Camp Nelson. Go there thurs day

Please send to me a check for seventy five $75 now due me   Thus oblige yours,

John G Fee

Please send to Berea[1]

1. Fee to Whiting, 14 Apr. 1868, AMAA 44540.

Afterword

Incredibly, all the Civil War era buildings, hundreds of them, have disappeared, except for one white house (the Oliver Perry House), now restored; most of the rest, almost all built of wood, were sold and moved or dismantled by the Federal government, and those that remained after that were mined for construction materials and fuel by locals, or they simply fell down and rotted into the soil

I drove to Camp Nelson this afternoon to walk around the site and think about the past there. After a winter storm last night, the dark, leafless trees were coated in white ice: ghosts of trees.

I visited a small cemetery on a bluff with a view of the Kentucky River Palisades, not the big U.S. cemetery, but a village plot where the people of Hall have buried their dead for generations. Most of the older tombstones are weatherbeaten and unreadable, but one has a clear inscription: W.S. Overstreet, Co. K, 124 U.S.C.I. (United States Colored Infantry); a little "street" in Hall is named Overstreet Lane. He was one of the black soldiers who stayed at Camp Nelson with his family after the war was over.

When I drove through Hall, an aged black woman with white hair, dressed in a winter coat, smiled and waved at me from the porch of her respectable little house; I suppose she is a descendant of Camp Nelson refugees, and I think she ran out of the house to see who was driving on the otherwise deserted road. There are not many houses in Hall, but lots of junked cars and some scattered trash. It's very out of the way, even hard to find. The streets are just country roads, blacktop leading to gravel turning to dirt roads and then dead ending, frequently without warning. There are lots of dead end roads in Hall, and many spectacularly beautiful glimpses of the Palisades. One of the roads leading to the village from Highway 27 is called Poortown.

I visited an old, dilapidated church (not the original building), perhaps on the site where Rev. John Gregg Fee organized the first congregation of Christians in Camp Nelson, where Rev. Gabriel Burdett preached for a decade after the war ended. In front of the church is a recently erected historical marker with pictures, all glazed over. I chipped off a layer of ice to see the picture of Fee staring resolutely at the camera, Bible firmly clenched in his hand. And I de-iced another picture: "A Street in Camp Nelson c. 1865," with African-American women, most of them slightly blurred because they moved when the photograph was taken, crowding a little road between rows of government-built cabins in the Refugee Home.

Except for some all-too-human eyesores, Camp Nelson is a beautiful site, beautiful now, beautiful then in the mid-1860s, as many observers agreed.

Select Bibliography

Only published, print resources that have been particularly helpful in this work and/or that contain direct references to Camp Nelson itself are included in this bibliography.

Adams, George Worthington. *Doctors in Blue: The Medical History of the Union Army in the Civil War.* New York: Henry Schuman, 1952.

American Missionary. Various numbers.

Bentley, George R. *A History of the Freedmen's Bureau.* 1955. Reprint, New York: Octagon Books, 1970.

Berlin, Ira, Barbara J. Fields, Thavolia Glymph, Joseph P. Reidy, and Leslie S. Rowland, eds. *Freedom: A Documentary History of Emancipation 1861-1867 Selected from the Holdings of the National Archives of the United States.* Series 1. Volume 1. *The Destruction of Slavery.* Cambridge: Cambridge U. Press, 1985.

Berlin, Ira, Joseph P. Reidy, and Leslie S. Rowland, eds. *Freedom: A Documentary History of Emancipation 1861-1867 Selected from the Holdings of the National Archives of the United States.* Series 2. *The Black Military Experience.* Cambridge: Cambridge U. Press, 1982.

Blackburn, George M., ed. *With the Wandering Regiment: The Diary of Captain Ralph Ely of the Eighth Michigan Infantry.* Mt. Pleasant: Central Michigan U. Press, 1965.

Blassingame, John W. "The Recruitment of Colored Troops in Kentucky, Maryland and Missouri 1863-1865." *The Historian* 29 (1967): 533-45.

Boatner, Mark Mayo. *The Civil War Dictionary.* New York: David McKay Co., 1959.

Bruner, Peter. *A Slave's Adventures Toward Freedom: Not Fiction but the True Story of a Struggle.* Oxford, Ohio: n,p., [1918?].

Buel, Clarence C., and Robert U. Johnson, eds. *Battles and Leaders of the Civil War.* 4 vols. New York: Century Co., 1884-88.

Burrage, Henry S. "The Retreat from Lenoir's and Siege of Knoxville." *Atlantic Monthly* 18 (1866): 21-32.

Calico, Forrest. *History of Garrard County, Kentucky, and its Churches.* New York: Hobson Press, 1947.

Collins, Richard H., and Lewis C. Collins. *Historical Sketches of Kentucky.* 2 vols. Covington, Ky.: Collins & Co., 1874. Reprinted as *History of Kentucky.* 2 vols. Frankfort, Ky.: Kentucky Historical Society, 1966.

Cox, Jacob Dolson. *Military Reminiscences of the Civil War.* 2 vols. Vol. 1, April 1861-November 1863. New York: Charles Scribner's Sons, 1900.

De Falaise, Louis. "General Stephen Gano Burbridge's Command in Kentucky." *Register of the Kentucky Historical Society* 69, no. 2 (Apr. 1971): 101-27.

Dyer, Frederick H.A. *A Compendium of the War of the Rebellion: Compiled and Arranged from Official Records . . . .* 2 vols. Des Moines: Dyer Publishing Co., 1908.

Fee, John Gregg. *Autobiography of John G. Fee, Berea, Kentucky.* Chicago: National Christian Association, 1891.

Gutman, Herbert G. *The Black Family in Slavery and Freedom, 1750-1925.* New York: Pantheon Books, 1976.

Heitman, Francis B. *Historical Register and Dictionary of the United States Army from its organization, September 29, 1789, to March 2, 1903.* 2 vols. Washington: GPO, 1903.

Howard, Victor B. *Black Liberation in Kentucky: Emancipation and Freedom, 1862-1884.* Lexington: U. Press of Kentucky, 1983.

Kinnaird, Dr. J. B. *Historical Sketches of Lancaster and Garrard County 1796-1924.* N.p., n.d.

Kireker, Lt. Col. Charles, Commanding. *History of the 116ᵗʰ Regiment U.S.C. Infantry . . . .* Philadelphia: King and Baird, Printers, 1866.

Kleber, John E., ed. *The Kentucky Encyclopedia.* Lexington: U. Press of Kentucky, 1992.

Lancaster Women's Club [Lancaster, Ky.], compilers and editors. *Patches of Garrard County: A History.* Danville, Ky.: Bluegrass Printing Co., 1974.

Litwack, Leon F. *Been in the Storm So Long: The Aftermath of Slavery.* New York, Alfred A. Knopf, 1979.

Long, E. B., and Barbara Long. *The Civil War Day by Day: An Almanac 1861-1865.* Garden City, New York: Doubleday & Co., 1971.

Lucas, Marion B. "Camp Nelson, Kentucky, During the Civil War: Cradle of Liberty or Refugee Death Camp?" *The Filson Club History Quarterly* 63 (Oct. 1989): 439-52.

———. *A History of Blacks in Kentucky. Volume 1: From Slavery to Segregation, 1760-1891.* Frankfort: Kentucky Historical Society, 1992.

Marrs, Elijah P. *The Life and History of the Reverend Elijah P. Marrs, First Pastor of Beargrass Baptist Church, and Author.* Louisville: Bradley and Gilbert, 1885.

Marvel, William. *Burnside.* Chapel Hill: U. of North Carolina, 1991.

McBride, W. Stephen. "Civil War Material Culture and Camp Life in Central Kentucky." In *Look to the South: Historical Archaeology and the American Civil War.* Edited by Clarence R. Geier Jr. and Susan E. Winter, 130-157. Knoxville: U. of Tennessee Press, 1994.

McBride, W. Stephen and William E. Sharp. "Archaeological Investigations at Camp Nelson: A Union Quartermaster Depot and Hospital in Jessamine County, Kentucky." University of Kentucky Program for Cultural Resource Assessment, Archaeological Report 241. Lexington: University of Kentucky, 1991.

McFeely, William S. *Yankee Stepfather: General O.O. Howard and the Freedmen.* New Haven: Yale U. Press, 1968.

Military History of Kentucky, Chronologically Arranged. Federal Writers' Project (Ky.). Frankfort: State Journal, 1939.

Morris, Robert Charles. *Reading, 'Riting, and Reconstruction: The Education of Freedmen in the South 1861-1870.* Chicago: U. of Chicago Press, 1981.

Newberry, John Strong. *The U. S. Sanitary Commission in the Valley of the Mississippi During the War of the Rebellion, 1861-1866.* [Final report of Dr. J. S. Newberry, Secretary Western Department.] Cleveland: Fairbanks, Benedict & Co., 1871.

Palmer, John M. *Personal Recollections of John M. Palmer: The Story of an Earnest Life.* Cincinnati: The Robert Clarke Co., 1901.

Peter, Frances Dallam. *A Union Woman in Civil War Kentucky: The Diary of Frances Peter.* Edited by John David Smith and William Cooper Jr. Lexington: U. Press of Kentucky, 2000.

Ramage, James A. *Rebel Raiders: The Life of General John Hunt Morgan.* Lexington: U. Press of Kentucky, 1986.

Redkey, Edwin S., ed. *A Grand Army of Black Men: Letters from African-American Soldiers in the Union Army, 1861-1865.* New York: Cambridge U. Press, 1992.

Report of the Adjutant General of the State of Kentucky. 2 vols. Frankfort: Kentucky Yeoman Office, 1867.

Scott, Robert Garth, ed. *Forgotten Valor: The Memoirs, Journals, and Civil War Letters of Orlando B. Willcox.* Kent, Ohio: Kent State U. Press, 1999.

Sears, Richard Duane. *Berea Connections: An Encyclopedia of Genealogy and Local History Related to Berea, Kentucky from 1854 to 1900.* Privately printed, 1996.

———. *A Utopian Experiment in Kentucky: Integration and Social Equality at Berea, 1866-1904.* Westport, Conn.: Greenwood Press, 1996.

Secretary of War. *Official Army Register of the Volunteer Force of the United States Army for the Years 1861, '62, '63, '64, '65.* 8 vols. Washington, 1865-1867.

Shannon, Fred Albert. *The Organization and Administration of the Union Army 1861-1865.* 2 vols. Cleveland: Arthur H. Clark Co., 1928.

Simpson, Joseph. *Letters from Joseph Simpson, Manchester [England].* London: Friends' Central Committee for the Relief of the Emancipated Negroes, 1865.

Smith, John David. "The Recruitment of Negro Soldiers in Kentucky, 1863-1865." *Register of the Kentucky Historical Society* 72 , no. 4 (Oct. 1974): 364-90.

Smith, John David, and William Cooper Jr., eds. *Window on the War: Frances Dallam Peter's Lexington Civil War Diary.* Lexington: U. Press of Kentucky, 2000.

Swint, Henry L. *The Northern Teacher in the South, 1862-1870.* 1941. Reprint, New York: Octagon Books, 1967.

U.S. War Department. *The War of the Rebellion: A Compilation of the Official Records of the Union and Confederate Armies.* 128 vols. Washington, D.C.: GPO, 1880-1901.

Warner, Ezra J. *Generals in Blue: Lives of the Union Commanders.* Baton Rouge: Louisiana State U. Press, 1964.

———. *Generals in Gray: Lives of the Confederate Commanders.* Baton Rouge: Louisiana State U. Press, 1959.

Western Freedmen's Aid Commission, Cincinnati, Ohio. *Report,* 1864.

Woodward, Elon A., ed. "The Negro in the Military Service of the United States, a Compilation of Official Records, State Papers, Historical Extracts, Relating to His Military Status and Service, from the North American Colonies." 7 vols. RG 94. NA: 1888. Also available in National Archives microfilm publication M858.

Index